STEVEN CANEY'S
ULTIMATE BUILDING BOOK

STEVEN CANEY'S
ULTIMATE
BUILDING
BOOK

By Steven Caney

RUNNING PRESS
KIDS

PHILADELPHIA • LONDON

Library of Congress Control Number: 2006923196

ISBN 13: 978-0-7624-0409-4
ISBN 10: 0-7624-0409-4

Cover illustration by Chris Butler
Cover design by Bill Jones
Typography: Baskerville, Lissen, and Times

This book may be ordered by mail from the publisher.
Please include $2.50 for postage and handling.
But try your bookstore first!

Published by Running Press Kids, an imprint of
Running Press Book Publishers
125 South Twenty-Second Street
Philadelphia, PA 19103-4399

Visit us on the web!
www.runningpress.com

Dedication

To my granddaughters
Lena, Hannah, and Serena

TABLE OF CONTENTS

Acknowledgements...ix

When I Was a Kid...1

Structures and Forms Are Everywhere................7

What Is a Structure?...8

A Brief History of Buildings and Structures.................................46

Clever Animal Architects and Builders.................................77

Getting Ready to Build.................................91

Gathering Materials, Parts, and Pieces.................................92

The Right Tools and How to Use Them.................................122

Good Design Is Good Form, Function, and Fun.................137

Building Plus Creativity Equals Invention.................................151

Space Frame Structures.................163

Understanding Space Frame Structures.................164

Building with Rods and Connectors.................207

Brick and Block Structures...349

Understanding Brick and Block Structures.................................350

Building with Bricks and Blocks.................................381

Panel and Plane Structures.................................443

Understanding Panel and Plane Structures.................................444

Building with Panels and Planes.................................465

Appendix: For Parents and Other Teachers.................................561

Glossary.................................585

Index.................................591

Credits.................................596

ACKNOWLEDGMENTS

In the spirit of my previous books, *Steven Caney's Ultimate Building Book* began as another endeavor about making fun toys and playthings from building systems that used common everyday materials. It turned out to be my magnum opus. From cover to cover, this book contains about three hundred thousand words, more than two thousand photographs, and almost seven hundred illustrations all packed into six hundred pages. The result was truly an "ultimate" effort that involved many people with special skills who continually revealed their genuine commitment and enthusiasm. Considering all the parents, teachers, kids and publishing professionals who helped bring my ideas to these pages, several hundred people contributed their talents in various ways. Although I'm sure I thanked each one that participated, a few were quite exceptional in both their on-going involvement and talent.

As the author, it was my idea to write a book that explained how various types of structures were built and then develop fun building systems and projects that demonstrated that knowledge. But the more I learned fascinating things about building, the more I wanted

to share them with others, and it soon became evident that this was going to be a very big book. In addition to writing the text and inventing the projects, I also took most of the photographs and participated in the design of the book. However, during the development from ideas to the pages you are now reading, these are the people I especially thank for helping me. Their special efforts were essential and made the many-year process enjoyable and rewarding.

Every author needs an editor to help guide a book's development. I was lucky to have Liz, an exceptional children's book editor from

Liz Encarnacion, editor

Running Press, who both understood and believed in the concept of such a mammoth work. I'm sure there were times when we both felt overwhelmed about the enormous amount of work remaining to be done, but by continually encouraging each other, we did it! Her suggestions, without exception, always resulted in improving the book.

Nearly every topic in this book required research that ranged from Internet savvy, to searching out copies of rare books, to sifting through the hoards of information that would hopefully reveal the "true" facts of the story. Jennifer's

Jennifer Myers, researcher

research not only included a focus on the information I requested, but also revealed discoveries that made the subject even more interesting. Jennifer's husband, Phil, who is a culinary guru, developed most of the recipes for homemade adhesives and mortars.

While writing text or responding to questions of fact or clarification from my editor, Liz, I often need immediate answers. Since Shelly's office is within shouting distance from mine, my queries were often answered within minutes: "How much does a medium-size bird eat in a day?" or "What is the ideal size of a butterfly net?" and literally a hundred other facts. Shelly also read everything I wrote just to make sure I got the facts right. She helped with so much more including hosting the design team to tea every afternoon at four o'clock.

Steven Caney,
author, photographer

Shelly Caney, researcher

Scott Kelly, project tester

As building systems and projects were being developed, Scott built models, tested our assumptions with kids, solicited their evaluations, suggested changes, and tested the results. Some projects never made it to print, and others were immensely improved by his insights. Scott's education in architecture was certainly a plus, and his enthusiasm with kids was contagious.

As I was inventing many of the building systems and experimenting with projects to build with them, many kids were engaged as testers. Kids from several schools throughout New England built, tested, and advised me on what worked and what could be better. However, the kids from the Fillmore Elementary school near Detroit, Michigan, became my official testers and critics. With the guidance of their teachers, they built my designs,

Kids from Fillmore Elementary, Sterling Heights, Michigan, project builders and testers

invented new variations, and presented their structures to me while making plenty of suggestions. I just loved working with them!

The RISD connection

It is not just a coincidence that the designers of the projects and pages in this book are all graduates of the Rhode Island School of Design. Each one of us may have our own interests and unique expressions of design (my degree is in Industrial Design and my passion is children's playthings), however, we all share a common education in the attitudes and methods of design. That connection was critical to the synergy we enjoyed and is demonstrated on every page. I can't imagine how this book could have been completed without them.

Lauren House, illustrator

Even though Lauren had just received her RISD degree in Illustration, her work and work style were immediately impressive. Nearly seven hundred illustrations needed to be sketched, revised, and painstakingly "inked" by pen. She often researched subjects for accuracy or built models for reference—and sometimes completed illustrations needed to be totally

redone (mostly because I changed my mind)—but Lauren always approached each one with a determination to make it just right. What a professional!

Noah Caney, principal book designer

Noah's degrees from RISD are in the Arts and Architecture, although he also has extensive skill and experience in graphic design. Noah's first involvement with this book was to help design some of the projects. He created all the Plastic Pipe Structures and brilliantly helped refine many others. Noah's primary task, however, was to lead the team that created the book design and executed page layouts. It is with enormous pride and satisfaction that I had the opportunity to share the development of this book with him.

Dan Freitas, book designer

Dan had just graduated from RISD with a degree in Illustration when he came on board to assist Noah with the design of this book. In addition to strongly influencing the many design conventions that give the book an orderly appearance, he was responsible for the monumental task of initially organizing the text, illustrations, and photos on every page. His design sensitivity and pleasant manner also turned arduous tasks into rewarding and enjoyable experiences.

I'm sure Marc would have been pleased with this book. He was my teacher and teaching colleague at RISD, my design mentor, and my friend. He inspired many, and I for one am grateful for his masterful insights and encouragement to continue learning by sharing. I hope

Marc Harrison,
design professor and mentor

this book helps to perpetuate his teachings. Certainly the content of every page is influenced by my understanding of his design philosophies and wisdom. I hope each reader and young builder is similarly stimulated.

And many helpers

During the development of this book, many others contributed their time and talents. I especially thank all the kids whose photos appear throughout these pages, and appreciate those who helped with photography, writing, research, model building, and inspirations, including…

Steve Boulter

David Foreman

Phillip Myers

Ginger Brown

Lauren Bello

Rick Culkins

Urszula Caney

Alex, Amy, and Jennifer Jemmery

Dick Dubroff

Peggy Laufer

Paul Eldridge

WHEN I WAS A KID

When I was a kid, I got underwear for my birthday. Well, maybe not always, but if I wanted something particular to play with, I usually just made it myself. My materials were the scraps of wood at a nearby construction site; old coffee cans full of metal parts and fasteners my father kept under the basement steps; an assortment of broken appliances stored in the garage; and a kitchen drawer stuffed full with twine, rubber bands, jar lids, and a lot of strange caps, clips, and containers that at some time my mother must have thought were valuable enough to save.

I never minded building my own playthings. In fact, I rather enjoyed planning and executing a building project and then playing with my contraption and trying to make it work. I didn't even mind fixing it when it broke or improving on the design when it didn't work just right. My only problem was not being able to figure out how to build the complicated stuff, like my own clock radio, a three-speed English bicycle, or an Erector set large enough to build a model of the famed parachute ride at Coney Island. Fortunately, I had a generous aunt who often fulfilled my wish list.

But much more important than possessing the playthings of my dreams was the help and encouragement I received from my many mentors who liked the things I built and showed me how to make them better.

About the time I was five, I discovered my grandfather's basement workshop. Down the basement stairs and to the left was a long wooden workbench up against the foundation wall (to the right was the dreaded furnace monster). Shelves above the bench held stacks of old cigar boxes, and each cigar box contained a giant assortment of metal, rubber, and plastic parts—parts taken from door locks and hinges, faucets and drains, kitchen appliances, and (to me) mostly unknown sources. Junk. The kind of broken stuff that gets saved just in case you need to replace a missing part someday. But to me, this was magical stuff and the inspiration for inventions.

The idea was to connect a bunch of parts together in some way that seemed to work, and then figure out what it was I had built. The contraption could be a tall and balanced tower, maybe a vehicle that rolled on wheels, or possibly just an assembly of moving parts that became one of my many "do-nothing machines." It was not so much that I planned what I built, it was more finding out what the combined parts wanted to make of themselves. If some small metal parts hanging on a string made a pleasant jingle, then I had just built a wind chime. If a hinge and rubber bands made a great spitball launcher, then I invented a target game and kept trying to improve my launcher. Most of the time I would just attach parts in ways they seemingly wanted to go together, and then try to figure out what I had invented.

Not all of my inventions worked, but it always seemed that just when I was about to give up, my grandfather would appear with the help and advice I needed. It would always start with the squeaky sound of the basement door opening and heavy footsteps descending the basement stairs. In just a moment, I would be asked what I was building, but before I could conjure up some feasible explanation for my half-baked contraption, my grandfather would open the folded newspaper he carried under his arm and begin to read aloud. "Secret invention being developed in basement on Washington Street. Steven Caney attempts to build first of its kind. Check tomorrow's paper for more news." Wow! Was I impressed and proud. My invention was so important that the newspaper had written about it. But how did they know so quickly what I was up to? (By first grade, I had figured that one out.)

My grandfather's basement was certainly an inviting place to build things with nifty tools and a big, old workbench that was already nicked, stained, and drilled into many times. And what a wonderful resource of materials I had to explore, full of things I could take apart, put together, bend, hammer, and even break— if that's what I wanted to do. But it was the encouragement I received from my grandfather that made this environment just about the perfect place for creativity, invention, and building to take place spontaneously. And it was big-time fun. He and I would add more parts and do more experiments all in a quest to make new discoveries, create interesting phenomena, and figure out what my invention really wanted to be. We never failed to make something I could proudly show off. It should be no surprise that later in life when I directed the design of the Boston Children's Museum, I created a hands-on exhibit space called Grandfather's Basement—soon followed by Grandmother's Attic.

By age eight, I was the neighborhood builder, inventor, and fixer of things among my peers. Over the next few years, I invented a bedspring suspension system for my roller-skate-clad soapbox racer, a remote shutter release for my Brownie camera (to take candid pictures of backyard birds), a mailbox that kept the rain out, and a whole bunch of things that propelled themselves or shot something through the air. If someone's toy broke, I could often figure out how to fix it. And if one of my friends wanted to pull a practi-

A remote-controlled camera invented by the author at age nine for photographing backyard birds

cal joke on someone, I was the one who invented the booby trap.

While practicing and improving my building and inventing skills, I was also learning ways to solve problems. Rather than just trying to think of a good solution, I would look for solutions that already existed. If I needed a way to attach two parts together in a certain way, for example, I would just look at all the things around me to discover how they were attached to something. Out of all these "sugges-

tions" would come the inspiration I needed for the right way to do it. I was giving myself options and then choosing the one I liked best. The more options I had to choose from, the better chance I would find the best solution. This method of giving myself lots of choices so I

could pick the best one was a process I could always count on for being creative.

When my third-grade teacher gave me a homework assignment to write a poem about an animal or a pet, I figured out an "automatic" way to generate the most rhyming words. "Oh I wish I had a dog." The first line was easy, but now I needed a word that rhymed with dog. So I wrote all the letters of the alphabet down the left margin on a sheet of paper. Then using each letter as the prefix to "og" I wrote a list of all the real words I recognized, like *fog, hog,* and *log.* And as I discovered each rhyming word, I would try to write the second line. "Oh I wish I had a dog to sit with me upon a log." Then I'd make up another line, "I'd take a stick and throw it far," and then go back to the alphabet list to find the best rhyming word to finish the line—*bar, car, tar,* or maybe *star*? How about " . . . but nowhere near the family car." I just kept going line after line, using my "process" until the poem seemed finished. It wasn't long before I became the class poet, meaning one of my poems would be published each month in the parents' and teachers' newsletter. This was fun, it was easy, and I had done something my parents could brag about.

OUR DANDELIONS
by Steven William Caney

All of a sudden and without warning,
our lawn turned yellow one April morning.

The field of flowers just kept growing,
no matter how much my dad kept mowing.

Then just as sudden and overnight,
all the flowers turned to white.

And if you blew with gentle care,
they'd disappear into the air.
Until next year.

When I graduated to the fifth grade, I was finally old enough to take the bus by myself to the local "Y" to go swimming after school. My father would pick me up on his drive home from work. While waiting for him one afternoon, I discovered a room on the third floor with a class of adult artists dressed in paint-smeared smocks. They were all standing behind easels and intensely studying a grouping of objects on a table at one end of the room. With a small wooden board held in one hand and a long thin paint brush in the other, each artist would alternately stare at the table-top objects and mix up a small puddle of paint on the wooden board that would then be applied to the picture they were painting.

Poking my head through the open door, I was curious to see what these pictures looked like, and the wonderful smell of oil paint and

linseed oil was reminiscent of some of my grandfather's projects. The class teacher not only invited me in for a look, he walked me past every canvas to show me that each painting was a different version of the same group of objects on the table. One was almost as real as a photograph, but most looked only vaguely like the actual objects. "I can do that good," I boasted rather glibly. With soft chuckles coming from all around, I was given an easel with a blank white canvas board, seven dabs of different color oil paints, and one of those long, skinny brushes. I had been invited to join the class, and I enthusiastically accepted the opportunity to mess around with paints!

My visual education took a gigantic leap that fortuitous afternoon. What I learned was not so much how to make paintings, but more so how to see. "Look at just a small part of the object, mix your paint to capture its color, then paint that small part of the object on your canvas. Now look back at the object and capture the color of a

small section next to the one you just painted. Just keep looking and painting, small section after small section, until you have captured the entire object." I quickly discovered that every part of the object I was trying to capture on canvas had its own unique color, even though at first I might have thought the entire object was all the same color. By learning to look closely at each part of the object, I was beginning to see what I had been missing, even though the colors had been there all the time.

Along with learning how to see the individual parts of an object, I was also becoming pretty good at visualizing things. That is, I was able to turn ideas expressed in words into pictures I could see in my mind. But in my neighborhood, that was nothing special, because every kid routinely practiced this skill of visualization. This was just before television first appeared in homes, so we had all grown up watching the radio. Yes, watching! After school and on Saturday mornings, my friends and I would gather

Painting of the Washington Street bridge in Wilmington, Delaware, by the author at age eleven

around the radio at one of our homes to listen to cowboy stories and adventure programs. Lying there on our stomachs and staring glaringly into the radio speaker, each of us would see our own mind pictures that depicted exactly what was happening in the story.

I went one step further and would practice coming up with my own stories so I could see whatever mind pictures I wanted. Those same skills also made it easy for me to figure out how to build things. Before I started the actual construction, I could first picture the design in my mind and imagine different changes until I liked what I "saw." Even so, most of my projects only started as I had imagined them and changed into whatever they suggested they wanted to be. That was another lesson I would formally learn later and strongly rely on. Be sensitive to what the design implies it wants to be.

In the seventh grade, I was first introduced to "shop class" where kids typically made metal ashtrays, candlestick holders, and small knick-knack trays for their parents. After demonstrating my skills at those feats of craftsmanship, the teacher gave me permission to create my own shop projects, and he suggested that I try using other materials and the tools needed to work them.

The projects that followed included a brass weather vane with some parts that were turned on a metal lathe, a transparent plastic mailbox that let you see what was inside, and a scale model of a grand piano

that played tunes using a miniature music box. I designed the piano from a picture in a catalog, made wood forms for bending the sides to shape, machined the white and black keys, laminated three layers of plastic to make the top and bottom pieces, turned the piano legs, put the whole piano together with plastic glue, hinges, and screws, and installed a wind-up music box that played "Oh Susanna" whenever the top was lifted.

In retrospect, the projects built in shop class were not nearly as important as the lessons learned about organizing and executing a building project. Each new construction started as a list of many project ideas that quickly narrowed to what really excited me—and what was practical to be built in shop class. (I never did make a working grandfather clock.) Once I did settle on an idea, it was time to sketch on paper how I was going to make it. Sometimes I was advised to first build a cardboard model or experiment with the materials I planned to use before beginning the actual construction. I also had to consider where to get the materials and what they cost. Did the shop have all the tools I needed, and would there be enough class time to complete the project?

I was now confident I could figure out a way to make, fix, or invent just about anything by applying all

these techniques of looking for options, visualizing solutions, planning the project, then building what I had designed. But was this really being creative? I somehow imagined that real creativity had nothing to do with techniques or processes. It would not be until my college years at the Rhode Island School of Design that many of these little tricks of creativity would be validated as legitimate design processes.

All eight fellow students in my sophomore photography course anxiously arrived at the first class ready to shoot pictures. The assignment for the afternoon seemed simple enough. "Take a walk around the block and photograph all the number sixes you can find." We decided to walk together just to assure no number sixes were missed. From every conceivable angle, we photographed the number six as it appeared on house addresses, license plates, and even the serial numbers on the telephone poles. In less than an hour, we were done, back in class, and ready for the next assignment. But in a rather incredulous directive, we were all instructed to go right back out to find all the sixes we had seemingly missed the first time around.

Our second walk was not proving to be very fruitful until one of my classmates scribbled a number six on the dirty hood of a parked car. As if that new number six was the most precious six to be found yet, we all rushed over to snap a picture. Wait a minute! If we could make a number six to photograph, what else might be allowed? How about Roman numeral VI for a six? How about twisting your body to create a shadow resembling the number six? How about cloud formations, branches, or a grouping of six oddly colored bricks in the wall? Who is in control of what constitutes a number six? We were. Each one of us was now off searching out our own definitions of what worked for an image of the number six.

Our second assignment was just as profound. After developing the film we had shot, and after looking through all the pictures of the number sixes we had captured, we were each simply asked to pick the one photo we liked best. No one had any difficulty narrowing down their pile of prints to a favorite. And no two favorite selections were alike. We had somehow experienced a way to generate our own creative options that went well beyond the obvious solutions and applied our own unique criteria to select the ones we liked best.

As a student of design, I was always being challenged to go beyond the obvious, to see alternatives inspired by nature, to borrow and adapt an existing solution to solve my unique problem, to understand the attributes of the materials I work with, and to learn what each tool wants to do and what each object wants to become. Today, as a teacher of design, I want to pass on the knowledge and skills that have served me so well through child-

hood and in my professional practice. And I know of no better way to teach and exercise those skills than through building. I now feel privileged to have had the materials, the space, and the encouragement to build the things I wanted and to do it my own way.

As you curiously search through the pages and projects in this Building Book, I hope you will be inspired to make the playthings and contraptions you like most. I also expect you will experience and learn the same lessons in creativity, design, and structure that have guided me, except I also know each young builder will create his or her own structures his or her own way

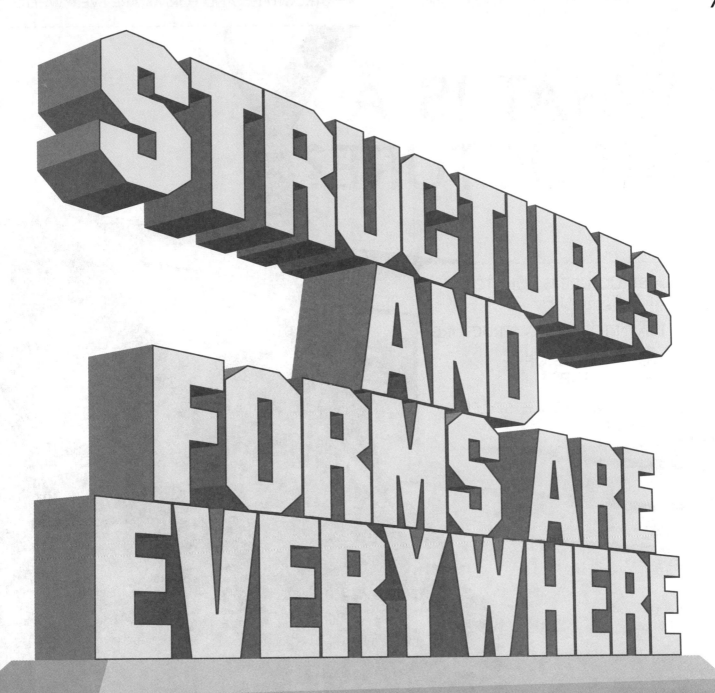

STRUCTURES AND FORMS ARE EVERYWHERE

WHAT IS A STRUCTURE?

A BRIEF HISTORY OF BUILDINGS
AND STRUCTURES

CLEVER ANIMAL ARCHITECTS
AND BUILDERS

WHAT IS A STRUCTURE?

A STRUCTURE IS BUILT TO KEEP ITS SHAPE

LEARN TO READ A STRUCTURE

THE ELEMENTS OF ARCHITECTURE

RECOGNIZING THE STYLES OF BUILDINGS

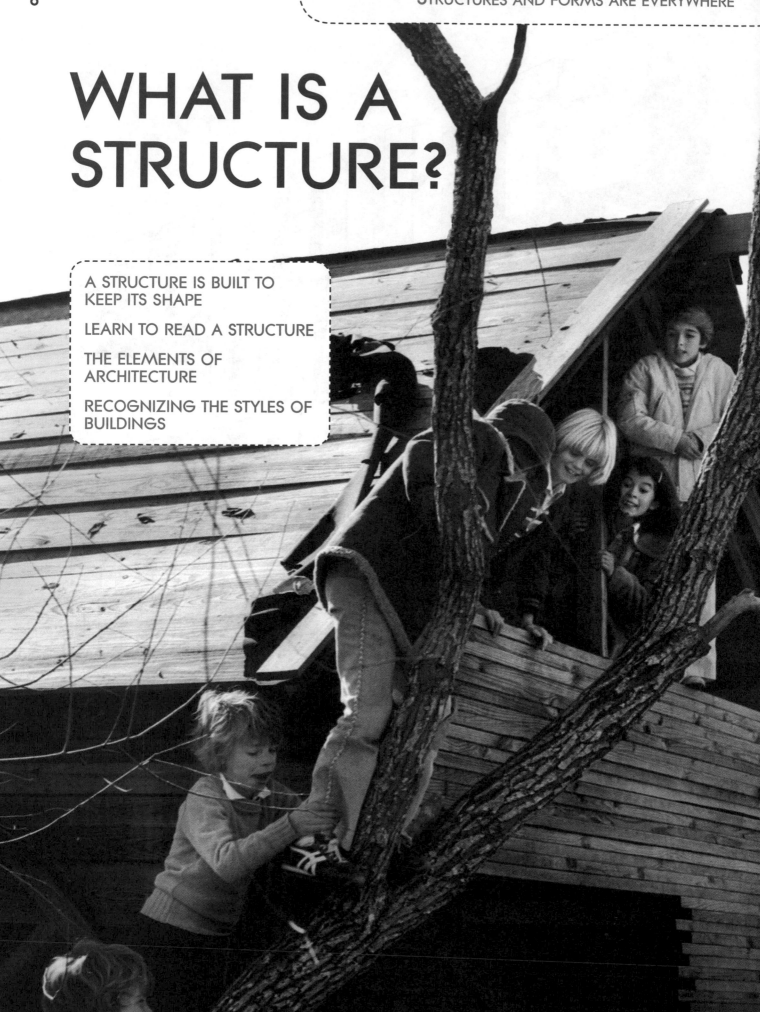

A STRUCTURE IS BUILT TO KEEP ITS SHAPE

Simply stated, a structure is a form that keeps its shape. Ice cream is a pretty good structure when it is cold enough to stay frozen, but it quickly loses its shape outside on a hot day. A single, flat sheet of paper isn't a very good structure because it easily bends and flops, but with a few creases the same sheet of paper becomes a rigid structure.

Structures are everywhere, both natural and human-made. Skeletons are the structure system of all vertebrates, including people, just as posts and beams are the structure system of some buildings. A spider's web is an intricate geometrical construction just as the structure of the space station or a bridge is made up of many connected geometrical units.

The structural components of a building, tower, or bridge are what keep it strong and standing upright. The simple pole frame of a tepee is a structure system that is used to support the outer covering, which is called the structure's skin. When a house, a factory, or a skyscraper is under construction, the structural framework is built first and then covered with a skin of some material to make walls, floors, and a roof. The skin of a building does the job of separating the outside from the inside, but the structure must make sure the building does not collapse, even when there are high winds, heavy snows, or soaking rains.

Some buildings use structure systems that do not need a skin because the structure itself is the skin. These buildings are usually made of bricks or stone blocks. An igloo made from blocks of snow, an adobe house made from mud bricks, and the great pyramids made from carved stones are good examples. And some structures, like most bridges and towers, don't need a skin covering and readily show off their structure system.

Throughout history, builders have experimented with and improved the structure systems they learned from earlier builders and their buildings. How could a greater distance be spanned, how could a structure grow taller without collapsing, or how could a dome be made larger? By trial and error, each builder discovered the limits of the structural systems he or she used. If the building collapsed during construction, it would either be a lesson to the builder about what went wrong and what to change, or a message that the builder had exceeded the potential of the structure system being used.

As structures evolved, they became larger and more complex. A better understanding of physics and science, plus stronger and lighter materials, have led to buildings that

are well over one hundred stories tall, bridges that span many miles, and domes that are wider than two football fields. These newer marvels of structural engineering and architectural design required enormous amounts of figuring out what works and what does not. The trial and error structure method of earlier builders isn't practical for building a skyscraper. Even if someone could afford building and rebuilding until it worked, the process could take forever. That is why many of today's modern structures could not have been built until the invention of the computer. Computers can simulate the building and rebuilding without the time and money it would take to build for real.

What is interesting to note is that most of the materials we use today for building simple or complex structures are the same materials that have always been used by builders. In more modern times, however, the traditional building materials of wood, stone, and bricks are often supplemented with concrete, steel, and plastics. Sometimes a new material allows a new type of structure system to be invented. Inflatable buildings, space-frame domes, and tensegrity tents are all structures that could only be built from modern materials. For example, the evolution of bridges has followed the availability of better materials and the knowledge of how to use them structurally. The earliest log bridges could only span a distance a little shorter than the length of the log. Rope bridges could span longer distances, but if they were too long, they swayed too dangerously. The Romans learned to build brick or stone arch bridges about one hundred feet long. And modern steel cables allow suspension bridges to span almost six thousand feet. That's over one mile!

Everyday Structures You Know

There are many structures you see or use everyday, and some may be more common than you think. Here are just a few.

Have you used any of these structures?

How many of these structures have you played with?

Have you been in or on one of these structures?

Did you know that these are also structures?

Have you seen any of these less common structures?

Understanding Tension and Compression

Tension is the force of pulling

Tension, the force of pulling, and compression, the force of pushing, are the forces that hold up a structure. Each time you tie a knot or tighten your shoelaces, you are applying the force of tension. The two teams in a tug-of-war are applying tension to the rope. If the rope was to break, you would say the rope failed in tension. The same terms can be applied to blowing up a balloon. As you inflate the balloon, the stretched rubber is in tension, but when it bursts, the balloon structure has failed in tension. Some other examples of tension include a kite string, a fishing line, a belt, the stem of an apple, the strings on a guitar, and the handle of a shopping bag.

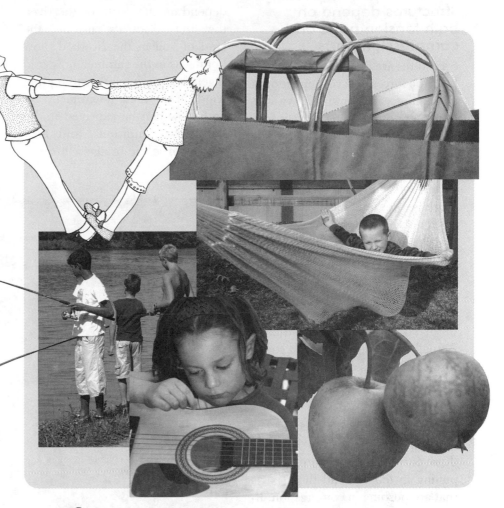

Compression is the force of pushing

In a pile of dishes stacked on a kitchen shelf, each dish is pushing down on the dish below it, and this pushing force is known as compression. In a similar way, your teeth are applying a force of compression when you bite and chew, and your legs are in compression as they hold up your body and push down against the ground. When you use a nutcracker to break open a nut, the nut is at first in compression, but when the shell breaks, the nut has failed in compression. Some other examples of compression include a pencil point while writing, any kind of clamp, the trunk of a tree, and any kind of ladder.

Structures depend on both tension parts and compression parts

Structures are designed and built to bear the forces of a certain amount of pulling and pushing without breaking or collapsing. This is true for all structures whether they be houses, skyscrapers, and towers or spider webs, beaver dams, and bee hives. A structure, like a building or a bridge, not only has to hold itself up, it also has to bear the weight of everything placed inside it or on it, including accumulations of heavy snow and the pushing power of strong winds. In some locations, a structure must also hold up under the shaking of an earthquake. Actually, one definition of a structure could be "something that can hold up under the forces of tension and compression."

The many forces that a structure has to deal with are shared between those parts of the structure that are pulling in tension and those parts that are pushing in compression. In every structure, each part does a special job in dealing with either the forces of tension or the forces of compression. It is the combination of both kinds of parts that gives a structure its ability to resist forces and stay erect. For example, in a simple playground swing set, the ropes of the swing are being pulled and are therefore the parts in tension. The swing set frame that supports the ropes is the part in compression because it is being pushed down against the ground.

When creating the best design for a structure, one of the first things to consider is what forces of tension and compression the structure will have to bear. The engineer who designs a bridge must first calculate the many forces the bridge will be subjected to. Those forces will depend on the depth of the river, the strength of its currents, the kind of soil in the riverbed, how hot it gets in the summer, how cold it gets in the winter, the strength of winds in the area, how much rain and snow can be expected under the worst conditions, and how much traffic the bridge will carry.

Taking into consideration all these forces of tension and compression, the engineer then figures out the best structure system and the best materials that can be used to build a bridge that will resist the strongest possible forces expected.

HOUSE BUILDING LESSONS FOR WINDY LOCATIONS
BY THREE LITTLE PIGS

"Straw, sticks, and bricks! Straw, sticks, and bricks!" the three little pigs chanted as they set off together, each pig looking for materials and a place to build a new home.

At the edge of the forest, they came upon a field of tall grass and straw where the first and youngest little pig stopped and exclaimed, "The two of you can go ahead, I'm going to build my house out of straw right here in this field."

"But straw is not very strong," said the second little pig as he pushed in on the two ends of a piece of straw. "You see, the straw just bends, buckles, and breaks."

"I know that," responded the first little pig, "but I can stack and weave the straw into a house that will be just right for me."

"Suit yourself," said the second little pig as he and the third little pig set off to find the perfect place to build their homes.

The first little pig got busy gathering straw into bundles, which he tied together with long grasses and stacked into walls. To cover the roof, the little pig wove some straw into a large mat, being careful to make the weave extra tight to keep out the rain. The little pig's tail wiggled with delight as he stood back and admired his handsome straw cottage shaped like a box with a door just big enough for the little pig to squeeze through.

I'll be safe, snug, and happy here, he thought, and the little pig stepped inside his new home to take a well-deserved nap. Suddenly a loud voice awoke and startled him.

"Little pig, little pig, let me in, or I'll huff and I'll puff and I'll blow your house down."

The little pig's heart began to thump with fear as he peeked through the little front door to see a hungry wolf taking a long, deep breath.

"N-n-n-no w-w-way you big, bad wolf,"

said the little pig, "I know you just want to catch me."

The wolf growled and started to blow.

The little pig thought he had woven the hay into a strong house, but the first big puff by the wolf blew down the front wall and sent the roof flying high into the air like a kite. The little pig was left standing there, eye to eye with the wolf.

"O-o-o-oh m-m-m-my," cried the scared, little pig as the wolf prepared to blow down the remaining walls. And when the wolf threw back his head to catch another big breath, the first little pig darted off into the woods to find his two brothers.

The little pig ran as fast as he could until he was nearly out of breath, when he came upon the second little pig gathering sticks and small branches.

"There's a big, bad wolf in the forest, and he just blew down my house made of straw," cried the first little pig, telling the whole story.

"The problem with your house," explained the second little pig, "is that you made it like a box with flat walls that catch the wind. Come look at my house made of sticks, and you will see it is round so the wind will easily flow around and over it. With a house like this, we'll be safe from that windbag wolf."

While the second little pig finished building the house frame and the front door by tying sticks together with long blades of grass, the first little pig helped by weaving straw mats to cover the stick frame walls and roof. It took all day to complete the handsome round hut, and when the two little pigs curled up on the floor to sleep that night, they both felt happy and safe.

But early the next morning, the two little pigs were rudely awakened by the fox, who had come across the second pig's house of sticks during his travels.

"Little pigs, little pigs, let me in, or I'll huff and I'll puff and I'll blow your house down."

"O-o-o-oh n-n-n-no, not again," cried the first little pig as his heart started thumping with terror.

"Go get lost, you big, bad wolf," ordered the second little pig with confidence. "This house of sticks is too strong and too round for you to blow down."

The wolf just growled, took a deep breath, and started to blow. His first big puff barely shook the little stick house as the wind slipped around its curved walls and over the round roof.

"The big, bad wolf can't blow our house in," giggled the two little pigs. "The round walls make the wind go spin, spin, spin!"

The wolf stepped a little closer to the stick house, put back his head to catch another breath, and blew. This time the

house shook a lot more and even began to lift off the ground. And on the wolf's third and biggest puff of all, the little hut shook so hard, it flipped over on its side and blew away.

"O-o-o-oh m-m-m-my," cried both the little pigs, and they scurried away to safety while the wolf was left trying to catch his breath.

The scared, little pigs kept running until they came upon the third little pig, who was making mud bricks by a small stream.

"There's a big, bad wolf in the forest," warned the first little pig.

"And he just blew down my house made of sticks," added the second pig.

"The problem with your stick house," explained the third little

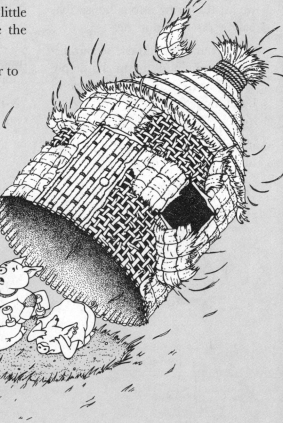

pig after the first two had finished describing what had happened, "is that you did not build it on a firm foundation. If you attached your house firmly to the ground, even a strong wind could not blow it away. Come and look at the house I'm building out of bricks."

The third little pig showed the other two how he made strong bricks in a brick mold by mixing mud with pieces of straw and letting it harden in the sun. The bricks could then be stacked and held together using more mud for mortar.

"That blowhard wolf will never blow down this house," bragged the third little pig, as he proudly showed off the handsome brick house he was building. "My house has a rounded, streamlined shape to deflect the wind, and the bottoms of the brick walls are buried deep in the ground so the house can't topple over."

All three little pigs worked the rest of the day to complete the brick house. The second little pig used sticks to make a framework for the

roof as well as a strong front door and shutters for the windows, while the first little pig collected bundles of straw to make a thatched, rain-proof covering for the roof.

"There may be a big, bad wolf around here," the third pig said, "but he won't be able to blow down my house made of bricks."

Just as the third little pig uttered those words of confidence, he heard a noise in the woods, and all three brothers spun around to see the wolf running toward them.

"O-o-o-oh n-n-n-no!" the first pig screamed, and all three little pigs dashed into the brick house and slammed the door shut.

"We'll be safe in here," said the third and oldest little pig.

What luck, thought the big, bad wolf, all three pigs inside one house. "Let me in, let me

in," he demanded, "so I can join you for din din din."

"We will never let you in," replied all three pigs.

"Then I'll huff and I'll puff and blow these walls in," answered the wolf.

"We dare you," the three said, grinning.

So the wolf took a deep breath and blew with all his might, but the round brick house with a strong foundation didn't budge an inch. Over and over again the wolf tried to blow down the brick house until he was so out of breath he couldn't blow any more.

And over and over again the three little pigs giggled with delight.

"Maybe the wolf will come back sometime," said the first little pig, "We could sure use a breeze on a hot summer night."

LEARN TO READ A STRUCTURE

Before trying to understand the technology of various types of structures, it is best to first learn just by looking at different structure systems—especially if the structures are in the process of being built. Many people feel almost compelled to look at construction in progress, from the hole being dug for the foundation to the framework being erected to the finish details. By observing a construction in progress, it is easy to see what materials are being used and how they connect to form a strong and rigid structure.

Some completed buildings and structures readily show their type of construction, especially those made of stone, brick, or uncovered steel.

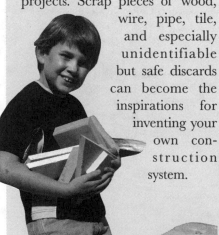
If you removed the outer skin shingles or siding from most other buildings, you would be able to see the structure system that holds the building up.

When you see a house or building under construction, notice that all the beams and braces are placed at very specific positions and angles that create a strong and rigid structure. Some structure systems have patterns that can easily be seen on bridges and tall towers. As you observe constructions, you'll notice that most architectural structure is geometric. The repeated triangle or curves of these structures have not been created just for style, they are the result of what builders and engineers have learned over time in creating very strong structures using only the minimum amount of material.

By knowing the basic concepts of structure such as tension, compression, shear, stress, and load, you will be able to read a structure and understand what work each part is doing, why it was built that way, and why many buildings look the way they do. But the structure system is not only making itself evident, it is also sending other messages to the observer. Some structures convey feelings of being strong or lightweight, balanced or unbalanced, economical or wasteful, elegant or confusing, beautiful or ugly. And so, in addition to reading the structure system, also try to appreciate the structure's design and creativity.

To be a good observer of structure, be curious. When you cross a bridge, ride by a tower, or see a big crane, notice how it is built and try to figure out why it is built that way. Do the same thing at a building site. Here are just a few of

the many questions you might ask yourself when reading a building under construction.

- What materials are used to build the framework, how are they connected, and what geometric patterns do they make?

- What material is used to make walls, and do the walls carry the weight of the roof and upper floors or just fill in the spaces between parts of a load-carrying framework?

- What patterns can be found in walls made of bricks, blocks, or stone?

- What is the structure and shape of the roof, and is it designed to shed the rain, carry heavy loads of snow, or maybe provide some shade?

- How many different types of fasteners are being used in the structure?

Be a Sidewalk Superintendent

A good way to see structure systems in action is to watch a construction project going up. Observers standing around a construction site are often called "sidewalk superintendents," an expression that began in New York City when skyscrapers were first being built. Because curious bystanders had a tendency to get dangerously close to the work in progress, the workers would build a wooden wall as a fence around the site to keep people back. However, these walls often had several round peepholes so anyone curious could still watch. When New York's Rockefeller Center was under construction, peephole onlookers were given wallet cards stating that the holder was a member in good standing of the Sidewalk Super-intendents' Club, along with the club motto, "The best pilots stand on the shore."

Is there is a new structure being built in your neighborhood, maybe a new house or addition, an office building or factory, a bridge, or a tower? See if you can figure out what structure systems are being used. Can you find posts and beams, triangles, or buttresses? What kind of materials and fasten-ers are being used? Where will the stairs be, or are there shafts for ele-vators? And if the structure has a roof, what type will it be?

If you hang around a con-struction site, you can learn a lot about struc-tures not only by observ-ing but by talking with the construction workers— and they usually love to show kids what they do and the ways they do it. But do be careful. Some construction sites can be dangerous, with large and noisy equipment moving around the site and poten-tially hazardous materials every-where. Maybe you can get a guided hard-hat tour from one of the con-struction workers, but otherwise stand back on the sidewalk, safely

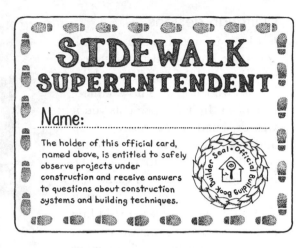

away from the construction, and just observe. Even without some-one to answer questions, there is a lot you can probably figure out on your own by using your intuition.

THE ELEMENTS OF ARCHITECTURE

Architecture Is Form, Function, Materials, and Style

Every day you can see works of architecture in the houses and buildings all around you. Before any one of these structures was built, someone had to first figure out what purpose the building would serve, where it would be best located, what form the build-ing should take, what materials would work best, and a whole lot of other things. In other words, a building needs to be designed before it can be built.

The landscape and local climate will partially determine how a building will look and feel, and so will the local building materials and construction techniques. Even the values of a society are usually reflected in their local building

style. But someone needs to com-bine all that information into a building that serves its intended use and is strong enough to withstand the forces imposed by humans and nature. Another objective for many people is a building design that is pleasing to look at. Someone also needs to design the rooms and fig-ure out where to put the doors and windows that will provide access and views as well as protection and privacy. The skillful result of that effort to design a strong, function-al, and pleasing building is called architecture, and the designer who did it is an architect.

The architect's design will often use a clever combination of

personal preferences and local building styles to provide the visual and emotional elements. For example, the architect knows that symmetry gives buildings a formal feeling and grandness, while an asymmetrical combination of ele-ments projects a comfortable, informal feeling. The architect knows that a tall structure can impose a feeling of strength and security (though not necessarily a welcoming look), while some hous-es made low and horizontal in a modern style can provide a feeling of open-ness and lightness.

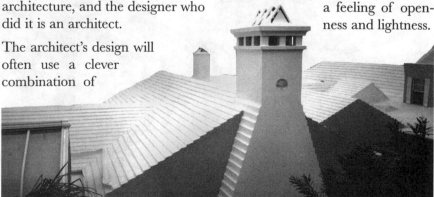

Utilitarian designs

Just looking at architecture will tell you something about the architect who designed the building and the people who use it. The architecture of an Indian tepee tells you it was designed to be easily set up and taken down, as well as transported from place to place. The heavy fortress walls of a castle and its tiny windows provide protection and give a massive, forbidding appearance to discourage an enemy. And the architecture of a factory usually emphasizes efficient and economical construction systems.

Emotional designs

But not all buildings are designed to provide just a utilitarian function. Architecture also fulfills the emotional needs of the user and the viewer. The pyramids were human-made versions of mountains that visually connected the earth and sky and gave Egyptians a sense of control in a world they found threatening. Greek and Roman temples used geometric forms to create pleasing patterns of grace and harmony. The Romans also created new, visually exciting architectural elements like arches, vaults, and domes. And churches of almost any era use large windows for grace, while pointed spires, arches, and roofs seem to connect the earth with the heavens.

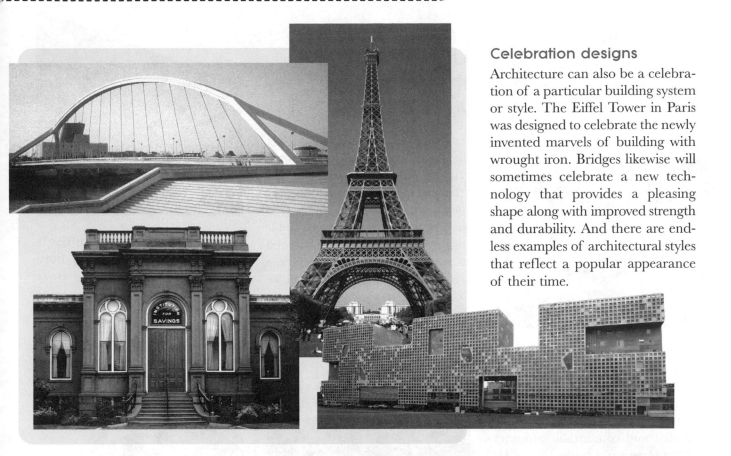

Celebration designs

Architecture can also be a celebration of a particular building system or style. The Eiffel Tower in Paris was designed to celebrate the newly invented marvels of building with wrought iron. Bridges likewise will sometimes celebrate a new technology that provides a pleasing shape along with improved strength and durability. And there are endless examples of architectural styles that reflect a popular appearance of their time.

House designs

Every type of building can be designed in one of many forms and styles. Just look at all the different designs for houses. All houses will have some things in common to meet the practical living requirements of a personal, private, and secure space. The simplest house is made up of walls, a roof, and a door. Next comes windows and maybe a chimney to vent an inside fire. Add a porch or a deck to extend the house outside. Dormer windows that project like eyebrows from a sloping roof can add light and space to an attic, and specialized outbuildings that complement the architecture of the main building can provide spaces for a garage, an artist's studio, a gardening shed, a barn, or maybe a guesthouse.

Depending on the design and the materials selected for construction, the architect might capture the look of a traditional building style or maybe project the image of a new style based on a new technology.

Architects frequently invent new ways to use materials and create new forms that reflect new attitudes, while some architects use contemporary materials and forms to capture the familiar and comfortable attitudes of the classic and traditional styles from the past. For example, a modern home does not need a fireplace, yet a large masonry hearth and chimney still remind people of warmth and comfort.

Over time, the basic elements of architecture (like a wall, roof, beam, or dome) have stayed the same, but as new materials become available, new and different styles are created. Proportions may change, conveniences may be added, new shapes may be created, or one big roof may be replaced with several smaller ones. But regardless of the architectural style, a building designed with pleasing proportions and balance, and constructed with an intelligent choice of materials, is pleasant to look at and just feels right. A beautiful house, a magnificent skyscraper, and a fascinating bridge are all structures that evoke feelings of pleasure and sometimes even passion. Architecture is often the ingredient that made them that way.

Understanding the Terms of Architecture

Architecture is like a language. Just as you use letters to make words and combine words to make a sentence, architecture uses materials to make structural components, and the components to create buildings. When selected and combined in some well-planned way, these basic components of architecture become a structure that clearly communicates the purpose and feeling for which it was designed.

Arch

A self–supporting, curved structure made of wedge-shaped blocks that span an opening. The wedge-shaped keystone block at the top of the arch is the last one to be inserted, locking the arch structure into place. Arches can be semicircular or pointed.

Beam

A horizontal structural section that spans the distance between two supports. Beams are usually made from wood, steel, or reinforced concrete, and typically support floors. A beam specifically meant to support a floor is called a joist. A supporting beam made of iron or steel is called a girder.

Buttress

A support structure, usually made of masonry, that is built up against the side of a wall to give it addi-

tional strength. A flying buttress is narrower and projects away from the wall as if supporting it at arm's length. The flying buttress was developed so windows in medieval cathedrals could be larger to permit more light.

Cantilever

A horizontal structural section (like a beam) that is firmly secured at one end and completely unsupported at the other. A good example is a swimming pool diving board.

Ceiling

The part of a building attached to the underside of a floor or roof that creates the upper surface of a room. The ceiling space in a home often contains only light fixtures, but in a commercial building, the ceiling may contain a maze of wires, pipes, and ducts.

Column/Post

Columns hold up building sections and can be made of any material. A line of columns used to hold up beams or arches forms an open-walled colonnade. Columns give buildings like banks, libraries, and museums the appearance of being orderly, solid, and important. A column that tapers toward the top gives the appearance of being taller.

Cornice

On the exterior of a building, the cornice is an ornamented horizontal band between the top of a wall and the roof. On the interior, the cornice is any molding at the top of a wall, usually between the wall and the ceiling.

Dome

A hemispherical-shaped roof that may be made from a variety of structure systems including blocks, space frames, reinforced concrete, or inflatables.

Dormer

A window for a room within the roof space that is built out at right angles to the main roof and has its own gable.

Eave

The underside of a roof where it overhangs the building's walls. Eaves provide shade and sometimes a shelter from rain.

Entry/Door

The shape and size of a door opening conforms to function, while the door design can imply a welcome or no trespassing.

Facade

The front side of a building, which usually contains the front door. This is the building's face and often best shows the building's personality.

Foundation

A flat platform or a walled perimeter used to firmly secure a structure to the earth and to carry and spread its weight over a larger area.

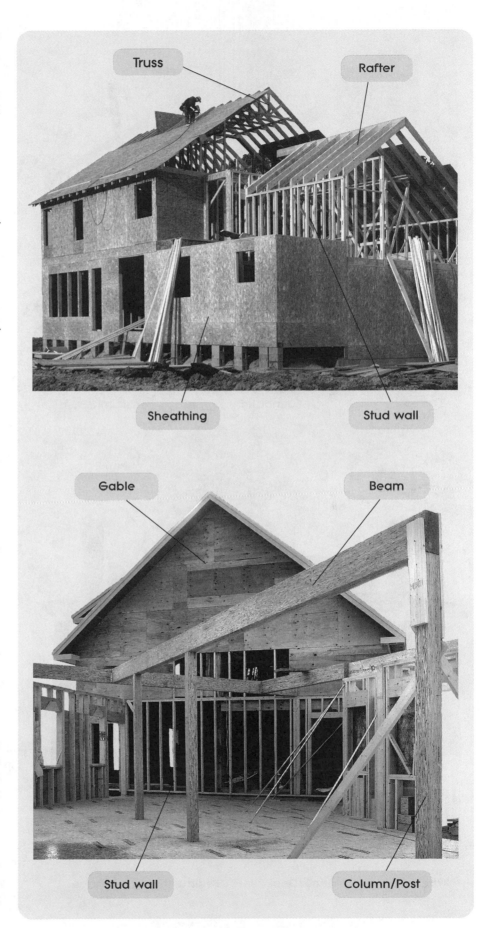

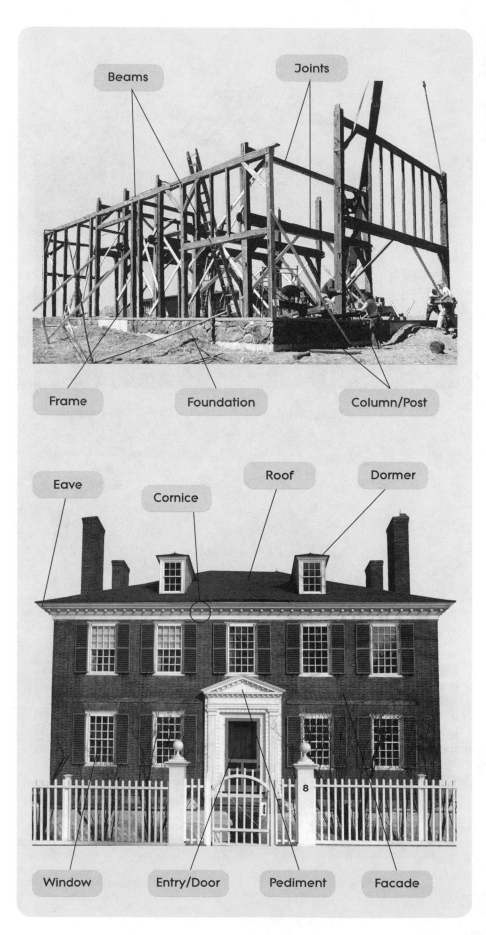

Foundations are usually beneath the ground and made of stone, bricks, blocks, or poured concrete.

Frame

The skeletal framework of a structure that is sometimes covered with an outer skin and sometimes left bare. Most houses and buildings reveal their frames in the early stages of construction before the outer walls are attached to the framework. Some structures reveal their uncovered framework on the inside (like in the attic or basement of a house) and some structures, like bridges and towers, usually keep their framework completely uncovered.

Gable

The triangular end portion of a pitched roof. A simple pitched roof would have a gable at either end. More complex roofs can have many gables as in the famous House of Seven Gables in Salem, Massachusetts.

Joint

The connection between two or more structural members. Depending on the materials to be fastened, the joint can be welded, bolted, nailed, or glued together, or designed in such a way that the structural members themselves interlock without additional fasteners.

Lintel

A horizontal beam that is placed across two upright posts to make a post and lintel (or post and beam) system of construction. Lintels are usually placed across the top of window and door openings.

Pediment

A broad triangular gable often supported by columns as part of a building's facade.

Rafter

The structural members (usually placed at an inclined angle) used to support a roof.

Roof

A covering over the structure to keep out rain, wind, snow, or sun. A roof can also provide shade to the building walls. The shape of a roof sometimes signifies its function or the building's importance, such as a state capitol's dome or a church steeple's spire.

Sheathing

The boards, plywood, or other material used to cover and enclose the outside of a building's framework.

Truss

A rigid framework of triangular structures made of beams and braces. A truss can be used to support a roof or to build a bridge spanning wide distances.

Walls/Stud wall

The portions of the structure with openings for windows and doors. Walls are built on the foundation and usually hold up the roof. Stud walls are constructed using evenly spaced vertical posts usually made from lumber.

Window

These are the eyes of a building for looking out and looking in, as well as the openings for letting in air and light. Windows can have many shapes for various functions and feelings and often give a building its character.

Understanding Steel Beams

How is your structural intuition?

When a skyscraper or other large building is under construction, its overall shape is first revealed by a structural framework of steel beams and columns. All these steel pieces are made in a factory, shipped to the building site, and assembled together with joint connectors made of steel angles and plates that are bolted, riveted, or welded in place.

Take a closer look and you will notice that the steel beams and columns come in several different shapes. If you were to cut through each type to see its cross section, these structural members would have shapes that resembled the letters "I," "L," "H," "C" (or "U"), and "T." You might also find round, rectangular, and square shapes. Each one of these shapes has structural properties that work best when it is oriented in a certain direction. Unless you know something about structural engineering, it may be difficult to figure out whether a C-shaped beam (also called a C-shape channel) should be placed with the opening in the C facing up, down, or to the side to make it stronger. If you were using a C-shape channel to make a bridge across two river banks, which way would you place it to support the most weight? Here's a hint. Your intuition is probably wrong!

You are right if you answered the opening in the C-shape channel should be oriented to face sideways—not up or down. You can prove this to yourself by making a C-shape channel out of paper and testing its strength with a bunch of large paper clips.

If you've already learned something about the forces of tension and compression in a beam, you can probably figure out why one orientation is stronger than another. If you use a structural shape as a vertical column, then orientation doesn't matter and you only need to be concerned with which shape is strongest in compression. Can you predict what orientation is strongest for other beam shapes? Here's a clue. Think of an "I" shape or an "H" shape as being two "C" channels connected back to back.

MAKING AND TESTING STRUCTURAL BEAM SHAPES

To make and test paper beams, you will need a few sheets of notebook or copier/printer paper, a pair of scissors, and about fifteen large-size paper clips.

Start with an 8 ½ x 11 inch sheet of paper, and fold the long edge over about one-half inch. Crease the folded edge by rubbing it with your finger.

Fold the same end over again another half inch and crease the fold, then fold it over one more time and crease. Unfold the paper and cut along the length of the last crease, the crease closest to the middle of the paper. Now you should have a paper strip with two creases that can easily be folded into a C-shaped channel with the same dimensions on all three sides.

To test its strength, support each end of the paper beam with a stack of books, or place it between two chair backs. To make a hook to hang the test weights on, refold a large paper clip to form a triangle that can be slipped over the middle of the paper beam. One at a time,

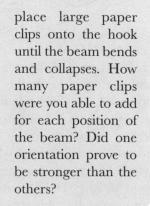

place large paper clips onto the hook until the beam bends and collapses. How many paper clips were you able to add for each position of the beam? Did one orientation prove to be stronger than the others?

The following are some of the most common structural shapes for beams.

W-beam

The "W" stands for wide flange, even though this shape looks much more like an "H."

S-beam

This letter designation may seem strange because the common name for this shape is an I-beam.

C-channel

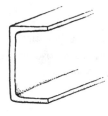

The two flanges of this shape can be wider, narrower, or the same width as the middle section.

L-angle

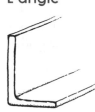

The two flanges, or the legs, of an angle can be the same or different widths.

WT-beam

Take a W-beam and cut off the bottom flanges to get a T shape.

TS-structural tubing

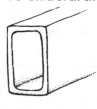

Beams that are box shaped come in several square and rectangular shapes.

The Jobs of Building

For big construction projects, it usually takes a team of many people, each with certain specific skills, to go from an idea to the completed structure. Most of these projects require an architect to come up with a design, an engineer to figure out how to build it, and a contractor to gather the right materials, hire the tradespeople needed, and do the construction. And there can be several other trades and professions involved in the design and building of all types of structures from sculptures to consumer products. If you could learn to do any of these jobs, which one do you think you would find most appealing?

Architect

An architect designs and oversees the construction of buildings and other types of structures in a way that achieves many different objectives. The architect creates a design that meets the functional and spatial requirements of the structure and is also a pleasing aesthetic design that complements the surrounding area. At the same time, the architect must follow building codes, zoning laws, fire regulations, and environmental laws that may limit what can be done. The many tasks and responsibilities of an architect include consulting with clients to determine their needs and likes, creating designs and building scale models, preparing scale drawings of the structure plus specifications for materials and construction methods to be used by the builders, and conducting inspections of the project during various stages of construction to be sure everything is being done as planned.

A drafter sometimes prepares the detailed drawings of architectural designs according to the specifications, sketches, and models provided by the architect. A landscape architect specializes in the design of land spaces like parks, gardens, recreational areas, playgrounds, backyards, front yards, and the areas around all types of buildings. In creating a pleasing design, the landscape architect must also address several functional concerns, including the proper drainage of rainwater, the use of plantings or structures as sound or visual barriers, and the type of plantings that are best suited for the climate and the terrain.

Engineer

Engineers use science and mathematics to develop practical solutions for all kinds of technical problems. Some engineers design the components used to build structures, some engineers design the machines to manufacture the components, and some engineers design the actual

structures. A civil engineer is concerned with the planning, design, and construction of buildings, bridges, highways, harbors, dams, tunnels, and many other types of structures that are a vital part of modern civilization. A structural engineer is responsible for the strength of the structure design so it can withstand all the types of loads it may encounter including wind and snow.

Contractor and subcontractors

The responsibility of the contractor is to build the structure and perform all specified construction work in accordance with the architect's plans as well as in accordance

with any codes, laws, or other restrictions. The contractor first estimates the cost of the materials and labor it will take to build the structure, then purchases the materials and hires various tradespeople or subcontractors to work on the project as they are needed.

When building a house, for example, a land surveyor might be brought in to measure distances, directions, and angles between points of land to determine property boundaries, exactly where the structure will be placed, and its elevation and orientation. Carpenters then cut, fit, and assemble wood and other materials to build floors, walls, ceilings, windows, doors, or whatever else is called for in the building plans. An electrician installs the outlets, lighting, and anything else electrical; a plumber installs the water lines and fixtures as well as heating and air conditioning systems; and a painter applies various finishes to the construction materials to both protect them from decay and provide color and texture. Depending on the type of house and the surrounding landscape, other subcontractors might include a bricklayer or a stonemason to build walls, fireplaces and chimneys, walkways, and stone walls. On bigger construction projects, ironworkers fabricate, assemble, and install structural metal parts like the steel framework of buildings, bridges, towers, and anything else made of metal including decorative railings and stairways.

Interior designer

An interior designer creates a plan for the interior layout of spaces in homes, office buildings, factories,

and retail stores. By designing or selecting the appropriate furnishings and other contents, then organizing them in an appropriate relationship, the interior designer creates spaces that are practically suited for their intended use and aesthetically pleasing. Interior designers need to know a lot about the way people interact with different types of spaces so the environment they create best supports the intended activities, like having plush, comfortable seating in a family living room while using easy-to-clean plastic seating in a fast-food restaurant. An interior decorator is not a designer but rather someone who is primarily concerned with appearance and creating a style or look for an interior space.

Industrial designer

The profession of industrial design, like architecture, is also concerned with aesthetic appearance, proper function, and structural integrity, but mostly for the design of manufactured products rather than constructed buildings or other large structures. Industrial designers are involved in the design of nearly every type of product imaginable from bird feeders to furniture to bicycles. Because of the many dif-

ferent types of things that can be designed, an industrial designer must often create like an artist, think like a structural engineer, and know all about various materials and manufacturing processes.

RECOGNIZING THE STYLES OF BUILDINGS

Clearly, not all houses look the same, even though they are all meant to provide sheltered spaces for living. Buildings, bridges, and other human-made structures also come in more than one design. Since prehistoric times, people have constructed buildings to suit their particular needs using the materials available and the structural techniques necessary to keep them standing. However, various peoples at various times and locations in history have built their structures in styles that also met their particular preferences for appearance.

Throughout history, there have been periods of design when certain styles were popular, only to replaced with different styles later. Most houses, buildings, bridges, and other structures provide visual clues about when they were designed and built. By just looking at the houses and other buildings where you live, you can probably tell which ones look old-fashioned or modern, or maybe even weird.

Over the centuries and decades, many building styles began to look more and more elaborate and highly decorated, which was often purposely done so the structures would appear to be less massive. As new building materials and construction techniques became available, designers and architects needed less decoration to disguise the function or size of the buildings, and many long-favored styles abruptly changed as buildings were built in a simpler and less ornate style.

In the more modern styles of building, the basic structure itself can provide a pleasing visual appearance. Using modern structural materials, buildings could now have steel skeletons to hold them up with walls made of glass panels. Architects could design free-form sculptural shapes made of concrete and roofs made from inflated balloon-like fabrics. Even

today, as new materials become available and as new discoveries are made in using them, architects, designers, and builders will continue to create new styles of buildings that are meant to please people's tastes. And some new materials and techniques will permit designs and styles that were not possible before.

Most of the houses, buildings, and other structures you see today were probably built in the last few hundred years, yet their appearances represent a wide range of popular styles. If you know what clues to look for, you can probably identify the style of the structure. But don't

be discouraged if you can't figure out the exact style of a particular building. For each style of building, there are many variations, and many buildings were built using a combination of styles. So it is not unusual to find a colonial-style house with Roman columns holding up the porch roof, or an international-style building with an Art Deco facade.

Here are some of the most popular building styles in America from past to present that you might see today.

Art Deco

A decorative style that was popular in the 1930s and is characterized by angular, geometric, and zigzag surface designs, as well as floral patterns. Art Deco skyscrapers often rise in steps and are topped with a tower.

International

This American and European "glass box" style can be seen in many skyscrapers and uses steel and concrete for the skeletal structure and glass for the outer covering. There is usually no decoration and no indication of any regional style. When applied to contemporary homes, the style incorporates a flat roof, a large expanse of windows, cantilevered balconies, and an asymmetrically balanced composition.

New England Colonial

The colonial style is a general term that refers to any style that was brought to America by the early settlers. This New England colonial has a simple box-like appearance with small windows and a prominent chimney. Sometimes the upper floor extended beyond the lower floor to create a slight overhang.

Southern Colonial

Usually a narrow house only one room deep with a steeply pitched roof. Massive chimneys on the gable ends and sometimes classical design elements help identify this style.

Dutch Colonial

A steeply pitched gambrel roof with deep overhangs flared beyond the front and rear of the house is the most identifying element of this style.

Georgian

The Georgian style is best characterized by a formal arrangement of the facade, often including a projecting pediment entry with columns and other classical elements. Windows can have many individual panes of glass in each sash.

Federal

Very popular in New England, this classical revival style is similar to Georgian but with less ornamentation. The entry may include an elliptical fan window above the door and narrow windows flanking the door. The Federal style often has a third story with short windows and a low-pitched roof.

Classical and Classical Revival

As the basis for many future styles, classical buildings originated in ancient Rome and Greece and are designed using a set of elements that combine to create pleasing shapes and proportions. Classical revival is a more modern version of classical style but still uses the same set of elements to create well-proportioned buildings.

Gingerbread

This highly ornamental and colorful style, closely resembling Victorian architecture, began in the nineteenth century and is still popular for homes in certain parts of the United States.

Gothic Revival

The Gothic style originated in Europe in the Middle Ages and was originally used for large cathedrals. The Gothic revival style adopts some design elements of the period, which can include pointed arches, rib vaulting, tall spires, exterior flying buttresses, extensive stained glass windows, and sometimes gargoyles projecting from the walls or roof. The most identifying characteristics of a modern example are steeply pitched roofs and dormers with gingerbread trim along the eaves, bay windows, and sometimes stucco walls.

Victorian

This decorated style became quite popular in the United States during the transition period from candle-lights to electric lights, from horse-drawn carriages to cars, from outhouses to indoor plumbing, and from fireplaces for heat to central heating furnaces. These houses were often as innovative in style as the inventions they had to accommodate. Many variations of the Victorian style ranged from the French chateau look with corner towers to the stick style with ornate decorations and several colors.

Italianate

This Italian villa style is characterized by low pitched but heavily supported roofs, asymmetrical and informal plans, square towers, and sometimes round arch windows.

Shingle

An American style popular in homes and hotels built between 1880 and 1900, it is characterized by the use of unpainted wood shingles for both the siding and the roof.

Brutalism

A modern style that almost always involves exposed, rough concrete, which is poured and left with little finishing. The structures are often large and chunky with elements that butt into one another.

Organic

Sculptural shapes and forms that harmonize with nature characterize this modern style and philosophy of design that began in the twentieth century and is still popular today.

Sculptural

Closely related to the organic style, sculptural designs use modern forms and shapes to create a pleasing composition.

Modernism

Similar to the international style but incorporating a much broader range of design elements, modernism is often a composition of clean rectangular forms organized to create balance and harmony. Ornamentation is minimal or totally absent.

Mechanical

In this "inside-out" style of architecture, all parts of the structure and its supporting mechanical systems are exposed as elements of the design.

ALL ABOUT

POMPIDOU CENTER

Pompidou Center
Paris, France
Designed by Renzo Piano and
Richard Rodgers, 1975

In a competition to design a new cultural center for French art, design, and music, the architects Renzo Piano and Richard Rodgers won with a plan that kept each floor as wide open as possible for museum exhibits and events. The architects of the Pompidou Center were so insistent on keeping each floor unencumbered by the building's infrastructure that they moved literally everything to the outside of the glass-walled building, including the space frame structural skeleton, the walkways, escalators, and elevators, the stairs, the air ducts, and even the bathrooms and plumbing.

There is no formal entrance to the building, and each side of the structure has its own unique style

and character. On one side, each element is color coded according to its function, so the elevators are painted red, the pipes and tubes for air conditioning ducts are blue, cold-water pipes are green, and electrical systems are yellow. On another side, the escalators are enclosed in transparent tubes that zigzag up all six floors. And even the roof is covered with large pods and ducts that contain systems for operating the building.

The building was not widely admired when it was first built, and many critics claimed it looked like an oil refinery. They were right, because it turns out that oil refineries were one of the inspirations the architects used for the design! However, others saw the colorful structure as a work of art. Because of its unusual appearance, the Pompidou Center has become one of the most popular attractions in Paris with up to twenty thousand visitors touring the building each day.

Types of Roofs
(and What They Do)

A roof provides the most basic type of shelter for protecting people and many other things from nature's elements. In some warm climates, a roof is all that is needed to provide protection from rain and sun.

In addition to providing protection, the roof on a home, building, or factory also has other work to do, depending on the local climate and the building's use. A specific type of roof may be required to hold up a heavy load of snow without collapsing, shed water quickly from thundershowers, collect water for drinking, support itself without interior columns, permit a high interior space, or maybe provide shade to outdoor areas. Each type of roof has features that are better for some purposes and possibly not suited for other conditions. Here is a photo guide to help identify many different types of roofs and understand the special features of each design.

Barrel or arch

- Carries heavy snow loads and resists wind forces
- Allows open interior space

Bermuda

- Ridges slow and direct rain to downspout and water storage tank
- White keeps roof and interior cool

Butterfly

- Allows taller windows
- Provides higher interior spaces

Clerestory monitor

- Allows additional windows and provides interior light
- Permits higher interior space or a second story

Folded plate

- Provides great strength to support loads
- Uses most material for the area covered

Hemispherical dome

- Resists wind forces
- Handsome shape but difficult to build

Geodesic dome

- Provides open and tall interior space
- Uses the least material to enclose a space

Polyhedral dome

- Often covering octagonal buildings

Onion dome

- Popular design for Russian buildings
- Handsome shape but difficult to build

Flat

- Uses least amount of material
- Is easy to build

Gable

- Strong triangular design
- Good runoff of rain and snow

Flying gable

- All the features of a gable roof
- Provides shade to end walls

Gambrel

- Variation of gable with steeper slope for runoff
- Allows higher interior space than a gable

Hip

- Designed for rain and snow runoff on all four sides
- Low, overhanging eaves provide shade on all four sides

Mansard

- A combination of gable and flat roof features
- Maximizes use of interior space

Pyramid

- Rain and snow run off in all directions
- Allows very high interior space

Shed

- Rain and snow run off in one direction
- Allows higher interior space on one side

Tent

- Allows quick or temporary shelter construction
- Covering can reject heat yet permit light from sunshine

The Typical American Stick-Built House

There is no one particular style or look for the typical American house, and just about any architectural style we may think of as being a typical American design probably had its origins in some other country. People from many countries immigrated to America, and with them came different lifestyles and different ways of building homes.

However, the problem facing many immigrants was that their new location in America was not the same as the one they left. Not only did a change in climate call for a different kind of structure that provided winter warmth or summer cooling, but the building materials commonly available in America were often much different than what the immigrant builders were used to.

By far, the most commonly available building material was lumber cut from America's great forests. At first, whole logs were used to construct simple post-and-beam house structures, which were later made with logs cut into building lumber. The standardization of

building materials into regular lumber sizes plus simple building techniques and tools for assembling the materials led to a new American way of building a wood-frame, or stick-built, house.

A complete house can be precut and partially assembled in a factory.

The American stick-built, wood-frame house can be constructed in any style or design, have one, two, three, or more stories, have any type of roof, doors, and windows, and sometimes even be covered with bricks or stone to look as if it had been built using some other material.

What is common to all these styles is the way the house frame is built with vertical posts holding up beams that support the floors and roof. Most often the house frame is constructed from materials that are cut and fitted at the building site, and sometimes all parts of the frame structure are precut and assembled in a factory and brought to the building site.

Here are several examples of American stick-built houses that can be found at various locations throughout the United States.

A-Frame

With a steep sloping gable roof that reaches to the ground, an A-frame structure is simple to build, but does not provide much usable floor space for the footprint it occupies. The entry and all windows are only on the gable ends.

Bungalow

An easy to recognize house style that uses wood, brick, or stucco walls, a gabled or hip roof (with the front entry on the gable end), large windows and sometimes dormer windows, an outside chimney, and a front porch with the entry covered by the roof

Colonial

Colonial is a general term that refers to any house design that was brought to America by the early settlers. Common examples include the New England colonial and Dutch colonial.

Contemporary

A "modern" looking house of a present or recent design trend that is often a pleasing or interesting composition of forms and shapes

Double decker

Two houses, frequently almost identical, stacked one on top the other. Triple deckers are also popular in some regions.

Ranch

A single-story and single-level house that may be built on a concrete slab or have a basement. Most ranches are varieties of a simple low-pitch gable roof design, although styles can range from log cabin to concrete contemporary.

Row house

One of several identical houses attached side by side in a row

Salt box

By extending the rear roof slope, the "salt box" shape increases the footprint of the house to provide additional interior space.

Semidetached

Two homes, the mirror image of each other, attached side by side with a common wall in the middle

Townhouse

Several houses attached side by side in a row, but the design or style of each house is different

Timber Frame Barns

The first barns were built in Europe as places to store crops of barley. In fact, the word *barn* means "a place for barley" in Old English. The idea of using barns to store crops came to America with the early settlers, but later generations of American farmers began also using the barn as a place to house cattle, protect farm equipment, and hold meetings, dances, and parties. Farm families value a strong, sturdy barn, and the design and construction of a barn often reflects the farmer's simple and honest values. It was (and still is) not uncommon for a farmer to put more care into building his barn than his house.

Almost all barns are rectangular with a simple gable or gambrel roof, but some are square, octagonal, or even round with other types of roofs. The earliest barns in America were box-shaped buildings made of stacked logs notched at the ends to overlap at the corners (similar to building with Lincoln Logs), and the gaps between the logs were left open for good air circulation. There are also early American barns built from stone or brick, though they are fairly rare because of the great expense and skill required to build them.

As better barn-building techniques were developed, the strongest and longest-lasting barns were made using a carefully fitted framework of timbers joined together with tapered wooden pegs tightly driven into drilled holes. The heavy hardwood posts and beams were attached at right angles with diagonal timbers notched into the intersecting corners to create a stable and self-supporting framework with great durability and flexibility. A good timber frame barn can withstand the twisting and bending forces of wind and snowstorms and resist the constant expanding and contracting of the wood through cycles of the seasons and heat of the sun. In fact, creaking noises in a barn are a good sign that the wood-pegged joints are tight, yet flexible to allow some shifting.

This post-and-beam or timber frame method of construction is much stronger and longer lasting than regular stud framing with 2 x 4 lumber. A stud-framed building (like most houses) gets its strength only after the outer or inner wall sheathing has been attached. In contrast, a barn's siding and roofing are only needed to enclose the space within the frame.

It usually took several years to build a timber frame barn. To make the timbers, the farmer first had to find trees that were just the right type and size. Then he waited until the cold winter months to cut them down, when they had less sap and better resistance to shrinkage and warping. Next, the round logs were cut into square beams and set aside for at least a year to dry out and season. In the spring, one year later, construction of the timber framework could begin.

A timber frame barn is built using a series of fabricated timber frames all lined up in a row to form the barn's framework and shape. The well-seasoned timbers are first cut to the various lengths and shapes needed to build the barn frames. Each frame, called a bent, is then fabricated and assembled flat on the ground somewhere near the proposed building site. The frames will later be moved into position and hoisted up from flat to vertical. The typical barn consists of four or five bents and would be called a four-bent or a five-bent barn.

Building the bents and finishing the timber framing required several hand tools to saw and chisel joints, drill holes, and cut slots so that each piece would tightly fit together like a puzzle. A mortise-and-tenon joint was the basic joint used in timber frame construction and provided a tight fit for a sturdy frame. Therefore, the mating parts of each joint had to be carefully carved to perfectly match. And since no two joints were exactly alike, the pieces of each joint were marked where they matched up with other pieces. That was necessary because the bents were frequently built and then disassembled into pieces until the barn itself was ready to be raised.

Using a heavy wooden mallet called a beetle, each timber was hammered into position. A hole was drilled through the assembled tenon in the mortise slot, and a wooden peg driven into the hole to tightly secure the joint. Wooden pegs make stronger joints than nails do, and they are longer lasting because nails and screws can rust. Wood pegs also expand and contract the same amount as the wood beams into which they are inserted, so the joint won't loosen over time.

While the timber was being seasoned and the bents for the barn were being prefabricated, a stone dry-wall foundation (with no mortar) was built around the perimeter of the footprint where the barn

was to be located. Depending on how the barn was to be used, the floor could be either plain earth or covered with boards that were carefully fitted and placed directly over the leveled earth.

When the foundation, the bents, and all the other pieces of the framework were ready, it was time to schedule the barn raising—a day when the farmer's friends and neighbors gathered to assemble the timber frame structure of the barn and then celebrate the achievement with a party. Each bent, one at a time, was moved into position

on the foundation and pushed up to a vertical position, using ropes, pulleys, and long poles with metal-spike tips. When the framework was all pieced together, the party began and lasted until sunset, when it was tradition for everyone to watch the sun setting through the framing of the new building.

Throughout the summer months, the farmer had time to complete the barn by putting on the roof and siding. The watertight roof was

constructed of rather conventional overlapping wood shingles. Loosely spaced vertical plank boards were preferred for siding because they didn't collect water and rot like the edges on horizontal boards. The last step for many barns was a traditional coat of red paint.

As farms grew, more buildings and barns were also needed. In New England, the barn was often connected directly to the farmhouse, so new barns and utility buildings were simply added on in a straight row or in an "L" plan. There might be a storage room attached to a main barn, then a shed for the farm wagons, a chicken coop, a small barn for more livestock, a pig sty, and a horse stable with a hay loft. By connecting all the barns together, the farmer could tend to barn chores without ever having to go outside in windy, rainy, or wintry weather. Of course, the inside of the barn was just as cold as it was outside, but it still provided shelter.

Many old timber frame barns can even now be found in the countryside in almost every part of America. Some barns are still being used for the job they were originally built to do, while others have been converted to other uses and a few have completely collapsed from too much use and the weathering forces of nature.

ALL ABOUT

BOB HOUSES

Every winter on the frozen fishing lakes of America, ice fishers set up small enclosures to protect themselves from the wind and cold. Each of these little houses, which have to be dragged on and off the ice each season, is unique in some distinctive way, often accommodating the particular needs and personality of its owner. They come in every type of design imaginable, from a simple one-person canvas tent to a small house complete with furnishings or a portable generator to supply power for a TV, and in one known case, even a hot tub.

Some ice fishing enclosures can be purchased from sporting goods stores, but most are built from scratch out of just about any material available, or converted from old sheds or car trailers. Despite all these differences in style, most bob

houses have a well-fitting door to keep out the wind, a hole in the floor through which to fish, and sometimes, the name the owner has given the hut or the owner's name painted near the front door. On some of the big fishing lakes, there may be hundreds of these tiny houses clustered into their own villages, connected by a maze of pathways plowed across the snow-covered ice.

In New Hampshire, these little ice-fishing shanties are called bob houses. According to one source, this name became popular because floating shacks and shanties were sometimes built on tidal waters in quiet bays. As the tide rose and fell, these small structures would bob with the tide each day. But ask an ice fisher, and you might get another explanation. According to one, the term *bob house* refers to the action of the fishing line as it bobs up and down through a hole in the ice. Since these holes are often located inside a small fishing shack through an opening in the floor, the shack became known as a bob house. And then there are other ice fishers who explain that if you don't remove your fishing shack from the ice before the spring thaw begins, you just might find it bobbing in the water.

There is no particular design best suited for a bob house. Indeed, its utilitarian function is only part of the intent of building one. Just as important is its architectural style, which can range from a clever concept, to a classic design, to a humorous spectacle. Here are a few of the more interesting bob houses that have adorned the fishing lakes of New Hampshire.

Keep-In and Keep-Out Fences

There is a popular expression attributed to the poet Robert Frost that "good fences make good neighbors." A good fence is one of the most important structures ever invented. Fences are a way people create order in their lives, to define personal spaces as well as property boundaries, edges, and limits. Fences are a way to keep things in and keep things out, a way to create a barrier against wind, noise, or visibility, and a way to manage the vastness of an area in organized units. And just like the many styles of current-day buildings, fences are built in a variety of styles that often reflect both the owners' particular needs and tastes.

The first fences appeared about six thousand years ago and were used as animal pens to contain livestock. People then began building different types of fences because they had other needs that ranged from defining a territory to providing privacy, to creating a barrier against enemies. The style and construction of a fence not only reflected the builder's intentions for its purpose,

but it also reflected the building materials available and the builder's choice of a particular design.

Today, fences are used for the same purposes, but the number of fencing styles to choose from and the building materials available are much greater. You have probably seen elaborate metal fences and gates surrounding expensive homes, metal chain-link fences around tennis courts, swimming pools, and ball fields, and barbed wire fences for containing cattle and other livestock. Even though these newer materials and styles may make fence building easier and provide a certain decorative look, the traditional types of wooden fences are still very popular and still serve their intended purposes quite well.

With a few exceptions, all fences share two common elements—vertical fence posts that are planted in the ground and horizontal fence beams that are attached across the posts. But even a casual observation of fences shows there are many variations to this basic structure. Here are some of the more popular types of fence structures and their particular attributes.

Zigzag fence

The zigzag fence is one of the few fence designs that does not use fence posts but takes a lot of material to construct. Most zigzag fences were therefore built when farmland was being cleared of trees to graze cattle or plant crops.

Farmers often took advantage of the abundant amount of timber harvested to build a zigzag fence because construction was easy and fast. Zigzag fences are made by stacking self-supporting rows of split rails that overlap at the ends by an angle of about 120 to 135 degrees. Today, very few new zigzag fences are built because they consume too much valuable material and the design also wastes too much space.

Post and split-rail fence

As techniques were created for splitting logs into thinner planks, or rails, the split-rail fence became an economical alternative to the zigzag design—at least as far as the amount of material was concerned. A post and split-rail fence uses two basic modules—the split

rails and the log posts—which have slots chiseled completely through to hold up the rails. Most designs use either two or three horizontal rails between evenly spaced posts. Although it takes some work to cut the slots and sink the posts, this design is quite sturdy and durable. A similar post-and-rail fence uses rails made of logs that are not split, but have been tapered at the ends to fit the holes in the posts.

Board fence

As lumber mills were established and machine-cut lumber became readily available, the board fence became a popular replacement for

the post and split-rail fence. Instead of cutting holes into posts to support the rails, boards could be simply nailed to the posts. Depending on its purpose, a board fence can have two, three, or more horizontal rails between posts.

Picket fence

Most picket fences are built to be more decorative than functional. A picket fence is usually low and friendly looking, so it is meant only to keep pets close to home (or out

of the garden) and help define property lines. Building a picket fence requires precision, patience, and a lot of material. In this design, posts hold up rails similar to a board fence, and then vertical slats, or pickets, are nailed to the rails to create the actual barrier. Much of the character of a picket fence comes from the design of the pickets, which can be cut to varying designs and heights, and spaced at different intervals for privacy or just to be decorative. In fact, the American picket fence has evolved to become mostly an artistic form, with highly imaginative designs that include fancy post-cap decorations, scalloped picket patterns, and fancy picket spacing.

Stockade fence

A stockade fence was originally built around the perimeter of a fort for protection from attacking

enemies. The stockade was therefore tall and solid, without any spacing between the vertical slats. Sometimes the slats were pointed at their tops to discourage someone from climbing over. The stockade structure is very much like a

tall, heavy-duty picket fence in which all pickets are tightly butted against each other. Modern stockade fences are built the same way and are typically used for security and privacy as well as to keep out wind and noise. Stockade fences are sometimes built along portions of highway to keep road noise from bothering nearby homes.

Wattle fence

The wattle fence is made of tree saplings and thin twigs and branches that are woven or arranged in a pattern between thin wooden posts. This type of fence was and still is

built in regions where there are few large trees. The actual pattern of the wattle varies greatly and usually reflects the builder's sense of decorative design. Even though the saplings are thin, a properly built wattle fence can be very strong and durable.

Lattice fence

This decorative design is made by overlapping narrow wooden slats at an angle that results in either a

square or diamond lattice pattern. The lattice is then attached to posts to create a fence that gives the impression of being a solid plane, yet allows light, wind, and sound to easily penetrate. Lattice fences and similar basket-weave fences are most often used for privacy or found in gardens to create a backdrop for plantings and to support climbing vines.

Barbed wire fence

When barbed wire was invented in 1868, cowboys found they could put up barbed wire fences a lot faster and cheaper than all-wood fences. Wire also proved to be more durable than wood. By using wire barriers strung from post to post to keep cattle from wandering, a long

fence encompassing tens or hundreds of acres could be quickly built and easily repaired. Most barbed wire fences for containing livestock use three to five horizontal strands stapled to the posts. Barbed wire became so popular that since its invention there have been over a thousand different designs for adding sharp barbs to a length of wire. Today, only a few barbed wire designs survive, with the most popular being the familiar two-point design. But because the sharp barbs can be a potential danger to people, they are not allowed in some residential communities.

Metal and wire fences

As metal and wire manufacturing techniques were adapted to create mass-produced fencing materials, many new designs began to emerge that proved less costly than wooden fence structures. Wire could now be woven into lattice designs and supplied to the fence builder in rolls that merely had to be unrolled and attached to vertical posts. Sometimes the woven fence mesh

is made of a strong and flexible plastic material instead of metal. There are virtually hundreds of woven wire designs available, with the most familiar being the popular chain-link fence. Metal is also used to create fences that mimic the design of several wooden fences, although the posts, rails, and pickets are thinner than wood because metal is so much stronger.

And many other types of fences

When a fence is needed, some builders are very creative in using whatever materials are readily available. Here are some rather unusual fences that also serve their purposes very well.

Tree House Getaways

There is something irresistible about a tree house. It is a place to escape from everything and yet still be adventurous. It is both indoors and outdoors at the same time. Anyone who has ever had access to one, no matter how simple or elaborate, knows that special feeling of having a getaway up off the ground that's the perfect place for hiding out, telling stories, watching wildlife, or quiet reading.

A most practical structure

When most people think of a tree house, they probably imagine a fun space for kids to play. But for many societies throughout history, a tree house structure has been, and still

is, an important part of practical living inspired by necessity. Shelters built in treetops were once a common way to seek protection from enemy intruders, wild animals, or floods. By building a tree house high above the forest floor, the dwellers not only had a strategic lookout post with a clear view in all directions, they could easily pull up the ladder so no one else could gain entry. And it was also easier to throw things down at an enemy who was attacking than for the enemy to attack from below by throwing things up.

For that reason, tree houses were sometimes used as a kind of fort. One such structure built in seventeenth-century England was capable of housing fifty soldiers. And the ancient Romans were known to build tree seats as observation posts.

Many tree houses built in earlier times were elaborate places to have fun. In sixteenth-century Italy, one prominent family built a tree house that included two stairways made of marble that spiraled up and around the supporting tree. Inside the tree house much of the furniture was also made of marble. In nineteenth-century Paris, France, a street lined with restaurants and large chestnut trees served dinner to their guests who were seated on platforms constructed among the tree branches. In fact, several three-hundred-year-old tree houses in France are still being used today.

Fun spaces for adults too

Today, some adults are rediscovering the tree house as an important part of their lifestyle. The art form of tree house building has even taken on its own identity, known as arboreal architecture, with styles ranging from a few planks of wood attached to branches to clever and even elegant examples consisting of two or more stories. Some modern-day American tree houses are used as vacation homes or full-time residences, while others may serve as a guest cottage or a blind for nature watching. But most of all, a tree house is designed to be a special, out-of-the-way place that is fun to be in. Adults who prefer living in a tree house rather than a conventional house say it reminds them of being young again.

ALL ABOUT

TREE HANGOUTS AND HIDEOUTS

No two tree houses are exactly alike, in part because each tree or stand of trees has a different configuration of trunk and limbs. Also, the materials used to build a tree house are often scrounged from throwaways or recycled from renovations or demolitions, and many construction decisions are made on-site. Each tree house is a unique design of its own circumstances, and many are considered works of art.

For those wanting to experience treetop living without building, there are now resorts featuring tree house cottages, with one being called a "treesort." And, for those really serious about the lifestyle, there is even a World Tree House Association that provides advice on construction and tree care.

One Canadian company manufactures and sells a portable two-story, tepee-shaped tree house that can simply be attached to the trunk of a single tall tree. These tree houses are often used in remote regions by forest workers who need to protect themselves and their food supply from animal invaders.

Modern tree house construction

A tree house must also be a sturdy and safe structure, so conventional methods of construction must be followed the same as when building a conventional dwelling. State, city, or local town governments are likely to have building codes that include regulations for the construction of tree houses. One town in New York State, for example, specified the thickness of everything from the platform flooring to the supporting branches. The code even specified the minimum size nails to be used and the types of access ladders that were acceptable.

The single most important component is finding the right tree or combination of trees growing close together to build in. It is also important to use proper building techniques that won't kill the tree. Depending on the size of the tree house to be built, most any type of sturdy and healthy tree with spreading branches will do fine. The strongest and best-suited trees for arboreal architecture include oak, maple, apple, fir, chestnut,

beech, willow, and hemlock. Tree trunks should be at least twelve inches in diameter, while load-bearing branches should be at least six inches in diameter.

It is better to drill holes through branches to attach beams with bolts and nuts rather than nailing directly into the tree. Also, under no circumstances should the bark be cut away from any part of the tree–that can kill a branch or the entire tree. The best way to fasten beams to branches is to lash them with strong nylon cord or metal cables; even then, the bark should be protected from injury by running the cables through cut lengths of garden hose wherever they wrap around bark.

The first part of the tree house structure consists of building a sturdy platform using floor joists and flooring. The platform of a kid's tree house might be constructed about six feet off the ground, while an adult one can be any practical height. In addition, the simplest of tree houses might include only a guardrail so no one accidentally falls off and a way of climbing up and down. Access to the tree house can be made by a rigid ladder or a rope ladder, both of which can be pulled up to exclude intruders. If the tree has several low-slung branches, access can be made by simply climbing the tree.

A more complete tree house structure might have a simple lean-to roof, as well as side walls, windows, and a door. The most elaborate tree houses are quite similar to a small cottage or a multistory house, with a few rooms, a loft, and a deck, except that everything is located up in a tree ▪

A BRIEF HISTORY OF BUILDING AND STRUCTURES

LEARN TO USE THE MATERIALS AVAILABLE

NATIVE AMERICAN STRUCTURES

NEW AND BETTER METHODS FOR FASTENING MATERIALS

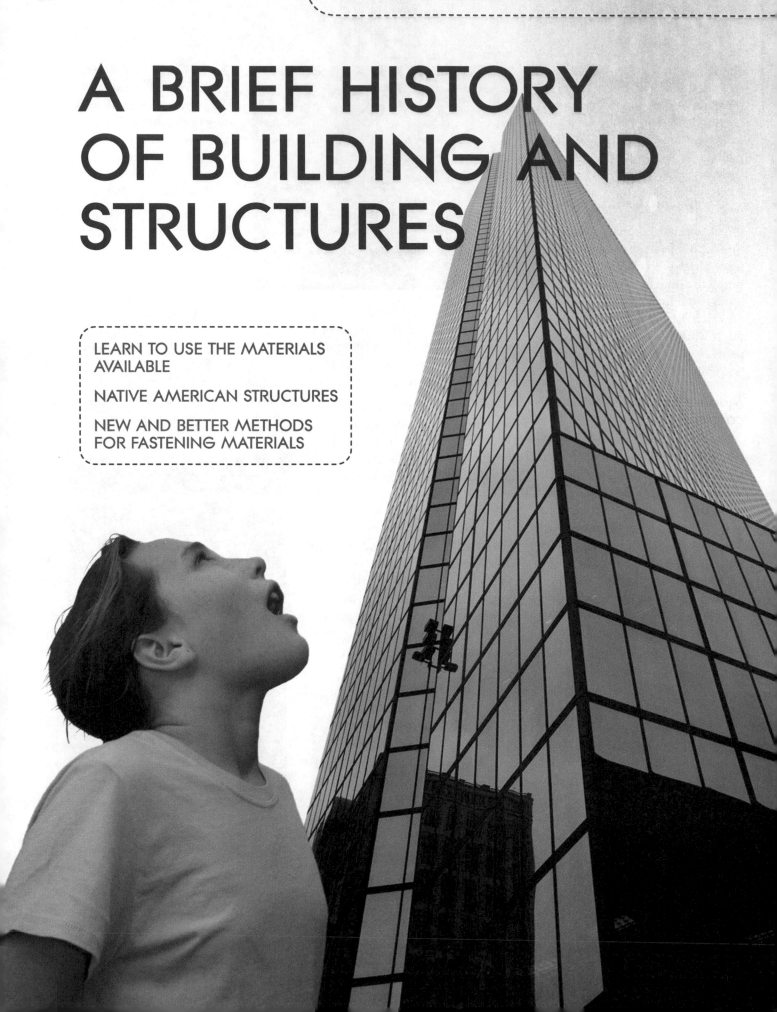

LEARN TO USE THE MATERIALS AVAILABLE

A building is most simply explained as a human-made structure of any shape or size that is able to support itself. Of course, in practical terms, a building also serves some purpose and has to withstand the forces of weather as well as gravity. The structure systems invented in premodern times were primarily used to build personal shelters made from whatever materials were readily available. If people lived near a forest, they would build with whole logs, logs cut into lumber, or even twigs. People living in the clear plains where there was little lumber often built with mud blocks strengthened by the twigs of bushes. The Inuit found a way to build ice-block structures. And nomadic Native Americans built portable tent structures using wood-pole frames covered with animal skins or a woven fabric.

These were simple and sensible structures. Each method of building required figuring out the best ways to use the materials. What size did the blocks, beams, or poles need to be strong enough? How should the materials be connected—by stacking, tying together, or gluing with adhesive? And what type of structure would be strong enough to last through wind and storms?

Experience Proves What Works Well (and what does not)

Contrary to the popular image, our earliest cave dwellers ancestors did not actually live in caves. Caves may have been used as temporary shelters for protection against severe weather and blistering heat, but the earliest buildings are believed to have been simple huts constructed by European hunters more than three hundred thousand years ago. These primitive structures were undoubtedly used for protection from wind, rain, snow, and sun, and maybe also from unfriendly wildlife. The designs varied, but most primitive huts were made using wooden frames covered with branches or animal hides. Where wood was scarce, the builder might have used long bundles of grasses or marsh reeds to build the framework, and sometimes the bones of large animals made excellent arches for hut structures.

About twenty thousand years ago, a primitive hut in treeless wilderness

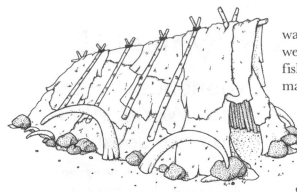

might have been built using the bones of a mammoth for structure and the hide for a covering.

The elegant and functional design of these early structures evolved over time. If something worked well, the builder and those builders that followed him kept on doing it and improving it. From repeated experience in learning what worked and what didn't, these ancient builders knew where to place these structures to gain the warmth of the sun and protection from the elements. They knew how thick to make the hut walls so the heat they absorbed from sunlight during the day would keep the hut

warm through a winter night— and in summer, transfer the coolness of night into keeping the interior pleasant during the heat of day. They knew how to build a straw roof that would block the heat of the summer sun and keep the heat inside during winter.

As people became more sedentary, they built more permanent structures for their homes, often with an indoor fireplace or hearth for

warmth and cooking. Areas that were particularly good for farming, fishing, or hunting tended to draw many settlers. Living near neighbors also provided better protection from attacks by enemies. An area with many houses soon became a village. As the village grew, so did the need for larger buildings for town gatherings. And, as people traveled between villages, they wore pathways that widened to become roads. Because

people also tended to build near freshwater rivers, streams, ponds, and lakes, going from village to village sometimes required building a bridge. The first simple footbridges were just long logs laid across a stream from bank to bank. To span wider bodies of water or a deep ravine, rope bridges made from vegetable fibers could be tied to trees or rocks on either side of the crossing.

The bigger a village grew, the more tradespeople, artisans, and others it attracted. More people meant more houses, more merchants meant more and bigger shop buildings, and all these structures required more space. Some villages and towns grew to become cities, and instead of just covering more land, many cities started building taller structures that enclosed greater spaces. Even several thousand years ago, builders had figured out how to make buildings several stories high. The Romans were capable of building large housing complexes that reached the incredible height (for that time) of ten stories.

Most of the buildings, bridges, towers, and other structures we see all around us were built to be strong and last a long time. The huge stone buildings of past civilizations are proof that even the earliest builders knew a lot about what materials and building techniques would endure. Even the temporary shelters of ancient peoples were made to be easily constructed and function well. So it is not surprising that some of those same materials and methods are still being used today.

NATIVE AMERICAN STRUCTURES

The most familiar dwelling of the Native American is probably the conical-shaped tepee. This masterpiece of elegant and functional design evolved over time to replace other types of Indian dwellings that were not as easy to construct or as comfortable to live in. Still, the homes built by the different Native American tribes all across North America were of many designs, shapes, and sizes that reflected the materials locally available, the climate of the region, cultural practices, and whether the tribe was migratory. Depending on the region, Native American homes might have been constructed using piled stones, bricks of dried mud, wooden frames with coverings, or cut planks of wood.

A temporary tent shelter to house a single family might be built from branches and bark in a matter of hours, while building a permanent communal structure to house a few hundred people could take months. Some Indian houses were built into the sides of cliffs or stacked on top of each other like apartments in a building. Some of these clusters of dwellings took years to construct, with new additions being added as needed. A few Native American structures were so enormous that one big building could cover an area the size of a football field.

Most Native American architecture was based on a few basic designs, although the exact styles and construction methods varied depending on the local climate and what materials were readily available. A framework dwelling in the hot regions might have a covered roof for shade and open walls to let breezes flow through. If the weather turned cold or rainy, the walls could also be covered quickly and easily.

Tribes along the fertile Pacific coast made round homes called lodges by constructing a roof of long redwood poles over an excavated pit in the earth. Inland from the coast on the woodless plains, the excavated lodges were covered with dome-shaped roofs made of packed earth. In the southwest, round adobe dwellings called kivas or hogans were typically constructed with a flat roof supported by horizontal poles.

Some western tribes built a unique version of the lodge that was constructed like a wigwam. But instead of being round, it was built in the shape of an "L" laid out flat. In the Yukon Territory of Canada, the double lean-to design favored by the Indians was constructed like an elongated tepee. And along the Southeast coast of America, where seashells were plentiful, huts were built with a shell and mud mixture called wattle and daub. But of all the different types and variations of dwellings built by Native American tribes in different regions of North America, the most favored structures were tepees, wigwams, longhouses, and pueblo villages.

Tepees of bark and buffalo hide

The Native American tepee was cleverly designed to be a comfortable dwelling that was easily erected and taken down, very durable, and highly portable. A Native American camp, typically located near a river or lake, might consist of fifty or more tepees with about four occupants living in each one.

Although all tepees have a familiar conical shape, the details of a tepee's design depended on how large it had to be and how long it needed to last. Some tepees built by bands of wandering Native American hunters could be quickly made on the spot using freshly cut poles from small trees and pieces of peeled bark for the covering. First, three poles were set up like a tripod, and then additional poles were added to form the upside-down, cone-shaped framework. Where the poles overlapped at the top, they were tied together with plant fibers, thin roots and

vines, or sometimes strips of rawhide. The thicker bottom ends of the poles were stuck in the ground for stability and to keep the tepee from blowing over in high winds.

Then, starting around the bottom of the framework structure and working up, pieces of peeled bark were attached between the poles until the framework was completely covered except for a "front door" opening and another opening at the top to let out smoke from the fire pit inside. Each row of bark overlapped the row below so the completed covering could shed rain. In very windy regions, a few additional poles might be added against the outside to keep the bark from blowing off. During winter, snow might also be packed over the bark to keep the cold winds from entering through cracks. When the occupants decided to move on to hunt a new territory, the bark-covered tepee structure was just left behind and a new one was built in the next location.

Strips of bark remained the most popular covering for a tepee until the first horses were brought to America by foreign explorers and settlers. Until then, Native Americans mostly traveled on land by walking. Once the horse became a common means of transporta-

tion for Native Americans, the tepee could be packed up to travel instead of being discarded when its inhabitants moved. However, the design needed to be modified somewhat so the tepee could be easily assembled, disassembled, and transported to the new hunting location. Rather than using a delicate bark covering that might easily crack and break in transit, most portable tepees were covered with animal hides.

These permanent and portable tents were made using at least thirteen poles to form a conical structure that could be anywhere from ten to twenty-five feet high. As with building a disposable tepee, the basic framework began by erecting either three or four poles to form the freestanding structure that could

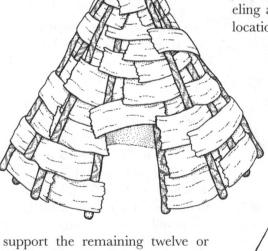

support the remaining twelve or more poles added to complete the shape. In fact, Native American tribes that lived in tepees were either known as "three-pole people" or "four-pole people," depending on their building technique for starting the structure.

The animal hide coverings were very durable, waterproof, and heavy enough to resist blowing away in the wind. It took about ten to twenty buffalo hides sewn together to make the semicircle-shaped covering that would be snugly drawn around the tepee frame. The actual number of hides needed depended on the tepee size, which typically ranged from twelve to eighteen feet in diameter at the base. The tepees of important Native American chiefs could be up to thirty feet in diameter. The smoke-hole at the top could be adjusted with a flap of hide that was positioned by a long pole to completely cover the opening or to shield the opening from a direct wind. The entrance was an opening about three feet high that could be closed with a drop covering made of an oval-shaped hide.

In most tribes, it was the women's responsibility to gather the materials and build the tepees (although men sometimes helped carve the long poles), and it was also the women's job to pack up the tepees for traveling and set them up in the new location—even though the tepee

could weigh a few hundred pounds or more. The portable Native American tepee design was so successful that the United States Army copied the concept to create their own version called the Sibley tent.

Wigwams covered with mats or bark

The wigwam's dome design was an improvement over the classic tepee in several ways. The dome shape has side walls that don't slope inward as quickly as a tepee and therefore provide more space for the inhabitants. And the roof of a dome is closer to the ground than a tall tepee, so it does a better job of keeping the occupants warm. Because a wigwam was more difficult to build than a tepee, it was usually intended as

a more permanent structure and was constructed to be lived in for many years. As families built their wigwams near one another for social and security reasons, clusters of wigwams formed small villages.

To construct a typical wigwam dome, poles were planted vertically in the ground around a large circle. Two poles, each on opposite sides of the circle, were then bent toward each other and attached to form an arch. Other pairs of poles around the circle were also bent and tied together in a similar manner to form arches of graduated

sizes until the framework of a dome was complete. To make the structure even stronger, a few rings of tree saplings formed horizontal bands around the dome. Long shavings of wood or bark and thin tree roots were used for lashing the framework together.

The covering used over the wigwam framework depended on the season and the available materials. Animal hide coverings provided warmth in winter, tree bark coverings were lightweight and easy to work with, and for wigwams located near swampy areas, woven mats made from the stems of cattails provided a windproof and waterproof covering. It was not unusual to see a wigwam that used all three coverings together, as well as layers of leaves, branch boughs, and snow for added insulation.

Tree bark, especially the bark from a birch tree, was an ideal material for covering the framework structure. Bark is naturally waterproof and lightweight, and was plentiful in forest areas. Pieces of bark were carefully stripped from the tree, softened by heat, flattened out, and sewn together with skinny roots to make a large bark mat.

The seams of the pieces could be sealed against rain, using tree sap and other waterproof gums. In cold climates, the wigwam structure might first have been covered with a layer of brush for insulation before the bark mat covering was attached. For all of its practicality, a covering of bark was highly flammable and somewhat delicate.

Northeastern longhouse

In places where Native Americans could grow crops, catch fish, or hunt a plentiful supply of wildlife, communities had no need to move about in a continual search for food, so they built permanent houses. In some northeast regions, multiple families—sometimes as many as twenty—lived together in one big long dwelling appropriately called a longhouse. Some of these longhouses were enormous structures, typically from fifty to one hundred fifty feet long and twenty to twenty-five feet wide. Some were up to four hundred feet long! Whatever the length, the height of the longhouse was usually the same as its width.

Building a longhouse was a community project. First, the footprint of the new building was drawn on the bare ground, and thick wooden posts were sunk in the ground at regular intervals around the perimeter.

To complete the outer wall framework, horizontal beams made of thinner tree branches and saplings were tied to the rows of posts. The roof structure was also made of branches and saplings and could either form a rounded arch or a pointed gable. The entire framework was then covered in slabs of elm tree bark that was layered like overlapping shingles to shed the rain.

More poles could be lashed over the bark covering to keep it from blowing away in strong winds. There was a door at either end of the longhouse, but no windows anywhere. Staggered holes in the roof let out smoke from fires in the fire pits that were located in the center of the building. A big, central passageway led down the middle of the building to a door at either end. Inside, along the side walls, animal skin curtains were used to divide the large space into private rooms for individual families. As families grew, as many as a hundred people might live in one house.

Southwest adobe pueblo

The pueblo dwellings of the southwest Native American tribes were built like a multilevel apartment building with many box-shaped, one-room units stacked together. A family might occupy one or more rooms, depending on their needs for living and storage space. Openings in the walls and floors connected the family's rooms. As communities grew, more units were added to existing structures. The largest of these communities had eight hundred rooms and could house a thousand people.

The box-shaped rooms had walls made of piled stone and adobe bricks. The bricks were formed from a sun-dried mixture of the local sandy clay and water fortified with pieces of straw and ashes. Once the bricks were laid to form the walls, any spaces between the bricks were filled with more adobe or plain mud. The few substantial trees available throughout the southwest region were made into wood beams and placed across the top of the walls to form a ceiling that would support the flat roof. Smaller poles were then placed over the roof timbers and covered with sticks or brush, then sealed with a coating of mud. The roofs of adobe dwellings served a dual purpose. In addition to keeping out the hot sun and bad weather, they were also used as decks where craft works were created outdoors and things were laid out to dry.

Most Native American pueblo structures had few windows and no doors. For protection from enemies, the entrance to the adobe structure was through a hole in the roof that was accessed by a ladder. One ladder rested against the outside wall, while another protruded from the opening. To keep someone out, the outside ladder was simply pulled up on the roof.

Everyone in the village helped in the construction. Men cut trees from the nearest forest, hauled them to the construction site, prepared the wooden roof beams, and installed them. Women made the adobe bricks and built the brick walls, then plastered the inside walls with a smooth coating of adobe finished with a white paint. Because heavy rain could soften and wash away adobe, it was not a very durable construction, and adobe dwellings needed constant maintenance and repair.

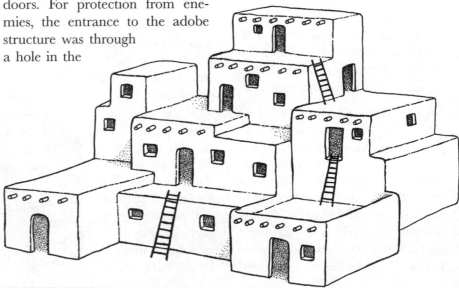

NEW AND BETTER METHODS FOR FASTENING MATERIALS

Some structures, like stone walls or the great pyramids, can be built by simply stacking material on top of itself and letting gravity hold everything in place. However, most every other type of building requires some system for fastening parts together. Over time, builders have developed new and better ways to fasten materials together.

Some of the earliest structures used rope or twine made from plant fibers to lash together building timbers. Many were covered with animal hides that had been sewn together using carved wooden sewing needles and thread made from animal guts. Early builders also discovered they could stick materials together using naturally sticky substances like beeswax, tree sap, and other substances from certain trees and plants that worked as adhesives. In time, better glues were created by mixing and heating a variety of substances from animal carcasses, plants, and earth minerals. To fasten stones and bricks, a simple mortar of clay and water was used; it was later improved by adding other earth substances like gypsum, limestone, sand, and even volcanic ash. As timber structures became larger and more permanent, wood pegs hammered through drilled holes became a way to keep the structure connected and rigid. Then came the invention of bronze and iron nails that replaced pegs. Once metal became a part of building, metal pegs called rivets were invented to hold steel beams together.

All of these fasteners were improved over time, and new ones are always being invented. Just look at the huge variety of screws, nails, bolts, mortars, tapes, adhesives, and other fasteners available at any hardware store, and you will quickly become aware of how important fasteners are to building.

As you learn about the basic types of structures that were built up until a hundred years ago, think of how impractical it would be today if we still just stacked stones and bricks or built only with wooden posts and beams. Builders are always looking for better materials and methods to build larger, stronger, and more complex structures. And today's craftspeople, engineers, scientists, designers, and architects have many sophisticated building systems to choose from—including these traditional "oldies but goodies."

Weaving and Thatching

Weaving the fibers of plants, straw, and grasses is one of the oldest skills in human history. Early humans learned to weave different shapes and sizes of baskets for storing and carrying things. Fishers knotted fibers to weave fishing nets, and some ancient peoples even learned to weave temporary shelters to protect themselves from the weather. More than eight thousand years ago, the people of Europe invented a type of weaving, called wattle, that used the long fibers from sugar cane woven between and around a series of upright stakes. When the wattle was coated with a kind of mud plaster called daub, the panels could be used to construct the walls of a building. The roofs of these slab-side buildings were typically made from overlapping bundles of straw or reeds called thatch. Some

builders of the time instead built the walls from bundles of reeds lashed together and made the roof from a woven reed mat. Weaving wattle and mud remained a practical way of building until just a few hundred years ago.

Wattle and daub walls

Modern thatch roof

Old thatch roof

Post and Lintel Construction

One of the earliest systematic building methods first appeared sometime before five thousand BC in the thickly forested villages of Europe where timber was plentiful. The farmers built their houses using vertical timber posts sunk into the ground with horizontal cross timbers called lintels connecting the tops of the posts. The timber frame was then covered as well as strengthened using lightweight woven branches. Sometimes clay or mud was used to fill in gaps to keep out the weather. And occasionally a stone foundation was used along with stone posts to support the wooden lintels. Post and lintel construction is still one of the most common methods for building the frame of a structure.

WATERWHEELS

A river becomes a constant supply of direct mechanical power when a waterwheel is used to harness its moving, or kinetic, energy. The waterwheel is a simple type of engine that consists of a paddle wheel with an axle. The water flow turns the wheel, which turns the axle, which turns pulleys, belts, and gears to power machines like a grinding mill, an irrigation pump, the blades in a sawmill, or manufacturing tools in a factory.

Another part of a waterwheel engine is the water-delivery system. Where the water approaches and drives the wheel determines the kind of wheel being used and how efficient it is in using the water energy available. Of the many designs for round and vertical waterwheels, the three most common are the undershot wheel, the overshot wheel, and the breast wheel. Their names imply where the water stream drives the wheel.

Although waterwheels have been used for thousands of years as a primary source of power for people throughout the world, in America today they are mostly used as quaint attractions by old riverside mills. However, their principle of operation did lead to the development of the modern hydroelectric turbine.

Undershot wheel

An undershot wheel, with a row of horizontal paddles, or blades, around its perimeter, is immersed just deep enough in a flowing stream so the water flow against the blades forces the wheel to turn. This is one of the simplest waterwheels to build, but it uses only about 30 percent of the water energy flowing through it.

Overshot wheel

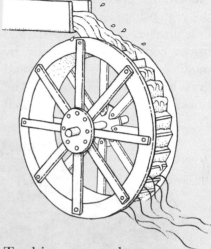

To drive an overshot wheel, the water flow is channeled to the top of the wheel. Both the force of the water flow and the force of the water falling onto the wheel's blades or shallow buckets cause the wheel to rotate with an efficiency of up to 90 percent.

Breast wheel

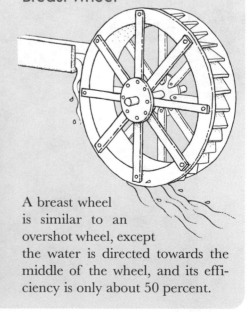

A breast wheel is similar to an overshot wheel, except the water is directed towards the middle of the wheel, and its efficiency is only about 50 percent.

Brick Construction

Because humans must have water to survive, people throughout history have tended to settle near rivers and lakes. A riverbed or lakeshore and the surrounding area were also excellent sources for mud, water grasses, and reeds. If the region happened to have very little timber or stone, hard mud bricks could easily be made by molding a mixture of mud and grass into uniform-size bricks. The bricks in their molds were then placed in the heat of the sun until dry and hard. For building, the bricks were stacked into thick walls and cemented with more mud. Because these early mud bricks were not very strong, the building walls needed to be quite thick, and even thicker wherever there was an opening for a window or door. In time, the structure would just crumble to dirt or be washed away by water from rain or floods.

Some people discovered that mud bricks would last much longer if they were baked in an oven at a high temperature rather than just dried in the sun. The Romans perfected the brick making process and made it an economical and popular building material. Today, modular bricks come in a large variety of materials and sizes and are still commonly used for all types of construction.

TALL CHIMNEYS

Relatively speaking, chimneys haven't been around very long. The earliest record of a home fireplace with a chimney dates back to 1347 in Venice, Italy. Before that time, it was common to just build a fire for warmth and cooking in a shallow pit usually located on the floor in the middle of a room. The smoke from the fire would rise to the ceiling and escape out an opening in the roof. Much of the time, though, black smoke would fill the room before finding its way out, depositing layers of dirty soot on everything in the room.

Smoke made a mess of everything, and even the architects and builders of Roman times complained that soot covered over their fine craftsmanship and painted decorations. Architects soon learned how to control the spread of smoke and direct it to the outside by building a tube, or flue, from the fire pit up through the roof. From that time on, chimneys became a standard part of most buildings, especially in colder climates. Chimneys are still used today to direct smoke away from people, homes, farms, and other nearby surroundings, even though modern fuels produce much less soot.

The tallest chimneys were built at factories, and the tallest chimney in the United States was built in 1909 at a copper and silver mining factory in Montana. It rose to a height of 506 feet (over fifty stories tall) and had a forty-seven-foot diameter at its base! Another tall chimney in New York City rose 353 feet tall and used more than two and a half million bricks to build. The largest chimney ever built is in Wales at a copper factory. Its enormous size of two miles is in length rather than height. The chimney runs up the side of a steep mountain, then continued vertically another one hundred feet above the summit. The entire chimney is so large that it can be seen from locations forty-five miles away.

Nearly all chimneys, both old and new, are constructed with modular bricks or blocks to form a tall structural tube. Here are some examples of tall chimneys that were built so well that they are still standing today.

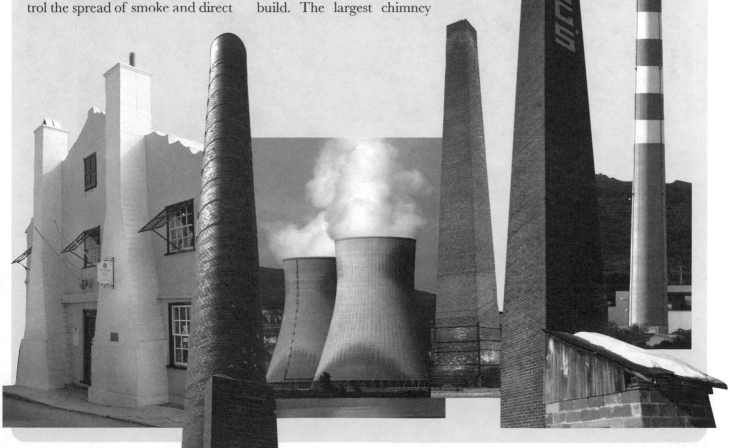

Stoneworking

Wherever there was a plentiful supply of stone and rock, that became the preferred material for building long-lasting structures. What is so surprising is how ancient peoples quarried, cut, and shaped rocks—sometimes even huge rocks—without the benefit of metal tools. Surviving ancient stone structures show workmanship of such astonishing accuracy that no mortar was needed between the rocks. In fact, there was absolutely no space at all for any mortar.

Early stoneworkers learned to drive wooden wedges into natural cracks in rocks. When the wood was soaked with water, the wedges would expand with enough force to crack the rock in two or break a slab off a boulder. Sometimes a fire would be set next to the face of a large rock, causing chips or slabs to break away and fall off. Harder pieces of stone were used as carving tools to chip away and shape a stone for building. Hard, flat stones could be used to polish the face of the building block. In more recent years, the introduction of metal stone-cutting tools, diamond-hard saws, and even laser cutting machines have made stone construction easier. However, the basic techniques of stone building remain unchanged.

ALL ABOUT

DRY STONE WALLS (MADE WITHOUT MORTAR)

Natural stone is one of the strongest, longest lasting, and best looking materials to build with. Many of the oldest structures ever found, and those still standing, were constructed of rocks and stones stacked on top of each other with nothing but gravity and friction to hold them together. Today, stacked-stone construction without mortar is still fairly common, especially stone-wall building in New England, where good stone is quite plentiful.

Building without mortar to hold the stones in place is called dry construction, but using only gravity and friction to keep the stones from falling out of place requires a special building technique. The most basic rule is "one over two," which means that each stone should rest on two stones beneath it. And since gravity works only downward, the wall should be built as vertical as possible.

It is also important to have as much contact between stones as possible, and that the stones always be positioned as close to horizontal as possible. The more flat and horizontal the bedding surface, the better gravity will help keep the stacked stones in place. Sometimes it is necessary to chip away a piece of a rock or use thin pieces of stone to make the surface as flat as possible for the next stone to be placed on top of it.

A few modern-day, dry-wall builders consider it okay to use a little mortar on the inside of their walls, as long as it cannot be seen (except for possibly finishing off the top of a wall between the stones to create a flat surface). However, if a stacked dry stone structure is built properly, it can be even stronger than any masonry structure using mortar to rigidly lock it all together.

Because no mortar is used to fill the gaps between the stones, each stone is able to shift a little without breaking its bond with surrounding stones and falling out of the wall. Having a certain amount of give and flexibility is especially important for stone walls that are subject to the forces exerted by frost-and-thaw cycles, the intrusion of roots, earth tremors, floods, and even clumsy, large animals.

The best stone to use

Several types of natural stone can be used for building masonry walls, including granite, marble, slate, limestone, sandstone, and bluestone, but only granite rocks are suitable for building dry stone walls. Granite is very hard and durable and comes in several shades of gray that depend on where the rock came from. As a general rule, the darker the granite, the harder the stone.

Granite rocks in all sizes from pebbles to boulders are typically found throughout the fields and hills of New England because the weather cycle causes them to be pushed up out of the ground. Each winter as the ground freezes and expands, the buried rocks get pushed up a little more until they ultimately appear on the surface.

New England farmers had to first clear their fields of rock before they could plow and plant crops. But there are limits to the size and weight of rocks that can be lifted without tools or machinery, so large granite boulders too heavy to be moved on horse-pulled stone sleds were split into smaller pieces that could be lifted. The stones the farmers collected were either stacked in mounds or used to build stone walls that defined the bound-

Freestanding walls

aries of their property. Stone walls also defined grazing pastures for farm animals or became the foundations for farmhouses, root cellars, and other buildings.

The art of the wall builder

Building a stone wall in New England is considered an art, and it is not uncommon to identify the builder of a wall by the particular way the wall is made. Although each individual rock must be positioned for strength, a stonemason will have his or her own way of mixing shapes and sizes to achieve a particular look and beauty. The signature pattern of a stone wall builder is often seen in the particular combination of shapes and sizes used, the way the top of the wall is finished, or the way steps and slopes are built into the wall.

Assembling a dry stone wall requires a good eye to see which rock in which position will best fit a space to be filled. A stonemason will typically spread hundreds of rocks on the ground next to where the wall is being built, then stare at them for a while, trying to remember each individual shape. The builder will have in mind which stones on the ground are flat for the top of the wall, which ones are good corner stones, which ones make good face stones, and which ones should be unseen in the center of the wall. As the stones are used, new ones are spread out and memorized.

Fitting a stone to a space can be done simply by tapping away pieces of the rock, using a stone chisel and a heavy mason's hammer, or rocks can be split in half by knowing where to tap the rock along its grain or an existing crack. Granite rocks are fairly uniform

Retaining walls

Breast walls

and show little grain, so splitting them often requires a different procedure of first drilling several holes along a straight line and then hammering wedges into the holes until the rock splits.

Some walls have rocks so tight fitting that it appears as if each has been cut to that particular shape, while other styles of dry wall building use small chinks of stone stuffed into the gaps between bigger rocks. Some wall builders show the flat sides of the rocks on the outside faces and top of a wall, while others may create an appearance with the rounded faces showing.

No matter what the individual builder's style, however, the basic principles of dry-wall construction have not changed since colonial times and even centuries before. Most experienced wall builders will agree that a dry stone wall will be strongest if the largest rocks are

placed at the bottom of a shallow trench. Smaller rocks are then used in the middle portion of the wall, and flat rocks are saved for finishing off the top surface.

In addition to the individual stones overlapping each other and the wall being built as vertical as possible with stones being as horizontal as possible, it is also important that the base of the wall be as wide or wider than the top. For stability, the base of a wall is usually at least two feet wide—wider for walls over three feet high. As a rule of thumb, many stonemasons figure the base should be two-thirds the height of the wall.

Most stone walls can be easily identified by their general type. A freestanding wall shows both sides and its top, while a retaining wall is butted up against the earth to hold it back. And a breast wall uses rocks simply laid into a slope to prevent erosion.

Cast Iron

By the end of the nineteenth century, stone became too expensive to use as a primary building material, especially with bigger and taller buildings becoming necessary. Cast iron components, which were easy to make and cheaper than stone, became the new construction innovation that eventually led the way towards creating modern bridges and skyscrapers.

At first, only a few cast iron shapes, like columns and window frames, were truly structural, while other cast iron components were mostly decorative. This was a time when highly decorated ornamental building components were popular, and just about any fancy design an architect created could be inexpensively molded in cast iron.

To create a cast iron building piece, a metal foundry first made a wood carving of the form, and then pressed the form into a bed of tightly packed damp sand. When the form was removed, it left an impression in the sand, which could then be filled with molten liquid iron. When the metal cooled and hardened, the cast iron piece was removed and assembled as part of a structure. Because these molds could be used over and over again to produce many more of the same part, cast iron architecture was very economical.

Decorative cast iron panels quickly became popular as coverings to renovate the facades of existing brick buildings. One of the appealing features to the building owner was that the cast iron panels could be cheaply molded and painted to look like expensive stone. Sometimes the only way to casually tell the difference was to actually touch the facade or to test the building with a magnet, since metal surfaces attract magnets unlike stone or wood.

Architects and engineers soon realized that instead of using cast iron panels to just cover an existing masonry structure, they could design new and taller buildings by using cast iron components for the building's structural frame as well. Inside the building, cast iron could also be used for making structural columns to support floors and staircases to go between them. Another feature and benefit was that sections of cast iron components could be preassembled at the factory to make sure they would fit correctly when installed, so in some ways, cast iron buildings were an early experiment in prefabrication.

Although cast iron was a brittle material, it was quite strong in compression but tended to crack and break in tension. By modifying the method for making iron, it was later discovered how to produce wrought iron that was more ductile and strong in both compression and tension. The structure of the Eiffel Tower, for example, is completely constructed of wrought iron parts.

LIGHTHOUSES

The purpose of a lighthouse is to prevent shipwrecks. Most lighthouses are built along the ocean coastline in dangerous places where ships heading for a port could be wrecked on a rocky shoreline, a small island, a coral reef, or a partially submerged rock. By sending a powerful beam of light far out to sea, the lighthouse warns ship captains to steer away from the shore.

To be clearly visible to ships at sea, lighthouses are usually built as tall towers with a light at the top and are situated on a coastal hill or a rocky bluff jutting out into the sea. These structures must therefore be extremely strong to withstand high winds, the relentless pounding of waves, and fierce ocean storms. Each lighthouse was built using whatever material and structure system was available to achieve the greatest strength.

The higher and brighter a lighthouse's lamp, the farther out to sea it will be visible. Some lights can be seen as far as forty miles away on clear, dark nights. However, one lighthouse in San Diego, California, was built on a cliff nearly five hundred feet above the ocean, but that was too high, because the light was often obscured by low clouds.

The Lighthouse of Pharos at Alexandria in Egypt was considered one of the Seven Wonders of the World and dates back to 280 B.C. It stood as tall as a forty-five story building and had a large wood fire burning at the top. Its shape was a stepped tower like a tall wedding cake, and the interior had a long spiraling ramp that provided a way to carry the wood to the top of the tower. Constructing the tower of heavy stone faced with white marble took twenty-five years. After it was finished, the lighthouse stood as the tallest stone structure in the world for nearly one thousand five hundred years. It finally toppled during an earthquake in 1326, but the materials from the rubble were used again to build a castle in the same spot.

Before lighthouses were electrified and automated, lighthouse keepers were needed to quickly get to the light just in case the oil lamp blew out during a storm. That is why so many older lighthouses also served as homes for the light keeper, or a small house was built nearby.

Even with all the computerized navigation technology available today, coastal lighthouses are still needed to warn ships of danger. Along the rugged, rocky coast of Maine (often called the "Lighthouse State"), there are sixty-eight lighthouses, each with a unique personality and rich history. Since several of these lighthouses are now automated and no longer require a light keeper, some have been turned into small inns where guests can imagine what it was like to spend the harsh winter months in isolation, keeping vigil over the sea.

Lighthouses are often recognized by the unique design of their structure or the pattern that is painted on them. But that doesn't help ships at sea that are too distant to recognize what particular lighthouse the light is coming from. Therefore, some lighthouses also emit their own patterns of light, which might be a constant beam, a rotating light, or a light that blinks at certain speeds.

Cast iron lighthouses

In the mid-to-late 1800s, cast iron had become a popular building material for fabricating large structures, and lighthouses benefited in a few unique ways. Compared to the typical masonry structure, a lighthouse constructed from cast iron panels bolted together was light in weight, watertight, and weathers well in a salt-air environment. And should the lighthouse become threatened by coastal erosion, it can be disassembled and reconstructed farther from the water.

Many cast iron lighthouses were later lined inside with brick. This not only added structural support to reduce sway in strong winds, but it also provided insulation against the winter cold and summer heat.

Gibbs Hill Light

This 117-foot tower built in 1846 on a hilltop in Bermuda is one of the first cast iron lighthouses in the Americas. The gleaming white tower of bolted metal panels can be seen from most anywhere on the island.

Biloxi Light

The conical form of this cast iron lighthouse, which strongly tapers to a narrow top, was typical of many other cast iron lighthouses built along the Gulf coast. The pleasant shape has also survived countless hurricanes.

Chatham Light

This U.S. Coast Guard lighthouse on Cape Cod, Massachusetts, was originally built using cast iron plates and later lined with a brick inner core. The light is an essential aid to local sailors and sits dangerously close to an eroding coastline.

Cape Hatteras Light

At 208 feet, Cape Hatteras lighthouse is the tallest brick light tower in America and is located at an extremely dangerous location where two strong ocean currents come together. Its black and white painted spiral design is unique.

Cape Canaveral Light

The curved and tapered design of the 145-foot cast iron tower is unlike any other lighthouse in the United States. In 1893, the structure was disassembled and reassembled more than a mile inland, where it is now safe from sea erosion.

Cape Henry Light

The last tall cast iron lighthouse built in America had a unique octagonal design emphasized by a distinctive black and white pattern. The lighthouse marks the entrance to Chesapeake Bay at Virginia Beach and remains in service today.

Portland Head Light

Portland Head Light is the oldest of sixty-three lighthouses that were built along Maine's dangerously rocky coast and was commissioned by President George Washington. The light is still in operation today.

Key West Light

The lighthouse at Key West, Florida, is a brick structure with eighty-eight cast iron steps to the top, and like most everything else in Key West, the lighthouse is "southernmost" in the United States.

Haig Point Light

The wooden two-story Haig Point lighthouse on Daufuskie Island, South Carolina, was built on the foundation of a destroyed plantation mansion. The light is no longer needed and has now become an elegant guesthouse.

Fowey Rocks Light

The unusual Fowey Rocks lighthouse structure at Cape Florida has a hexagonal steel framework and was considered a marvel of engineering when it was built in the late 1800s.

West Quoddy Head Light

The West Quoddy Head lighthouse is located on the coast of Maine at the easternmost point in the United States. The distinctive red and white stripes of the tower give the appearance of a big candy cane.

Colchester Reef Light

This post-and-beam lighthouse was originally built in 1871 on Lake Champlain and moved inland in 1952 to the nearby Shelburne Museum in Vermont, where visitors can explore the structure.

Harbor Town Light

This lighthouse on Hilton Head Island in South Carolina is built of wood frame and wood siding as a symbol for the Sea Pines Plantation resort. It is claimed to be one of the most recognizable lighthouses in America.

Steel

The ability to make structural components from steel was an important turning point in the design of buildings, bridges, and towers. Using lessons learned in cast iron architecture, architects and engineers realized even taller buildings could be constructed with internal steel frames that acted much like a skeleton. These buildings could be built so tall they seemed to reach the clouds, and they quickly became known as skyscrapers. Cast iron, which is a close relative of steel, is brittle and not malleable like steel, so it could not be used for skyscraper frames.

Steel is an excellent material for making structural beams for a building's skeleton frame, because it is much stronger in both tension and compression than stone or wood, which were previously used to build huge structures. But, until the middle of the nineteenth century, steel was able to be produced only in small batches, which made it too expensive to use in large building projects. When new tech-niques were invented to inexpensively produce high-quality steel in larger amounts, steel beam construction became a major innovation in architecture and engineering.

The first large-scale structure built with steel was the Firth of Forth railway bridge in Scotland. It was completed in 1889 and is still in use today. The Empire State Building in New York City, although it is no longer the world's tallest skyscraper at 102 stories tall, represented the extraordinary possibilities of using steel for higher and higher con-structions.

Empire State Building

Firth of Forth railway bridge

ALL ABOUT

TALL AND INTERESTING TOWERS

A tower is a freestanding structure whose height is at least several times the diameter or diagonal of its base. The most commonly seen towers include radio and television broadcasting towers, water storage towers, forest lookout and observation towers, electric wire towers, and bell towers. Some tall chimneys, lighthouses, and silos might also be considered types of towers. Several famous towers include the Washington Monument in Washington, D.C., the Eiffel Tower in Paris, France, and the Leaning Tower of Piza in Italy.

What differentiates each of these structures from tall buildings is that a tower is not intended as a place for people to work or live. Most of the world's tallest towers were built as monuments to commemorate a person or an event, as defensive battlements, or, in the case of more modern towers, to support communications antennas. Many towers, like the Eiffel Tower, were built with no other purpose than to give visitors a "ladder to the sky… to climb up and have a look around." These grand observation towers present a view from them that is just as important as the view of them.

Even nature produces towers, especially in mountainous regions where the ice ages have left large spires of rock that can reach up thousands of feet. Devil's Tower in Wyoming rises 1312 feet from the desert floor. It is fifty million years old, and even has a sculpted exterior with naturally formed polygonal shapes.

The tallest freestanding human-made tower (and structure) in the world is the CN Tower in Toronto, Ontario, which reaches a total height of 1815 feet from ground level to the top of its antennas. That's equivalent to a skyscraper more than 180 stories tall. Several radio and communications masts are even higher, such as the Warszawa radio mast near Plock, Poland, which was 2120 feet tall until it came crashing down in 1991, and a TV tower near Fargo, North Dakota, at 2063 feet tall. But these tall structures are not self-supporting and must be guyed, which means they are held upright by taut wire cables anchored to the ground. Self-supporting towers have no guy wires and instead are usually splayed out at the bottom for stability.

Towers are built in a large variety of unique designs, but they are typically constructed with the same materials and methods used for tall structures and skyscrapers. In fact, very tall towers could be built only

Devil's Tower

after the introduction of iron- and steel-frame construction as well as special ways of using reinforced concrete.

The pride and bragging rights for claiming the new tallest tower are usually short-lived. It seems as though taller towers are always being built to support the communications antennas needed by modern-day radio, television, and wireless phone technology. And, to build ever taller communications towers, engineers have found that concrete construction works much better than a steel space-frame structure for several reasons.

Concrete is more rigid than steel, reducing the amount the tower will bend in the wind. Also, the more rigid the tower is, the higher the quality of the radio waves being transmitted from the antenna. Sometimes the metal struts of a steel tower will vibrate in the wind, causing a resonance that interferes with the clarity of the transmitted signals. A concrete structure is more aerodynamic to greatly muffle the sound of the wind and does not produce a harmful resonance. Metal towers need to be painted every eight to twelve years to protect against rust and corrosion, but concrete towers are usually left unpainted and need much less maintenance. And finally, building a tower of concrete is less expensive than using steel.

The following are some of the tallest and most interesting towers still standing around the world today.

CN Tower

The CN Tower, rising over a third of a mile high, is the tallest free-standing structure in the world. The tower was built using a special technique for molding its core support structure in concrete. The hollow, Y-shaped core, which keeps the tower steady in high winds, is like a tall chimney that tapers gently as it rises. The tower stands almost perfectly straight, with the tip of its spire only one inch from where it is supposed to be. The CN Tower's seven-story main pod is located two-thirds the way up. In addition to containing TV broadcasting equipment, the pod also

houses a revolving restaurant and two observation levels. Even higher up, there is another observation level with a view of one hundred miles in all directions. To get to the pod and observation levels, visitors take elevators that are glass fronted and operate on the outside of the building for a great view of the city.

Ostankino Tower

For many years, the Ostankino communications tower in Moscow held the title of the tallest structure in the world. The steel tower is considered a "vertical cantilever structure" because of the way its base is constructed to keep the tower standing. Under strong wind conditions, however, the spire at the top of the tower can bend nearly twelve feet from center. The uniquely sculptured steel tower not only supports television, radio, and communications antennas, it is also a popular tourist attraction. A fifty-eight-second ride to the observation deck at 1105 feet provides a view of all of Moscow, and just below the observation deck there is a restaurant with three revolving dining rooms.

Emley Moor Mast

This transmitting tower is actually the third tall structure to be built on this site. The first was a guy-wired 445-foot high antenna mast built in 1956 that somewhat resembled a skinny Eiffel Tower. That mast was replaced in 1964 with a 1265-foot-tall, guy-wired mast made of tubular steel. Unfortunately, ice would form and accumulate on the steel structure during winter storms, and the falling ice damaged several nearby buildings. Then, on March 19, 1969, the weight of the ice and

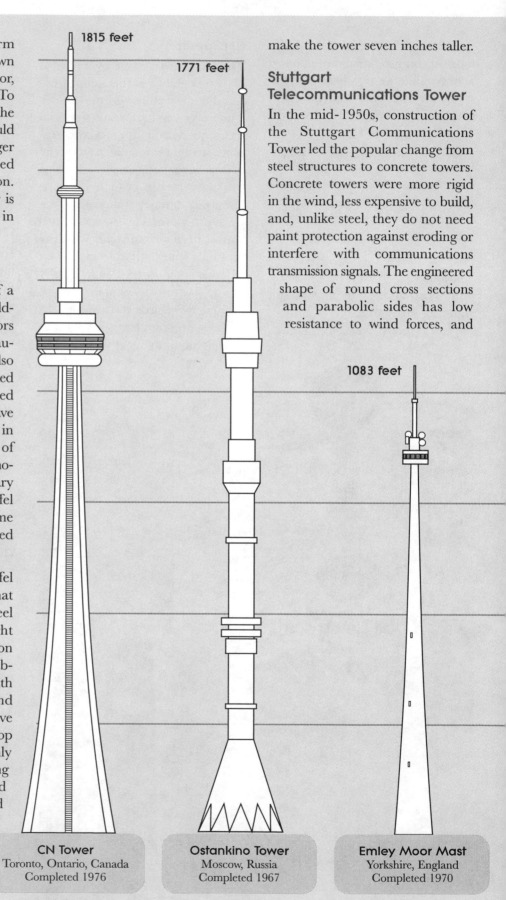

the strong winds from a storm brought the mast crashing down near the village of Emley Moor, destroying a local church. To replace that mast, and to assure the villagers that the new tower would present no future danger, a stronger concrete structure was designed and built in the same location. This newest Emley Moor tower is the tallest freestanding mast in Britain and all of Europe.

Eiffel Tower

The Eiffel Tower is something of a cross between a bridge and a building, with elevators that take visitors to observation platforms, a restaurant, and a small theater. It is also the first tower ever to be constructed using wrought iron struts assembled in a space-frame lattice. Gustave Eiffel won a design competition in Paris to create his "symbol of industry and science" to commemorate the one hundredth anniversary of the French revolution. Eiffel designed the tower using the same exposed-structure methods he used for designing bridges.

The legs and structure of the Eiffel Tower rise up in a curve that means none of its 18,038 steel parts come together at right angles. And since wrought iron cannot be welded, all these prefabricated pieces were drilled with holes, perfectly positioned, and assembled using two million five hundred thousand rivets. The top of this rigid iron tower may only lean about three inches in a strong wind, but the heating and expanding of the metal caused by the hot summer sun can bend the tower as much as six inches off center and

make the tower seven inches taller.

Stuttgart Telecommunications Tower

In the mid-1950s, construction of the Stuttgart Communications Tower led the popular change from steel structures to concrete towers. Concrete towers were more rigid in the wind, less expensive to build, and, unlike steel, they do not need paint protection against eroding or interfere with communications transmission signals. The engineered shape of round cross sections and parabolic sides has low resistance to wind forces, and

1815 feet

1771 feet

1083 feet

CN Tower
Toronto, Ontario, Canada
Completed 1976

Ostankino Tower
Moscow, Russia
Completed 1967

Emley Moor Mast
Yorkshire, England
Completed 1970

the smooth concrete surface doesn't howl in the wind. Besides its practical design and use, the tower also has a restaurant and observation deck with its railing tilted inward so visitors might feel less dizzy.

Washington Monument

This obelisk memorial is the world's tallest freestanding masonry structure and is constructed of stacked granite and marble blocks with no metal supports. In fact, the only metal in the entire structure is a small nine inch cast aluminum pyramid at the tip. (Aluminum was a rare metal in the 1800s.) And, even though buildings and structures in other cities today routinely exceed five hundred feet, federal law states that the Washington Monument will forever be the tallest structure in Washington, D.C.

The project began in 1833 when the newly formed Washington National Monument Society asked all Americans to donate one dollar (worth about sixteen dollars today) to build a memorial to the first president of the United States, George Washington. On the Fourth of July in 1848, the cornerstone was laid with a time capsule inside, and construction was started. After six years of building, construction abruptly stopped at 156 feet and did not resume until after the Civil War. On December 6, 1884, more than thirty-six years after it had been started, the aluminum-tipped marble capstone was set on top of the obelisk, and the tower was completed. Since then, the monument has become one of the most popular attractions in Washington, D.C., and it now has an elevator to take visitors to the top.

Leaning Tower of Pisa

Construction of the bell tower to the cathedral of Pisa, Italy, was begun in 1173, and work on the cylindrical stone and marble tower progressed nicely for the next five years. The tower was originally designed to be 328 feet high, and construction stopped and then started again several times over the next 150 years (mostly because of wars) until the structure began to tilt. Since it was impractical to continue building on a sinking foundation, the tower was considered finished in 1350 at a height of only 185 feet. Since then, the tower has continued to tilt farther each year, and now it is about fourteen feet out of plumb. (If you dropped a rock from the top edge of the tower, it would land fourteen feet away from edge of the base.) The inclination is increasing about one inch every twenty years, and if a fix is not found soon, the tower may collapse.

In 1934, engineers decided to shore up the foundation with concrete, but that attempt at stopping the tilt has since been blamed for actually making it worse. And in 1995, in an attempt to begin tilting the tower back upright, 830 tons of lead were added to the north side. So far, the tower has corrected its tilt by a little more than an inch.

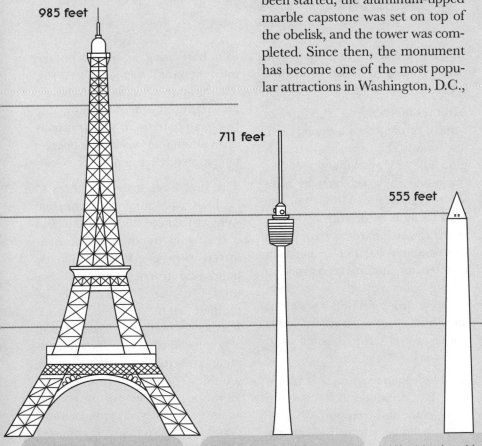

985 feet

711 feet

555 feet

185 feet

Eiffel Tower
Paris, France
Completed 1889

Stuttgart Telecom Tower
Stuttgart, Germany
Completed 1955

Washington Monument
Washington, D.C.
Completed 1884

Leaning Tower of Pisa
Pisa, Italy
Completed 1350

Reinforced Concrete

The development and improvement of reinforced concrete over the past one hundred years has revolutionized architecture, and today it is the most commonly used structural material. Before concrete is poured into a form that will give shape to the material, steel bars are laid in a pattern at the bottom of the form. The reinforcing steel bars that are molded into the concrete come in several different diameters and are called "rebar" for short. Rebar typically has ridges on its surface to bond better with the concrete. When the concrete hardens with the bars inside, the steel will handle the tension forces of a load placed upon the form, and the concrete on top will carry the forces of compression. This is a perfect balance of tension and compression forces, which results in the strongest structures. A solid slab of concrete that does not contain a steel framework can bend under its own weight, or the weight of a load, until it cracks and breaks.

Reinforced concrete is an excellent material for constructing buildings and other structures because it is fireproof, waterproof, soundproof, easy to make, and inexpensive. Concrete is also what is

called "plastic," meaning that before it hardens, it can be formed into any shape desired.

Most concrete is a mixture of cement combined with stones, sand, and gravel. The cement acts as a glue to hold everything together (including the steel bars in reinforced concrete). Most concrete used today is made with hydraulic cement, which hardens even if it is wet or under water. This makes it possible to continue construction during rainy periods or to build concrete structures under water. In fact, the longer concrete stays under water, the harder and stronger it gets.

The concrete mixture is usually prepared at a concrete plant and transported to the building site in big cement trucks with revolving tubs. These constantly turning tubs keep the cement well mixed and prevent it

from hardening before it is poured into prepared forms at the site. The temporary walls of the forms are removed once the concrete begins to harden, or set. It usually takes about four weeks for concrete to completely harden.

The first large-scale structures to be built with reinforced concrete were at first considered a fad. But it was soon discovered that reinforced concrete buildings made handsome structures, and architectural ornaments could easily be molded right into the forms. Further experiments and testing also proved that reinforced concrete structures were extremely durable, comparatively free from vibration, and good protection against the forces of tornadoes and floods. Today, reinforced concrete is a very popular building material used in a large variety of structures that includes all types of buildings, bridges, and towers.

FARM SILOS

The tall, cylindrical structures that stand next to or are attached to many barns are familiar sentinels of the farm landscape. Silos are used for storing certain harvested crops as they undergo a fermentation process that prepares the grains for becoming animal feed. Although some older silos in New England states were built square in shape, the more common round column shape of a silo has proved to be an elegant design for several reasons. A round silo is easy to clean because it has no inside corners, the round shape deflects the forces of the wind, and the structure is rather easy to construct.

For centuries, farmers have been finding ways to store grain, but only in the last 150 years have silos been built to resemble the tall structures commonly seen today. Early silos were just large pits dug into the earth and filled with grain, and some farmers stored piles of grain inside their barns. But no storage method worked as well as a tall, round cylinder. The first upright wooden silo in America appeared on an Illinois farm in 1873, and by the early 1900s, both wooden and fieldstone silos were a common rural sight. Although the cylindrical shape is now common to all silos, the materials and methods used for building the structure have evolved to also include bricks, blocks, metal, and concrete.

The earliest wooden silo structures were made by stacking wood hoops atop each other, but the hoops often sprung apart. The next generation used vertical wooden boards held together with metal hoops—similar to the construction of a wooden barrel. The design of the silo roof varied greatly from flat to pitched to cone- or dome-shaped. You might notice these buildings are rarely plumb, or perfectly vertical, and usually lean the way the prevailing wind pushes them.

By the early 1900s, there was a widespread change to masonry construction. Silos built with bricks, cast tiles, or cinder block were more durable than wood and better able to withstand both moisture and the outward forces of the silo's contents. Welded steel panels also proved to be more rigid and durable than wood. At the same time, the first concrete silos were being built using massive, formed concrete rings poured atop each other, and held in position by metal bands and turnbuckles. Today, reinforced concrete silos are built using a variety of methods, but typically have a poured concrete dome to cap the tower.

Pneumatics and Inflatables

Air is used as part of a structural system in many familiar objects, including bicycle tires, basketballs, and balloons. Air pressure is pumped inside these air-inflated objects to give them stiffness and form, then the inflated structure is sealed so the air can't escape. If any of these items were to lose air pressure, it would just deflate and collapse, and all that would be left would be its soft outer membrane.

Sometimes air is used to fill up and fill out a formed membrane shape that is not completely sealed, like hot air filling out a hot-air balloon or the wind filling out the sails of a

Air-inflated structures

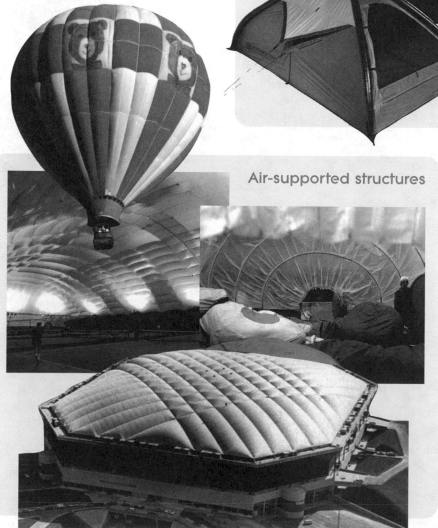

Air-supported structures

sailboat or the surfaces of a kite. Rather than being totally inflated and sealed, these air-shaped forms get their structural stiffness from a constant source of air pressure like a fan, and are called air-supported structures. Both air-inflated and air-supported forms are grouped into one building category known as pneumatic structures.

During the early twentieth century, when blimps and dirigibles were being developed as practical flying machines, engineers began to realize that an air-inflated balloon structure could also be used as a building system. However, this was not the first attempt at building a practical air-inflated structure. As long ago as 1000 B.C., boatmen on the rivers of Egypt had figured out a way to shape animal skins into air-inflated balloons that could be used like pontoons to float cargo rafts. And more recently in the 1930s, bathers were offered the first inflatable floatation devices made of a rubberized material.

Today, air-inflated rafts and beach toys are as popular as ever, and air-inflated architectural structures are typically used for large advertising balloons, novelty playground equipment, and some rather interestingly shaped enclosures.

During the 1950s and 1960s, air-supported pneumatic architecture began to become popular. The first practical application of the idea was an air-supported roof enclosure for radar systems. That was quickly followed by designs for air-supported roofs to cover large sports stadiums, worlds-fair pavilions, and other large spaces that needed to be wide-open inside without the interference of roof supports. In these structures, the shape of the roof membrane is made from large sheets of a rubberized or plastic material sealed together and air-supported by fans that continually blow air into the building and create the air pressure necessary to fill out and support the roof. But if the fans should stop working, the entire building would totally and quickly collapse.

One of the biggest benefits of pneumatic architecture is that even extremely large enclosures need no other support from posts or beams. In fact, pneumatic architecture is the only type of structure that is totally in tension—without any compression. However, even though pneumatic structures are considerably less expensive to build than conventional roofs and enclosures, most of them are only expected to last fifty years or less.

AN AIR-SUPPORTED RADOME

In the rural farmlands near Andover, Maine, there is an enormous, dome-shaped, air-supported structure that encloses an antenna and ground station for receiving and sending signals to global communications satellites. In order to operate properly, the antenna has to be protected from wind, rain, and snow, and yet no other type of enclosure is practical. Not only would a conventional type enclosure of steel and concrete be extremely expensive, the structure's materials would interfere with the signals sent and received.

Although the air-supported radome is well over one hundred feet tall and uses one hundred twenty thousand square feet of thin, rubber-coated fabric weighing over sixty thousand pounds, it only requires one or two small fans (each the size of a hair dryer) to keep the dome shape filled with air. On windy days or during snowfalls, the fabric is kept taught by turning on one or more additional fans to increase the interior pressure.

Since an air-supported structure can cover such a large area without any interior supports, some designers, engineers, and architects believe farms and even small cities may someday be covered with similar domes. The climate within such a dome could be completely controlled, allowing farmers to regulate ideal growing conditions, and people could live in perpetual spring-like weather regardless of the actual location. Oranges, olives, and palm trees could be grown in northern Canada, while homes in Florida would not need air-conditioning.

ALL ABOUT

FUTURE FANTASIES FROM THE PAST

Futuristic structures conceived but never built

Designers and architects frequently try to imagine how structures will be better and different in the future. Sometimes they only conceive new ideas in sketches, sometimes they build models of their futuristic designs, and every once in a while, one of the designs is actually built. Even if a futuristic concept is never built, the process of trying to imagine new designs for structures and the application of new materials and building methods is what ultimately leads to improvements and designs that better meet our changing needs.

Here are some futuristic structures that generated a lot of interest when they were first conceived, but for various reasons, none were ever built.

Fargo-Moorhead Cultural Center Bridge

Fargo, North Dakota, and Moorhead, Minnesota, are twin cities separated by the Red River. When it came time to replace an old bridge that connected the two cities, architect Michael Graves suggested a bridge with a cultural center in the middle that would both physically and symbolically link the two communities. The plan called for an art museum spanning the bridge and connecting to a concert hall and public radio and television stations on one side with a history museum on the other. The greenhouse-like structures looking out onto the river were an attempt to make a connection between the items being exhibited in the museums and their derivation from the land outside.

Walking City 1964 by Ron Herron, collage of vehicles in New York East River   © 1964 by Ron Herron

Walking City

Perhaps one of the most bizarre proposals in futuristic architecture was the Walking City. The concept was developed by Ron Herron, who was a member of a group of architects called Archigram. These futuristic thinkers experimented with all the possibilities of architecture, using an approach that did not limit their ideas to what was practical, safe, or even needed. In his plan, Herron conceived of huge walking machines, with each machine containing an entire city. A self-contained city could then walk all over the world, stopping wherever the inhabitants wanted. People of this society would live in house modules that could be plugged into one of the large walking machines that happened to be going their way.

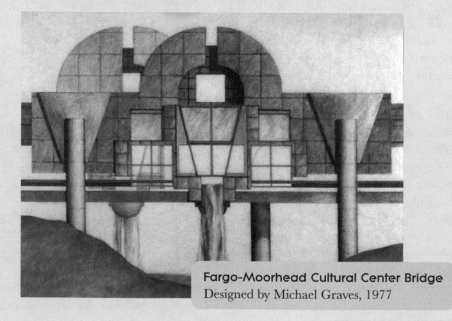

Fargo-Moorhead Cultural Center Bridge
Designed by Michael Graves, 1977

3D Jersey

The architect Paolo Soleri is best known for what he calls *arcologies*, a word he coined that is a combination of "architecture" and "ecology." To create arcologies, Soleri tried to design structures that did not harm or destroy the environment. One way to achieve his goal was to design "high density" buildings that could house a lot of people in a small area. That way much of the surrounding land could be left unbuilt, preserving the environment for people to enjoy.

In the late 1960s, Soleri began designing an arcology called 3D Jersey that was planned to be located in New Jersey somewhere between Philadelphia and New York City. In his proposed circular design, the main structures would cover an area of about one square mile and rise to a height of one-half mile. Within those structures would be the homes, schools, stores, and everything necessary to comfortably support a population of one million people. Industrial and warehouse buildings would radiate out from the main structure and would be covered with parks and gardens. A circular airport runway would ring the entire site.

Sky City
Designed by Buckminster Fuller, 1962

Sky City

The architect and engineer who invented the geodesic dome, Buckminster Fuller, constantly experimented with ways to apply this clever structure. Not only could a geodesic dome enclose open areas without columns for support, the structure made from rods and connectors could be built to almost any size. One of Fuller's ideas was to build a huge, transparent geodesic dome to cover all of midtown Manhattan in New York City. That would require the dome to be about two miles in diameter and cover an area of more than five hundred city blocks! The primary benefit of a covered city would be protection from bad weather, environmental pollution, and natural disasters.

Philadelphia City Hall Tower

Beginning in 1952, the architect Louis Kahn began designing a building that would have used concrete in a new way. The idea he proposed for a new Philadelphia City Hall Tower was a geodesic skyscraper made of tetrahedrons. In his design, rather than pouring concrete into molds to form structural walls and panels, molds would be used to form long concrete rods.

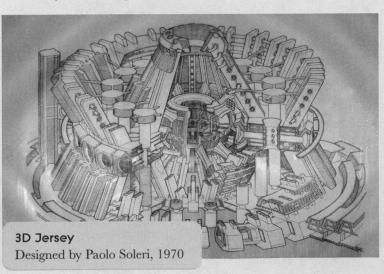

3D Jersey
Designed by Paolo Soleri, 1970

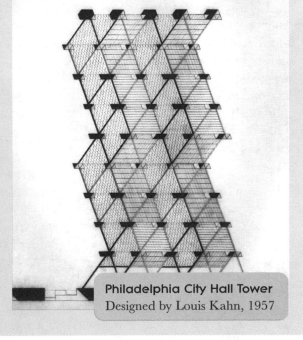

Philadelphia City Hall Tower
Designed by Louis Kahn, 1957

The rods would then be used with connectors to build tetrahedrons, and a configuration of tetrahedrons would create the structural skeleton that surrounded the outside of the building. The futuristic concept was not only visually exciting for the time, but also provided a lot of completely open spaces without columns or walls

Kahn considered creating spaces one of the most important functions of architecture. He referred to his proposed method of using concrete rods as "building with hollow stones," with spaces defined by the structural members. He also explained his concept for an exterior skeleton by claiming that "Space is architecture when the evidence of how it is made is seen and comprehended."

Mile High Skyscraper

Some architects have a fantasy to design the next tallest building in the world. But to architect Frank Lloyd Wright, the purpose of an enormously tall building was to address certain social, economic, and environmental issues. Wright believed that people in crowded cities needed more contact with nature and open spaces. His idea was to build a skyscraper that would rise one mile high and contain 528 stories. It would have been five times as tall as the world's tallest structure at that time, the Empire State Building.

The proposed building was so tall that an entire city with a population of over one hundred thousand people could live in the skyscraper instead of being spread out in houses on the ground. Wright even described the structure as "an upended street." And, because the building's footprint occupied so little ground space, it would free up the surrounding land that could be turned into parks and recreational spaces.

The building was designed to include six million square feet of living space, five levels of covered parking with enough room for fifteen thousand cars, and a helicopter landing pad on the roof that could accommodate one hundred helicopters. To move people quickly throughout the building, the elevators were five cars long.

The framework of the structure was designed like a tree, with a center column of concrete mimicking the tree trunk and the branches being recreated through the cantilevered floor slabs. Even the foundation was designed to be like the roots of a tree so the tall building would be safe from falling over in the high winds.

The concept of a mile high skyscraper was not intended to be just an exercise in futuristic design. Wright actually expected it to be built. To many other architects and engineers, the design seemed physically impossible, but Wright reassured everyone that such a building could be safely built. "It's a tetrahedron in form," he claimed, "It's really a tripod, so from whichever direction the wind comes, two of the sides stand braced against it."

In celebration of the remarkable design, the mayor of Chicago (the city where the building was expected to be built) pronounced September 17, 1956, as Frank Lloyd Wright Day. And on that day, Wright unveiled his plans for the mile high skyscraper with drawings that were twenty-six feet tall. In the end, however, the mile high skyscraper was never constructed because no one had enough money to build it.

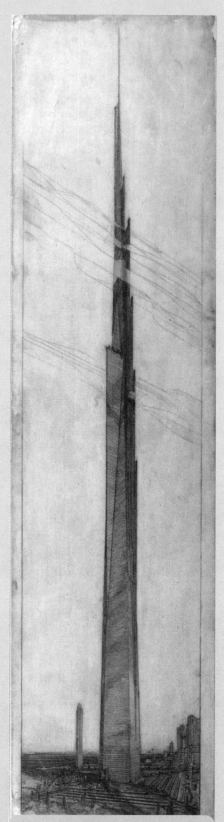

Mile High Skyscraper
Designed by Frank Lloyd Wright, 1956

CLEVER ANIMAL ARCHITECTS AND BUILDERS

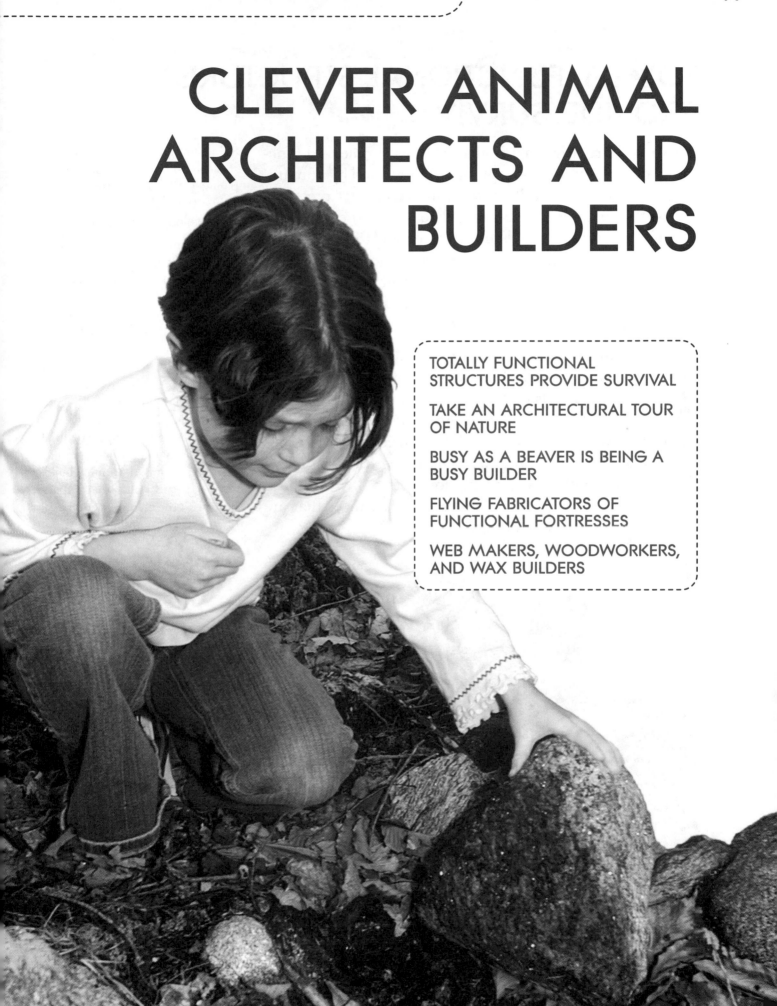

TOTALLY FUNCTIONAL STRUCTURES PROVIDE SURVIVAL

TAKE AN ARCHITECTURAL TOUR OF NATURE

BUSY AS A BEAVER IS BEING A BUSY BUILDER

FLYING FABRICATORS OF FUNCTIONAL FORTRESSES

WEB MAKERS, WOODWORKERS, AND WAX BUILDERS

TOTALLY FUNCTIONAL STRUCTURES PROVIDE SURVIVAL

Building a structure that is elegant in its simple and functional design is not a concept that was invented by humans. Long before cave dwellers, back to the earliest creatures on earth, structures were being built to protect their builders. Just like humans, animals need protection from the cold, rain, snow, and sun. Animals also need a home that is hidden or protected from enemies so they can safely sleep and raise their young. If an animal is to survive, it had better be a good builder.

Structures in the world of nature are always good examples of how the form and the method of construction are dictated by the needs of the builder. Bird nests come in a large variety of specialized designs, intricate spider webs are perfectly suited for the work they need to do, termites build huge "paper" houses as well as long tunnels that let them travel safely away from home, and beavers have learned how to build their homes with entrances that are accessible only by swimming under water.

Some animal dwellings are constructed only for the builder's occupancy, while others are meant to house the builder's family or an entire colony of many families.

In creating their magnificently functional structures, the only tools available to the animal builder are the parts of its body that can push, grab, bite, and chew. What is even more interesting is that each animal builder is also acting as an architect. That is, each animal goes through an instinctive and well-disciplined process of building that begins with selecting the best site and gathering the proper materials. Then, through a series of perfectly executed actions, the animal builder creates a safe home that expertly deals with the environmental issues of temperature and humidity control, protection from wind or rain, and even keeping out pollution.

TAKE AN ARCHITECTURAL TOUR OF NATURE

One of the ways an architect gets inspirations for new ideas is to look at the structures created by master architects, and that includes structures in nature as well as human-made ones. You have only to go outside and look around to see the results of nature's famous builders. There's even a good chance you'll get to see some of the world's greatest builders in action. Each animal construction can reveal many marvels of design, but only if you know something about the builder's reasons for making the structure that way.

Know Where to Look

It's easy to spot animal structures once you know where to look for them. Remember that an animal's home is probably built in a protected place.

So look in areas that might be out of reach to other animals. Look up in the trees for nests, look down at the ground for holes that might be entrances to homes, look in wood piles and rock piles, and, since animals need water to drink, look near streams, rivers, and lakes.

Look for ants building a mound and what you will see is the entrance to an elaborate maze of tunnels and chambers they are constructing underground. Look at a bird picking up a twig or pecking away at a mud puddle to gather materials to build a nest. Look for holes burrowed in the ground and you've probably found someone's home—maybe a rabbit, a mole, or a fox. Look up under the eaves of a house and you might see a many-

celled wasp's nest, a hornet's nest, or at least a spider web. If you're lucky, you might even see a bee-hive, which can be the home of hundreds of bees. Should you see a mound of sticks and branches piled up in a pond with small clouds of mist rising above it, you have discovered a beaver lodge and a sure sign that a beaver is inside. One of the easiest builders to catch in the act of building is a spider. Most spiders begin rebuilding a web every night, so early in the morning is a particularly good time for viewing the completed work.

Some animals are not such enthusiastic builders, so they may just improve a ready-made structure that nature, humans, or other animals have provided for free. Some birds look for a nest another bird has abandoned, then fix it up to their liking. Bears find a cave to live in and often add makeshift doors to the entrance by piling up dirt and leaves. Coyotes often move into abandoned badger holes, some crabs live in empty seashells, and bats look for a warm, dark, protected space where they can hang upside-down and sleep the day away. And

OBSERVING NATURE

- Remember to just observe nature; never disturb any animal's dwelling. Many tiny creatures, like insects, will let you approach them, but just about every other animal will be scared away if you get too close.

- If you happen to get too close to an animal's nest or off-spring, it could attack instead of running away. So when viewing larger creatures, keep a safe distance away.

- If you have a camera, bring it along to photo-

graph the structures you find.

- It's also a good idea to bring along a paper bag just in case you find the abandoned home of an animal to take with you.

just look under any rock and you will probably find some creature that has taken up residence.

Certain animals come with built-in mobile homes they carry everywhere they go, including snails, turtles, and clams. In fact, every empty shell you find at the beach was once the mobile home of some animal. One sea animal called coral is like a small jellyfish with a hard external skeleton to protect it. But instead of traveling, coral connects itself to other coral to form large communities called coral reefs. Sometimes these communities are huge—the Great Barrier Reef off Australia is over a thousand miles long.

BUSY AS A BEAVER IS BEING A BUSY BUILDER

A beaver is the undisputed king of animal architects. Beavers don't just build homes, they are skilled loggers at cutting down large trees and hauling the wood away, they are flood-control experts with the ability to construct dams in rivers to create their own private ponds, and they are master builders in constructing their water-bound fortresses called lodges. Beavers are such incredibly good builders that there is speculation that early human civilizations learned how to harvest timber and build dams by watching beavers at work.

Each family of beavers lives in its own pond, and it is usually a pond the beavers have created by damming up a river or stream. The first step in selecting a new home site is finding a stream with clean running water and plenty of trees along the banks. The trees will be used for food as well as for a building material. After choosing the exact location for the dam, it's time to start building.

All beavers are born with built-in construction tools. Their teeth are sharp and chisel-like, allowing them to gnaw through tree trunks, peel off bark, and nip off branches. Working in pairs from either side of the tree, the adult beavers in the family gnaw notches in the trunk and rip out the chips of wood between them. This process is repeated all around the trunk until the tree falls—beavers also know to get out

of the way when the tree is about to topple. Next, they gnaw off the branches and chop up the tree into building pieces, and, while doing so, the beavers eat the peeled bark.

Now comes the job of getting the building materials to the construction site where the dam and their new house are to be built. To start the dam, the beaver family members carry branch boughs to the site by gripping them with their teeth. Beavers are great swimmers, with tails shaped like broad paddles and webbed hind feet, so they find it much easier to move materials through water than over land. If the fallen tree is too far inland from the water, the beavers will dig a canal to the tree so the material can be floated all the way to the building site. These canals in themselves can be quite elaborate constructs extending far inland to tree stands and having their own small dams to maintain water levels.

To build the dam, the beaver pulls branch boughs down under the water and attaches them to the

bottom in very particular positions, using rocks and mud. On top of that, they pile up more boughs, sticks, mud, and grass until the dam spans the stream and stops its flow. A typical beaver dam is only a few feet high, but it may need to be anywhere from a few feet to a few hundred feet wide in order to contain the rising water that floods the riverbanks and forms the beaver pond. The newly formed beaver pond not only serves the beaver family, but it serves as a reservoir in times of drought, provides an ideal breeding ground for fish and other water life, and can even help stop a forest fire from spreading.

Using more trees, branches, bushes, reeds, and mud, the beavers build a huge mound somewhere near the middle of the pond. These conical-shaped structures can be up to twenty feet in diameter, beginning at the bottom of the pond and extending up to ten feet above the water. (Adult beavers are fairly large animals, about three to four feet long and weighing between fifty and a hundred pounds, so a family of beavers can take up quite a lot of space.)

To form the lodge's living quarters, the beavers next tunnel into the mound from underwater, burrow a hole to the upper part of the mound, and hollow out a cavern inside. This large, single room is inside the mound but completely above the water surface. As the beavers carve out their lodge, they don't just discard the excavated material. Instead, they shred the sticks and reeds into soft matting and spread it like a carpet on the floor. Beavers are always wet when

Beavers also build dams to create ponds.

they come up through the underwater entrance, and the shredded carpet acts like a drain, allowing the excess water to seep through the floor. A small area in the top of the mound is purposely not packed tight with mud so the loosely woven branches can provide ventilation.

The completed structure is a warm, dry home that can be entered only from underwater and is protected on all sides by the pond, like a castle surrounded by a moat. A hungry wolf might know the beavers are home inside, but there is no way he can get to them. In winter, when predators might cross the frozen pond on foot, they will find the lodge frozen tight by the cold, with the beavers safely inside. Beavers can still leave the lodge and swim under the ice to retrieve branches and green foliage they have kept in underwater storage for the winter months' food supply.

In all, a family of beavers will divide up the building tasks so that certain beavers are responsible for cutting down trees, trimming branches, transporting materials, making mud mortar, piling the material in place, applying the mortar, and packing the structure tightly by beating it with their big tails. There is even a beaver that seems to play architect and direct the work.

Beavers are born with the instincts and knowledge to build dams and lodges, and part of that innate ability is learning from building mistakes. Beavers will routinely examine their structures to look for weakness and damage and quickly make repairs. If the water level should rise and threaten to flood the lodge, a beaver will intentionally make a hole in the dam to drain off excess water to lower the pond.

Sometimes problems don't get better despite the beaver's best efforts. For example, mud, silt and other particles that would normally wash away downstream may gather in the dammed-up pond, making it dark and murky. Eventually, it may silt up entirely, forcing the beavers to move downstream to build yet another dam and another new home.

FLYING FABRICATORS OF FUNCTIONAL FORTRESSES

Almost all birds build nests, and nearly every type of bird builds with its own unique elements of architecture. Considering there are well over eight thousand species of birds, that's a lot of different nest designs. Some nests are quite simple, consisting only of stacks of random weavings of twigs, grasses, and found debris. The American eagle makes simple piles of sticks and branches to build an enormous elevated platform about as big as a bathtub, while the ostrich barely scratches a hole in the ground for its nest.

More complex nest building is done with mud or mud and straw masonry. The straw holds the mud together and keeps it from cracking apart if it becomes too dry. The barn swallow can build a hollow, bowl-shaped nest entirely out of mud balls and straw. The magpie also builds a bowl-shaped nest out of mud balls, but then covers it with woven twigs and lines the inside with soft grass.

Some birds are quite skilled at weaving very intricate nests from human-made fibers or grasses, while a few birds can build their entire nests by using only threads of their own saliva, which hardens on contact with the air. A delicacy known as "bird's nest soup" is made from these nests. The African weaver bird has the remarkable ability to tie grasses into a half-hitch knot and a slip knot by using its bill like knitting needles. In a thatched nest, the bird builder just keeps sticking pieces of straw into its haystack nest. And the common names of some birds reveal their unique building techniques, including the woodpecker, who pecks out splinters of wood to carve a hole home in a tree trunk, or the rufous-breasted castle builder, who builds a tiny fortress among the leaves.

Some birds are very particular about the materials they use. They seek out certain plants because they are strong and waterproof. Other birds will use materials provided by other animals. One type of hummingbird likes to use a spider's web to make its nest. Another kind of bird uses a snake's skin. Some members of the bird family, including ducks and geese, make their own nest-building materials. They grow a special kind of feather, called down, which is so fluffy that it acts as a blanket of insulation. These birds pluck the down feathers from their own bodies to line the inside of their nests. Down is such a good insulating material that we use it in winter coats and sleeping bags.

Robins Are Master Mud Makers

The robin, with its familiar red breast, is probably the most well-known bird in America and one of the best makers of mud plaster. To protect the robin's helpless newborn chicks, its nest is a strongly woven and heavily plastered cup shape that provides protection from every direction except directly above. Building the nest on a branch too low or close to the trunk would make the robins vulnerable to squirrels, but putting it too far out on a limb might send the nest crashing to the ground.

Once the site is chosen, the female robin gathers grass, straw, string, leaves, and small twigs, then she weaves the materials into a flat-topped ball. To form the ball into a nest, she sits on top of the ball and pushes out to the sides with her wings. This action is repeated over and over again as the robin rotates her body a little each time to mold the nest into its familiar cup shape. Meanwhile, the male robin's job is to stand guard over the project (scaring off any predators) and to supply food for the female builder. On some occasions, the male may also help gather the building materials.

After the nest is woven, it is heavily plastered with mud, and this is where the robin excels. If there is a mud source available, the robin will repeatedly pick up pellets in its beak, carry them back to the nest, and plaster the walls. The mud greatly strengthens the nest and provides extra insulation. The robin is also quite a resourceful builder. During a dry period, the robin will fill its mouth with dry soil and then fly to the nearest water source to dip its beak and make mud. And in some instances, the robin will wet its wings at the water source then shake the water off onto dusty soil to make mud.

The Baltimore Oriole Is a Clever Weaver

Of the birds that build their nests by weaving, the Baltimore oriole is one of the best. For protection from predators, orioles choose incredibly perilous building sites for their nests, such as the end of a skinny branch overhanging a rushing river or maybe directly over a busy highway. Even though the nest is in plain sight, it's beyond the reach of hungry animals. To make sure the nest can't be blown or shaken down, it is built strongly and firmly attached.

The oriole uses its beak as a needle to do the intricate weaving. The male may sometimes help, but it is the female's responsibility to build the nest. Using plant fibers and found pieces of string, thread, yarn, or hair, she first attaches several long strands to the end of a tree branch. Each strand is securely fastened with a knot. The oriole then adds more fibers and found materials to weave two walls that she

then stitches together to form a six-inch pouch with a small opening. Working like a weaver, the oriole secures each fiber or thread by knotting long strands to the structure and repeatedly pushing smaller strands and loose ends into the constructed mesh. Most of the weaving is done from within the open-topped pouch, which helps to both shape and smooth the inside.

WEB MAKERS, WOODWORKERS, AND WAX BUILDERS

Compared to their size, insects build the biggest buildings in the world. There are ants that build dirt mounds three feet high, others that carve tunnels through entire tree trunks, and termites that can build hollow towers of mud eighteen feet tall. While some insects like spiders prefer to do their home building alone, others, including ants, bees, and hornets, work in well-organized groups. In fact, insect builders are the most efficient work force on the planet. Each insect has a specific job to do, which could be gathering or making the building materials, constructing the nest, guarding it, finding food, or some other necessary task to ensure the nest gets built. These hard-working insects begin working immediately after they are born. Each insect knows exactly what to do without being taught and never seems to complain.

Spiders Make Webs in All Shapes and Sizes

A spider's web is perfectly designed to be both its home and a fresh-food catcher. Spiders have poor eyesight, so they just spend the day sitting on their web homes waiting for the next unsuspecting airborne insect to become trapped—soon to be food for the spider's next meal. Sticky goo over the spider's capture web keeps the flying prey from getting away once caught. The web structure works quite well, but not all webs are built the same way. There are actually thousands of different spiders, and each species

builds a web of its own unique design. Some webs look like a miniature hammock or the cobwebs in the corner of a ceiling, while others look more like crumpled balls of silk or even hollow tubes. But the most familiar spider web design is the orb shape, with its many concentric rings and spokes radiating from the center.

In producing an orb-shaped web, the spider is most efficiently using the least amount of thread to make a large and durable web. The silk strands that a spider secretes and weaves are actually stronger than nylon thread the same size and have

twice as much stretch. That means the spider's web can be blown in the wind without breaking. And even more important, it means the web can trap fast-flying insects and bugs and absorb the shock of their momentum without breaking.

The female spider usually does the building, and she works alone. The "main cable" of the web is first strung across two attachment points where the web will hang. Because there will be a lot of tension pulling down on this thread, she reinforces it by making it extra thick, like the main cable on a suspension bridge. (In many ways, the design of an orb-shaped web is very similar to the structure of a suspension bridge.)

Next, the spider hangs several silk strands from regularly spaced points on the main cable and joins the strands at the center of the web. More spokes are then put in place from the center to other attachment points. She then spins heavy, sticky strands across the spokes until the web is complete.

HOW TO COLLECT AND PRESERVE SPIDER WEBS

If you can get near enough to an interesting spider web for a close-up view, you might want to collect it. There is a simple way to remove and preserve the delicate web, using spray paint and paper. Don't worry about the spider. As long as you leave the spider behind and don't injure it, she will build another web, usually within a day.

The procedure for finding and collecting spider webs involves some knowledge to identify harmless spiders and some spray painting technique. Therefore, this project may require the assistance of an adult. For the best viewing and collecting of spider webs, first put together a kit of these materials.

- Baby powder—can be used to better see a web

- Spray paint—black or white spray enamel works well

- Heavy paper—use a paper color that contrasts with the paint color

- Scissors—for cutting paper and cutting the web support strands

Begin by looking for interesting spider webs. Look outside around the nooks and crannies of your home and between the branches of trees and bushes. Remember that you are looking for webs and not necessarily spiders, but it's still a good idea to know if there are any dangerous spiders living in your area so you can avoid them. When you locate a web worth dusting or collecting, be sure to first chase away any spider that may be residing there. Gently blowing on the spider will often cause her to leave the web for better protection elsewhere.

If you want to get a better look at a web but do not want to collect it, a light dusting of baby powder will stick to the silk strands and vividly reveal the web pattern. Just put a little powder in the palm of one hand, then clap both hands together to create a dusting cloud next to the web.

For collecting a web, follow these directions.

1. Cut a sheet of heavy paper to a size large enough to capture the entire web but small enough to be maneuvered into place behind the hanging web. Construction paper works well in colors that contrast with the paint color you will be using.

2. Sometimes it is possible to capture a web without it first being spray painted. You might try skipping this painting step and see if the natural stickiness of the web will allow it to stick to the paper. However, most of the time paint will better adhere the web to the paper and make the pattern clearly visible.

Shake and mix the spray paint following directions on the can. Hold the can about ten to twelve inches from the web, aim the spray nozzle, and lightly spray the web with paint, using a smooth back-and-forth motion. Don't allow the nozzle to get too close or the spray pressure could break the web. Also, don't apply a heavy coat of paint that could cause the strands to droop and break. Two or three light coats of paint, applied one right after the other, work best. Try to avoid spraying nearby structures and plants by protecting them first.

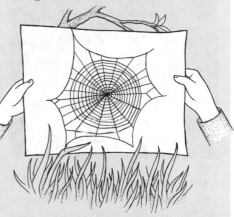

3. Quickly and carefully, before the paint has a chance to dry, place the paper sheet directly behind the painted web and move the paper into the web, lifting it onto the paper. Keep lifting until the support strands break away, or cut them with a pair of scissors.

4. As the paint dries, the web will remain stuck to the paper and the woven web pattern will be preserved, although it will still remain quite delicate. To keep and store preserved spider webs, you can apply a clear plastic laminate over the sheet or slip the sheet into a clear plastic sheet protector. Both laminates and sheet protectors can be found at office supply stores.

But if the strands were all sticky, the spider would get caught in its own web. The spider's secret is that she is able to produce both sticky and not sticky strands, and she uses both kinds when constructing the web. So when the spider runs out on the strands to collect her freshly caught prey, she clearly knows which strands to walk on. The orb-shaped web design also includes an escape route to a fortified shelter somewhere near an edge. This small enclosure and shelter is usually woven from small pieces of leaves and provides protection from predators and bad weather.

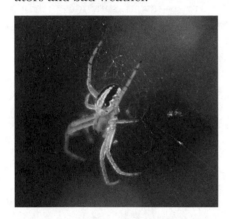

During the day, the spider uses the web as her parlor, sitting in the middle, waiting for flies and other flying insects to get caught in her "invisible" trap. She feels the web with her legs, and if the strands begin to vibrate, she knows an insect has become stuck. By the vibrations, the spider can also tell what kind of creature it is. If the vibration is strong, it's probably something dangerous like a bee. In that case, she would leave it alone or possibly cut it free. Smaller, lighter vibrations tell the spider that a meal has arrived.

Sometimes a bird flies into the web. When that happens, the whole thing is usually torn to pieces. Some spiders spin a thick chunk of white silk in their webs so that birds can see and avoid them.

Termites and Ants Are Dedicated Construction Workers

To most people, termites are destructive pests more noted for the damage they cause than for being skillful builders. Maybe that's because termites tend to hide themselves while they go about building their home nests, and they also travel in tunnels so they won't be seen. What people do sometimes see is the result of a termite feast on their wooden houses.

Wood is the preferred diet of these termites, so they are quite skillful at building tunnel enclosures that go from their underground homes up and over the house foundation and to the wood frame structure above. Inside these tubular tunnels made of wood fibers and soil, the termite workers travel undetected back and forth from their home to their plentiful source of food. Given enough time, termites have been known to make it all the way to the attic of a three-story house in search of still more fresh wood. You might never know termites have invaded a house until some of the visible wood starts to crumble away, or you spot one of their tunnel tubes.

Another type of termite lives in Africa and builds its home as a huge mound that can rise to ten, fifteen, or more feet above the ground. To build the mound, the termites mix soil and saliva to make adobe-like particles that they stack up, one by one. Termites work in large groups and are very fast builders. Each termite works on a small area of the larger structure, adding particle after particle until the shape is complete. A hard outer

Termite mound

shell covers the mound and is made from several compacted layers of mud with bits of material that act like reinforced concrete. This hard outer shell not only serves as protection from the many animals who would love to feast on fresh termites, but it also helps regulate the temperature inside the mound.

Inside the mound, the termite workers build an ingenious ventilation system designed to maintain a high level of humidity that preserves the termite's food and helps the young termites grow. Other inside structures might include a type of spiral staircase and several underground passages that lead to various locations outside the mound, so at night the termites can wander out to collect food and building materials.

Unlike termites, who work undercover, ants do a lot of their work

Ant hill

out in the open. The ants you're probably most familiar with are the ones that build small mounds of soil above the entrance to their nest. These little hills may rise up only an inch or two, but they're usually easy to spot because of all the ant activity going on around the entrance. Even in cities, ant mounds can be spotted on the cracks in sidewalks.

Some relatives of the common ant build mounds that can rise up several inches or several feet. These large anthills work like solar houses. Since the sides of the mound are steeply slanted, they get direct sunlight in the early morning and late afternoon when the sun is low in the sky. The ants open and close ventilation holes at the top of mounds to regulate the air temperature. When it's cold, they close all the entrances.

Carpenter ants, like termites, also bore through wood, but they don't actually eat the wood. Instead, the carpenter ants just chew at the wood and spit it out as they carve the tunnels that will become their new home.

Leaf-cutter ants, found mostly in tropical lands, including parts of the southern United States, excavate the soil to form large rooms under the ground that are mostly

Carpenter ants

used to make and store food. The actual ant nests are separate flat-top mounds interconnected to each other and to the food warehouse rooms by a maze of underground tunnels. Some of these cutter ant colonies contain hundreds of rooms and cover an area the size of several football fields.

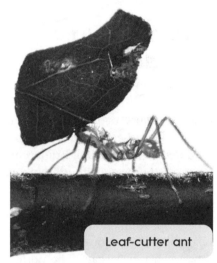

Leaf-cutter ant

But what is most interesting about the leaf-cutter ants is watching the way they collect the food to be stored in the rooms. As many as a half-million cutter ants may attack a small tree and cut off all its leaves in just a few hours. Using their jaws as scissors, each ant cuts off a piece of leaf, then carries it vertically over its head back to one of the storage rooms. Because the piece of leaf is so much bigger than the ant carrying it overhead, these ants are sometimes called "parasol" or "umbrella" ants. The pathway of these leaf-carrying ants walking single file can be hundreds of feet long. When the ants reach home, the leaf pieces are chewed to pulp and stored in rooms where the pulp grows a fungus that the ants can eat.

Honeybees Honeycomb Homes

Different types of bees build different kinds of homes. The bumblebee constructs a nest using found feathers and sticks them together with a sugar-like substance. Some bees build hives similar to the way wasps fabricate their paper. But, among all the bees, the honeybee takes credit for being the most ingenious builder. The well-guarded honeycomb structure they construct with wax is both their home and the storage site for the honey they produce.

Honeybees are very particular about finding the right location for building their honeycomb homes. It might be an existing hollow in a tree, under the protective eaves of a building, or maybe in a human-made beehive someone has purposely provided because they want to collect the honey. Once a location is established, construction proceeds quite rapidly as young female worker bees produce the wax and build the honeycomb cells. Even though the hexagonal-shaped and nested cells are fabricated with precise mathematical accuracy, the finished shape and appearance of the large multicelled structure can be somewhat arbitrary.

To produce the building wax, a group of the worker bees starts by eating as much honey as they can ingest. A young female worker bee has special glands that make wax from some of the honey, but it takes about six times as much honey to make one flake of building wax. The gorged bees then attach themselves to each other in long chains, which become all tangled to form a large, dense mass that might include hundreds of bees. The honeybee cluster warms up to 95°F, which is the temperature needed for the bees' bodies to produce wax. The wax is secreted in small flakes from each bee's abdomen and then scraped off

using her hind legs. The bee mixes the wax with her saliva and applies the flake to the hexagonal-shaped cell she is building. As the wax cools, it hardens, so the bees have to work quickly.

The hexagon shape is the perfect shape for making clusters of compartments because it gives the greatest amount of space for the least amount of building material used. Consider the other options. Instead of using hexagonal-shaped cells, what if the bee were to build the same size structure using triangular-shaped cells (three-sided) or square-shaped cells (four-sided)? All these structures will hold the same amount of honey, but the hexagonal-shaped cell has the smallest circumference, and that means

less material is used to build the hexagon structure than the square or triangle. If the cells were round, pentagonal (five-sided), or octagonal (eight-sided), there would be wasted spaces between cells and not many common cell walls, which means the structure would take extra material and extra work.

Wasps Build Wonders with Mud and Paper

Like the variety of construction styles other insects exhibit, wasps of different species build different types of homes. A mud dauber wasp, as its name implies, builds a home of mud, as does the organ pipe wasp, with a home design that resembles the connected long tubes of a pipe organ. The potter wasp builds a home that resembles a tiny, round clay pot. But among the most intriguing builders are the several species of wasps that build their homes out of a paper-like material they produce themselves. Using their sharp teeth as scrapers, the wasps collect wood fibers from

This papermaking wasp is starting a nest.

building boards, trees, and shrubs, then chew the fiber until it is soft and pulpy and ready to build with.

Papermaking wasps build their structures upside-down, attached to some secure structure by a thin stem. At the end of the stem, the wasp first builds the top floor of the home, which consists of several cells. When the top floor of the wasp apartment building becomes filled with eggs or newborns, the workers build another floor below

Papermaking wasps keep building one floor below the previous one.

the first. The floors are held together by vertical paper pillars, and the floors are connected to each other by paper ramps. This building of one floor below the previous one goes on for as long as more space and cells are needed.

Surrounding the layers of cells, the wasps then fabricate an outer paper skin or envelope. These "roofer" wasps make the outer covering by first producing the paper pulp and then pressing and sticking the soggy mass onto the structure by spreading it into long, thin strips with their forelegs. Walking backward, the wasp then pats the paper with its feelers to measure thickness and further flattens out

The completed nest is covered with paper-like strips.

any thick areas. Working from the bottom of the structure up, the strips of paper cover the open cells

in overlapping rings like roof shingles. Air spaces between the paper sheets help insulate the nest.

The ultimate size of a wasp nest structure can be as small as a grape or as big as a refrigerator. Even after the nest is covered and finished, the resident wasp population could decide to make it bigger by adding more floors of cells and expanding the size of the floors already built. But that means the roofer wasp builders must tear down the existing walls and construct a new and larger outer covering. One group of wasps simply works from the inside tearing down the old wall, while another crew on the outside builds the new wall envelope ▪

GETTING READY TO BUILD

GATHERING MATERIALS, PARTS, AND PIECES

THE RIGHT TOOLS AND HOW TO USE THEM

GOOD DESIGN IS GOOD FORM, FUNCTION, AND FUN

BUILDING PLUS CREATIVITY EQUALS INVENTION

GATHERING MATERIALS, PARTS, AND PIECES

MODULAR SCRAP MATERIALS MAKE BUILDING FUN

COLLECTING A RESOURCE OF BUILDING MATERIALS

SOME MATERIALS YOU MAY NEED TO PURCHASE

ADHESIVES, TAPES, AND MECHANICAL FASTENERS

PAINTS, BRUSHES, AND ROLLERS

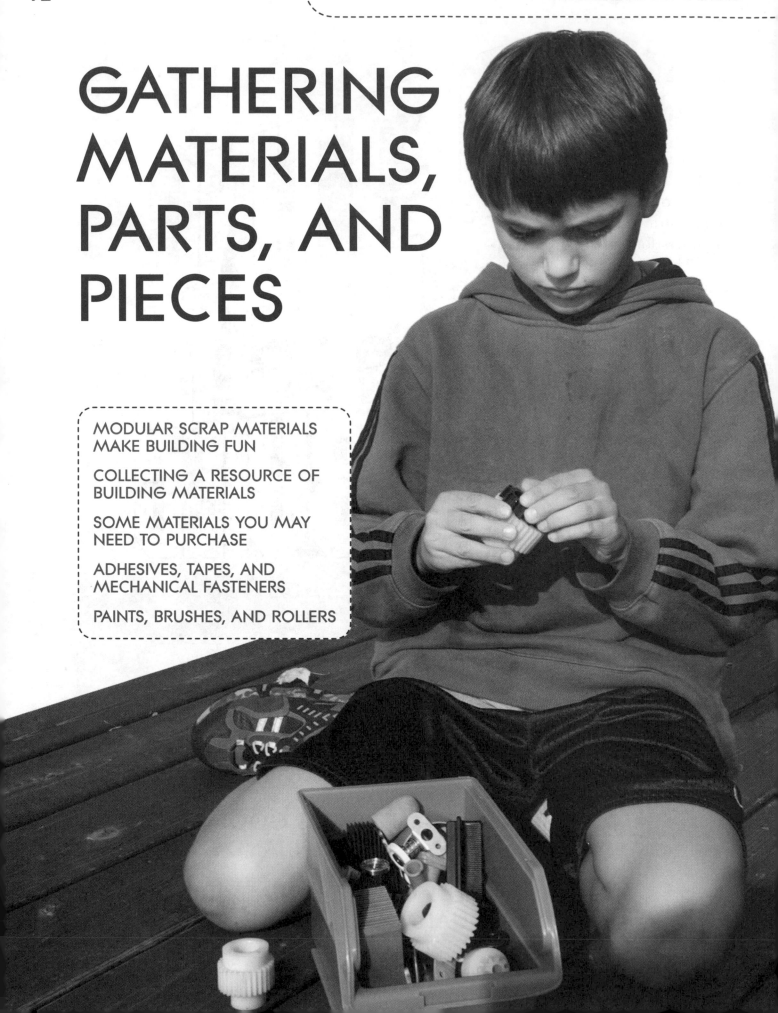

MODULAR SCRAP MATERIALS MAKE BUILDING FUN

Many of the common objects and materials you probably already have around your home can be used as building modules to make all kinds of fun structures. With enough drinking straws and paper tubes, you can build the trestles and chutes for a model roller coaster or maybe a "space station" bird feeder. Or, by using a bunch of empty peanut shells as bricks cemented with some flour and water "mortar," you can construct model buildings, towers, and sculptures. Even different pasta shapes can be used to build all kinds of models, including vehicles with pasta wheels. Almost any plentiful scrap material in which the pieces come in modular sizes, or are relatively identical, can become building parts. A starter list of modular-part possibilities might include buttons, paper plates, paper cups, paper clips, drinking straws, spaghetti, pipe cleaners, Popsicle sticks, tongue depressors, index cards, aluminum foil, and toilet paper tubes.

One of the big advantages of building with scrap materials and common ingredients is that you have the option of keeping the completed construction, disassembling it to reuse the parts, or even throwing it away. And it's also no problem if the finished construction accidentally gets broken. You made it, so you certainly know how to fix it—and there's bound to be more scrap material available. A good building project doesn't need to last forever; it just has to be fun.

The Secret of Putting Modular Parts Together

The real challenge of a homemade modular building system is inventing how to fasten one part to another. Some modular parts, like paper clips, pipe cleaners, and clothespins, can easily be fastened to themselves. But most homemade or scrap modular parts need a second element to fasten them together. Common fasteners include rubber bands, staples, tape, stickers, string, thread, and glue. Sometimes the fastening system is created by altering the module itself—for example, cutting a slit, poking a hole, folding, or bending.

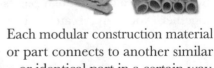

Each modular construction material or part connects to another similar or identical part in a certain way, repeating piece after piece until the structure takes shape. Some parts allow more freedom in building than others because they can be connected together in multiple ways or at several different angles. Others are quite limited in the ways they connect unless special parts are added to the system. The most elegant building systems are those with a single type of module that can be assembled into the most varied number of shapes.

Systems with the fewest different kinds of modular pieces are the easiest to build with, but are often the most limiting in the shapes and forms of structures they can produce. A deck of cards, sugar cubes, toothpicks, Q-tips, or paper clips can all be modular construction systems with a single type and size of module. That is, each piece of the system is virtually the same as all of the other pieces in the system.

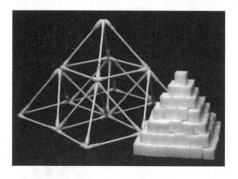

A slightly more complex modular system might include a second variable, such as size. For example, using drinking straws as the modular material, you could cut the straws to different lengths. Or, if you were building with dough bricks, you might make double-sized or half-sized bricks. Sometimes by combining a few modular pieces together, you can create a new

modular form. Three drinking straws threaded with string and tied to form a triangle would make a triangle module. Several triangle modules could then be tied together to create structures. Six straws tied to form a tetrahedron would create a three-dimensional version of the triangle module.

More sizes, shapes, and accessories being added to a module may greatly increase the flexibility of what the system can build, but it can also make the system more difficult to build with. Younger builders will find it easier to start with a simple single-unit modular construction system. Experienced builders will want to begin adding other materials to their constructions and take on more complex constructions and construction systems.

The construction systems and projects in this book are made from a variety of common objects and materials that can be used for modular construction. Some builders may want to find or create their own modular

building systems. Just remember that the real elegance of a building module is in discovering or inventing a simple way to fasten one part to another.

COLLECTING A RESOURCE OF BUILDING MATERIALS

You should have no problem finding the materials used in this book's projects. Most of these "treasures in the trash" are common discards left over from our daily consumption of stuff, and some are found in everyone's kitchen or home workshop (or the kitchen drawer that serves as a workshop toolbox in many people's homes).

Every day you probably throw away perfectly good construction materials without being aware of it. Paper tubes from toilet paper, paper towels, and kitchen wraps can collect quite quickly if you have a regular

place to store them. Milk cartons and other containers can be rinsed out and saved in bags or boxes (where the bags and boxes also are collected as building materials). Accumulating household odds and ends can be an activity in itself. How many toilet paper tubes do you generate in a week? How many plastic drinking straws can you collect in a day? If you didn't throw away cardboard boxes, what range of sizes would you have?

Another plentiful source of building materials is the stuff inconsiderate folks leave behind at camp sites, on beaches, or just throw out into the street or road. If only the polluter knew what to do with it, a soft-drink can could become a great raft, a plastic bag a kite, or a plastic bottle a squirt gun. (They also make pretty good shoes for walking on hot sand.) But since you do know how valuable all that stuff can be, take advantage of the opportunity and go on a materials search and collection mission. To give you some idea of what you can

expect to find, look at the list below. Each year, on one day, volunteers around the United States collect and count all the trash they can find on our coastal beaches. In a one-day count, this is what they typically find:

- 348,000 plastic bags
- 250,000 plastic bottles
- 35,000 six-pack holders
- 192,000 drinking straws
- 125,000 plastic-foam cups
- 235,000 glass bottles
- 107,000 bottle caps

To build certain structures, however, you might have to search the shelves at the food market or hardware store for the specific materials required. Searching through stores to find the right stuff will teach you much about the kinds of materials, fasteners, and specialized tools that are available. One of the best ways to find materials for solving a construction problem is to conduct a scavenger hunt through the store shelves, keeping the problem in mind and asking, "How can this material solve my problem?" If a salesperson asks if you need help, say, "I'm just inventing." Sometimes he or she will join in the hunt.

What to Get and Where to Get It

It's a good idea to keep a wide variety of building materials on hand, and plenty of them. The actual materials needed will depend, of course, on what you are building. But just having a large collection of materials will inspire solutions to problems. Most of the stuff you collect will probably come from common household materials and leftover scraps. Lots of parts also can be found in discarded items such as broken toys and old appliances. Here is a list of useful modular parts and where to find them.

Nature

stones
shells
branches
sticks and twigs
clay
mud
snow
water
acorns and pinecones
sand
grass and reeds
birch bark

Pantry or supermarket

graham crackers
paper plates
paper cups
Q-tips
pipe cleaners
toothpicks
drinking straws
plastic food wrap
aluminum foil
wax paper
twist ties
paper grocery bags
corrugated boxes
pasta
popped corn
sugar cubes
cakes of soap

Office supply store

rubber bands
paper clips
string
paper sheets
foam board
index cards
file folders
poster paperboard
balloons
pushpins
packaging tape
mending tape
paper rolls
construction paper
markers
labels and stickers
glue sticks
easel pads
envelopes
bubble wrap
shipping boxes
cardboard tubes

Waste, leftovers, discards, and extras

cardboard
fabric
incomplete deck of cards
old blankets and sheets
drinking straws
milk cartons
egg cartons
empty cans
paper and plastic cups
product packaging
plastic containers
plastic bottles
wire coat hangers
six-pack holders
paper tubes
magazines
newspaper
paper bags
bobby pins
empty cans
ribbon
yarn
string
wire
buttons

Hardware store

screws, nails, bolts, and nuts
Velcro
wood dowels
magnets
springs
tubing
plastic pipe and connectors
thin wire
fishing line
glue
hot-melt glue sticks
wax
wire screening
plastic drop cloth
wallpaper
shoelaces
rope
chain
duct tape
plaster
concrete
plywood
lumber
sheet metal
sheet plastic

Scrounged parts from . . .

small appliances
construction site discards
toys
lamps
and other things

Music-Making Materials

Have you ever noticed that when a nail, a spoon, or some other piece of metal falls on a hard surface like a table or floor, it makes a ringing sound? Or that pieces of different sizes and shapes each make sound at their own particular pitch? Almost anything will make a musical sound if you can figure out how to play it, and that usually means knowing where and how to tap it, pluck it, or blow it. Here are a few classic music-making materials and simple instruments you can build and play.

No lessons and no talent are required to play these basic and rather crude homemade musical instruments. They are not intended to make really good music (or really bad music, either), but music-making materials are fun to build to see what sounds and notes you can make using everyday objects. Rhythm instruments, like sandpaper rhythm blocks, pencil and fingertip drumsticks, or the jug and bottle base horn, can be played to experiment with different beats, to mimic familiar sounds, or to play in rhythm to recorded music or even your own singing. Can you tap, blow, scrape, or beat out the rhythm of your name? Can you play the same rhythm on different instruments? And can you mimic the rhythm from the sound of a pile driver, a sewing machine, a woodpecker, or a thunderstorm?

If you happen to have a "good ear" for music, try to pick out tunes or make up your own melodies on musical nails or a glass bottle xylophone. Those who are really musically ambitious could get some friends or family to join in and form a jug band.

Musical nails and bolts

Musical nails can either be played as an instrument or hung outdoors as a wind chime. Begin by gathering a collection of large nails in different sizes. Nails produce a pleasant, chime-like sound, but large bolts will also produce nice sounds. If you cannot find all the large nails you need by looking around your home, buy an assortment of nails at the hardware store, trying to get at least six or eight sizes. You will also need some very thin string or nylon sewing thread. String that is too heavy will make the nail chimes sound dull.

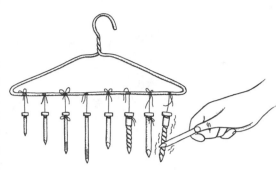

Tie a length of string or thread around the head of a nail and suspend the nail from the string. Do the same with the other size nails and arrange them in order from the lowest to highest sounding note by tapping each nail with a mallet, like another large nail, a pencil, or a spoon. The longest and fattest nail should make the lowest tone. Now find a place to hang the musical nails, for example, from a railing, the rung or back of a chair, a coat hanger, or the edge of a table.

Striking the nails in order will probably not produce a clear octave of notes, like a piano has, but you can still try to play simple songs and invent your own. If you want to tune the nails to exact notes, the pitch of any nail can be raised by filing off some of its length. If you spend enough time filing and testing, you can make a pretty good musical-nail xylophone.

Glass bottle xylophone

Find a place to build where spilled water won't cause damage, such as a kitchen counter. Line up several glass bottles or drinking glasses. To make a full-octave, eight-note xylophone you may need to use eight glasses in a combination of shapes and sizes. They must be made of glass (plastic won't work), and the thinner the glass is, the nicer the tone will be. Test the pitch of each empty glass by flicking it with your fingernail or by striking it gently at the rim with a pencil or spoon. Each differently shaped glass will produce its own unique ring. Replace any glass that does not

produce a clear, one-note tone. To lower the pitch of any glass, play it over and over again while slowly filling it with water until you get the note you want.

To make a tunable xylophone, begin by lining up eight empty glasses in a row in front of you. Arrange the glasses in order from the lowest pitch on the left to the highest pitch on the right. Fill the glass on the left end nearly completely to the top with water and then tap the rim. The note you get will be the first note, or *do*, on the musical scale. Now pour water into the next glass until you get a clear second note, or *re*, and continue with the rest of the glasses in order, filling each just enough to get *me, fa, so, la, ti,* and *do*. You might need another instrument or person to help with the tuning. When your glass bottle xylophone is properly tuned, try to play or pick out a simple tune by tapping out the notes on the musical glasses. Advanced players should try adding more notes and playing with both hands.

T.P. paper tube kazoo

The kazoo is a good instrument for experimenting with musical sounds because it can be played instantly by anyone who can sing a melody in "doo-doo-doo-doo-doos" (kind of a cross between humming the melody and singing the lyrics). Once you understand how to make the

right sound, it's very easy to play any song you know in the high-pitched, raspy sound of a kazoo.

The kazoo is considered a real instrument, and this one, made from a piece of wax paper, a rubber band, and a toilet paper tube, really sounds good.

Begin by wrapping a single thickness of wax paper pulled tautly over one open end of the tube, and hold the paper in place with a rubber band. Aluminum foil will also work instead of wax paper, but the sound will be higher pitched and not as loud. Next, using a pointed pencil, punch a hole through the side of the tube closer to the end with the wax paper. To play the kazoo, hold the open end around the outside of your mouth, pucker your lips, and

begin singing or humming a song in "doo-doos." Try a little improvisation like "doo-doo-doodle, doo-doo-doodle-oodle, doo-doo-doodle-oodle-doo." Now try kazooing to the music of a CD or radio.

Sandpaper rhythm blocks

This is a very simple but very effective rhythm instrument that can produce the sound effects of a steam engine train, rainfall on a roof, or wind rustling tree branches. All you need is medium or fine grit sandpaper and a pair of small, empty packaging boxes in a size you can hold in one hand, like a toothpaste box, a box that holds a bar of soap, or the box from an individual serving of cereal. Small wooden blocks will also work. Fold,

crease, then tear the sheet of sandpaper to fit the width of the box, leaving the length long. With the sandpaper side facing out, wrap the strip around the box and tape the overlapping edge to the two exposed box ends. Using the leftover sandpaper, do the same thing with the other box.

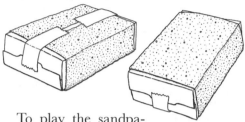

To play the sandpaper blocks, hold one in each hand by grasping the sides like a brick, and brush the flat sandpaper faces gently back and forth against each other in a steady rhythm. Play a song and try keeping rhythm to it, varying the sounds you make. By experimenting with different rhythms and different grit sandpaper, you might be able to create some interesting sound effects.

Rubber band and box banjo

There is no melody instrument that is easier to make or play than a rubber band and box banjo. Simply stretch several rubber bands around an open box and pluck away. The secret of making a good instrument is finding the right box, one that will be a good amplifier of the notes and not collapse its sides from the combined force of the rubber bands. See what sturdy, small boxes you can find, or use a small, rectangular plastic food container with the lid removed.

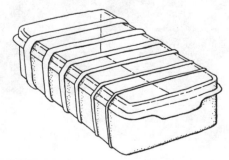

Rubber bands of different lengths, widths, and thicknesses will produce different sounding notes. And because the tension on the rubber band also affects the pitch of the note it plays when plucked, you can slightly change the pitch by adjusting the tension of the rubber band across the box opening. However, don't expect a rubber band banjo to keep its tune to any particular notes. At best, the twangy sound can accompany a song to add emphasis to the music.

Cartons and cans
washtub bass

A jug-band style washtub bass made from a sturdy corrugated box, an empty metal paint can, or a plastic bucket may not sound as good or as loud as one made from a metal washtub, but it will work well enough to play a simple melody or to pluck out a rhythm of bass notes that harmonize with other music. For the neck of the instrument, use a straight section of a branch or a wooden dowel sized proportionally to the container. If you use a large box or bucket, make the neck about as long as the distance from the floor to your shoulders. For an empty gallon-sized paint can, a smaller neck, roughly eighteen inches long, is about right. Turn the container open side down, and punch a small hole in the center of the bottom, using a nail and hammer.

Thread one end of a thin nylon cord or heavy fishing line through the hole into the container, and tie a twig or something similar to the end of the cord to prevent it from pulling back up through the hole. Next, rest the fatter end of the long stick on the edge of the container, and tie the free end of the cord to the top of the stick so it is taut when the stick is held straight upright. To play the

washtub bass, stand or sit behind the neck and put one foot on the top of the container to keep it from sliding. Hold the neck in one hand and pluck the cord with the other hand. You can raise or lower the pitch of the notes by how much you pull back on the neck to slightly tighten or loosen the cord.

Pencil and fingertip drumsticks plus anything drums

Have you ever found yourself beating out the rhythm of a song by tapping your feet or fingers, or drumming a pencil on the table, or jingling the change in your pocket? Notice how the sound depends on what surface and object you are using. Just about any hard surface or container can be used to make drum-like sounds. Try large, empty tin cans like the ones used for coffee or paint. See what sounds you can get from an empty flowerpot, cooking pot, cake pan, or even a car hubcap or a metal can lid. Tap each one with your fingers and with the eraser end of a full-length pencil to see which drumstick makes the most pleasant sounds.

Usually, the larger the object, the easier it is to play and the louder the sound it will make. Select the drum sounds you like best, and practice tapping out rhythms by combining different drum sounds.

Jug and bottle bass horn

Any jug or bottle with a skinny neck and opening can make a good wind instrument with a note that sounds like a foghorn. Large soft-drink bottles and plastic jugs work well. The larger the jug, the lower note it will sound, and vice versa. To play a note, hold the rim of the bottle or jug against your puckered lips so that your bottom lip is pressed against the side of the

neck and flush with the opening, and your top lip is slightly arched over the opening. Now blow across the opening—not too hard, but not too softly. Practice adjusting your lips slightly as you blow until you get a deep, vibrating note. After experimenting with different jugs and bottles, you will learn how to change the way you pucker and place your lips for different sizes and types. To play the bottle bass horn to music, just blow a note in time to each beat of the song. If you want to change the note, either use a different size of bottle or jug or partially fill the one you're using with water.

SOME MATERIALS YOU MAY NEED TO PURCHASE

Some building projects require specific materials that are hard to find as scraps and discards. Thin foam board with paper attached to either side is excellent for building models and is readily available at office supply stores. A walk through a lumber yard or a home improvement store will reveal a vast resource of materials that can be used for building projects, and some are so inexpensive that they should be considered as worthwhile additions to the builder's materials resource center. Plastic piping, for example, may be made for plumbing, but it also makes excellent space-frame construction material, with rods that can be cut to any length and snug-fitting connectors that come in several angles. Lumber and wood products are some of the most common building materials that may need to be purchased if the right scraps and discards are not available.

Wood and Lumber

Wood comes from large, fully grown trees that started out as small seedlings. Every year a new layer of wood grows around the tree trunk and branches (just under the bark), and the tree gets fatter. Maybe you have seen the annual growth rings on the cut end of a log and counted them to determine the age of the tree. Each layer of this annual growth is made of wood fibers that generally grow from the bottom up in the direction necessary to make the tree grow taller and the branches grow longer.

These wood fibers and the direction in which they grow can easily be seen on a piece of bare wood by looking at the pattern of the wood's grain. When looking at the growth rings, you are looking at the end grain. The grain pattern on the other sides of a piece of lumber may appear as parallel lines, squiggles, or ovals and will depend on which part of the log the piece was cut from.

The various patterns of wood grain produced by different types of trees and different cuts of lumber are often considered aesthetically pleasing, but grain direction and pattern serve a much more important purpose for selecting a cut of wood. Lumber that has a grain pattern running lengthwise from end to end will serve as a much stronger beam than a cut in

which the grain runs across the narrow part of the board. Try this experiment to demonstrate the important relationship between grain direction and strength.

When making anything from lumber, use the material's grain to create strength where it is needed most. For example, think of which direction the wood grain would go if you were using a piece of wood for a broom handle, a bookshelf, or a fence post. Most lumber already comes with the grain running lengthwise from end to end. However, when using smaller pieces of wood, short boards, and odd-shaped pieces, make sure the grain is placed in the right direction for maximum strength. And if you plan to whittle or carve the wood, a little experimenting will

EXPERIMENT

UNDERSTANDING THE STRUCTURE OF WOOD GRAIN

Make a square piece of "toothpick and tape" lumber. Lay out two strips of masking tape side by side with the sticky side up (other types of tape can also be used). Now line up toothpicks side by side across the tape until a square is formed.

You can also use drinking straws, pencils, or pasta to form the square if toothpicks aren't available. Fold

the tape ends over the toothpicks and you have a simulated piece of lumber with the toothpicks forming the grain.

Handling this small square board quickly reveals that it bends easily in one direction but not in another. If you were to use this square plank as a bridge over a river, in what direction would the grain go—from one bridge support to the other or in the same direction as the river?

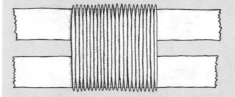

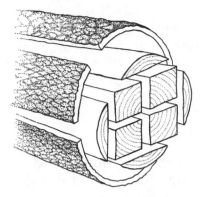 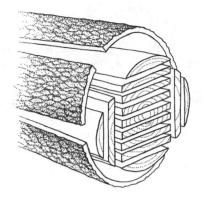 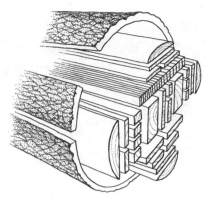

show you how difficult it can be to cut or sand across the end grain. So try to lay out the work to do most of the cutting in the same direction as the grain running along the sides of the wood piece.

Types of lumber

Wood is divided into two general types—hardwoods and softwoods. As their names imply, hardwoods like oak, maple, mahogany, cherry, and walnut are harder than softwoods like pine, fir, spruce, cedar, or redwood. For building projects, the softwoods are much easier to cut, sand, nail, screw, and glue. The availability and cost of certain softwoods will depend on where you live. In the northeastern United States, pine is quite plentiful and inexpensive (Maine is called the "Pine Tree State"), and redwood is quite expensive everywhere except northern California, where it is grown. If the building project is to be used outside, some softwoods, including pine, fir, and spruce, will require a protective finish of paint to resist decay. Other softwoods like cedar and redwood are naturally resistant to decay and do not need a finish.

Lumber is purchased by size and grade of quality, but getting the size you want could take a little figuring. "Milled lumber" is usually cut to the exact size you ask for, so a two-inch-thick piece of pine that is four inches wide by twenty-four inches long will be exactly that size.

However, "dimension lumber," typically used to frame houses and other structures, is actually smaller than the "nominal" size by which it is sold. The two-inch by four-inch board you want to buy may have started out that dimension when it was cut from a tree, but through drying and shrinkage and planing to make it smooth, the so-called "two by four" ends up actually measuring $1\,5/8$ inches thick by $3\,1/2$ inches wide. On the other hand, the length of the board will exactly match what you ask for because the length is cut after the lumber has been dried and planed.

The other piece of information you may need to tell the lumber store is what grade of lumber you want. Grading lumber can be confusing because combinations of numbers and letters are used to describe the surface of the wood, including whether knots and imperfections are present and how noticeable they are. Lumber is also graded as common—which is typically used for general construction purposes and for fabricating structure systems, and select—which is

often used for finer woodworking projects like building furniture and models. The easiest way to understand lumber grading is to remember that select grades are better than common grades, and the lower the number the higher the quality. Any piece of select grade lumber is excellent for most beginners' building projects because it is smooth, relatively free of knots, and easy to paint. For a piece of common lumber, a No. 1 grade will have the fewest knots and surface blemishes, and a No. 5 grade will be very rough with possible gauges, splinters, and lots of knots and knotholes.

Pine is a good all-purpose wood for many kids' projects because it is easy to work with. The very best clear grades of pine have no knotholes. A No. 2 grade piece of pine costs a lot less, but it contains knots that are very difficult to carve, cut through, or sand smooth. In some regions, you might be able to get blocks of sugar pine that are especially clear and easy to whittle and carve.

Plywood

Plywood comes in large, thin sheets and is a highly versatile building material, especially for big projects. Plywood is made by layering several thin sheets of wood, called veneers, one on top of another like a sandwich or a layer cake. Each veneer is placed so that the direction of its wood grain is at a right angle to the veneer below it, and the veneers are then glued together.

This layered fabrication gives plywood several advantages over solid dimension lumber. Plywood has strength in all directions, it has better resistance to warping, it is less likely to split or crack and, because it comes in large sheets, it is easy to install and less costly.

However, the same qualities that make plywood stronger than solid wood also make it more difficult to cut. The alternating grain patterns can also make cuts look messy. A handsaw or power saw with fine teeth will make the smoothest, straightest cuts in plywood. One way to make cleaner cuts is to first place a length of masking tape on both sides of the plywood right in line with the cut. When you cut through the wood, the tape will keep the surface veneers from splintering.

As with regular lumber, plywood made from both softwoods and hardwoods is available, as well as special types for exterior use made with weatherproof glues. Hardwood plywood is expensive and mostly used for making furniture and cabinets. Softwood plywood, usually made from Douglas fir, is the type used in most construction and structure-building projects. It comes in four-foot by eight-foot sheets and its thickness is typically between a quarter of an inch and one inch.

Plywood is also rated on different grades of quality that refer to the amount of imperfections on both surfaces. On many plywood projects, only one side of the material will be seen, so sheets of softwood plywood will often have a combination letter grade like "A-C" or "C-D" to indicate a different grade for the surface on each side. A sheet with large knotholes will have a lower letter grade than one without any knotholes. Here is a listing of some of the most common grades of plywood.

Grade A

Smooth and paintable surface with a few neatly made repairs

Grade B

Smooth and paintable surface with some tight knots and several repair patches

Grade C

Surface has knots, small knotholes, and some splits

Grade D

Large knots and knotholes, and some splits

Dowels

Most wooden dowels are made from maple or birch woods and come in thirty-six-inch lengths with diameters ranging from $1/8$ inch to one inch. Thinner dowels are also available, but they are more likely to be found at a crafts store than a

hardware store. Larger diameter and longer wooden closet poles are available at most lumber stores. Dowels are commonly cut into short lengths and placed between the two pieces in matching drilled holes to strengthen the joints in wooden building projects. But because they come in several diameters and can be cut to various lengths, dowels are also excellent for a wide variety of building projects, especially for making axles, wheels, rollers, struts, and columns.

Hardboard, fiberboard, and other composite boards

Hardboard and fiberboard, like plywood, come in large, stiff, four-foot by eight-foot sheets. But instead of using many thin layers of wood veneer, these composite boards are made from small wood chips, sawdust, or wood fibers held together by hardened glue. The scrap wood material is heated with the glue, and the mixture is compressed into large, flat sheets. Fiberboard is made from wood or vegetable fiber and is relatively soft in comparison to hardboard or plywood.

Hardboard, fiberboard, and other lumber-like composites have no knots or direction of grain. They are typically harder and more dense (heavier) than plywood, and they have smooth or evenly textured surfaces. Some of these boards are easy to cut and shape, but the hard glue used to make the material can quickly dull regular cutting tools. And composite boards do not hold a fastener very well, making it difficult to nail or screw anything into the material. In construction, nails or other fasteners are driven through the composite board into a piece of lumber behind it.

ADHESIVES, TAPES, AND MECHANICAL FASTENERS

Regardless of what materials are being used in a building project, individual pieces need to be attached to other pieces using some type of fastener that is appropriate for the structure being built. Just look around you to see how many different ways pieces are fastened together using nails, tape, zippers, paper clips, bolts, cement, and so on. Each method of fastening was probably selected because it worked well with the material and the way the parts fit together.

Some joints are meant to be fastened forever, while others might need to be taken apart later. That is usually the first decision to make when figuring out what adhesive or fastener will work best with the material you are using.

THE INVENTION OF GLUES AND ADHESIVES

Glues and adhesives are a common part of everyday life. Glues are used to seal envelopes and attach postage stamps, to assemble the parts of a model kit, to reassemble broken parts, and to build many things. Glues are used to stiffen fabrics, attach the layers of plywood, and assemble the parts of shoes. And as better glues and adhesives are created, they continue to replace more conventional ways of fastening materials together.

In addition to screws, bolts, and welds, a typical car now uses nearly thirty pounds of glue to keep parts together, and a large airplane uses more than a thousand pounds of adhesive. These glues are often stronger than the fasteners they replace. Special adhesives are now used by doctors to set broken bones or in place of sutures for stitching up wounds.

But not all glues are a recent invention. Glues were used by some civilizations at least five thousand years ago, and up until the 1930s, the process for making glue had not changed very much. The Egyptians boiled animal bones, hides, and other animal parts to create a thick, gooey substance that made things stick together. Technically speaking, only animal-derived sticky materials are actually considered glues. Most modern day synthetic glues are derived from chemical processes and are more accurately called adhesives. For practical purposes, however, both glue and adhesive are used interchangeably to refer to any type of adhesive.

All glues and adhesives work by surface attachment, that is, by hooking onto both surfaces being attached. You can't see the hooks—the microscopic molecules of the adhesive are what physically attach themselves to the molecules of the materials being joined. When first applied, most glues are liquid so they can penetrate or conform to the material's surface. When dry, the molecule hooks harden into a strong film. Water-based glues dry when the water within them evaporates, which could take several hours. Many nonwater-based glues use solvents that evaporate more quickly—a few even instantly.

Some modern chemical adhesives are incredibly strong. In an advertisement for one brand of super glue, a crane was shown hoisting a car in the air with only a single drop of glue carrying the entire weight. Another brand of glue displayed a similar ad but used an elephant instead of a car. Technology has also been developed to produce adhesives that are meant not to stick well at all, like sticky notes, and adhesives meant to stick and be unstuck over and over, like some closures on packaging. In the future, you can expect to see other types of adhesives that will replace more current-day fasteners and even allow new inventions, like sticky-bottom shoes that don't slip on ice.

Sometimes you will have several good choices for the type of fastener to use with your material, and your selection may depend on which fasteners are most available, which ones are the easiest to use, or maybe even which type you think would look best. For example, two pieces of wood can be fastened together with nails, screws, bolts, or glue. Or, depending on the type of joint needed, those same pieces of wood might even be fastened with twine, tape, rubber bands, hinges, Velcro, or aluminum foil.

Other criteria for selecting a fastener might include the age, skills, and interests of the builder. It is a lot faster and takes much less skill and patience to hold two parts together with a piece of tape than to drill a hole through them for a bolt and nut. Of course, the most important building criterion is that the fastener selected does the job intended. What follows is a listing of the most common building fasteners and the typical materials that work best with each. If your first choice of fastener isn't handy, experiment with other types and some scrap pieces to adapt whatever fasteners are available.

The Best Glues for Building

A properly glued joint can be stronger than the materials being glued together—as long as the right glue is used correctly. And to do their job well, certain commercial glues and adhesives are formulated to bond specific types of materials and to provide certain desirable properties like good holding power, quick drying time, waterproof joints, or easy cleanup.

For most constructions, fast drying time is the most important criterion.

It's a lot more fun to keep building without waiting hours for a joint to dry before continuing the project. Some glues harden by drying, some by cooling, and others by chemical reaction. For white and yellow glues, drying takes place as the water in the glue evaporates. These water-based glues are very safe and relatively easy to clean up, but they take a long time to dry completely. Most of the other glues commonly available at a hardware store are made with ingredients and chemicals that make them fast drying as well as poisonous or irritating to the skin. So always be sure to read the warning labels and follow all the instructions for safety.

Some common glues that make strong and fast bonds require some skill to apply correctly, and some are too difficult for young builders to use safely. Several types of super glues bond a variety of materials together almost instantly, but that can also mean accidentally supergluing your fingers together instantly. Epoxy glues are good for filling gaps as well as bonding almost anything, but the two epoxy chemicals have to be mixed just before using (sometimes within minutes), and they can irritate or burn skin. And, although a hot-melt glue gun makes fast, firm, and waterproof joints between most all materials, especially plastics, corrugated paperboard, and odd-shaped pieces, applying hot glue requires a plug-in tool with a heating element inside. For older kids, a hot-melt glue gun can be quite handy for

building quick structures because the glue hardens by cooling within a few seconds.

Here are some general tips for any type of gluing.

• Select the right glue for the job. Consider the materials to be joined and whether or not the joint should be waterproof, needs to be fast drying, or the parts can be clamped or taped together while drying.

• For most glue joints, a thin layer of glue and a tight glue joint will make the best bond.

• Make sure both surfaces to be glued are clean and dry. It doesn't do much good for the glue to bond to surface dirt or oil instead of the material.

• The warmer the temperature, the faster most glues will dry. Always try to keep the temperature above 70°F if possible.

• The end grain of wood quickly absorbs glue and makes a poor joint. If you must glue the end grain, first give it a preliminary, or first, coat of glue and let it set a while before adding a second coat of glue and fastening the pieces.

White glue

This safe and easy to use water-based glue is a favorite for gluing wood, paper, cardboard, fabric, and many other porous materials because the glue soaks into the surface, giving it a strong hold once it dries. However, it is not good for nonporous materials that do not allow liquid to pass through, like plastic, glass, or metals. Although the glue looks white when wet, it dries clear and transparent. White glue can also be thinned with water to make a paintable glaze, or clear coating, to seal the surface of wood or to stiffen paper constructions. A small amount of sand or sawdust can be mixed into the glue to make a texture. And a little food coloring will give the glue a pastel color after it dries.

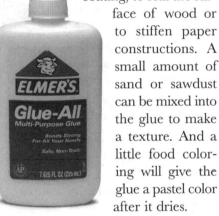

Apply white glue directly from the applicator tip of the bottle and spread the glue around the entire surface to be joined. Use your finger for spreading, or use a special glue brush with stiff bristles (regular paint brushes have bristles that are too soft for applying glue). White glue sets in about one hour and is completely cured to full strength after twenty-four hours.

White glue is nontoxic and easy to clean up. To remove fresh glue that is still white, just wipe it up with a damp sponge or paper towel. Glue that has already dried clear can usually be peeled off in a strip. In really tough cases, like when glue has dried on clothing, put the object in the freezer and later try picking off the brittle, frozen glue.

Yellow glue

Yellow glue, also called wood glue, is very similar to white glue, but it has two additional features. Yellow glue can easily be sanded once it has dried, and it is also stronger and more water resistant than white glue—but it's not waterproof. Although yellow glue is a yellow color when wet, it dries hard and

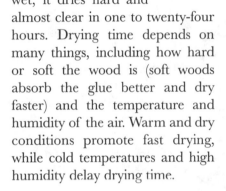

almost clear in one to twenty-four hours. Drying time depends on many things, including how hard or soft the wood is (soft woods absorb the glue better and dry faster) and the temperature and humidity of the air. Warm and dry conditions promote fast drying, while cold temperatures and high humidity delay drying time.

Like white glue, yellow glue is non-toxic, nonflammable, and doesn't stain; it can be tinted with food coloring, and it is most easily cleaned up before it sets.

Rubber cement

Rubber cement was once commonly used in schools, but now it is restricted to home use under adult supervision. Warning: Rubber cement is a flammable adhesive that can be harmful or fatal if swallowed. Carefully read the warnings on the rubber cement container before using this adhesive.

Rubber cement is an excellent adhesive for making either removable or permanent bonds between paper and paper, and in some creative applications, it can be used to bond stones, shells, straws, or Q-tips. Rubber cement is easy to apply and spread, it is very fast drying, and it

rubs off easily once it has dried. Just rub the dried cement with your fingers or use a special rubber-cement eraser sold in office supply stores to remove it.

For easily removable bonds, coat one side evenly (a brush is usually attached to the inside of the jar cap) and immediately join the coated and uncoated pieces of paper. While the glue is still wet—it starts drying in less than a minute—you should be able to reposition the pieces of paper as you like. If, after the glue has dried, you want to separate the two pieces, slowly peel one from the other, starting at an edge.

For stronger or more permanent bonds, evenly coat both of the surfaces to be bonded and let them dry before firmly pressing them together. Be careful while positioning the two pieces because once the two glued surfaces touch, the bond cannot be pulled apart or repositioned without causing damage to the paper.

Contact cement

Contact cement is good for bonding almost any kind of material to any other material, or to hold together large, flat pieces like sheets of corrugated paperboard, plywood, and all kinds of laminates. It is also quite suitable for bonding hunks of plastic foam, pieces of hardboard, metal, and leather to wood, or any soft porous materials to one another. Contact cements do not bond as securely as glues, so they are best used where high strength is not important. Contact cement is also water resistant but not waterproof.

SUPER SIMPLE HOMEMADE PAPER PASTE

For some simple paper or cardboard constructions where great strength is not necessary, a homemade paste mixed from safe kitchen ingredients may be used instead of—and may even work better than—a commercial paste. Here's the recipe.

Tools

Medium-size mixing bowl
Mixing spoon

Ingredients

White flour
Water
Salt

Recipe

To one handful of white flour in a medium bowl, add small amounts of water until the mixture is gooey. Then add a pinch of salt and mix.

To use, spread the paste thinly on the piece to be glued, then press it in place on another piece of paper or cardboard. After play, discard any unused paste.

For homemade paste that is stronger, smoother, and can be stored in a covered container in the refrigerator for a week or more, make the same recipe but add more water so the paste is a little bit thinner. Then heat the mixture slowly for five or ten minutes while stirring constantly.

Warning: Most types of contact cement are very flammable and give off noxious fumes. They also require special solvents for cleaning up drips on surfaces and fingers, and they leave a stain when dried. However, there are also a few latex contact cements that are nontoxic, nonflammable, easy to apply, and easy to clean up with water. For young builders, latex-type contact cements are always preferred, but may be only available in large containers of a pint or more.

To use contact cement, the adhesive is applied separately to both surfaces to be joined and allowed to dry and get tacky, usually for ten or twenty minutes. Then the two pieces can be instantly joined upon contact, but be careful in handling the pieces before contact. You get only one chance at correct alignment, and once the pieces touch, they are joined.

Plastic glue and cement

Glues made specifically for joining plastics are solvent glues that contain volatile chemicals and components, so they are only suited for older builders. Plastic glue can also be used for bonding wood, fabric, leather, glass, and other materials to one another or to a piece of plastic, but the attachment may be weak. The advantage of using plastic glue on plastic-to-plastic joints is that the glue actually melts the pieces together, and, with some plastics, the joint has some flexibility so it doesn't easily break. Beware, however, as this type of glue does have a tendency to shrink when dried, so it isn't good for filling gaps.

Plastic glue works best for attaching lightweight pieces of plastic to each other. The two pieces being joined need to be clamped, taped, or held in position until the glue begins to set, which could take a few minutes to an hour or more. Cleanup requires a special solvent called acetone that can also be purchased as nail polish remover. Just like the glue, the cleaner is a flammable poison with toxic fumes, so it should be used only outdoors or in a well-ventilated area.

Other adhesives

There are many other types of adhesives commonly available that are excellent for building but require special application techniques. For example, cartridges of construction adhesive applied with a caulking gun take the place of nails, but can bond most anything to anything. Epoxy glues and super glues will also attach most anything to anything—including your fingers!

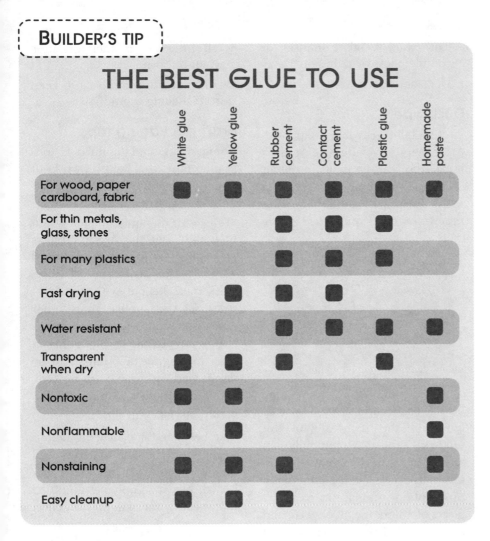

THE BEST GLUE TO USE

	White glue	Yellow glue	Rubber cement	Contact cement	Plastic glue	Homemade paste
For wood, paper cardboard, fabric	■	■	■	■	■	■
For thin metals, glass, stones			■	■	■	
For many plastics			■	■	■	
Fast drying		■		■		
Water resistant			■	■	■	■
Transparent when dry	■	■	■		■	
Nontoxic	■	■				■
Nonflammable	■	■				■
Nonstaining	■	■	■			■
Easy cleanup	■	■	■			■

A Tape for Every Purpose and Project

Tape is one of the fastest, easiest, and, in some cases, best ways to attach two pieces—especially when the joint is not meant to be permanent. If you want to quickly try out a construction idea, temporarily hold something in place, make a simple hinge, cover up a gap, or perform an emergency repair, tape is often the best fastener to use. And there are hundreds of different kinds of tape meant for different fastening purposes.

Tape typically consists of a long, narrow strip of material with a sticky adhesive on one side. The material can be paper, fabric, plastic, or even thin metal, and the adhesive can be temporary or permanent. Tapes with a permanent adhesive usually take a day or longer for the adhesive to cure and develop its full bonding strength. Certain types of mounting tapes have adhesive on both sides and are used between two objects.

All of the common tapes described in this book are safe, although chemical cleaners may be required to remove residue adhesive where a piece of tape has been peeled away from something valuable like furniture or woodwork. Working with some tapes can be easy even for younger builders, while other tapes require skill and technique to apply them neatly. Remember that for any tape, you have only one chance to position it correctly.

Each time a piece of tape is applied, peeled back, and applied again, it loses much of its stickiness and its ability to hold.

Transparent mending tape

This thin, clear cellophane tape (commonly known as Scotch tape) is probably the most common household tape, but its use in building projects is limited to light-weight connections or paper-to-paper applications where it is important to see through the tape. When stuck to paper, the bond is usually permanent, but when applied to other materials, the bond is only temporary and the tape can be easily peeled away. Transparent mending tape comes on rolls in several widths that range from about a half inch to one inch but is usually found on a small plastic dispenser with a serrated edge for tearing the tape to length.

Advantages

- Transparent and sometimes almost invisible
- Water resistant once stuck
- Excellent for paper attachments

Disadvantages

- Sticks only one time so it cannot be removed and reused
- Does not stick well to wood, metal, or fabric
- Difficult to tear, so scissors or a special dispenser are needed

Masking tape

Masking tape was invented and first used to mask, or cover, areas of cars that were not to be spray painted. Since then, masking tape has become one of the most universal fasteners of project building. This strong and waxy tan paper tape with a tacky adhesive on one side sticks well to almost anything and is often used to temporarily hold parts together while another

fastener is being fitted or a glue is drying. Masking tape comes on rolls in several widths that range from a half inch to three inches and even wider.

Advantages

- Can be easily hand torn to length
- User friendly because it isn't too sticky
- Good for a wide variety of temporary or weaker attachments

Disadvantages

- Heat causes adhesive to melt away from tape so residue bonds to surface
- Cold temperatures or moisture

can cause weak adhesion or complete loss of adhesion

- Does not attach well to fabrics

Duct tape

This metallic-gray fabric tape with a very aggressive adhesive was first created to seal the joints in the air ducts used in some buildings, but today duct tape is used more commonly for other purposes. There

have even been entire books written about the many uses of this universal tape that seemingly can attach (or reattach) any two items. Duct tape can be used to mend rips in plastic and fabrics, to attach pieces of wood, metal, or glass, and to connect sheets of corrugated cardboard or even plywood. And sometimes duct tape is used as the primary material itself as pieces of tape are stuck to each other to fabricate thin shell structures and other shapes. Duct tape comes on rolls of various lengths, but all duct tape is about two inches wide. Other kinds of fabric tape work much like duct tape, but come in narrower widths as well as many bright colors.

Advantages

- Good strength in tension
- Flexible and can be formed around parts
- Aggressive adhesive sticks to almost anything

Disadvantages

- Hard to tear unless a slit is first cut at the edge

- Often leaves a sticky residue when removed
- Difficult to handle and keep from sticking to itself

Kraft packaging tape

Sometimes called gummed carton-sealing tape, this light brown kraft paper tape comes in both regular and reinforced varieties. Regular kraft tape can easily be torn or cut to length, but the much stronger kraft paper tape that is reinforced with crisscrossing strands of fiberglass must be cut with a pair of scissors. And, unlike most other tapes that unroll with their adhesive ready to stick, the gum on kraft packaging tape must first be dampened by water to become sticky, much like the gummed flap of an envelope.

The best use for packaging tape is to tape together the material used for corrugated cartons and cardboard boxes. Applying gummed tape takes some skill and practice.

Using too little or too much water will cause the tape not to stick, and once dampened, the tape must be applied quickly before the gum adhesive starts to dry. A simple technique is to dampen a sponge with warm water, slightly squeezing out excess water. Cut the tape to length and pull it gum-side-up under the sponge. After applying the tape, smooth it down with your fingers or a balled-up cloth.

Kraft packaging tape comes in rolls of various lengths, but is often three inches wide. There are some narrower rolls available, but wider is better for most corrugated-board building projects. Special tape widths or shapes, when needed, can easily be cut from wider rolls.

Advantages

- Gum adhesive makes a strong bond when it dries
- Designed to work best with corrugated cardboard
- Reinforced tape creates connections and joints that won't tear

Disadvantages

- Application takes skill and practice
- Water source must be available
- Adhesive can melt and detach under wet or humid conditions

Plastic packaging tape

An alternative to gummed packaging tapes that must first be dampened, plastic packaging tape comes ready to use with a very sticky adhesive on one side. These tapes are made from a very thin but tough plastic film that is often clear or tan, but is also available in a variety of colors. For some building projects, a clear or colorful transparent tape may provide some unique benefits to the builder. Another advantage is that plastic packaging tape will aggressively stick to most anything. However, because of that, it can be difficult to manage and messy to remove if

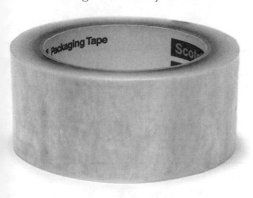

accidentally stuck to the wrong place. Plastic packaging tape comes on rolls of different widths and lengths, although a common width is about two inches.

Advantages

- Resists tearing from an edge
- Can be applied and used in warm, cold, or damp conditions
- Available in clear or colored varieties

Disadvantages

- Must be cut with scissors
- Difficult to handle and keep from sticking to itself
- Easily rips once a tear has started

Filament tape

Imagine masking tape made out of strong filaments of fiberglass instead of paper, and you have an idea of what filament tape is like. Because of its tremendous strength in tension, filament tape is typically used to wrap around shipping cartons or to bundle pieces of pipe or lumber. In order to take advan-

tage of its strength, filament tape must be used primarily as a wrap that goes completely around the parts to be fastened and is then stuck back onto itself. Filament tape adhesive is a bit more aggressive than that of masking tape, but it tends to dry out over time and completely lose its adhesion. Filament tape comes on a large roll and is one inch wide.

Advantages

- Extremely strong for heavy-duty bundling

- Sticks to both smooth and rough surfaces
- Resists moisture once applied

Disadvantages

- Can only be cut with a knife or scissors
- Difficult to handle long pieces that want to curl and stick together
- Ages and becomes brittle, often leaving an adhesive residue

Vinyl electrical tape

The best feature of this black plastic tape is its ability to stretch and wrap tightly around the parts to be joined. Electricians use electrical tape to insulate joined wires, but it

is commonly used like twine to wrap any number of parts together, with the advantage of not having to tie a knot. The completed tape joint is both waterproof and immune to changes in temperature, and the tape can often be removed without leaving any adhesive residue. Electrical tape is about $3/4$ inch wide and comes on rolls of various lengths. Electrical tape is sometimes available in red, white, and green as well as the standard black.

Advantages

- Stretches and forms to shape
- Waterproof and weatherproof
- Moderate adhesion makes it easy to use and remove

Disadvantages

- Must be cut and can't easily be torn to length
- Good only for wrapping-type fastening
- Somewhat difficult to handle without getting stuck to itself

Nails and Screws

Finding the right fastener and using it properly is an important part of building successful structures. Many times, more than one type of fastener will do the job well, so you might select the fastener with the best appearance or the easiest one to install. Whichever type of fastener you choose, be certain it will keep your structure together and be able to support more than the heaviest load that might ever be placed on it.

Nails

Different types of nails are available for general purpose fastening of wood and for many special applications like attaching upholstery, roofing shingles, or flooring boards. There are even nails with two heads that are easy to remove from temporary constructions.

THE SIZE OF NAILS

Each type of nail comes in a variety of sizes, and there are also various ways to describe the size of a nail. Some nails are measured by their length in inches plus a gauge number for their diameter. But common flathead nails and finishing nails use their own unique "penny" scale for describing overall size. Look at a box of common flathead nails and you will see the size of the nail described as a number and the lowercase letter d, such as 2d, 6d, or 10d. Each number stands for the length of the nail, but that does not mean a 2d nail is two inches long. In fact, a 2d nail is only one inch long, a 6d nail is two inches long, and a 10d nail is three inches long. So, what is the connection between nail sizes and actual nail lengths?

It all started with the British, who sold nails by the hundred. Back then, one hundred one-inch nails cost two pennies, so a one-inch nail was called a two-penny nail. And because one hundred two-inch nails cost six pennies, that size was called a six-penny nail, and so on. The symbol for an English penny is abbreviated as d, so a two-penny nail would be written as 2d. Of course, prices have increased tremendously in the past few hundred years, so a hundred nails now cost more than a few pennies, but the system of measurement still remains. Here is a list of d-penny nail sizes and their lengths in inches.

Size	Length (in.)	Size	Length (in.)
2d	1	10d	3
3d	1 1/4	12d	3 1/4
4d	1 1/2	16d	3 1/2
5d	1 3/4	20d	4
6d	2	30d	4 1/2
7d	2 1/4	40d	5
8d	2 1/2	50d	5 1/2
9d	2 3/4	60d	6

Common flathead nail

This general-purpose nail, with a large nail head that is easy to hit, won't pull through wood, and is easy to grip for removal.

Finishing nail

The small head of a finishing nail is meant to be hammered into the wood to leave a smoother surface finish. However, the head is difficult to grip for removal, and the thin body easily bends.

Roofing nail

The large nail head resists pull-through and is good for nailing down roofing shingles and other thin materials including fabric, corrugated cardboard, and some plastics.

Brad

A small and thin wire-type nail that is good for attaching small parts and is less likely to split wood.

Tack

This small nail with a large head and a short shank is ideal for attaching thin sheet material (such as cloth or paper) to wood.

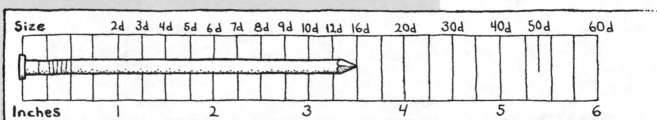

Corrugated nail

This corrugated metal strip with a very sharp edge is good for making quick, but weak, corner joints and T joints. A corrugated nail is very difficult to remove.

Screws

Fastening with screws has two significant advantages over using nails—screws hold better than nails, and screws can be easily removed to disassemble parts. However, selecting the right screw for the job will depend on the materials being fastened and the type of screwdriver you have.

First, there are two basic types of screws: wood screws and sheet-metal screws. Wood screws have relatively fine threads that go from the point to about two-thirds up the screw body. Wood screws often need a drilled hole for easy inserting to avoid splitting the wood.

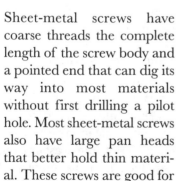

Sheet-metal screws have coarse threads the complete length of the screw body and a pointed end that can dig its way into most materials without first drilling a pilot hole. Most sheet-metal screws also have large pan heads that better hold thin material. These screws are good for fastening to softwoods, plywood, particleboard, and even corrugated cardboard.

Next, there are two basic types of screw-head slots that fit two different types of screwdrivers. Straight-slot heads fit blade screwdrivers, and cross-slotted screw heads fit Phillips-head screwdrivers. Phillips screws are best for young builders' constructions because there is a smaller chance of a Phillips screwdriver slipping out of the crossed slots. Both slotted and Phillips type screw heads are available in a variety of shapes for different types of applications.

When purchasing wood screws, first decide what type of screwdriver you will be using, bladed or Phillips, and then what style screw head. The other information you need to know is the length and diameter. Length is measured in inches, and the diameter is specified as a gauge number from six (small) to fourteen (large). Select the proper screw length so that two-thirds of the screw will be in the base piece to which you are fastening. The larger the diameter, the stronger the screw—but the harder it will be to screw into the material. For most projects, use the smallest diameter screws that will successfully do the job.

Roundhead

The most common head for general-purpose fastening of wood, this type of screw accepts a washer, and its head protrudes above the work piece.

Flathead

The head of this screw can be driven flush with the work piece, but it may require drilling a tapered recess, or countersink, in the top piece of the material to accept the screw head.

Pan head

Similar to a roundhead but flatter, a pan head screw has special sheet-metal threads that are excellent for holding in plywood.

Lag head

Found on super heavy-duty screws that come in large sizes, this square head is driven with a wrench instead of a screwdriver.

Bolts, nuts, and washers

A combination bolt and nut fastener holds two or more pieces of material together with a squeezing force. Unlike nails and screws that dig in and bore into the material being fastened to, a bolt must pass through predrilled holes in each piece of material. Unless the holes already exist, you will also need a drill and a drill bit that is a little larger in diameter than the body of the bolt. You will also need special tools for tightening bolts and nuts, but the specific type and size of tools will depend on the type and size of the bolt and nut being used.

The top, or head, of a bolt is bigger around than its body, so the head cannot pass through the hole in the first piece of material being fastened. The underside of the head that rests against the surface around the hole is called the bolt's shoulder. After the bolt is passed through the holes in all of the pieces to be fastened, a nut is threaded onto the protruding body of the bolt and tightened. Very often, a washer is fitted between the shoulder and the piece and another between the nut and the piece. Washers help distribute the squeezing forces, to keep the head and nut from digging into or pulling through the material.

There are hundreds of bolt types and sizes available, with each one having a particular combination of head design, body diameter, type of threads, and length. For a bolt and nut to fit together, the threads on the bolt and the threads inside the nut must match, and they must also be the same diameter. Thread types can be especially confusing because there are both "coarse" threads and "fine" threads available for the same diameter bolt and nut, as well as SAE-type threads (what we commonly use in the United States) and metric-type threads (used by most other countries). And there is even a choice of nuts and washers that come in a variety of designs to help the fastener do its job better. Here is an illustrated guide to the most common bolts, nuts, and washers used in project building.

Bolts

Machine bolts

Also called machine screws, these are the most common type of threaded bolts. They are available with many different heads and in lengths up to 12 inches and more. Smaller size machine screws often have head designs similar to wood screws, but machine bolts with bodies 1/4 inch in diameter and larger come with square head, hex head, or cap-screw (Allen-screw) heads.

Carriage bolts

These bolts with a rounded head and a square shoulder underneath are meant to fasten lumber. The square shoulder digs itself into wood as the nut is tightened, keeping the bolt from turning. Body diameters range from 3/16 inch to 1/2 inch in lengths up to 12 inches or more.

Stove bolts

Stove bolts are available in diameters from 1/8 inch to 1/2 inch and are shorter than most machine bolts and carriage bolts, rarely exceeding 6 inches in length. All stove bolt heads are round and slotted, and come in button-head design or a countersunk head. Stove bolts were originally used to hold the pieces together in metal stoves.

Nuts

Square nut

This square-shaped nut is tightened or loosened with an open-end wrench or an adjustable wrench.

Hex nut

Short for "hexagon" nut, a hex nut has six sides and is best tightened or loosened with a box wrench or a socket wrench.

Wing nut

Two protrusions that look like wings extend out from this nut to allow tightening or loosening by hand. Wing nuts are ideal for fastenings that will frequently be disassembled or adjusted.

Acorn nut

An acorn nut is used to cover the threaded end of a bolt, and, as its name implies, this nut is shaped like an acorn. Since the threads do not go all the way through, the nut can be threaded only a short distance onto the bolt.

Washers

Flat washer

This flat, circular disk with a hole in the middle for a bolt to pass through distributes the pressure generated by the squeezing of nut and bolt. Washers may be placed under the bolt head, under the nut, or next to the materials being fastened.

Fender washer

These special washers have normal-size holes for bolts, but extra large diameters for even better distribution of the bolt and nut squeezing force. Fender washers keep the bolt head and nut from pulling through soft or thin materials.

Spring lock washer

Lock washers are circular rings with a twisted break in one place, something like one loop of a spring. The cut ends of the washer compress and lock into the material being fastened as the bolt and nut are tightened. The compressed spring action keeps the fastener from easily loosening.

Internal-tooth/external-tooth lock washer

This design for a lock washer uses a ring of teeth, around either its inside or outside diameter, to lock the fastener to the material so it will not accidentally loosen.

Builder's Hardware

For every special fastening requirement, there is a special fastener designed to do the job best. A walk through any hardware store will reveal a huge variety of builder's hardware and is the best way to find the special fastener that will work best on your project.

Hinges

Butt hinge

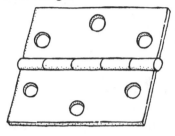

Piano hinge

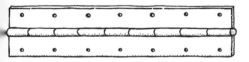

Strap hinge

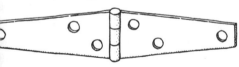

Angle irons and mending plates

Straight mending plate

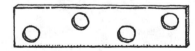

T-angle iron

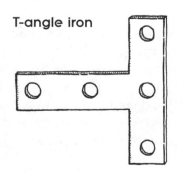

90-degree angle iron

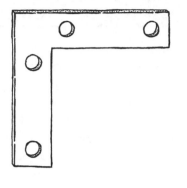

Corner brace

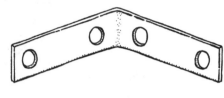

Screw and bolt hooks

Screw hook

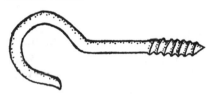

Screw eye

Screw eye and ring

Square screw hook

Hook and eye

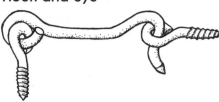

Eyebolt

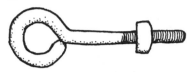

U-bolt

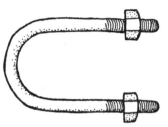

Turnbuckle

Other Handy Fasteners

Plastic ties

Cotter pin

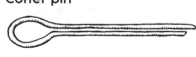

Velcro

Rubber bands

These are the most popular sizes of rubber bands that are commonly available.

Size	Width (in.)	Length (in.)
8	$1/16$	$7/8$
10	$1/16$	$1 1/4$
12	$1/16$	$1 3/4$
14	$1/16$	2
16	$1/16$	$2 1/2$
18	$1/16$	3
19	$1/16$	$3 1/2$
27	$1/8$	$1 1/4$
29	$1/8$	$1 3/4$
30	$1/8$	2
31	$1/8$	$2 1/2$
32	$1/8$	3
33	$1/8$	$3 1/2$
62	$1/4$	$2 1/2$
63	$1/4$	3
64	$1/4$	$3 1/2$

INVENTION

THE OTHER USE OF RUBBER BANDS

The common rubber band hasn't changed much since Stephen Perry of London, England, who owned a company that made rubber products, patented the invention in 1845. The story about these small loops of vulcanized rubber used for banding things together would probably have gone no further had it not been for another inventor who discovered a different use for the stretchy bands—a way to power small model airplanes.

In 1871, thirty-two years before the Wright brothers first sustained controlled, powered flight, Alphonse Penaud invented a rubber band-powered model airplane toy he called a planophore. Before then, most flying toys were simple gliders or balloons, but Penaud's twenty-inch-long toy airplane was the first known example of stable, powered flight.

A rubber band airplane motor is made by fixing one end of the band to the back of the plane and twisting up the other end at the front of the plane, where it is attached to a propeller. Turning the propeller in the opposite direction from the direction it would rotate for flight causes the rubber to stretch tighter and tighter until it wants to unwind. When the propeller is released, the rubber band rapidly unwinds and spins the propeller for several seconds, which powers the plane.

Penaud's first model plane was a little different and had the propeller in the back to push the aircraft rather than pull it. His rubber band engine ran for 11 seconds and carried the plane a distance of 131 feet.

During most of the late 1800s, both adults and children became fascinated with rubber band-motored planes, and the toy is credited with being an inspiration to young scientists and engineers of that era who wanted to develop a flying machine that would carry a person in flight. Indeed, after seeing Penaud's flying toy planes, Orville Wright (age 8) and his brother Wilbur (age 12)

built their own first flying machine, a rubber band-powered helicopter. It would be another 24 years before their early experiments with rubber band-powered toys would inspire the Wright brothers to invent powered flight for people.

PAINTS, BRUSHES, AND ROLLERS

There are two basic reasons for painting something: to protect it and to make it look better. Painting bare wood seals its porous surface to prevent swelling or rotting, and a coat of paint on metal will stop it from rusting. And adding color to a construction can draw attention to certain features, create an illusion that the object is bigger or smaller than it actually is, or give a visual unity to a hodgepodge of parts and materials. Regardless of why you choose to paint your construction, you may think of painting either as another fun part of building or as a time-consuming, messy, and boring job. But for nearly everyone, there is something quite satisfying about the final results of a project after giving it a fresh coat of paint.

Before beginning any painting job, be sure you have gathered all the tools and materials you will need.

Once you've started a job, it could be difficult to stop and look for something else that is needed—the paint on the brush could start to dry and restarting could leave visible stop-and-start streaks. Here is a checklist to remind yourself of what tools and materials you will need.

- Sandpaper
- Sanding block
- Paint scraper
- Dusting brush
- Masking tape
- Drop cloth or newspaper
- Enough paint to complete the job
- Can lid opener
- Mixing paddle (or stick)
- Empty cans
- Brushes
- Roller
- Cotton rags
- Solvent for paint used

Paints and Other Finishes

Of the many paints, stains, varnishes, oils, waxes, polishes, and other finishes available, certain ones are best suited for wood, while some are meant to be applied to metal, some to plastic, and some only work on paper and cardboard. Many paints are specifically labeled for just interior use or exterior use. Each type of paint and other finishes also have properties that determine how easy or difficult they are to apply, how long it takes for the finish to dry, whether the dried finish is glossy, flat, or somewhere in-between, and what solvent is used to clean up drips, brushes, and yourself.

Not only does the type of paint you use somewhat depend on the material to be painted, but so does the preparation for the paint job. To paint something like a puppet theater made from a corrugated box or a paper-plate dome, there is very little preparation needed. Just apply the paint to the paper material with a brush or roller and wait for the paint to dry. However, before painting anything made of wood, you may want to sand away any rough, sharp, or splintered edges. Before spray painting a plastic-pipe construction, you should first lightly sand and roughen the smooth, shiny plastic surface so paint will adhere better. Always use sandpaper to remove the rust from metal, and before painting just about anything, make sure its surfaces are clean of dirt, grease, and oil.

A solvent is a liquid used to thin or dissolve the paint, and only certain solvents will work with certain paints. Water is a safe and

PROPER PAINTING TECHNIQUES

Without using proper techniques, painting can get messy with sloppy-looking results. And some painting materials are potentially dangerous. So follow these tips for a neater, safe, and better looking job.

• Most paints and finishes need to be shaken or stirred well before using. Stir with a wooden mixing paddle or stick, and use it to scrape the bottom and mix in any paint pigment that has settled.

• Paints that are too thick to apply smoothly can be thinned with the appropriate solvent. Add only a small amount at a time, stir, and test the new mixture. But be careful not to add too much solvent—there is no practical way to make paint thicker once it has been thinned.

• Many paints emit fumes when the paint is wet and while drying, so if you are painting indoors, be sure the room is well ventilated.

• It is easier to paint from a half-filled container than from a full one. So, when opening a new can of paint, carefully pour half the paint into an empty, clean container with a lid. Pour the paint back into the original container when you need more or when you have finished the job.

• Hold a paintbrush handle with a grip that feels most comfortable to you. Hold the handle of a large paintbrush or roller in your fist the same way you would grip a bicycle handlebar.

• When dipping a brush into any paint or finish, dip the length of the bristles only half way in and don't wipe the brush over the edge of the container to remove any excess paint. Instead, tap both sides of the paint-filled brush on the inside wall of the container.

• Don't paint in a dusty area, as the dust will stick to the freshly painted surface. It is also a good idea not to paint outside on windy days when things can be blown onto the fresh paint.

• The brighter the work area, the easier it will be to see drips, notice missed areas, and paint borders.

• Most paints are easiest to apply and dry best at temperatures between 60°F and 80°F, and that applies as well to the temperature of the object being painted.

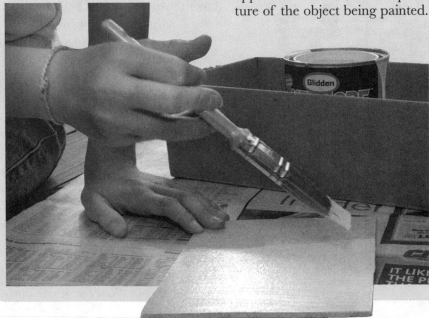

easy-to-use solvent, but it works only with water-based finishes like latex paint, poster paints, and watercolors. Most other solvents and paints are toxic and flammable, so either avoid them or carefully follow all the precautions and warnings listed on the paint and solvent containers. These are the most common paints and other finishes and how to use them.

Primer

To achieve the most durable finish when painting bare wood or bare metal, first apply a paint primer. Primers are special paints that produce a good foundation for the overlying coats of paint. A wood primer is usually a thick white paint that both seals the wood surface and fills in small imperfections. Metal primers are usually gray, red, or brown and help keep the metal from rusting.

Shellac

When painting wood with many knots showing on the surface, like a knotty pine board, you must first paint over the knots with a coat of shellac if you don't want them to show through the paint. Shellac is available as a powder or in flakes that should be mixed with alcohol just before using. A mixture of shellac can quickly spoil, causing it to not dry properly.

Latex and acrylic paint

Latex and acrylic paints are water-based finishes that are easy to apply, quick drying (less than one hour),

fairly odorless, available in different types for indoor use and outdoor use, and come in a variety of finishes from flat to semigloss to high gloss. Latex paint can be applied to most materials and is very easy to clean off brushes and hands using plain water and soap. However, cleanup must be done before the paint dries. Dried latex or acrylic paint must be removed with harsh chemical paint removers.

Oil-based and alkyd paints

Although both interior and exterior types are available, these paints are usually used for outdoor projects. They have more "hiding power" than latex paints and often

only one coat is needed to cover up dark marks or other colors. Oil-based paints are very slow drying and have a strong odor, whereas alkyd paints use a synthetic oil for faster drying and have much less smell. Both types provide very tough coatings that adhere well to most materials. Oil-based and alkyd paints can be thinned and removed (before drying) with turpentine, paint thinner, or mineral spirits.

Varnish

Varnish is a clear, slightly yellow

finish that is mostly used on wood that will be exposed to the weather. It is also a common finish applied over wood stains. Varnish for exterior

use contains oil and is relatively slow drying. Varnishes for interior use contain faster drying synthetic materials and are often called polyurethane, alkyd, or phenolic varnish. For the best job, apply varnish in a dust-free room at room temperature as varnish will not dry properly in cold or damp conditions. If possible, use a natural-bristle brush made especially for varnish. Several coats of varnish (with drying time and light sanding between coats) are usually needed to achieve a high-gloss finish. Clean the brush in paint thinner or turpentine.

Stains

Stains are used to enhance or add a color tint to the appearance of wood grain. Stains come in many shades of brown, from light tan to nearly red, plus a few bright colors. Plain stains, those not combined with another fin-

ish like varnish or oil, do very little to seal and protect the wood, so an overcoat of clear finish, like wax, oil, or varnish, is usually applied over the stain. Some stains are used to make one type of wood look like another type, and they are named accordingly, such as light walnut, dark cherry, oak, or mahogany. Stains can be applied with a brush, cotton rag, or sponge, and cleanup depends on whether the stain is water-based or oil-based.

Linseed oil

If you like the appearance of bare wood and natural looking wood grain, a clear oil finish will penetrate and protect the wood while subtly enhancing the color and appearance of the wood grain.

Linseed oil is non-toxic and an especially good finish for wood that can be safely chewed by younger children. Unlike paints, oil finishes do not crack, chip, or peel off. Linseed oil can be applied with a brush or cloth, working back and forth in the direction of the wood grain. Don't allow the oil to puddle, and after thirty minutes or so, wipe off any oil that has not soaked into the wood. Clean up with turpentine or paint thinner.

Floor wax

Wax is the easiest finish to apply to bare wood and will usually not change the color of the wood. Follow any precautions listed on the container, like wearing protective gloves, and use a cotton rag or a sponge to apply just a light coat of liquid or paste wax to the wood. Rub the wax into the wood, wipe off any excess, and allow the wax to dry. Depending on the type of wax used, it might dry to a glossy finish on its own or it may require polishing with a clean, dry cotton rag. The wax will seal the wood surface and keep it from getting dirty. Use soap and water for cleaning up.

Poster paints

These thick, water-based paints are best suited for young painters because they clean up so easily.

Wet or dried paint can be removed from clothes, faces, furniture, or almost anything else using only water or a damp cloth. A selection of brightly colored poster paints typically comes in jars or small tubs, and are best used for decorating indoor constructions made of paper or corrugated board.

Watercolors

Small, hard tablets of watercolor pigment become paint when daubed with a wet brush. A selection of six or more watercolor

paints often comes in a long, narrow tin container, and they are applied with a small, soft watercolor brush. Watercolors are meant more for applying decorative designs to paper projects than for painting surfaces. Cleanup with water is very easy.

Felt-tip markers

Although not really a paint or finish, felt-tip markers are very convenient for adding color to delicate constructions made of toothpicks, Q-tips, pasta, paper, and lots of other small materials. Markers are

available in a wide variety of colors and come either with watercolor inks that wash off and clean up easily or with indelible inks that are permanent on many materials and difficult to remove from hands. If soap and water does not remove the marker ink, try rubbing alcohol.

Spray paint

Spray painting has a lot of advantages. The fine paint spray can produce a smooth, even finish and is excellent for painting items that have complex shapes or lots of pieces, parts, nooks, and crannies. Most spray paints dry to the touch in about twenty minutes, and spray painted items can be handled and used in an hour. Another big benefit to spray painting is not having to clean brushes, rollers, or paint trays. But spray painting also has a few disadvantages. It takes some practice to get good results; over spray, the paint spray that misses the painted object and goes somewhere else, can be messy; and the aerosol spray is flammable. Never attempt to puncture a can of spray paint, even an empty can, and never dispose of a spray-paint container in a fire because it might explode.

A can of spray paint contains a pressurized aerosol propellant that forces the paint through a tiny spray nozzle when the valve on the top of the can is pressed. Several types of paint in a variety of colors are available in aerosol spray cans. The most common include very fast-drying lacquers that require lacquer thinner for cleanup, and alkyd paints that take a little longer to dry and use mineral spirits or paint thinner for cleanup. Both types are usually available only in a glossy finish, although black, white, and a few colors are available in a flat or semigloss finish.

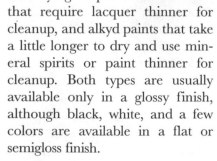

To protect the surrounding area from over spray, place the object to be painted on sheets of newspaper or some type of drop cloth. Over spray can travel several feet, so protect all nearby furniture, floors, and yourself. Also, be sure to open doors and windows for good ventilation. It is okay to spray paint outdoors, but only when there is absolutely no wind. Even the slightest breeze will deflect and ruin the spray. Also, don't spray paint when it is very humid or when the temperature is below 50°F.

Brushes and Rollers

Paintbrushes

There is a size, shape, and type of paintbrush available for every painting job, and it is important to use the right one or you could have trouble painting or ruin the brush. Both the kind of paint being used and the size and shape of the area to be painted will determine which type and size of brush is best for the job. When considering what quality of brush to buy, remember that a cheap brush can turn a fun painting project into a messy and sloppy job. A good-quality brush will hold more paint without dripping, apply the paint more smoothly, and keep its shape, and will not lose bristles while painting.

The size and shape of the brush you choose may depend on your preference in addition to the size and shape of the surfaces to be painted. But the type of bristles used in the brush must also be appropriate for the paint being used. Polyester, nylon, and other synthetic-bristle brushes are meant for use with water-based paints. Natural-type bristle brushes, including hog bristle, china bristle, and horsehair bristles, should be used only with oil-based finishes and can be ruined by latex paint. Some synthetic-bristle paintbrushes are designed to work well for all finishes and can be used with either oil-based or water-based paints. Each type of brush is available in several shapes and a range of sizes from about one-half inch wide to about 6 inches wide. Here are some of the most common types and sizes of paintbrushes.

Trim brush

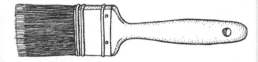

Beveled trim and sash brush

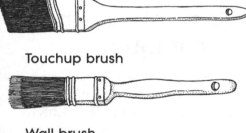

Touchup brush

Wall brush

A good-quality paintbrush is worth keeping in good condition. Brush cleanup with warm water and soap is easy when using water-based paints, but cleaning brushes used with oil-based paints and other finishes requires the correct chemical solvent for the type of paint used. After cleaning a brush in solvent, wash the bristles with warm water and soap. Whatever type of paint is used, it is always best to thoroughly clean a brush as soon as you are through painting. To keep the brush well shaped, wrap the damp bristles in a paper towel.

SPRAY PAINTING TECHNIQUES

Before using a can of spray paint, the paint must be stirred by shaking the container up and down and around for a few minutes. A small steel ball inside the container helps do the mixing. Follow the spray-painting instructions described on the container. For nearly all spray paints, the best technique is to hold the container parallel to and about ten to twelve inches away from the surface to be painted, and begin the job by painting across the edge closest to you.

Start the paint spray by firmly pressing down on the nozzle or valve while aiming just off the edge of the object. Using a smooth and steady motion, move the paint spray all the way across the surface to just past the object, and release the valve to stop the paint. Now press the nozzle and start spraying again at the point where you just finished, and paint another stroke across the surface in the other direction, again releasing the spray valve just past the edge of the painted object. For each pass back and forth across the painted surface, move the spray forward enough to overlap the previous

"stroke" by about one-third. If you are painting a large surface, stop every minute or two and shake the can a few times to stir the paint before starting again.

It takes practice to spray paint correctly and do a good job. If the stroke is too slow or the nozzle is too close to the object, the paint can drip, run, or sag. If the spray nozzle is too far away or the stroke is too fast, the finish will not be uniform and can have streaks or an uneven, rough texture. To get a smooth, evenly painted surface, it is much better to apply several thin coats of spray paint (with five or ten minutes drying time between each coat) than to apply one heavy coat of paint. Using several thin coats also makes it easy to reposition the object between coats so all surfaces receive paint.

When you are finished painting (or if you are going to be waiting longer than ten minutes between coats), clear the spray nozzle of paint so it doesn't clog. Turn the container upside-down and aim the nozzle away from yourself and at scrap newspaper or some other waste material held vertically. Depress the spray valve and keep spraying only until just the propellant and no paint comes out. If a nozzle does become clogged with dried paint, you can try to clean it with a pin, but it is often easier to remove and replace the nozzle with a clear one from another can of spray paint.

Watercolor brushes

The very soft bristles of a water-color brush are trimmed to a point, which makes the brush suitable

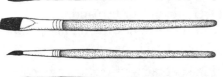

only for painting on paper with watercolor paints. Watercolor brushes are not good for applying a coat of paint to surfaces.

Paint rollers

Rollers are most handy for quickly painting large, flat areas and for achieving a smooth, even finish without drips or sags. A complete paint-rolling kit includes a roller handle, a roller cover, and a roller

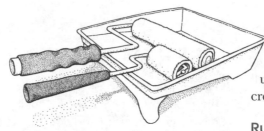

paint tray. A roller handle is matched to the width of the roller cover. The most common roller and handle widths are three, seven, and nine inches. There are also special roller shapes for painting in corners or around posts.

The fuzzy material used on the roller cover must be suitable for the paint being used (latex or oil-based) and the surface finish you like. The label or wrapper on a new roller will describe what paints it can be used with and the surface texture it will produce. Usually, the shorter the nap or pile of the roller cover,

the smoother the finish will be. Long-nap rollers are best for painting rough, irregular, or uneven surfaces—or to purposely create a bumpy, textured finish.

Rubbing cloth

Oil finishes can be applied with a cotton cloth and then buffed with another cotton cloth after the oil has soaked into the wood. Pieces of an old bath towel work well. If you use a rubbing cloth with an oil-based finish, remember this warning: Under certain uncommon conditions, an oil-wet cloth can spontaneously catch fire, so be sure to leave all oil-soaked cloths outside to dry, then throw them away.

Special Painting Techniques

Instead of painting in solid colors, there are several special painting techniques for blending the effects of two or more different colors. Here are three basic methods for creating interesting visual effects. And with a little experimenting, you should be able to create many more.

Scumbling

Paint the object or area with a base color and let it dry. Then apply a second color over the first, and while the second coat is still wet, use a crumpled wad of newspaper to daub the surface (but don't rub). Repeated daubing will remove some

---

BUILDER'S TIP

USING PAINT ROLLERS

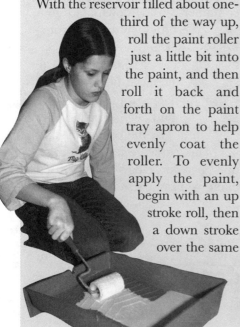

To properly use a paint roller, don't completely immerse the roller cover in the paint tray reservoir. With the reservoir filled about one-third of the way up, roll the paint roller just a little bit into the paint, and then roll it back and forth on the paint tray apron to help evenly coat the roller. To evenly apply the paint, begin with an up stroke roll, then a down stroke over the same

area without lifting the roller. Continue to roll the same area using both up-and-down and side-to-side strokes. Next, roll another fresh load of paint on an adjoining area, always starting on an unpainted surface, then overlap the previously painted section. Roll with a smooth, steady motion. If you spin the roller too fast, the paint will splatter.

Thoroughly cleaning a roller when finished can be difficult, even when using water-based paints, and the cleanup job can be more messy than it is worth when using oil-based finishes. So, unless your project requires a high-quality professional finish that only an expensive lamb's wool or mohair roller cover can provide, use inexpensive roller covers and just dispose of them when the job is finished.

of the wet topcoat and leave an interesting pattern. For large areas, keep replacing the newspaper wad.

Splatterdash

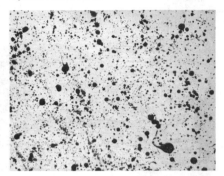

Protect all surrounding areas with a drop cloth or newspaper, because this can be a messy process. Paint the object or area with a base color and let it dry. Then apply splatters over the base coat in a contrasting color or as many colors as you like. To get the splatter effect, use a stiff bristle brush (it can be a small whisk brush or scrub brush rather than a paint brush) and dip it about an inch deep into the paint. Holding the loaded paintbrush in one hand, aim at the area you want to splatter and rap the base of the brush briskly against your other hand. Continue the technique until the desired area is completely splattered.

Oil slick

This patterning technique works only with oil-based paints. You will also need some turpentine and a large bowl or deep pan with a surface dimension larger than the

BUILDER'S TIP

PREPARE AHEAD FOR EASY CLEANUP

Paint and painting can be messy, even when you try to be very careful. Sometimes paint can splatter or drip when being mixed, stirred, brushed, or rolled, and paint often drips down the brush handle and the outside of the paint can. It is not easy to avoid drips and splatters, so always apply the golden rule of painting: It's easier to cover up first than to clean up later. Here are a few tips for preventing a mess and for easy cleanup in case you do.

- When opening and mixing a can of paint, do it inside a corrugated box (one with the top flaps removed or folded inside).

- When using a roller and tray, line the inside of the tray with a piece of plastic (a small plastic garbage bag will do).

- Wear latex or rubber gloves when applying a finish with a cloth.

- To keep a small can of paint from accidentally being knocked over, put the small can inside an empty gallon-sized paint can.

- When storing a partially used can of paint, blow into the can just before putting the lid on tightly. Your exhaled breath replaces the oxygen in the can with carbon dioxide, which will help keep the remaining paint from skimming over.

- Use salad oil to remove fresh oil-based paints and varnishes from your hands. Salad oil is much kinder to skin than chemical solvents are.

object you intend to paint. Fill the bowl with cold water, then thin a small amount of oil-based paint with a little turpentine and pour it onto the surface of the water in the bowl. Because oil is lighter than water, the oil paint will remain floating on the surface. You can stay with just one color or add more colors. Use a small stick or a drinking straw to swirl the colors into an interesting pattern. To transfer the paint and pattern to one surface of the object you are painting, carefully lower and barely dip the surface into the floating paint, pause a moment, then slowly raise it out of the paint. Turn the painted object over and place it on newspaper to dry ■

THE RIGHT TOOLS AND HOW TO USE THEM

ONLY REAL TOOLS WORK SAFELY

EQUIPPING A BASIC TOOLBOX

A TOOL FOR EVERY PURPOSE
BEYOND THE BASICS

SOME POWER TOOLS ARE SAFE
AT ANY SPEED

What's wrong with this picture?
See pages 125 and 129.

ONLY REAL TOOLS WORK SAFELY

Tools are an important part of building and an important part of learning how to change things to meet your specific needs. Only with tools can you take things apart that have been built with tools. Tools allow builders to measure things, cut materials, apply and remove fasteners, grip things tightly, make holes, and apply finishes. In fact, there is a tool available to do just about anything easier, safer, and better, but that doesn't mean you need them all. It's best to start with a basic set of building tools and learn to use each one safely.

You don't need to buy the most expensive, industrial-quality tools because you won't be using them every day. Simple hand tools of good quality are not very expensive and will last for years of safe building. By using real tools, you will develop a respect for how well each tool helps you do a job, which should also encourage you to take care of them.

However, even though good-quality tools are safer tools, each tool has certain ways it wants to be used—as well as ways it doesn't! A builder should know how the tools being used were designed to be used and, even more important, what not to do with them. Someone who is experienced in using tools can be very helpful in showing how a tool works and maybe in demonstrating why it could be dangerous if used in other ways.

Whether you acquire just a few tools or a complete set all at once, learn how to use them one tool at a time. When you have demonstrated a good understanding of how that tool is used safely, begin practicing with the next tool. Always remember that even though you may know how to safely use tools, they could pose a serious danger to others, especially inexperienced builders and younger brothers or sisters. Your first tool should also be accompanied by a toolbox to keep it in—and to keep it away from others.

Safe Building Is Knowing What's Dangerous

Eventually, every builder's finger will get pinched, hit, or accidentally cut. That's a normal part of building. The lesson learned from any accident should be not to repeat it. Most accidents occur because something happens that was not expected. A saw blade skips off the wood and across a finger, a nail is hit off square so the nail goes flying and the hammer hits a finger, or pliers slip and pinch a hand instead of a bolt. The best way to avoid building accidents is to know what tools and materials could present a potential danger and how they might hurt you, and then take precautions against getting injured. In time, every builder learns safety from experience, but for young builders who are just acquiring new experiences, the potential dangers may be more difficult to recognize.

A good rule of safety is to use only the tools you are familiar with and accustomed to operating. If you have never been shown how to use a particular tool and haven't been told of its potential dangers, ask someone experienced to give you a lesson. Then have that person watch you practice using the tool just to make sure you understood everything correctly. Even with precautions, however, accidents still happen, so it's a good idea to keep a first-aid kit handy.

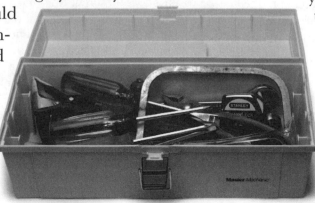

EQUIPPING A BASIC TOOLBOX

Most tools can be classified into three types. There are tools that move things, like a screwdriver or a wrench, tools that shape material, like a saw, a knife, or a file, and tools that mark or measure. A basic starter kit of tools should contain all three types and begin with the following.

Tools That Move Things

Screwdrivers

Even good quality screwdrivers are inexpensive, so you should start with a set of screwdrivers matched to the most common screw sizes and types. No one size of screwdriver will work for every project. If the

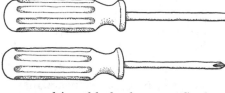

screwdriver blade does not fit the screw, it will slip out of the screw groove or slot, causing damage. For most building projects, a set of two flat-bladed screwdrivers and two screwdrivers with Phillips-type blades will do, along with an assortment of wood screws and machine screws with nuts to practice with. The larger the diameter of the screwdriver handle, the easier it will be to tighten (and loosen) screws.

Pliers

Bare hands are not very good for tightly gripping small bolts, nuts, or wires without the help of a tool that provides secure attachment and some leverage or mechanical advantage. That is what pliers do.

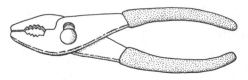

They hold onto the material while you pull it, twist it, bend it, or turn it. Pliers can also be used to squeeze or crimp things. Depending on the size and shape of what you need to hold, there are several types and sizes of pliers available. By far, the most common and most useful type for the budding builder is slip-joint pliers. This familiar tool can be adjusted to two positions for different size jaw openings and to fit various shapes. But do not use pliers on medium or larger size bolts and nuts because the pliers will have a tendency to slip off—and that often causes pinched fingers

and marred parts.

Adjustable wrench

It is always best to use a wrench that is meant to fit the exact type and size of the nut, bolt, or fastener being installed or removed, but that could mean needing hundreds of special tools. An adjustable wrench is second best and can be

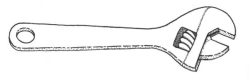

made to fit both square-headed and hex-headed bolts and nuts in a wide range of sizes. A small adjustment wheel makes the jaws of the wrench narrower or wider, up to a certain limit, to fit the fastener. Adjustable wrenches come in different sizes, with larger ones hav-

BUILDER'S TIP

SCREWDRIVER SUGGESTIONS

- A screw should first go through the thinner material being joined and then into the thicker material.

- Coating or lubricating a screw with candle wax or hand soap will allow it to be driven into the material more easily.

- To start a wood screw, first make a small pilot hole using a nail or a pointed tool called an awl. The starting hole only needs to be an indentation deep enough so the screw threads will grab when the screw is turned into the hole by hand. With the screw already started, you will avoid poking your hand with the screwdriver as you might if you were holding the screw and the screwdriver slipped.

- To fix a screw hole that is too large, or "stripped," stuff the hole with a small piece of steel wool or a piece of a toothpick, and reinsert the screw.

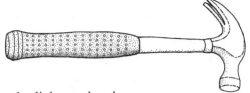

BUILDER'S TIP

AVOIDING PINCHED FINGERS

When driving small nails or screws, protect your fingers from being pinched, pounded, or poked by holding the nail or screw in position, using a scrap of paper or cardboard. Simply push the nail through the paper and hold onto the paper "handle" while hammering the nail or turning the screw into the material. Once the nail or screw is well started, simply rip the paper away. With a little practice, a pocket comb can also be used for holding nails and screws.

ing rocks. The best all-purpose hammer for young builders is a lightweight curved claw nail hammer. This hammer is designed to drive nails straight into wood and to pull them out, as well as for doing other pounding jobs. Claw hammers are sized by weight from about seven ounces to twenty ounces. A seven-ounce hammer is perfect to start with, but a builder who wants to nail two by fours and construction lumber will need a heavier hammer of about a thirteen ounces. A model builder may need a tack hammer, which is even lighter than

the lightest claw hammer.

To properly hammer a nail into wood, hold the hammer in one hand near the end of the handle. With the other hand, hold the nail between your thumb and pointer finger. Now position the nail on the wood and gently tap the head until the nail stands up by itself when you let go. By flexing your arm and wrist up and down in a firm and steady rhythm, drive the nail completely into the wood. If the nail bends or starts

BUILDER'S TIP

HAMMER HINTS

When attaching two pieces, always drive the nail through the thinner piece into the thicker one.

Only use the face of the hammer head for striking. Never strike with the side of the hammer, the claw, or the handle. And don't use a nail hammer to strike metal or rock. That could cause dangerous chips of material to go flying right in front of you.

Even if you use a hammer properly, it's a good idea to wear protective safety goggles or glasses. These are inexpensive and available at all building supply and hardware stores.

For strong joints, the nail should be at least three times as long as the thickness of the thinner piece.

Coating or lubricating a nail with candle wax or hand soap will allow it to be driven into the material more easily.

Driving the nails of a joint at different angles (rather than all at 90-degree angles) will give the best holding power.

For better nail pulling leverage or to pull out long nails, put a small block of wood or some other thick scrap of material under the middle of the hammer head.

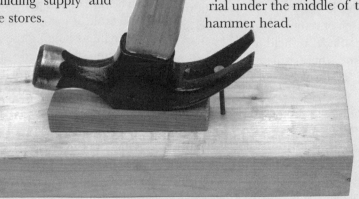

ing larger opening limits. A good starter-size wrench would be a six-inch adjustable wrench, which is named after its handle length and has an opening that will adjust up to $3/4$ of an inch, or even an eight-inch adjustable wrench with an opening that adjusts up to one inch. For safe control of any wrench, position yourself so that you are pulling on the wrench handle and not pushing it.

Curved claw hammer

There are several types of hammers for different types of work that range from pounding nails to break-

going in crooked, use the claw end of the hammer to pull it out.

Tools That Shape Things

Coping saw

One of the safest and easiest saws to use is the coping saw, designed for making straight or curved cuts in thin woods, plastics, and other materials. Blades come in a variety of types and can easily be changed in the saw frame. Thin, round, wire-like blades are even available for cutting intricate patterns. The finer the saw teeth, the smoother the cut, and the more coarse the saw teeth, the faster the cutting action. For younger builders, fine-tooth saw blades with the most teeth per inch

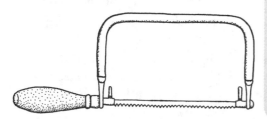

are safer and less likely to cause accidental cuts than blades with larg-er and coarser teeth even though the cutting will take a little longer.

To safely use a coping saw, first make sure the blade is not loose. On most coping saws, the blade is tightened by twisting the handle (twist in the opposite direction to loosen or remove the blade). Because the blade is held in a U-shaped frame, there is a limit to how far the saw will cut into the material. However, the saw blade can also be positioned at different angles in the frame to allow the saw to cut side-ways. The blade can be installed with the teeth pointing in either direction, for cutting on the push stroke or the pull stroke (the blade is meant to cut in only one direction).

DRILLING STRAIGHT, CLEAN HOLES

- When starting to drill into any material, keep the bit from wandering by first making a shallow starting hole with the point of a nail or a pointed awl or punch.

- Firmly hold, position, or clamp the work piece so it won't wiggle while being drilled.

- Hold the drill handle so you can apply light to medium pressure directly in line with the drill bit. A comfortable and balanced position will keep the drill bit cutting straight and prevent slipping.

- Be careful not to bend or wobble the drill bit to avoid breaking it.

- For small holes, drill at a fast speed, and use a slower speed for larger holes.

- When drilling completely through something, clamp the material to a piece of scrap material so you'll drill through it instead of the worktable or floor.

- To do a neat job when drilling through wood and especially metal or plastic, apply less pressure as the drill bit is just about to break through the material.

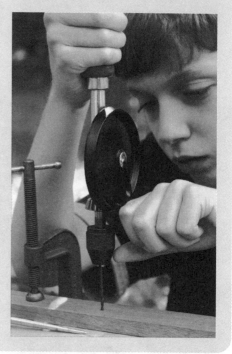

The easiest and safest cutting, however, is with the teeth slanted toward the handle for cutting on the pull stroke.

Since a coping saw is meant for lightweight and intricate cutting, the material to be cut can usually be held firmly in place on the edge of a table, using one hand with the other hand holding the saw to cut on the downward stroke. Of course, be careful not to cut into the tabletop. The material can also be clamped in place to the tabletop or held in a vise.

If the building project calls for cutting through a bolt, a nail, or any other piece of metal, the metal-cutting hacksaw is also relatively

safe. As with the coping saw, there are many blades available for a hacksaw, with the finer-toothed blades being the safest against accidental hand cuts.

Hand drill

A hand drill, sometimes also called an eggbeater drill, is easy and safe to use for drilling small holes up to 1/4-inch diameter in wood, plastic, and thin metal. For most projects, that is a good size range for drilling bolt holes and pilot holes for screws. The hand drill is operated with a crank handle attached to a large gear that turns a smaller gear and the cutting bit at a higher speed (about three to four revolutions of the drill bit for each complete rotation of the hand crank). The straight-shank, twist-drill bits used in a hand drill are available in many sizes that come in sets or separately. A good starter set might include drill diameters of $1/16$ inch, $1/8$ inch, $3/16$ inch, and $1/4$ inch. On the drill, an adjustable chuck has jaws that can be tightened down to hold the drill bit from slipping.

To drill larger diameter holes requires another type of hand drill called a bit brace. These large drills with big crank handles provide a lot of turning force. With the proper drill bit, a brace can drill through almost any material—it just may take a lot of turning and a long time.

Scissors

A good pair of workshop scissors is an indispensable tool for cutting cardboard,

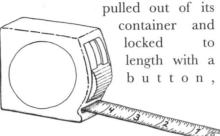

thin metal, rope, small gauge wire, rubber, tubing, fabric, and lots of other materials. Although they may look somewhat similar, workshop scissors are not the same as common paper cutting shears. Instead, they are rather heavy-duty scissors that have blunt tips and sometimes feature serrated cutting edges and a special notch for cutting wire and cord. For cutting heavy-gauge wires like wire coat hangers and small nails, use a pair of wire cutters.

Tools That Mark or Measure

Measuring tape

For projects that require measur-ing to make parts and fit them together, a retracting, roll-up steel measuring tape is indispensable. On most tapes, the markings indi-cate both inches and feet, and there is often a special marking every sixteen inches because that is a common unit of length in large construction projects. Different amounts of the coiled tape can be pulled out of its container and locked to length with a button,

depending on what you are measuring. The locking feature allows for one-handed measuring. Releasing the button causes the tape to retract (sometimes quickly and with force) and coil back up in its container.

Most roll-up steel measuring tapes make it easy to take inside meas-urements, like the inside length or width of a box or a drawer, by adding a specific number of inch-es to the measured length indicat-ed on the tape to take into account the width of the tape case.

And because the tape's curved shape allows it to be either rigid or flexible, a metal tape can be used to measure straight distances or around shaped objects. Measuring tapes come in several lengths and widths, with the wider tapes being the easiest to use. A convenient length is twelve feet, with a $3/4$-inch-wide tape. Longer and wider automatic retractable tape meas-ures are available up to about twenty-five feet in length, and hand-cranked retracting reel tapes for measuring big projects come in lengths of fifty feet and a hundred feet and have a flat and flimsy tape rather than a curved and rigid one.

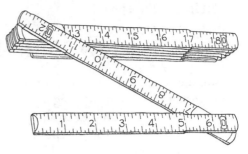

Folding wooden rule

Another common measuring device is the folding wooden rule, some-times called the zigzag rule because of the way it is opened. Folding rules are typically made from sev-eral six-inch or eight-inch wood sections that are hinged together so the rule can extend rigidly to a length of six feet or fold up to fit in a pocket. Folding rules are not as practical and durable as measuring tapes, but they will work and can be fun to play with.

Builder's square

For many construction projects, it is very useful to have a 90-degree right-angle tool to help get things squared up, or draw square cor-ners, and to check that things are vertical. Of the several types of squares available, the simplest to use is the try square, which is avail-able with a 6-, 8-, or 12-inch-long steel-blade ruler attached to a wood block exactly at a right angle. This tool is handy for meas-uring and marking, to test

the squareness of adjoining sur-faces, or to mark a straight right-angle line for cutting. And to test for true flatness, simply place the edge of the blade on the surface and see if any light comes through.

A combination square does even more, with additional features that include a 45-degree angle for

MEASURING WITH FINGERS AND FEET

Building often requires measuring and using rulers or measuring tapes. But if your measurements do not have to be exact, you might find using your fingers, hands, and feet a pretty good tool for measuring proportions and relative sizes like twice as long, three times as high, or one-and-a-half times as thick.

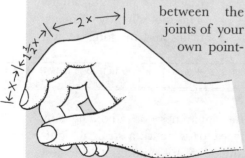

For example, the end of your pointer finger (the last joint to the tip) is about half as long as the distance between the knuckle of that finger and the middle joint. And the middle section of that finger is about one and a half times as long as the tip section. Or think of it this way. The end of your finger is one unit long, the middle section is one and a half units long, and the largest section is two units long. You can measure the distance between the joints of your own point-

er finger to see how long each unit is in actual inches. Interestingly, the length of the tip of an adult's pointer finger is about one inch long, so an adult's pointer finger pro-

vides a convenient way to readily measure multiples of one inch, one and a half inches and two inches.

If you spread out the fingers of your hand as wide as they will go, the distance between the tip of your thumb and the tip of your little finger will be about eight units long. This can be another "handy" tool for measuring or determining length.

For measuring long distances, you can use several methods. For measuring distances on the ground, place each of your feet alternately in front of the other (heel to toe) and count off "1 foot, 2 feet, 3 feet, 4 feet," and so on. If this sounds like a familiar unit of measurement, it is because that is how English units of measuring were first invented. The length of a large adult foot in shoes was considered to be twelve inches long. Measure the length of your own shoe from heel to toe to know how long your "foot" really is.

If you have really long distances to measure, you might try "walking it off" by counting the steps or paces as you walk from one point to another. The actual length of each step you take while walking at a normal pace is usually about three times the length of your foot. So if your foot were an actual 12 inches long, a 3-foot pace would equal 36 inches (or one yard) for each step.

But since your foot is probably shorter, your pace will also be shorter than a yard and will need to be measured for actual length.

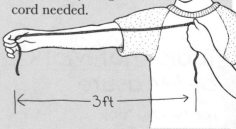

To measure a long length of string, rope, or any type of cord, hold the end of the cord in the fingers of an outstretched arm off to the side, and draw the cord taut to the middle of your chest with the other hand. For an adult, that distance is also about one yard. Again, you will have to measure the actual length of your own reach. Multiples of that distance can then be used to measure out any length of cord needed.

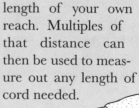

measuring and marking, a sliding ruler to measure the depth of holes and depressions, and sometimes even a built-in bubble level.

A large but simple framing square is best for measuring and marking cut lines on building lumber and for squaring up structure components during assembly of really

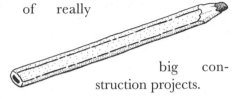

big construction projects.

Carpenter's pencil

This large, flat-sided pencil with a large, flat lead is a bit more difficult to use than a regular pencil (especially for drawing curved lines), but the lead never breaks, no matter how hard it is pressed, and it takes a long time for the point to wear down. When it does, the only way to resharpen a carpenter's pencil to a fine, flat edge is to whittle it with a knife.

Other Basic Tools

Clamps

Using clamps to hold parts together while gluing or just working on them is like having extra hands with a super strong grip. Having many small clamps is especially handy when fabricating projects with several pieces that have to be held in position just right, or if you want to keep building without having to wait for pieces to dry. C-clamps, named for their curved shape, have a thumbscrew that can be tightened to

change the clamping force between firm and very tight depending on how much clamping force the job needs. C-clamps come in many sizes, with the widest opening starting at one inch and the largest C-clamp having a maximum opening of about eight inches. C-clamps sometimes mar the material being clamped unless small scraps of wood or cardboard are placed between the jaws and the material.

A faster and simpler way to hold pieces together is with a spring clamp, although there is no adjustment of the clamping force. These clamps range in size from about four inches long with a jaw that opens to $7/8$ inch to eight inches long with a three-inch opening. For most projects, the smaller sizes are most useful. The bigger size clamps have springs so powerful that it takes two hands with a wide grip to squeeze them open.

Safety goggles

Whenever you are building and there is a possible danger of something hitting your eye, you should wear a pair of safety goggles or glasses. That safety rule includes

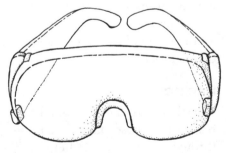

almost anytime you are hammering or cutting. Most safety goggles and glasses are inexpensive and made from shatterproof and scratch-resistant plastic, but the quality, clarity, and comfort varies greatly among the choices available. If you can't see clearly through the lenses or if the fit is

uncomfortable, you probably won't want to wear them even though you should. So find a pair of goggles or glasses you really like, and that might make it easier for you to remember to wear them when needed.

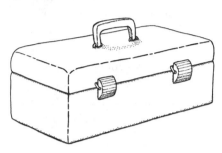

Toolbox

If there is one place where you regularly do building projects, like a table in your bedroom or a workbench in the basement, it may make sense to keep your tools there, ready to use. Some builders like to put a sheet of pegboard on their workshop wall and hang many of their tools on it in plain sight, using pegboard hooks. That certainly makes it easy to quickly find a tool when you need it. Just make sure the displayed tools can't be reached by anyone who doesn't know how to use them. A more common way to store tools is in a toolbox. Not only does a toolbox help organize your tools, but it makes them easily portable to any job site—indoors, outdoors, or a friend's home.

Toolboxes come in a large variety of types and sizes, but all you will probably need is a small (but good quality) plastic toolbox with a comfortable handle and a removable tray inside. Bigger tools are placed in the bottom of the toolbox, and smaller tools like screwdrivers, pliers, and a measuring tape are kept in the upper tray. In some toolboxes, the tray has a special narrow compartment for socket-wrench sockets, but that area is also a

A TOOL FOR EVERY PURPOSE BEYOND THE BASICS

The tools you add to your toolbox will depend on the type of building you are doing. Model builders will need small clamps, carving knives, a coping saw, and maybe tweezers. The mechanically inclined builder might need wrenches and sockets, wire cutters, and a hacksaw. The outdoor builder could need a garden spade, a bucket, and a wood saw.

In some ways, the tools you have might even influence the type of building you do. A simple set of sockets and a socket wrench make it tempting to remove bolts and nuts to take things apart and maybe reassemble them in some way other than the original configuration. And similarly, a saw invites cutting, and a drill will make drilling holes irresistible.

Sketching and drawing can help you figure things out on paper before committing an idea to construction. So it's a good idea to have simple drawing tools, including a pad of graph paper, a 45°/90° plastic triangle, a 30°/60°/90° plastic triangle, a one-foot ruler, a drawing compass, and, of course, a pencil. If you have never used some of these tools, experiment with them or ask someone to show you how they work.

Although a particular building project or special interest may dictate what tools you need next, there are some basic add-ons that are most useful.

Keyhole or compass saw

To make small cutouts anywhere on sheet material or curved cuts in thick materials and lumber requires a saw with a narrow blade but without a frame (a coping saw or a

hacksaw can only make cuts from an edge to the depth of their frames). Like the coping saw, a compass saw and a keyhole saw can accept different types of blades for cutting through different materials and thicknesses. A keyhole saw is smaller than a compass saw and was originally used for cutting small keyholes in wooden doors. The compass saw is more like a smaller and thinner version of the carpenter's crosscut saw with the same aggressive-cutting teeth. Starting from a drilled hole, both of these saws can be used to cut openings and shapes anywhere within the material without starting from an edge.

These saws can also be used to cut from an edge using backward strokes. Use the teeth of the saw blade closest to the handle, and make several short pull strokes until a groove is formed to guide the saw blade. If you try to start a cut with a push cutting stroke, the blade will have a tendency to skip to the side and possibly hit the hand holding the material.

Hacksaw

A hacksaw has a fine-toothed saw blade that is best suited for cutting through metals (including nails and screws) and plastics. The fine-toothed blades come in many interchangeable types with teeth designed for cutting specific materials and thicknesses. The long, narrow blades with a small hole at either end are meant to fit in a rigid hacksaw frame and handle with the teeth positioned to cut on

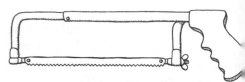

the push stroke. Mounted in the frame, the cutting edge of the hacksaw blade can be positioned facing up, down, or sideways, according to what is needed to make the cut. To prevent breakage, make sure the blade does not easily twist and flex by tightening the wing nut that pulls the blade taught. And even though a hacksaw has only one handle, it is meant to be held with two hands—one on the handle and the other holding the front of the frame.

The teeth of a hacksaw can sometimes catch and pull the material out of your hands, so whenever possible, mount what you are cutting in a vise or clamp it down over the edge of a worktable. When cutting very thin materials, angle the blade so you are cutting more on the surface of the material than across the edge. A hacksaw is not very good for cutting wood because the small teeth will easily clog and make cutting slow and tedious.

Crosscut saw

A crosscut saw is designed to cut lumber and boards across the wood grain and can also be used to cut plywood as well as other sheet materials in any direction. The crosscut saw has fewer and larger teeth than a coping saw or hacksaw, usually from seven to twelve teeth, or points, per inch. The fewer the teeth, the faster the cutting and the rougher the cut. Hold the saw at a 45-degree angle, and start the cut on a backstroke at the butt end of the blade near the handle. Use several pull strokes until a good starting groove is formed to keep the blade from skipping on the push strokes. The blade of a crosscut saw is designed to cut on both the push stroke and the pull stroke, so keep a light but firm cutting pressure on the saw for strokes in both directions. If you are cutting off a large piece of material, be sure to support the cutoff as you make the final strokes. Otherwise, the weight of the cutoff can break, bend, or splinter the material before it is completely cut through.

There are special ripsaws with teeth designed specifically for cutting wood parallel to the grain, like sawing a long board lengthwise. But a ripsaw is not nearly as versatile as a crosscut saw, which can occasionally be used to also make cuts in the direction of the grain.

Bench vise

A bench vise can either be a bolt-on type if you have room for it on a workbench or a clamp-on type that can be temporarily mounted on the edge of a worktable. Both types are especially useful for holding work firmly in place for planing, sawing, sanding, or chiseling. You also have a choice between a woodworker's vice with large, flat jaws that protrude over the edge of the workbench or a mechanic's

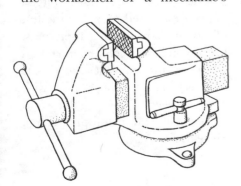

vise that rests on top of the workbench and has both flat jaws for clamping down on most shapes and rounded jaws for holding pipe, poles, and tubes.

Level

A level comes in handy when building big structures to check if the sides are perfectly vertical and if one side is higher or lower than another. The actual level is a small, liquid-filled glass tube with an air bubble inside. Usually, at least two of these bubble vials are fixed within a rigid frame with flat edges.

One is for checking horizontal surfaces, and the other indicates true vertical (which is called plumb).

Levels come in three basic types. A line level, used for long horizontal spans, is only a few inches long and is hung from a taut string line. A torpedo level is only about eight or nine inches long, but is very handy for most building projects and for getting into tight spaces. A carpenter's level is usually from two feet to four feet long.

Knife

For carving wood, cutting through corrugated boxes, and many other building tasks, a sharp knife is an essential tool. Knives come in a large variety of shapes and sizes designed to do specific types of cutting. Craft knives are small, razor sharp, and come in many configurations for cutting intricate shapes and patterns. Using craft knives requires developing technique and a lot of care, so they are not well-suited for younger builders. Kitchen knives of any size should also not be used for

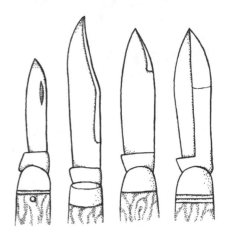

building projects unless the project calls for slicing up food. And hunting knives or fishing knives should never be used to cut wood and other construction materials.

The best first knife for a young builder is a folding pocketknife or clasp knife in which the blade closes into the handle. Pocketknives come in several styles with blades of different shapes and sizes. The smallest is the penknife, which usually has two or more blades, none being more than three inches long. A jackknife usually has only one large blade between three and a half and five inches long, and sometimes one or two smaller blades.

Both penknives and jackknives are available with blades shaped to do certain types of cutting and carving. Knives with narrow, pointed blades are good for getting into corners and carving intricate designs, while blades with wider ends are good for carving holes, making grooves, chipping wood, and other kinds of cuts. The most common types of pocketknife blade shapes are the pen, a larger version called the spear, the more pointed clip, and the sabre spear.

Any knife used for building projects must be kept sharp! That is the number one safety rule for knives. The sharper the knife blade, the safer it is. Some adults may think that a dull knife blade is safer for kids to use, but a dull blade requires far more pressure to make

WHITTLING WOOD FOR FUN AND FANCY

The best wood for whittling

The type and particular piece of wood you select will greatly determine how hard or easy it is to whittle. For the beginning whittler, there are several easy-to-cut woods that are soft, straight grained, and free from knots. Some are readily found or bought at a lumberyard and include balsa, northern white pine, basswood, redwood, sugar pine, and willow. Common yellow pine is unsuitable because it is very knotty and splinters easily. After some practice at whittling, you might want to try a harder wood such as mahogany, oak, birch, or elm. And make sure the wood you select is seasoned

and dry. A "green" branch or any freshly cut wood is very difficult to carve. Wood from downed trees that have naturally dried and seasoned can be excellent for carving, unless the wood has become too old and soft or rotted.

How to whittle

First comes safety. The general rule for safe whittling is to always cut with the blade moving away from you and away from the hand holding the wood. That way, if the knife should skip or slip, you will not accidentally cut yourself. And be sure to keep the knife blade sharp. A dull blade requires more force and gives you less control.

Before starting some ambitious whittling project, practice your knife technique by just chipping away at a scrap of wood. You will soon develop a feel for the knife and how it carves the type of wood you are using. Next, practice whittling knife control (and make something practical at the same time) by making a fire-starter fuzz stick.

Begin with a piece of a dry branch, and make lots of slices around the stick and along its length. Each slice should create a chip that curls out but stays attached to the stick—something like the look of a pinecone. Try making more fuzz sticks, each with a unique pattern of cut chips. If you've created some pleasant carvings, you may want to keep your practice fuzz

sticks to start a whittling collection, or use them for starting fireplace fires or campfires.

After some more practice, you may be ready to whittle a specific shape or object. Select an appropriate piece of wood, and draw the shape to be carved on one side of the wood. If the shape is complex, also draw the rear, sides, top, and bottom views. It is easiest when you start with a piece of wood about the size of the object you want to whittle.

Find a comfortable place to sit and begin to cut away at the wood slowly and carefully, carving out the shape chip by chip, cutting only small chips. Remember that once a chip is whittled off, it can't be replaced. So don't try to make big cuts, but gradually work the wood down to the lines you have drawn. Roughly whittle out the entire shape before carving any details. As you are carving the wood, try to keep a mental picture of the shape or object you are making.

Here are a few whittling tips. When roughing out a shape, hold the knife in your fist with your thumb on the back edge of the handle. For finer cutting, move your thumb forward onto the dull back edge of the blade.

What to whittle

Nothing that you whittle has to be practical, and actually most whittled items are created more for the fun of doing than for their usefulness. Once you have become hooked on whittling, there are several classic carvings you might try, starting with a single piece of wood (balsa wood is easiest if you're still practicing). Here are a few.

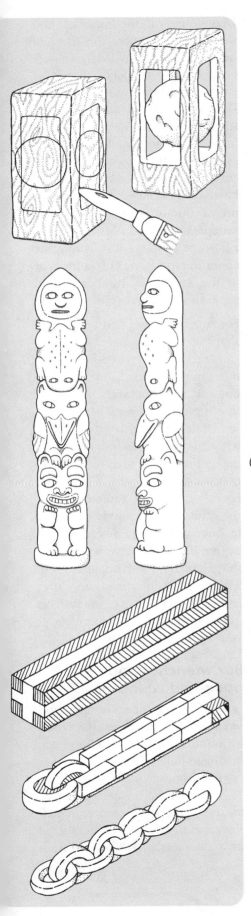

a cut and is therefore more likely to slip and scar the material, refuse to cut where you want it to, split the wood, or possibly snap shut while cutting. The sharp edge of a knife blade will begin to wear dull as soon as you begin to use it. And even a brand new knife may require finer sharpening before it can be used for carving or cutting. The blade is made sharp by grinding both sides of the blade edge on a sharpening stone.

Utility knife

A utility knife is very useful for cutting or scoring corrugated board. A cut score is a shallow cut that does not go completely through the material. When you score something, it makes it easier to bend at that specific point. Utility knives are available either with a

replaceable fixed blade that protrudes about an inch from the handle or with a retractable blade that can be adjusted to a few different cutting depths.

Metal and wood files

Files come in a very large variety of shapes, lengths, and cutting surfaces and are used for shaping and smoothing metal, wood, and plastics and to enlarge holes and slots. The process of finding the right file for a job starts by selecting the proper shape for the result wanted and the correct coarseness for the material. The file shape is described by its surfaces and can be flat, round, half-round, square, or triangular. Half-round shapes are good choices for general purposes. The cutting surface of a file consists of lines cut into the hardened steel, and the deeper the lines,

the more coarse the file. If the lines go in one direction, the file is called a single-cut, and if the lines go in two directions, the file is called a double-cut. A special type of file intended just for wood is called a rasp. Instead of having lines cut into the surface of the steel, a rasp has small, sharp teeth that cut into the wood and allow sawdust to clear away without clogging the file.

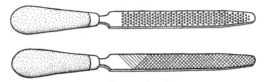

One end of a file has a tang to which a plastic or wood handle can be attached.

For proper filing, hold both ends of the file and move it back and forth over the work. For some types of filing, you may be able to hold the file only by one end. Whenever possible, hold the work in a vise or clamp it down, especially if the material vibrates or chatters while being filed.

Sandpaper

Sandpaper is not made of sand at all, but rather from four other common granular materials that all have special abrasive properties good for sanding specific things like metal, wood, plastic, plaster, or paint. Each type of sandpaper is identified by its type of abrasive and a grit number, or coarseness rating, which is printed on the back of the sandpaper sheet. Grit grades can range from number 12, which is very coarse, to 600, which is extremely fine.

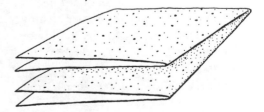

SHARPENING A KNIFE

If a blade has become very dull from neglect or if the blade edge has become chipped, it may need to be sharpened on a grinding wheel with help from an adult. But if the blade edge has become slightly dulled from cutting, you can regrind the edge by using a sharpening stone and oil.

There are several types of sharpening stones, varying from coarse to smooth, with flat to rounded shapes. If you don't have a sharpening stone, find a smooth, flat rock or stone, and put a few drops of machine oil on the flat surface. Lay the blade almost flat on the stone with the back edge raised slightly. Gently stroke the blade so that the knife edge is pulled across the stone. Turn the blade over and stroke the other edge. Continue stroking and turning the blade over alternately until it is sharp. Don't press hard against the stone—only a gentle, steady pressure is needed. If you have a chance, watch a wood craftsperson use a sharpening stone. There are several individual hand techniques, and developing a technique will make sharpening much easier.

To finish the sharpening job, draw the blade several times, as you have been doing, across a piece of leather or cardboard. This technique removes any slightly rough wire edges, or burrs, that are sometimes caused by the sharpening stone. To test a whittling blade for sharpness, draw it across the edge of a piece of paper. The blade should cut the paper cleanly and easily. If the paper bends or tears, the blade still needs sharpening. Don't let the blade become too dull. Whenever things feel harder to cut, stroke the knife a few times across the stone. Here are more tips to help keep your whittling knife sharp and safe.

- Never hammer on a knife or use the knife as a hammer. The steel of the knife blade is hard and brittle, and can break or shatter if hit.

- Never use a knife on material that is very hard and could dull or break the blade. Also, watch out for knots and nails when whittling in old lumber.

- Never heat the blade in a fire. The metal will discolor and lose some of its hardness.

- Never use the blade as a screwdriver to pry things open or for throwing into the ground.

- If the blade gets wet, wipe it dry and lightly oil the hinge.

- When not using a knife, close the blade with the palm of your hand and put it away. Never carry the knife with the blade open.

Depending on the material and shape to be sanded, the sheet of sandpaper can be folded into a pad, cut into strips or special shapes, or wrapped around a sanding block. For flat-surface sanding jobs, use a small block of wood you can comfortably grip in your hands. Use a cylinder-shaped object for sanding curved surfaces. For many irregular-shaped surfaces, it is easiest to use a one-quarter-size sheet of sandpaper just held in your hand. For some sanding jobs, it may be easier to tape a sheet of sandpaper to the top of a workbench and move the work across it.

For rough sanding and shaping, sandpaper can be used across the grain of wood, but for medium and fine sanding, always sand back and forth with the direction of the grain. When it is necessary to start with course sandpaper, resand the surface, progressively switching to finer grits. Remember that the degree of smoothness depends on the grit of the last sandpaper used. The best test for smoothness is to run your fingertips over the surface. Your fingers will feel imperfections your eyes can't easily see.

Box wrenches and open-end wrenches

A set of box wrenches or open-end wrenches are indispensable tools for removing and assembling large hex-head bolts and nuts. Wrenches come in sets according to the type of fastener they are used on (SAE for most American fasteners in inch sizes and metric for fasteners sized in millimeters). Each set covers a

range of the most popular sizes from about $1/4$ inch to $3/4$ inch and 4 mm to 19 mm. A box wrench is meant to fit securely over the bolt head or nut, and an open-end wrench can slip onto the head or nut from the side. Some sets are available with combination wrenches in which each wrench size has a box wrench on one end of the handle and an open-end wrench on the other end. Always make sure the wrench snugly fits the fastener or the wrench could slip off the bolt head or nut. A loose wrench might also damage and round off a bolt head or nut.

Socket wrenches

If you want to speed up the removal and installation of bolts and nuts or if you need to access a fastener in a tight space, use a socket wrench with the proper attachments. Sockets come in the same SAE and metric sizes as box wrenches, and they fit over the bolt head or nut the same way (except sockets are deeper). Each size socket in the set can be attached to a common ratchet handle either directly or with an extension between them. The ratchet mechanism of a socket wrench allows tightening (or loosening) in one direction and free rotation in the other direction. In cramped or obstructed spaces, that allows you to turn the fastener by moving the wrench handle repeatedly back and forth over a very short range. Socket wrenches and sockets are sold in sets based on a particular driver size. One-quarter inch and $3/8$-inch drivers are best suited for most household mechanics, and $1/2$-inch and larger drivers are commonly used for large automotive and industrial fasteners.

SELECTING THE RIGHT SANDPAPER

To help select the right sandpaper for the job, these are the most common types and their characteristics.

Flint paper

- best for coarse sanding of wood and removing old finishes
- least expensive but not very durable
- easily identified by its typical beige color

Aluminum oxide

- best for coarse to medium hand sanding of bare wood, plastics, and fiberglass, plus stainless steel, other types of steel, and bronze
- cuts fast and is very durable even with hard materials
- usually light brown in color

Garnet paper

- excellent for hand sanding bare wood from coarse to very fine
- cuts fast, but not very durable or long lasting
- reddish to golden brown in color

Emery cloth

- for polishing many kinds of metals
- slow cutting and not very long lasting
- heavy blue cloth with a black abrasive

Silicon carbide

- extremely durable abrasive can be used wet or dry
- best used wet on brass, copper, aluminum, and plastic, and for smoothing sharp edges of glass and ceramics; use dry for finishing wood
- blue gray or charcoal in color, waterproof backing paper

To help select the right sandpaper grit for the job, determine how coarse or fine the sanding needs to be. Most hardware and paint stores commonly carry sandpaper with grits that range from 50 to 220. These grit-number grades also have name designations.

Extra coarse

Grade 50 or 60 for removing thick coats of paint and heavy rust

Coarse

Grade 80 for quick and rough shaping of wood

Medium

Grade 100 for lightly shaping wood, removing rust from metal, and general sanding

Fine

Grade 150 for final finishing before painting

Very fine

Grade 220 for sanding between coats of paint

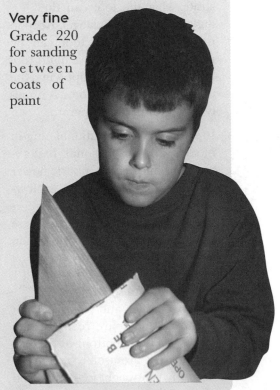

SOME POWER TOOLS ARE SAFE AT ANY SPEED

Older builders with plenty of experience using hand tools may want to consider adding one or more power tools to their workstations. It is not so much that a power tool will do the job faster; some power tools are just much better at doing the job. A power saber saw, for example, could make intricate and curvy cuts that would be very difficult or even impossible to do with any kind of handsaw. And because it makes the job so much easier, a power tool can inspire you to take on more complex projects and experiment with different ideas.

Remember, the same safety rules apply to hand tools and power tools. Always learn from someone with a lot of experience who can explain and demonstrate what the tool can do and how it can be a danger. Keep in mind that a power tool can be more dangerous than a hand tool because a motor is supplying the power, and the tool motor is usually stronger than the operator.

In addition to conventional plug-in models and professional battery-powered models, most basic power tools are also available in low-powered and low-cost, battery-operated models. Some of these power tools can cost little more than hand tools, but there is often an additional cost for a separate battery charger, and you may want to purchase a spare rechargeable battery. These bottom-of-the-line power tools are usually meant for relatively lightweight jobs—the kind of building construction young

builders typically do. The low power of the tool makes it easier to control, and battery power is safe. Depending on the kind of building projects to be done, these are the first battery-operated power tools to consider.

Saber saw

In addition to making straight and curved cuts in plywood, thin boards, and other sheet materials, a battery-powered saber saw is an excellent tool for cutting shapes from corrugated-paper boxes and board—and much safer than cutting corrugated board with a knife. There are several types of removable saw blades available intended for cutting different materials, and some models have convenient options including several speeds and a scroller that lets you change the direction of the blade while cutting without turning the saber saw.

Power drill

Battery-powered drills come in a wide range of power options, with a low battery-voltage rating indicating a lower-powered drill. Only low-powered drills are appropriate and safe for young builders because more powerful drills develop a lot of torque, or twisting power, that can twist the drill out of even strong hands. In addition to drill bits, a power drill can take several types

SAFETY FIRST

Remember to keep baggy or loose clothing away from power tools and machinery. Also, pull back long hair

and remove any jewelry before starting to work on a project.

of accessories, including a sanding disk, a polishing pad, a grinding wheel, and even a paint stirrer.

Compact rotary tool

For avid model builders, a compact rotary power tool with accessories is indispensable for building on a small scale including cutting, drilling, grinding, etching, polishing, and carving. The battery-powered versions of this tool

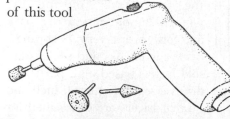

are quite safe, yet plenty powerful and extremely versatile. Especially consider a rechargeable model with adjustable speeds ■

GOOD DESIGN IS GOOD FORM, FUNCTION, AND FUN

EVERY BUILDER DEVELOPS PERSONAL PREFERENCES

GOOD DESIGNS ARE HERE TO STAY

NATURE PROVIDES THE BEST CLUES TO GOOD DESIGN

DEVELOPING A VISUAL VOCABULARY

EVERY BUILDER DEVELOPS PERSONAL PREFERENCES

Almost anything you build may be a complement to your creativity and invention skills, but is it well-designed? What is good design as opposed to bad design? What is ugly and what is good looking? And how does someone create good design? As you grow older, your changing likes and dislikes affect your opinions, choices, and demonstrations of what is good design and what is not.

Given several options, nearly anyone can pick the one design they like best, although individual choices may vary greatly. That's because each person responds to a design on many levels. How well does the design do the job it was made for? Is the design inherently good-looking or fashionable? Is it impressive, fun, colorful, sleek, or funky? For most people, the best design is the one with the most attributes that address their own particular needs and likes. Through creative building and inventing, you will have plenty of opportunities to develop your own personal sense of design and the skills to create good design.

Design Is Not the Same As Style

Recognizing and appreciating the features that contribute to good design are necessary to learning how to create good design. However, the evaluation of any design should begin with the understanding that a design's structure, form, and appearance are related to its function. For any design to be appealing, it must be fit for its purpose, that is, it must do what it was designed to do. After making sure the design has functionality, there is often plenty of opportunity for the builder to adjust parts of the design's appearance. Clearly, not all bridges look alike even though they are all designed to achieve generally the same purpose. The same is true for the many designs of fences and houses. Even a design created for pure function, like an antenna tower, a bus-stop rain shelter, or a camping tent, can take on a variety of appearances that reflect the individual designer's preference for building techniques and visual appearance.

However, when elements of a construction are applied for the sake of appearance only, the word *style* should be substituted for *design*. Style focuses on the way an object's appearance is meant to generate an emotional response and is usually added to a design. Just look at all the different styles of cars, furniture, and clothing available to understand the concept of style and to realize that style does not necessarily reflect a good design.

What is considered attractive today will likely be replaced soon with

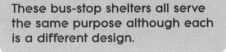

These bus-stop shelters all serve the same purpose although each is a different design.

something thought to be even better looking. Our popular culture always seems to be restyling itself with something different that will gain appeal, even if only temporarily. Styles are meant to last only a short time and then be replaced with different, but not necessarily better, ones. That's fine as long as styling or any added decorations do not interfere with the functional performance of the design. An inherently good—and long-lasting—design, by contrast, is usually simple and without added styling, achieving a pleasant appearance that grows out of the design's elegant functionality.

Although a functional approach to design addresses essential needs without styling adornments, the design does not have to be boring.

A design that fully achieves its purpose in a minimal construction is often seen as being a beautiful thing. But to recognize and appreciate the beauty of the object's form and function, the observer must have an understanding of how the design is used. For example, until you use one, you might not appreciate the structural beauty of a good umbrella, a backyard swing set, or a director's chair.

THE DOO-WOP MOTELS OF WILDWOOD

The Wildwoods Vacation Resort, located south of Atlantic City on the southern shore of New Jersey, is the location of America's best-preserved collection of 1950s stylistic architecture. Each of the more than one hundred highly styled motels is uniquely and flamboyantly decorated with architectural elements and themes that reflected the popular culture of the times. Elaborate neon signs, plastic palm trees, twinkle lights, futuristic shapes, and references to exotic locations throughout the world were all exercises in decorative styling designed to attract visitors.

It all began in the mid-1950s when Wildwood learned a lesson from its successful neighbor to the north. Atlantic City had come up with the idea of naming its streets after American states like Delaware Avenue, Connecticut Avenue, Wisconsin Avenue, and so on, so visitors from outside New Jersey would feel right at home. That concept, plus a boardwalk along the beachfront, proved to be quite popular, and tourists flocked to the seaside resort.

So the Wildwoods decided to reinvent itself as another up-to-date tourist resort and came up with its own idea to attract visitors. They would build motels styled after the popular themes of the times. Within just a few years, motels sprang up on nearly every street corner, and each one seemed to try and outdo the others with amazing names and themes—like the Pyramid Motel, which had gable ends that resembled a pyramid shape; the Tahiti Motel, with a lavish array of plastic palm trees; the Singapore Motel, with a five-tiered pagoda; and the Royal Hawaiian, which had an enormous flying-saucer-like structure atop its roof. And, in case visitors did not immediately associate the architectural elements of the structure with its theme, a glowing and flashing neon sign by the curbside or on the roof boldly announced the motel's name.

This modern style of architecture, with its butterfly and boomerang roofs, futuristic forms, and popular themes, also reflected the growing popularity of rock and roll music, leading to the name doo-wop design. Ironically, the structures underneath all the added styling elements and glitz were all nearly the same.

Many of these 1950s and early 1960s motels have been carefully restored to their original designs so that Wildwood, New Jersey, can now claim to be the doo-wop architecture capital of the world.

GOOD DESIGNS ARE HERE TO STAY

When you look at any building, structure, or product, there are many design clues that reveal its age and era. You can tell if the structure looks old-fashioned, contemporary, or maybe even futuristic. You might observe that many older designs still look pretty good today, while others seem dated and are no longer appealing. Good design will usually endure, while poor design quickly loses its appeal. On the other hand, a new design is not necessarily a better one.

Look at the houses, factories, churches, fences, towers, and other structures in the historic district of a city or town. Why do you imagine we still find so many of these structures pleasing? And what do you think happened to the old

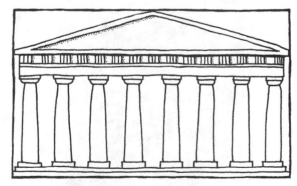

structures that were not such good designs? The same fate will be true for the designs being created today, so that in time, only those structures both pleasing in appearance and capable in their function will survive.

Observe the design of a bridge, a tall tower, a bicycle, a shovel, or any tool. These must be good, functional designs or they wouldn't still be around after decades. Yet there is always the possibility of making them better. Good design can certainly go beyond basic structure and function to include smaller changes in shape and form, color, and applied graphic designs. Even these seemingly arbitrary elements can improve the design's function, enhance its use, and add visual appeal. Would a bicycle be a better design if it were painted a color that could be easily seen in the day and glowed at night? And would a screwdriver, handlebars, or a pot handle work better if their grips were molded to perfectly fit the shape of the user's hand?

Sometimes a design will attempt to show and predict the next evolution of good design. These futuristic structures are guesses of how our culture will be changing, but in hindsight, they almost always look somewhat silly. The most outrageous of these designs, however, often take on another attribute called nostalgia, or kitsch, that endears them to many even though their styling overwhelms any purpose or function. Of course, if the primary purpose of an overdone design is to generate a giggle, then functionality has been achieved.

The Golden Rectangle

The most aesthetic proportions for a shape are usually determined by eye, with the designer trying different proportions of height and width until one looks just right. Although each person may have his or her own preferences, likes, and dislikes when it comes to design, there are some shapes that nearly everyone finds aesthetically pleasing. And when it comes to

rectangles, there is one particular shape that seems so perfect to most people that it has become known as the golden rectangle.

FINDING GOLDEN RECTANGLES

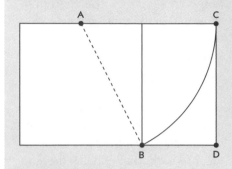

How many objects today can you find that have the pleasing proportions of the golden rectangle? First, you'll need to create a viewing frame the proportions of a golden rectangle. Start by drawing the precise rectangle on a sheet of paper, using paper and pencil, a right angle (the cardboard back of a notepad will do), a ruler to measure, and a drawing compass.

1. Using the right angle as a template, draw a square box (with right-angle corners and the same dimension on each side) and then extend the lines of the top and bottom edges to one side.

2. Measure the middle point of the square at the top edge A and use that as the position for the compass point. Open the compass to the circle radius A B and draw an arc from B to C.

3. Using position C as a corner, draw a right-angle line from C to D to complete the perimeter of the golden rectangle.

It is interesting to note that if you now removed the original square from the golden rectangle, the area remaining would be a smaller golden rectangle.

Cut out the golden rectangle shape from your sheet of paper, and use the remaining frame to view objects through the opening. Which ones nicely fit those proportions? Try looking at window shapes, decks of cards, books and magazines, tabletops, photographs, and paintings. And what about the proportions of things in nature like a seashell or a pine tree? Now do you also agree that the golden rectangle has the most pleasing proportions of any rectangle?

The architects of ancient Greece used geometry to calculate what they believed was the most pleasing relationship of height to width, and therefore the perfect proportions for a building. They found the length of a perfectly shaped rectangle to be 1.6 times its height. Many buildings from ancient history, like the Parthenon in Greece, used the proportions of the golden rectangle in their architecture, and their shapes still seem pleasing today.

Subtractive Design Is Better Than Additive Design

The objective of a good design is not only to make the creation work as planned, but to make it work using the smallest number of parts that will do the job well. This usually means eliminating unnecessary parts or combining two parts into one until the simplest functional structure remains.

If a simple and elegant design is the result of reducing parts, or subtractive design, then additive design occurs when the designer thinks of some other feature or function that should be added after the basic design has been completed. There is nothing wrong with changing your mind midstream or thinking of a better way to do something after you have already done it. But don't try to modify an existing design to accommodate the new features. Go back to the beginning and rethink the solution, this time using the new criteria added. Only when all the features and objectives of the design are clearly understood at the outset can an elegant design be achieved.

BRIDGES OF THE MERRITT PARKWAY

In the southeastern portion of Connecticut, there is a length of highway called the Merritt Parkway that has sixty-eight bridges crossing over it. That in itself is not too unusual. More unexpected is the fact that even though they were all engineered to be simple, segmented steel arches with concrete abutments, each is decorated in a different style. Some look like they are made of stone, some steel, and some concrete. Some have lots of decoration, and some are rather plain. And some look modern, while others are done in the art deco style that was popular when the bridges were being designed in the mid-1930s. Each bridge is an exercise in additive styling.

Because the bridges are so different in appearance, there is a popular belief that each one had its own designer or that the bridge designs were the ones selected in an engineering competition. Neither story is true; in fact, all the bridges were designed by the same person, George Dunkelberger. After engineers in the Connecticut Highway Department figured out the structural plans for the bridges, George had the job of taking them and "dressing them up" to be less monotonous to parkway drivers.

Connecticut state representative Schuyler Merritt, for whom the parkway was named, thought that "a beautiful parkway should be constructed so as to add beauty to the landscape and, therefore, help to attract desirable residents." So that became George Dunkelberger's

mission as he tried to come up with sixty-eight different ways to give each bridge covering, or veneer, a style that complimented and beautified its surroundings.

Despite the grand plans, only three of the bridges are covered in stone. When the whole project looked like it was going to be too expensive to complete as planned, the highway department decided that those towns along the route willing to pay for it could have the more expensive designs that used stone. Only three towns were willing to pay for their stone-covered bridges. The rest of the bridges vary in design from interesting to eclectic with no particular common theme.

Unfortunately, much of the fine detail found in the designs cannot be seen while passing in a moving car—unless, of course, there is a traffic jam!

NATURE PROVIDES THE BEST CLUES TO GOOD DESIGN

To see the ultimate examples of beautiful and functional design, just look at nature. How functional as well as pleasing in form are a seashell, a spider web, a bird's nest, a bee's honeycomb, or a cactus? Nature always seems to build with just the right materials (and only the minimal amount needed), fashioned into just the right form, with just the right features suited for the application.

In attempting to achieve the same elegance of design, many structure systems have been invented using human-made materials that attempt to imitate nature. To the designer, that means looking to nature for design clues and patterns that may become inspirations for creating a particular form to achieve a particular function. If you want to design an umbrella that doesn't break in a strong wind, the solution might be inspired by the branches and leaves of a tree or maybe by a mushroom. If you want to find modular shapes that fit together in interesting patterns, you might look at several types of crystals. Or if you want to create a pattern that gives the feeling of order and balance, look at the symmetry of leaves, flowers, seashells, or even snowflakes.

Architects and designers often use shapes and forms in nature as a reference for their own designs. What other forms in nature might be used as a reference for making a human-made structure? Can you imagine a beehive apartment building, a day-lily umbrella, or an alligator tail lawn mower?

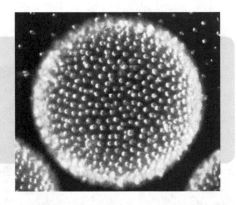

Buckminster Fuller's geodesic domes were influenced by the similar structure of some living cells.

The roof of the opera house in Sydney, Australia, is similar to the shape of some seashells.

Frank Lloyd Wright's Johnson Wax building is like being on the bottom of a pond looking up at lily pads floating on the water's surface.

A Ferris wheel is very much like the structure of a spider's web.

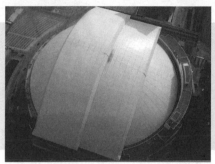

The Roger's Centre in Toronto, Canada, has a roof that was modeled after the overlapping plates of a lobster's tail.

The repetition of a single form in this beehive and apartment building create a regular pattern.

Both a propeller and a maple seed are shaped for flight.

The triangular treads of a spiral stair mimic the sections of a half grapefruit.

DEVELOPING A VISUAL VOCABULARY

Learning to recognize the visual relationships in the design of a structure requires a special knowledge about the different ways shapes or forms can be combined to produce different effects. It also requires a visual vocabulary and some practice in being able to describe why one structure may look balanced, well-proportioned, orderly, and particularly pleasing, while another seems awkward, unstable, boring, or chaotic.

There are special words and concepts in a visual vocabulary that help describe how we respond to and feel about the appearance and relationship of certain shapes and forms. Here are a few of the most common attributes in a basic visual vocabulary, along with visual exercises to help you better recognize, understand, and create structures with pleasing visual designs.

Order

Many common structures have a regular order, or arrangement, like the steps of a staircase, the spokes of a wheel, or the rungs of a ladder. Looking at a brick wall in which all the bricks are the same shape and size and are placed in a regular pattern, you can easily see there is a regular order to the bricks. Once you understand their particular order, you know exactly where each brick should go. If

Regular order

some of the bricks were a bit too long or too tall, it would mess up the regular pattern, and there would be disorder. In a similar way, there is an order to the pickets in a picket fence. All of the pickets are typically the same size and shape and placed exactly the same distance from each other, or in a pattern that repeats itself. If a few of the pickets were too short, too tall, too wide, or out of order, they also would mess up the regular pattern to create a disorder.

But to have a design with a regular order does not necessarily mean that all elements of the structure need to be the same. When you count from one to five, there is an order to the numbers—each successive number is one more than the one preceding it. Since you understand the order, you can determine what number comes

next. After five comes six, then seven, eight, nine, ten, and so on. If you count by twos (as in 2-4-6-8), or by fives (as in 5-10-15-20), there is also an order that you understand, so the next number in the order is predictable.

There are many objects and things that have this type of regular order, in which each element of the structure is a progression of units larger or smaller than the preceding one. Look at the regular progression of sizes in the stacked layers of a wedding cake or in the stepped pyramids of Mexico. Even though each element of the structure is a different size, order comes from all elements being the same shape and in an order that is regular and predictable.

Sometimes a structure has a regular order, but you have to look closely to figure out what it is. Again using numbers to demon-

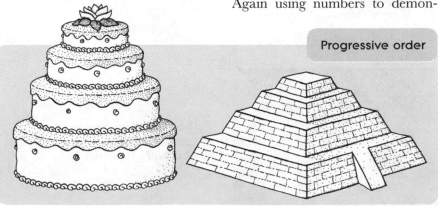

Progressive order

strate order, what is the next order-ly number in the sequence 1-2-4-7-11? If you said 16, then you figured out that 1 was added to the first number in the sequence, 1, to make 2, then 2 was added to the second number, 2, to make 4, then 3 was added to the third number, 4, to make 7, 4 was added to the fourth number, 7, to make 11, and 5 was added to the fifth number, 11, to make 16. If you kept on going, the next numbers in the sequence would be 22-29-37. A structure with elements using this or any regular progression will also look orderly.

Pattern

Whenever elements are repeated in a regular order, the result is a pattern. In a regular pattern, the same elements are repeated in the same way over and over again. The individual design or element can be a geometric shape or form (like a rectangle or cube) or even an arbitrary shape or form, as long as multiples of the element are all identical. These all-alike elements are often called modules. The bricks of a building, the triangles of a space frame, or the hexagon cells of a beehive are all modules that, when combined, make up all kinds of different shapes, forms, and patterns, even though each module is the same.

When the elements of a structure are similar in some attributes but different in others, there can still be a pattern, but it is considered to be an irregular pattern. For example, the rocks in a fieldstone wall are all rocks, but each one is a unique shape and size. When combined to build a wall, however, the rocks fit together to create a pleasing irregular pattern.

These patterns are created by the regular order of modular identical components.

These patterns appear to be regular even though they are created using irregular components.

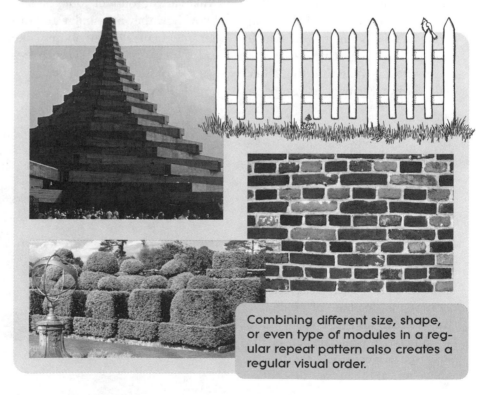

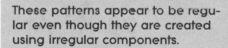

Combining different size, shape, or even type of modules in a regular repeat pattern also creates a regular visual order.

The arrangement and order of a repeat pattern can also provide a visual rhythm to the structure that is very similar to an audible rhythm in music. For example, a song in 4/4 time could have a rhythm that puts an emphasis on every fourth note, such as da-da-da-DA, da-da-da-DA, and so on. What if you used that same musical rhythm for building a picket fence? You might use a taller, wider, or different color board for every fourth picket.

Elements that are not alike can also be combined to create a module that by itself may not seem to have any particular order, but when that same arbitrary design is repeated over and over again in a structure, the result is a pattern that can help provide a pleasing visual order to a structure that might otherwise appear too complex and visually confusing.

structure seems stable with elements on one side in balance with elements on the other side.

Contrast

Purposely making some element of the structure visually different than the other elements tends to make it stand out because it is in contrast to the rest of the structure. Compared to a regular pattern that looks the same throughout, a contrasting element to the monotonous pattern causes your eye to stop and focus on it.

Contrast can be created many ways, including a change in size, shape, form, or color. But too much contrast can be busy or chaotic, just as too little contrast can be ineffective in drawing attention. Sometimes contrast can add a stylistic interest to a structure that would otherwise look too plain. And sometimes contrast can draw

attention to an element of the structure for a practical purpose, like emphasizing the entrance of a building so it is easily found.

Balance

Another way to create a visual order is through balance. The most common form of balance in structures is symmetry, in which one half of the structure is the exact mirror image of the other half. However, two halves of a

design do not have to be identical opposites for the structure to achieve a feeling of balance. Balance can also be created using asymmetry, in which no part of the structure is necessarily the mirror image of another, yet the entire

ALIKE AND NOT ALIKE

Take any group of objects and show how they are similar and different. Consider attributes like color, shape, size, thickness, material, flat or curved, rough or smooth, fragile or sturdy, symmetrical or asymmetrical. How are these objects alike and not alike?

Proportion

Every shape and form has a size. One common way to describe the size of a structure is by comparing it to something most people already know the size of. You might say something is as small as or as big as yourself, a car, a house, or any other familiar object or structure. But in using comparative sizes, something can be called huge and actually be very small or, conversely, very large, depending on what it is and what it is being compared to. For example, compared to the size of you, a huge nail is still pretty small, and a tiny house is still pretty big.

When you compare the actual sizes of two things, the relationship can be described as a proportion. Proportion is a mathematical relationship (called a ratio) that can be used to make the sizes of elements in a structure relate to each other, both physically and visually. For example, a common brick is twice as long as it is wide, so it has a length-to-width proportion that can be expressed as "two to one" or written as 2:1. That is also the same proportion for a standard 4′ × 8′ sheet of plywood. Modular components of proper proportions are designed to fit together perfectly and make construction easier. That is why the length, width, and thickness of all types of modular building blocks

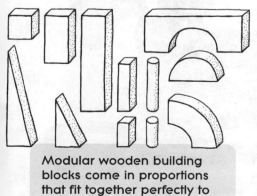

Modular wooden building blocks come in proportions that fit together perfectly to make pleasing patterns.

EXPERIMENT

SYMMETRY AND ASYMMETRY

Which of these structures are symmetrical or asymmetrical? Which structures look or feel balanced, and which ones seem unbalanced? Which designs do you find most pleasing or interesting?

The architectural elements of a structure appear pleasing when they are in proportion and may seem strange when they are out of proportion.

come in proportions such as 1:1, 2:1, 3:1, and 4:1. Using elements of pleasing proportions that relate to each other in pleasing patterns also creates a pleasing visual order.

Proportion is also used to describe individual shapes and forms that make up a complete structure, as well as the relationship of those forms to the complete structure. When looking at a house, for example, you might like or not like the proportions of the windows (the width of a window compared to its height). You might find the

windows too large or too small for the house, or the front door might seem too small for a large facade. And when looking at the entire house, you might comment that the house looks too tall or too short in relation to its width. When the proportions of something seem right, it can be called in proportion, and when they don't seem right, it is out of proportion.

Scale

The visual concept of scale is also about size and proportion. Scale is another way people see the size of one thing in proportion to another. Much of the time the most pleasing scale is considered in relationship to the person viewing or using the structure. A young child sitting in a big, overstuffed chair will seem even smaller (or the chair will seem even bigger). And a tall basketball player will appear dwarfed standing next to an ocean liner in port. Things that seem to be the right size in proportion to everything else can be described as being in scale, and those that don't are called out of scale.

The person viewing or using a structure can best tell if it is in scale or out of scale.

THE VISUAL POWER OF CONTRAST

Place several small common objects on a sheet of paper in any arbitrary arrangement. Use whatever is handy like paper clips, coins, pencils, a shoelace, a bottle cap, or a spoon. Does any one particular object stand out among the rest and draw your eye to it? Without removing any of the objects from the paper, change the arrangement so that some other object stands out among the others.

IN AND OUT OF PROPORTION AND SCALE

Which of these individual objects has shapes, forms, or parts that seem in proportion to each other? Which objects have parts that seem out of proportion—and what would you change to make them look more in proportion? What groupings of objects are in scale with each other?

BUILDING PLUS CREATIVITY EQUALS INVENTION

TRYING NEW IDEAS LEADS TO BETTER SOLUTIONS

HOW TO GET INSPIRATIONS FOR INVENTION IDEAS

TRYING NEW IDEAS LEADS TO BETTER SOLUTIONS

Creativity is the special ingredient that often turns building projects into inventions. Just about everything you encounter from toys and tools to gadgets and games is an invention that someone first thought of and then built. But a creative idea can only become an invention when someone figures out how to build it. Proving that an idea really works is one of the requirements for patenting an invention, along with showing it is something no one has ever done before and that it serves some useful function.

For our purposes, however, these requirements can be eased a bit. Any construction that demonstrates a creative solution previously unknown to you, the builder, can be considered an invention. In that spirit, nearly every construction, every model, and every experiment has an element of the invention process. Something new is tried, and something new is learned from the results. The experiments that work are repeated and added to your growing vocabulary of building techniques. In some ways, every time you build something, you are acting like an inventor. But to really develop your skills and spirit for building inventions first requires an understanding of how inventors think.

Learn to Think Like an Inventor

Most inventors have a passion for messing around with materials, building contraptions, conducting experiments, observing how things work, figuring out better ways to solve problems, being inspired by clues others don't see, and then force fitting their good ideas into usable solutions. To help figure out how to make an invention idea work, the inventor must develop a special creative attitude for looking at everyday things from different perspectives. Nearly anything can be considered a possible clue in the mental hunt for the right combination of ingredients to make an invention idea work. For example, suppose the invention problem was building something to catch houseflies. What clues might the inventor get from considering the attributes of duct tape, a piece of cheese, plastic wrap, paper cups, molasses, or ice cubes? How about a combination of these items like a cup and molasses, or cheese and duct tape? A look around the room or a walk around the block will usually reveal all kinds of clues for ways to make any idea work.

Once the inventor has a solution in mind, the process of building an invention is neither to build randomly nor to build according to a plan. Instead, the inventor's work is to build and test, rebuild to improve and test again, and keep on rebuilding until the invention works. Older builders are often able to make sophisticated models of invention ideas with parts that really work, and it's okay for young builders to make simpler and sometimes nonworking models that come with explanations of how the inventions are supposed to work. This is also the invention process at work. Builders must understand that unsatisfactory results should not be seen as failures, but rather as necessary experiments on the way to solving the invention. Therefore, inventions in progress should be built more for testing functionality than for final appearance. Once you figure out how to make it work, the design can be refined.

A normal part of inventing is getting stuck and then finding ways to get unstuck. One of the best ways to get new input for solving an invention problem is for the inventor to present the work-in-progress to others—but do it this way. Begin the presentation by stating what the invention is supposed to do, and then show what has been accomplished so far. This will at least give credit to the inventor for solving part of the problem. Next comes the explanation of what doesn't work or where the process has stalled. At this point, you can always count on the others present to spontaneously offer a flood of suggestions for what to do next. The inventor can then decide if any new ideas are worth trying.

HOW TO GET INSPIRATIONS FOR INVENTION IDEAS

Not all inventors work the same way or the same way all the time. Sometimes the inspiration for an invention comes from a personal need or the awareness of a need that others have. Fifteen-year-old Chester Greenwood invented earmuffs in response to other kids laughing when he wore his grandmother's scarf to the ice-skating pond. And a teenage Levi Strauss is credited with putting rivets at the corners of pants pockets so they wouldn't rip when gold miners stuffed their pockets with nuggets.

These are good examples of the common expression "Necessity is the mother of invention." And these types of planned inventions require a clear understanding of what needs to be accomplished. The more the problem is discussed, the more ideas for solutions will be generated, and the closer the inventor will get to finding the best one. In other words, a problem that is well-defined will directly lead the inventor to the best solution.

But sometimes necessity is *not* the inspiration for invention. Many inventors are inspired by the discovery of some interesting phenomenon. They then use creative thinking to see how that phenomenon might solve some other problem. The inventor of Velcro was inspired by the way barbed burrs from bushes would stick to his pant legs when he walked through the woods. A very young George Ferris's fantasy of taking a ride on a huge waterwheel later led to his invention of the Ferris wheel. And after seeing empty pie-baking tins being used in a backyard game, somebody invented the Frisbee.

Discovering a phenomenon by seeing things from a new perspective is what inspires inventions and is one of the most useful skills an inventor can learn. For example, an inventor might look at a paper drinking cup and begin to imagine other things it might be used for. In the mind of the inventor, this is simply figuring out "What else does it want to be?" In some ways, it's like conducting an interview of the object, asking questions that begin with *who, what, when, where, why,* and *how.*

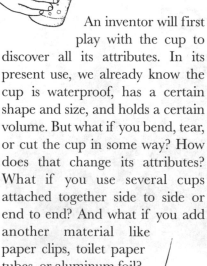

An inventor will first play with the cup to discover all its attributes. In its present use, we already know the cup is waterproof, has a certain shape and size, and holds a certain volume. But what if you bend, tear, or cut the cup in some way? How does that change its attributes? What if you use several cups attached together side to side or end to end? And what if you add another material like paper clips, toilet paper tubes, or aluminum foil? By messing around with all the attrib-

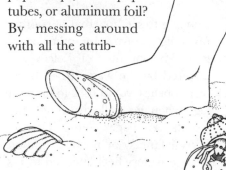

utes of a paper cup and asking a lot of "What if?" questions, the inventor will learn what else that paper cup wants to be—and even more clearly what it doesn't.

Considering each of these attributes, the inventor will then figure out all the other things the cup might be used for. Because the cup is waterproof to hold liquids, what else could it hold that needs a waterproof container? Maybe fill a cup with soil and use it to start seedlings. The cup may be designed to hold things, but what if it is turned upside down? Maybe it then becomes a protector of some kind, a translucent shell over small delicate seedlings planted in a garden, or a bare-toes cover for walking on a hot beach. If one of these ideas or some other application is exciting enough to inspire the inventor, it might be further developed into a new invention.

Playing with a material or an object to discover new perspectives and learn what else it wants to be is a technique that can also be used to find creative solutions to well-defined problems. Let's say you want to invent and build a toy sailboat and the only materials available are common discards and disposables. The inventor might start by thinking about what attributes are important for a floating model and then look around the house for scrap materials and things that are waterproof and can also float. The results of that might include empty plastic jugs, paper and plastic

drinking cups, storage containers with snap-on lids, empty milk cartons, balls and balloons, and probably lots of other stuff.

This is like a scavenger hunt with the inventor looking at each object as it is encountered on the search and asking "Is it waterproof? Will it float? How can I turn it into a sailboat?" By looking closely at each object, by handling each one and seeing how it might be made into a boat by cutting, tearing, bending, or doing something to it, each material will begin to reveal if it wants to (or doesn't want to) become a sailboat.

Indeed, one kid inventor discovered that an empty milk carton cut on three sides across the diagonal makes a great floating catamaran boat. When the cut milk carton is folded open, it forms two pontoon hulls in the shape of a "W." To turn it into a sailboat, the inventor made a slit in the middle of the "W" hull and added a paper plate as a sail. This milk carton sailboat cannot only sail swiftly with the slightest breeze, the twin hulls can be loaded with cargo. In this example, the invention process was elegant and so was the final design.

WHAT ELSE DOES IT WANT TO BE?

Nearly every material, every component, and every product that was created for one particular purpose can also be used to do something else. Sometimes these new uses are even more exciting than the original use. If you mess around with stuff in enough ways, you might discover that paper tubes can become musical instruments, plastic wrap and water make a giant magnifying lens, a length of hose makes a good short-distance telephone, a paper clip bent a special way becomes a building module, and a plastic six-pack carrier can be used to blow streams of big bubbles.

The idea is to learn what else the object wants to be by imagining what it might do differently if it floated on water, if it were three times as big, or if it glowed in the dark. The more ideas you try out, the better chance you will find—or actually invent—an exciting, new use for the object. To help in the discovery process, here is a list of words you might start with to see what else an object might want to be. It helps to have the object with you to try out the idea as you think of it—being able to look at the object and handle it also helps generate new ideas.

What else could this be if it could . . .

float in air?

float on water?

be giant size?

be miniature in size?

fly?

roll?

change color?

be worn?

be carried?

be upside down?

be sideways?

get hot?

get cold?

be hung?

move by itself?

become invisible?

last forever?

be soft?

be hard?

be smooth?

be rough?

glow?

be fuzzy?

emit sounds?

be unbreakable?

be thrown away?

be used to build with?

hold something?

protect something?

be a toy?

be connected to something else?

be cut in pieces?

smell good?

smell bad?

be sticky?

have wheels?

be waterproof?

be eaten?

be a work of art?

save time?

be used by pets?

How could you use the object in different places, like . . .

in your bedroom?

at school?

in a hiding place?

in a car?

on a bicycle?

in a specific room?

on the floor?

on the wall?

on the ceiling?

at a restaurant?

in bed?

on a table?

on a boat?

at the beach?

at the park?

Frank Lloyd Wright and His Froebel Blocks

At the 1876 Centennial Exhibition in Philadelphia, a small exhibit introduced the Froebel System of Kindergarten—a progressive series of toys, activities, and games designed to encourage young children to experience the attributes of various objects, colors, textures, causes, and effects through play, while teaching them an appreciation of what Froebel called the unity of all things in nature. Mrs. Anna Lloyd Wright of Weymouth, Massachusetts, was attending the exhibition when she became fascinated with the demonstrations of children playing with the Froebel materials. The Froebel kindergarten playthings were not ordinary novelty toys, or building crafts, or competitive games. Instead, they were simple shapes, forms, and plain construction materials with very specific exercises for producing abstract patterns and structures. These fabricated designs, depending on their loose association with familiar shapes in nature, might be called a flower, a bird, a tree, or some other form.

Mrs. Wright watched as the children created geometric forms and designs from small wooden blocks, cut, folded, and wove pieces of colored paper, assembled structures from toothpick-sized sticks, using peas for connectors, and modeled shapes in clay. She had always wanted her young son, Frank, to become an architect, and these Froebel Gifts seemed to be the perfect play materials to encourage his creativity and architectural curiosity. And even though Frank was already nine years old and well past kindergarten age, Mrs. Wright stocked the family playroom with the complete set of Froebel Gifts.

Later in life when he had become one of America's most celebrated architects, Frank Lloyd Wright credited his early play with the Froebel Gifts as being the greatest influence in forming his sense of design. If you look at any Frank Lloyd Wright building, the geometric patterns, symmetries, shapes, and forms of the structure are very reminiscent of the designs created by the Froebel materials and exercises.

The Froebel Gifts

By 1873, the Milton Bradley toy company of Springfield, Massachusetts, began manufacturing and selling the twenty "Kinder-Garten Gifts," which were also advertised to be fun constructions and games that fulfilled a child's natural curiosity.

All of these toys could be used for free play without instruction, but each gift came with illustrated lessons showing how the pieces could be used to create three categories of designs—forms relating to nature, forms based on science and technology, and forms evoking a sense of beauty. Each successive gift drew upon the lessons learned in the previous gifts and presented the next lesson in the progression.

Gift 1. Balls

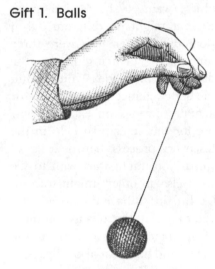

The first gift consisted of six hand-crocheted wool balls in six rainbow colors. The balls were about the size of small Christmas tree ornaments, and each had a string attached that could be used to hang the ball, pull it, spin it, or move it in many other ways described in the lessons. Other exercises included grasping a ball, rolling it, dropping it, and hiding it. The set of balls was also used for counting, simple math, color experiments, and organizing the balls into pleasing designs.

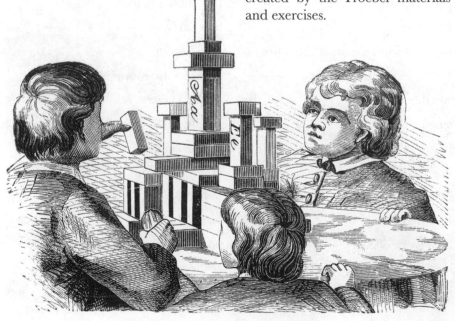

Gift 2. Sphere, Cylinder, and Cube

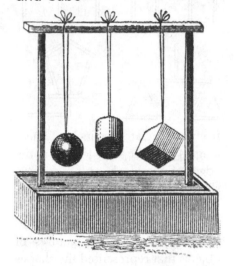

The stacking of a wooden cube, cylinder, and sphere became the image most often associated with the Froebel kindergarten system. Each of the three blocks had several small metal loops located at different points so a short string could be attached for hanging, swinging, pulling, and spinning the block. And each of the three block forms also had a small hole drilled completely through, from one side to the other, for accepting a small wood dowel that turned the block into a spinning top. The rectangular wooden box that packaged the second gift became a base for two vertical posts and a crossbeam from which the forms could be hung. In addition to following pages of illustrated experiments, the forms were also used to teach arithmetic and basic geometry, and at story time they were used to represent people, animals, buildings, or any form in nature.

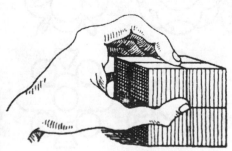

Gift 3. Blocks

Block building is probably the most lasting contribution of the Froebel kindergarten system. This third gift included eight small, one-inch cubes fitted together to make a larger two-inch cube and packaged in a small wooden box. Among many

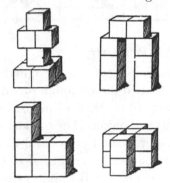

other lessons, this set of blocks tried to implicitly teach the concept of the whole in relation to its parts, and vice versa. Simple manipulations of the blocks taught the concepts of inner and outer, modularity, scale, divisibility, and complementary form. The blocks could also be laid out in patterns or abstract pictures that fostered an aesthetic sensibility, or stacked in different ways to create representations of buildings, bridges, trees, or forms the child wanted to mimic. To that end, Froebel insisted that all the blocks in the set be used for whatever was being built.

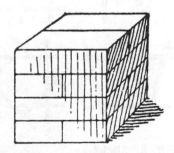

Gift 4. Building Blocks

In this next gift of the learning progression, eight identical brick-shaped blocks were fitted together (in the same size box as the third gift) to form another two-inch cube.

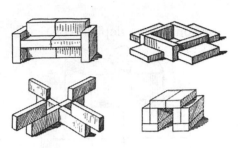

The brick shapes, however, unlike the one-inch cubes with identical sides, have sides with modular dimensions. Each brick block is one-inch wide, two-inches long, and one-half-inch thick. Using the eight rectangular blocks, compared to cubes, allowed more elaborate two-dimensional patterns and pictures and a greater variety of three-dimensional forms.

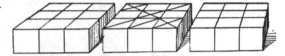

Gift 5. Blocks

Forming a three-inch cube, these blocks consist of twenty-seven one-inch cubes, with three of them cut into halves on the diagonal to make six prism-shaped blocks, and three more of the cubes cut into quarters on crossing diagonals to make twelve smaller prism blocks—totaling thirty-nine blocks in all. With the addition of triangular-shaped prism blocks, more lifelike structures could be built including crystal shapes, snowflake patterns,

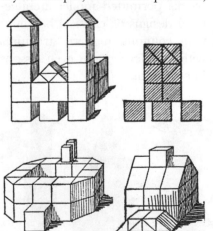

or houses with sloping roofs.

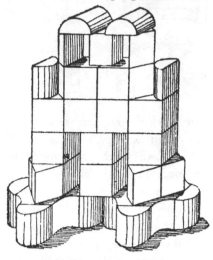

Gift 6. Blocks

The three-inch cube in the wooden box is formed by thirty-six modular blocks consisting of eighteen bricks (identical to the brick shape

in Gift No. 4), twelve half cubes (each half the size of a brick), and six column blocks. These additional blocks permitted model architectural designs of classical buildings with columns, modern structures with cantilevers, and even lessons in cube roots.

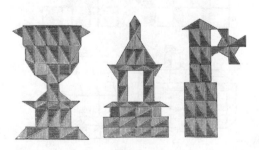

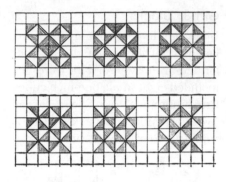

Gift 7. Parquetry

The seventh gift was designed to create two-dimensional pictures rather than three-dimensional forms and objects. The original set of natural-wood or colorful cardboard parquet pieces included several each of five flat and modular shapes—one-inch squares, half-square isosceles triangles, equilateral triangles, half equilateral triangles, and obtuse triangles. A few years later, circles and semicircles were added. The parquet shapes were also available in paper with gummed backing so they could be pasted in place on sheets of paper. Exercises using the geometric shapes included hundreds of arrangements to create both pattern designs and pictures of things.

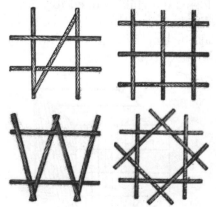

Gift 8. Sticks

A set of skinny wooden sticks introduced the first linear elements for building with lines and making outline drawings. The gift box contained several hundred toothpick-like sticks in five modular lengths

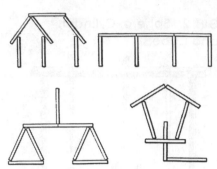

from one inch to five inches. These lengths were the same lengths as the edges of the blocks and parquetry shapes of earlier gifts. Exercises started with outlining letters and making words, then progressed to making patterns and pictures of objects that represented the shapes found in "knowledge, nature, and beauty."

Gift 9. Rings

The rings provided another way to design a variety of patterns and came in a set that included several each of whole rings, half circles, and quarter circles. And each of the

circle shapes came in three incremental sizes. Rather than building or drawing with straight lines and angles as in the previous gifts, the heavy-gauge wire rings could be used alone to create designs of arcs and circles, or added to the previous gift to add curves to the drawings made with sticks.

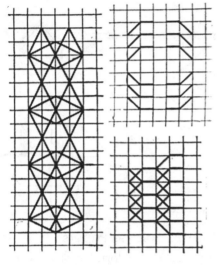

Gift 10. Drawing

The drawing gift included several items, starting with a book of blank pages, except that each page had a printed grid of squares to be used

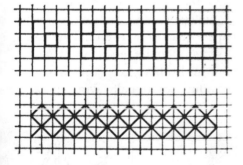

as a guide for drawing geometric patterns, alphabet letters, and recognizable forms. Slate pencils and a drawing slate with an etched grid of squares were also included for practice copying designs and making test patterns that could be erased or easily changed. Another book had lessons for drawing designs on a grid including "ornament and tile work, leaves, flowers, fruits, and

animals."

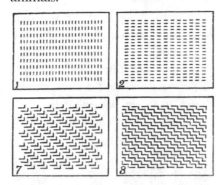

Gift 11. Pricking

This was another technique for making pattern designs and drawings on a preprinted grid. However, instead of drawing with lines, the design was created by punching many tiny holes through a sheet of white paper, using the point of a pinpricking tool. First, a thick felt perforating cushion was placed on the table, then a blank sheet of paper was placed over the felt, and another sheet of paper with a preprinted or drawn design was placed over the blank sheet. The pricking tool was used to punch holes through both sheets of paper following the lines of the pattern. When finished, the pattern was discarded, and the pinhole drawing could be held up to a light or taped to a bright window to reveal the sparkling star picture. Pieces of colored tissue paper could also be sandwiched against the backside of the prick-hole drawing to create a twinkling-rainbow effect.

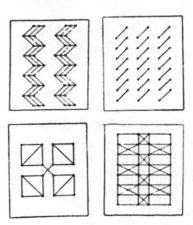

Gift 12. Sewing

Sewing was considered another type of drawing that taught diversity—or yet another way to form patterns that mimicked the shapes of nature and everyday life. This decorative embroidery exercise used a needle and colored thread plus grided cards with prepunched holes to sew patterns of colorful crosses, squares, zigzags, and other geometric shapes.

Gift 13. Cutting Papers

Color and transformation were the primary lessons learned from these cutting exercises. Square sheets of paper in a variety of colors were

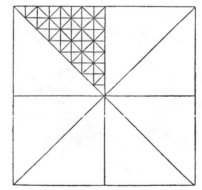

used for cutting free-form shapes of familiar things as well as symmetrical shapes, designs, and patterns. To begin, a single sheet was folded in one of a number of ways, then small pieces were cut away from the folded edges. When the paper was unfolded, the result was a perfectly symmetrical pattern of an object, or something like a snowflake design, a doily, or a chain of paper dolls.

Gift 14. Weaving

Weaving patterns with colored strips of paper provided lessons in counting, progression, composition, and creativity. Long, narrow strips of paper were woven in pre-slit weaving mats made of heavier paper with parallel slits across the entire sheet (except for the borders).

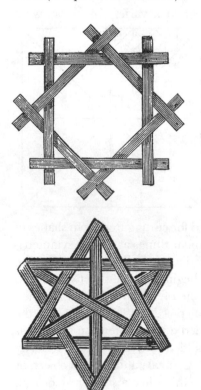

Gift 15. Slats

Similar to Popsicle sticks, the slats were flat wooden sticks all the same length, available in plain or painted wood. The slats were used to weave patterns and to "draw" shapes in space, as well as to teach lessons in tension and compression.

Gift 16. Jointed Slats

Very much like a carpenter's folding rule, the jointed slats consisted of a linear series of flat slat sticks joined end to end by brass hinges. Although each individual slat was the same length, the jointed slats came in several different lengths from four to sixteen sections. Various geometric shapes could be formed and several lessons in geometry could be demonstrated by folding, unfolding, overlapping, and adjusting the jointed slats.

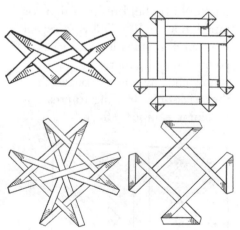

Gift 17. Interlacing

The long strips of colored paper that came in this gift were used to make outlines of geometric and abstract shapes. Because the paper strips could be bent, folded, woven,

interlaced, or twisted at any point, these materials offered many more design options than the slats or joined slats.

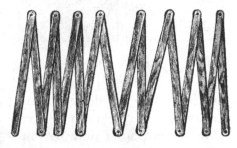

Gift 18. Folding Papers

A package of colorful square sheets of paper provided material for folding forms and shapes similar to origami. But unlike the three-dimensional birds, animals, and people forms made in traditional origami, these exercises used a sequence of folds to transform the paper squares into two-dimensional designs of multiple squares, triangles, and other geometric shapes, including rotationally symmetrical pinwheels.

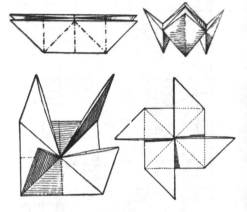

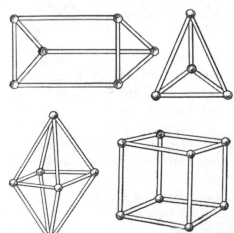

Gift 19. Peas Work

Both two-dimensional shapes and three-dimensional forms could be constructed using these small wooden toothpick-like sticks and pea connectors. The peas had to be soaked in water to soften, and sometimes small balls of clay or wax were used instead as the connectors. First, flat triangles, squares, polygons, alphabet letters, and patterns were constructed using full-length or cut-to-length sticks. Then geometric shapes were joined to make cubes, pyramids, crystals, and other polyhedrons. These "drawing in space" with sticks exercises helped reinforce the concepts of volume and structure.

Gift 20. Modeling Clay

Modeling clay was the last gift, and molding the malleable material into virtually any shape was considered the concluding exercise in the sequence of lessons learned in the previous gifts. Instead of being given a ball, cylinder, and cube as in the second gift, the forms could now be made in clay with an even greater understanding of their attributes. And any shape or form that was modeled from a hunk of clay could easily be remodeled and transformed into something else. A clay sphere might become a model of a clay flower, then a clay duck, two clay pyramids, and so on. This final lesson in transformation provided even greater evidence to Froebel's belief that there is a unity to all forms in nature

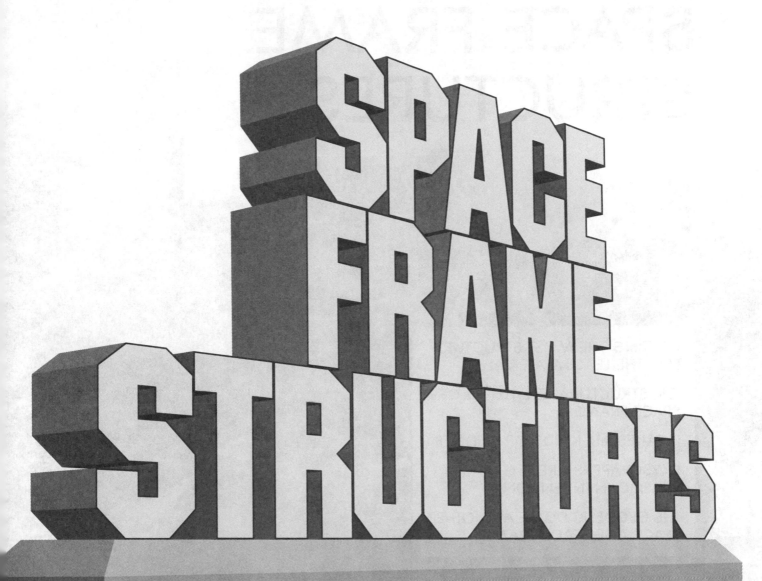

SPACE FRAME STRUCTURES

UNDERSTANDING SPACE
FRAME STRUCTURES

BUILDING WITH RODS AND
CONNECTORS

UNDERSTANDING SPACE FRAME STRUCTURES

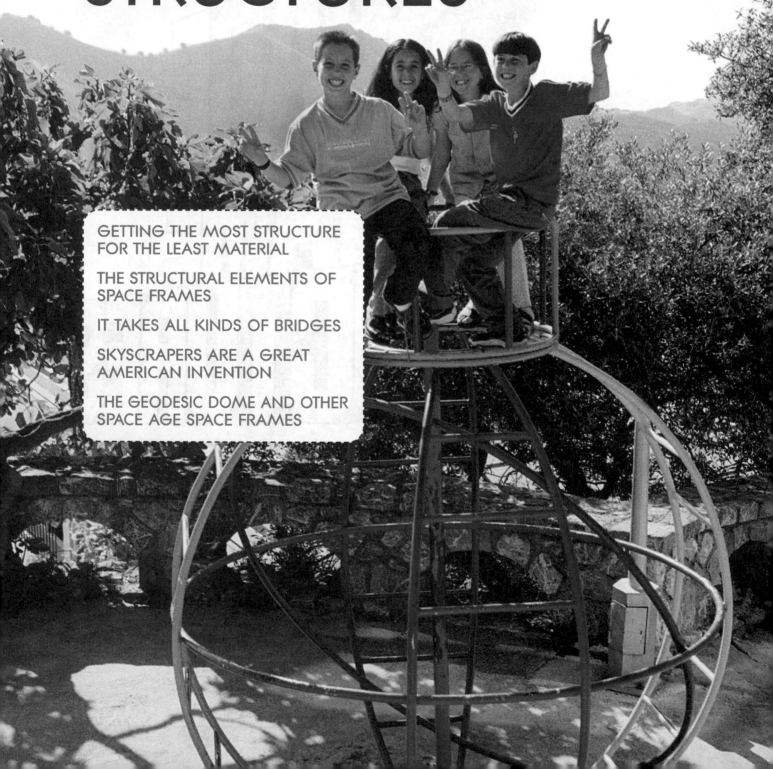

GETTING THE MOST STRUCTURE FOR THE LEAST MATERIAL

THE STRUCTURAL ELEMENTS OF SPACE FRAMES

IT TAKES ALL KINDS OF BRIDGES

SKYSCRAPERS ARE A GREAT AMERICAN INVENTION

THE GEODESIC DOME AND OTHER SPACE AGE SPACE FRAMES

GETTING THE MOST STRUCTURE FOR THE LEAST MATERIAL

If you could look under the outer covering of most modern buildings and other large constructions, you would probably see a complex framework made up of three-dimensional geometric patterns. Sometimes the intricate structure is left visible without an outer covering, like the structure of a large bridge. It is the combination of all these triangles, squares, and rectangles that give the structure its strength and form.

The complete three-dimensional framework structure made of geometric shapes is called a space frame. A space frame is one of the most economical structures used in modern construction. That is, you get the most structural strength for the least amount of material used to make the structure.

Notice that every space frame structure has its own unique framework pattern. If you look closely, you can see that the large space frame pattern is made of many smaller, interconnected shapes, and each three-dimensional geometric shape is made of several long, straight pieces. These pieces that make up the framework are called rods or struts, and they are connected to each other at their ends. Depending on the particular geometric shapes used in the space frame design, the struts may all be the same length or several different modular lengths.

Space frame construction is a modern technology that requires machine-made parts and engineered building systems. Although solid geometric shapes have been used for thousands of years to build shelters, bridges, and monuments, you will not find many human-made examples of space frame construction before the twentieth century.

Unlike bricks, stone, timber, or any previous method of building, space frame structures are very light in weight compared to their size and strength. For example, the classic masonry arch is difficult to build in large scale because stone and brick are very heavy. In space frame technology, the arch can be replaced with a space frame truss that is considerably lighter in weight and can span a much greater distance.

It is that unique combination of being lightweight and strong that allows space frame buildings and structures to take new shapes and larger scales. Today, space frame construction is commonly used to build our most modern buildings and structures, including the International Space Station.

The special features of space frame construction include:

- Extremely lightweight in proportion to size

- Strong and rigid structure

- Open structure allows light and air to pass through

- Modular struts and connectors permit quick construction of any form

- Framework can be covered in a variety of different "skins"

- Space frame members can support loads in both compression and tension

THE INTERNATIONAL SPACE STATION

A space frame laboratory for exploring outer space

The International Space Station, also called the ISS, is one of the most complex engineering projects ever attempted. The ISS is being designed and built by a partnership of sixteen nations that include the United States, Canada, the eleven member countries of the European Space Agency, Russia, Japan, and Brazil. When the ISS is completed, it will be the largest spacecraft ever built and the greatest international space venture ever accomplished.

The plan is to build and operate this permanently inhabited, Earth-orbiting research facility to learn how we can improve the environment and the quality of life on planet Earth. To do that, scientists need to learn how various species from Earth, including humans, can adapt to the extreme environments in space. Not only is there a lack of oxygen to breathe in outer space, but temperatures can alternate between unlivable freezing cold and searing hot in just a matter of hours. The results of these and other experiments will provide information about building new spacecrafts that can travel to the planets in our solar system—and maybe beyond.

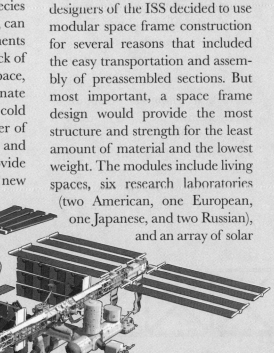

The design of the ISS consists of several modules, all mounted to a 356-foot-long central girder called a space frame truss. Engineers and designers of the ISS decided to use modular space frame construction for several reasons that included the easy transportation and assembly of preassembled sections. But most important, a space frame design would provide the most structure and strength for the least amount of material and the lowest weight. The modules include living spaces, six research laboratories (two American, one European, one Japanese, and two Russian), and an array of solar power panels for providing electrical energy to operate the ISS.

Altogether, more than one hundred preassembled sections of the ISS are being built and tested on Earth before they are launched about 250 miles up into space. The first component was launched into orbit in 1998, and at least three types of rockets, including the U.S. Space Shuttle, the Russian Soyuz, and the Russian Proton, will dock with the ISS to deliver all the parts. As each part arrives, it will be assembled to the space frame truss by astronauts "walking" in space or by using special robotic arms.

The completed International Space Station will require forty-three space flights to deliver all the preassembled sections and will cover an area about the size of a football field, weigh over one million pounds, and provide living and working areas for up to seven astronauts in spaces equal to the size of three average American homes.

THE STRUCTURAL ELEMENTS OF SPACE FRAMES

Sometimes the best way to understand how a structure works is to build a model. Even in small-scale form, the model will act pretty much the same way as the full-size structure. For that reason, most builders craft and test an exact model before full-scale construction begins.

The building systems and projects in this book not only make some fun and amazing structures, they also demonstrate the building characteristics of real structures and systems in a smaller form. By

experimenting with these systems and projects, you can understand how buildings and other structures stand up, hold weight, and resist the forces of wind and even earthquakes.

Here is an explanation of the structural principles you will find in all space frame constructions, along with simple building experiments to illustrate their special features. These principles will also help you design your own structures using the rods and connectors building systems in the next chapter.

Triangulation

The special geometric property that makes space frames both lightweight and strong is called triangulation. The triangle is one of the most common and successful shapes for building strong structures. A space frame structure will always have a three-dimensional framework mostly made of triangles, and sometimes it will be constructed completely of triangles. That is because a triangle will hold its shape even when forces are applied to it from any or all directions.

In fact, a triangular structure is stronger and more rigid than a square one that uses more material. The triangle is a geometric shape that will remain rigid even if its three joints of attachment are all hinged. The shape of a triangle can be changed only by either

shortening or lengthening its sides. Therefore, if you create a structure made up of triangles, it will be very rigid.

In most space frame structures like towers, bridges, and building frames, the idea is to create the form entirely of triangles. When squares are necessary, they are often divided into triangles by adding a diagonal rod. If you think about it, the space frame of some buildings is very much like the structure of a bridge that has been turned on its end and attached to the ground. Or you might think of a bridge as being like a tall skyscraper laid on its side.

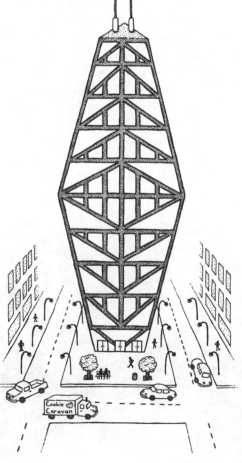

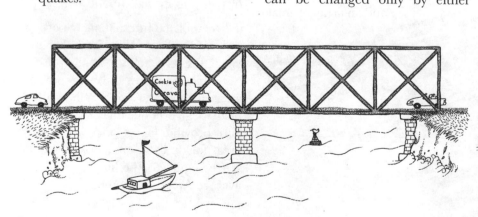

TINKERTOY

As a young man back in 1904, Charles Pajeau went to work in the family business of building stone monuments, but in his spare time, he liked to build toys and simple inventions. One day Charles noticed some local children playing with pencils and wooden sewing-thread spools. A pencil could be slipped through the hole in one or more spools to make a stacked tower or something with wheels that rolled. Charles was impressed by the way these children would stay fascinated with building and unbuilding simple constructions over and over again. Suddenly, he had an idea to make the pencils and spools plaything even better.

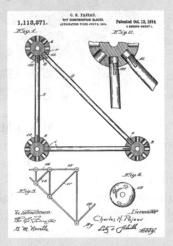

Back home in his toy-making workshop, Charles began to experiment with a way to connect several wooden dowels to one wooden spool. He began by drilling eight evenly spaced and shallow holes around the curved edge of the spool (which already had a hole through its center) so that dowels could be inserted around the spool at angles, and the dowel rods could be connected to the spools to form triangles—the basic building block of space frame structures.

But Charles went even further. Using his knowledge of math and the Pythagorean theory, he was able to calculate the correct rod lengths necessary to create a series of progressively larger right triangles. (The longest side, or hypotenuse,

of one triangle becomes the smaller side of a bigger triangle, and so on). That geometry allowed his construction system to build more types of structures than any toy he had ever seen. However, Charles still had one more problem to solve.

To keep constructions from falling apart, the dowel rods needed to fit snugly into the spools, and yet young children needed to easily assemble the pieces and take them apart.

After months of tinkering and lots of failed experiments, Charles finally developed the simple idea of cutting a slot in the ends of the rods. The slot allowed the ends of the rods to compress slightly as they were inserted, but also maintained enough friction inside the holes to keep the rods from falling out.

Nearly ten years after Charles had begun his construction-toy experiments, he and a business friend decided to start a company to manufacture Tinkertoy—The Wonder Builder. In that first year of 1914, Tinkertoy sold for fifty cents and consisted of seventy-three wooden spools and rods, eight cardboard blades (for building a windmill), and complete instructions for making all kinds of structures.

As a way to catch people's attention, some toy stores set up elaborate Tinkertoy displays that included a huge Tinkertoy Ferris wheel that was kept turning by a hidden electric fan. The displays and the building-toy-in-a-can became so popular so quickly that the Tinkertoy factory couldn't keep up with the demand from customers even though it made nearly a million sets in just one year.

Over the years, the original Tinkertoy set has gone through many changes, including the shape of the spools. Also, the spools are now made of plastic instead of wood, and they come in a variety of colors. Altogether there have been more than fifty variations of the Tinkertoy geometric construction set, including the ones you can buy today.

Scaffolds

When the walls of some buildings are being constructed or are under repair, the workers first set up a separate and temporary space frame structure alongside the wall so they have a place to stand at any height while working. This box and cross-braced framework is called staging or scaffolding, and it's a simple structure that makes it easier to build another structure.

A typical scaffold building system consists of metal pipe struts with clamp connectors that quickly and easily assemble into a framework. Because the scaffold must be very stable without wiggling or swaying, the structure requires a lot of cross-bracing struts to form rigid triangles. Planks of wood for the workers

TRIANGLE VS. SQUARE

To better understand the great strength of triangulation, try this experiment using drinking straws and string. By building a triangle with three straws and a square with four straws, you will be able to compare and determine which shape is stronger when you try to twist each one out of shape.

1. Thread four full-length straws onto a single length of string. Bring the two ends of the string together and tie a

knot so the string is taut and the straws form a square.

2. By pushing and pulling on any of the four sides or corners, you can easily change the shape of the square into a tall diamond, a wide diamond, and many parallelogram shapes in between. Because the square does not want to hold its shape, it is a weak form to build with.

3. Now thread only three straws onto a length of string and knot the ends of the string to form a triangle instead of a square. No matter which way you pull or push, the triangle remains unchanged. When a force is applied to a triangle, all three sides work together to hold its shape.

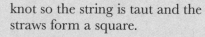

to stand on are then straddled across the horizontal struts at whatever standing height is needed. Scaffolding can be erected either completely around the building under construction or placed in a particular location where and when it is needed, and then moved to the next location.

Even though today's pipe scaffolding is constructed as a modern space frame structure, scaffolds were a necessary part of building many ancient structures as well, especially large walls, arches, and domes. In Roman times, a scaffold structure was constructed pretty much the same way as today, except wood beams or bamboo poles were used instead of pipe, and they were temporarily tied together using long reeds or twine.

FORCES IN A SPACE FRAME

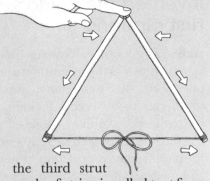

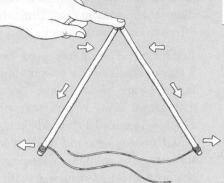

A space frame must transfer all the forces of its own weight plus the weight of any loads through its struts. These forces will cause some struts of the space frame triangles to be in compression (pushing together from the ends) and others to be in tension (pulling apart from the ends).

To better understand how tension and compression affect space frame structures, try this experiment using drinking straws and string.

1. Thread two full-length straws onto a single length of string. Keep the two straws butted end to end by wrapping the string around the other ends of the straws.

2. Bend the joint where the two straws are butted to form two sides of a triangle, and hold the triangle on a tabletop. With your other hand, place a fingertip on the peak of the hinged joint.

As you press down, the straws are in compression. Notice that the bottom ends of the straws are being pushed away from each other in opposite directions, while the straw ends at the joint are pushing together—and pinching your finger!

3. Now unwrap the string from the bottom ends of the straws and tie the strings together to form a complete triangle. Again try pressing down on the peak and you will find the structure is quite rigid. Notice that as you press,

the third strut made of string is pulled taut from both sides. This third strut of the triangle is in tension.

Because the two sides of the triangle forming the peak are in compression, they must be made of rigid struts. However, the third side of a triangle in tension needs only to be strong, not necessarily rigid. In actual construction, the triangular member in tension may be identical to the other struts or it can be made of a lighter material like cables or thin rods.

Trusses

A truss is a two-dimensional version of a space frame that is made of several triangles attached in a rigid chain. Most trusses are used to span distances because they are very light in weight and strong compared to other methods of creating a span. Look at highway bridges, railroad bridges, or open ceilings like attics, and you will probably see many examples of truss construction.

The structure and strength of a space frame comes from connecting many trusses together in all directions. Whatever shape you build using two-dimensional or three-dimensional trusses, you will be getting the maximum structural strength for the material being used.

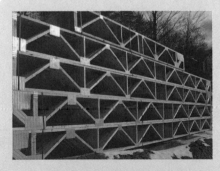

Tetrahedron Kites
and how Alexander Graham Bell almost invented the world's first airplane

Although Alexander Graham Bell is best known as the inventor of the telephone, he has many more inventions to his credit, including the tetrahedron. Although today the tetrahedron shape is commonly seen in space frame construction, it was first used by Bell nearly one hundred years ago in a design for a kite.

From the time he was a young boy growing up in Edinburgh, Scotland, Alexander Graham Bell was fascinated with the idea of being the first person to invent a mechanical flying machine—a heavier-than-air, motor-driven aircraft in which people could safely ride. At that time, most people thought the idea of flying was absurd, and anyone who talked of inventing such a machine was considered to be a bit crazy.

But Graham Bell, as he was called by friends, had an idea. He figured that a properly constructed kite should be capable of being a flying machine and therefore a good flying machine should be capable of

being flown as a kite. So Bell set out to make a kite that was stable in flight and could also lift the weight of a man. For ten years he conducted experiments to find the effective but elusive design.

Bell's first experiments used box kites, but as the kites were built larger to carry more weight—some as big as a living room—they did not fly very well. The box design was based on squares and was structurally weak. Making it stronger required a lot of bracing, which

added weight and interfered with flying. Bell was not much of a scientist and he preferred to invent by trial and error. What he learned from building large box kites was something known as "the law of cubes and squares," which means that a structure built twice as big as a model will weigh eight times as much as the model. And so, as soon as Bell's kites were big enough to lift a person, they were too heavy to fly.

In the winter of 1901, Graham Bell had a breakthrough that outwitted the law of squares and cubes. He invented the tetrahedron, a simple form composed of four equilateral triangles having four triangular faces bounded by six equal edges. It was the

perfect engineering form, combining extremely low weight with great strength.

The tetrahedron proved to be the perfect shape for a kite. The first small tetrahedron kites designed by Graham Bell looked and flew "like a flock of birds." To give the kite more lifting power, he attached several small tetrahedron kites together to make a larger kite. Bell's six-foot-wide kite had to be flown with a manila rope towed by an athletic worker, and his fifteen-foot-wide kite was towed by a heavy rope tied to the collar of a galloping horse. Bell was so captivated by the tetrahedron shape that he even built a simple wooden shelter in the shape of a perfect tetrahedron where he and his elderly father would sit and observe the kite experiments.

Now that Bell was convinced his tetrahedron kite could fly no matter how large it was, he set out to build a kite that could carry a man aloft. It was the year 1907, and the Wright brothers had just proven that manned flight was possible when Graham Bell was ready to test

his 42 ½-foot-wide, man-carrying tetrahedron kite he called Cygnet. Before he added an engine and propeller to the kite, which would have made it a true airplane, Bell decided to test its flight worthiness and had the enormous kite towed behind a steamship. With the test

pilot on board, the kite lifted up gracefully and soared high in the sky. Then, for some reason, the kite suddenly began to lose altitude until it crashed and was dragged through the water. The pilot escaped, but the kite was completely wrecked, and Graham Bell's experiment was over.

EXPERIMENT

TETRAHEDRON VS. CUBE

After testing the strength of triangles and squares, try a similar experiment—but this time in three dimensions. Using drinking straws and string, construct and test the strength of a tetrahedron structure made up of four triangles versus a cube made from six squares.

1. Thread four full-length straws onto a single length of string. Bring the two ends of the string together and tie a knot so the straws form a square. Build a second square the same way.

2. Use four more straws and four lengths of string to connect the corners of the two squares to form a cube.

3. By pushing and pulling on any of the eight corners of the cube, you can easily change its form. Because the cube does not want to hold its shape, it is a weak form to build with.

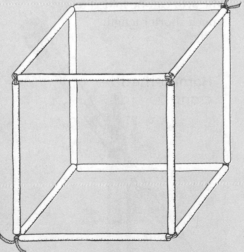

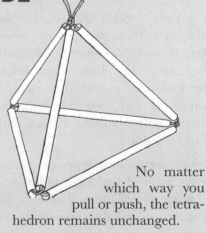

4. Now build and test a tetrahedron. Thread three straws onto a length of string and knot the ends of the string to form a triangle instead of a square. Add two more straws to one long end of the string to create an adjacent triangle. Now add a sixth straw with a length of string to create the tetrahedron form.

No matter which way you pull or push, the tetrahedron remains unchanged.

Although both the cube and the tetrahedron are made from straws of the same length, the triangular tetrahedron is far stronger than the cube, even though the cube uses many more straws. When you are creating any space structure, remember this experiment and the important principle of triangulation—triangles are strong and squares are weak!

Cranes

Cranes were designed to hoist and move large loads from one location to another. They are especially useful in the construction of tall buildings to carry mortar, bricks, materials, and sometimes the workers to various levels of the structure.

The crane seems to have evolved from the wooden arm attached to the mast of a sailing ship and commonly used for loading and unloading heavy cargo. In medieval times, wooden-arm cranes that rotated on pivots were used to hoist heavy stones when building castles and tall cathedrals.

Since then, many types of cranes have evolved for doing many different types of lifting. However, all cranes need to have a very strong yet lightweight arm called a boom, so it is common to build them using a truss-like, space frame structure.

A crawler crane is perhaps the most common type of crane with its boom attached to a rotating body mounted on a truck with wheels or caterpillar tractor treads. The steel cable and hook going over the outer end, or head, of the boom can be reeled in or out by a power-operated mecha-

Crawler crane

Crawler cranes use wheels or caterpillar treads to position the boom.

nism, and the boom itself can also be raised or lowered. Large, heavy weights on the back of the truck counterbalance the heavy loads being lifted. When the crane truck is being moved to a new job site, the arm can be folded to a much shorter length.

Another common type is the tower crane, sometimes called a hammerhead crane, which is assembled at the construction site and has a fixed, vertical space frame post supporting a long horizontal boom. The cantilevered boom with counterbalancing weights on the

Hammerhead crane

Tower and hammerhead cranes have rotating booms with trolleys that can be positioned higher as the construction grows taller.

short side can usually rotate in a complete circle and has a trolley that slides back and forth along the horizontal arm. With the ability to move the crane's cable and hook up and down, all around, and in and out on the trolley, a load can be picked up, positioned, and unloaded just about anywhere near the site or on the building. Instead of a horizontal boom and trolley, some tower cranes use a conventional angled boom without a trolley.

Gantry crane

Gantry cranes are used mostly for loading and unloading materials and shipping containers.

Whenever you see a tower crane being used to construct a new building, you might also notice a small evergreen tree at the top of a crane. Construction workers consider it to be a good-luck tradition.

A gantry crane uses a horizontal bridge truss instead of a boom, with a trolley that can be positioned anywhere along the bridge. The bridge is rigidly supported by legs, and the two movable legs can move back and forth on wheels or fixed rails.

There are many other types and variations of cranes for different types of hoisting, but most use a space frame boom or a bridge and trolley system. When you see a crane in action, try to figure out how many different movements it can make. Trace the forces from the load through the structure. Where do they go? And how is the weight of the load counterbalanced?

Other types of cranes

Other types of cranes are usually variations designed with specific movements to do specific jobs.

BIOSPHERE II

A space frame building for a space age experiment

Biosphere II was a grandiose experiment in the Arizona desert that was designed to help us learn more about Earth's environment and also pioneer the research needed for humans to live self-sufficiently on some other planet. Biosphere I, by the way, is planet Earth.

The space frame structure of Biosphere II, designed by British architect Margaret Augustine, consists of two linked space frame structures covered in glass. The structures, which look like two huge greenhouses, were capable of producing a completely sealed environment so that inside, scientists could create their own ecosystem— one that provided all the food, water, and air needed to keep eight people alive for more than two years.

Inside the five-story-high Biosphere II structures, there are many environments that try to duplicate conditions on Earth, including a desert, an ocean with tides and a coral reef, a tropical rain forest, and agricultural areas, as well as many species of birds, insects, reptiles, and small animals. Other spaces inside are used for living quarters, laboratories, workshops, libraries, recreation areas, and communications systems.

To maximize the amount of sunlight entering Biosphere II, the construction system needed to be mostly transparent to the outside. And, to enclose nearly seven million cubic feet of space (that's five hundred times as large as the average house), the system needed to be very strong. Yet another objective was to make the entire structure completely airtight. The ideal solution was a space frame building.

Space frames are inherently stronger than traditional structures, use less material, and can be built in many different shapes. The Biosphere II space frame structure is made of steel tube triangular shapes with panes of glass sealed directly to the steel with a silicone adhesive. One of the two space frame structures in Biosphere II, the agricultural space, consists of several circular vaults,

while the other is shaped like a pyramid. Both buildings sit on concrete foundations that have been covered with a thin, stainless steel liner. The liner curves up at the edges of the building to form a seal to the glass-covered space frame walls so the entire structure is airtight.

Here are some other facts about Biosphere II.

- Built from 1987 to 1990, about forty miles north of Tucson, Arizona.

- The structure and environment are expected to last one hundred years.

- The buildings cover 3.1 acres, and the highest point of the structure is eighty-five feet.

- Inside there are about 3800 species of plants and animals.

- The experiment began September 26, 1991, when eight "biospherians" sealed themselves inside.

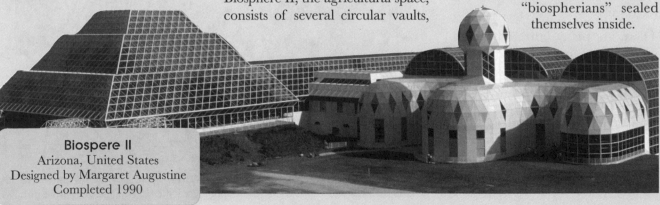

Biospere II
Arizona, United States
Designed by Margaret Augustine
Completed 1990

IT TAKES ALL KINDS OF BRIDGES

Bridges can be found wherever there are rivers, valleys, gaps, or other obstacles that need to be crossed. Just about everywhere in the populated world there are simple footbridges to walk across and roadway bridges for vehicle traffic, but depending on where you live, you might also see a wooden covered bridge, a mechanical drawbridge, a railway trestle, a stone arch bridge, or maybe even a majestic suspension bridge. If you are really observant, you might also find a few special-purpose bridges meant for carrying pipelines, snowmobiles, or farm animals.

Altogether there are over a million bridges in America. Considering the fact that a span must be at least twenty feet long to officially be called a bridge, there are probably at least twice that number if you also count the smaller ones.

Many bridges—both those built over the last thousand years and the ones being built today—are not only engineering marvels, but they are also considered magnificent works of art. In fact, many bridges have gained lasting fame not necessarily for having the longest span, the tallest towers, or being of the newest design, but because of their timeless beauty. There will always be a longer bridge to be built and a newer method of bridge construction that gives a different look to bridge design. But the enduring beauty of a Roman arch bridge, the impressive design of the Brooklyn Bridge in New York, or the glistening sparkle of the Golden Gate Bridge in San Francisco still draw long stares and admiration from everyone who sees them.

The Earliest Bridges

The first bridges were used for the same reasons that bridges are needed today—to make it easier to get from one place to another. When humans first walked across the open land to hunt and gather food, they often encountered fast-flowing streams or wide and deep rivers that couldn't be crossed on foot. Sometimes steep mountains or deep ravines impeded their way, making the journey much longer to go around the obstacle, or even impossible.

The earliest bridges across these impediments were probably nothing more than natural occurrences. A tall tree blown down by the wind that accidentally landed across a small gorge or a stream became a simple footbridge for those who found it there. A few stones that happened to be spaced just the right distance apart across a streambed became stepping stones from one bank to the other side. A strategically located hanging vine might have been used to swing across a ravine. And there were other natu-

ral bridges created by rock formations and erosion that allowed early humans to cross spans that were too far apart to step over or jump across, shortening the distance to be traveled.

But what if there was no natural bridge, no fallen tree across the stream, no rocks in the streambed, or no convenient vine hanging by the ravine? In time, humans began to imitate the natural bridges they found by building similar bridges

where they were needed from materials available nearby. A simple beam bridge could be made by cutting down a tall tree, removing the branches, and placing the tree trunk across an open span so that it rested on a support at each end. The support could be just the banks of the crossing, or piers could be constructed from more logs or nearby rocks.

Some early bridge builders purposely placed stepping stones across a riverbed, then learned to make higher piles of walking stones when the river level rose in the spring. The next improvement came when bridge builders discovered that placing a log across two piles of stones created a pathway that

was easier to walk on. And a wider bridge could be built by simply using two parallel timbers with many branches or boards laid across them as planking for the pathway.

In some locations where there were no trees or rocks or other practical ways to construct a solid bridge, long ropes made from vines were probably used to swing over and across obstacles. It was later discovered that a single taut rope firmly connected at both ends of the crossing could be traversed by swinging hand over hand.

A later version of the rope bridge (but one that was not much better) used two ropes—a lower rope for walking on and an overhead rope for hanging on to keep balance. The next improvement used two parallel ropes for the walkway with woven grass mats tied across them to cover the gap. These early sus-

pension bridges still needed an overhead rope or a side rope to hold onto for balance.

The builders of these early bridges learned from experience how to build a structure that would not collapse when being crossed and could survive high winds and rushing waters. Every time a bridge failed in use or was destroyed by some event in nature, another

stronger and safer bridge was built to replace it. Over time, the design, engineering, and construction of bridges gradually improved to span greater and greater distances, to carry heavier loads, and to dazzle us with their beauty.

INVENTION

COVERED BRIDGES

Using practical American ingenuity

The earliest bridges in America were made of simple wooden trusses holding up a wooden roadway that spanned the banks of narrow rivers and streams. If the river was too wide for the length of one truss bridge, a piling or pier was built in the middle of the river so two bridges could be joined end to end. But building a pier in the middle of some rivers proved dangerous because the pier could be hit and knocked down by a boat or even swept away by fast-moving currents.

A better design was needed, and a self-taught architect named Timothy Palmer came up with a solution. Palmer's design used huge timbers curved into long arches that spanned a river from bank to bank. A Palmer bridge could span a river nearly 250 feet wide—wide enough so that when an even longer bridge was needed, huge strong piers could be built in the river to connect two or more bridges called spans. Because the spans were so long and the river so wide, these piers were safe from being washed away or interfering with boat traffic. Palmer's longest bridge had several piers and was over 1350 feet long—about one quarter of a mile!

However, the problem with building a bridge, or any other structure, out of wood is that wood holds up well only when it is either always wet or always dry. When wood is subjected to alternating conditions of being wet and then dry, it begins to rot away. So in 1805, when Palmer built a three-span, 550-foot bridge across the Schuylkill River in Philadelphia, a local judge suggested covering the bridge with a wooden timber roof to protect it from rain, snow, and sun, and to make it last longer. If the roof rotted away, it could be replaced, but the bridge itself would be protected and remain strong.

Palmer wanted to leave the bridge uncovered so his pleasing arched design would be visible, but he agreed to test the idea that a covered bridge would last longer. The concept worked, and Palmer's first covered "permanent bridge" lasted forty-five years before it was replaced.

Palmer bridge design

Soon after that discovery, most new wooden bridges were designed to have roofs, and many existing bridges were covered as well. This was especially true of wooden bridges built in New England and other cold climates, where the bridges not only got a roof, but also side coverings to help keep out the blowing snow. Many of the earliest covered bridges even looked like longhouses straddling a river from bank to bank.

People soon discovered many other advantages of covered bridges. If someone was caught outside in a storm, a nearby covered bridge would provide shelter. The shade of a covered bridge provided a cool place to rest a horse in summer. And it was easier to herd animals across a covered bridge because they couldn't see the water below and become frightened.

The individuals and communities that paid for the building of bridges also recognized several advantages in covering their bridges. Since covered bridges lasted longer, they were a better investment, and the sides of covered bridges were excellent places to sell advertising for products—just like today's billboards.

Palmer's arched covered bridge remained popular until Theodore Burr of Connecticut came up with an even better design. The roadway

Town lattice truss design

on a Palmer bridge followed the curve of the arched timbers that supported it, which meant that anyone crossing the bridge first had to go uphill and then downhill. Burr invented his own type of arched truss, called the Burr truss, which had a flat roadway.

Soon, covered bridges using either Palmer's design or Burr's design were being built across the streams and rivers of many Eastern states. Although these early covered bridges were pleasant to look at and structurally sound, both designs required massive timbers and skilled craftspeople to build them.

One of those craftspeople, Ithiel Town, decided that a better and simpler covered bridge design was needed that didn't rely on big timbers and could be built by ordinary carpenters. Town invented a new type of bridge truss, called Town lattice truss, which used a series of crisscrossed diagonal beams fastened together with wooden connecting pins at the places they overlapped. Although Town's lattice design required a lot of fastening, it used much smaller timbers and was easy to build. Rather than build the bridges himself, Town received a patent and charged other builders one dollar for each foot of bridge that was built using his design. Because he sold his design to builders across the American countryside, Town's covered bridges soon became the most popular type of bridge in America.

Other improvements were made in the design of bridge trusses, especially by an engineer named William Howe of Spencer, Massachusetts. Howe's design for covered bridges used iron rods along with wood beams. His use of iron eventually led to the use of steel, concrete, and other materials that eventually replaced wood altogeth-

Burr truss design

CLEARANCE 8 FEET

er. When wood was no longer used to build bridges, there was no need for a roof covering, and the era of the covered bridge ended.

There are over a thousand covered bridges still being used in America, and about seventy of them are in the small New England state of New Hampshire. These handsome structures are so treasured by local townspeople and visitors alike that they are kept in good repair and even replaced, when needed, exactly as originally built.

CORNISH-WINDSOR BRIDGE

Built in 1866 at a cost of $9,000, this is the longest wooden bridge in the United States and the longest two-span covered bridge in the world. The fourth bridge at this site, the 460-foot structure was built by Bela J. Fletcher (1811-1877) of Claremont and James F. Tasker (1826-1903) of Cornish, using a lattice truss patented by architect Ithiel Town in 1820 and 1835. Built as a toll bridge by a private corporation, the span was purchased by the state of New Hampshire in 1936 and made toll-free in 1943.

WALK YOUR HORSES OR PAY TWO DOLLARS FINE.

The Three Categories of Bridges

Despite the wide variety of bridges built in the past plus the newest designs being planned today, there are only three basic categories of bridges—beam bridges, arch bridges, and suspension bridges, although there are many variations of each. The most significant difference among the three categories is the way each bridge displaces the forces created by the weight of the bridge plus the load of traffic on the bridge. In beam bridges, which

include truss and girder bridges, each end of the beam simply rests on a pier or the ground, and the forces of compression are directed straight downward. An arch bridge exerts its forces of compression outward to its abutments, and a suspension bridge uses cables in tension that are held firmly by anchorages at each end of the bridge.

There are many factors to be considered when deciding which type of bridge is best for the use intended. For example, is the bridge going to cross a river, a gorge, or a high-

way? Does the surrounding landscape and shoreline consist of mountains, flatlands, rocky coast, or wet swamps? What is the bridge going to carry—vehicle traffic, foot traffic, or trains? What has to go under the bridge—boats, trains, cars, or nothing? And what materials are conveniently available and affordable—wood, steel, or concrete?

Of course, each category of bridge has many variations, and some modern bridges combine two or all three types in one design. New materials can also affect the engineering and appearance of a bridge,

but underneath its concrete or steel exterior, or upon close examination of its structure, every bridge can be classified as a beam, arch, or suspension bridge.

There are probably many bridges you commonly see, especially if you live in or near a city with rivers, railroads, and highways running through. Try to identify the category of each bridge and figure out why it is best suited for where it is and what it has to do. To better understand and discuss all categories of bridges, these are the names of their most common parts.

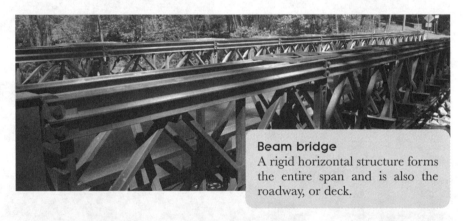

Beam bridge
A rigid horizontal structure forms the entire span and is also the roadway, or deck.

Arch bridge
A curved structural span supports the deck from below or above.

Suspension bridge
The deck is supported from above by cables hanging from towers.

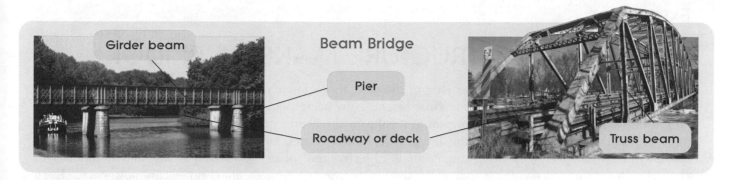

Beam Bridge

Girder beam · Pier · Roadway or deck · Truss beam

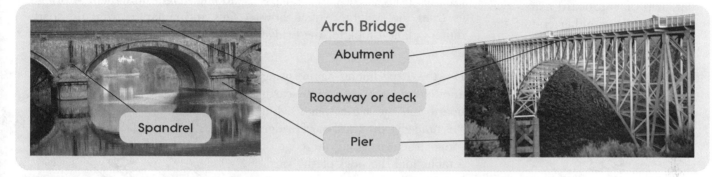

Arch Bridge

Abutment · Roadway or deck · Pier · Spandrel

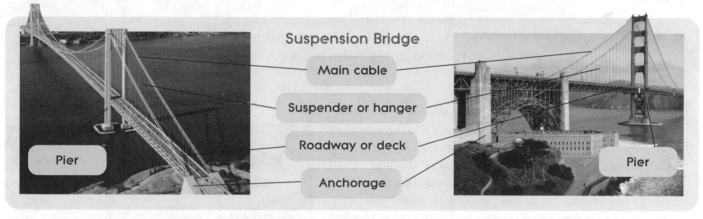

Suspension Bridge

Main cable · Suspender or hanger · Roadway or deck · Anchorage · Pier

Understanding the Parts of Bridges

Abutment
End support for the horizontal forces of an arch bridge

Anchorage
The secure attachment of the cable ends of a suspension bridge

Beam
A rigid horizontal structure that can also be the deck of a beam bridge

Deck
Another name for a roadway

Girder
A very large beam made of steel or concrete

Hanger
Another word for the suspenders of a suspension bridge

Main cable
A cable hung from the towers of a suspension bridge

Pier
The supports between bridge spans

Roadway
The surface that supports traffic crossing the bridge

Spandrel
The area of an arch bridge between the top of the arch and the deck

Suspender
A vertical element linking the cable to the deck and supporting the deck

Tower
A vertical structure that supports the cables of a suspension bridge

Truss
A rigid space frame with members in tension and compression

A SIMPLE STRUCTURE MAKES A BRIDGE

The real strength of a bridge comes from its structural design and not necessarily from what it is made of. If you want proof, try this experiment.

To make a simple bridge, place a flat strip of cardboard across two supports, one at either end of the strip. Anything will do for supports—like two books or two shoe boxes—

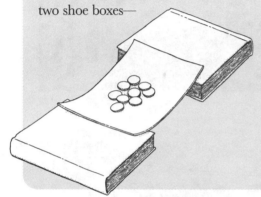

as long as they are approximately the same height. Now begin placing some weight on the center of the bridge. Use coins, stones, or other small objects, and place them on the bridge one at a time until the bridge bends and collapses from the weight. Notice how much weight it took for the bridge to fail.

Do the experiment again using another piece of the same cardboard and the same weights, but this time give the cardboard bridge some structure. Using the edge of a table, fold the sides of the cardboard strip into a U-shape as shown. This new shape is called a channel, which is one of the shapes used to build a girder bridge.

Now place your new bridge across the same two supports at the same distance apart, and begin loading it with the weights. You might be amazed at how much more weight the bridge can now carry. Keep adding weight until the new bridge fails and collapses from the load. Try placing the bridge on its pier supports with the sides of the channel facing up, down, to the side. Which way works best?

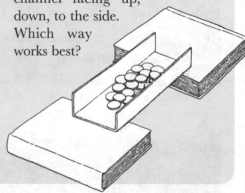

Beam Bridges

A simple beam bridge is constructed of any solid beam or horizontal structure supported by a pier at either end. The earliest beam bridges were made of solid logs or timbers

and could rarely span distances between piers greater than about fifty feet—usually much shorter. Early bridge builders learned that a tree or a wooden plank that was long enough to span a wide gap might not be strong enough to support the traffic crossing over it. If the span was too wide or the tree not strong enough, the bridge could break in the middle under the load of traffic or eventually sag and collapse because of its own weight.

So, to span a divide that was greater than the length a single tree-trunk beam could handle, more stone piers were built all in a row, and logs were placed end to end across the piers to form a continuous chain

of individual bridges. In time, as stone, blocks, bricks, mortar, and other building materials and methods became available, stronger and taller supporting piers could be built, and longer spans could be constructed on top of them.

Still, the length of any single-beam span was limited to the longest and strongest tree that could be found. So when the masonry arch bridge was invented—a bridge that could span a much greater distance—the

simple solid beam bridge was used for only the shortest of spans. Then, about four hundred years ago, bridge builders began to experiment with beam bridges made of structural trusses instead of solid horizontal timbers.

It was discovered that long wooden bridge beams and, later, steel girders that would normally sag under a heavy load could be braced and strengthened with trusses. During most of the 1800s in America, truss-beam construction was the most popular way to build a bridge. Not only could relatively lightweight trusses span distances nearly comparable to arch bridges, but builders soon learned that it was much cheaper and much faster to build a truss bridge than a masonry arch bridge.

The most basic truss bridge used timbers leaning against each other, tip to tip, in the shape of an upside-down V with a horizontal roadway completing the triangle. To build a longer basic truss bridge, a vertical timber supporting the middle of the roadway was hung from the tip of the inverted V. The addition of the vertical tim-

ber to the triangular truss created two triangles from one, which also made the entire bridge stronger. To make an even longer truss bridge was then just a matter of figuring out how many and what combination of triangles would be needed for the span to be crossed.

Over time, bridge builders began to invent new and better truss designs that spanned ever-greater distances, all based on a combination of triangles. The most popular timber truss designs were the king post truss and a variation called the queen post truss. Other common truss designs used for bridge building included the Burr truss, Howe truss, Pratt truss, Long truss, and Town lattice truss, all named for their original inventor builders.

Bridge engineering and the art of designing bridges took gigantic leaps in the nineteenth and twentieth centuries. The rapid growth of railroads across America led to the

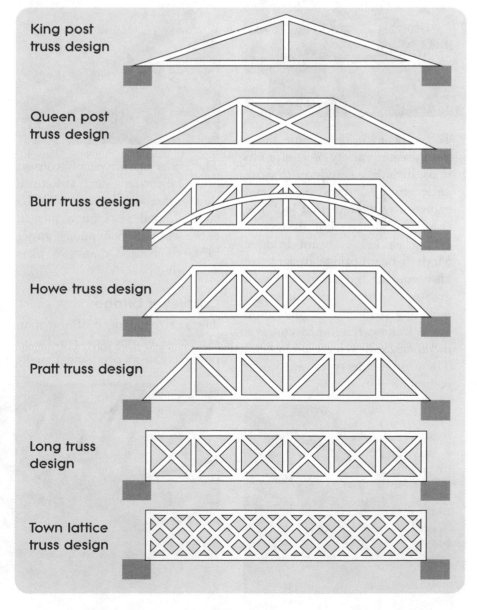

King post truss design

Queen post truss design

Burr truss design

Howe truss design

Pratt truss design

Long truss design

Town lattice truss design

construction of many interesting truss bridges, and the invention and fast-growing popularity of the automobile created a need for more roads, which often needed bridges. Many of the early wood-truss designs were reengineered to use iron and then steel girders. The Howe truss became widely used for building steel railroad bridges, along with a few newer designs that were rather complex and only possible with iron or steel.

Today, beam bridges come in an even greater variety of configurations, including cantilever designs, girder bridges, drawbridges, and cable-stayed designs that look like suspension bridges but are techni-cally classified as beam bridges. Modern beam-bridge designs are also constructed from an even greater variety of materials, including steel trusses, aluminum space frames, reinforced concrete members, and welded steel plates. These are some types you might commonly see.

Simple beam bridge

The bridge span is made of one or more horizontal logs, planks, or other type of solid beams that simply rest on vertical supports called piers.

Single girder bridge

The bridge span typically consists of a fabricated steel structural shape, often an I-beam or a U-channel, that rests on a pier at either end. A continuous girder bridge has more than two piers supporting it.

Cantilever bridge

The horizontal deck of the span extends out from its vertical sup-port to create an overhang. Usually

two cantilever sections, each sitting on a pier, are joined to form one continuous bridge.

Plate girder bridge

The structural shape of the bridge girder is fabricated from steel plates that have been welded or riveted together.

Truss bridge

There are many types of truss beam bridges. In a deck bridge, the roadway is above the supporting truss structure, in a suspended bridge, the deck is below the sup-porting structure, and in a through bridge, the deck runs between the top and bottom of the trusses.

Moving bridges

There are several types of moving bridges usually constructed where taller bridges can't be built high enough for ships to pass beneath them. A few types include the swing bridge that pivots horizon-

tally to move out of the way, a lift bridge in which the deck is raised straight up and lowered down like an elevator, a bascule bridge, which is the typical drawbridge design with either one or two decks that pivot up and down, and others.

Cable-stayed bridge

The world's smallest drawbridge is in Bermuda and creates an opening only seventeen inches wide, just enough to allow the mast of a sailboat to pass through.

The floor or roadway of the span is a continuous girder bridge that gets additional structural stiffness and support from diagonal cables hung from one or more towers. The roadway is not, however, completely held up or suspended like the deck of a suspension bridge.

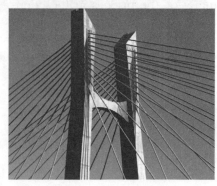

BAILEY BRIDGES

The Bailey bridge is named for its British inventor, Sir Donald Bailey, an obscure civil engineer who liked to build model bridges. Using parts from a toy Meccano set (the British version of America's Erector set), he began experimenting with simple bridge trusses by assembling flat rectangular panels with diamond shapes inside. He then attached several of these modular panels together to form bridge walls and decking. The model bridges he built using this system were extremely strong, yet simple to build. Also, changing the size and length of his bridge was a simple matter of adding or subtracting panels.

Bailey believed the simplicity, strength, and adaptability of his model bridge design was better than any existing design for a full-size bridge. So, in the 1930s, he patented his idea, but plans to actually design and build a real load-carrying bridge were delayed until 1940, shortly after the start of World War II.

As the war progressed, the armies defending Europe discovered that many of the bridges in the countryside were not strong enough to support heavy tanks, trucks, and other weapons. In fact, Britain had secret plans to build a new, super-heavy tank, and they were going to need temporary bridges strong enough to support it. Enemy troops were also destroying bridges every day to slow down the allied armies.

At the time, Donald Bailey was working as a civilian designer for a branch of the British War Office called the Experimental Bridge Establishment, and he suggested that his design for a modular bridge structure could be the solution for quickly building new bridges and rebuilding destroyed bridges anywhere the army needed them. In December 1940, the War Office gave Donald Bailey approval to construct a prototype of his portable bridge system, and one year later it was built and approved.

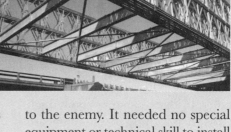

The full-scale Bailey bridge was almost identical to his model, so it looked like a giant-sized Erector construction. The walls and deck were made of several identical panels attached with bolts and nuts, and the length, width, or strength of the bridge could easily be changed by altering the number of panels, end to end or side by side.

Its simplicity, portability, strength, and easy assembly made the Bailey bridge ideal for warfare, since bridges were often built at night when the workers could not use lights or noisy equipment that might reveal their position

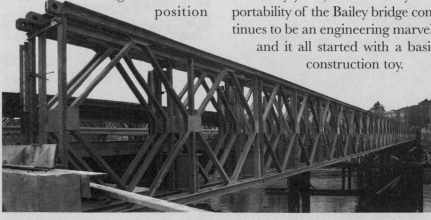

to the enemy. It needed no special equipment or technical skill to install quickly. Each panel section was light enough to be carried by a few men and assembled by feel.

During the last three years of the war, so many Bailey bridges were built that, laid end to end, they would have measured more than two hundred miles. Indeed, the Bailey bridge was credited with helping to win the war, and Bailey was knighted in 1946 for his contribution.

Today, Bailey bridges are still used by armies in trouble spots around the world, but they are even more popular in civilian construction. In the United States and elsewhere, Bailey-type panel bridges are commonly used for emergency repairs, planned detours, pedestrian crossovers, and utility bridges that carry pipelines over water. After more than sixty years, the versatility and portability of the Bailey bridge continues to be an engineering marvel, and it all started with a basic construction toy.

Arch Bridges

The most significant improvement in early bridge building was the development of the arch, which allowed the piers at either end of a single-arch bridge to be placed much farther apart than the greatest length of any single beam. That also meant a long, continuous span, consisting of several arches end to end, could be built using fewer piers than a continuous beam bridge. Since the piers were often the most difficult part of the bridge to build, arch bridge construction quickly replaced beam bridges for all but the shortest spans.

The first type of arch used in bridge building was the corbeled arch, which resembled two sets of upside-down steps meeting in the middle. Bricks or stones were placed on top of each other, with each layer projecting farther than the one below it until the two sides met in

the middle. But the corbel arch bridge had many limitations that made it impractical to span distances even as long as a simple beam bridge.

In time, the structure of arch building was refined, and longer and stronger arches were built using wedge-shaped stones called voussoirs. The masonry arch bridge was the only practical construction for spanning distances greater than about fifty feet. However, building a "true" arch bridge made of wedge-shaped stones first required building a temporary wooden support structure called the falsework.

Starting at both ends and working towards the middle, the tapered stones were laid over the falsework until the final wedge, known as the keystone, was set in place at the top, or crown, of the bridge arch. The falsework could then be removed, and sidewalls called spandrels were built up between the arches, filled with rubble, and covered by a deck, which could be either curved or flat.

By the time of the great Roman civilization, the art of building arch bridges had evolved from simple wood-arch structures, to corbeled-arch stone constructions, to true stone arches, to elegant arched

spans made from bricks and mortar. Many of the Roman arch bridges built 2500 years ago are still being used today. (Of course, they have often been repaired and sometimes even rebuilt.) The Romans were also well-known for building magnificent arched aque-

ducts, which were bridges specially designed for supporting the troughs and pipes that brought water from the distant mountain lakes to the populated cities.

The masonry arch bridge continued to be a practical structure for centuries (and in some applications, still is today), using essentially the same materials and building techniques.

The most significant evolution in masonry bridge construction was the ability of engineers to design arches that were flatter and less

When the Sounding Arch Bridge was built, it had the widest and flattest masonry arch in the world.

round so the span of the arch could be made wider without increasing the height of the bridge. In 1838, a brick arch bridge was constructed over the Thames river in England that for its time had the widest and flattest arch in the world. Each of its two brick spans is 128 feet wide with a rise of only 24 feet. When the falsework was being removed, everyone except the bridge designer expected the structure to collapse. It did not, and the bridge is still in use today.

A building boom in Europe during the Middle Ages provided further opportunity for new arch-bridge designs, and some included small shops, chapels, and roadside resting places for travelers. Some bridges supported homes and even castles, while many had iron gates that could be lowered to block the roadway during an attack.

By the late 1700s, the first non-masonry arch bridges were being built out of cast iron ribs held together with cast iron bracing, supporting a cast iron roadway. Although these relatively lightweight arches still used massive stone block abutments, they were cheaper and faster to build than masonry arches. The only problem was that they were not as strong. Frequent use weakened the joints of iron bridges, and many collapsed—some causing terrible disasters.

It was not until the late 1800s that steel became both affordable and available for construction, and it quickly replaced iron for building arch bridges. Steel was much stronger and more flexible than iron, and pieces of steel could eas-

ily be cut to shape rather than being cast in molds. Steel arches could also be built much larger than iron or masonry arches, so steel bridges could span greater distances. Steel arch construction also did not require constructing falsework, which could block river traffic for years while a masonry arch was under construction.

A steel arch bridge was typically built by constructing the arch in two halves, starting at each base of the arch and building up at an increas-

ing angle until they meet in the middle. Instead of using falsework, temporary wire cables anchored from the shore were used to help support the two space frame sections before they joined in the middle to complete the arch.

The first examples of iron and steel arch bridges had the roadway above, being supported by the arch underneath. A few used a main roadway on top of the arch and a shorter roadway at the bottom of the arch, which also tied the base of the arch together and lessened the need for strong abutments. In the early 1930s, when a steel arch bridge was being built over Sydney Harbor in Australia, a different design was used, with the roadway suspended below the arch by steel hangers. At the same time, a similar steel arch bridge with the roadway beneath was being constructed in Bayonne, New Jersey, just outside New York City. With an arch span of 1652 feet, the Bayonne bridge was two feet longer than the Sydney Harbor Bridge—although the Sydney Harbor Bridge claims to be the widest bridge in the world and capable of carrying the heaviest load. Both bridges were half again as long as any previous arch bridge.

The most modern arch bridges are now made from reinforced concrete, although masonry block and steel frame construction are still quite common.

Arch bridges can be built many ways and support the roadway from above or below.

Suspension Bridges

By the early 1800s, new bridges were being built almost everywhere people lived, worked, or wanted to go, and engineers were inspired to design longer and stronger bridges. They were also challenged to develop cheaper ways of building bridges that were both functional and good-looking. Bridge engineers began to experiment with ways to span the greatest distances using the least amount of construction material for the distance covered. The only viable solution was a suspension bridge.

The concept of suspending a pathway from overhead ropes was not new, but suspending a roadway over a wide river would take more modern engineering. The benefits seemed worth the effort, because a suspension bridge uses the materials it is made of more efficiently than any other type of bridge.

Some of the earliest suspension bridges used chains to support the roadway. Chains were stronger than rope, but not as strong as the steel wire cables that replaced them. John A. Roebling refined the engineering of suspension bridges and the fabrication of wire cables when he designed the Brooklyn Bridge in New York City. When completed in 1883, it was the longest bridge in America, and it held that record for the next twenty years.

By the early 1900s, both building technologies and materials had improved to the point that a suspension bridge could span a gap two to three times wider than the greatest span of an arch bridge. And a suspension bridge could also be built so high that the tallest ships were able to pass beneath it.

Early bridges often used chains for the main cables.

The wooden roadway of this early bridge swings freely.

The three most important parts of a suspension bridge are the towers, the anchorages, and the cables, which are also constructed in that order. It is the combination of cables, towers, and the roadway that gives a suspension bridge its unique shape, character, and structure.

Towers have been made of wood, stone, and steel, but the towers of most modern suspension bridges are made of reinforced concrete. Wide piers that support the bridge towers must often be built underwater in specially constructed work chambers.

The main cables of a suspension bridge drape over the towers and support the roadway from vertical suspender cables. Because the suspended deck or roadway is free hanging, it must be engineered to be very heavy or very stiff to resist swaying and twisting under heavy loads or high winds.

Before the main cables can be put in place, strong anchorages that will firmly hold them in tension must be built at either end of the bridge. Natural bedrock that goes deep into the earth makes the best and strongest anchorage to hold the main cables, but massive masonry constructions and reinforced con-

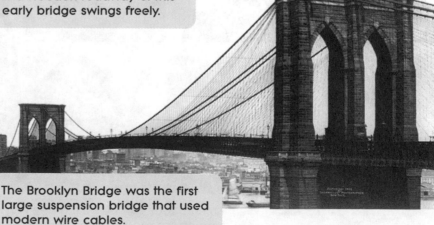

The Brooklyn Bridge was the first large suspension bridge that used modern wire cables.

The rigid space frame structure of a modern suspension-bridge roadway keeps it from twisting and swaying.

crete blocks are also commonly used as cable-end attachment points.

Each of the main cables is made by stringing thousands of thin steel wires from one anchorage point, across both towers, to another anchorage at the opposite side. When a suspension bridge is being built to cross water, the first few wires of the main cables are usually transported from one bank to the other by boat. The first wires are then hoisted by crane to the top of the towers and set at their anchorages to determine the actual curves the length of cable will take. A footbridge or work platform is then built along the unfinished cable to allow workers to add the remaining wires while bundling them together to create one large-diameter cable. Each of the main cables of the Golden Gate Bridge in San Francisco is a little over three feet in diameter and contains 27,572 individual strands of wire.

The engineering and design of suspension bridges continued to evolve throughout the twentieth century as every "longest suspension bridge ever built" was replaced by an even longer bridge somewhere else. In fact, the world's longest, tallest, and most famous bridges are all suspension bridges. Note that the length of a suspension bridge (as well as other types of bridges) is

Brooklyn Bridge
1595 feet

George Washington Bridge
3500 feet

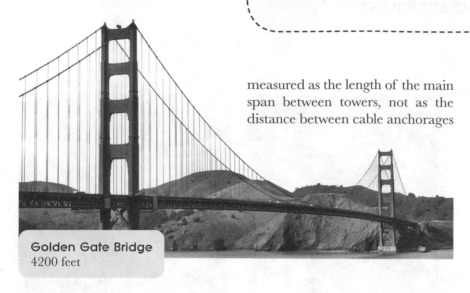

Golden Gate Bridge
4200 feet

Verrazano-Narrows Bridge
4260 feet

Humber Bridge
4626 feet

measured as the length of the main span between towers, not as the distance between cable anchorages or the total length of the roadway, which also includes approaches. The Brooklyn Bridge with a span of 1595 feet, the George Washington Bridge in New York City at 3500 feet, and the Golden Gate Bridge at 4200 feet all are a significant part of bridge history and are still important to the cities they serve.

In 1965, the Verrazano-Narrows Bridge, connecting New York's boroughs of Brooklyn and Staten Island, set a new world's record for the longest center span at 4260 feet. At that time, most people believed it was "the bridge to end all bridges." The bridge was so long that engineers had to consider the curve of the earth's surface and build the towers two inches farther apart at the top than they are at the base.

However, by 1981, the Humber Bridge in England had set yet another new record with a main span of 4626 feet, and today, the Akashi Strait Bridge in Japan is the current record holder at 6529 feet. In this century, even longer bridges will undoubtedly be built, but will the world's next record breaker be a suspension bridge or some new type of structure?

Akashi Strait Bridge
6529 feet

INVENTION

ERECTOR SET

While glancing out the window of the train he was riding, a young man named Alfred Carlton Gilbert kept noticing cranes along the railway that were erecting steel girders for bridges and towers. He was intrigued by the intricate joints and patterns made by the intersecting steel parts of these structures. Suddenly, A.C. Gilbert had an idea. Why not make a toy construction set using miniature steel girders to build working models of cranes and bridges, as well as many other mechanical things?

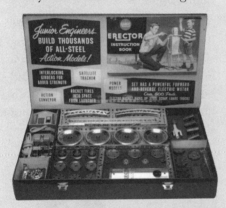

That evening, back in 1911, Gilbert and his wife sat at the kitchen table carefully cutting small girders out of various lengths of cardboard. He then had the paper girders duplicated in metal. Using those girders and lots of little bolts and nuts, Gilbert began building small versions of every kind of structure that might interest young boys as well as himself. He figured out ways to assemble the parts to build models that resembled windmills, airplanes, amusement rides, bridges, trucks, and hundreds of other things.

Gilbert already owned a business that manufactured magic tricks, and in 1913, the first Erector Structural Steel & Electro-Mechanical Builder set was introduced as the perfect toy for boys. Each set came with an Erector manual of illustrations showing how to assemble the parts to build all kinds of things from a simple wheeled cart to a complex machine with motion. Illustrations also showed builders how they could construct models of the Eiffel Tower in Paris or the Brooklyn Bridge in New York, plus many other engineering marvels of the early twentieth century.

To further encourage creativity, Gilbert issued certificates of recognition to young builders, bestowing on them "degrees" as "Engineer" or "Master Engineer." And, to get new ideas for his popular Erector building manuals, Gilbert held competitions that encouraged boys to create new designs. The winners were awarded substantial prizes like a canoe, a pony, or money.

New kits were soon added, offering different numbers of the basic parts, or special parts to build a dirigible and a drawbridge. One of the biggest kits had so many parts that it came in a wooden crate and weighed over one hundred pounds. And when an electric motor with a gearbox was added to several of the larger sets, kids dreamed of someday being able to build the motorized Ferris wheel that was more than four feet in diameter, or the spinning merry-go-round with painted metal horses that moved up and down on poles.

By the mid-1950s, Erector sets were capable of building steel-girder versions of walking robots and rocket launchers. But even though these were the fascinating machines of the time, the popularity of Erector building was quickly beginning to wane as kids began wanting toys that looked more like the machines of the future they saw on TV shows.

After fifty-four years of manufacturing more than thirty million Erector sets, the A.C. Gilbert Company went out of business in 1967. Today, another company makes Erector toys, but each set is now a small kit with only the special parts needed to build one specific model. Collectors and builders who want the older sets with lots of standard parts often find them at flea markets and garage sales.

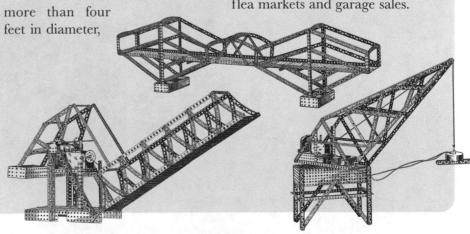

SKYSCRAPERS ARE A GREAT AMERICAN INVENTION

Until the late 1800s, there was a limit to how high a building could be built. Masonry structures made of bricks and stone required thick, massive walls to support the weight of the floors above plus the roof on top. The taller the building, the thicker the walls at the base needed to be. When a masonry building got to be more than eight or nine stories tall, the walls of the first few floors had to be so thick that the remaining space used for rooms inside was greatly reduced. The tallest masonry building ever constructed with load-bearing walls had sixteen stories and needed walls ten feet thick at the base.

In addition to limiting the amount of usable interior space, even the thickest load-bearing walls were not strong enough to support really tall buildings without crumbling under the weight. But since most people didn't care to

walk up more than a few flights of stairs anyway, there was no incentive to build tall buildings.

As the populations of America's largest cities swelled in the 1880s and businesses grew larger, more buildings were built and spread out over the remaining land until there was very little space left in many downtown areas. The only practical solution that would allow cities to keep growing and provide as much space as needed was to find a way to build taller buildings with thinner walls in the same amount of space.

A few architects in Chicago had a theory that tall buildings could be constructed using an iron framework to support the floors, the same way engineers of that time were building long bridges using iron-frame trusses to hold up the roadway. The basic difference was that the horizontal bridge structure would be built vertically.

The first few iron-frame buildings constructed were indeed designed to hold up the floors above, but the framework did not support the exterior walls. These buildings still had self-supporting masonry walls that limited how high they could be built without crumbling under their own weight. To build taller buildings would require both a new method of construction and a way to get people up to the higher floors without having to walk too many flights of stairs.

Architects soon began to realize that a metal framework was strong enough to hold up the walls of a building as well as the floors. And because the thin "curtain" walls hung from the framework were not structural and only needed to cover the framework, they

could provide much more usable space within the building, Windows could also be larger and allow more light into the building. To add to these impressive benefits, engineers calculated that a building with a skeleton frame and curtain walls could be built more quickly and at a lower cost than a masonry building.

It was also quite fortuitous that around this same time, Elisha Otis invented a reasonably fast and safe elevator that made the idea of taller buildings seem more practical. Being lifted up and transported to the top floors of a tall building seemed quite appealing at the time, since most people had never been more than a few stories off the ground. It wasn't long before architects began to publish sketch-

es of their ideas in magazines showing what tall skeleton-frame buildings might look like, and people began to imagine what it would be like to be that high up in a "cloud scraper" building.

Before the expression "cloud scraper" had a chance to catch on, an architectural writer of the early 1880s referred to several of these newly proposed tall buildings as "skyscrapers." Interestingly, the name skyscraper had been used several times previously when, for example, referring to the topsail on a clipper ship, a high baseball pop-up, and even a tall hat. But the term seemed most appropriate for buildings that promised to be taller than anyone had ever seen, and taller than most people imagined anything could ever be built.

Starting with the First Skyscraper

Chicago was the first American city bounded by a limited amount of land to really need tall buildings, and one architect convinced a local insurance company to build their new office building as a skeleton-frame structure with thin curtain walls. Completed in 1885, the ten-story Home Insurance Building in downtown Chicago is considered by most architectural historians to be the first skyscraper ever. It was the first building to have a metal skeleton frame to support both the floors within as well as the surrounding masonry walls. From

The Home Insurance Building in Chicago was the first skyscraper.

the outside, the Home Insurance Building may have looked like a conventional masonry building with load-bearing walls, but the outer brick skin was actually supported by the building's metal-framework core.

When construction of the Home Insurance Building began, the framework of the first six stories consisted of cast iron columns bolt-

Skyscrapers are the largest (but not the tallest) structures built on planet Earth.

ed to wrought iron crossbeams. The cast iron columns were produced by pouring hot molten metal into forms, which results in a very strong part when used in compression, but also a brittle part that could break when bent. That is why the crossbeams between the columns were made from wrought iron, which is even stronger than cast iron but more flexible and less likely to break. Wrought iron is made simply by hammering a heated piece of cast iron into the final shape needed.

However, during construction, the architect decided to switch to steel beams for building the framework of the remaining four floors because steel was even stronger and less expensive than wrought iron. Steel beams had already been successfully used in the construction of bridges, train rails, and large ships, but this was the first time steel had been used for the structure supporting a building.

The Home Insurance Building established the definition of a skyscraper and began the evolution of a new building technique. Since the weight of each floor in a skyscraper is evenly distributed over the framework instead of depending on the exterior walls for support, the nonstructural walls can be made of relatively thin and cheap materials like glass, terra cotta, stainless steel, and stone tiles.

Architects throughout America quickly adopted steel-frame construction, which gave them a whole new vocabulary for design and permitted buildings to be constructed vastly higher than masonry structures. By the end of the nineteenth century, skyscrapers were popping up in many American cities, and the tallest buildings not only offered more space, but they also brought their owners great prestige and a lot of attention.

The first skyscraper in New York City

The first true skyscraper to be built in New York City was the Flat Iron Building, which was completed in 1902. At that time, it also won the title of the tallest building in the world. When looking up from the sidewalk at its twenty-two stories, some New Yorkers feared the structure's tall and narrow triangular shape might make it topple over, so the building's owner boldly claimed it to be the "strongest building ever erected." It was this shape, which resembled a hand iron used for pressing clothes, that gave the building its name.

Flat Iron Building

The Flat Iron Building not only used an all-steel framework, but it was the first skyscraper to have elevators. Without the invention of the Otis "safety elevator," a building that tall would not have been practical for people to use. By 1902, the design of the Otis passenger elevator had greatly improved;

The invention of a safety elevator by Elisha Otis first made skyscrapers practical.

it now used an electric motor to wind and unwind cables that hoisted a passenger car up to higher floors and lowered it down again. But most important, the new Otis elevator featured a safety brake to prevent the passenger car from falling if a cable broke.

A competition to build the tallest skyscraper

Over the next several years, taller and taller skyscrapers continued to be built and new records were set for the world's tallest building—from twenty-two stories, to forty-five stories, to sixty stories, to seventy-one stories, and beyond. By the end of the 1920s, there were 377 skyscrapers over twenty stories tall across America, with 188 of them located in New York City. Still, New York needed more office space, and architects and their corporate clients became fascinated with the idea of building the next world's tallest building.

One of the most interesting (and unofficial) competitions occurred in the late 1920s between three New York City buildings then under

Bank of Manhattan Building

Chrysler Building

Empire State Building

construction—the Empire State Building, the Chrysler Building, and the Bank of Manhattan building. As all three buildings were being planned and built, no one revealed exactly how tall each skyscraper would ultimately be.

Originally, the more classic and conservatively designed Empire State Building was intended to stop at 1000 feet, and the design for the Bank of Manhattan Building topped out at 927 feet. So the designers of the elaborately deco-decorated Chrysler Building modified their plans to extend the height even farther. A tall spire was secretly built and hidden inside a fire shaft at the top of the Chrysler Building. Even though it seemed that the structure had been completed, the spire was later hoisted up through the dome roof to increase the building's total height to 1048 feet—temporarily giving it the status of the world's tallest building.

By then, the completed Bank of Manhattan Building had already lost the competition by 121 feet, but when the owners of the still-unfinished Empire State Building learned of the change, they decided to add five more stories to bring their skyscraper up to 1050 feet, topping the Chrysler Building by a mere two feet. However, they were still concerned that the architects of the Chrysler Building would do something to one-up them again, so a two hundred-foot-tall mooring mast for dirigibles was added to the top of the Empire State Building, giving it the undisputed status of being the new world's tallest building for the next forty years.

Interestingly, there were only two attempts to actually moor a dirigible to the tall mast, but strong winds at that altitude made the maneuver much too dangerous. During the second attempt, as high winds dangerously buffeted the airship around, the crew had to dump tons of ballast water overboard, soaking the pedestrians a quarter of a mile down on the sidewalks.

The world's tallest skyscraper

The desire to build the tallest building did not end in 1931 with the Empire State Building scraping the sky at 1250 feet. In 1972, the twin towers of New York City's World Trade Center set a new record at 1368 feet, and two years later, the Sears Tower in Chicago rose to 1454 feet. That is where the record stood for the next twenty-four years, until 1998, when the twin Petronas Towers located in Kuala Lumpur, Malaysia, a country in Southeast Asia, reached a record height of 1483 feet.

However, this successor to the title of World's Tallest Skyscraper was mostly constructed of reinforced concrete instead of the steel frame construction that had became the standard method for building tall skyscrapers in northern American cities with cool climates. A steel skeleton framework has the ability to expand and contract with changes in seasonal temperatures,

Sears Tower

and it also resists the shaking forces of an earthquake. But Malaysia is located very near the equator in a consistently hot climate, and in an area where there are no earthquakes. So the architect and engineers of the Petronas Towers

The Petronas Towers in Kuala Lumpur are true skyscrapers even though they are constructed from reinforced concrete rather than a steel framework.

decided to use a special type of extra-strong reinforced concrete rather than a steel skeleton frame for the skyscraper's structure.

Reinforced concrete combines the best structural features of concrete and steel, allowing buildings to be even taller and stronger. Some modern skyscrapers use a hybrid construction with a reinforced concrete core in the center of the building, surrounded by a steel skeleton frame that extends out from the core. The hollow core often houses elevators and stairs plus electrical wiring and air ducts.

The two identical Petronas Towers sit on a six-story podium base and are each eighty-eight stories tall, linked by a steel-framed bridge at the forty-second floor. Combined, the floor space inside both tall, tapered, concrete towers equals nearly fifty football fields. Sixty-seven high-speed elevators travel up and down so quickly that they have to be pressurized so the riders won't be affected by the rapid changes in altitude.

The unusual design of the towers has a basis in traditional Islamic geometries. A cross section of either tower reveals a plan based on two interlocking squares to form an eight-point mosaic, which is the most basic design concept in the Islam religion.

Covering the concrete structure is an outer skin made of over four million square feet of polished stainless steel. The continuous horizontal ribbons of windows on each floor are shaded from the hot sun by protruding shades or awnings that look like large stainless-steel teardrops or eyebrows. The shades also shed rain away from the building and windows—and in Kuala Lumpur it rains in downpours at least half the days of the year.

Just one year after the Petronas Towers were completed, construction began in Taiwan on an even taller skyscraper named Taipei 101. Taipei is both the city where the structure is located and an abbreviation for "Technology, art, innovation, people, environment, and identity." The 101 in the name refers to the 101 floors to the top. The steel and glass pagoda-style structure was completed in 2004 and with its spire rises to a height of 1667 feet—tall enough to be the next building to claim the title of World's Tallest Skyscraper.

Taipei 101 in Taipei, Tawain

The exterior of Taipei 101 resembles segments of bamboo, with eight stories to each segment, which are shaped like scepters. The building design includes large replicas of ancient coins on the exterior of the twenty-sixth floor to give this modern building a Chinese style. Taipei 101 also has the world's fastest elevators, which can transport passengers to the eighty-ninth floor observatory in only thirty-nine seconds.

Official calculations for measuring skyscraper height include only the distance from the ground floor sidewalk entrance to the roof at the top of the building's structure. Spires do count in determining total height, but antennas and other additional structures placed on the roof do not count. If they did, the Sears Tower in Chicago would still claim the "tallest" title over Taipei 101.

By 2008, the Shanghai World Financial Center in Shanghai,

China, could set yet another record for skyscraper height at 1700 feet or taller. And the colossal Tower of Dubai in the United Arab Emirates will reach a new height record of over 2300 feet! But no doubt, the competition to see who can build the next tallest building will continue as even bigger skyscrapers are needed in crowded cities with growing populations. And someday there may even be a building as tall as Frank Lloyd Wright's proposal for a 528-story, mile-high skyscraper.

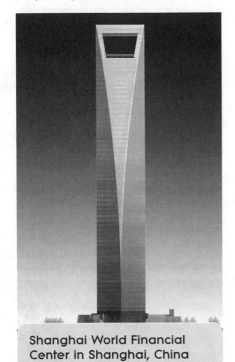

Shanghai World Financial Center in Shanghai, China

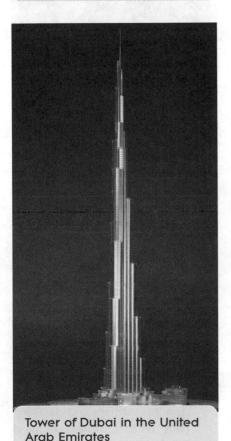

Tower of Dubai in the United Arab Emirates

	Date completed	Stories high	Feet tall
Tower of Dubai Dubai, United Arab Emirates	2009	167	~2314
Shanghai World Financial Center Shanghai, China	2008	97	~1700
Taipei 101 Taipei, Taiwan	2004	101	1667
Petronas Towers Kuala Lumpur, Malaysia	1998	88	1483
Sears Tower Chicago	1974	110	1454
World Trade Center * New York City	1972	110	1368
Empire State Building New York City	1931	102	1250
Chrysler Building New York City	1930	77	1046
Woolworth Building New York City	1913	60	792
Metropolitan Life Tower New York City	1909	50	700
Singer Building* New York City	1908	45	612
Flat Iron Building New York City	1902	22	285
Home Insurance Bldg.* Chicago	1885	0	180

* These buildings are no longer standing.

Skyscraper Foundations

Why heavy buildings don't sink in the ground

The steel-frame skeleton of a skyscraper must carry the full weight of the structure itself plus everything placed inside the building, including the people who occupy it—and the ground on which the structure is built must be able to support the building. But types of ground can vary greatly from solid rock to muddy soil, so the foundation that a building needs to keep from sinking must be designed for the particular type of earth the building will rest on. If the foundation is weak or the wrong type, the building can tilt and maybe even fall over.

The best possible foundation for a skyscraper is solid rock, and large, heavy buildings can be built directly on rock that reaches the surface of the earth. Sometimes the rock is excavated if the building is to have one or more floors below ground level.

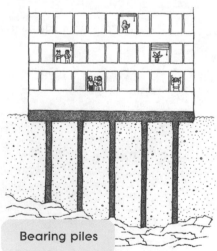

Bearing piles

In soils with a bed of rock underneath, wooden or metal bearing piles that look like long telephone poles are driven into the soil until they reach the rock beneath. Sometimes piles are made by drilling holes in the earth down to the rock bed and filling them with reinforced concrete. If there is no bed of rock below the compact soil, the piles need spread footings much larger than the diameter of the piles to spread the weight being supported over a larger surface area.

Spread footings

When a building site doesn't even have compact soil, a large slab or floating raft made of reinforced concrete or steel is built to float on the surface of the ground as a foundation for the building. Another way to support a building on soft ground with no rock bed beneath is to excavate the earth to a depth several stories below ground level, removing an amount of earth equal to the weight of the entire building. Sinking the building's structure into the soft earth, like planting a pole into the sand, keeps the building upright and solidly supported.

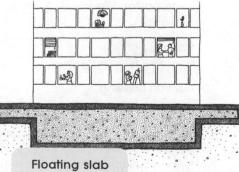

Floating slab

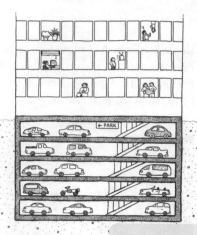

Excavation

In addition to supporting the weight of the building, a foundation must also resist the additional forces created by winds pushing against the sides of a skyscraper. So, rather than swaying with the wind (which

The crisscross bracing on the outside walls of the John Hancock Center in Chicago greatly stiffens the structure and transfers wind pressures to the foundation.

could cause the building's occupants to get motion sickness), the rigid skeleton framework of a skyscraper transfers the load to the ground pushing against its foundation—just as you would resist someone trying to push you over by standing stiffly and pushing back with your legs planted firmly against the ground.

THE GEODESIC DOME AND OTHER SPACE AGE SPACE FRAMES

Suppose you were asked to design a covered stadium big enough to seat fifty thousand people. If you decided to build a structure with a flat roof spanning such a large area, the roof would need to be supported with many columns. Can you imagine a stadium with a hundred or more columns growing up out of the playing field and spectator seats? Picture a football, hockey, or basketball game with the players trying to avoid the columns and the spectators trying to see around the posts. A large, flat roof might also be vulnerable to collapsing from heavy snows, windstorms, and earthquakes.

A better way to cover a large stadium without using posts might be to build a structure called a geodesic dome. A geodesic dome is made from many struts that are joined to form triangles, and the triangles are connected to each other to form a dome-shaped structure. The num-

ber and scale of the triangles determine how large the dome will be.

Depending on how the dome will be used, the dome framework can be covered with a variety of materials, including rigid panels, fabric, transparent plastic, or any material that will keep out rain, snow, wind, and cold. Since the covering does not contribute to the strength of the structure, the materials used can be very thin and light in weight.

A geodesic dome can enclose the largest amount of space with the least amount of material when compared to any other method of building ever invented. Some geodesic domes are large enough to cover an entire city block, and the space within them is completely open and uncluttered with columns. Smaller geodesic domes are also quite practical and often used for personal dwellings, greenhouses, storage sheds, garages, and play spaces.

Geodesic Structures Do More with Less

The geodesic dome was invented in the late 1940s by Buckminster Fuller, an American designer and architect. Actually, the first known geodesic dome was designed and built in Germany more than twenty years earlier as the roof of a small planetarium. But it was Fuller who developed the details of a practical system for building geodesic domes, and in 1954, he received a patent for his dome invention.

Fuller devoted his life to making the world a better place to live, and his geodesic dome design demonstrated ways he believed architecture could improve housing for people all over the world. His idea was simple—do more with less. Devise a construction system to provide the greatest amount of liv-

ing space for the least amount of material needed to enclose it. In practical terms, that meant finding a way to build strong yet inexpensive structures.

By using combinations of triangles formed into modular pentagon and hexagon shapes, Fuller was able to create domes with a spherical form, which is the most efficient building system ever invented. The more triangles used to create the structure, the more closely the dome resembles the form of a true sphere. Fuller used the Latin term *geodesic* to describe his dome, which means, "earth dividing," and refers to the symmetrical divisions of a sphere.

The classic geodesic sphere is a hollow icosahedron, although geodesic dome designs can be based on several other spherical polyhedral forms, including an octahedron and even a simple tetrahedron. An icosahedron consists of twenty equilateral triangles, and each triangle can be further divided into smaller triangles. Those triangles can continue to be divided into even smaller and smaller triangles to further approach the roundness of a sphere. But interestingly, the resulting pattern will always contain twelve pentagons of five triangles each with any remaining triangles organized into hexagons. And although the three sides of

triangles used in a geodesic dome have nearly equal lengths, none are exactly equilateral triangles.

Understanding dome frequency

In technical terms, the design of a geodesic dome or sphere is described as being of a certain frequency. Frequency relates to the number of triangles into which the dome is divided. Specifically, frequency (which is represented by

the letter "v") is the number of parts into which any one side of an icosahedron triangle is divided. And the triangle can be divided and further divided two basic ways.

When the basic triangles of an icosahedron are further divided into triangles, the dome becomes more rounded so that a four-frequency dome has many more triangular components and is more smoothly curved than a one-frequency dome that barely resembles a sphere

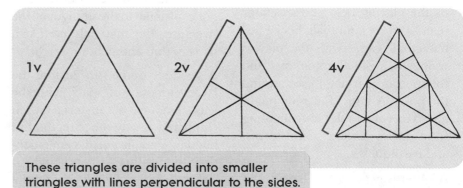

These triangles are divided into smaller triangles with lines perpendicular to the sides.

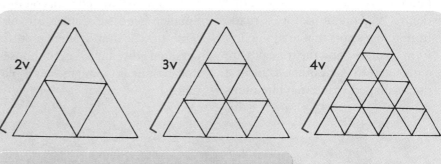

These triangles are divided into smaller triangles with lines parallel to the sides.

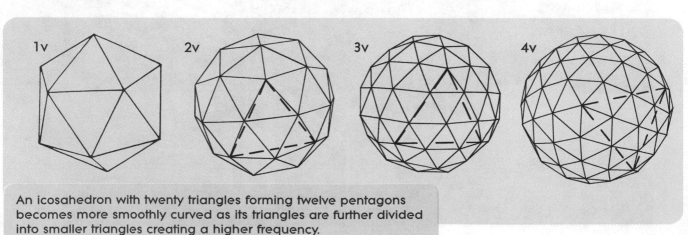

An icosahedron with twenty triangles forming twelve pentagons becomes more smoothly curved as its triangles are further divided into smaller triangles creating a higher frequency.

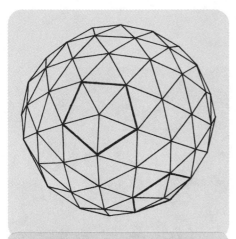

There are four triangles from the centers of adjacent pentagons, so this is a four-frequency geodesic dome.

Another way to determine the frequency of a dome you may be observing is to count the number of triangles (or strut sections) directly from the center of one pentagon to the center of an adjacent pentagon. The number you count is the frequency of that dome.

Although a geodesic dome can be completely round like the Spaceship

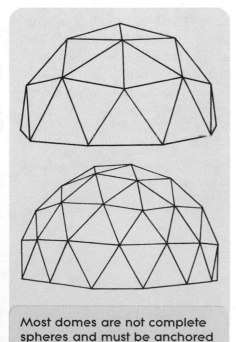

Most domes are not complete spheres and must be anchored to a base or the ground to complete a rigid structure.

Earth dome at Disney's Epcot Center in Florida, most domes are only partial spheres and are generally referred to as half spheres, three-quarter spheres, or whatever approximate portion of the sphere is being used as the dome.

Dome designs are here to stay

Buckminster Fuller's dome captured the imagination of designers, architects, engineers, and hobbyists all over America, and by the 1960s, geodesic structures were showing up everywhere as homes, backyard sheds, kid's climbers, planetariums, and even the roofs of round oil-storage tanks. A dome structure is not only strong, but its shape makes it capable of withstanding heavy winds and storms. Dome structures are also relatively inexpensive to construct, and they assemble quickly. It is also possible to disassemble and relocate the dome, making it a good temporary or emergency shelter in all climates.

Living or working in a geodesic dome building has several practical advantages compared to conventional rectangular buildings. Since a dome interior has no corners, heating and cooling the space is much more efficient and air flow is better. Heat loss is also reduced because there is less exterior surface for the amount of interior space. The unobstructed dome interior allows an even distribution of light and sound, and keeps out more unwanted noise than other designs. In fact, light is actually amplified by the interior wall surfaces and seems brighter inside a dome.

Geodesic dome structures have several other fascinating characteristics. The larger the dome structure, the stronger it becomes and the more efficiently it uses materials to enclose a geometrically larger

amount of space. And really large geodesic domes, like those that cover sports stadiums, can be so light in weight compared to the heated space enclosed that they begin to act like hot-air balloons and actually want to lift up. If the structure were not secured to the ground, a giant geodesic dome about a half mile in diameter would

theoretically float in the air when the temperature inside the dome was only one degree warmer than the outside air. Although the flurry of geodesic dome building mostly ended in the 1970s, geodesic domes are still being built for the same practical and aesthetic reasons that first made them popular.

SPACESHIP EARTH

The first completely spherical geodesic dome building

The most striking building at Epcot in the Walt Disney World Resort in Florida looks like an enormous geodesic golf ball. In fact, it is a geodesic structure, but unlike most domes, this one is a complete sphere. The dome, called Spaceship Earth, encloses several exhibits including one that takes visitors on a spiraling ride past major events in the history of civilization.

The structure is not only the first completely spherical geodesic dome building ever constructed, it is the world's largest spherical dome at eighteen stories tall. The sphere itself is 165 feet in diameter and rests on three pair of steel legs that raise it fifteen feet above the ground.

The framework of the geodesic dome was constructed from 1450 steel struts, and each strut was wrapped with a waterproof neoprene covering. The framework was then covered with a skin of nearly one thousand triangular aluminum panels bolted to the struts. The Spaceship Earth dome was engineered and built to withstand wind speeds up to two hundred miles per hour, because Florida occasionally experiences hurricane-force winds.

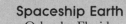

Spaceship Earth
Orlando, Florida
Designed by Walt Disney World
Completed 1982

BUILDING WITH RODS AND CONNECTORS

- SPACE FRAME TOYS AND DISCOVERY PLAYTHINGS
- PERSONAL-SIZE SPACE FRAMES AND PLAY PLACES
- NEW AND NOVEL SPACE FRAME SYSTEMS

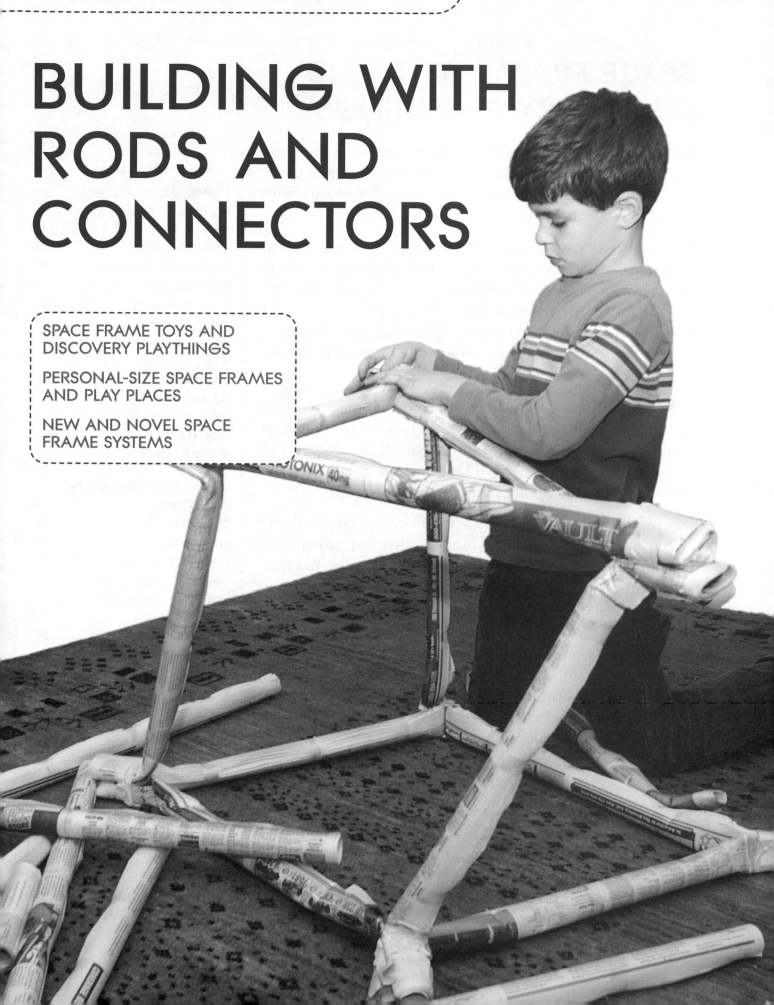

SPACE FRAME TOYS AND DISCOVERY PLAYTHINGS

Building a space frame toy can be as simple as stringing together a few drinking straws to make an indoor golf game or as complicated as building a marble roller coaster with lots of twists and turns all around your room.

The instructions for each space frame building system show you how the system uses its rods and connectors to create geometric space frame structures. They also describe the features that make each building system suitable for certain types of constructions. Following each building system are toys, games, or other playthings that can be built using that system.

Most of these space frame toys can be built and played with by a single builder, while a few could use a third hand to help with the assembly. And some space frame games, like Magnetic Battle Bugs, Clip Hangers, and Sticky Triangle Dominoes, require another player to compete with.

For model builders, the Pasta Pieces and Paste building system has a special, fast-drying adhesive and enough different pieces to build a miniature building, bridge, or other space frame structure. Space frame building systems can also make Classic Kites, a Bird Feeder Space Station, and many other favorite playthings. Tub Tube Toys are great for building floating structures, and you can't buy anything like them in stores. Some projects, including Pyramid Power, Bubble Frames, and the Mosquito Chamber of Doom, will introduce you to fascinating discoveries in nature and science. If you happen to be a math whiz, keep in mind that nearly all the space frame building systems can make every known kind of polyhedron form.

Choose the building systems and build-it projects that inspire you the most. And, of course, builders are always encouraged to invent and build their own projects.

BUILD IT

STRING AND STRAW STICKS	209
POLYFORM KICKBALL AND INDOOR GOLF	211
PYRAMID POWER	213
WATER LENS MAGNIFIER	216
PORTABLE POCKET SCOPE	218
SPACE FRAME TERRARIUM	221
STICKY Q-STICKS	224
STICKY TRIANGLE DOMINOS	226
BUBBLE FRAMES AND 3-D PLANES	229
POLYGON PUZZLES AND POLYHEDRON PLAYTHINGS	232
PUNCH AND POKE STICKS	235
MARBLE COASTER TRACKS AND TRESTLES	237
BIRD FEEDER SPACE STATION PLATFORM	242
CLASSIC KITES	244
WIND WHIRLIES	249
TINKER TOOTHPICKS	251
GEODESIC DOME BUG HOUSE	254
MOSQUITO CHAMBER OF DOOM	256
TOOTHPICK TANTALIZERS	259
QUICK STICKS	263
BUTTERFLY NET	267
TRI-STICK STOOL	269
TUB TUBES	271
TUB TUBE TOYS	273
PASTA PIECES AND PASTE	275
TRIANGLE TRUSS BRIDGES MODEL BUILDING	279
ROTELLE RATTLER AND OTHER PASTA SNAKES	282
NOODLE NOVELTY TWISTERS	285
CLIP GRIPPERS AND STRAW STRUTS	290
CLIP HOOKS AND HANGERS	292
MAGNETIC BATTLE BUGS	294

STRING AND STRAW STICKS
BUILDING SYSTEM

Space frame structures made with String and Straw Sticks can quickly grow quite large and yet be very light in weight. That feature makes this construction method ideal for building polyhedral forms of any size. In this space frame building system, the straws are the struts, and strings threaded through the straws are the connectors. Because the strings are tied together with knots, String and Straw Sticks are best for building permanent structures and projects that you don't intend to take apart.

Using only full-length plastic drinking straws, you can easily make single and multiple tetrahedron constructions similar to the kite frames built by Alexander Graham Bell (who is better known for inventing the telephone). By cutting the straws to various modular lengths, you can build other types of polyhedron shapes as well as free-form structures.

Construction

Builder's age
7+

Materials
☐ Plastic drinking straws
☐ Lightweight string

Tools
☐ Scissors

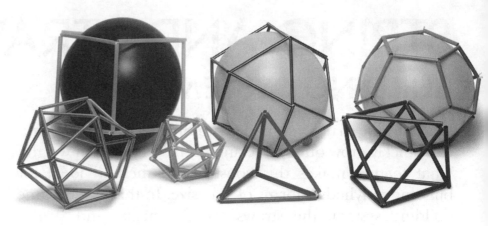

Building techniques

First, decide what form you plan to build, and collect the number of straws needed. If your construction requires straws of different lengths, they must be cut to length with scissors before assembly. Assembling the straws is like putting together a puzzle and requires some planning.

There are two ways to thread string through the straws: you can push it through or suck it through. For full-length straws, sucking works best if you don't mind getting a mouthful of string. Place one end of the string into one end of a straw and suck it through the other end. If you are using fat straws, it helps to tie a knot at the end of the string you insert into the straw. For some constructions, you might need to thread two or three strings through the same straw. In that case, it's easier if you suck them through all at once. Be careful not to suck too hard or you might find yourself swallowing the string.

Follow these instructions to build a simple String and Straw Stick tetrahedron space frame, and then use the same techniques to build other forms.

1. Start with a length of string about four to five feet long, and thread it through three straws, then fold them to form a triangle. Tie a knot where the two unconnected straw ends meet. When tying the straws together, pull the string tight and tie a good knot that won't loosen.

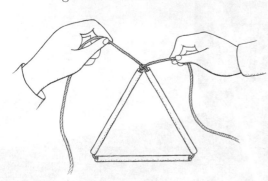

2. Add two more straws on the same string to connect a second triangle to the first (with both triangles sharing one common straw). Tie a knot to secure the second triangle.

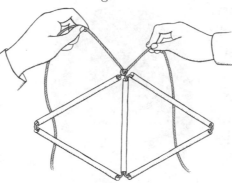

3. Now fold the two triangles toward each other and use a shorter length of string and two knots to connect them with a final straw to form a tetrahedron.

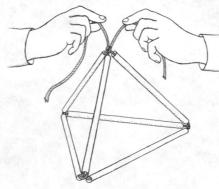

To build larger structures, use a longer length of string and keep adding straws or make several separate structures and fasten them together using more straws and string. To keep the structure sturdy by minimizing joint movement, tie off the string whenever you come to an intersection of three or more straws. If you need shorter struts, just cut the straw to the length needed and thread it on the string.

Experiment with combining triangles, squares, and odd shapes to see what types of space frames this system can make. How large can you build a structure and still keep it rigid? How tall can you build a skyscraper frame?

STRING AND STRAW STICKS BUILD-IT PROJECTS

POLYFORM KICKBALL AND INDOOR GOLF

PYRAMID POWER

WATER LENS MAGNIFIER

PORTABLE POCKET SCOPE

SPACE FRAME TERRARIUM

POLYFORM KICKBALL AND INDOOR GOLF

In some places, it was a common sight to see a kid walking to school while kicking a stone ahead, catching up to the stone, then kicking it again, over and over. The idea of each kick was to send the stone as straight and as far as possible, but it didn't always go where the kicker wanted. If the stone went too far off course (like into the street), it was simply abandoned and the next stone encountered was kicked ahead.

Instead of rolling in a straight line like a ball, stones are shaped irregularly with facets, curves, and points that cause them to go off course. But that is the fun part—not knowing exactly where the stone will go even though the kicker is trying to aim the kick.

It's still fun to kick stones, but here's a version of the game designed specifically for indoor play. The multifaceted Polyform Kickball is guaranteed to behave erratically no matter how well you aim, and the ball is designed not to go very far, no matter how hard it is kicked. Also, the kickball is so light that it's guaranteed not to break anything it hits, including other players.

Construction

Building system
String and Straw Sticks

Builder's age
7+

Player's age
5+

Materials
☐ 3 to 8 drinking straws, each cut into four equal lengths
☐ 6 feet of string

Tools
☐ Scissors

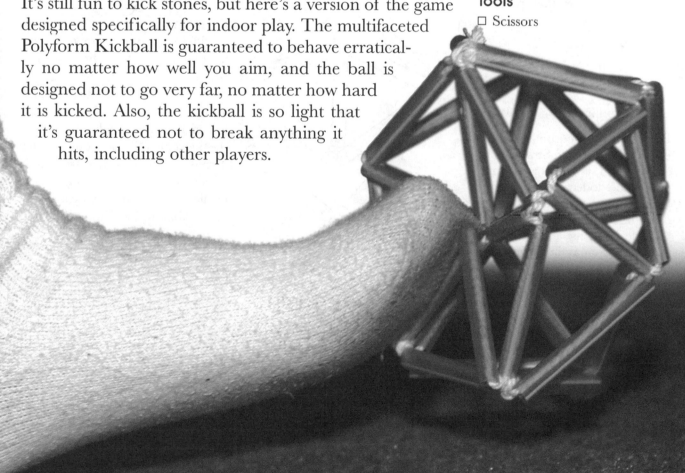

Building instructions

Using String and Straw Stick construction, there are several polygon forms that make good kickballs. The more facets, the straighter and smoother the ball will roll across both carpeted and hard floors. Kickballs made of polygons with fewer facets will bounce around more unpredictably on carpeted floors, but on hard floors, they may just slide straight ahead on one facet. For really interesting action, build a small polygon first, then build a slightly larger one around it.

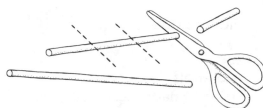

1. Decide which Polyform Kickball you want to build, and cut the number of quarter-length straw struts needed for that polyhedron.

Octahedron	12
Icosahedron	30
Dodecahedron	30
Square Antiprism	16

2. Build the polyhedron structure using the String and Straw Sticks construction system. For all forms except the dodecahedron, begin by threading three straw struts onto the string and form a rigid triangle by tying a knot. Don't cut off the remaining string.

   For the dodecahedron, begin with five straw struts forming a pentagon.

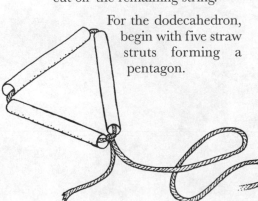

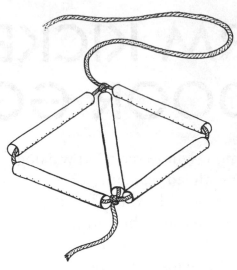

3. Refer to the Appendix for the polyform polyhedron design you are building, then thread more straw struts onto the string to create an adjacent triangle or pentagon and tie it off. Continue to add straw struts (and added lengths of string as needed) to complete the shapes that make up the finished form.

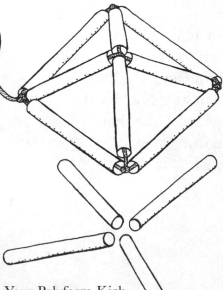

Your Polyform Kickball is now ready for testing. Experiment with different ways of kicking to develop techniques for distance and accuracy. If you want to build a larger or smaller kickball, or build a ball within a ball, use struts that are a little longer or shorter. Another variation that will change the way the kickball behaves is to wrap the kickball in aluminum foil so the foil conforms to the polyform.

Kickball Indoor Golf

The kickball is designed for just kicking around indoors and trying to get the ball to go where you want it to go. You can also use a Polyform Kickball to play an interesting zigzag version of indoor golf. Pick target "holes" all around

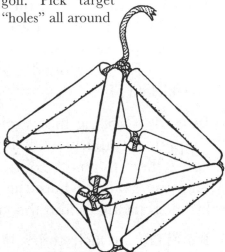

the room or in different rooms. Targets can be table and chair legs, the base corners of furniture, and even books or shoes that you strategically locate on the floor. Now see how few kicks you can take to bounce the kickball off each one of the targets, going in order from one target to the next. You might also challenge someone to play a round of Kickball Indoor Golf with you.

PYRAMID POWER

The theory of pyramid power began when archaeologists discovered that chambers inside Egyptian pyramids contained animal and plant matter that had not decayed even though it was thousands of years old. One of the theories is that the shape of the pyramid helps focus some type of energy from the universe to a particular point within the pyramid structure.

The idea may sound strange or even supernatural, but for centuries people in several countries have used pyramids to sharpen dulled knives and keep dairy products from spoiling. Someone has even patented a pyramid-power sharpener for razor blades. And some people believe a pyramid-shaped hat will relieve headaches or even make the wearer more intelligent.

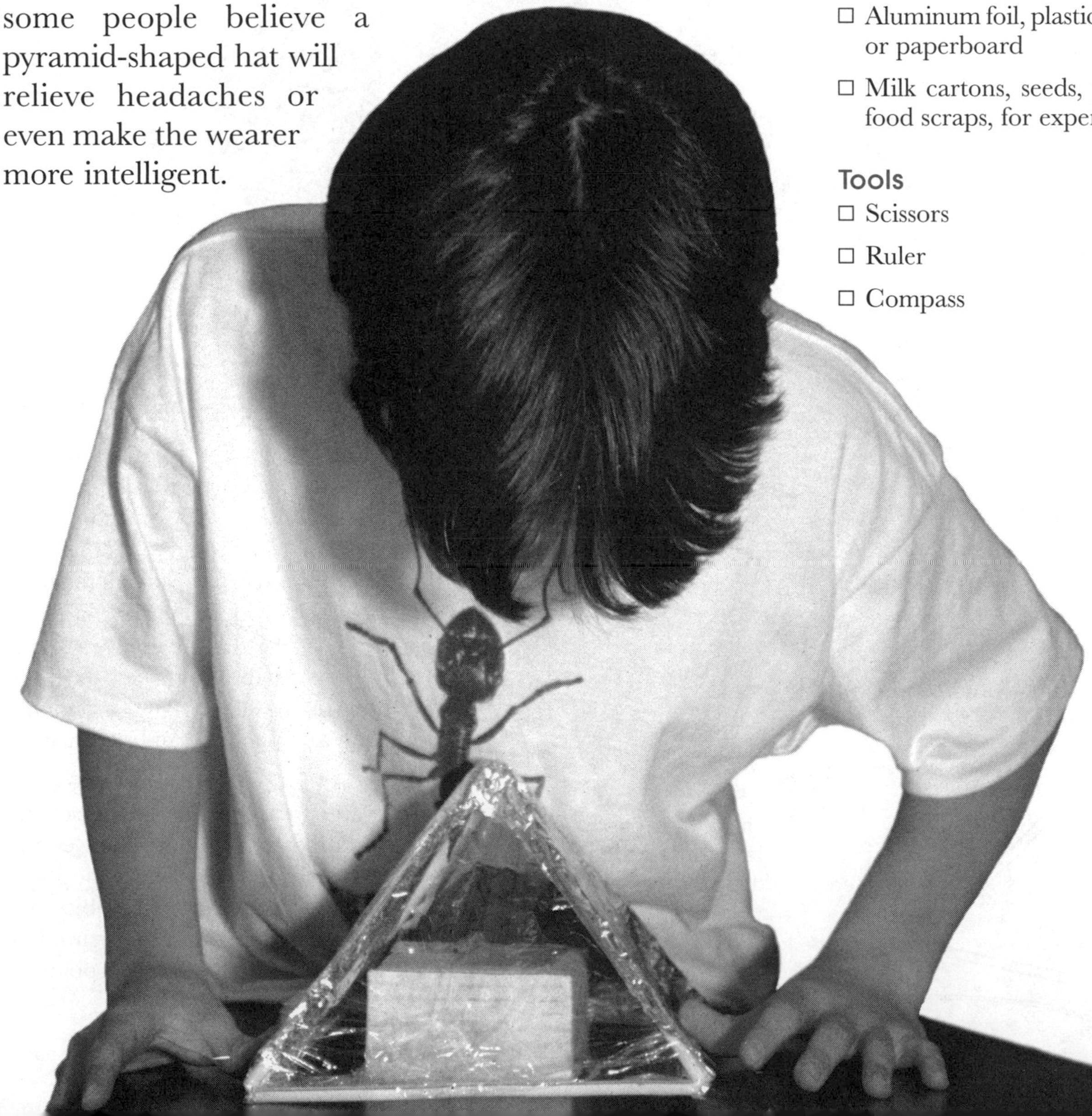

Construction

Building system
String and Straw Sticks

Builder's age
7+

Player's age
6+

Materials
☐ 8 drinking straws
☐ 8 feet of string
☐ Aluminum foil, plastic food wrap, or paperboard
☐ Milk cartons, seeds, pencil, and food scraps, for experiments

Tools
☐ Scissors
☐ Ruler
☐ Compass

Building instructions

To generate pyramid power, the size of the pyramid is not important, but the exact geometric proportions are critical. The angle of the pyramid sides should be exactly fifty-one degrees, and the platform inside the pyramid used to hold objects must be positioned at one-third of the height from the base to the pointed top. You should be able to come pretty close to those specifications using a few different lengths of Straw and String Sticks to build a space frame pyramid with a square base. Because the angle of the pyramid sides must be exact, two different lengths of straws are needed.

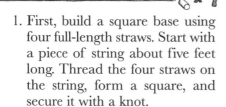

1. First, build a square base using four full-length straws. Start with a piece of string about five feet long. Thread the four straws on the string, form a square, and secure it with a knot.

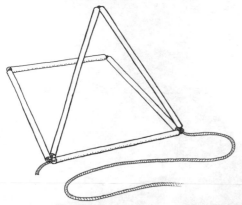

2. Measure and cut one-quarter of an inch from each of the remaining four straws. Add two of these shorter straws on the same string used for the square base, and form a triangle side with one of the base straws, then secure it with a knot.

3. Use a separate piece of string and the remaining two shorter straws to make the opposite triangular side, and tie it all together to make the pyramid frame.

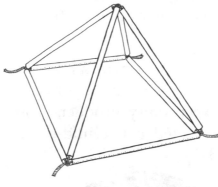

4. The four triangular sides of the pyramid should be covered using any flat sheet material. You can use the pyramid frame as a template and cut pieces of paperboard or aluminum foil to be taped to the frame. Clear plastic food wrap makes a transparent covering so you can look inside the pyramid without lifting it up. The covering does not have to fit the frame exactly and can overlap on the frame edges, but do try to keep the sides flat.

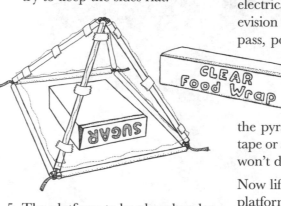

5. The platform to be placed under the pyramid can be made from a found object or several objects stacked to achieve the correct platform height. The bottom of an empty milk carton cut off to the right height works well. To determine the correct platform height for your pyramid, measure the overall height of the pyramid straight up from the middle of the base to the top pinnacle, then divide that measurement by 3. If the drinking straws used for constructing the square base were a standard eight inches long, then the height of the platform would be just a little less than two inches.

Experiments with pyramid power

The first step to generating pyramid power is correctly positioning the pyramid. Find a tabletop or other flat surface away from all

electrical appliances, including television sets. Using a magnetic compass, position the pyramid so that one of the four sides faces magnetic north. Carefully mark the position of the pyramid, using small pieces of tape or another marking system that won't damage the table surface.

Now lift up the pyramid, place the platform in the exact middle of the pyramid footprint, and lower the pyramid to its original position. Whenever you place an object on the pyramid platform, be sure it is centered with its long axis pointing north and south.

To see if your pyramid has special powers that affect objects, try the following experiments.

Sharpening objects

Find a short, stubby pencil and sharpen the tip. Draw a few lines on a piece of paper to slightly wear down the pencil lead. Now put the pencil inside the pyramid with the tip in the exact

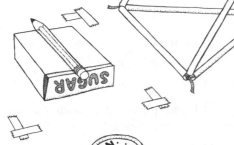

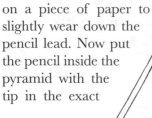

middle of the platform, pointing north. Depending on how dull the tip is, the resharpening process might take a few weeks to several months—or it might not happen at all. The focused energy of the pyramid is supposed to invisibly vibrate the edge of the object, causing the molecules to realign and make the object sharper.

Germinating seeds

Some experiments have shown that placing seeds in a pyramid may cause them to sprout more quickly than if planted in the usual

way. Seedlings started in a pyramid are also supposed to produce better flowers and crops when transplanted in the garden.

To do a controlled experiment that tests this theory, make or find two identical containers or cups just a little taller in height than the platform in the pyramid. To make planting cups, you might try using the bottoms of empty milk cartons or cutting down the tops of paper cups. Fill both cups with soil, then plant the same type of seeds in each. This is important—the seeds in one of the cups should be planted in the center of the cup's surface soil so they are all facing the same direction. Now put that cup inside the pyramid in place of the platform. The other planted cup should be placed nearby, but outside the pyramid. The seeds do not need light to sprout, so the pyramid covering can be opaque. Keep both seed cups watered and see what happens. Did the seeds in one cup sprout more quickly than those in the other?

Drying and preserving

Pyramid power is supposed to cause rapid dehydration, which prevents decay and rotting. To see if the process works, try placing some organic matter on the center of the pyramid platform, lined up from north to south. You might try a piece of fruit, flowers, cheese, or even a casualty from the fish tank. It may take as long as a few weeks for the matter to completely dehydrate. You can periodically look under the pyramid to check progress, but don't disturb the object on the platform. If

the experiment starts to smell bad, the pyramid isn't doing its job and you should throw the organic matter away.

Pyramid-Power Panama Hat

After conducting a few pyramid-power experiments, and if you truly believe in the power of the pyramid, you might also try wearing it as a hat. Face north as much as possible while wearing your pyramid hat. Maybe it will make you smarter. The tapered sides of the pyramid hat allow one size to fit all.

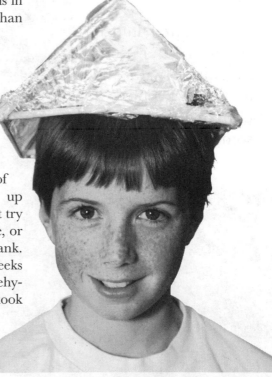

WATER LENS MAGNIFIER

Have you ever looked through a magnifying lens or a microscope to see objects and details that appear larger than life? It can be an awesome experience. The images produced by a homemade water lens may not be as greatly magnified or as clear as those produced by precision-made optics, but a water lens is certainly as much fun to use because you get to make the lens and experiment with magnification as well as begin to understand how a magnifying lens works.

Maybe you have already experienced the magic of a water lens by looking through a clear glass that's full of water and seeing the magnified image of a cereal box or something else behind it. Or maybe you have noticed that the texture of the table seems much larger when seen through an accidentally spilled drop of water.

A String and Straw Stick space frame structure can easily be converted into a simple water lens magnifier with the addition of a piece of clear plastic wrap and some water.

Construction

Building system
String and Straw Sticks

Builder's age
7+

Player's age
4+

Materials
☐ 12 drinking straws
☐ 10 feet of string
☐ Clear plastic dry cleaner's bag or clear plastic food wrap
☐ Tape
☐ Elastic loop or rubber bands (optional)
☐ Water

Tools
☐ Scissors

Building instructions

The water lens is made using an octahedron frame with a piece of transparent plastic sheeting covering the top, open facet of the structure. Water added to the plastic panel causes it to sag and creates the magnifying lens.

1. Build the octahedron structure using String and Straws Sticks. Begin by threading three straws onto the string and form a rigid triangle by tying a knot. Don't cut off the remaining string.

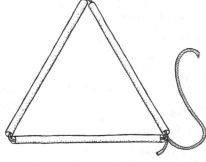

2. Thread and connect two more straws to each side of the first triangle, making three more triangles. Tie off each triangle as you make it.

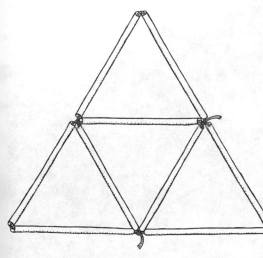

3. Thread and connect a straw to each corner as shown in the illustration. To form the octahedron shape, tie the unfastened ends of the straws to an opposite corner.

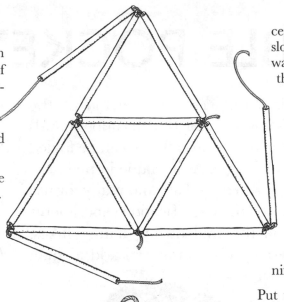

4. Cut a piece of plastic wrap a few inches larger all around than one of the triangle openings in the frame. Be generous—the size does not have to be exact. Clear food wrap will work fine, but the clear plastic wrap from a dry cleaner's bag will work better because it will stretch more easily when the lens is later filled with water.

5. Put the cut piece of plastic loosely over the triangular space frame opening and secure it in place with a few pieces of tape. To hold the plastic in place more securely, you can also use a snug-fitting loop of elastic or a loop made from several rubber bands knotted together.

6. To turn your space frame structure into a magnifying lens, just add water. With your fingers, make a slight depression in the center of the plastic wrap and slowly pour room-temperature water into it from the outside of the structure. Cold water will fog the lens. The weight of the water will cause the plastic to sag and take the shape of a plano-convex lens that is flat on the top side (the surface of the water) and curved on the other side (where the water is making the plastic sag). The more water you add, the more the plastic will sag and the stronger the magnification will be.

Put the objects you want to view under the lens through the openings in the side of the structure. Raise or lower the objects as needed to put them into focus.

Because the water lens will probably spill, it should be used only in water play areas like the bathtub, sink, backyard, beach, or on the porch.

If you're curious enough to experiment a bit further (and not afraid of the potential mess and cleanup), you might try using other clear liquids instead of water to make the lens. For example, try using cooking oil or corn syrup to see how they affect the amount of magnification.

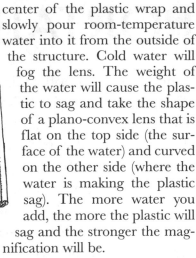

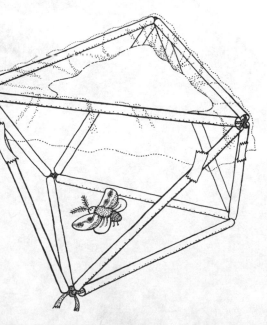

PORTABLE POCKET SCOPE

This is really cool! It is a reduced-scale version of the Water Lens Magnifier that is assembled with rubber bands instead of string so that the octahedron frame can be folded flat into a small compact triangle. As its name implies, the Portable Pocket Scope can be carried around ready for use when you want it for conducting magnification experiments in the sink or tub, or on the trail during nature hikes. Simply unfold and pop-open the frame and add a small amount of water to activate the scope's magnification properties. The magnified images it produces may appear a bit wavy and fuzzy, but it does do the job.

Construction

Builder's age
9+

Player's age
6+

Materials
- [ ] 6 drinking straws (or 12 of the bendable kind)
- [ ] Clear plastic wrap
- [ ] 14 No. 19 rubber bands (3 $\frac{1}{2}$" x $\frac{1}{16}$")
- [ ] Water

Tools
- [ ] Scissors
- [ ] Jumbo paper clip

Building instructions

Making a paper-clip pull tool

This construction requires bending a jumbo paper clip into a special tool to help thread rubber bands through the drinking straws. Simply unbend and straighten the first two bends of a jumbo paper clip (a regular size paper clip is too short) leaving only the small

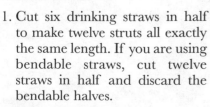

half-loop. Bend the small half-loop completely around to form a complete loop—that also forms a small hook. The paper clip should be completely straight except for the small loop hook. Test the paper-clip pull tool by placing a rubber band on the hook, then feeding the tool through a half-length drinking straw to pull the rubber band through.

Making the octahedron frame

The octahedron frame is made by stringing half-length, drinking-straw struts onto a chain of rubber bands to form triangles. Notice that each time the instructions call for adding rubber bands and struts to the chain, there is always one rubber band for each strut, and at the end of the construction step, there will always be one extra rubber band at the front of the chain without a strut.

1. Cut six drinking straws in half to make twelve struts all exactly the same length. If you are using bendable straws, cut twelve straws in half and discard the bendable halves.

2. Make a chain of four rubber bands by looping one to the next. In this construction, No. 19

rubber bands are the perfect size for half-length drinking straws (which are about a half-inch longer than the rubber bands).

3. Use the paper-clip pull tool to thread the rubber band chain through three straw struts, then form a triangle by threading the chain through the loop of the first rubber band, which is at location A. There should be one unthreaded rubber band.

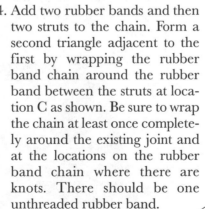

4. Add two rubber bands and then two struts to the chain. Form a second triangle adjacent to the first by wrapping the rubber band chain around the rubber band between the struts at location C as shown. Be sure to wrap the chain at least once completely around the existing joint and at the locations on the rubber band chain where there are knots. There should be one unthreaded rubber band.

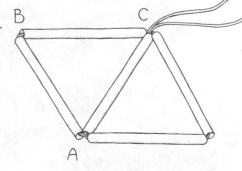

5. Make two more adjacent triangles the same way by adding two rubber bands and two struts at a time. At this point, you should have four adjacent triangles, and there should be one unthreaded rubber band as shown.

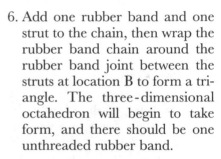

6. Add one rubber band and one strut to the chain, then wrap the rubber band chain around the rubber band joint between the struts at location B to form a triangle. The three-dimensional octahedron will begin to take form, and there should be one unthreaded rubber band.

7. Add one rubber band and one strut to the chain, then wrap the rubber band chain around the rubber band joint between the struts at location D to form a triangle. There should be one unthreaded rubber band.

8. Add one last rubber band and one last strut to the chain, then wrap the rubber band chain around the rubber band joint between the struts at location A to form a triangle and complete the octahedron form. Tie the remaining unthreaded rubber band in a simple knot around the joint.

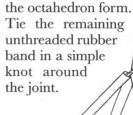

Before completing the pocket scope, you may want to practice folding and unfolding the frame. To collapse the octahedron, push any corner into the opposite corner to form a single pyramid, then fold the pairs of triangles into a single stack. The rubber band loop remaining at one of the corners can be looped around the stack to hold it together. To pop open the frame, just reverse the procedure.

Completing the pocket scope

9. Cut a piece of plastic wrap about one inch larger all around than one of the triangle openings in the frame. Clear food wrap will work fine, but the clear plastic wrap from a dry cleaner's bag will work better because it will stretch more easily.

10. Put the cut piece of plastic loosely over one triangular face, and secure it in place with a single No. 19 rubber band. With your fingers, make a slight depression in the center of the plastic wrap. The frame can still be folded flat and unfolded with the plastic wrap in place.

11. To turn your pocket scope into a magnifying lens, place it on a flat surface and add water. Position the objects you want to view under the pocket scope through the openings in the side of the structure. Raise or lower the objects as needed to get them into focus.

Because the pocket scope will probably spill, it should be used only in water play areas like the bathtub, sink, backyard, beach, or on the porch.

DRINKING STRAWS

The invention of the drinking straw goes back to 1888, when Marvin Stone of Washington, D.C., figured out a way to drink a cold glass of lemonade through a straw without ruining the lemon flavor and without getting a lemonade seed in his mouth.

On hot summer days in Washington, it was quite fashionable to sip a cool drink through a hollow piece of grass straw. This was supposedly done so the drinker would not have to hold the glass and thereby warm it with his or her hands. But any small benefit of a colder drink was offset by the terrible grassy taste the straw gave to the drink. Then Marvin Stone had an idea.

Marvin Stone was a manufacturer of small, short paper tubes used as holders for cigarettes. He figured that the same way he made paper-tube cigarette holders, he could make a long, artificial drinking straw. His first exper-

iment was to wind a long strip of paper into a spiral around a pencil and fasten the edges of the tube with a little glue so the paper would not unravel. His paper-tube artificial drinking straw seemed to work just fine. To produce his invention commercially, Marvin Stone used a wax-coated manila paper so the straw would not get soggy when placed in the drink. He also calculated the best diameter for the tube so a lemon seed would not get sucked up or become lodged in the tube.

Stone patented his invention, and pretty soon people throughout America were using "lemonade straws" for sipping all kinds of cold beverages. The demand for paper straws became so great that Stone had to enlarge his factory several times to hold more and more workers winding paper tubes. By 1906, a steam-powered machine was invented that could automatically wind the paper straws.

Today, it is much easier to manufacture a liquid-proof drinking straw from plastic, although in some places, you will still find people who prefer using a well-made paper drinking straw.

SPACE FRAME TERRARIUM

A terrarium is a miniature greenhouse for growing plants indoors, away from their natural environment. Even if the growing conditions where you live are unfavorable for certain plants, they might grow successfully in the controlled environment of a terrarium. A flourishing terrarium not only provides a close-up view of nature, but it can also be an interesting living decoration in your room.

Three conditions are necessary for maintaining a healthy terrarium—moisture, temperature, and light—and this Space Frame Terrarium is designed to manage all three. An ideal weather-tight enclosure for growing plantings can be made using String and Straw Sticks plus some clear plastic food wrap. Depending on the diameter of the planting container you choose, the enclosure can be a small space frame tetrahedron, a medium-sized, square-base pyramid, or a large-sized pentagonal pyramid. All three enclosures are constructed of equilateral triangles.

Construction

Building system
String and Straw Sticks

Builder's age
7+

Player's age
4+

Materials

- ☐ Waterproof container 10 to 14 inches in diameter with a depth of 1 to 2 inches, such as an old soup bowl, a serving dish, a baking pan, or a terra cotta saucer
- ☐ Gravel or sand
- ☐ Soil
- ☐ Stones
- ☐ Small native plants
- ☐ Water
- ☐ Activated charcoal (optional)
- ☐ 6 to 10 drinking straws, depending on the pyramid design
- ☐ 8 feet of string
- ☐ Clear plastic food wrap
- ☐ Clear mending tape

Tools

- ☐ Garden trowel or tablespoon
- ☐ Scissors

Building instructions

Decide what to plant in the terrarium

What you grow in the terrarium depends mostly on the native plants available in the region where you live. Find a damp, shady spot in a nearby woods or park, and use a small garden trowel or a tablespoon to gently dig up small plants and seedlings to fit in the planting dish of the terrarium. Be sure to dig deep enough to remove the roots, and keep the plants moist by placing them inside a plastic bag until you replant them. Also, dig up enough extra soil to fill the container you plan to use for planting.

Some common plants that grow quite well in a terrarium include ferns, ivy, lichen, moss, wildflowers, grasses, and small seedlings of trees. Of course, if you live in a hot, dry climate, you will be more likely to find and grow small desert plants in a sandy soil.

Prepare the planting dish

Select a planting container that's between 10 and 14 inches in diameter, or the right diameter and depth to fit the pyramid covering you plan to build. Place a quarter inch of gravel in the bottom of the container, then nearly fill the rest of the container with soil taken from the ground where you gathered the terrarium plants. Use a few stones to create a terraced look, complete with miniature rock ledges.

As a precaution against fungi growth in the garden, you could mix a small amount of activated charcoal into the soil. Activated charcoal can be purchased at pet stores.

Carefully transplant each small plant into the container. First, poke a hole in the soil with your finger, insert the plant roots into the hole, and then carefully backfill the soil to fill the hole. Try to arrange the plants so the tallest ones are in the middle and the shorter ones are closer to the perimeter of the container.

When you're finished planting, moisten the soil by sprinkling it with water, but don't make the soil muddy. It will take a few days for the plants to become accustomed to their new environment, so don't be disappointed if the new plantings begin to wilt and droop a little at first.

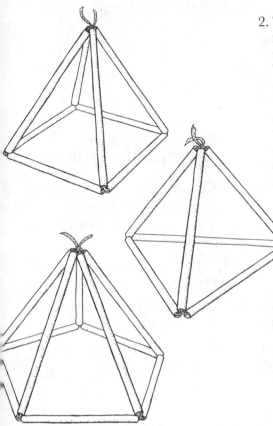

Make the pyramid enclosure

The base of the pyramid enclosure must fit within the sides of the planting container so that it rests directly on the soil. Using full-length straws, see what base shape (and therefore what pyramid form) fits the container best—a triangle (tetrahedron), a square (square-base pyramid), or a pentagon (pentagonal pyramid).

1. Build your chosen pyramid structure using String and Straws Sticks to make combinations of six, eight, or ten equilateral triangles. Begin by threading three straws onto the string and form a rigid triangle by tying a knot. Don't cut off the remaining string. Thread and add two more straws to form a second adjacent triangle, and tie it off.

2. To make a tetrahedron, add one more straw to the two triangles to complete the form as shown. To make a square pyramid enclosure, add three more straws to the two triangles as shown. Be sure to tie off each triangle as you make it. To build a pentagonal enclosure, add five straws to the two triangles in the order shown.

3. Completely cover all sides of the pyramid with clear plastic wrap, except the base that sits on the planting container. Cut pieces of plastic wrap a few inches larger than the section of the frame you are covering, and tape them in place. Try to use the largest pieces of plastic possible without the wrap bunching or having big wrinkles. It is also important that the covering have no holes or gaps for moisture to escape.

4. When completed, just rest the pyramid enclosure directly on top of the garden, and gently gather soil around the outside of the pyramid base to create a seal.

How to care for terrarium plants

Because the Space Frame Terrarium is a closed system, moisture cannot escape and the plants will need to be checked for dryness only occasionally. If the plants or leaves show signs of wilting, you will know that it is time to add a little water.

It is just as important that the environment not be too wet. If big droplets of moisture form inside the plastic covering, remove the pyramid enclosure for a short time to allow fresh air to circulate around the plants. Occasionally airing the plants will also help prevent the formation of fungus.

Maintaining the correct terrarium temperature is also very important. Most terrarium plants grow best at room temperature or warmer. So keep the terrarium in a warm room where the temperature is reasonably constant.

All plants require light energy to survive, but don't place the terrarium in direct sunlight. Filtered light or shade is best for most terrarium plants throughout the year. The perfect location for the terrarium is close to a window with shaded sunlight on the south side of your home.

Here are a few more tips for maintaining a healthy terrarium.

- Remove dead leaves because they usually breed mold.

- Replace any plant that has outgrown its environment.

  - Only add water when the plants are clearly dry.

    - Prune back plants that become too tall.

STICKY Q-STICKS
BUILDING SYSTEM

This elegant strut building system takes advantage of two special features. The cotton swab tip coated with rubber cement makes a flexible tip-to-tip joint that can be positioned at any angle. Also, the joint can be taken apart and repositioned over and over again. Best of all, Sticky Q-Sticks assemble very quickly to build large or small structures.

Even though the swabs are all the same length, the many types of space frame structures you can build can have very interesting shapes. Sticky Q-Sticks are especially well-suited for building many types of polyhedrons, including a dodecahedron, cuboctahedron, and rhombicuboctahedron. These forms are fun just to display, or you might adapt a polyhedron to become a toy or game.

SYSTEM FEATURES

- Cotton-tip swabs are readily available and inexpensive
- Tip-to-tip joinery is flexible to any angle
- Joints are strong yet can be easily pulled apart
- Small and large structures can be built quickly
- Sticks can be reused over and over again

Construction

Builder's age
5+

Materials
☐ Cotton-tip swabs

☐ Rubber cement

☐ Wax paper or drinking straws or pencils

Tools
☐ Hands only

Making the building pieces

Make Sticky Q-Sticks in small batches as you use them. Start with at least twenty-five. Although all cotton-tip swabs are about the same length, your structures might be easier to build if all the swabs you use are the same brand.

1. Begin by making a place for the dipped sticks to dry. Lay out a piece of wax paper or use two parallel drinking straws or pencils.

2. Dip the cotton-tipped ends of a cotton-tip swab into rubber cement while twirling the stick with your fingers. Dunk each end only far enough into the cement to coat the cotton—not the stick.

3. Place the stick on the wax paper or across the straws or pencils to dry. Continue to make more struts the same way.

The Sticky Q-Sticks will be ready for use after drying for about three to five minutes, or whenever the rubber cement is no longer wet. If a cotton tip should ever loose its stickiness, just coat it with more rubber cement.

Put the top back on the rubber cement as soon as you are done to keep the fumes from spreading and the glue from drying up. If the weather is pleasant, you might consider using the cement outdoors.

Building techniques

To build with Sticky Q-Sticks, firmly press the end of one stick to another at any angle you like. Even when attached, the joints are flexible, so the angle will adjust itself to the geometry you are building.

The structures and projects built with Sticky Q-Sticks will be quite rigid and sturdy if you form mostly triangles or use combinations of triangles and squares. And yet, the sticks can be easily pulled apart and the structure completely disassembled and reused to build something else. When pulling the sticks apart, grasp the cotton tips with your fingers to keep the cotton from pulling off the stick.

Sticky Q-Sticks are best for quickly building models

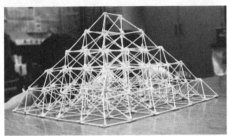

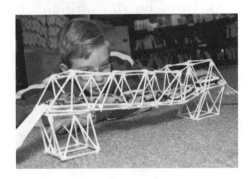

rather than constructing more permanent projects. Experiment to see how large or tall a structure you can make without it collapsing from its own weight. The record to beat is eleven feet high.

During very hot weather, a few rubber cement joints may slip or come apart and cause the structure to sag. If this happens, simply attach them again. When not being used, the sticks should be stored in a sealable plastic bag.

STICKY Q-STICKS
BUILD-IT PROJECTS

STICKY TRIANGLE DOMINOS

BUBBLE FRAMES AND 3-D PLANES

POLYGON PUZZLES AND
POLYHEDRON PLAYTHINGS

STICKY TRIANGLE DOMINOS

If you have ever played a game of dominos, you will quickly catch on to this sticky and colorful variation that uses triangular-shaped game pieces made from Sticky Q-Sticks. Building the game pieces is a project in itself, and playing the solitaire game can be easy or tough depending on the rules you choose.

If you're looking for an even harder game, try playing 3-D Dominos. And, for the ultimate challenge— and maybe the ultimate frustration—you might attempt 3-D Pyramid Dominos. Whichever version of the game you choose to build and play, the result is always an interesting and colorful space frame design.

Construction

Building system
Sticky Q-Sticks, slightly modified so that the cotton swab tips are first colored before the rubber cement is applied.

Builder's age
7+

Player's age
5+

Materials
☐ Cotton-tip swabs, box of 100

☐ Rubber cement

☐ Wax paper

☐ Coloring in four colors. Colored felt-tip markers are easy to use for coloring the cotton ends of cotton-tip swabs, but watercolors and food coloring produce more vibrant game pieces. (A package of food coloring usually includes four colors: red, blue, yellow, and green.)

Tools
☐ Hands only

Building instructions
Making the triangle-domino game pieces takes a little planning. Each triangle is made of three Sticky Q-Stick rods, and each of the three corners of a triangle game piece can be any color, but the two tips that make up each corner must be the same color. Here is one mass-production method you might try for making an entire set of Sticky Triangle Domino game pieces.

Protect the work surface with wax paper or several layers of newspaper. Using food coloring, markers, watercolors, and rubber cement can get messy. And plan ahead. Felt-tip markers using permanent ink will usually dry in a few minutes, but watercolors, food coloring, and markers with washable inks can take a very long time to dry, and you might not be able to continue the project the same day you start.

Place three plain swabs in the shape of a triangle with ends touching. Decide which of the four colors you want one corner to be, then dye or paint the pair of cotton tips at that corner with the same color. Pick a color (the same or a different color) for another corner of the same triangle, and paint the pair of cotton tips at that corner. Then pick a color for the third corner of the triangle, and paint that pair of cotton tips.

Leave the three swabs in their triangle position while the color is drying, and keep on making more triangles, using any combinations of the four colors in a variety of three-color corners. Be sure to make some triangles with two corners or all three corners the same color. Using all four colors, there are eighteen possible triangle color patterns. Younger builders can start with just three colors, making ten possible triangle color patterns, which also makes the game easier to play.

When the colored tips of the game pieces have dried, you can begin the rubber cement dipping process. Be sure to keep each set of three rods in their triangle positions (but with their tips not touching) so the rod positions and color matches don't get mixed up while the glue is drying. When the rubber cement has dried, you can begin putting the rods together to make the triangle-domino game pieces.

Rules of the game
To play a simple game of Sticky Triangle Dominos, you will need about sixteen triangles (forty-eight Sticky Q-Sticks). With more triangles, you can play competitive games, and if you're really looking

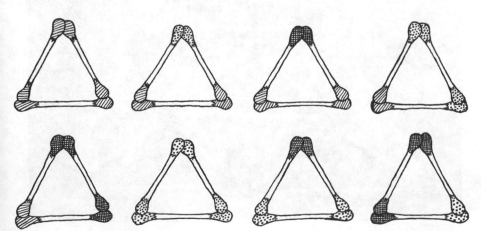

for a challenge, try playing the game using three-dimensional tetrahedron (pyramid-shaped) dominos.

Solitaire Triangle Dominos

Arrange the dominos in any flat pattern, side connected to side, adding one triangle piece at a time. However, you must follow one simple rule: The two color tips on the side of each triangle domino must match the two colors of the side of the triangle it is connected to.

The object of the game is to see how many dominos in your set you can connect so that all the connected colors match. The best play, of course, is to use all the domino triangles so none are left.

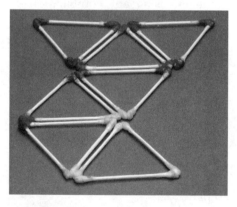

For another version of the game, change the rule so that the connecting colors between domino triangles must be different. Do you think this makes the game easier or more difficult?

Bigger triangles

Using the regular rule that connected colors must match, you can connect the triangle dominos either side by side (edge to edge) or only tip to tip. Four triangle dominos side by side form the shape of one larger triangle. Add five more matching dominos to make an even larger triangle. With enough matching pieces, you could continue to try to make the next largest triangle.

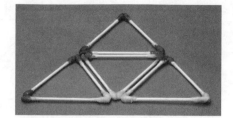

Instead of connecting game triangles side by side, you can form larger triangles faster and easier with fewer pieces by connecting the triangles only tip to tip.

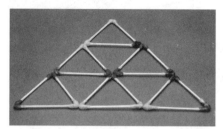

When there are still game pieces remaining but none match your game construction, simply disconnect and reconnect the struts of the remaining pieces to make the correct matching pieces you need.

3-D Dominos

This variation of Solitaire Triangle Dominos lets you connect and build the dominos tip to tip in all directions, including up. Matching the colors of all connecting dominos in a 3-D form can be really tough, so you might

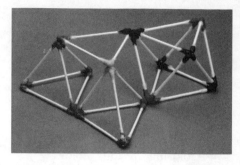

need to reconstruct some of the game pieces for correct color matchups, or use the reverse rule that no connecting colors can match.

3-D Pyramid Dominos

This is as tough as it gets. Instead of making flat triangular dominos, use six Sticky Q-Sticks to make each game piece in the shape of a tetrahedron, a pyramid with a triangular base, with one common color at each of its four corners. Make at least ten tetrahedron game pieces and then connect them tip to tip to build a larger tetrahedron, matching color to same color at all common connection points. Remember that you may be able to reassemble the struts of any remaining tetrahedrons to create the pieces and color matchups you need. How many more perfectly fitting tetrahedron game pieces would it take to make an even larger pyramid?

BUBBLE FRAMES AND 3-D PLANES

Instead of blowing bubbles into the air, dip these bubble frames into soapy water to see some pretty amazing flat-sided bubbles. The transparent prisms, cubes, and other soap-film forms created within the Bubble Frames are an interesting phenomenon that uses soap-film planes to build unique flat-sided figures.

Each combination of planes and forms connects all edges of the dipping frame to all its other edges, always using the least amount of surface area possible. And the Bubble Frame creates the forms automatically, always perfectly arranging the film planes into the most economical pattern possible. You can even blow traditional bubbles if you like before dipping the frame in the soap solution again to see if you get the same result each time.

It is also interesting to note that the film of soap that makes up the planes is one of the thinnest things that can be seen without a microscope—it's actually about five thousand times thinner than a hair from your head!

Construction

Building system
Sticky Q-Sticks

Builder's age
7+

Player's age
4+

Materials

- ☐ Cotton-tip swabs
- ☐ Rubber cement
- ☐ Glue (any fast-drying type)
- ☐ Wax paper, drinking straws or pencils
- ☐ Liquid dishwashing soap
- ☐ Glycerin (optional, but makes much better bubbles; safe and available at drug stores)
- ☐ Water

Tools

- ☐ Mixing bowl, pot, or other container deep enough to completely submerge the tallest Bubble Frame
- ☐ Mixing spoon

Building instructions

Making the Bubble Frames

These are the simple geometric solids you can make using rods that are all the same length. Because the frames will need handles for dipping, each construction requires one more Sticky Q-Stick rod than it takes to build just the frame.

Connect the Sticky Q-Stick rods to form an outline of each polyhedron according to the illustrations. After building a frame, connect one more rod to any corner to be used as a handle for dipping the frame into the bubble solution. Because the Q-Stick handle is attached at only one end, it could easily pull off, so use any fast-drying glue to more securely attach it.

Form	Number of rods
Cube	13
Tetrahedron	7
Octahedron	13
Triangular Prism	10
Square Base Pyramid	9

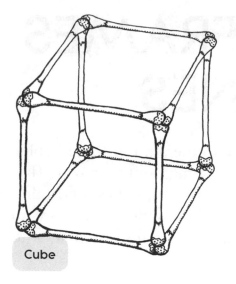

Cube

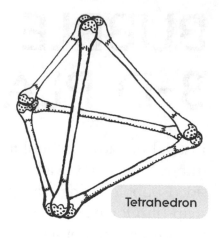

Tetrahedron

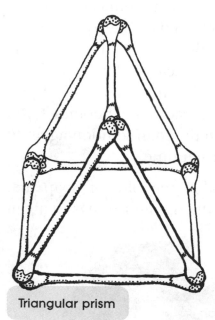

Triangular prism

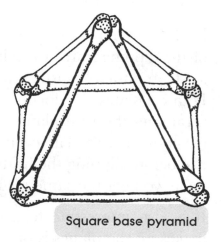

Square base pyramid

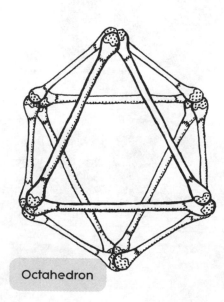

Octahedron

Making the soap bubble solution

There is a basic formula for making a good soap bubble solution that includes liquid dishwashing soap, water, and glycerin. Soapy water alone will make pretty good bubbles, but a little bit of glycerin added to the mixture makes the bubbles last longer.

Start with this recipe, and mix the solution gently so you do not make a lot of suds. Use a container that's deep enough to completely submerge the tallest hanging Bubble Frame (the cube), but not so large to require making a double batch of soap bubble solution.

1 quart (32 ounces) water

10 ounces dishwashing soap

4 tablespoons glycerin

You might try experimenting with different brands of dishwashing soap (Joy and Ivory work particularly well) and different proportions of water to soap to glycerin.

Doing the dipping

Dip any one of the geometric-form frames completely into the bubble solution, holding the frame by its handle, then slowly remove the frame and you will immediately see the three-dimensional geometric forms within your Bubble Frame. Keep dipping the frames to get slightly different pattern variations. Sometimes big and small bubbles will become part of the film plane structure.

After some use, the cotton-tipped corners of the Bubble Frames can become waterlogged and the dipping handle may break off. You can also use your fingers as the handle by pinching a corner of a Bubble Frame for dipping, but it does get a bit messy.

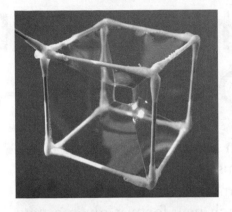
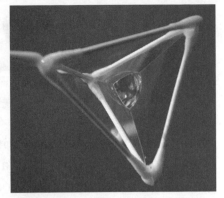

More information for the curious

In addition to always producing bubbles with flat surfaces, the film planes created within the Bubble Frames demonstrate several other interesting qualities. If you are scientifically minded, see if you can observe these phenomena.

- There can never be more than three film surfaces meeting at an edge.

- There can never be more than four edges meeting at a point.

- There can never be more than six film surfaces meeting at a point.

- All the film surfaces and edges can meet only at equal angles.

Sometimes a Bubble Frame will momentarily create a film pattern that breaks the rules, but the unstable forms will quickly slide over one another, changing positions until they do conform and become stable. It's amazing!

POLYGON PUZZLES AND POLYHEDRON PLAYTHINGS

Since ancient times, polygon forms (called polyhedrons) have fascinated mathematicians as well as kids. Some of the greatest achievements in geometry have been the creation of new polyhedral forms. Each new form is given a new descriptive name that is usually quite complicated. For example, have you ever heard of or seen a small rhombicuboctahedron or a great rhombicuboctahedron?

Polygon frames can be constructed using most any space frame construction system. Many polygons require struts of two or more different lengths, while some can be constructed of struts that are all the same length like Sticky Q-Sticks.

The completed polyhedron Q-Stick form can be used as a decorative display piece or as part of another project. Many of the ball-shaped polyhedrons can be rolled or even bounced. To see the solid form of a polyhedron, cover the frame with facets of paper, aluminum foil, or clear plastic wrap. You can even attach several polygons together to make super-sized constructions.

Construction

Building system
Sticky Q-Sticks

Builder's age
5+

Player's age
5+

Materials

- ☐ Cotton-tip swabs
- ☐ Rubber cement
- ☐ Wax paper
- ☐ Aluminum foil, plastic food wrap, or stiff paper (optional)

Tools

- ☐ Hands only

Building instructions

The simplest polyhedrons to make are those constructed with all equilateral triangles, like a tetrahedron or an octahedron. After a little practice, you might try something a bit more complicated, but watch out. The more complicated the polyhedron, the more the construction design becomes a puzzle you have to figure out. Even if you're not the mathematical type, you might try to invent (and name) your own unique form.

The number of Sticky Q-Sticks required depends on the polygon you build. Both a three-dimensional drawing and a flat construction plan are provided for each polygon to help you figure out the pattern. And remember, all of these polyhedrons can be constructed using struts that are all the same length.

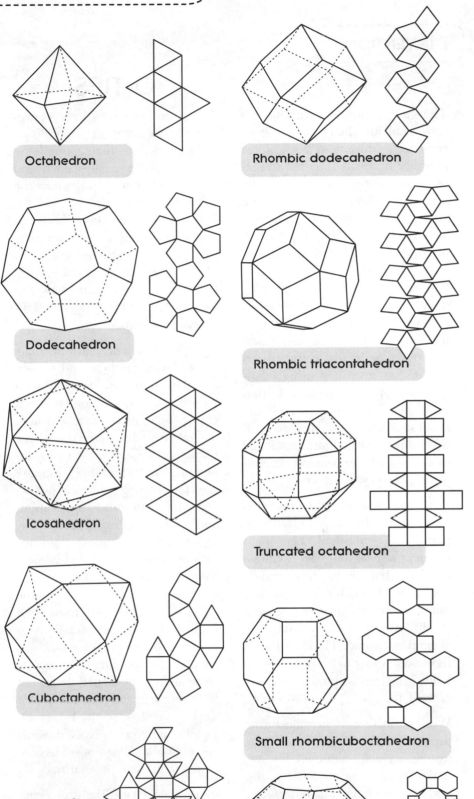

Octahedron

Rhombic dodecahedron

Dodecahedron

Rhombic triacontahedron

Icosahedron

Truncated octahedron

Cuboctahedron

Small rhombicuboctahedron

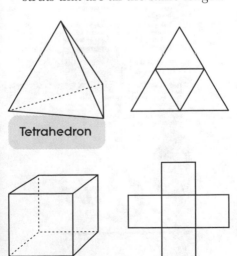

Tetrahedron

Cube

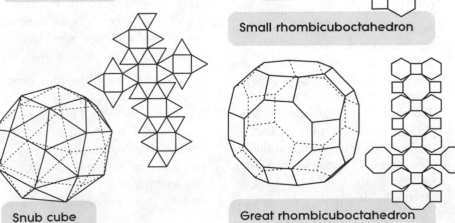

Snub cube

Great rhombicuboctahedron

INVENTION

Q-TIPS

The short, little sticks with a small cotton ball attached to one or both ends are an invention born out of practical necessity. The inspiration occurred more than eighty years ago when Leo Gerstenzang, a young immigrant businessman, watched his wife apply a small wad of cotton to the end of a toothpick and use it to clean the ears of their baby daughter. Gerstenzang immediately had an idea. Instead of having to take the time to make up the swabs, what if mothers could just purchase ready-to-use cotton swabs? And instead of using a dangerously pointed toothpick that could poke or splinter, what if the small stick had blunt ends? Now all he had to do was figure out a way to easily and inexpensively manufacture the new product.

Within a few months, the Leo Gerstenzang Infant Novelty Company was established. Leo spent the next several years developing a machine that would automatically take a blunt-end birch wood stick (birch doesn't splinter) and wrap a small ball of cotton uniformly around each end. He also had to figure out a way to keep the cotton balls from easily pulling off the ends of the stick.

While perfecting the manufacturing process, Gerstenzang decided he needed a catchy name for his new and safer cotton-tipped ear swabs, and his first choice was Baby Gays. He soon changed that name to Q-Tips Baby Gays, adding the letter "Q" to stand for quality. But the product quickly became familiar to most people by the shortened name, Q-Tips, so the Baby Gays part was eventually dropped.

Q-Tip cotton swabs were conveniently packaged in a sterilized, sliding-tray box that allowed the package to be easily opened and closed with one hand (while the other hand was used to hold the baby), and the swabs to be taken out one at a time. And because the manufacturing and packaging of Q-Tips was accomplished entirely by machine, Gerstenzang began to use the advertising slogan "Untouched by human hands."

Q-Tips were not only an immediate success with mothers and babies, but they were also popular with handymen and homemakers, craftspeople, mechanics, and anyone else who discovered one of the hundreds of uses for the handy little swabs. In fact, more Q-Tips are used for cleaning in crevices, applying glue, and other applications (including, of course, making Sticky Q-Stick constructions) than for their original purpose of cleaning a baby's ears. Other uses for the swabs became so prevalent that at one point, Gerstenzang introduced a swab with bigger cotton balls on a longer stick. The giant-size swab was intended for cleaning large surface areas and oddly shaped items, but most people already had acceptable ways to do that, so the bigger Q-Tip was not very successful, while the original smaller-size swabs continued to grow in popularity.

By the late 1950s, the prosperous Gerstenzang Company had become known simply as Q-Tips, Inc., and it continued to expand its production capacity by purchasing a company in England that manufactured paper sticks for the candy and ice pop industries. The idea

was not to go into the candy business, but rather to offer the Q-Tip with a softer, safer, and less expensive paper stick. All the machinery was shipped to the United States, where the Q-Tip company began manufacturing and offering their swabs with a choice of either paper or wooden sticks. Eventually, only the paper-stick Q-Tip survived.

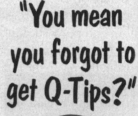

"You mean you forgot to get Q-Tips?"

You buy peace of mind when you buy 'Q-Tips' swabs . . . you know your baby couldn't have safer, surer, more loving care.

Can't irritate—superfine cotton at both ends; never leaves lint. Swabs can't slip or come off.

Hygienically clean. Sterilized right in the package by the best hospital method.

Ask your doctor. It's true: More doctors and nurses recommend and use 'Q-Tips' than any other prepared swab!

Do what the film stars do

Hollywood's loveliest actresses apply their make-up with 'Q-Tips' . . . it blends on beautifully, easier too. Try these handy swabs for all your grooming jobs—to apply bleaches, oils, lotions, to remove smudges or nail polish the neat way.

The original cotton swab—in the famous blue box.

Q-TIPS

Q-TIPS®... Made by Q-Tips Inc., Long Island City, N.Y.

108

PUNCH AND POKE STICKS
BUILDING SYSTEM

What's so neat about this construction system is that it requires only one material—drinking straws—for both the rods and the connectors. No separate fasteners are used. Using ordinary, regular-size drinking straws that are $1/4$-inch in diameter, plus a standard-size paper hole punch that makes a $1/4$-inch diameter hole, you can insert one straw through another straw to make a secure connection. And even though the connections are all at right angles, the straws can be cut to any length and inserted at any position around another straw. You will be amazed at the variety of large-scale and sturdy space frame structures that can be created.

Because plastic drinking straws are waterproof, space frame constructions made from them, like bird feeder stations or outdoor toys and models, will weather fine in rain or snow. However, like many other plastics, drinking straws will eventually weaken, crack, and break if left too long in direct sunlight.

SYSTEM FEATURES

- Straws are the only material
- Straws are available in colors
- Straws are easily cut to lengths
- Constructions are rigid
- Makes waterproof structures
- Good for large-scale models
- Modular parts can be reused
- Easy to make repairs

Construction

Builder's age
8+

Materials
☐ Drinking straws, ¼" diameter (Nonbendable straws work best.)

Tools
☐ Paper hole punch, ¼" diameter

☐ Scissors

Building techniques

Attaching straws at right angles

A Punch and Poke Sticks straw can be connected to another straw in only two ways: at a right angle or end to end. For right angle connections, punch a hole in one straw and push another straw through the hole. It may take a little practice to punch holes in the exact center of the straw so the sides stay intact.

1. First, select the location along the length of a straw where you want to punch a hole, and flatten the straw between your fingers just enough that the flattened straw will

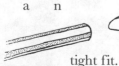

easily slide into the hole punch.

2. Before punching the hole, look, or sight, down the length of the straw, and carefully align the straw and the punch so the hole will be in the middle of the flattened area. Try to not punch too close to an edge or punch through the edge of the flattened straw.

Sighting down the length of the straw is also helpful when punching two or more holes to make the inserted straws parallel. If the holes are

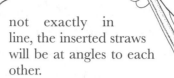

not exactly in line, the inserted straws will be at angles to each other.

To avoid getting a straw caught or stuck when inserting it into a hole in another straw, it helps to spin the straw as you push it through.

Attaching straws end to end
There are three good methods for attaching straws end to end.

3. You can

f i r s t insert, push, and twist the pointed end of a pencil or ballpoint pen into the end of one straw to slightly enlarge the opening, then another straw can be securely pushed in a b o u t

an inch for a tight fit.

4. Another method is to fold the tip of one straw so it will start to fit into the end of another. Then push the two straws together so they overlap about a n

inch for a tight fit.

5. The third way to connect straws end to end is to use a pair of

scissors to cut the end of a straw on the diagonal, then put that pointed end into the end opening of another straw.

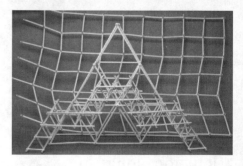

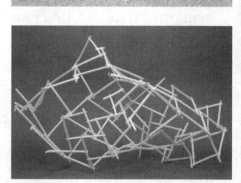

PUNCH AND POKE STICKS BUILD-IT PROJECTS

MARBLE COASTER TRACKS AND TRESTLES

BIRD FEEDER SPACE STATION PLATFORM

CLASSIC KITES

WIND WHIRLIES

MARBLE COASTER TRACKS AND TRESTLES

For many kids, a roller coaster is a thrill magnet they can't get enough of, while others would prefer to stay grounded and just watch. This marble coaster is a model roller coaster that you get to design, build, test, change, and perfect. And, for those who would rather just observe the action, there is much to learn about the concepts of gravity, friction, structure, turns, and trajectory.

A marble coaster consists of a paper-tube track that starts from some high place in the room and follows a twisting and dropping course all the way down to the floor. At strategic points along the course, the track is supported by Punch and Poke Stick trestles that resemble the wooden support structures once used for roller coasters. The track system is designed for marbles, but you can also try using similar-size ball bearings or beads. You might even be able to run a miniature vehicle down the track if it is steep enough and there are no severe turns.

Construction

Building system
Punch and Poke Sticks

Builder's age
9+

Player's age
5+

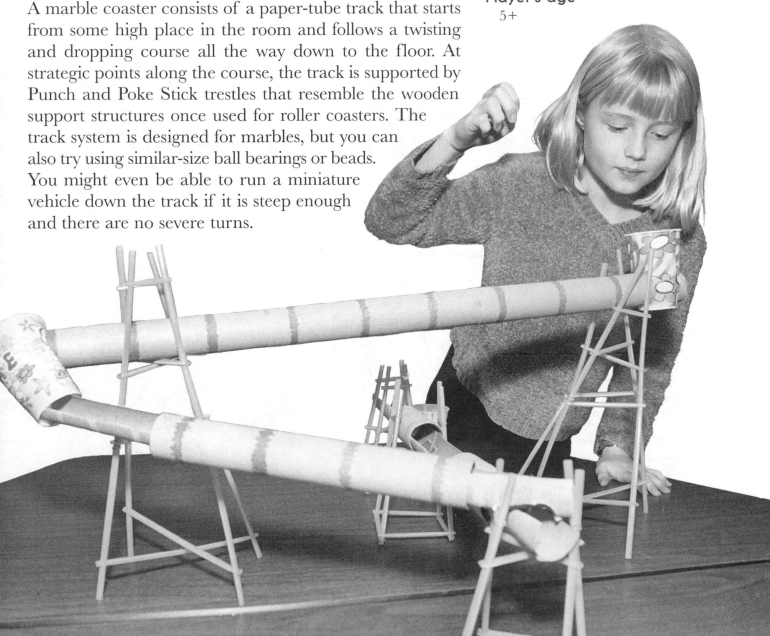

Materials

☐ Drinking straws, ¼″ diameter

☐ Paper tubes (Collect tubes from toilet paper rolls, paper towels, and food wraps, plus long tubes the same diameter as toilet paper tubes from gift-wrapping paper.)

☐ Masking tape

☐ Marbles or marble-sized bearings and balls

Tools

☐ Paper hole punch, ¼″ diameter

☐ Scissors (Tubes can also be cut with a taped-handle hacksaw blade, a coping saw, or a serrated bread knife.)

Building instructions

Making trestles

Before building the trestles, review the instructions for working with Punch and Poke Sticks.

Sections of the marble coaster track are supported by trestles that can be constructed in graduated heights. The standard trestle design has the ability to make minor adjustments for height, plus can be used with extension legs that more than double the height.

1. The standard trestle uses full-length straws (typically 7 ½-inches long) cut to specific lengths and hole punched as shown in the plan. Cut and punch the straws, and make sure that whenever two holes are punched in a straw, the holes are in alignment with each other.

   Full-length straws with no holes

   4 ⅋ ⊏━━━━━━━━━━━━⊐

   Half-length straws with a hole at each end

   6 ⅋ ⊏◎━━━━◎⊐

   Quarter-length straws with a hole at each end

   2 ⅋ ⊏◎━━◎⊐

2. Assemble the twelve straw sections into a standard trestle by following the three steps shown.

   A. Form four of the half-length straws into a square, overlapping the holes at each corner, and insert the four full-length straws into the corner intersections.

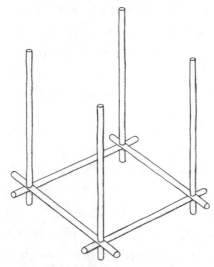

   B. Use the two remaining half-length straws to form a cross brace near the middle of the long straws. This should cause the full-length vertical straws to lean toward the center.

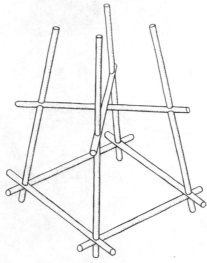

   C. Install the two quarter-length straws on top of opposite pairs of the full-length straws to form a cradle support for the track.

   Notice that as you move the cross bracing down the vertical straws, the cradle narrows. You

can also adjust the cradle straws up or down to hold the track snugly or make minor changes to the height of the track.

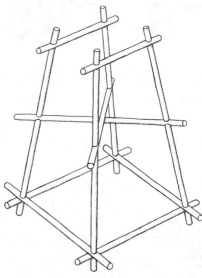

3. To extend the legs of the standard trestle and increase its height, insert an unpunched straw into each leg of a standard trestle. Then punch a hole in each end of two full-length straws as shown, and use them to form a cross brace near the base.

   4 ⅋ ⊏━━━━━━━━━━━⊐

   2 ⅋ ⊏◎━━━━━━━◎⊐

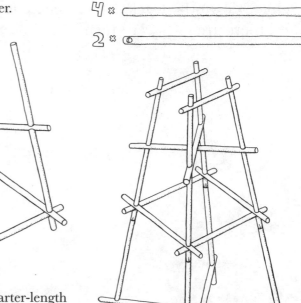

Making tracks and track connectors

The marble coaster course is constructed by joining sections of straight track with straight or angled connectors. Both the track sections and the connectors are made from paper tubes, like the tubes from toilet paper rolls, kitchen towels, and food wrap, so the first task is to gather a large quantity of tubes. The tubes can be any length, but all should be about the same diameter. The more tubes you collect, the more exciting the coaster course will be.

Thin paperboard tubes can be cut to length, cut lengthwise, or notched using sharp scissors. Some builders may want to make neater and more accurate cuts using a serrated bread knife or a fine-tooth saw.

Straight tracks are made by cutting paper tubes in half the long way so that each tube becomes two half-round sections of track. Scissors should be sufficient to cut most tubes lengthwise. If you can, vary the length of the track sections from several inches to several feet long by using everything from short toilet paper tubes to longer gift-wrap tubes.

Straight connectors are simply lengths of straight tubes. These connectors do not have to be long (although they can be), and toilet paper tubes, or similar-size sections cut from longer tubes, work fine.

Angle connectors are made by cutting out an angled section from the center of a straight connector and folding the tube to form a corner, then using a piece of masking tape over the joint of the folded tube to hold it in place. The angle of the section removed will determine the angle of the folded connector. So a bigger section removed will result in a sharper corner at the connection point. Make lots of angle connectors, and vary the angle from a slight bend to a sharp right angle.

To assemble the track sections using connectors, push a section of track into a connector only as far as it needs to go to hold firmly. If the fit seems too loose, use a piece of tape to hold the track and connector together.

Setting up the coaster course

Assembling a marble coaster course usually takes more than one pair of hands, so ask someone to help.

Build several standard and extended trestles, and have a good collection of tracks and connectors ready to assemble. You can build additional tracks and trestles as you need them.

Think about how you would like to set up the marble coaster course. The course could go around and around like the shape of a Christmas tree spiral, or descend back and forth like the ramps in a tall parking garage, or take twists and turns anyway you like until it reaches the bottom—and the end of the ride.

Look around for books, boxes, chairs, wastepaper baskets, and other objects to prop up the trestles. The track must be supported anywhere it sags, which is usually at the connectors. If the tallest trestle is still too short for a location where it's needed, build up a base of props to make the trestle taller.

Start the course by placing the first trestle at a conveniently high location, such as the top of a tall dresser, and then add trestles to support the track as it descends the course you are creating. Fewer trestles will be needed if you use masking tape to secure the track sections to the connectors.

For the marble to roll smoothly down the course, all tracks and connectors must slant downward. Depending on the speed at which you want the marble to travel, the slope can vary from almost horizontal, to a gentle downward slant, to a nearly vertical drop. You might decide to make a steep and fast course that's also long and complex with lots of turns to make the ride last a long time. Or you could make the slope just steep enough so the slow-moving marble doesn't get stuck in sharp-turn connectors. You can also experiment with the angle of the tracks and connectors to build jumps, drops, and spins.

Test the course each time you add a section. Regular-size marbles require a rather steep and fast drop to avoid getting caught inside a connector. A larger shooter-type marble or a large, round bead will run smoothly on a more gently sloped track. However, the added weight of a large marble can cause it to gain too much momentum and roll off the track unless the track is banked, or angled, correctly. The idea is to build then test and experiment with each added section until the marble rolls smoothly.

During the process of making and testing the raceway, most construction issues can probably be solved best through trial and error. For example, you will most likely discover the

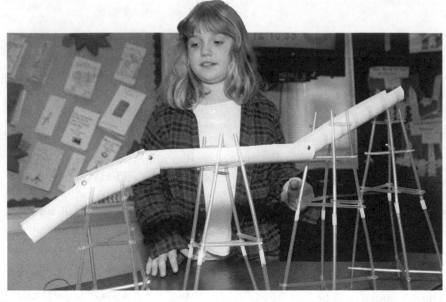

answers to these questions as you build and test the course.

- How can you control the speed of descent?

- How much should you bank a turn to keep the marble on track?

- Should you forcefully push the marble down the starting track or just gently release it?

For a grand finish, you can run the last chute section into a wide-mouth, empty glass jar. This will produce a ringing sound at the end of the coaster ride and prevent the marbles from rolling away on the floor.

After play, the tracks and trestles can quickly be taken down and the parts disassembled and stored to be used again. However, some builders will want to continue adding sections to the track and trestle course over several days or even longer.

And more thrills!

If you want to build a super coaster, try experimenting with the tracks and trestles by adding a parallel track for racing, a switch track to divert the marble to an alternate track, and a cross-over intersection between two courses. Give yourself challenges and goals. For example, can you build a coaster course from one side of the room to the other? What about a course that goes around the perimeter of the room so that the marble will travel the entire distance nonstop?

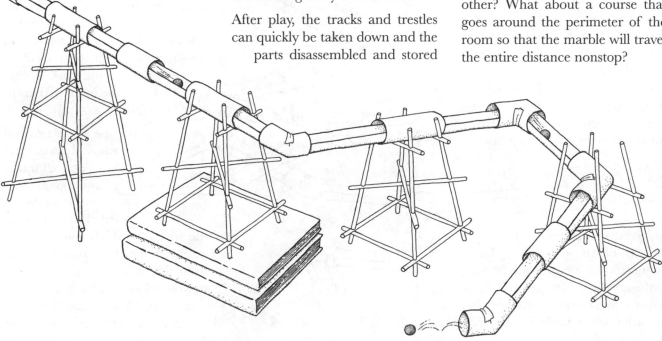

ROLLER COASTERS

When the gates to the first roller coaster opened in 1884, the line to get onboard literally stretched for miles. To the eager crowd waiting, this new contraption promised thrills and excitement far beyond anything they had ever seen. The new ride was built at New York's Coney Island Amusement Park by a man named LaMarcus Adna Thompson, and he called it the "Gravity Pleasure Railway."

Thompson had always wanted to build something others would consider the ultimate amusement ride, and he knew that the sensation of speed would draw a big crowd. The idea of sliding down an incline while in a sitting position was not new. For over a few hundred years, many public amusement parks in Russia had icy slopes that people rode down on toboggans. And after seeing one of those ice slides, a Frenchman was inspired to build his version of the amusement. But instead of an icy slope (the climate in Paris, France, was too warm), he built a long sloping conveyor belt that looped around rollers. Riders would sit on their toboggans as they rode the conveyor belt down "Russian Mountain."

Thompson's new amusement ride was different in many ways, and especially faster than an icy slope or a chunky conveyor belt. The Gravity Railway had tracks and wheeled cars, like a small train. Riders would climb up a tower to get into the cars, and powered by gravity alone, they rolled down a series of small hills to the end of the tracks. The passengers would then get out of the cars, climb another tower, and ride a second car on a second set of tracks back to the starting point. At each end, the riders waited at the top of the towers as a crew of strong men hauled the cars up the hills to the loading platforms.

The Gravity Railway was the success Thompson had hoped for, and he quickly became rich. He also worried that someone else would build a bigger or faster amusement ride, and before the 1884 season was even over, another coaster was built at Coney Island, and this one had a more exciting circular layout. It wasn't long before the crowds rushed to the new circular ride and Thompson's Gravity Railway was abandoned.

To handle the crowds of riders, a second circular ride was built the following year and called the "Coney Island Coaster." It used a motor-driven chain to haul cars up the initial incline and became the new "ultimate" amusement ride. But Thompson didn't give up trying to invent an even better coaster, and two years later, he introduced his new amusement ride, the "Scenic Railway."

This innovative version of a coaster ride had dark tunnels filled with special effects meant to scare riders, then moments later the ride entered another tunnel filled with electric lights that lit paintings on the walls. The electric lights were a thrilling surprise for the riders, most of whom still used candles at home. Thompson wasn't sure the riders would like the scary part of the coaster ride as he waited nervously for the first passengers to board. From the shrieks of terror to the relief of laughter that Thompson heard, he could tell they loved it.

In addition to its new entertaining surprises, the Scenic Railway also introduced new coaster technology. The track was laid out in a large oval supported by wooden trestles, and in addition to a motor-driven lift chain to haul the cars up the initial incline, there were special motorized cables with hooks that grabbed the cars at strategic points along the track to give them a fresh burst of speed. It was the second successful "ultimate" design for Thompson, and as a result, he was commissioned to build Scenic Railways all over the United States.

The inspirations that first challenged Thompson to build a better thrill ride are still the principles used today for building high-tech roller coaster rides. The illusions of speed, excitement, and danger attract riders. The one thing that has not changed, unfortunately, are the long lines of people waiting to get onboard.

BIRD FEEDER SPACE STATION PLATFORM

Although you don't really keep them, wild birds can make interesting pets. The same birds will come back to your feeder year after year if they know where food will always be available, giving you the responsibility of caring for a living thing.

Punch and Poke Sticks are the perfect material for building an outdoor bird-feeding platform. This design uses one or more space frame platforms to build a variety of feeder shapes. The sturdy structure will withstand the weather nicely, and the diameter of the straws is just right for perching birds. You can also adapt the station to fit an outdoor windowsill, deck rail, or tree branch. The Bird Feeder Space Station Platform can also be hung outdoors from a variety of places. Just be sure to keep it away from any place that cats and squirrels might reach.

Construction

Building system
Punch and Poke Sticks

Builder's age
8+

Player's age
Any age

Materials

- ☐ 15 drinking straws for each platform, ¼″ diameter. Extra straws may be needed for connecting multiple platforms
- ☐ Several 5-ounce (or smaller) disposable drinking cups
- ☐ String, for securing to surface or hanging (optional)
- ☐ Bird seed

Tools

- ☐ Paper hole punch, ¼″ diameter

Building instructions

Depending on where you intend to place it, a Bird Feeder Space Station Platform can consist of one or more basic platform modules.

1. The space frame for the feeder station platform module requires three types of straw struts—full-length straws with no holes (A), full-length straws with four evenly spaced holes (B), and one-third length straws with a punched hole at each end (C). Make seven A struts, four B struts, and twelve C struts as shown in the illustrations.

A ⬯

B ⬯

C ⬯

2. Assemble four A struts through two B struts to form a grid.

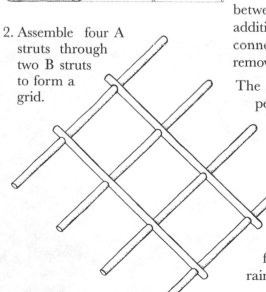

3. Following the connections shown in the illustration, assemble all twelve C struts to the ends of the A struts and then attach the B struts over the A struts to complete the top grid.

4. Use the remaining three A struts to connect the bottom opposite pairs of C struts. Adjust all struts so the nine squares on the top of the grid are all about the same size. The basic platform structure is complete

Combine two or more space frame modules as shown to build the best size for the location you have chosen. Some connections between modules require additional struts, and some connections may require removing a few struts.

The seed cups should fit perfectly into the structure of the platforms. If the cups are too large to fit the grid squares, remove one of the B struts to make a grid of six rectangles. Use as many or as few seed cups as you like. If the feeder will be exposed to the rain, use a pencil to poke a small hole through the bottom of each cup for water drainage.

If you are placing the feeder station on a flat surface, tie it down with string or use a small rock for weight so it won't blow away. If you are hanging the feeder station, make a string harness that keeps the space frame from spinning.

Feeding instructions

Once you do start feeding the birds, you have an obligation to keep them supplied with food, especially during the winter months, because some birds will learn to rely on your feeder as their only source of food.

Different kinds of birds like different types of food, and some are attracted to hanging feeders, while others like to eat off the ground. So not all local species will feed at your space station. One of the best

foods to attract the largest variety of birds is sunflower seeds—particularly the "black oil" kind. If you want to attract woodpeckers, tie a piece of suet to the feeder. Put the feeder in a place that will let you watch the birds and also make it easy to refill. It might take a few days for the birds to find your feeder, but once they do, they will keep coming back.

CLASSIC KITES
DIAMOND, BOX, AND SLED

The earliest kites made strictly for fun did not appear until a few hundred years ago. The first toy kites were diamond-shaped structures that flew pretty well but required a lot of attention to keep them up in the air. A little over one hundred years ago, the box kite was invented, and it was much more stable and easy for kids to fly, as long as there was enough wind. In more recent years, air-foil kites called sleds have made successful kite flying almost guaranteed, even in the lightest breezes.

These miniature Punch and Poke Stick versions of the three most popular classic kites won't fly as well as bigger ones made from wood struts and nylon fabric, and they are certainly not as durable. But building them is quick and easy, they can be flown in a fairly small area, and they offer plenty of opportunities to experiment.

Construction

Building system
Punch and Poke Sticks

Builder's age
8+

Player's age
6+

Materials

- ☐ Plastic drinking straws, ¼″ diameter
- ☐ Thin plastic sheeting, cut from plastic trash bags, dry cleaner bags, shopping bags, or grocery bags
- ☐ Kite string or lightweight monofilament fishing line
- ☐ Transparent mending tape

Tools

- ☐ Paper hole punch, ¼″ diameter
- ☐ Scissors
- ☐ Ruler
- ☐ Felt-tip marker, crayon, or ballpoint pen that will write on the plastic sheeting you use

Building instructions

Making the kite frame

Decide which kite you want to build, and follow the appropriate illustrated plan below to assemble the kite-frame struts. All kite frames use full-length straws. Use the plan to figure out where to punch holes in the straws and how to attach the straw struts together.

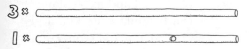

Diamond kite

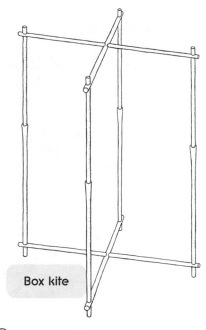

Box kite

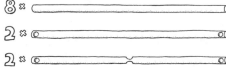

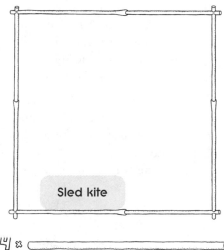

Sled kite

Double-length straw struts are made by placing the crimped end of one straw inside the fully open end of another straw. Connected straws should overlap at least one inch. For more detailed information on hole punching and building techniques, refer to the instructions for the Punch and Poke Sticks Building System.

Covering the kite

The best kite coverings are both strong and lightweight. The thin plastic materials that most trash bags, shopping bags, and grocery bags are made from are strong and lightweight, as well as easy to cut, handle, and tape. Plastic-film food wraps also make quick kite-frame coverings without even needing to be taped, but the clingy plastic film can be very difficult to handle.

Using material from large plastic trash bags, cut the plastic kite covering to the correct pattern, being sure to allow some extra room for taping the covering over the frame. When taping, use several short one- or two-inch lengths of tape rather than one long piece. It makes the taping job much easier.

To make the covering pattern for the Diamond Kite, use the kite frame as a guide, and cut the plastic sheeting about one-quarter inch bigger than the diamond shape on each side.

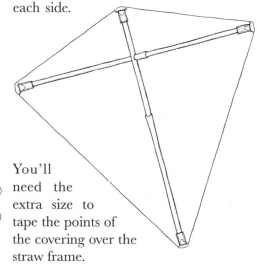

You'll need the extra size to tape the points of the covering over the straw frame.

For the Box Kite coverings, cut out two identical rectangular pieces of plastic sheeting. The height should equal one-third of the height of the kite frame, and the length should be a little longer than the perimeter around the kite frame. You'll need the little bit of extra length to tape the ends together. One band

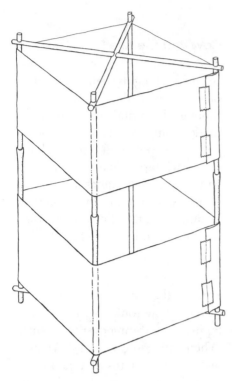

of covering wraps around the top of the frame and the other band wraps around the bottom, leaving the middle of the frame open.

The size of the covering needed for the Sled Kite is equal to the height of the frame by one and a half times the width of the frame. So the width of the plastic sheeting should be about one straw length longer than the width of the frame. The covering attaches only to the sides of the frame to form a floppy plastic arc.

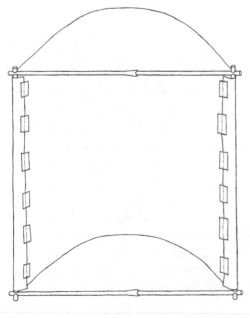

Attaching the bridle

The purpose of the bridle is to position the kite to the wind at just the right angle so the kite "finds" the wind and is lifted up. But for a kite to fly at all, the bridle must be just right for the shape of the kite and the wind conditions in order to create enough lift-ing power.

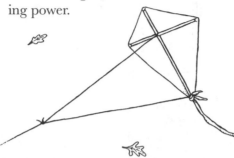

The simplest bridle to make is a two-legged cord attached to the kite at two points along the center vertical spine. Usually, the top leg is attached about one-quarter of the way down from the top of the kite, and the bottom leg attaches to the bottom of the kite. The kite string is then knotted to the bridle where the "V" comes together.

Once you have built the kite, locate the two attachment points and measure the distance between them. Cut a length of kite string for the bridle that is

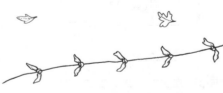

four times that distance. The Sled Kite requires two identical bridles brought together where they attach to the kite string, as shown in the illustration.

Attach each end of the bridle to its attachment point by tying the string around the straw. At some attachment points, you may first need to poke an access hole through the plastic covering.

When attaching the kite string to the bridle, the length of the top leg should be a bit shorter than the longer bottom leg, but the actual difference will depend on the type of kite you build and the strength of the wind you are flying in. When the bridle is set at the wrong angle for the wind, the kite will behave erratically by diving, flut-tering, spinning, or wobbling from side to side.

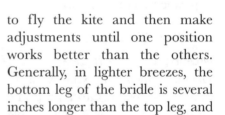

The easiest way to determine the best angle for the bridle is to fly the kite and then make adjustments until one position works better than the others. Generally, in lighter breezes, the bottom leg of the bridle is several inches longer than the top leg, and in the strongest breezes, both legs of the bridle are clos-er to the same length.

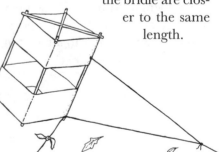

Since you will be mak-ing frequent adjustments to the bridle angle, tie the kite string to the bridle line in such a way that it is firmly attached but can also be slid to a new position.

Adding a kite tail

A kite tail attached at the bottom of the kite frame helps to stabilize the kite and keep it from spinning, twisting, and diving. Both the weight of the tail and its resistance to the wind stabilize the kite and keep it facing the right direction

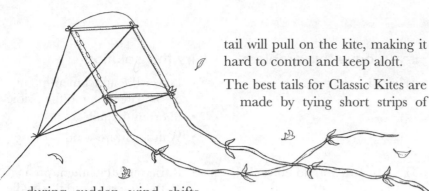

during sudden wind shifts and gusts. The kite may sway a bit, but the tail will straighten it out and set it flying right again.

To properly counteract the turbulent forces of the wind and still allow the kite to soar, the tail must be the proper weight and length for the particular kite design. If the tail is too short, it will be ineffective, while if it is too long and heavy, the tail will pull on the kite, making it hard to control and keep aloft.

The best tails for Classic Kites are made by tying short strips of plastic bag material to a length of kite string like a chain of bow ties. Start by cutting many strips about one inch wide by three or four inches long, then tie the string around the center of each strip, positioning them about six inches apart.

Another way to make an effective tail is by cutting longer strips of plastic bag material and tying them together end to end. Be sure to use the thinnest bag material you can find, or the tail could be too heavy for your kite. When using more than one tail on a single kite (like the Sled Kite), these long, knotted strips are less likely to snag and tangle together than bow-tie tails.

Start by trying a kite tail that is about four times the length of the greatest dimension of the kite. For example, a fourteen-inch-tall diamond kite or box kite would need a tail at least fifty-six inches long. In lighter breezes, you can probably shorten the tail a bit and allow the kite to fly higher.

KITES FOR POMP AND PRACTICAL PURPOSES

A kite was probably the first true human-made aircraft in history. Ancient records show that ceremonial kites were being used in China several thousand years ago. In other earlier civilizations, kites were used to send signals to others far away, and even for taking fishing lines far off shore well beyond where a fisherer could cast.

Over the following centuries, kites became bigger and stronger with more lifting power that made them suitable for all kinds of practical uses. Some kites were large enough to carry a person aloft to spy on the enemy during wars. Not too many years ago, kites were commonly used to send weather instruments and cameras aloft. And today, kites are part of the survival gear in a military life raft so shipwrecked sailors and airmen can raise a radio antenna and signal for help.

Decorating the kite

You can draw designs, words, or pictures on the plastic covering, but do not add any decorations that will add weight. The lighter the kite, the higher it will fly and the less wind you need to keep it in the air. Try using felt-tip markers, ballpoint pens, and crayons on a few scraps of the plastic covering material to see what marks best.

Kite-flying techniques

How easy or difficult it is to get your kite in the air will depend on the force of the breeze, the design of the bridle, and your skill as a kite flyer. After some practice, you'll learn which techniques work best for different kites and different conditions.

In a strong breeze, you may need to do nothing more than place your back to the wind, hold the kite up to catch the wind, and let out the kite string. To get the kite up in a lighter breeze, you may have to run into the wind, pulling the kite behind you while slowly letting out the string. Breezes just twenty or thirty feet above the ground are usually stronger and more steady than those at ground level. Once your running has lifted the kite high enough, you should be able to stop and stand in one location without the kite dropping.

Once the kite is aloft, slowly let out the string until you have reached an altitude where the kite flies steadily, but not so high or far away that you can't see it clearly. Several small tugs on the line while letting it out may help the kite to climb and gain altitude.

With an adequate breeze, most kite-flying problems can be fixed by making adjustments to the bridle and the tail. Here is a guide to help you adjust your kite for the best possible flying.

If you have this problem	Try this solution
Kite flies too low	• Lower the attachment point of the kite string to the bridle • Shorten the tail • Wait for more wind
Kite rotates and nosedives	• Raise the attachment point of the kite string to the bridle • Lengthen the tail
Kite darts from side to side	• Raise the attachment point where the top leg of the bridle is tied to the frame

Reading the breeze

The best conditions for flying a small kite are a gentle to moderate breeze. Too little wind, and the kite will just keep falling to the ground. Too much wind, and the kite will fly erratically and out of control, often crashing hard into the ground. So how can you tell if the wind is just right for a Classic Kite? Observe the wind conditions around the kite-flying area, then use this chart to determine the wind speed.

Observations	Wind Condition	Wind Speed
Smoke rises straight up	Calm	0 to 1 mph
Smoke drifts but leaves are still	Light air	1 to 3 mph
Leaves rustle and wind is felt on face	Light breeze	4 to 7 mph
The best conditions for flying Classic Kites		
Leaves and twigs are in motion, and a light flag extends and flutters	Gentle breeze	8 to 12 mph
Loose paper and dust blow about, and small branches wave	Moderate breeze	13 to 18 mph
Small trees sway, and standing water forms wavelets	Fresh breeze	19 to 24 mph
Large trees sway, power lines whistle, and umbrellas are difficult to use	Strong breeze	25 to 31 mph

WIND WHIRLIES

Hang a Wind Whirlie outside, and it will spin in the gentle breeze. Hang one inside over a radiator or by a sunny window, and it will spin in the air currents caused by the rising warm air. Or just walk past a hanging Whirlie, and the air movement may be enough to slowly spin it.

Wind Whirlies are made from Punch and Poke Sticks, which are commonly used to build space frame structures. In this construction, however, the struts are spaced so closely together that they form a solid plane, and that plane can be twisted to form and hold a spiral shape. When hung from a string, air currents and breezes will cause the spiral to rotate and spin. Build several Wind Whirlies using different designs to see which shapes spin best and which ones look best.

Construction

Building system
Punch and Poke Sticks

Builder's age
8+

Player's age
3+

Materials

☐ Drinking straws, ¼" diameter. The number of straws needed will depend on the design and size of the Wind Whirlie. The smallest Whirlie needs only about 12 straws, and a big Whirlie about 50 straws.

☐ Short length of sewing thread

Tools

☐ Paper hole punch, ¼" diameter

☐ Scissors

Building instructions

1. To build a basic Wind Whirlie, start with one full-length straw for the axle, and cut twelve straws exactly in half to make twenty-four cross struts.

2. Punch a hole through the center of all but one of the cross struts.

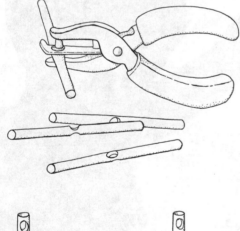

3. Punch a hole through the axle straw at each end. Each hole should be close to the end of the straw, but the two holes do not have to be in alignment with each other.

4. Assemble the Wind Whirlie by first putting the one unpunched cross strut through a punch hole at one end of the axle straw. Center the strut. Now put all the punched cross struts onto the axle straw above it.

5. By aligning all the stacked cross struts with one directly on top of another, you will give the Whirlie the shape of a flat plane. But if you slightly rotate each straw so it is slightly offset in position from the one below it, the plane will take on a spiral twist in the shape of a screw thread.

It is the spiral shape that will catch breezes and air currents and cause the Wind Whirlie to spin. By using different amounts of offset between the cross struts, you can change the pitch of the spiral. Experiment to see what spiral pitch works best for different air conditions.

6. Tie a length of sewing thread to the top hole in the axle straw, and hang the Wind

Whirlie in a location where it will catch indoor air currents or outdoor breezes.

Since the Whirlie is so light in weight, it can be attached indoors to a ceiling or wood molding with a pushpin or a small piece of tape. Outdoors, hang the Whirlie where it can easily be seen through a window. Unless there is a handy branch or overhang nearby, you may have to devise some type of a bracket for hanging the Whirlie.

Design variations

Once you get the knack of building a Wind Whirlie, there are several design variations you can quickly try.

• Build Whirlies using shorter- or longer-length cross struts.

• Build a cone-shaped Whirlie using graduated-length cross struts. Start with a short strut at the bottom and make each successive strut incrementally longer.

• Build longer Wind Whirlies by attaching two or more straws end to end to make a longer axle.

• Experiment with combinations of different color straws to create spiral patterns.

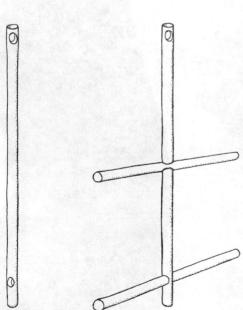

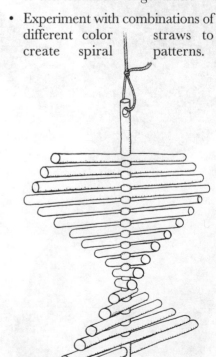

TINKER TOOTHPICKS
BUILDING SYSTEM

A basic space frame construction system consists of many building struts with connectors to fasten the struts together at any angle. Round, pointed toothpicks make excellent building struts because they are lightweight and strong, they are about the right size for models, and the pointed ends can be stuck into several types of connectors. By using peas, cranberries, raisins, or jelly beans for connectors, you can easily stick as many as five or more toothpicks into one connector, each at any angle needed.

Tinker Toothpicks are especially well-suited for making domes and other space frame geometric forms that use struts of the same length, including any of the forms made with Sticky Q-Sticks. The shapes you create can be used as ornaments, mobiles, toys, or whatever else you imagine. You might also try building free-form structures resembling animals or objects, or maybe even an art sculpture.

SYSTEM FEATURES

- Easy to assemble and inexpensive
- Many different types of connectors can be used
- Structures can be temporary or permanent
- Toothpicks are available in colors and can be reused
- Appearance can be whimsical to geometric

Construction

Builder's age
7

Materials
☐ Round, pointed toothpicks

☐ Connectors. Use this chart to choose the best connector or combination of connectors for your construction.

Tools
☐ Hands only (except a bowl of water when using whole dry peas as described below)

	Easy to use	Appearance	Build strength	Dry strength
Cranberry	Excellent	Excellent	Excellent	Fair
Raisin	Good	Fair	Fair	Excellent
Jelly bean	Fair	Excellent	Excellent	Fair
Whole pea	Good	Good	Good	Excellent

Building techniques

Toothpicks will easily penetrate and hold in any of the connectors suggested, however, each type has its own unique characteristics. Which connector you choose will depend on what you plan to build, the appearance you like, and how long you want the construction to last.

Most of the connectors have enough flexibility to allow some twisting and bending that might be necessary to make struts and connectors meet. Some connectors, in time, will create a tight bond with the struts, making a strong and rigid structure.

For temporary structures, the toothpick struts can be used and reused over again, although new connectors should be used each time a Tinker Toothpick structure is built.

Using cranberries

Cranberries are colorful, large, and firm, and a single one can firmly hold several struts without splitting. In a week or so, however, cranberry connectors will begin to get soft and lose their grip on the toothpick struts. But if left to dry and harden over a month or two, the cranberries

will shrivel up and the structure will be rigid. The more holes poked in a cranberry, the sooner it will dry up and harden. The hardened structure might also be deformed a bit because the dried cranberries will shrink and slightly change shape.

Builder's note

If you want to build larger scale structures, a cranberry connector is large enough and tough enough to accept wood skewers, which are longer, instead of toothpicks.

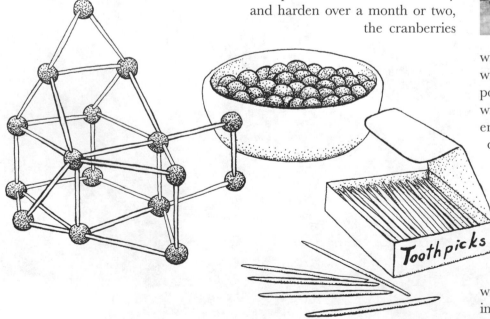

Using raisins

When first attaching struts to the raisins, the connections are weak and wobbly. Because the toothpicks and connections pull apart so easily, it is best to build small structures when using raisins. After a day or two, the raisins will begin to harden, and the toothpick struts will become solidly connected. If you want to build large structures, use raisins that have already turned stale and started to harden.

Using jelly beans

It is a little more difficult to insert a toothpick strut into a jelly bean than into other types of connectors. The outer coating of a jelly bean is hard, and the tip of the toothpick can slip or break if it is not pushed in straight. The smaller size jelly beans have somewhat thinner coatings than large ones and are easier to use. Once you get the hang of it, jelly beans make strong and colorful connectors. Over time, the punctured jelly bean connectors will become harder and not easily accept new toothpick struts.

Using dry whole peas

The peas must be prepared ahead of time. Pour only a part of a package of dried whole peas into a large bowl of water. Make sure the water covers the peas by an inch or more. Let the peas soak at least six

hours. The soaking will soften the peas just enough to allow the toothpick struts to be stuck in without splitting the pea. There is little problem with soaking the peas too long (although after a few days they may begin to sprout). If a pea does split, just replace it. The smaller peas seem to split least and hold the best. When a construction is finished, put it aside to dry. In a day or two, the peas will dry out and shrink, making the joints tight and the structure quite rigid.

TINKER TOOTHPICK
BUILD-IT PROJECTS

GEODESIC DOME BUG HOUSE
MOSQUITO CHAMBER OF DOOM

GEODESIC DOME BUG HOUSE

If you are going to collect bugs to observe their behavior, let them be happy bugs. With a few leaves and blades of grass placed inside, this airy bug house comes a lot closer to the creature's natural environment than the traditional glass jar and perforated lid. However, after studying the captive creatures for a while, let them go in time for their next meal.

A geodesic sphere is the perfect structure for a space frame bug house because it can create an enclosure of any size using far fewer materials than an ordinary box-shaped structure. Tinker Toothpicks are perfect for building the framework, and a piece of pantyhose fabric works great as a breathable covering. The completed Geodesic Dome Bug House also has a simple "trap door" to easily put bugs in and take them out, yet it seals well enough to keep the creatures from escaping.

Construction

Building system
Tinker Toothpicks
(Any connector will work.)

Builder's age
7+

Player's age
5+

Materials

☐ 30 toothpicks

☐ 12 connectors, plus some extras (Cranberries, raisins, jelly beans, or dried peas will work fine.)

☐ Pantyhose fabric

☐ Short length of string, a wire twist tie, a small rubber band, or a piece of tape

Tools

☐ Scissors

Building instructions

In technical terms, the Geodesic Dome Bug House is a one-frequency icosahedron. An icosahedron is a polyhedron shape that can be built with all equal-length struts.

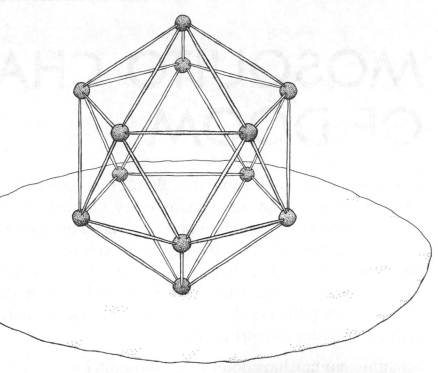

1. Follow the plans for laying out the struts and building the connecting triangles to make two identical pyramids with pentagon bases.

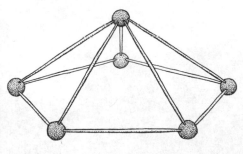

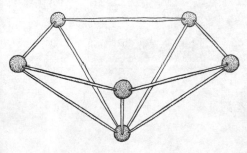

2. With the two pentagon bases facing each other, add the remaining ten struts to form a complete icosahedron.

3. Cut a flat, round piece of pantyhose large enough (when stretched) to wrap around the entire frame. The lighter the color of the pantyhose, the better you will be able to see inside the bug house. Place the frame in the center of the pantyhose piece and pull the fabric up around the sides to the top of the sphere. Pantyhose has a lot of stretch, so the fabric should lay pretty flat against the facets of the icosahedron form. Where all the fabric comes together, cinch it with a knotted string, a wire tie, a rubber band, or a strip of tape. Now cut off the excess pantyhose. The icosahedron sphere should be completely covered.

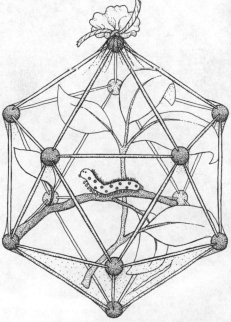

Make a "door" opening into the bug house by cutting a slit in the fabric panel that covers one of the facets on the bottom. To place leaves, blades of grass, or a bug inside the bug house, just lift the sphere and slip it in the door. As long as the sphere rests on the door facet, nothing can escape.

MOSQUITO CHAMBER OF DOOM

It is probably safe to assume that almost everyone dislikes mosquitoes, especially since many carry diseases. There are many kinds of mosquito repellents to keep the buzzing insects away from you, but the best solution is to get rid of the mosquitoes so they don't even get the chance to bite. The Mosquito Chamber of Doom might only attract and kill a few mosquitoes each day, but that's still a fewer number of mosquitoes to torture you.

Scientific studies have found that mosquitoes are highly attracted to sugar, petroleum jelly, beef bouillon cubes, the color black, and Lemon Fresh Joy dishwashing detergent. So, to have the best chance of attracting mosquitoes, the clever design of the Mosquito Chamber of Doom incorporates all five ways of attracting mosquitoes, plus a pool with a special ingredient that helps catch the insects as they try to fly out of the chamber.

Construction

Building system
Tinker Toothpicks

Builder's age
9+

Player's age
6+

Materials

☐ 26 toothpicks

☐ 12 jelly bean connectors, plus some extras

☐ Black pantyhose fabric

☐ Tape (masking tape, duct tape, or any tape that sticks well to pantyhose)

☐ Beef bouillon cube

☐ Petroleum jelly, such as Vaseline

☐ Soup bowl or deep dish (See instructions for sizing description.)

☐ Lemon Fresh Joy dishwashing detergent

☐ Water

Tools

☐ Scissors

☐ Stapler (optional)

Building instructions

The frame of the Chamber of Doom is a small dome based on an icosahedron and made from Tinker Toothpicks and jelly bean connectors that contain the sugar that helps attract mosquitoes. Inside the dome hangs a strut that suspends an extra connector covered in petroleum jelly, and the dome is covered with a piece of black pantyhose. And if that isn't enough to get a mosquito's attention, the dome sits just inside a soup bowl that contains a shallow pool of water and a bouillon cube. The water is also laced with a little lemon-scented detergent that helps to attract insects and trap the legs of any mosquito who touches it.

1. Looking at the illustration, use all but one of the toothpicks and one of the connectors to build connecting triangles to form the geodesic framework of a three-quarter icosahedron. Start with a pentagon-base pyramid of five triangles, then add the remain-

ing ten triangles. Because the dome is not a complete icosahedron and only three-quarters of a full sphere, the completed structure might be a bit wobbly. After attaching the pantyhose covering, the entire structure will become stronger.

Notice that hanging straight down from the top connector of the dome is another toothpick strut with a jelly bean connector on its other end. This connector will later be covered with petroleum jelly, which is one of

the baits. You may find it easier to attach this last strut after covering the dome chamber.

2. Find a soup bowl or a deep dish that is the right diameter for the dome structure. The dome chamber should sit on the inside sloping edges of the bowl, not on the flat bottom. That will allow spaces between the dome and the bowl (and above the water) where the mosquitoes can fly into the chamber.

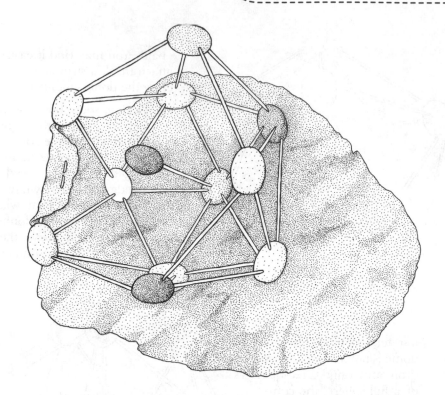

pick to the top center connector of the dome.

5. Fill the bowl with water to a depth that is just below the base of the dome when it is resting in the bowl. Add a teaspoon of dishwashing detergent to the water, and stir very gently, trying not to make soap bubbles. Add a bouillon cube to the bowl of soapy water.

The completed Chamber of Doom can be placed outside near a wet or damp area where mosquitoes are likely to be. Then check the trap every few days to see how many pests you have eliminated. Don't be surprised if you also catch some moths and other insects, because mosquitoes are not the only creatures that will like the bait.

3. Cut a flat, round piece of pantyhose large enough (when stretched) to wrap around the entire geodesic frame. The darker the color of the panty hose, the better it will attract mosquitoes.

Rest the geodesic frame upside down in the center of the pantyhose piece, and pull the fabric up around the sides of the frame. Pantyhose has a lot of stretch, so the fabric should smoothly cover the sides. Wrap the fabric over the edges of the base and secure the fabric in

place with short strips of tape. With some technique and practice, you can use a stapler instead of tape.

The sides of the dome should be completely covered, and the bottom should be completely open. Trim away any excess fabric.

4. If you haven't done so already, attach an extra connector to an extra toothpick, then coat the connector with petroleum jelly. Hang the bait inside the dome chamber by attaching the tooth-

TOOTHPICK TANTALIZERS

There are some pretty challenging games you can play and constructions you can make using only a box of toothpicks. Start with an easy puzzle to give yourself some practice in creative thinking before trying to solve the more difficult ones. You'll need it!

Either round or flat toothpicks will do, although the flat type are easier to use because they don't roll around. To also keep the toothpicks in place, work on a napkin, a table cloth, or some other nonslip surface. To solve the puzzles, the toothpicks cannot be bent or broken into shorter lengths and cannot be doubled-up side by side. Just in case you do get stuck, solutions are given on the following pages.

Construction

Player's age
Geniuses of any age

Materials
☐ Box of toothpicks (Flat works best.)

Tools
☐ Hands only

Somewhat easy puzzles

Four to Three Puzzle

Arrange twelve toothpicks to form a square composed of four squares. Move (but don't remove) three toothpicks so there are only three squares remaining and all twelve toothpicks are used with none overlapping.

Six to Three Puzzle

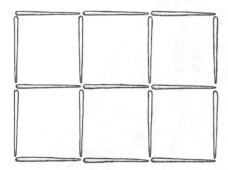

Arrange seventeen toothpicks to form a rectangle of six squares as shown. Remove five toothpicks, leaving the remaining toothpicks in place, to make three squares.

Wagging the Tail

Arrange ten toothpicks that overlap in a zigzag exactly as shown. Notice that the first toothpick is closer to the third toothpick. If the layout is right, the second toothpick will wag up and down when you press down on the tenth toothpick.

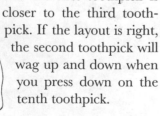

More difficult puzzles

Squares and Triangles

Use eight toothpicks to form a shape containing two squares and four triangles.

Only Triangles

Use six toothpicks to form four equilateral triangles. Here's a clue: In what dimension are you thinking?

Nine to Two Puzzle

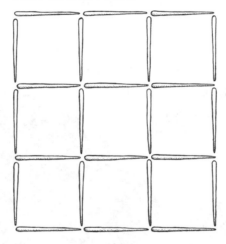

Arrange twenty-four toothpicks to form a square of nine squares as shown. Remove eight toothpicks, leaving the remaining toothpicks in place so that there are only two squares. If you want a clue now, continue reading: The two remaining squares do not have to be the same size.

Very challenging puzzles

Six to Nine Puzzle

Place six toothpicks parallel to one another as shown. Without moving any of them, add five more toothpicks to make nine. There is an important clue in these instructions, so read them carefully.

Three to Two Puzzle

Use twelve toothpicks to form three separate squares side by side as shown. Remove two toothpicks and rearrange only three toothpicks to leave two.

Bridge Building Balancing Act

If you have a lot of patience for doing delicate work, build this arch bridge by laying out the twenty-two toothpicks in the exact order and position shown. Good luck.

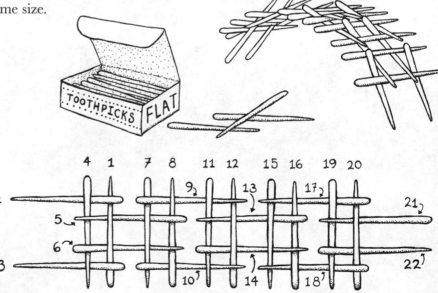

For puzzle solutions, turn to page 262.

WOODEN TOOTHPICKS

How the tiny town of Strong, Maine, became the toothpick capital of the entire world

Look at a box of toothpicks in more than one hundred countries around the world, including America, and the odds are quite good that it came from the Forster Company toothpick factory in Strong, Maine. Forster makes more toothpicks than any other company in America, and maybe even more than anyone in the world. The manager of the factory claims the number of toothpicks they make in just one year, laid end to end, would circle the entire earth nearly thirty times.

The birth of the toothpick business in America began around the time of the Civil War with a young American merchant named Charles Forster who happened to be working in South America. One day a trading ship arrived with a cargo of whittled wooden toothpicks that had been handmade by European craftspeople. The idea of a toothpick wasn't new, but toothpicks were usually made from slivers of ivory or bone. Some toothpicks were even made of gold or silver with inlaid precious stones.

But a carved wooden toothpick was new, and Forster thought it was a great idea. A wooden toothpick was not only less expensive to make, but it softened with use and was gentle on the gums. And it was cheap enough to be thrown away after being used only one time. Forster liked the carved wooden toothpicks so much that he bought a box and sent it to his wife in Boston. Perhaps her own fascination with the gift inspired Forster to return to the United States and start his own toothpick business.

However, Forster decided to first take a job in a manufacturing plant near Boston so he could learn as much as possible about production methods. Forster soon realized he would have to devise a machine to make toothpicks both quickly and inexpensively. Fortunately, Forster's employer let him use the company's machinery to help figure out a way to cut wood blocks into small slivers of wood. After a few years of experiments and after solving a lot of production problems, Forster had designed a successful wooden-toothpick manufacturing machine that could produce as many toothpicks in one minute as a carver could whittle in a whole day.

Charles Forster had realized his dream. He had invented a way to make machine-carved toothpicks and started a small factory to produce them. But now there was a new obstacle to overcome. It seemed that many first-time customers never became second-time buyers because they thought the wooden toothpicks "tasted too much like a tree." Just like the bone, gold, or silver toothpicks people were already used to, the ideal wooden toothpick should have hardly any taste at all.

Forster needed a wood that was not too hard for his machinery to cut, not too soft or the toothpick would easily break, and with no splinters that would make the wooden toothpick unsafe to use. In his search, Forster must have tried oak, pine, and other local woods until he eventually tested and tasted wood from the white birch tree. This was the perfect wood for toothpicks. White birch was just soft enough for the machinery, hard enough not to break, and it had a nice white appearance with a clean grain and no splinters. Birch logs were also easy to cut, and the bark easily came off the logs like peeling paper. And best of all, white birch is utterly tasteless!

Forster's improved wooden toothpick was well received by customers, and his business was a success. By 1887, twenty years after he had started, demand for Forster toothpicks was booming, so Charles Forster moved his factory from Boston to the woods of Strong, Maine, where he would be right next to his plentiful supply of beloved white birch trees. Today, the Forster Company is still operating in the same town and making more toothpicks

than any other single manufacturer anywhere. And that makes Strong, Maine, the "toothpick capital of the world."

Making wooden toothpicks

The Forster factory now uses machinery that is remarkably similar to Charles Forster's original invention, except today's equipment is operated by computers. But the process of making toothpicks still begins with selecting the right trees. Loggers search the huge forests of Maine for mature white birch trees and deliver the logs to the factory free of any branches.

A mechanical robot arm picks up a birch log from the wood pile and places it on a conveyor belt that goes to the saw room. The long tree log is then cut into smaller logs called bolts that are about twenty inches long. The wooden bolts then proceed through a peeler that cuts off the bark. All the bark and any scrap pieces of logs are sent to the boiler room where they are used to fuel an electric generator that runs the plant. The scrap wood and bark are also burned to heat the building and make steam for the next step in the operation.

From this point on, no hands ever touch the wood again until someone actually uses a toothpick. The debarked bolts are placed in a steam pit and left to get hot, soggy, and mushy enough to be easy to

cut, which takes about sixteen hours. Each soft wooden cylinder bolt is then sliced into a long sheet of veneer, which is then slit with knives into long, thin, floppy, spaghetti-like strips. Next, it's on to a slicer where the wooden strips are cut into short toothpicks. Finally, the toothpicks are heated, dried, and polished in a big tumbler, and each end is pointed. Before another robot arm packs them up in small boxes, some toothpicks are colored red, blue, yellow, or green, and some toothpicks are given a mint or cinnamon flavor.

Not including the day it takes to steam the wood, the entire manufacturing process from log to toothpick takes just a few hours. Here are a few more facts about wooden toothpicks and the Forster toothpick factory. Each twenty-inch wooden bolt makes about fifty thousand toothpicks, which means an average size birch tree can yield well over one million toothpicks. In a single workday, this one factory (with only eight people actually making toothpicks) can produce over thirty million toothpicks, which is more than enough to keep Americans supplied with the thirty billion toothpicks they use each year. And considering there are 250 toothpicks in a small box and 800 in a large box, the Forster company claims each box count is accurate to within five toothpicks.

Toothpick Tantalizers solutions

Four to Three Puzzles

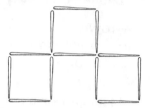

Six to Three Puzzle

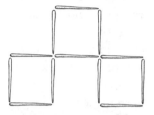

Squares and Triangles

Only Triangles

Nine to Two Puzzle

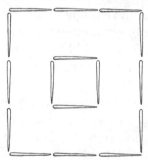

Six to Nine Puzzle

Three to Two Puzzle

QUICK STICKS
BUILDING SYSTEM

Quick Stick building rods are perfect for fast and easy, large-scale, temporary space frame models and experiments where precision craftsmanship isn't needed. The modular-length rods are simple to make from quarter-inch wooden dowels, and for the connectors, you can choose any one of four different fastening systems. Hook and Loop Rods have Velcro ends for quick temporary connections. Tubers and Dowels can connect several dowels at a single point and at any angle. Thingama-Dowel-Jig fasteners offer the most attachment options for structures that don't require precision. Rubber Band Wraps are made by simply wrapping rubber bands around intersecting rods.

SYSTEM FEATURES

- Good for temporary models
- Makes large-scale structures
- Very fast assembly
- All parts are reusable
- Aids in structure experiments
- Four fastening systems available
- Rods can be cut or adjusted to length

Construction

Builder's age
9+

Materials
☐ ¼″ hardwood dowels in 36″ or 48″ lengths

☐ Refer to the fastening system you plan to use for other materials needed

Tools
☐ Measuring tape
☐ Pencil
☐ Coping saw or hacksaw
☐ Medium or fine sandpaper
☐ Refer to the fastening system you plan to use for other tools needed.

Building techniques

Making the rods

All four Quick Stick construction systems use ¼-inch-diameter wooden dowels for connecting rods. Dowels typically come in three-foot lengths (sometimes four-foot lengths) and are available at most hardware stores and lumberyards.

One-quarter-inch-diameter wooden dowels are made from hardwoods that can easily be cut with a coping saw or a coarse hacksaw blade. Mark the length to be cut, then cut and sandpaper the edge of the cut end until it is smooth and slightly rounded.

You can cut dowel rods to length as you need them for a particular construction, or you can make a starter set of modular-length rods to have handy for quick structures. This twenty-four-piece starter set uses twelve thirty-six-inch-long dowels (or nine forty-eight-inch dowels) cut to these rod lengths. Lay out the cuts so you use the entire length of each dowel without any leftover scraps.

Rod length (in.)	Number of rods (pieces)
36	6
18	6
12	6
6	6

Making the connectors

You have a choice of using any one of four connector systems that range from simply wrapping rubber bands around rods to manufacturing multiples of a specialty fastener. Choose the type of connector that works best for you or the structure you are building.

Hook and Loop Rods

These sticks have Velcro ends that are meant to make temporary connections. Space frame structures built with this system will not be very strong, but they are most useful for quickly testing ideas and conducting structure experiments.

Materials

☐ ¼″ dowels cut to lengths needed

☐ ⅞″ Velcro hook squares and loop squares

☐ White glue, yellow glue, or plastic glue

Tools

☐ Hands only

Building techniques

Velcro squares are sold already cut to the perfect size and are available at hardware stores and building centers. The starter set of dowel rods will require twenty-four pairs of hook and loop squares.

Wrap and stick a hook square of Velcro around one end of each rod and a loop square around each opposite end. It is easiest to first place the end of the rod on the sticky middle of the square, then wrap the Velcro around the dowel. Press the Velcro firmly in place so it sticks well, and let the Velcro adhesive harden overnight before using the rod. To be sure the Velcro ends do not unstick and unwrap from the rods, apply a small amount of adhesive to the seams where the two edges of the Velcro come together.

To build with Hook and Loop Rods, just attach a hook end to a loop end and keep on adding rods the same way. Any number of rods can be joined at a single connection point—in fact, the more rods connected, the stronger the connection.

Tubers and Dowels

The connectors of this system are made from thin-wall vinyl or polyethylene tubing that can accept two, three, four, or five dowels of any length and at any angles to build large and complex models of space frame bridges and towers, as well as full-size kites.

Materials

☐ ¼″ dowels cut to lengths needed

☐ Thin-wall, flexible, clear vinyl or polyethylene tubing with a ¼″ inside diameter (ID). This size of tubing is commonly available at most hardware stores, hobby shops, and building supply centers.

Tools

☐ Kitchen scissors or heavy-duty scissors

☐ Paper hole punch, ¼″ diameter

Building techniques

Because this system can use rods of any length and the flexible connectors can join up to five rods at a single point, it is well suited for building large, complex space frame models. And because Tubers makes the most precise constructions of all the Quick Stick fastening systems, you can also use Tubers and Dowels to build kite frames.

The Tuber connectors are made from thin-walled vinyl or polyethylene tubing that has a ¼-inch inside diameter. The tubing is cut to short lengths of about two inches, and some tubing connectors also have a hole punched in the middle.

To make a basic two-way connector, use scissors to cut a piece of tubing about two inches long.

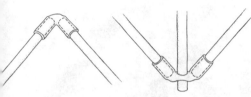

To make a basic three-way connector, cut a piece of tubing about two inches long, then punch a hole through the middle of the tube, using a paper hole punch.

Because a paper hole punch is designed for punching holes in paper, not plastic tubing, a special technique is needed. Pinch and flatten the cut piece of tubing in the middle so it will fit in the jaws

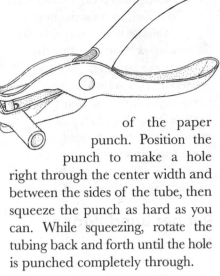

of the paper punch. Position the punch to make a hole right through the center width and between the sides of the tube, then squeeze the punch as hard as you can. While squeezing, rotate the tubing back and forth until the hole is punched completely through.

Build structures by placing the ends of dowel rods into the ends of the tube connectors and by sliding rods through the holes punched through the connectors. Don't push the rods all the way to the middle of the connectors, but do leave enough empty tubing in the middle so the connectors can bend to any angle.

Make a four-way connector by tightly wrapping a small plastic tie or a knotted piece of strong string around the middle of two basic two-way connectors positioned side by

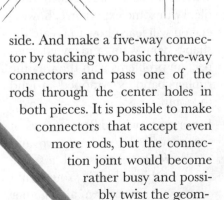

side. And make a five-way connector by stacking two basic three-way connectors and pass one of the rods through the center holes in both pieces. It is possible to make connectors that accept even more rods, but the connection joint would become rather busy and possibly twist the geometry of the structure.

Thingama-Dowel-Jig

This unique connector can accept any number of dowel rods at any location on a dowel, and rods can be angled in any direction or adjusted to any length. But the joints are very imprecise, making this system best suited for sculptures and garden trellises.

Materials

- ☐ ¼″ dowels cut to lengths needed
- ☐ Scrap polyethylene plastic

  Sources include food tubs and lids, detergent jugs, and other pliable plastic containers.

  Or you can use scrap rubber cut from the inner tube of a bicycle tire.

Tools

- ☐ Kitchen scissors
- ☐ Paper hole punch, ¼″ diameter
- ☐ Ballpoint pen

Building techniques

Find a three-inch-round object to use as a guide for drawing circles. A soup can, the lid of a spray-paint can, or the mouth of a drinking cup will all work fine. Use a ballpoint pen to trace a three-inch-diameter circle on a scrap of plastic or rubber, then cut out the disk with a pair of kitchen scissors.

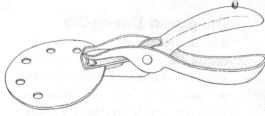

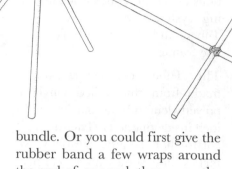

Use a paper hole punch to punch holes all around the perimeter of the disk. The holes should be spaced about ¾-inch apart (does not have to be exact) and not too close to the edge. If your paper hole punch has enough reach, also punch a few more holes closer to the center of the disk. A starter set of connectors will require about eighteen disks.

Because a paper punch is designed for punching holes in paper, not plastic, a special technique is needed. Position the punch where you want to make a hole, then squeeze the punch as hard as you can. While squeezing, rotate the disk back and forth until the hole is punched through the plastic.

To build with Thingama-Dowel-Jigs, insert the end of a rod through any two adjacent (or available) holes in a disk. Although these connections hold the dowel rods firm and secure, the appearance of the joints is pretty clunky-looking, and the alignment of the rods is somewhat imprecise.

You can keep on adding rods to a disk as long as there are available holes, and you can twist portions of the disk to make any angle of connection you want. If you need more holes or holes in a different location, just punch them where needed. With some experimentation and experience, you will learn the best ways to make different types of joints.

Rubber Band Wraps

Connections are made by simply wrapping a fat rubber band around the intersection where two or more dowels meet.

Materials
☐ ¼″ dowels cut to lengths needed
☐ Rubber bands

All ⅛″-wide rubber bands work well, especially the longer sizes (No. 31, 32, and 33).

Tools
☐ Hands only

Building techniques

Every time you make a rubber band joint, there will be forces on the rods that might make them twist and turn in odd directions. Until all the rods of your space frame structure are in place, this system can be cumbersome to handle. With some experience, however, you will learn how to create the shapes you want and avoid connection problems with the way the rubber band is wrapped around the joint.

Experiment with different ways of connecting the ends of two and more dowel rods with a single rubber band. You could group them all together and wrap the rubber band around the

bundle. Or you could first give the rubber band a few wraps around the end of one rod, then wrap the second rod, and so on for more rods. To finish the joint, loop the

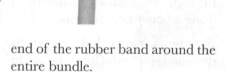

end of the rubber band around the entire bundle.

Also, experiment with making connections along the length of a dowel rod. Connecting the end of one rod anywhere along the length of another is pretty easy to figure out, but you will have to plan ahead to connect two rods that cross along their length. Just wrap the two rods at their ends, then slide the rods through the rubber band wrap into whatever positions you like.

QUICK STICKS
BUILD-IT PROJECTS
BUTTERFLY NET
TRI-STICK STOOL

BUTTERFLY NET

Butterflies are commonly seen in sunny areas where they are attracted to flower nectar, and watching butterflies flutter from one flower to another is a popular hobby for many kids. Although butterfly collectors catch and mount various species for display, most watchers use a butterfly net only to capture the insects for examining them up close and then let them go.

The ideal butterfly net should have a big opening and a long handle for easy catching, a large, soft net that won't damage the butterfly's delicate wings, and one you can easily see through for examining the butterfly before releasing. This Butterfly Net made from Quick Sticks meets all these requirements, and it is also lightweight and easy to use. When you spot a butterfly you want to catch, approach it quickly and swing the net to trap it inside. Observe the butterfly while it is in the net, but don't touch it. The fine powder-like substance that covers its wings actually helps the butterfly to fly.

Construction

Building system
Quick Sticks—Tubers and Dowels

Builder's age
10+

Player's age
5+

Materials
- Three, 48″-long ¼″ dowels cut to lengths needed
- 1 foot of thin-wall, flexible, clear vinyl or polyethylene tubing with a ¼″ inside diameter
- 48″ (or larger) square of polyester or nylon netting
- Heavy-duty sewing thread

Tools
- Paper hole punch, ¼″ diameter
- Measuring tape
- Marker
- Shears, wire cutter, or hacksaw blade to cut dowels
- Kitchen scissors
- Blunt-tip tapestry needle (The needle eye must fit through the netting mesh.)

Building instructions
Building the frame

1. Two of the dowels are used full length. Measure, mark, and then cut from the third dowel one piece fourteen inches long and one piece twelve inches long. Quarter-inch dowels can be cut with heavy-duty shears, wire cutters, or a hacksaw blade. Save the remaining length of dowel for making any needed repairs.

16"   12"

2. Using scissors, shears, or wire cutters, cut the length of tubing into six pieces, each about two inches long. Two of the tuber connectors are punched with a single hole through the middle, and one connector is punched with a hole near each end. Three connectors are not punched. Remember that it takes some technique to punch the holes with a paper hole punch. Bend and flatten the tubing to fit, position it between the jaws of the hole punch, and twist the tubing back and forth as you apply pressure to the handles of the punch.

× 3   × 2   × 1

3. Attach two full-length dowels end to end, using one of the connectors without a hole, then fold the dowels parallel as shown.

4. Attach the remaining five connectors to the two dowels as shown. First, place the two-hole connector onto the two dowels, through the holes, and slide it down the sticks to within about eight inches of the folded end. Place a one-hole connector onto each of the dowels and slide them down the sticks to about fourteen inches from the sticks' tips. Place the remaining connectors on the tips of the two dowels.

5. Insert one end of the fourteen-inch-long dowel into one of the tip connectors, fold the dowel at the joint, and insert the other end into the other tip connector. You will need to bend the connector to line up with the dowel.

6. Complete the Butterfly Net frame by inserting the twelve-inch-long dowel into an end of each of the remaining two connectors.

48"
48"

Making the net

Fine-mesh netting is available at fabric stores and typically comes in widths from about fifty inches to sixty inches. Polyester netting is softer than nylon netting and also easier to work with. Cotton netting is also soft, but ravels and tears easily.

7. Start with the largest square of netting you can find. Fold the square in half, then fold it again into quarters. Using the double-folded corner as the center, use a marker to draw a quarter circle as shown. You can carefully draw the quarter circle by eye, or use a measuring tape as a guide.

8. Using scissors, cut through the four layers of netting on the quarter-circle line. Unfold the netting to form a large circle, and draw four evenly spaced marks around the perimeter of the circle.

Attaching the net to the frame

The edge around the netting is sewn to the rectangular portion of the frame, using a blunt-end tapestry sewing needle and heavy-duty sewing thread. One-quarter of the edge (the length between two marks) is sewn onto each of the four sides.

9. Tie an end of the sewing thread around one corner of the rectangular frame.

10. Starting at the same corner, fold the edge of the netting over the dowel, from the outside of the frame to the inside, so it overlaps about an inch, and sew the netting to the frame with a loop. Continue to fold the netting over the dowel and sew it in place with a loop about every inch. When you run out of thread, tie the end onto the frame, and rethread the sewing needle to continue.

Continue to sew the netting to one side of the frame until you reach the quarter-mark on the netting, then turn the corner and sew the netting to the next side. Because the length of the edge to be sewn onto each side of the frame is much longer than the frame side, you will need to bunch up the netting on the dowel as you sew. The Butterfly Net is complete when the netting has been sewn to all four sides of the frame.

TRI-STICK STOOL

Maybe you're watching a game at the ball field but don't want to sit on the damp ground, or maybe you're camping and want to sit by the campfire. If you've ever needed a seat, but didn't have a chair handy, knowing how to make a Tri-Stick Stool can be a very convenient skill. This low-to-the-ground seat is quite strong and deceptively comfortable.

Using three found sticks and a piece of rope, a Tri-Stick Stool can usually be built right on the spot in only a few minutes. The stool also folds closed for carrying. That means you can take it away with you or you can make one beforehand to have ready when you need it. And there is even a way to convert a spare pair of jeans into a seat cushion.

Construction

Builder's age
7+

Player's age
4+

Materials
☐ 3 fat sticks, each about 2 to 3 feet long (See instructions below.)

☐ A few feet of rope

Tools
☐ Knife (to cut the rope)

Building instructions
Collect three fat sticks all about the same thickness and all about two to three feet long. Exact size is not important.

1. There are many kinds of sticks that can be used to make a Tri-Stick Stool depending on whether you make it on the spot or in a workshop. Fallen branches about two inches in diameter make good sticks as long as the wood is sound and not rotted. A fancier and more furniture-like version of the stool can be built using fat wooden dowels or a cut-up wooden closet pole instead of sticks. Wooden stakes (the two-inch by two-inch size) commonly available at building centers are very inexpensive and can also be cut to stool length. And three baseball bats make excellent "sticks" for building a stool.

2. Hold the three sticks together in a bunch, wrap the rope around the center of the bunch, and knot the rope. A few turns of a heavy rope will do, but thinner ropes like clothesline should be wrapped around the bundle at least four or five times before knotting.

How loose or how tight you make the rope will determine how much the stool will spread when you sit on it. Experiment by starting with the rope wrapped loosely.

3. Following the illustrations, spread two of the sticks apart to form an "X." Then, spread the third stick to rest in the fork of the other two sticks. Test the stool by sitting in the "pocket" formed by the three sticks. Put each cheek of your bottom on a stick with the third stick at your back.

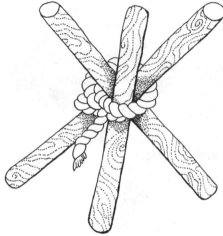

You will find that the stool spreads out a bit more and lowers a little when you sit on it, but it should be springy and reasonably comfortable. Tighten the rope if the stool is too low. When you are satisfied with the stool's height and comfort, cut off any excess rope, or use it to form a loop to make a handle for carrying.

Making a seat cushion
If you plan to be sitting on the stool for a while or if you would just like a more comfortable seat, consider putting a cushion in the seat pocket. If you have a small cushion or pillow handy, try using it. However, in the same build-it-on-the-spot attitude as the Tri-Stick Stool itself, a spare pair of denim jeans can easily be used to make a seat cushion sling.

The jeans do not have to be cut or altered in any way and will be fine for wearing again. You can also use any size jeans, although waist size will determine the size of the cushion and seat.

Begin by fastening the waist of a pair of jeans and closing the zipper. Open the Tri-Stick Stool and place it where you will be sitting. Place the waist band of the jeans over the top of the three sticks and pull it down several inches. Fold one pants leg and then the other into the center of the seat.

When you sit on the stool, the sticks will spread a bit more also causing the jeans to spread and creating a sling seat for even more comfort. Using this seat cushion, you may find sitting most comfortable when your legs straddle one stick and you sit back against the other two sticks.

TUB TUBES
BUILDING SYSTEM

It is always fun to add a little soak-time play to the bath routine, and this super-simple kit of modular parts is especially suited for young builders. The big foam tube struts easily attach and detach from large plastic connectors, and all the rod and connector pieces float—as do the constructions built with them. It takes only a few minutes to build a complete boat, raft, or any floating structure. And sometimes it's fun to just put parts together and then see how the structure floats to decide what it is or what parts to add.

A set of big, soft Tub Tubes is easy to make, very durable, and the perfect size for tub play. They can also be used at the beach, in a sandbox, in a wading pool, or just on the play-

SYSTEM FEATURES

- Perfect for young builders
- Building system tubes are easy to make
- Easy to cut to any length to make modular-size components
- Materials and constructions are durable and weatherproof
- Tubes and fasteners easily connect and disconnect
- Tubes, connectors, and constructions float
- Tubes bend to form curves

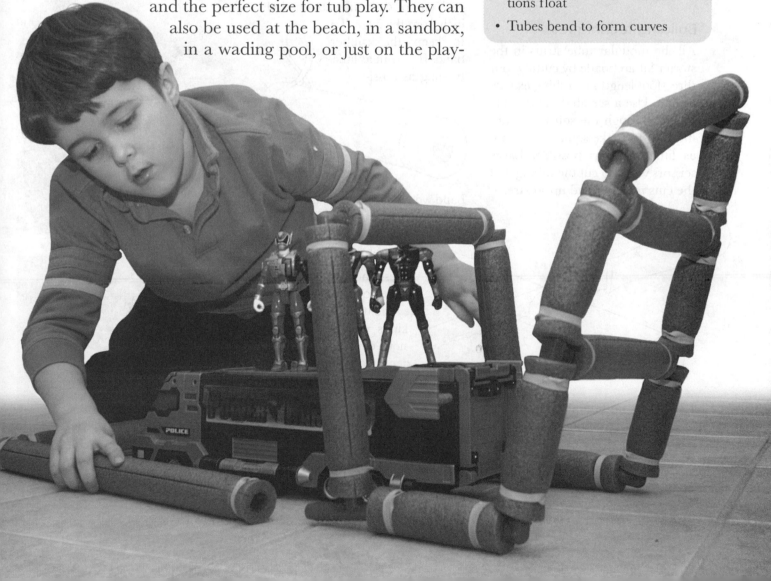

Construction

Builder's age
8+

Materials (for starter kit)
- ☐ Four 3-foot lengths of foam insulation tubing for ½″ copper pipe (Be sure the foam tubing is not slit all the way through along its length.)
- ☐ 28 No. 64 rubber bands (3 ½″ × ¼″)
- ☐ ½″ size plastic tubing connectors:
  - 8 Elbow 90° connectors
  - 6 "T" connectors

Tools
- ☐ Serrated bread knife or large scissors

Building techniques
All the modular tube struts in the starter kit are made by cutting four three-foot lengths of tubing exactly in half. Use a serrated bread knife to saw through the soft foam tubing. Try to make square cuts with as little angle as possible. Large scissors will also cut the tubing, but the cuts may not end up square.

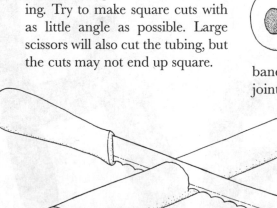

1. Start by cutting all four whole-length tubes into halves.
2. Cut six of the pieces into halves again to make twelve one-quarter lengths.
3. Cut four of the quarter-length pieces into halves again to make

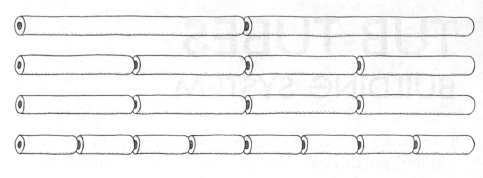

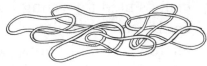

 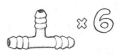

eight one-eighth lengths. You should end up with:

2 pieces ½ length

8 pieces ¼ length

8 pieces ⅛ length

Double up a rubber band over each end of each tube about a half inch from the edge. Try to keep the rubber bands flat, with as little twisting as possi-

ble. A No. 64 rubber band works best to keep assembled joints snug (and also keeps the tube from splitting open along the tube slit).

Test each of the plastic tube connectors to see if they float in water. Some kinds do and some do not, depending on the density of the plastic they are made from. A connector can easily be made to float by jamming one or two small pieces of foam tubing inside, to the center of the connector. You may have to sacrifice one of the small tube struts to make enough floatation plugs for all the connectors in the kit if they don't float naturally.

To build with Tub Tubes, just dump all the floating pieces into the bath water, select the parts to assemble, and push the connectors into the tube struts. The things you build will also float.

TUB TUBES
BUILD-IT PROJECT

TUB TUBE TOYS

TUB TUBE TOYS

There are many simple structures you can build using only the parts in a starter set of Tub Tubes. In addition to your own floating creations, these Tub Tube Toys are designed for the soak-time activities kids like most. For tub readers, there's a Floating Magazine Stand to keep your arms from getting tired. (Don't try this with a book, though!) For gamesters, the Ring Toss has an adjustable target that moves from easy to impossible. Sailors will certainly want to adjust the mainsail on the Sailboat (or turn it into any other type of vessel). And pretend players can imagine that the huge Water Bug is really a friendly creature. Or you might quickly build all the Tub Tube Toys just to get ideas for your own toy inventions. How about a water-walking sea creature?

Construction

Building system
Tub Tubes

Builder's age
9+

Player's age
2+

Materials

Starter set of Tub Tubes consisting of

☐ 2 half-length Tub Tubes
☐ 8 quarter-length Tub Tubes
☐ 8 eighth-length Tub Tubes
☐ 8 Elbow 90° connectors
☐ 6 "T" connectors
☐ 36 rubber bands

Tools

☐ Hands only

Building instructions

Using only the pieces in the starter set, you can build these Tub Tube Toys and many of your own constructions. You can also add more pieces to the set to build larger and more grandiose designs.

Magazine Reader

Part	Quantity
$1/4$-length strut	4
$1/8$-length strut	8
Elbow	6
"T"	4

Sailboat

Part	Quantity
$1/2$-length strut	2
$1/4$-length strut	5
$1/8$-length strut	6
Elbow	4
"T"	5

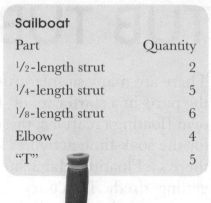

Ring toss

Part	Quantity
$1/4$-length strut	7
$1/8$-length strut	5
Elbow	7
"T"	3

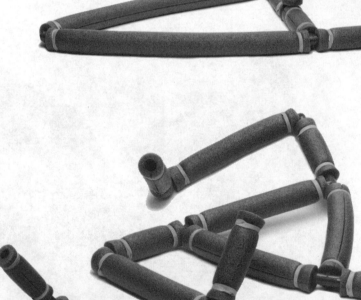

Waterbug

Part	Quantity
$1/4$-length strut	6
$1/8$-length strut	6
Elbow	6
"T"	3

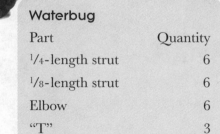

PASTA PIECES AND PASTE
BUILDING SYSTEM

The most versatile or "open ended" space frame building systems have modular components that come in several shapes and sizes to build models of almost any form and design. In many ways, Pasta Pieces and Paste is that perfect construction system with lots of beams, rods, tubes, and wheels, as well as many specially shaped parts you might need for just the "right" details. And to fasten all these parts together, there is a safe, quick-drying, Super Pasta Paste that's easy to make. To start building with Pasta Pieces and Paste, all you need is a selection of dry pastas from a grocery store and a box of gelatin powder to make the pasta paste.

The types of structures you build can be anything from skyscrapers and cranes to model creatures and cars. And this building system is so inexpensive that you can build lots of neat stuff and not ever have to take your projects apart or reuse the pieces.

SYSTEM FEATURES

- Choose from a large selection of inexpensive pasta pieces
- Beams and rods can be easily broken to any length
- Builds all types of space frames and other type structures
- Gelatin glue is safe (even edible) and dries quickly
- Pasta Piece structures and playthings look terrific
- Completed structures can be colored with markers or paints

Construction

Builder's age

6+ (Adult supervision is needed for cooking the pasta paste.)

Materials

- ☐ Variety of pasta shapes. See the list of pasta pieces for many of the pasta shapes that may be available.
- ☐ 1 quarter-ounce packet of unflavored gelatin
- ☐ 1 cup of water
- ☐ String, paperboard, aluminum foil, and other scrap materials (optional)
- ☐ Felt-tip markers or water-based paints (optional)

Tools

- ☐ Cooking pot and stirring spoon
- ☐ Small brush for applying the paste (optional)

Building techniques

The constructions you build using Pasta Pieces and Paste can take on almost any form. But the strength of the structures you build will depend on how well you apply the principles of space frame design. Remember that using triangles and trusses will give you the strongest structure for the least material.

Many pasta pieces can be used as is right out of the box, and long, thin pastas can be broken to any length you need. See what types of pasta are available at the grocery store and start with a few types of both tubular pasta and pasta strands. Think about what you might want to build. You can use rotelle for wheels, lasagna for roadways, roofs, and train tracks, and fettuccine for framing models. After gathering the pasta shapes you

plan to use, it's time to make a batch of Super Pasta Paste.

Making Super Pasta Paste

Because making the paste requires cooking, adult supervision or permission is required.

First, dissolve a packet of gelatin powder in water, but do not follow the instructions on the package. Use this recipe instead. Add one envelope of unflavored gelatin (1/4 oz) to one cup of cold water. Stir the mixture in a saucepan over medium heat until the gelatin is completely dissolved. Continue to

cook the mixture until it almost boils, and then remove it from the heat. If you use a microwave oven instead of a stove top, try cooking the mixture at full power for about 1 1/2 to 2 minutes. The pasta paste is ready to use in about fifteen minutes or as soon as it is cool enough to touch.

Fastening pasta pieces

To apply the pasta paste to pasta pieces, you can use your finger, a scrap piece of pasta, or a small brush. Any pasta paste you get on your hands or clothes will easily wash off with water.

To fasten pasta pieces together with the pasta paste, apply a small amount of paste to one of the parts, then put it together with another part and hold the two pieces in place for a minute until the glue begins to set. The larger the area of contact between the two parts, the stronger the joint will be.

As each glued joint begins to set, you can continue to work on the structure, attaching more pieces in place, but be gentle. The glue bond will take several hours to fully harden. To reposition a part or if a piece breaks loose, just add another drop of pasta paste.

If your pasta joints are too weak, use less water in the mixture. If your supply of pasta paste gets too thick or turns to jelly, a little heat will make it thinner again. Any unused pasta paste can be stored in a closed container at room temperature to be later warmed up and used again.

Here are a few more tips for working with pasta paste: The more paste you use, the longer the joint will take to harden. A little paste will dry hard enough in a few minutes so you can handle the parts and build structures quickly. In a few hours, the adhesive bonds will become their strongest. You can later add more glue for added strength. And you will also find that some types of pasta stick together much better than others.

Making pasta bundles

Many dry pasta shapes will break if bent too much, especially spaghetti and other long, thin noodles, so build with care. If you need an extra-strong rod, paste together several strands of spaghetti to make a "bundle beam." Hold a small bundle of pasta tightly together with the ends flush, and dip each end of the bundle in the pasta paste. For an even stronger beam, spread some pasta paste along the length of the bundle. To connect the bundles, use elbows, ziti, rigatoni, or mostaccioli (whichever fits best).

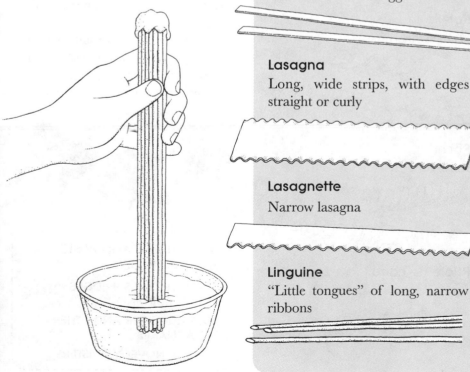

ALL KINDS OF PASTA PIECES

Pasta comes in a huge variety of shapes that inspire building different types of structures. Ribbons and strands can be used like miniature pieces of lumber, tubes can be attached side by side like round bricks or to form vertical tube walls, and the many special pasta shapes can add wheels, bows, and other special features to your pasta construction. Some pasta names actually describe the pasta shape in Italian. Fettuccine, for example, means "little ribbons," and vermicelli translates into "little worms." Not all types of pasta may be available at your local grocery store unless you live near an Italian food market. But any type of hard pasta will work fine for building with Pasta Pieces and Paste.

Ribbons

Fettuccine
"Little ribbons" of egg noodles

Lasagna
Long, wide strips, with edges straight or curly

Lasagnette
Narrow lasagna

Linguine
"Little tongues" of long, narrow ribbons

Pappardelle
One-inch-wide noodles with straight or pinked edges

Tagliatelle
Egg noodles a bit wider than fettuccine

Strands

Capelli D'Angelo
"Angel's hair," very thin pasta

Cappellini
Thin strands, slightly thicker than angel's hair

Fusilli
Twisted or spiral-shaped strands

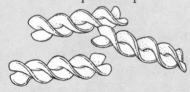

Spaghetti
Long, round, thin strands

Spaghettini
Very thin spaghetti

Vermicelli
"Little worms," or thin strands slightly thicker than cappellini

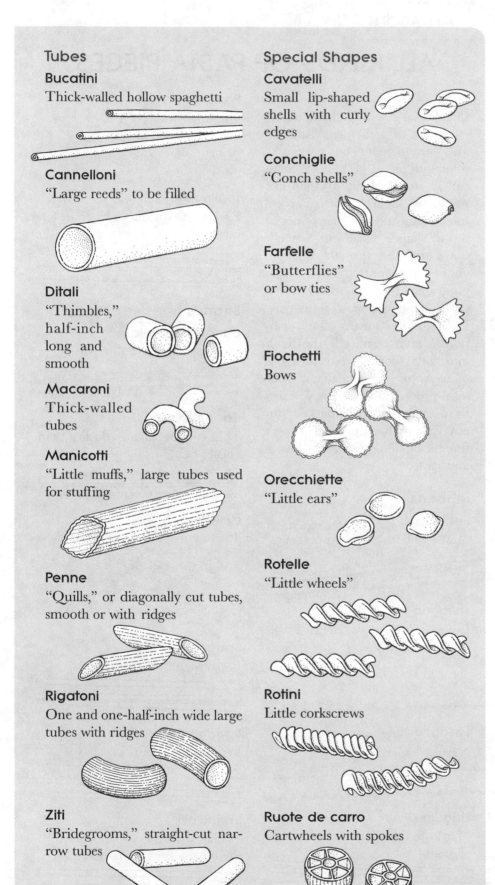

Tubes

Bucatini
Thick-walled hollow spaghetti

Cannelloni
"Large reeds" to be filled

Ditali
"Thimbles," half-inch long and smooth

Macaroni
Thick-walled tubes

Manicotti
"Little muffs," large tubes used for stuffing

Penne
"Quills," or diagonally cut tubes, smooth or with ridges

Rigatoni
One and one-half-inch wide large tubes with ridges

Ziti
"Bridegrooms," straight-cut narrow tubes

Special Shapes

Cavatelli
Small lip-shaped shells with curly edges

Conchiglie
"Conch shells"

Farfelle
"Butterflies" or bow ties

Fiochetti
Bows

Orecchiette
"Little ears"

Rotelle
"Little wheels"

Rotini
Little corkscrews

Ruote de carro
Cartwheels with spokes

Making Pasta Piece playthings

With a variety of pasta pieces and some pasta paste, you can construct just about any shape or form or type of space frame structure from a detailed model to some kind of working contraption, or maybe a sculpture that looks like nothing. And you can always just mess around with the pasta pieces to see what wants to connect with what. Just use your imagination and build whatever your fantasy can conjure up—and imagine whatever you build can be anything.

For builders who want to follow building plans or need inspirations, look through the instruction booklets that come with construction toys and building sets, then figure out how to build what you like using the Pasta Pieces and Paste building system. Photos from magazines and catalogs are also a good source of ideas for things to build.

You decide what you want to make and how you want to construct it. For some constructions, you may want to add other materials like string for cables on cranes or riggings on ships. Pieces of thin cardboard can be used for roadways on bridges or roofs on houses. And if you want to color the pasta pieces, try using wide felt-tip markers or any water-based paint.

PASTA PIECES AND PASTE BUILD-IT PROJECTS

TRIANGLE TRUSS BRIDGES
MODEL BUILDING

ROTELLE RATTLER AND OTHER PASTA SNAKES

NOODLE NOVELTY TWISTERS

TRIANGLE TRUSS BRIDGES MODEL BUILDING

Many of the highway and railroad bridges that traverse great distances are constructed of trusses formed by lots of struts. The fact that there are different types of trusses used in bridge making usually means that each particular truss design was best suited for certain uses like long spans or short spans, and heavy loads or light loads. However, sometimes the truss design selected for a covered bridge just happened to be the favorite of the builder.

Using Pasta Pieces and Paste construction, you can fabricate the beams, struts, and roofing panels needed to build models of several types of truss bridges and covered-bridge designs. And with watercolors, you might paint the pasta pieces to look like wood or add roof shingles and other realistic details. The bridges you build may be too delicate for active play, but they are perfect for display.

Construction

Building system
Pasta Pieces and Paste

Builder's age
8+ (with adult supervision for cooking the paste)

Player's age
8+

Materials
☐ Fettuccine (for struts, beams, roadway, roofing, and siding)

☐ Linguine (optional for making struts)

☐ Lasagna (for quickly making roadways, roofing, and siding)

☐ Paperboard (optional for roadways)

☐ 1 quarter-ounce packet of unflavored gelatin

☐ 1 cup of water

☐ Plastic wrap or wax paper (to protect the work surface)

Tools
☐ Cooking pot and stirring spoon

Building instructions

Select a truss design

Choose the truss bridge design you want to build. All the trusses shown have been used for uncovered bridges, but most covered bridges use a Burr truss, a Howe truss, or a Town lattice truss.

Next, decide how large the bridge will be. You can build a truss the same size as the plans shown here by placing a piece of clear plastic wrap (or wax paper) over the plan you select, then place the pasta struts in position over the plan and paste them together. Building the trusses on plastic wrap will keep the structure from sticking to the book.

Instead of working directly on the book and trying to keep it flat, it may be easier to first make a copy of the plan—if you have access to a copier. Using a copier, you can also change the scale of truss to make it larger or smaller.

Making bridge beams and struts

Make an inventory of the beams and struts needed by carefully breaking the pasta to the proper lengths. Most truss designs use only a few different strut lengths. For accurate length pieces, mark where you want to break the pasta strut, and break it on the mark over the square edge of a table.

The heavy "wooden" beams and struts of a covered bridge truss are

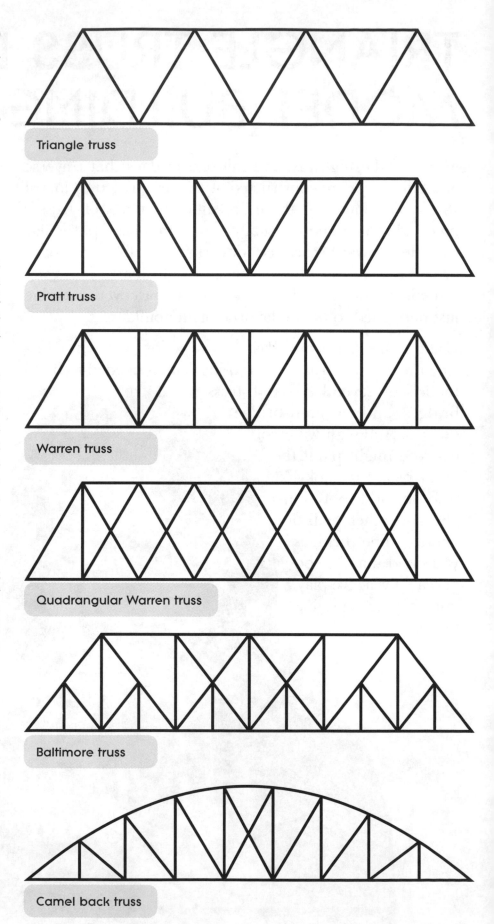

Triangle truss

Pratt truss

Warren truss

Quadrangular Warren truss

Baltimore truss

Camel back truss

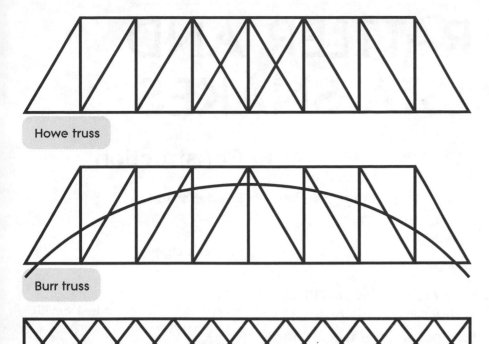

Howe truss

Burr truss

Town lattice truss

Building the truss structure

1. Mix up a batch of pasta paste. For the paste recipe and gluing tips, see instructions for Pasta Pieces and Paste.

2. Build the sides of the bridge first. Follow the pattern carefully and build two identical trusses. Building the trusses on a piece of plastic wrap will keep the structures flat and from sticking to the work surface or plans.

3. When the pasta paste is dry, carefully remove the two trusses from the work surface and position them side by side and spaced apart as wide as you want the bridge to be. Make several crossbeams (made like struts) the width of the bridge, and glue them in place across the top and bottom of the trusses as seen in the models shown.

Covering the roadway, roof, and sides

The basic truss bridge you have designed only needs a roadway to be complete. You can convert any truss bridge into a covered bridge by also adding a roof and sides. And like most covered-bridge builders, you get to design the roof structure, which is usually a simple gable but can also be a flat or shed roof.

The roadway, roof covering, and bridge siding can all be built using lengths of fettuccine pasted side by side. But that could take a lot of pasta planks and a lot of time for gluing. As an alternative for faster building, you might try using a wider flat pasta like lasagna.

4. Using the truss plan or the truss bridge you have built, fabricate more pasta pieces to the proper lengths needed for building a roadway plus a roof and siding (if you are building a covered bridge), and paste the pieces in place.

made by stacking and laminating two or more equal lengths of pasta. Struts require only two stacked pieces, but beams can be made using three, four, or more stacked pieces. To fabricate a laminated beam or a strut, first break as many pieces of pasta as needed to the

proper length, then laminate the pieces in a stack, using pasta paste. Allow the laminated stack to dry and harden before using it to build a truss.

Fabricate all the proper length beams and struts needed to build two trusses.

ROTELLE RATTLER AND OTHER PASTA SNAKES

Making a long, squiggly play snake that can cause adults to back away and shiver can be very satisfying. You can easily make many different types of articulated "snakes" by stringing together pieces of pasta. And it's just as easy to create colorful snakeskin patterns using paints, food coloring, or markers.

There are many shapes and sizes of tube-like pasta that can be used for making many different kinds of snakes. But if you happen to string rotelle pasta (little wheels) into the length of a rattlesnake, you'll get a Rotelle Rattler. What kind of a snake would you get using penne, ziti, or ditali pasta?

Construction

Builder's age

5+

Player's age

3+

Warning: Play by young children should be supervised. Small pasta pieces can be a choking hazard.

Materials

☐ Selection of dry pastas

☐ String or package twine

☐ Watercolor paints and paint-brush (optional)

☐ Color markers (optional)

☐ Food coloring and water (optional)

☐ Glue and glitter or glitter glue (optional)

☐ Paper towels, wax paper, or news-paper if using food coloring

Tools

☐ Scissors

☐ A bowl if using food coloring

Building instructions

1. Select the pasta. The kind of pasta you use will affect the shape and size of the snake you make. Of course, the pasta must be some tubular shape or be able to be strung. Having several kinds of pasta will let you combine shapes to define the different looks of the snake's body, head, and tail.

For the snake's body, you might choose a smooth or ribbed tube pasta. Rotelle is shaped like little wheels and can be easily strung to make a round snake body that twists and bends somewhat like a real snake. Pasta tubes cut at an angle, like penne, are good for making "rattler" tails, and any larger tube pasta can be used for the head.

Here's a builder's tip: If you know the type of snake you are going to make and have the design of all the pasta pieces planned, you may want to paint the pasta before you start stringing.

2. Thread the string through the pasta pieces. Cut a length of string several inches longer than you plan to make your snake, and tie one end to a piece of pasta used for the snake's tail.

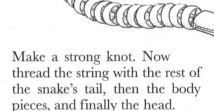

Make a strong knot. Now thread the string with the rest of the snake's tail, then the body pieces, and finally the head.

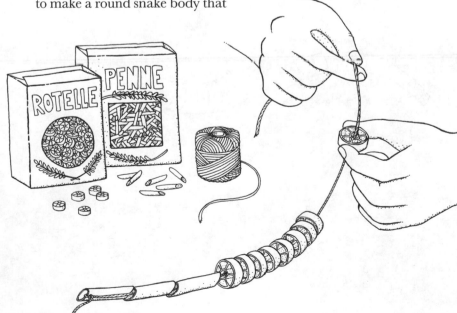

Make sure all the pasta pieces are pulled snugly onto the string, and tie the string in a knot around the last piece threaded for the head. To make a tongue, thread the string end through the snake's head and out its mouth, then trim the string to a few inches.

3. Paint the snake with a colorful pattern. Many snakes have very colorful skins with interesting patterns you can copy for your pasta snake. You can either paint the pasta pieces before stringing them together (easier to do), or paint the snake after it is made and hang it to dry by the head or tail string. Remember to paint the tongue string red.

Watercolor paints and felt-tip markers work well on pasta. For the most brilliant colors, soak batches of the pasta pieces (before stringing) in different food colorings that have been thinned with a little water. After five to ten minutes, remove the pieces and spread them to dry on a stack of paper towels, wax paper, or old news-paper. The longer the pieces have soaked, the deeper the colors will be.

Whatever method used to color the pasta, you can apply spots, stripes, and other markings to the pieces with contrasting color paints or markers, and maybe use glitter glue to give your snake sparkling eyes and a shiny rattle.

Snake pattern coloring guide

Snakes come in a huge variety of sizes, patterns, and combinations of colors. You might conduct a lit-tle research to see what these and a few other colorful snakes actually look like, or make a copy of the page and color the illustrations using the numbered colors listed in the chart.

Banded Rock Rattlesnake

Southwestern states

Two feet long

Greenish gray with brown or deep gray rings

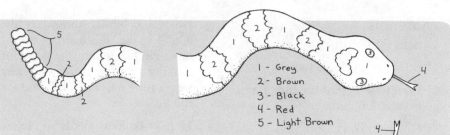

1 - Grey
2 - Brown
3 - Black
4 - Red
5 - Light Brown

Death Adder

Australia

Sixteen to twenty inches long

Brown to red alternating rings

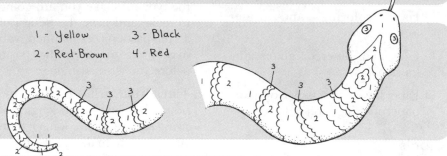

1 - Yellow 3 - Black
2 - Red-Brown 4 - Red

Arizona Coral Snake

Southern Arizona

Twenty inches long

Alternating bands and rings of red, white, and black, with the red bands always bordered on each side by white rings

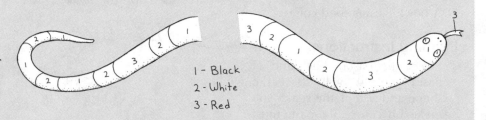

1 - Black
2 - White
3 - Red

Green Tree Python

Australia and New Guinea

Seven feet long

Generally bright green with light blue patches and white spots

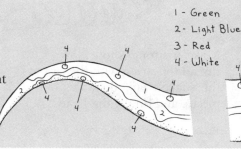
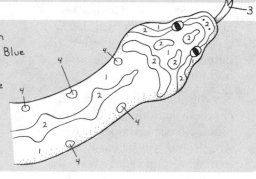

1 - Green
2 - Light Blue
3 - Red
4 - White

Southern Coral Snake

South America

Three feet long

Repeating sequence of bands and rings, red-black-white-black-white-black-red, and so on

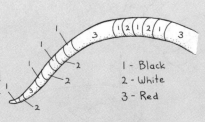
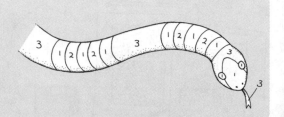

1 - Black
2 - White
3 - Red

Hairy Bush Viper

West Africa

Two feet long

Pale to dark yellowish green spiked scales

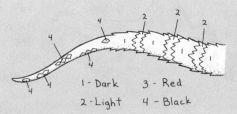
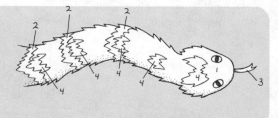

1 - Dark 3 - Red
2 - Light 4 - Black

NOODLE NOVELTY TWISTERS

String a bunch of short pasta tubes onto a long chain of rubber bands to make a Noodle Novelty Twister that will hold the shape you put it in until you twist it into something else. Using several long strings of pasta, you can twist them together the way a clown twists balloons into familiar objects. You can also start with a rubber band skeleton to make a Noodle Novelty Twister into a stick figure with movable joints, or maybe build some arbitrary form just to fiddle with. For added fun, the pasta pieces can be decorated to create colorful patterns or special creature features.

The idea behind Noodle Novelty Twisters may sound simple, but making these articulated toys takes planning before you start building and figuring out some things as you assemble the pieces. The instructions are only meant to get you started with a few projects without ending up in a tangled mess. Once you catch on to the building techniques, see what other twisters you can make.

Construction

Builder's age
7+

Player's age
7+

Materials
□ Rubber bands (No. 19 and other long, thin rubber bands work best.)

□ Tube pasta (dry)

    Rigatoni

    Penne

    Ziti

    Ditalini

    Elbow macaroni

    Rotelle

□ Optional coloring

□ Food coloring

□ Watercolor paints and brush

□ Markers

Tools
□ Paper clip (standard size)

Building instructions

Create a design and select the pasta

Depending on what you plan to build, select one or more types of dry tubular pasta. For younger builders and beginners, larger pasta tubes like rigatoni are easier to handle. If you have something particular you plan to build, lay out the design, using the actual pasta pieces.

Start with an easy-to-make design like a long string of pasta tubes. After learning the methods of creating rubber band "skeletons" and attaching the pasta tubes together, build the more complex Mobility

Figure. Once you've become a pro, try assembling the Fidget Cube.

Make a rubber band skeleton

Long, thin rubber bands are easier to thread through noodles and secure around noodles. Size No. 19 (3 1/2 inches long by 1/16 inch wide) works very well and is commonly available. Most Noodle Novelty constructions will require various lengths of rubber bands that can be made by linking, or chaining, two or more rubber bands end to end.

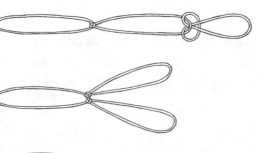

If you just want to experiment with twisting a single strand of pasta tubes into a few simple designs, begin with a chain of three or more rubber bands. If your design is more complex, with several connections and endings, it may be easier to first lay out the complete rubber band skeleton before stringing the pasta tubes. Follow these illustrations for the different ways to connect rubber bands to each other.

String pasta onto the skeleton

A paper clip bent out into the shape of a letter "J" makes a handy needle for pulling a rubber band through pasta tubes, especially when the rubber band is in tension. Leave the small loop of the paper clip for the hook and use the tool like a sewing needle. First, attach the end

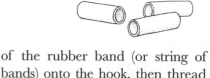

of the rubber band (or string of bands) onto the hook, then thread the other end of the tool through a noodle and pull the rubber band completely through.

To string elbow macaroni and other small-diameter tube pasta, you might need to narrow the width of the hook by squeezing it using pliers. The paper clip tool can also be bent into a curve (use your fingers for bending) to easily pass through curved tubular noodles.

To string any simple or complex strand of pasta, you need a way to prevent the rubber band from pulling completely through the first pasta piece. And at the end of any string of pasta pieces, you need a way to attach the end of the rubber band to the last piece. Follow these illustrations for one way to begin and end a simple string.

Wherever you end a string, the rubber band must be in tension. You can either add enough pasta tubes to use all the length of rubber band available, or tie off the end of the rubber band to make it shorter.

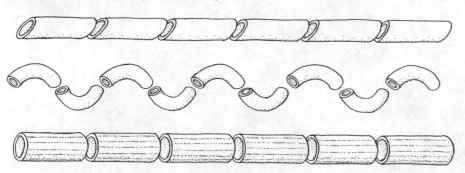

Decorating pasta pieces

The easiest time to color the pasta tubes is before you string them onto rubber bands. Felt markers and craft paints work well, but the fastest and easiest method is to soak the pasta pieces in diluted food coloring.

Fill a bowl with one-fourth cup of water and five to ten drops of food coloring (pick the color or colors you want), and soak the pasta for about five minutes. Don't soak the pieces any longer or the pasta will become soggy and lose its shape. Use a fork or tongs to remove each piece of pasta, and lay them out individually to dry on a plate, cookie sheet, or wax paper. The food coloring will create beautifully bright colors.

Things to build

Here are two projects to help you get started. Once you've gotten the hang of it, invent your own simple Noodle Novelty Twister designs for familiar things like an airplane, a car, a boat, a spider, and all the letters of the alphabet plus the numbers zero through nine.

Mobility Figure

Depending on the pasta tubes you use, there are many designs possible for making all kinds of Noodle Novelty mobility figures, and you might want to invent your own figures. This one uses a variety of pasta shapes plus five No. 19 rubber bands to make a stick figure with movable arms, legs, and head. Even the hands and feet can rotate. The pasta pieces you need are two rotelle, four penne, four ziti, and two macaroni.

1. To make the head and body, connect the two rotelle by looping one rubber band around both of them, then over one as shown.

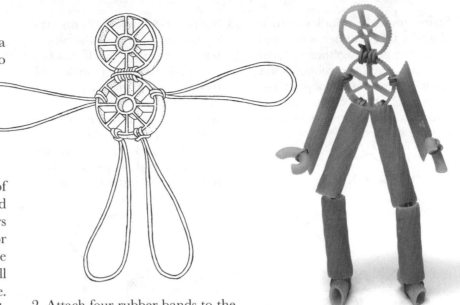

2. Attach four rubber bands to the rotelle body in the best positions for arms and legs.

3. Make arms by stringing one penne onto each arm rubber band, and end each loop with a macaroni noodle hand. The angled ends of the penne will allow the arms to angle downward.

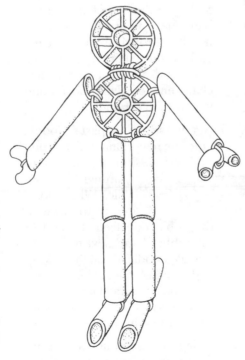

4. Make legs by stringing two ziti noodles onto each leg rubber band, and end each loop with a penne noodle foot.

Fidget Cube

To build a Fidget Cube, you will need twelve straight ziti noodles and six No. 19 rubber bands. Sort through the ziti to find twelve reasonably straight pieces that are all about the same length. What you will get is a loosey-goosey cube that can be twisted, bent, and flipped in ways only a fidgeter can figure out. Assembly will be easier if you use two paper clip pulling tools.

1. String four ziti noodles onto a chain of three rubber bands and bring the ends together to form a square. Feed the rubber band chain through the loop at the beginning of the chain and pull firmly so the rubber bands are slightly in tension.

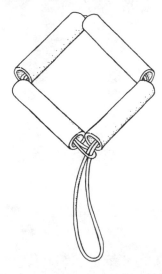

2. Attach a rubber band to each of the other three corners and string one noodle onto each one.

3. String two noodles on the remaining portion of the rubber band chain, and while holding the chain with the hook tool, feed the end of the rubber band at an adjacent corner (with a single noodle) through the loop at the end of the chain. Remove the hook and attach it to the new chain end (which is the rubber band you just fed through).

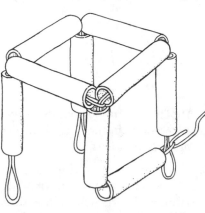

4. String a pasta noodle onto the new chain end and pull the chain end through the noodle. While holding it there with the hook tool, feed the end of the rubber band next to it (with a single noodle) through the loop at the end of the chain. Remove the hook and attach it to the new chain end of the rubber band you just fed through.

5. Again, string a pasta noodle onto the new chain end and pull the chain end through the noodle. While holding it there with the hook tool, feed the end of the rubber band next to it (with a single noodle) through the loop at the end of the chain. Remove the hook and attach it to the new chain end of the rubber band you just fed through.

6. String the last pasta noodle onto the new chain end and pull the chain end through the noodle. To form a cube and finish off the end of the chain, stretch the rubber band so you can hold it

while removing the hook. Thread the rubber band around the last corner of the cube, then loop the end back over the last pasta piece it came through.

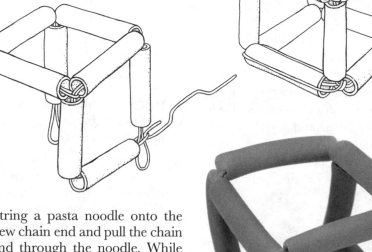

Other fidget forms can be made in a similar way by stringing ziti on rubber band chains.

PASTA

Did you ever wonder why Yankee Doodle ". . . stuck a feather in his hat and called it macaroni"? Back in the days of the American Revolution, macaroni (and all other types of pasta) was considered a very special luxury eaten only by those wealthy enough to afford it. Rolling and cutting pasta by hand was hard work, and the special durum wheat used to make noodles was expensive. So when pasta was occasionally served during an elegant dinner party, it was eaten for dessert.

By the late eighteenth century in England, the word *macaroni* had come to mean perfection and elegance, and the expression "That's macaroni" was used to describe anything especially good. So in the British soldier's song "Yankee Doodle," the feather he put in his hat was simply being called elegant.

Pasta is made by mixing flour and water into a paste that is then formed and dried into many different shapes. Although it is unclear which ancient culture actually invented pasta, China and several Arabic countries have legends about its beginnings. The first actual mention of pasta was in a Roman cookbook from the first century A.D., which gives the recipe for making lasagna. Wealthy Romans of the time were also eating ravioli and fettuccine pasta dishes.

Pasta remained a luxury in many European civilizations right up to the eighteenth century. Even Thomas Jefferson, who was America's ambassador to

France in 1789, brought home a spaghetti-making machine and used it to serve pasta to the distinguished visitors who came to his Virginia home, Monticello.

In nineteenth century Italy, man-powered machines were invented

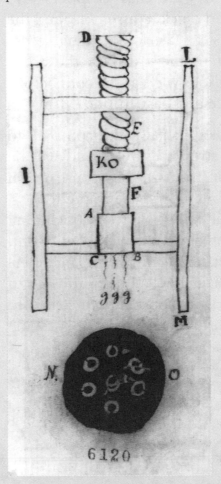

for kneading and pressing dough, meaning that pasta could be made faster and cheaper. It also encouraged more farmers to grow the special types of wheat needed for pasta making. With machines for mass producing pasta, this once expensive treat quickly became more commonly available and much more affordable. By the end of the century, pasta had become the national staple of Italy.

The discovery of electricity in the early 1900s made life even easier for pasta makers. Electric-motor-powered machines mixed and shaped dough on their own. The complete pasta-making process that used to take weeks could now be done in just a few hours. As pasta became a common addition to many family meals, pasta makers began to experiment with different types of wheat and a lot of new pasta shapes.

Today, there are more than one hundred fifty varieties of pasta cut and formed into nearly every conceivable shape. In Italy, where most of these were invented, there is even the Museo Storico Degli Spaghetti (Historical Spaghetti Museum), a special museum dedicated to the history of pasta.

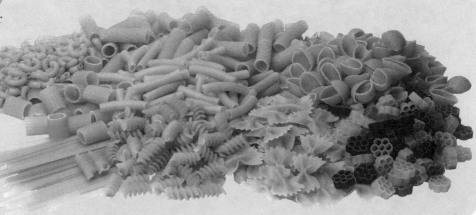

CLIP GRIPPERS AND STRAW STRUTS
BUILDING SYSTEM

Space frame structures made with Clip Grippers and Straw Struts are super easy and quick to assemble, and the pieces can be taken apart just as fast for building something else. In this building system, the straws are the struts, and paper clips are used in various ways as the connectors. Both materials are inexpensive and easy to find.

Because paper clips and drinking straws can combine to make rigid connections, the structures you build will be fairly strong and lightweight for their size. This construction system is especially good for building space frame towers, truss bridges, skyscrapers, all kinds of roofs (including domes), and just about any polyhedron you can figure out. Sometimes it is fun just to start connecting straws of different lengths and using the clip fasteners in different ways to see what kind of forms result. If any part of your structure is flimsy or weak, just add triangular braces to provide more rigidity.

SYSTEM FEATURES

- Perfect for quickly building large-scale, space frame constructions
- Paper clip connectors can be bent to join straws at any angle
- Constructions are sturdy, yet can be easily taken apart
- Plastic straws are lightweight and strong
- Straws are easy to cut to make modular-sizes
- Makes good-looking, colorful structures
- Uses inexpensive materials or discards

Construction

Builder's age
6+

Materials
☐ Plastic drinking straws, ¼″ diameter

☐ Paper clips (Standard size)

Tools
☐ Scissors

Building techniques

If you have a particular shape or structure you plan to build, collect the number of straws needed. If your construction requires straws of different lengths, they can be measured and cut (and trimmed even shorter if necessary) during construction. To make struts longer than a normal-length straw, connect two or more straws together, end to end, by squeezing and forcing the end of one straw into the open end of another straw. If you don't have a building plan to start with, just begin attaching straws to straws and invent the structure as you go. Here are some clip fastener methods to get you started.

The first three connectors each use only one paper clip bent open into the shape of the letter "S." For a straight connector, slightly bend out each of the two loops to slightly open them up. Then push each loop into the end of a straw. Bending out a loop makes the paper clip fit snugly inside the straw.

An angled connector works the same way, except the opened clip is bent in the middle to create an angle.

Types of clip connectors

Straight connector
Joins two or more straws in line

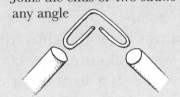

Angled connector
Joins the ends of two straws at any angle

Slider connector
Connects the end of a straw at any point along the length of another straw

Swivel connector
Creates a flexible joint at the end connections of two or more straws

For a slider connector, the larger loop is not bent out and is hooked over a straw, while the smaller loop is bent out slightly and inserted into the end of another straw.

To make a swivel connector, start with one clip, and hook one or more clips onto it. Then push each clip into a straw.

As you build with clips and straws, it may be necessary to fit more than one clip into one end of a straw. Three clips inserted into one end is the maximum, since a fourth clip will cause the straw to crack. If you have to connect the ends of several straws at one point, use a swivel connector, which only requires one clip per straw regardless of how many ends come together.

Experiment with combining triangles, squares, and odd shapes to discover the types of space frame structures this system builds best. How tall a structure can you build and still keep it strong and rigid? How long can you build a span that doesn't collapse? Or how big of a polygon can you make?

CLIP GRIPPERS AND STRAW STRUTS BUILD-IT PROJECTS

CLIP HOOKS AND HANGERS
MAGNETIC BATTLE BUGS

CLIP HOOKS AND HANGERS

This is one of the only building toys that starts at the top and builds downward. By bending paper clips into one or more modular hook shapes, you can hang the clips from each other to form an intricate wire sculpture. The completed design can be hung anywhere, but to show it off best, hang the sculpture by a sunny window to reflect the sparkling light from the shiny metal or colored clips. And, if you are the competitive type, you might try playing a game of Clip Hangers with a friend. The idea is to see which of you has the most skill in keeping the hanging structure balanced—and which one has added one clip too many. Oops!

Construction

Builder's age
  6+

Player's age
  6+

Materials

☐ Paper clips, at least 50

Jumbo or standard size, shiny metal or colored (Bigger clips are easier to work with.)

☐ String

Tools

☐ Hands only

Building instructions

There are many ways to bend paper clips so they can be connected and hung from each other. These are some of the best bent shapes that make good combination hooks and hangers.

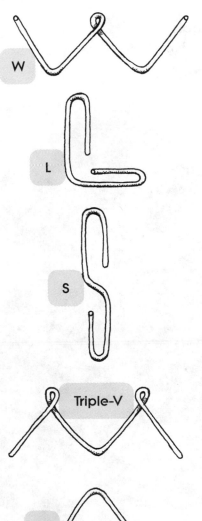

The "S" and the "C" shapes allow only building straight down, while the other bent shapes allow the sculpture construction to expand wider or become narrower. You can also choose to use all the same type of bent-shape clips in a hanging sculpture (but not with "S" or "C" hooks), or mix all the different types of hooks and hanger clips.

Start the hanging construction by tying one "W" Clip Hook and Hanger to a dangling piece of string. Then hang two clips from the first, and so on, building downward. The different combinations of bent clip shapes will produce unique sculptural patterns and forms. Experiment to learn what each bent-clip shape can do. For example, when building down with "W" clips, attaching clips with the loop facing up will cause the sculpture to grow wider, and with the loop down, the form will narrow. But watch your balance. If the hanging sculpture gets too lopsided, the whole thing could come crashing down.

Playing Clip Hangers, or the one-too-many game

In this game, which can be played by two or more participants, there can be only one loser, and everyone else is a winner. The rules are simple. Starting with one hanging clip, each player in turn adds a bent clip to the sculpture. As the hanging-clip structure grows, it will also become tipsy and easy to unbalance. The player who adds the clip that causes all or part of the structure to fall is the loser. With more than two players, you can also divide the players into two teams.

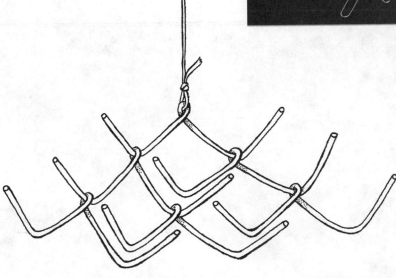

MAGNETIC BATTLE BUGS

In less than a minute, you can build some pretty amazing and weird bug-like creatures simply by attaching a bunch of bent paper clips to one or more small magnets. Just toss some bent paper clips at the magnet to see what kind of bug you get. The magnet will hold all the paper clips together to create its own sculptural form. The creatures you build can also include paper clip parts that you add, like legs and antennae. To make a pair or more of Magnetic Battle Bugs that will be ready for competition, simply add bent paper clip weapons like claws and hooks. Then, following the rules of Magnetic Battle Bug combat, you and your friends can determine which bug is the best warrior.

Construction

Builder's age
5+

Player's age
5+

Materials
- ☐ Small magnets (either disk or bar shaped)
- ☐ Paper clips (jumbo or standard size)

Tools
- ☐ Hands only

Building instructions

To build Magnetic Battle Bugs and other bug-like creatures, use regular- or jumbo-size paper clips. The bigger clips are easier to work with, but regular-size clips come in shiny metal as well as different colors. Using one or more disk magnets or

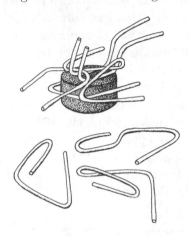

a bar magnet for the bug's body, simply bend several paper clips into a variety of shapes and place them on the magnet. As you add clips, try to shape the bug's body and appendages. Bend and arrange the paper clips around the magnet "body" to create bug legs, antennae, pinchers, stingers, hooks, and other bug-like stuff. You can then display the creatures you build and easily change them by just rearranging a few parts.

To build a winning Magnetic Battle Bug, you must securely attach many appendages to the bug's body, and bend the end of each appendage into a V-shaped hook. When you have built two battle bugs, it's time to do battle and see how many clips each bug can hook and pull off the other. As clips are pulled from one battle bug, they usually attach to the other. Any loose clips on the battlefield can be hooked by any battle bug. The battle bug with the most clips attached to its body is the winner.

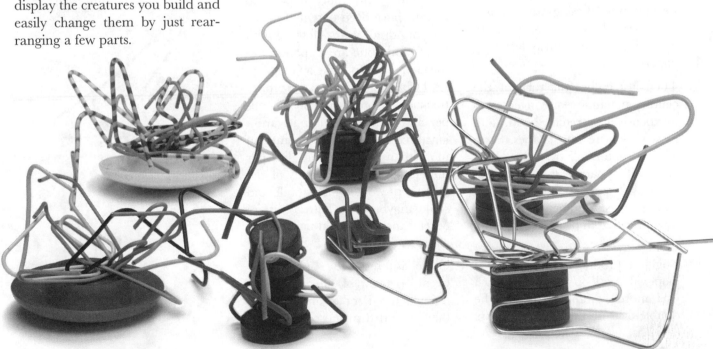

PAPER CLIPS

To many people, the simple, common, bent-wire paper clip represents design perfection. Its form is both elegantly simple and highly functional. In addition to clipping pages together, the paper clip now has hundreds of other uses that range from making chain necklaces to being the recommended tool for releasing stuck disk drives on some computers.

The first method used for fastening several papers together began in the thirteenth century, when a ribbon was threaded through a few parallel slits cut in the upper left-hand corner of the pages. That method soon evolved into using a combination of wax and ribbon.

Nothing much changed for the next six hundred years until 1835, when a New York physician named John Ireland Howe designed and built a machine for mass producing straight pins. Besides their many other uses, these pins were specifically sold for temporarily fastening papers together.

Then just before the turn of the century, machines were invented to inexpensively stretch, bend, and twist steel wire into shapes. Soon after, inventors all over the world began filing patents for all kinds of metal-wire paper clips having all kinds of twists and bends that were now practical to produce.

Gem Manufacturing Ltd. of England produced the first oval loop-within-a-loop paper clip, which was more commonly called the double-oval or the double-U clip.

Oddly enough, the Gem clip—which became the most popular type—was never patented. Instead, in 1899, William Middlebrook of Waterbury, Connecticut, patented the machine that produced the Gem clip.

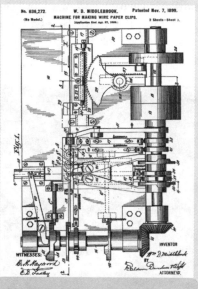

Middlebrook's patent drawing for a machine to make Gem paper clips.

Although many more paper clip designs have been patented in the last hundred years, few remain today, and none are as popular as the Gem clip. To make a Gem clip, steel wire is stretched to the proper thickness, coated with tin or copper, and then twisted into its familiar three-oval spiral at a rate of more than two hundred clips per minute per machine. Many of the other clips worked just as well, and some maybe even better, but no other paper clip could be made as easily as the Gem clip.

Quite interestingly, only about twenty percent of all paper clips manufactured today are used for their intended purpose—to fasten papers together—and half of those are consumed by the United States government. The rest are used for bookmarks, money clips, staple removers, poker chips, toothpicks, dress-hem holders, curtain holders, and fingernail cleaners, as well as for making all sorts of bent-wire toys. And many clips are simply played with and twisted into new shapes by office workers (typically while making telephone calls). There is even a paper clip art gallery that includes the best of these bent-clip sculpture inspirations. These are reproductions of a few.

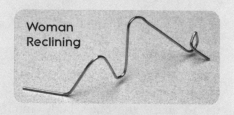

Woman Reclining

Citadel

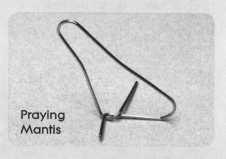

Praying Mantis

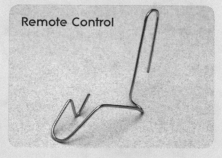

Remote Control

PERSONAL-SIZE SPACE FRAMES AND PLAY PLACES

It is always exciting to build big constructions that are full-scale versions of kid-size structures. Most construction sets and building systems are best suited for making small-scale models of large objects like a tall tower, a small building, or maybe a creature from outer space. But, with large struts and large building modules, you can construct large-scale versions of the same things. Some personal-size space frames are large enough to become actual play places to crawl into or gigantic sculptures that nearly fill a room.

For easy, quick, inexpensive, and temporary large space frames, long struts of almost any length can be made from rolled sheets of newspaper and quickly assembled (and disassembled) with large rubber bands. With enough newspaper, you can build a Personal Pyramid Play Space or an Indoor Circle Dome, several types of Four-Poster Roof-Canopy Beds, or maybe a larger-than-life creature of your own design. Just remember to keep Newspaper Struts and Poles construction indoors, out of the rain.

The Plastic Pipe Dreams building system is perfect for building permanent structures that can be used indoors or outdoors in any weather. And although building full-size working playthings and play spaces with plastic pipe requires time and craftsmanship plus the cost of the components, the results are impressive. Some constructions, including the Pipe Sculpture Sprinkler, the Cozy Cat Playground, and the 3-D Blind Marble Maze are unique products that can't be found anywhere else.

BUILD IT

NEWSPAPER STRUTS AND POLES	298
PERSONAL PYRAMID PLAY SPACE	301
ONE-KID TWO-KID TEPEE	303
FOUR-POSTER ROOF-CANOPY BEDS	305
INDOOR CIRCLE DOME	307
PLASTIC PIPE DREAMS	309
PLASTIC PIPE ART EASEL	312
CLASSIC LEMONADE STAND	315
3-D BLIND MARBLE MAZE	318
PLASTIC PIPE PLAYHOUSE	320
GARDENER'S GREENHOUSE	322
PIPE CHABLES	325
COZY CAT PLAYGROUND	327
PIPE SCULPTURE SPRINKLER	330

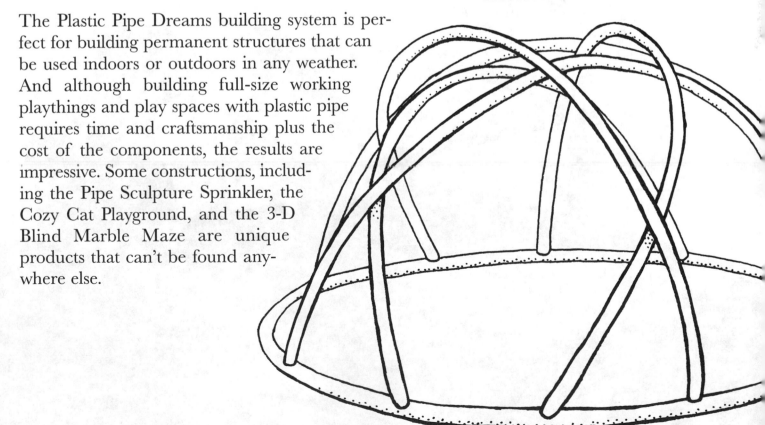

NEWSPAPER STRUTS AND POLES

BUILDING SYSTEM

Most of the space frame construction systems in this book use struts that are only a few inches long. Although these systems are fine for building models and small-scale projects, they are too short, thin, and lightweight for making large structures. To build kid-size space frames, you need a system that uses long, rigid struts.

Newspaper Struts and Poles are just the right length and strength for building structures big enough for you to get inside them. Once you have made a bunch of struts, you can quickly assemble them into a structure by just taping or tying the tube ends together. Struts that are tied together using string or large rubber bands can be disassembled just as easily to build something else. To complete your Newspaper Struts and Poles structure, and to provide some privacy for its inhabitants, the open framework can be covered with a bedsheet or blanket.

SYSTEM FEATURES

- Good for building large, kid-scale structures
- Old newspapers are plentiful and free
- Struts are easily made to any length
- Strut ends can be bent and connected at any angle
- Craftsmanship is not required
- Modular struts can be reused

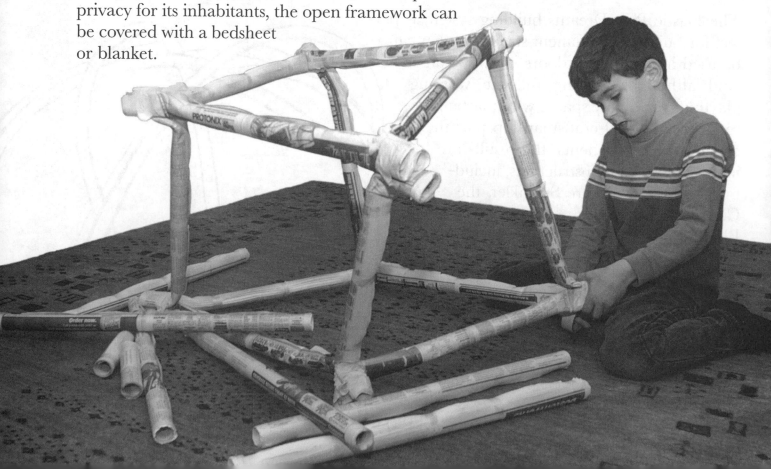

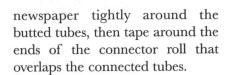

Construction

Builder's age
8+

Materials

☐ Newspaper

Regular-size sheets, tabloid-size, or both can be used. Don't underestimate the amount of newspaper you will need. A single newspaper tube uses 12 to 32 numbered newspaper pages. Even simple newspaper tube structures will require about ten daily newspapers or a few fat Sunday editions.

☐ Masking tape, ¾″ or 1″ wide

☐ String (optional)

☐ Shoelaces (optional)

☐ Large rubber bands (optional)

Tools

☐ Broom handle (optional)

Building techniques

There are three ways to roll sheets of newspaper into tubes to make rigid space-frame building struts and poles. Experiment with all the methods to see which one works best for the structure you are building. Generally, straight-rolled tubes are best for making short struts, and overlapping or spiral-wound tubes make better long-length struts. The secret of making a strong newspaper tube is to use the right amount of newspaper and to roll the tube tightly. Loosely wound tubes make weak structures.

Method No. 1: Straight-rolled, unit-length tubes

Find a large cleared table or a large area of the floor to work on.

The basic tubular strut and pole module is started by opening flat and then neatly stacking eight full sheets of newspaper (four numbered pages per sheet). Starting at one of the wide sides, roll the stack of pages into a tight tube. The hole formed in the center of the tube should be no larger in diameter than your

thumb. The larger the hole in the tube, the weaker it will be, and the more likely the tube will bend.

Keep the rolled-up newspaper tube from unrolling by wrapping three or four strips of tape around the tube along its length.

It may take a little practice before you become good at rolling tight tubes. Often, the hardest part is starting the tightly wound roll. You might find it easier to roll the newspaper sheets around a broom handle and then remove the handle just before the roll is taped.

For building some structures, you will need struts or poles longer than a single newspaper tube. You can make longer newspaper-tube struts by connecting two or more tubes end to end with more newspaper. Start by laying out and stacking four open sheets of newspaper, then lay two completed newspaper tubes end to end on the open sheets. The butted ends of the tubes should be centered on a narrow side of the stacked paper sheets. Roll the

newspaper tightly around the butted tubes, then tape around the ends of the connector roll that overlaps the connected tubes.

Continue to add on newspaper tubes in the same manner until the strut or pole is as long as you need it to be. For most newspaper tube constructions, strut or pole lengths of one, two, or three tubes are all that is needed.

Method No. 2: Overlapping, continuous-length tubes

Start with a single full sheet of newspaper (four numbered pages) and keep it folded once. Starting from the folded edge, begin tightly rolling up the newspaper (like a straight-rolled tube) until you are about halfway. Hold the half-rolled newspaper

to keep it from unrolling while placing another folded sheet over the unrolled portion and overlapping the length of the first roll about halfway. Continue rolling until the second sheet is half rolled, then add a third sheet and roll, adding additional sheets in this way until the roll is as long as you need it to be. When you have

rolled up the last sheet, fold the ends of the tube over and tape them in place to keep the tube tightly rolled. Because the tube has less newspaper rolled at both ends,

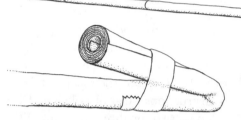

folding the ends also gives more strength to the weakest part of an overlapping tube. If your newspaper tube is more than a few feet long, wrap strips of tape around the tube in a few more places along its length to keep the sheets from unrolling.

Method No. 3: Spiral-wound, continuous-length tubes

As with making overlapping tubes, spiral-wound tubes are made by rolling folded newspaper sheets, but in this method, the sheets are rolled

on the diagonal. Additional sheets for more length are added one sheet at a time as the previous sheet is rolled about halfway. When you have rolled up the last sheet, fold over the ends of the tube and tape them in place. Tape around a few more places along the length of the tube to keep the sheets from unrolling.

Connecting Newspaper Struts and Poles

The ends of each newspaper strut or pole can be flattened and bent to any angle for connecting to the ends of one or more other struts.

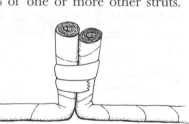

The joint of two or more gathered ends can be held together by wrapping the joint with tape (for permanent connections) or by tying the ends together with string, shoelaces, or large rubber bands (for removable connections).

When needed, a newspaper strut can be sharply bent anywhere along its length to create an angled joint. Also, the flattened tab end of a strut can be taped or tied to another strut anywhere along its length.

NEWSPAPER STRUTS AND POLES BUILD-IT PROJECTS

PERSONAL PYRAMID PLAY SPACE

ONE-KID TWO-KID TEPEE

FOUR-POSTER ROOF-CANOPY BEDS

INDOOR CIRCLE DOME

PERSONAL PYRAMID PLAY SPACE

Some people believe a square-base pyramid has special powers derived from the proportions of its shapes and the direction in which the pyramid is oriented. Although there is controversy about the existence of pyramid power, some scientists believe a pyramid can focus energy in a manner similar to the way a lens can focus light. The focal point in this case is inside the pyramid.

To test these theories yourself, you can build a large pyramid framework big enough for you and a friend to fit inside, and cover it with a blanket, sheet, or corrugated paper panels to make a personal pyramid tent. There are no specific ways to prove the powers your pyramid may have. Just get inside and see if you feel smarter, more creative, less tired, or stronger. Some people even believe their singing sounds better inside a pyramid enclosure.

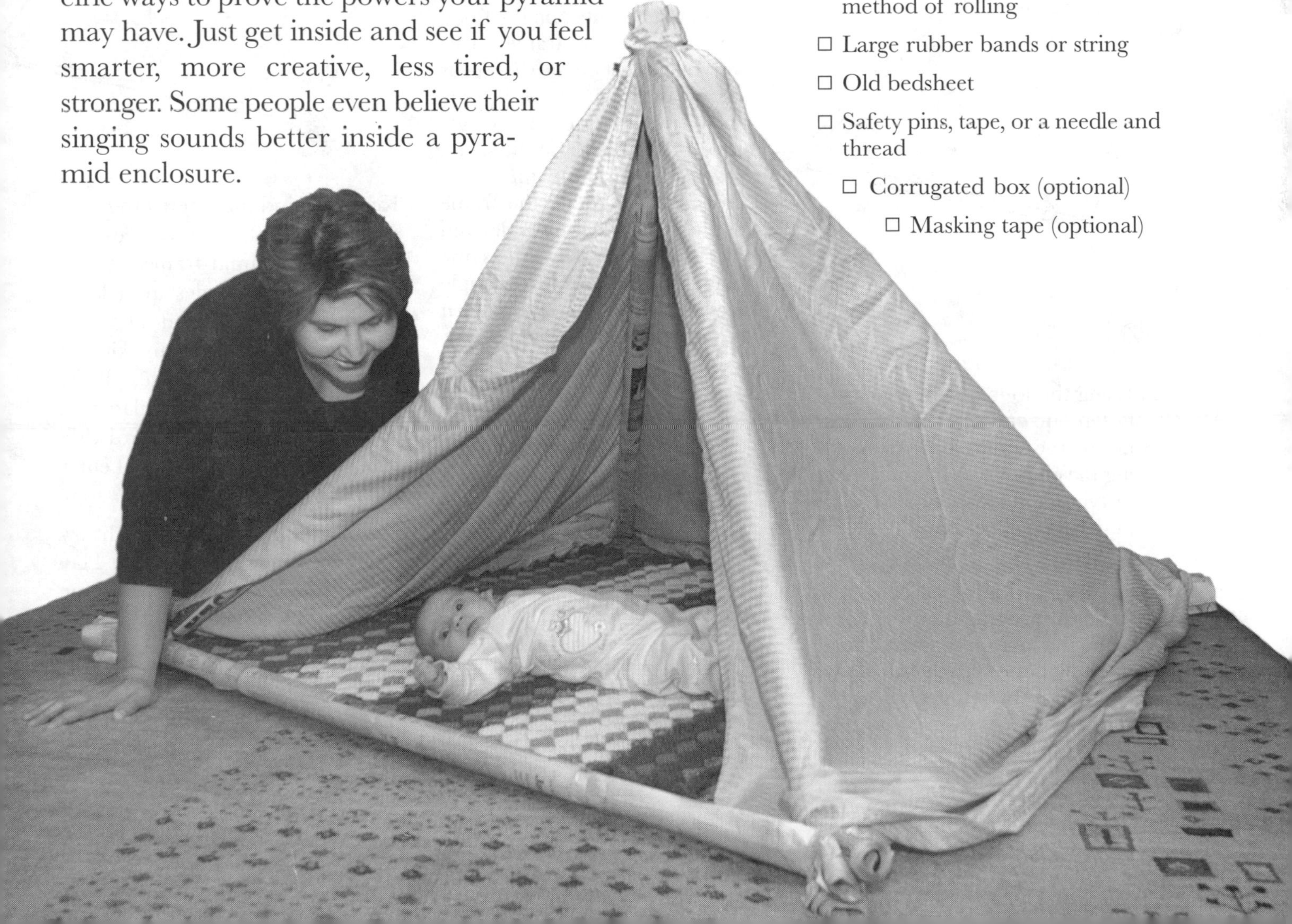

Construction

Building system
Newspaper Struts and Poles

Builder's age
8+

Player's age
Any age

Materials

- ☐ 8 newspaper double-length or triple-length struts, using any method of rolling
- ☐ Large rubber bands or string
- ☐ Old bedsheet
- ☐ Safety pins, tape, or a needle and thread
  - ☐ Corrugated box (optional)
    - ☐ Masking tape (optional)

Tools
☐ Scissors

Building instructions

You can make almost any size of pyramid you want or have the space for. A one-person pyramid starts with a square base that uses struts the length of two straight-rolled newspaper rolls on each side. A two-person pyramid uses struts that are three newspaper rolls long on each side.

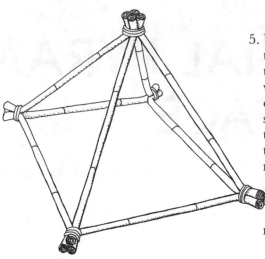

1. First, position the four double-length or triple-length struts that make up the square base. To fasten the corners of the base, bend the ends of the poles (either outward or inward) and join them together with tape, string, or large rubber bands.

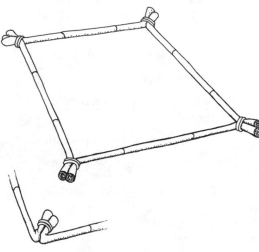

2. Using the four remaining struts, fasten one end of each to a corner of the square base by bending the end of a strut and taping or tying it in place, or slipping it under the rubber band.

3. Bring the unattached ends of the four struts together in the center above the square to complete the pyramid form. Bend the newspaper strut ends down and fasten them together.

   Note that it is a little easier to fasten the poles together by bending all of the pole ends out-ward instead of inward. The structure is the same size and just as strong, but the pyramid will have a "bump" on the outside of each corner.

4. To cover the four triangular sides of the pyramid frame, you will first need to make a pattern. Begin by smoothly laying out an old bedsheet on the floor. Turn the pyramid frame on its side and place it on the sheet near one of the corners. Using any kind of marker, trace the triangle shape of the frame on the sheet. Now, without lifting the structure, carefully rotate the frame to the next adjacent side and trace that triangle. Do the same thing with the last two triangle sides so that you have a pattern of four connected triangles.

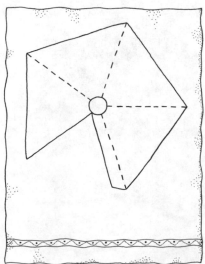

5. Using a pair of scissors, cut out the pattern around the perimeter, but do not cut out the individual triangles. Fasten the two ends of the cover together using safety pins, tape, or a needle and thread. Then just drape the custom-fitted cover over the pyramid frame and your Personal Pyramid Play Space is complete. To enter the pyramid, just lift the structure or one of the fabric sides, and crawl under it.

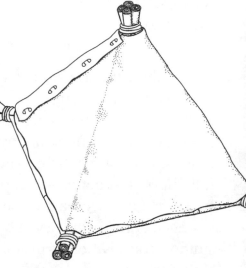

Keep in mind that there are many other materials you can use to cover the pyramid frame, including cut-to-fit triangles from large corrugated boxes and attached with tape. Avoid using any kind of plastic sheeting because plastic does not allow air to circulate and could pose a choking hazard to a very young player who might enter the pyramid.

For more variations, you might try building a Personal Pyramid Play Space using a tetrahedron frame made of triple-length poles. And, instead of bending the ends to form corner joints, try threading heavy string or light cord through the hollow center of the tubes, and assemble the tetrahedron frame like String and Straw Sticks.

ONE-KID TWO-KID TEPEE

With a few well-rolled and extra-long Newspaper Struts and Poles plus a cut-up bedsheet, you can make a tepee just big enough for you and a friend. The construction is quite simple, and the design does not have the many unique features of a true tepee dwelling, but you can play games, read, or have privacy (with the entrance closed) inside your personal portable tepee.

The size of this tepee depends on the size of the bedsheet you start with, and the size of the sheet determines the number of newspaper poles you need and how long they should be. With a few colorful markers, you can further personalize your cone-shaped play space.

Construction

Building system
Newspaper Struts and Poles

Builder's age
8+

Player's age
3+

Materials

☐ Newspaper tube poles

☐ Old bedsheet (A twin bedsheet makes a one-kid tepee and needs five poles. A queen or king bedsheet makes a two-kid tepee and needs six poles.)

☐ Safety pins

☐ String or cord

☐ Tools

☐ Scissors

☐ Felt-tip markers (optional)

☐ Latex paint (optional)

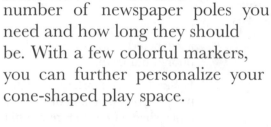

Building instructions

1. Find an old bedsheet that you can cut up, and lay it flat on the floor. Make a large compass for drawing a circle by tying a length of string to a felt-tipped marker or crayon. Hold the marker at one corner of the sheet and have someone hold the string taut at the center of the long edge of the sheet while drawing a semi-circle on the sheet.

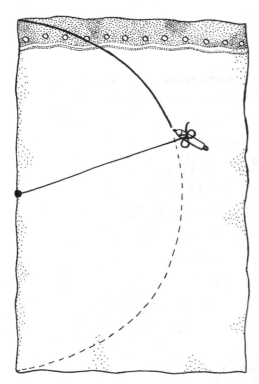

2. Using a pair of scissors, cut out the semicircle shape from the sheet.

3. Make the number of newspaper poles needed (either five or six) for the size sheet you used. All poles should be the same length and about one foot longer than the radius of the semicircle shape. (The radius is the length of the compass string used.)

4. Gather the poles in a tight bundle, and tie them together loose-ly by wrapping string or cord several times around the bundle about one foot down from the top.

5. Spread the poles out at the bottom, roughly in a circle, to form the tepee frame.

6. Cover the tepee frame with the semicircular sheet by placing the center of the straight edge at the point where the poles are tied, then wrap the sheet around the rest of the frame. Where the sheet comes together, along the edge that overlaps the other edge, fasten the upper two-thirds with safety pins. The bottom third should be left open to be used as an entrance.

7. Spread the poles out even more as needed until the sheet fits snugly around the frame. The poles will hold their position

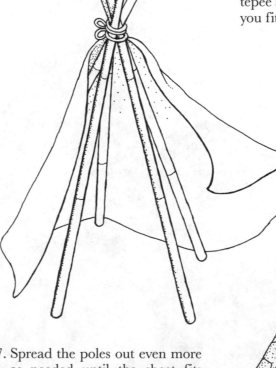

better if you place the tepee on a carpeted floor or use it outdoors on a lawn.

8. Using felt-tip markers or latex paint, you can decorate the tepee sheet either before or after you fit it to the frame.

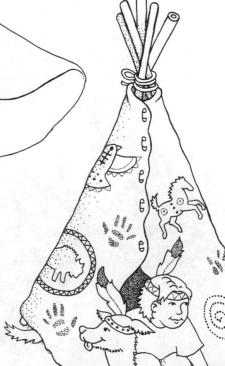

FOUR-POSTER ROOF-CANOPY BEDS

There is something very special about sleeping in a four-poster bed with a canopy covering the top. If you'd like to have the experience, it's easy to temporarily convert many regular beds into covered beds by using a framework made of Newspaper Struts and Poles and covering it with a bed-sheet. But if you want to make a bed canopy that's something special, build the framework into the form of your favorite style roof. You may prefer the modern look of a simple flat-roof or shed-roof canopy, the sophisticated design of a rounded-arch or pavilion-roof canopy, the elegance of a mansard-style canopy, or maybe the appearance of a New England-style gable roof.

Construction

Building system
Newspaper Struts and Poles

Builder's age
8+

Player's age
5+

Materials

☐ Newspaper tube poles (The number and length of the poles needed will depend on the structure being built.)

☐ Masking tape

☐ String or cord

☐ Old bedsheet

☐ Tools

☐ Scissors

☐ Felt-tip marker

Building instructions

1. Decide what style of roof canopy you want to build, then copy the design shown. You can also invent your own canopy roof design.

2. Make or gather a supply of several newspaper tube poles and more newspaper for lengthening the poles as needed. Also have masking tape handy for fastening joints.

3. Begin the framework by attaching an upright pole or post to each corner of the bed. Depending on the design of your bed frame, you might be able to tie the newspaper poles to existing bedposts or to a metal bed frame. Another method for attaching the uprights is to bend one foot of the length of each pole to a right angle, and slip it under the mattress. Lengthen the poles to make each upright the same height and as tall as needed for your canopy design.

4. Make two poles, each the length of your bed, and two more poles, each the width of your bed. Assemble the four new poles around the top of the four vertical poles to complete the basic frame. At each corner, flatten both ends of the connecting poles, overlap the flattened ends, and wrap the

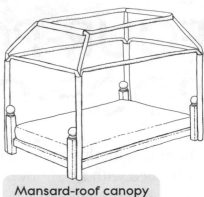
Flat-roof canopy

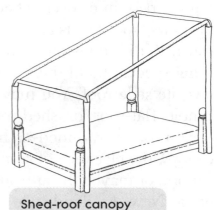
Mansard-roof canopy

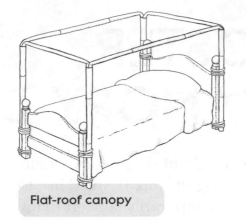
Gable-roof canopy

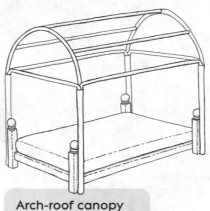
Shed-roof canopy

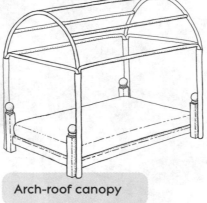
Arch-roof canopy

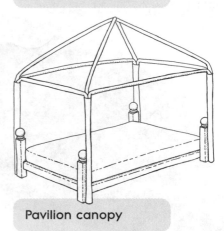
Pavilion canopy

joint with a few turns of masking tape to hold it together.

5. Follow the plan of the design you have chosen and connect the additional poles needed. Tape each joint as you build until the structure is finished.

6. Carefully drape a large bedsheet over the frame, and use safety pins or masking tape to gather and secure excess fabric while fitting the sheet to the form of the canopy framework.

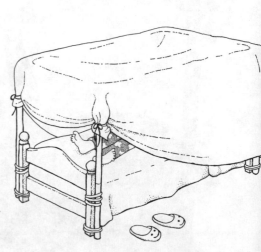

INDOOR CIRCLE DOME

Most domes are built using unit-length struts and connectors to create a polyhedral, many-faceted structure, but a Circle Dome is quite different. Instead of assembling struts to build triangles, the form of a Circle Dome is created using one big, circular-shaped newspaper tube pole for the base and five semicircle arched poles to form the "ribs" of the hemisphere framework.

Newspaper Struts and Poles are strong enough to make any size dome you like. A four- or five-foot-diameter Circle Dome covered with a sheet makes a cozy one-kid "tree house" you might build and use on your bed. An eight-foot-diameter covered Circle Dome on the floor makes a "cave" large enough for two or three kids to crawl inside.

But don't be too ambitious. Just the base ring of a five-foot-diameter dome will require a single newspaper tube pole about sixteen feet long! So you might first try building a much smaller, three-foot diameter Circle Dome, and cover it with a clear plastic (polyethylene) drop cloth to create an indoor mini-greenhouse for plants only.

Construction

Building system
Newspaper Struts and Poles

Builder's age
8+

Player's age
5+

Materials
- Newspaper tube poles, loosely rolled (The length of the six poles needed will depend on the diameter of the dome to be built.)
- Masking tape
- Old bedsheet
- Safety pins
    - Tools
        - Scissors
        - Felt-tip marker

Building instructions

Although building a Newspaper Struts and Poles circle is easy, construction can take a very long time. It's a good idea to have a helper or two to assist with rolling the long newspaper tubes and to hold the floppy tubes in place while the joints are being taped.

Because the rather large completed structure will be difficult to move without the tubes breaking or the joints coming apart, it's best to build the dome right in the place where you plan to use it.

1. Decide what diameter dome you want to build, and calculate the circumference of the base circle (circumference = diameter x 3.14). That will also be the length of the newspaper tube you make for the base circle. Remember that the height of a Circle Dome will be one-half of its diameter.

   Because the very long newspaper tubes must be bent into circular shapes, this is one Newspaper Struts and Poles project that actually benefits from slightly looser, less rigid, and larger diameter tubes. You may need to experiment a little to get the tubes just right so they can be bent in an arc without being too floppy and flimsy.

2. Form one long newspaper tube (or several shorter-length tubes joined) into a complete circle to form the base ring. Use masking tape to fasten together the overlapping ends.

3. Use a felt-tip marker to mark ten equally spaced points around the base ring. To calculate how far apart to space the points around the ring, simply divide the circumference of the base by 10.

4. The five semicircular ribs that form the dome framework are all the same length, equal to one-half the circumference of the base circle. Make the five newspaper tubes to that dimension plus a few extra inches in length for securely taping the ends of the ribs to the base ring.

5. Install the first rib in a circular arc from one position mark on the base ring to the position mark directly opposite it. Use a helper or two to hold the rib in position and to keep the structure from collapsing while the joints connecting the rib ends to the base ring are being taped together. Tape the joints well, because they will be under a lot of stress.

6. Notice in the illustration that each of the five ribs is set at a slight angle leaning to the side and not perfectly verti-

cal. Continue to add each of the remaining four ribs to the base ring, using opposite pairs of location marks, the same slight angle of lean, and the same method of attachment.

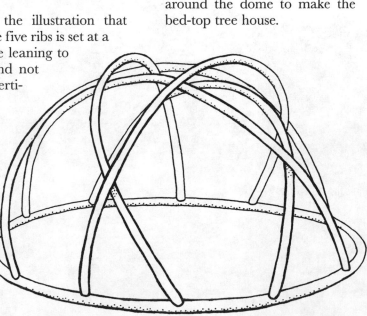

The structure will seem quite flimsy and difficult to manage until the last rib has been taped in place. To complete the structure and make it more rigid, the newspaper tubes must also be taped together wherever they cross.

7. Use an old bedsheet or light blanket to cover the structure. You can just toss it over the framework for a cave effect, or use safety pins to fit the sheet around the dome to make the bed-top tree house.

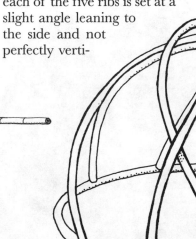

PLASTIC PIPE DREAMS
BUILDING SYSTEM

Some of the most exciting playthings to build are kid-size structures made of large-scale building components. Plastic Pipe Dreams uses common and inexpensive plastic plumbing pipe for making space frame rods that can be quickly and easily assembled using perfectly fitting molded plastic connectors that come in a variety of configurations.

The builder can play architect to create a walk-in playhouse, an outdoor greenhouse, a lemonade stand, or just about any type of space frame or post-and-beam structure. Playing engineer or designer, you can even build bridges, tunnels, furniture, and all kinds of big play vehicles. You can also use the system to create abstract sculptures and games. The connections made with this plastic pipe building system can either be snugly fitted together to later take apart for reuse in another project, or permanently cemented together.

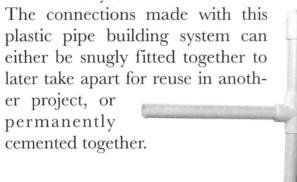

Construction

Builder's age

10+

Materials

☐ PVC plastic pipe

Rigid plastic pipe for plumbing (white) comes in several sizes that are designated by their diameters, which range from one-half inch all the way up to four inches. However, the inch size designation is much smaller than the actual outside diameter of the pipe. Most Plastic Pipe Dreams structures can be made with ½-inch pipe (which has an actual outside diameter of slightly less than one inch). Plastic pipe is readily available in ten-foot lengths at hardware stores and building supply centers. You might ask to have the pipe cut in half lengths for easier carrying. Two ten-foot lengths of ½-inch pipe makes a starter set.

☐ PVC pipe fittings

There are many types of regular and special fittings available to make most types of simple joints. Determine the type and number of joints needed for a specific project or use the ones suggested for a Plastic Pipe Dreams starter set.

☐ PVC cement (optional)

A special plastic cement can be used for making permanent connections, but adult supervision is absolutely required. The cement typically comes in a small can or jar with a brush attached to the inside of the cap for applying the cement.

Warning: Although PVC cement is harmless when dry, in its liquid state, the cement is extremely flammable, with vapors that can ignite and be harmful to eyes. The liquid cement can also irri-tate skin and be fatal if swallowed. These are the same warnings that appear on a tube of plastic model cement, which is nearly the same as PVC pipe cement.

Tools

☐ Plastic pipe shears, pipe cutter, or hacksaw

A pipe cutter or a hacksaw can be used to cut plastic pipe to the lengths needed. However, a special pair of plastic pipe shears is easier, faster, safer, and more accurate, plus the cut ends will not have to be sandpapered to remove burrs.

☐ Measuring tape

☐ Pencil or marker

☐ Sandpaper or file

Building techniques

Although ½-inch plastic pipe is relatively inexpensive and suitable for all the Plastic Pipe Dream projects, large structures requiring lots of pipe fittings or structures using larger diameter pipe can cost a lot.

Any of your own structure designs meant for sitting, climbing, or bearing any heavy weight should be made from ¾-inch or 1-inch plastic pipe. And if your design calls for even larger rods and connectors, plastic pipe (with a more limited selection of fittings) comes in 1 ¼-inch, 1 ½-inch, 2-inch, 3-inch, and 4-inch sizes.

If you already have plans for the structure you are building, cut all the pipe struts to the lengths needed and gather the quantity of each type of connector required. If you intend to invent and create a structure or a sculpture as you go, begin with a starter set of modular-length rods along with a variety of connectors.

15 feet of PVC plastic pipe, ½-inch size

Pieces suggested for a starter set (in.)	Quantity
24	4
12	8
6	4
1 ½	6

PVC pipe fittings

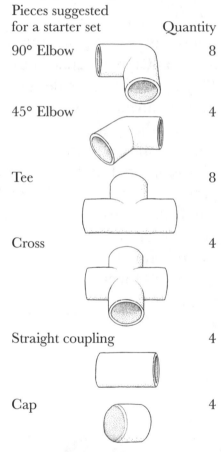

Pieces suggested for a starter set	Quantity
90° Elbow	8
45° Elbow	4
Tee	8
Cross	4
Straight coupling	4
Cap	4

Cutting plastic pipe

Cutting plastic pipe with pipe shears is simple. Just measure and mark the length to be cut, position the shears on the mark, and squeeze the shears. The cut pipe is ready to use.

To use a pipe cutter, open the cut-ter jaws wide enough to slip over the pipe, line up the cut mark with

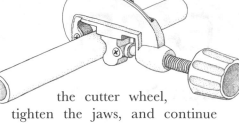

the cutter wheel, tighten the jaws, and continue tightening the jaws as you rotate the cutter around the pipe. Keep tightening and turning until the pipe splits in two pieces. The cut pipe is ready to use.

If you are using a hacksaw to cut the plastic pipe, it is much easier to get a square-cut end if you also use a simple miter box to align the pipe squarely with the saw. You can easily saw through plastic pipe in seconds, but the rough burrs around the cut edge will need to be removed with sandpaper or a file.

Connecting the pipe rods

To connect a rod at a joint, simply push the rod into the selected connector, using a back-and-forth

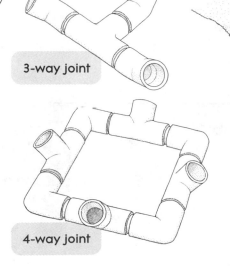

twisting motion. The rod will firmly bottom out when it is in all the way. Friction in the joint should hold the rods and connectors together for some constructions. If a joint is too loose, roughen up the pipe end just a little using pliers, coarse sandpaper, or the edge of a file.

To make permanently glued structures, it is very important that you cut and fit all pieces

together before you begin to glue anything. Then, when everything fits well, begin undoing, gluing, and rejoining one joint at a time, always checking to be sure the structure shape does not change. Use PVC cement outside if possible, or indoors in a space that is very well ventilated. Plastic cement begins to dry rather quickly, but fumes can linger. So wait at least a few hours before bringing the structure inside.

Special types of connectors

The types and combinations of connectors used will determine the possible space frame shapes that can be built. Some structures, however, may require rod angles and joints that are more complex than the connections allowed by a single elbow, tee, or cross fitting. Experiment with combinations of connectors joined by short lengths of pipe to see if you can create the joint you need. Here are examples of a simple three-way joint, and a complex four-way joint that allows rods to connect at different angles.

3-way joint

4-way joint

For advanced builders, these are some of the accessories you can make to increase the versatility of Plastic Pipe Dreams structures. The hold-down J hooks are used to

anchor a frame to the ground so the structure is not easily knocked over. Hinges can be used to build opening and closing door and window frames. Tube clips allow loose fabric or plastic sheet coverings to be easily attached to the plastic pipe framework.

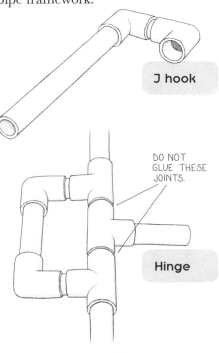

J hook

DO NOT GLUE THESE JOINTS.

Hinge

Tube clip

PLASTIC PIPE DREAMS
BUILD-IT PROJECTS
PLASTIC PIPE ART EASEL
CLASSIC LEMONADE STAND
3-D BLIND MARBLE MAZE
PLASTIC PIPE PLAYHOUSE
GARDENER'S GREENHOUSE
PIPE CHABLES
COZY CAT PLAYGROUND
PIPE SCULPTURE SPRINKLER

PLASTIC PIPE ART EASEL

The Plastic Pipe Art Easel is double sided, so two kids can draw and paint without getting in each other's way. Or, for the solo artist, the two sides can be equipped with different art media by putting markers and a newsprint pad on one side, and watercolors, brushes, and a roll of white wrapping paper on the other side.

Whichever way you use it, this versatile and sturdy art easel has many other convenient features. Each side contains five paintbrush or marker holders. The holders also provide support for a large pad of paper or a roll of paper. A simple U-shaped cardboard tray can be placed in the trough formed by the holders to make a shelf for paints and small water cups. And the whole easel folds flat for storage in a closet or under a bed.

Construction

Building system
Plastic Pipe Dreams

Builder's age
10+

Player's age
3+

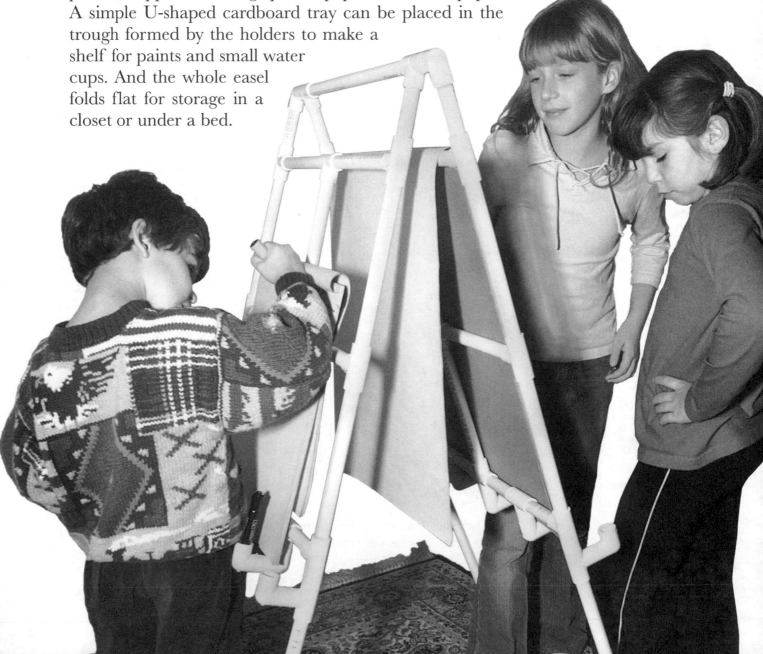

Materials

☐ 36+ feet of PVC plastic pipe, ½″ size

Strut	Length (in.)	Pieces
A	21	2
B	20	4
C	18 ½	1
D	10	20
E	4 ½	8
F	4	2
G	2 ½	2
H	1 ½	24

☐ PVC pipe fittings, ½″ size

Type of Fitting	Pieces
90° Elbow	22
45° Elbow	2
Tee	24
Cross	4

☐ PVC cement

☐ Masking tape

☐ Packaging cord, twine, or nylon cord about two feet long

☐ Corrugated box board (optional for making paint shelf) cut to 3″ x 24″ inches with corrugations lengthwise

Tools

☐ Pipe shears or cutter

☐ Measuring tape

☐ Pencil

☐ Sandpaper or file

Art supplies

☐ Newsprint or other paper with a stiff backing board, any size from 18″ x 24″ to 24″ x 36″

☐ Roll of white wrapping paper about same width as pad

☐ Art paints and brushes

☐ Art pencils, crayons, and markers

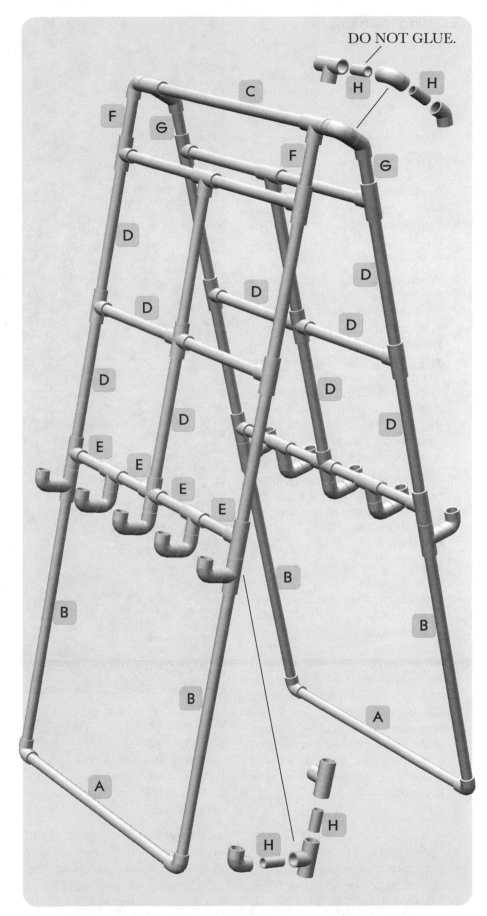

Building instructions

1. Cut all the pipe struts to the lengths needed and gather the quantity of each type of connector required. For cutting, fitting, and gluing techniques, refer to the detailed instructions for the Plastic Pipe Dreams building system.

2. Follow the assembly drawing and fit all pieces together before you begin to glue anything. You can temporarily wrap short strips of masking tape around any loose or twisting joints.

3. When everything fits well, begin undoing, gluing, and rejoining one joint at a time, always checking to be sure the glued joints do not loosen while drying and the shape of the structure does not change. You can also use small strips of masking tape to hold joints together and aligned while they dry. Be sure to make any adjustments necessary before the adhesive starts to harden.

   Notice that the outer ends of the two top tee fittings *do not* get glued so they can act as hinges and allow the easel to fold flat.

4. When all the glued joints have hardened, set up the easel with the two sides spread open to an A-shaped angle so that the structure is stable. Tie a length of strong cord across the center of the easel from side to side. You can simply tie loops at both ends of the cord and then slip the loops over the brush-holder posts, or wrap and knot the cord to the opposing center struts. The tie cord keeps the easel from continuing to spread open past the proper angle.

Equip the easel with the supplies you want. Pads of paper can be placed directly on the trough created by the brush holders. Individual sheets of paper or roll paper will require a flat, rigid backing board, which can be a paper pad or the leftover backing from another large pad. In a pinch, you can use a piece of corrugated box board even though the surface isn't perfectly smooth.

If you want to place small jars of paints in the trough, you will first need to make a U-shaped liner, using a strip of corrugated box board. Cut the strip to size with the corrugations going lengthwise, then fold the strip lengthwise along the corrugations to form the U-shaped liner. Insert the liner into the trough formed by the brush-holder posts.

If you are concerned about small items falling into the brush holders and down inside the frame, just wad up a small piece of tissue to stuff into each holder down to the bend.

CLASSIC LEMONADE STAND

There is nothing more typically American than a kid manning a sidewalk lemonade stand on a hot summer day. All it takes to be in business is a little entrepreneurial spirit plus a simple sign, a pitcher of ice-cold lemonade with a stack of paper cups, and a box or table to put all of it on.

But if you're interested in setting up a more professional— and more profitable—business, you can build a more permanent and professional looking Classic Lemonade Stand, using plastic pipe. Of course, you'll also need to learn and follow some basic business guidelines, and most of all, you'll need a recipe for making great-tasting lemonade. The good news is that all the information you need is right here.

Construction

Building system
Plastic Pipe Dreams

Builder's age
10+

Player's age
4+

Materials

☐ 44+ feet of PVC plastic pipe, 1/2″ size

Strut	Length (in.)	Pieces
A	32 1/2	2
B	28	2
C	24	1
D	22	4
E	20 1/2	4
F	18	2
G	12	8
H	10	2
I	6	2
J	4 1/2	2
K	1 1/2	12

☐ PVC pipe fittings, 1/2″ size

Type of fitting	Pieces
90° Elbow	6
45° Elbow	4
Tee	16
Cross	2

☐ 8 tube clips

☐ PVC cement

☐ Wood board 12″ x 32″

☐ Old sheet or other fabric cut to size

    1 piece 12″ x 32″

    1 piece 24″ x 32″

Tools

☐ Pipe shears or cutter

☐ Measuring tape

☐ Pencil

☐ Sandpaper or file

☐ Felt-tip markers

Building instructions

Making the lemonade stand

1. Cut all the pipe struts to the lengths needed and gather the quantity of each type of connector required. For cutting, fitting, and gluing techniques, refer to the detailed instructions for Plastic Pipe Dreams.

2. Follow the assembly plans shown, and fit all the pieces together before you begin to glue anything. Make any adjustments necessary. If needed, temporarily wrap short strips of masking tape around any loose or twisting joints.

3. When everything fits well, begin undoing, gluing, and rejoining one joint at a time while always checking to be sure the glued joints do not loosen while drying, and the shape of the structure does not change.

4. The countertop can be made from a length of pine shelving, or cut to size from a piece of ply-

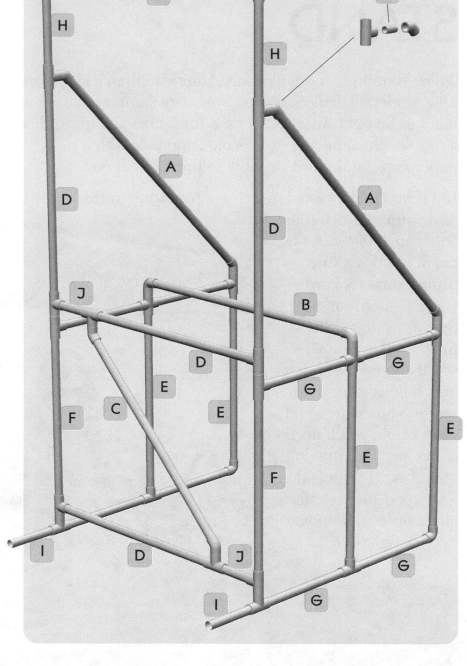

wood or hardboard. The countertop is held in place by the plastic pipe structure.

5. To complete the lemonade stand, cover the base of the bottom front and sides of the frame with a piece of cloth cut from an old bedsheet, and use another piece of sheet to make the sign across the top of the stand. Before attaching the cloth panels to the structure using tube clips, draw your advertising message on the fabric with felt-tip markers. In big, bold letters, the sign should say something like "Cold Lemonade," "Steve's Fresh Lemonade" or just plain "Lemonade." Also, include the price. For added appeal, draw a picture of a big yellow lemon on the sign or on the base covering.

Warning: Be careful on windy days so the stand does not blow over. The cloth draping and banner could act like a sail and catch the wind, so it's best to remove them if there is more than a breeze.

Making lemonade

Here is the recipe for making American Classic Lemonade either by the cup or by the gallon. Be sure to test the lemonade recipe before you open for business. Lemons can vary greatly in both taste and strength of flavor. Start with the fewest number of lemons and tablespoons of sugar listed in the recipe, and add more of either ingredient as needed

Tools

☐ Knife for cutting lemons

☐ Cutting board

☐ Juicer for squeezing lemons

☐ Long-handled spoon for mixing

☐ Large pot and serving ladle (for the gallon recipe) or quart jar with lid (for the 16-ounce, by-the-cup recipe)

☐ Measuring spoons

☐ Pitcher of water (for the 16-ounce, by-the-cup recipe)

Recipe

1. First, assemble all the ingredients and the tools you will need.

2. Cut the lemon(s) in half. Squeeze the lemon(s) on the juicer, and pick out the seeds with a spoon. Put the lemon juice and pulp in a 16-ounce drinking cup or a pot.

3. Add the sugar, ice cubes, and enough water to nearly fill the cup, or the amount specified for a gallon.

4. Stir thoroughly and serve.

Business tips for success

Location

Besides locating your stand on the sidewalk in front of your home, think about other locations nearby where a lot of people may be passing or gathering—places like yard sales, car washes, playing fields, and other outdoor events.

Advertising

It pays to advertise your business, so put up a few signs in the neighborhood during the hours you are open. The sign can just say something like "Cold, Fresh Lemonade" with an arrow pointing in the direction of your stand. Here's another way to advertise. Distribute flyers around your neighborhood that tell people how your lemonade stand would be a good attraction at their next yard sale.

Finance

To earn a profit, the price you decide to charge for a cup of lemonade should be more than the cost of the ingredients to make it. So do a little math to add up the total cost of the amount of lemon and sugar per cup of lemonade plus the cost for one paper drinking cup. Your selling price should be about three times that cost, which gives you one-third to cover those direct costs, one-third to help pay back the cost of building the lemonade stand, and one-third for profit. For example, if the total cost of ingredients and materials for making each cup of lemonade is 26 cents, the price you charge should be 3 x 26 = 78 cents. You could round that off to 75 cents so it is easier to make change.

American Classic Lemonade recipe

Ingredients	To make a 16-ounce cup	To make a gallon
Lemons	1/2	4 to 8
Granulated white sugar	2 to 3 level tablespoons	1/2 to 1 cup
Ice cubes	3	24
Water	Enough to fill cup	3 quarts

3-D BLIND MARBLE MAZE

What's so interesting about this marble maze is that you can only hear where the marble is going. You can't see it! That's because this puzzle is made from a jumble of pieces of opaque plastic pipe all interconnected into a three-dimensional maze of passageways. Put a marble into one of two or more open tubes (Start) and see if you can follow the right passageways so the marble comes out another open tube (Finish). Along the way, there can be lots of turns that lead to dead ends, so you'll probably do a lot of backtracking before discovering the correct route–and that's true even if you designed and built the maze yourself.

Construction

Building system
Plastic Pipe Dreams

Builder's age
7+

Player's age
5+

Materials

☐ Scrap lengths of PVC plastic pipe, ½" size

☐ All types of PVC pipe fittings including caps, ½" size

☐ PVC cement (optional)

☐ Masking tape (optional)

☐ Marble or ball bearing (A small marble works best, but any small, round ball that will easily slide through the pipe and joints will do.)

Tools

☐ Pipe shears or cutter

☐ Sandpaper or file

Building instructions

There is no specific plan for the design of the maze, in fact, it's pretty difficult to figure out what to do until you actually start building. You can just begin connecting scrap lengths of pipe to other pieces of pipe, creating several passageways that twist in a spiral, turn up and down or across, and branch out to more pathways. When you're done, cap all the open tube ends except for two that will become the start and the finish points. Later, you can completely change the route of the correct passageway simply by moving the end caps to create a different start and finish.

1. Gather all the scrap lengths of plastic pipe you have. Longer lengths and full-length pieces can be cut to smaller pieces as you need them. Also, collect all types of connectors, especially crosses and tees that will allow your maze to branch out and look complicated (that's good!). And you will need lots of caps to create the dead ends.

2. Start attaching short scrap lengths of pipe to one connector, add connectors to the other ends of those pipes, put pieces of pipe in those connectors, and so on, trying to build the maze in as complicated of a three-dimensional pattern as you can. Cut longer lengths to shorter pieces as you need them. For cutting, fitting, and gluing techniques, refer to the detailed instructions for Plastic Pipe Dreams.

3. When you're satisfied with the tubular maze structure you have assembled, put caps on all but two of the open tube ends. Either one of the open tubes can be the starting point and the other the finish.

4. If the pipes and connectors fit real snugly, you may not need to use any PVC cement to hold the joints together. If the joints are loose and tend to come apart, you might try taping each pipe and connector joint. You can also glue the joints together, either while you are assembling the pieces, or after you're finished with the maze design. *Do not*, however, glue on the caps. You may later want to change their locations to change the route of the maze.

5. Now try out the maze, using a small marble, a metal ball bearing, or any small ball that will easily slide through the pipe and joints without getting stuck. In a pinch, you might try using a small, round pebble, but that will make it more difficult to maneuver through the maze. It's a good idea to find a marble or ball that rolls smoothly through the tubes before you test one in a maze that has already been glued together.

PLASTIC PIPE PLAYHOUSE

Most playhouses this size are constructed of lumber, which makes them much too heavy to move from place to place, however, this Plastic Pipe Playhouse is exceptionally light, very strong, easy to move, and can be used indoors or outdoors.

This playhouse frame is specifically designed to use folded sheets of newspaper for the exterior siding and paper grocery bags for the roof shingles. If you plan to build and use the playhouse outdoors, you may need to paint the newspaper covering to waterproof it for rainy weather—or just recover the frame with fresh newspaper and paper bags when needed. That part of the construction is easy and fast.

Construction

Building system
Plastic Pipe Dreams

Builder's age
10+

Player's age
3+

Materials

☐ 136+ feet of PVC plastic pipe, ½" size

Strut	Length (in.)	Pieces
A	45 ¼	6
B	40 ¼	15
C	18	4
D	10	20
E	9	12
F	7 ½	12
G	5 ½	4
H	1 ½	28

☐ PVC pipe fittings, ½" size

Type of fitting	Pieces
90° Elbow	16
Tee	80

☐ PVC cement (optional)

☐ Lots of newspaper

☐ Paper grocery bags

Tools

☐ Pipe shears or cutter

☐ Measuring tape

☐ Pencil

☐ Sandpaper or file

☐ Scissors

Building instructions

1. Cut all the pipe struts to the lengths needed and gather the quantity of each type of connector required. For cutting, fitting, and gluing techniques, refer to the detailed instructions for Plastic Pipe Dreams.

2. Follow the assembly plans shown, and fit all the pieces together before you begin to glue anything. Make any adjustments necessary. Temporarily wrap short strips of masking tape around any loose or twisting joints.

3. When everything fits well, begin undoing, gluing, and rejoining one joint at a time while always checking to be sure the glued joints do not loosen while drying, and the shape of the structure does not change.

4. The horizontal frame struts on the sides of the playhouse are spaced to hold folded sheets of newspaper as a covering. For each piece of siding, use a section of newspaper consisting of about sixteen numbered pages. Hang each folded newspaper shingle

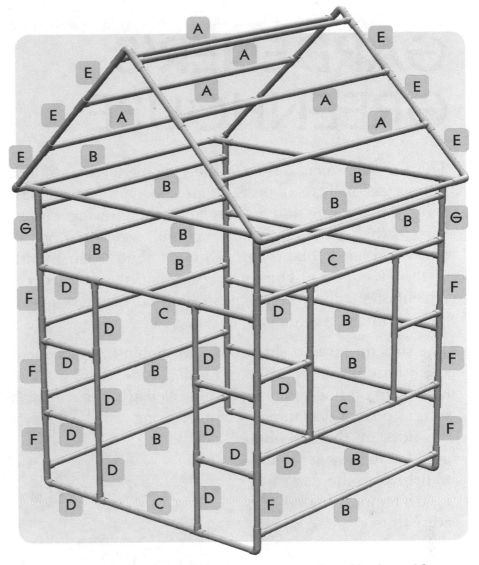

over a section of horizontal framing so that it straddles the frame pipe it is hanging on as well as the frame pipe below it. Begin applying the newspaper siding from the bottom row and work up. Slightly overlap the siding sections that are side by side.

5. The horizontal frame struts across the roof are spaced to hold paper grocery bags for the roofing shingles. Simply hang the bottom of each folded bag on a section of the horizontal roof framing. Begin applying the roof shingles side by side completely across the bottom row, then continue applying bag shingles across the next row up. If you need a narrow shingle to finish off a row, cut the bag to the width you want.

GARDENER'S GREENHOUSE

This kid-size greenhouse has many of the features found in a professional greenhouse. It's great for starting seedlings early in the spring and for extending the growing season beyond the first frosts for flowers and vegetables. Some herbs and hardy plants can be grown almost year-round in the greenhouse. During the summer, the Gardener's Greenhouse will protect plants from many hungry pests, harsh sunlight, and damaging rains.

The structure uses a shed roof and should be positioned against an outside south-facing wall. Inside, there is a kid-height potting bench and a sun-filled area for several pots and planters. Flaps covering the sides of the greenhouse can be adjusted to provide ventilation and to help keep the inside temperature from getting too hot.

Construction

Building system
Plastic Pipe Dreams

Builder's age
10+

Player's age
6+

Materials

☐ 78+ feet of PVC plastic pipe, ½″ size

Strut	Length (in.)	Pieces
A	40 ¼	5
B	26	6
C	21	2
D	19 ½	8
E	18 ½	4
F	18	4
G	12	4
H	10	10
I	9 ½	4
J	1 ½	22

☐ PVC pipe fittings, ½″ size

Type of fitting	Pieces
90° Elbow	6
45° Elbow	6
Tee	38

☐ Special fittings

   Hold-down hose clips, about 20

   Hold-down "J" hooks, about 6

☐ PVC cement

☐ Heavy-duty, clear-plastic drop cloth

☐ 10″ pine shelving, one piece 43″ long for each shelf (optional)

Tools

☐ Pipe shears or cutter

☐ Measuring tape

☐ Pencil

☐ Sandpaper or file

☐ Scissors

Building instructions

1. Cut all the pipe struts to the lengths needed and gather the quantity of each type of connector required. For cutting, fitting, and gluing techniques, refer to the detailed instructions for Plastic Pipe Dreams.

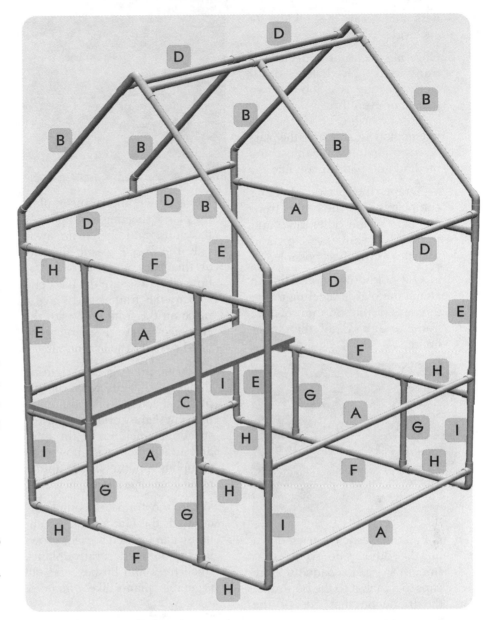

2. Follow the assembly plans shown, and fit all the pieces together before you begin to glue anything. Make any adjustments necessary. You can temporarily wrap short strips of masking tape around any loose or twisting joints.

3. When everything fits well, begin undoing, gluing, and rejoining one joint at a time while always checking to be sure the glued joints do not loosen while drying, and the shape of the structure does not change.

4. When the structure is complete and the glued joints have hard-ened, move the greenhouse to an outdoor location against a southern-facing wall. Positioning the greenhouse against an outside wall will provide some protection from it being blown over. When choosing a location, remember to consider early morning and late afternoon shadows. The more sun the greenhouse gets, the better the plants inside will grow.

When you are satisfied with the location, secure the bottom of the frame to the ground using hold-down "J" hooks at the corners and near the middle of each side.

5. Covering the frame with clear or translucent polyethylene drop-cloth sheeting is a job for two people or even three, so get help before you begin. This is the easiest method for attaching the plastic covering, but you can use any method and pattern you like.

a. Drape the plastic sheeting completely over the frame, from one side to the other side, and smooth out any overlaps and wrinkles as much as possible.

b. Use hold-down hose clips to attach the plastic sheeting to the tubing on the bottom of the frame at one side of the greenhouse.

c. Pull the plastic covering down on the other side so it is as smooth as possible, and use hose clips to attach it to the bottom of the frame on that side of the greenhouse.

d. Use more hose clips to attach the covering to the corners of the frame and anywhere else needed to keep the covering smooth and reasonably taut.

e. With a pair of scissors, trim away all extra plastic sheeting around the base of the greenhouse only.

f. You can cover the front and back gable ends in any one of three ways. The easiest method is to just gather the loose plastic sheeting at either end, and weight it to the ground with a rock or board.

For a better appearance, allow the plastic sheeting to drape over the ends, and then trim away only the excess plastic sheeting at the sides and bottom. Use hose clips to secure the back end flap to the frame, and leave a place on the front end (with the entrance) where the flap can be lifted to enter the greenhouse.

If you are pretty good at figuring things out, trim away all the plastic sheeting from both ends, then cut slightly oversized plastic-sheeting panels to fit the ends and attach them with hose clips (doubling up the plastic under some hose clips already in place).

When the frame is completely covered, the Gardener's Greenhouse can be used as is for growing tall potted decorative plants, small trees and bushes, and tall vegetable plants like tomatoes.

Just place the potted plants on the ground inside the greenhouse and care for them as you would if they were planted in a garden. Sufficient ventilation should be provided by the spaces at the bottom of the two sides and the loose-fitting plastic sheeting covering the entrance end.

If you plan to grow smaller potted plants or start seedlings, you can also place the planters directly on the ground or add shelves to the greenhouse. The frame is designed to support three shelves, one at the back and one on either or both sides of the greenhouse.

Each shelf is made from a forty-three-inch long piece of ten-inch-wide pine shelving. To keep a shelf from slipping off its frame support, nail wood cleats under both ends of the shelf as shown. Cleats can be made from scraps of wood or ten-inch long pieces of 1 X 2-inch lumber. Before nailing the cleats to the underside of a shelf, mark their positions so both cleats will fit snuggly against the inside sides of the frame.

Once built, it's up to you to stock your greenhouse and learn how to care for the plants you grow.

PIPE CHABLES

If one structure is both a chair and a table, then maybe it should be called a *chable*. This Plastic Pipe Dreams piece of furniture can actually be adjusted to any height you want just by changing the length of its four legs. The same basic chable design can be built as a low stool, a table, a chair, a high stool, or a stand-up counter.

These tables and chairs may be kid-sized, but they are sturdy and strong enough to support anyone. You can sit directly on the chair frames, or the seating area can be made much more comfortable by adding a small pillow or a small folded blanket. A tabletop surface to place on the plastic pipe frame can be as simple as a big piece of corrugated box board, or as permanent as a cut-to-size piece of plywood.

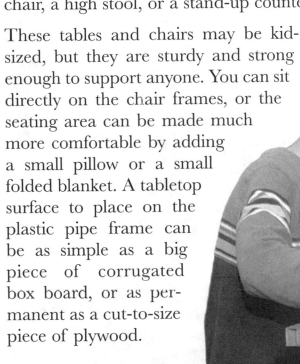

Construction

Building system
Plastic Pipe Dreams

Builder's age
10+

Player's age
3+

Materials

☐ 12-20 feet of PVC plastic pipe, ½" size

Strut	Length (in.)	Pieces
A	14 ½	3
B	10	4
C	6, 12, 18, 24, or 30*	4
D	4 ½	4
E	1 ½	4

*or any leg height. The total frame height will be two inches more than this dimension.

☐ PVC pipe fittings, ½" size

Type of fitting	Pieces
90° Elbow	8
Tee	6
Cross	1

☐ PVC cement

☐ Small pillow or small blanket (optional)

☐ Tabletop approximately 20" x 20". Use double-wall corrugated box board, hardboard, or plywood

☐ Duct tape

Tools

☐ Pipe shears or cutter

☐ Measuring tape

☐ Pencil

☐ Sandpaper or file

Building instructions

1. Decide what height you want the chable to be, cut all the pipe struts to the lengths needed, and gather the quantity of each type of connector required. For cutting, fitting, and gluing techniques, refer to the detailed instructions for Plastic Pipe Dreams.

2. Follow the assembly plans shown, and fit all the pieces together before you begin to glue anything. Make any adjustments necessary. You can temporarily wrap short

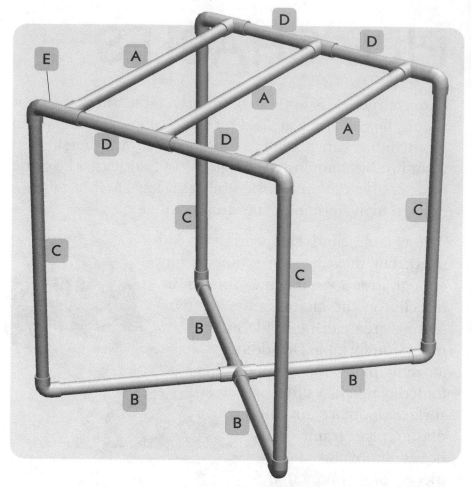

strips of masking tape around any loose or twisting joints.

3. When everything fits well, begin undoing, gluing, and rejoining one joint at a time while always checking to be sure the glued joints do not loosen while drying, and the shape of the structure does not change.

4. For a chair or stool, the structure is complete unless you want to add a cushion or a folded blanket to the seat for more comfort.

5. Depending on what material you choose for the tabletop, use the proper tools to cut it to size. Lumberyards and home centers always have a bin of plywood and hardboard "cut offs" where you might find a piece already cut to the right size.

6. Center the tabletop over the base frame, and use several strips of duct tape to fasten the underside of the tabletop to the frame.

COZY CAT PLAYGROUND

Kittens and cats just love having their own playground, especially one that's designed for cat climbing, cat acrobatics, nail scratching, and, of course, napping. This plastic pipe structure is based on modular cubes and square panels, so you can easily change the design to create different playground spaces and arrangements.

Square panels cut from carpet samples make horizontal platforms and cozy hammocks, and carpet squares mounted vertically as wall panels or angled as ramps are good for climbing and can be arranged around platforms to make private cat spaces and places to keep cat toys. And, if you need a bigger Cozy Cat playground, you can probably figure out how to add more modular plastic pipe cubes.

Construction

Building system
Plastic Pipe Dreams

Builder's age
11+

Player's age
Kittens and cats of any age

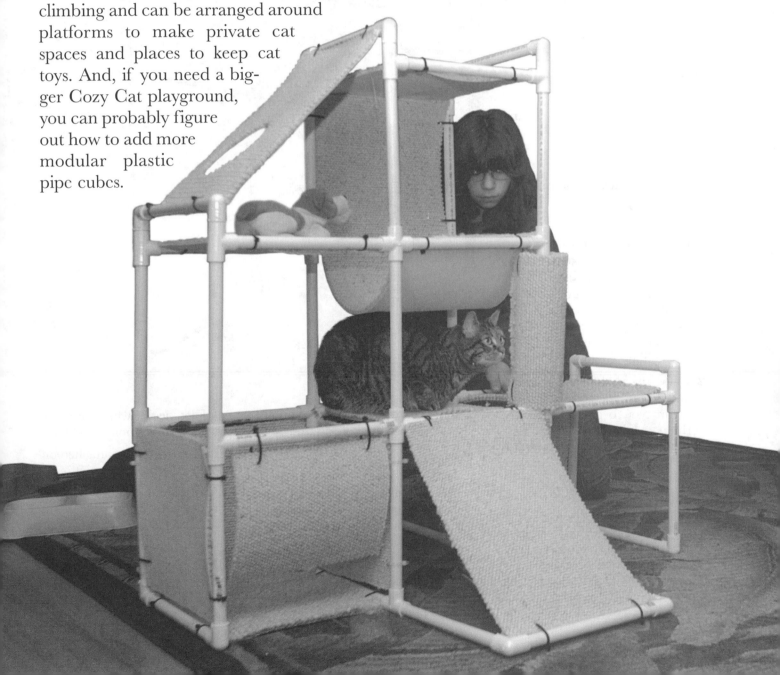

Materials

- □ 48+ feet of PVC plastic pipe, ½″ size

Strut	Length (in.)	Pieces
A	12	44
B	1 ½	8

- □ PVC pipe fittings, ½″ size

Type of fitting	Pieces
90° Elbow	16
Tee	16
Cross	6

- □ PVC cement
- □ Carpet swatches, to be cut to 12″ squares
- □ Plastic ties (8″ size or longer)

Tools

- □ Pipe shears or cutter
- □ Heavy-duty shears or carpet knife
- □ Scratch awl
- □ Carpenter's square
- □ Pencil or black felt-tip marker
- □ Sandpaper or file

Building instructions

1. Cut all the pipe struts to the lengths needed and gather the quantity of each type of connector required. For cutting, fitting, and gluing techniques, refer to the detailed instructions for Plastic Pipe Dreams.

2. Follow the assembly plans shown, and fit all the pieces together before you begin to glue anything. Make any adjustments necessary. You can temporarily wrap short strips of masking tape around any loose or twisting joints.

3. When everything fits well, begin undoing, gluing, and rejoining one joint at a time while always checking to be sure the glued joints do not loosen while drying, and the shape of the structure does not change.

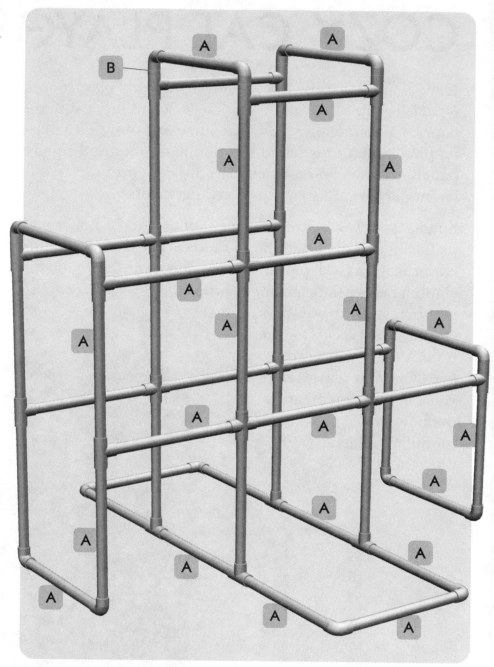

4. Using a carpenter's square and a pencil (or marker), lay out a twelve-inch square on the back side of each carpet swatch. Then cut out the squares, using shears or a carpet knife. Carpet stores usually give away old sample swatches, and they might even cut them into squares for you.

5. The carpet squares are attached to the pipe framework, using plastic wire ties fed through holes punched through the carpet. First, decide where and how you want to position a square.

- A horizontal square attached on all four edges makes a platform.

- A horizontal square loosely attached on two opposite edges makes a sling.

- A vertical square attached on all four edges makes a wall.

- A vertical square attached only at the top edge makes a hanging door.

- A sloped square attached diagonally at the upper and lower edges makes a ramp.

Most carpet squares will be stiff enough to be supported by two wire-tie loops on each attached edge. If the carpet is flimsy, you may need to add a third wire tie in the middle of each edge.

On the back side of each carpet square, locate and mark the position of each attachment point one inch from the edge and about two inches from either end. Then carefully use a scratch awl to punch a hole all the way through each point. It is pretty easy to punch holes with a scratch awl, so don't try using a drill of any kind, which can easily twist up the carpet pile and get tangled.

At each attachment point, thread a plastic tie through the hole and around the pipe frame, then fasten and tighten the wire tie as needed. Trim off any "tails" with shears or a wire cutter. If a sling or a ramp panel requires plastic ties longer the ones you have, simply attach two or more ties together, end to end.

Making a cozy cat environment

Here are some things cats like that you might consider including in your cat playground.

- Cats develop certain habits and likes that you can observe, and they are often particularly selective about where they like to sleep. Many cats like to nap in places that are warm and offer a view of the room. Try to duplicate those preferences for surface texture, color, and confinement (open or enclosed).

- Carpet-covered scratching posts should be tall enough for the cat to fully stretch out its upper body and front legs.

- Cats enjoy several different private spaces for sleeping, lounging, hiding, and scratching. Create different environments to see which ones are preferred.

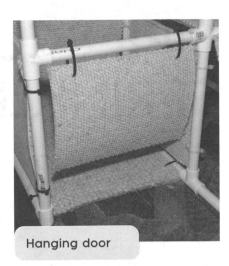

Hanging door

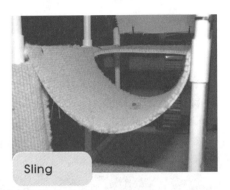

Sling

Ramp

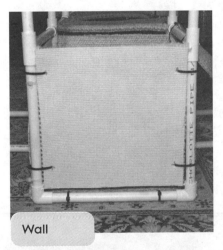

Wall

Scratching post

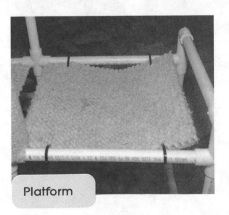

Platform

PIPE SCULPTURE SPRINKLER

By connecting a garden hose fitting to a special Plastic Pipe Dreams structure, you can build an outdoor sprinkler that shoots many streams of water for great distances in all directions—or whatever direction and distance you want. The Pipe Sculpture Sprinkler is perfect for cooling down on a hot summer day, or maybe for creating a water sculpture with lots of streams shooting in all directions. And there are no exact plans to follow and no specific lengths to cut. Just follow a few easy instructions for building a stable structure, drilling the nozzle holes and capping the tubes, then let your building creativity take over.

Construction

Building system
Plastic Pipe Dreams

Builder's age
10+

Player's age
3+

Materials

- ☐ PVC plastic pipe, ½″ size or larger

  Use scrap lengths left over from other projects, or cut whatever lengths are needed as you build.

- ☐ PVC pipe fittings, ½″ size or same as pipe

  Use whatever type of fittings you may have, or purchase several of each type including elbows, tees, and crosses. You will definitely need several caps to seal off the ends of all open tubes in your construction.

- ☐ PVC pipe garden-hose coupling, ½″ size

  This special fitting allows a garden hose to be attached to ½″ plastic pipe

- ☐ PVC cement

Tools

- ☐ Pipe shears or cutter
- ☐ Measuring tape
- ☐ Pencil
- ☐ Sandpaper or file
- ☐ Hand drill or battery power drill with a ¹⁄₁₆″ bit

Building instructions

1. Use existing scraps of plastic pipe, or cut each piece to length as you build. Also, gather several of each type connector. For cutting, fitting, and gluing techniques, refer to the detailed instructions for Plastic Pipe Dreams.

2. Build as simple or as complicated a structure as you like, but make sure to incorporate a way for it to stand up. You could create a tripod base, maybe attach a few short tubes in the right places for stability, or use one of the sprinkler's pipes as a spike and just stick it into soft earth.

3. Attach the special garden-hose fitting somewhere near the bottom of the structure, and place a cap over every tube with an open end. Fit all the pieces together before you begin to glue anything. Make any adjustments necessary. You can temporarily wrap short strips of masking tape around any loose or twisting joints.

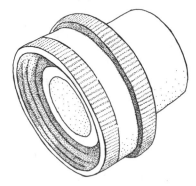

4. When everything fits well, begin undoing, gluing, and rejoining one joint at a time, always checking to be sure the glued joints do not loosen while drying, and the shape of the structure does not change.

5. The size and number of holes you drill in the pipes will determine how far the water jets will squirt, and where you drill will determine their directions. Making holes in plastic pipe with a ¹⁄₁₆-inch drill is easy, so you can use a hand drill. If you use a power drill, make sure it is the battery type. Do not use a plug-in power drill around water.

Start by drilling only three or four holes into the pipes. The locations and the angles of the drilled holes will determine the directions of the water spray. Be sure to angle some holes so the water jets spray up.

Make sure the sprinkler is positioned and stable where you place it outside, then attach a garden hose, turn on the water, and see what kind of water jet you get. Turn off the water, and

drill a few more holes in the pipes to create additional water jet spray wherever you want them, then test the system again by turning the water on again. Continue to drill more holes with the water off, just one or two at a time, and test the results until you get the water jet sprinkler pattern you like.

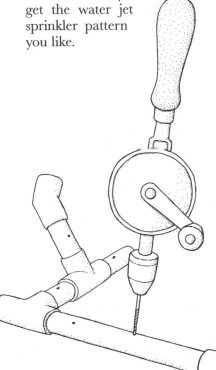

NEW AND NOVEL SPACE FRAME SYSTEMS

New materials and new technologies often become the inspiration for inventing new building systems. Sometimes the materials we use every day can be used in different ways that were not originally intended or even considered. When ordinary coat hangers are combined in a special way to make a geometric sphere, when scrap discards are combined any way you want to build a working contraption, or when pencils can be used as building struts without any pencil touching another, that too can be considered the invention of a New and Novel Space Frame System.

The Caney Trihanger Module building system is so new that much of what it could build has not yet been discovered. By experimenting with various combinations of the basic triangular building module, builders might figure out ways to make large trusses, spheres, and domes that would then become big playthings and play spaces.

Universal Modularity building systems presents a new approach for connecting anything to anything to make whatever you can imagine, so there is plenty of opportunity to create gizmos and gadgets that probably never existed before you created them. Maybe the best use of a universal building system is to create a Rube Goldberg contraption that demonstrates how complicated a machine you can make to do a simple task like ring a bell.

To see how one designer created a unique space frame building system using struts that never touch each other, try building a Tensegrity Thing, and then try to figure out how the structure might be used as a toy or for other practical applications. Considering what you have already learned about different types of space frame structures, maybe you can discover how to convert other everyday materials into elegant new and novel building systems.

BUILD IT

CANEY TRIHANGER MODULE 333

TRIHANGER PYRAMIDS, SPHERES, DOMES, AND TRUSSES 336

MOTH MAGNET MOVIES 338

TENSEGRITY THING 340

UNIVERSAL MODULARITY 343

RUBE GOLDBERG INVENTIONS 345

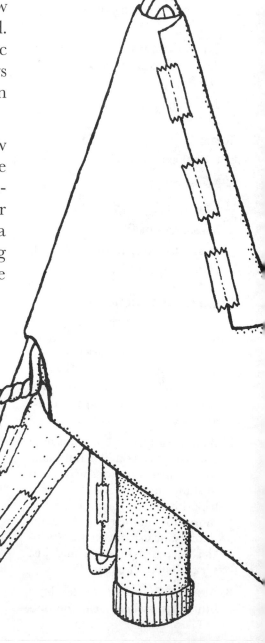

CANEY TRIHANGER MODULE
BUILDING SYSTEM

Have you ever thought about what happens to the billions of coat hangers produced each year? An even more difficult mystery is what to do with all the extra coat hangers you may have hanging around your home. Now, after years of experiments searching for an elegant way to turn ordinary coat hangers into a space frame building system, the Caney Trihanger Module (named after the author of this book) represents a unique solution with several special features. And the handsome, triangular module uses simple wire or plastic coat hangers, as is, without bending, cutting, or changing their shape in any way.

Caney Trihanger Modules are best suited for constructing space frame polyhedrons, domes, trusses, and pyramids that use all triangular components. And because combinations of the basic Trihanger Module can make increasingly larger triangular modules, the size of the structures that can be built is almost unlimited.

SYSTEM FEATURES

- Makes large-scale space frames to any practical size
- Uses inexpensive (or free) components
- Suitable for indoor structures and outdoor uses
- Basic modules combine to make larger modules
- Modules combine either side to side or tip to tip
- Appearance varies with the type and color of coat hangers
- System invites experimentation and unique designs

Construction

Builder's age
9+

Player's age
3+

Materials
☐ Wire or plastic coat hangers, all the same type and size

12 hangers build a small tetrahedron

60 hangers build a small icosahedron

☐ Plastic ties, 6″ or 7″ size

Estimate needing two to three ties for each coat hanger used in the completed structure.

Tools
☐ Wire cutters, shears, or heavy-duty scissors for cutting the plastic ties

Building techniques
Either wire or plastic coat hangers will work, but all the hangers used in any one structure should be of the same type and size. No cutting or bending of the coat hangers is required for building the modules or for assembling the modules into larger constructions.

Wire coat hangers from a dry cleaners work well, but they must be the type made entirely of wire, and it may take some time to accumulate all you need. Plastic hangers typically cost less than ten cents apiece at discount stores, and they build very sturdy (and colorful if you like) all-weather structures.

The basic Trihanger Module is a tetrahedral-like triangle made from three identical coat hangers. When combined with other identical Trihanger Modules, the building sys-

tem can create trusses, polyhedrons forms, and other space frame structures that use all triangles. Basic modules can also be combined to create larger scale modules up to any practical size.

Making basic modules
Building Trihanger Modules and structures is a lot easier with a helper to hold parts in position while they are being fastened together.

1. Arrange three coat hangers in a triangle as shown in the illustration, being sure the hooks come together all facing the same direction of rotation.

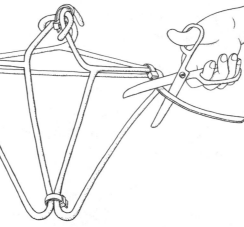

2. Use plastic ties to fasten the hangers at each corner of the triangle and use one around the combined hooks. The basic module is complete.

To build modular space frame structures using the triangular modules, simply fasten the triangles side to side or corner to corner, using plastic ties. Any form that can be built using equilateral triangles can be built with basic Trihanger Modules.

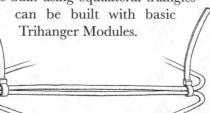

You can build larger scale Trihanger structures by just using larger size modules. The next largest

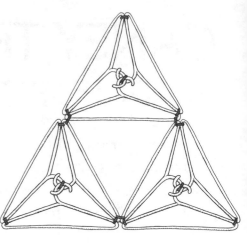

Trihanger Module uses four basic modules and covers four times the area of one basic module. And by combining four of the larger modules in a similar way, you could make a gigantic module, and so on.

It may take a long time to make all the modules needed for many structures, so start with something relatively small and easy. A four-module, twelve-coat-hanger tetra-

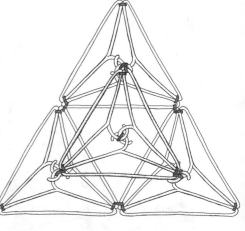

hedron with the modules fastened side to side can be built quickly and will demonstrate how strong a Trihanger structure actually is. Four tetrahedrons attached corner to corner will make a kid-high pyramid (and take four times as long). And a large icosahedron with twenty-five triangular faces could take an entire day.

Trihanger structures that are hollow, including all polyhedrons, can be built with the coat hanger hooks facing inwards for a less complicated exterior shape and a cleaner appearance, or with the hooks facing outwards for a more technical appearance and more space inside the structure.

INVENTION

WIRE COAT HANGERS

One winter afternoon back in 1903, Albert J. Parkhouse arrived back at work from lunch to find there were no vacant hooks available to hang his coat. There often were not enough coat hooks for all of the employees at the Timberlake Wire and Novelty Company in Jackson, Michigan, and so this wasn't the first time he'd had to hang his good coat on the back of his chair.

But that day, when his coat once again got crumpled and wrinkled, Albert came up with an interesting solution—a sort of portable clothes hook that could be used almost anywhere. He took a piece of his company's wire and twisted it into two loops that would fit inside the arms of his coat. He then bent a second piece of wire into a hook and attached it to the middle of his coat-hanger device. The invention worked so well that Parkhouse continued to experiment with wire forms until he figured out a way to bend the entire hanger out of a single piece of wire.

When Parkhouse's invention became popular with other employees, the owner of the Timberlake Wire and Novelty Company realized that the wire coat hanger could become a hot new product for his company. In those days, it was common, and legal, for employers to patent the inventions created by their employees, and that is what the Timberlake Company did. Albert Parkhouse never received a penny for his simple-but-brilliant idea, and the Timberlake Company went on to make millions and millions of wire coat hangers.

Today, one hundred years after its invention, practically nothing about the wire coat hanger has changed except for the way people use them. In addition to hanging clothes, wire coat hangers are often used as an extension for reaching things beyond an arm's length, to unlock car doors when the car keys have been locked inside, and to build toy structures.

TRIHANGER PYRAMIDS, SPHERES, DOMES, AND TRUSSES

Building space frame structures using Trihanger Modules is limited only by the time and space you have for building. Making a big, lumpy, and bumpy icosahedron sphere might inspire a game to play with the structure or could suggest another use, like a place for birds to perch.

A Trihanger pyramid or truss in a bright color could be used as a garden trestle for vines and flowers and would also be a safe perching place for birds. A large, kid-sized dome turned into a personal play hut might take several days to build, but it could last for several years as a permanent part of your landscape. The same large-module dome might also become a minigreenhouse, a spacious doghouse, or a wild bird sanctuary. And those ambitious builders looking for a whole summer's worth of work could build a dome pavilion the size of a small garage.

Construction

Building system
 Caney Trihanger Module

Builder's age
 9+

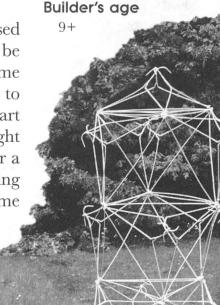

Player's age

4+

Materials

☐ Wire or plastic coat hangers, all the same type and size

12 hangers build a small octahedron with modules corner to corner

24 hangers build a small octahedron with modules side to side

45 hangers build a small, truncated icosahedron dome

60 hangers build a small icosahedron sphere

180 hangers build a large, truncated icosahedron dome

30 hangers build a small square-base pyramid with modules corner to corner

120 hangers build a large-module square-base pyramid with modules corner-to-corner

About 4000 hangers build a room-size dome

☐ Plastic ties, 6″ or 7″ size

Estimate needing two to three ties for each coat hanger used in the completed structure.

Tools

☐ Wire cutters, shears, or heavy-duty scissors for cutting the plastic ties

Building instructions

There are several ways to combine Trihanger Modules to create a particular form. The basic modules can be connected side to side for a very strong structure that has a dense and complex appearance. You may be able to connect modules corner to corner, which uses fewer modules to build big structures and has a lighter, less complex appearance. Using either building method, the modules can be connected with the coat hanger hooks facing outward for a knobby surface look, or with the hooks facing inward for a smoother, more rounded appearance.

If you already have an idea for building a Trihanger structure, choose the building method that best meets your needs. A smoother outer surface (hooks inward) for a dome is easier to cover, and the hooks could be used for hanging things inside the structure. A Trihanger construction that positions the hooks on the outside offers multiple attachment points for hanging the structure or connecting one Trihanger construction to another.

One of the most impressive structures to build with Caney Trihanger Modules is an icosahedron sphere or dome. A small dome uses only forty-five coat hangers, and with some modifications to provide a covering and entrance, the structure could become a small doghouse or a tiny greenhouse. Adding another five basic modules (fifteen more coat hangers) will create a full icosahedron sphere that you might use for a game or another product you invent. A large, truncated icosahedron dome uses 180 coat hangers and is just the right size for you and a friend to play in.

1. To build a small dome, make a total of fifteen basic modules. For a large dome, make fifteen large modules. Building is faster and easier if you have a helper to assist in making the modules and fitting them together.

2. Combine five triangular modules to form the pentagon-shaped top of the dome. Use plastic ties wrapped around adjoining hangers to connect the modules together.

3. Attach the remaining ten modules around the pentagon top to form a dome. Because the icosahedron is not complete (that's why its called truncated), the structure will only be sturdy when sitting on the ground. If you try to pick up the dome or move it, the structure will be wobbly. Once positioned, you may want to create an entrance by removing one of the modules around the base.

4. The completed dome can be left with the structure exposed, or you can figure out ways to cover it using a blanket or a bedsheet draped over the framework. You might also use triangular corrugated-box panels cut to size and taped to the module triangles on the smooth side.

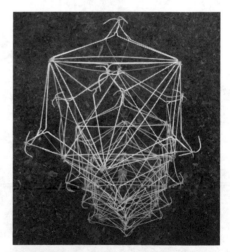

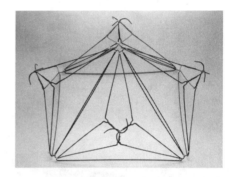

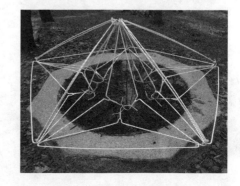

MOTH MAGNET MOVIES

On a warm summer evening, you have probably seen moths flying and fluttering around an outdoor light and casting their shadows on nearby walls. Unlike butterflies that fly about during the day, moths tend to hide while it is daylight and do their flying at night. For some reason not clearly known, moths are especially attracted to bright white lights.

By building a Moth Magnet Movie projector, you are providing both the light source to attract moths and a three-sided movie screen for viewing the moths' dancing shadows. The Moth Magnet Movie projector is especially good for viewing moths without capturing them, because keeping a live insect in a proper environment requires lots of care. When you turn off the movie light, the moths will just fly away in search of another light magnet.

Construction

Building system
Modified version of the Caney Trihanger Module

Builder's age
8+

Player's age
4+

Materials
☐ Three wire coat hangers

☐ White tissue paper (if you don't have the type of wire coat hangers already covered with white paper)

☐ Transparent mending tape

☐ Flashlight

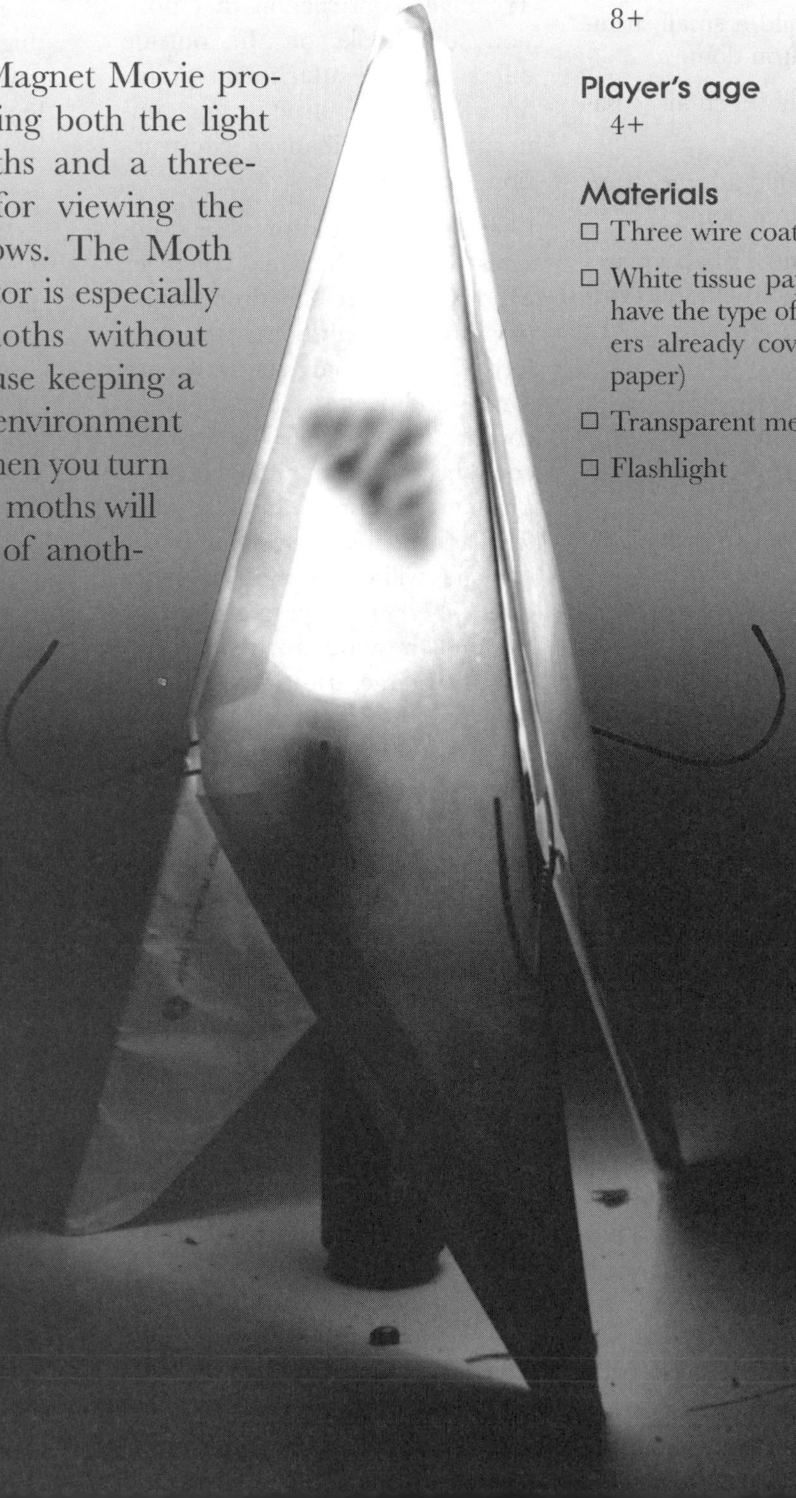

Tools

☐ Pencil

☐ Scissors

Building instructions

To build the three-sided moth movie screen, first build the coat hanger frame, then cover each of the three coat hangers with tissue paper.

1. Arrange three hangers in a pyramid shape as shown, and tape the structure together.

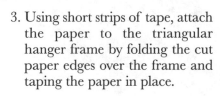

3. Using short strips of tape, attach the paper to the triangular hanger frame by folding the cut paper edges over the frame and taping the paper in place.

4. Position the flashlight under the three-sided screen so it is pointing up under the center of the screen. When positioned properly, the flashlight will illuminate the three screens, causing a white glow that will attract moths (and probably a few other kinds of insects as well). Make sure the flashlight batteries are fresh and the bulb glows brightly. Moths will not be attracted to a dim or yellow-tinted light.

2. Trace the shape of one full coat hanger on the tissue paper and cut it out, leaving an extra inch of paper all around the perimeter of the traced shape.

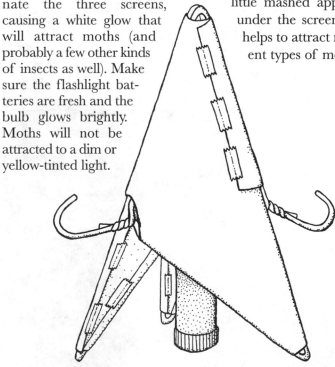

Watching moth movies

The best time to see a moth movie is during a warm summer evening, when moths are most active and easily attracted to light.

Try to find a location where there are no brighter lights to attract the moths away from yours. You can set up the screen and flashlight on an outdoor table or even on the ground.

Give the nearby moths at least a half hour after darkness to locate your light magnet. Some moths attracted by the light will fly around the outside of the pyramid, and a few moths will fly under and up into the three-screen structure, casting "dancing" shadows and patterns on the paper-covered surfaces.

Some moths are also attracted to sugar and other sweets. Sticky sugars like molasses will attract some moths, but they can also catch a moth's delicate legs. Try putting a little mashed apple or banana under the screen and see if it helps to attract more or different types of moths.

TENSEGRITY THING

Don't even think about building a Tensegrity Thing unless you have excellent dexterity, good coordination, and a lot of patience. The difficult part of making it is keeping all the pieces in their correct positions while connecting them to each other. And, as this three-dimensional structure takes form, it becomes even more difficult to handle until the last connection is made. But if you do get it right, you will have built a tensegrity tetrahedron in which the six struts interweave in a complex-looking pattern so that no one strut directly touches any other strut. It almost seems as if the struts are floating in space, yet the structure is still fairly rigid and will always return to its original shape even after being twisted.

Tensegrity structures can be built to mimic the forms of several polyhedrons, including an octahedron and a dodecahedron, but the complexity of those tensegrity constructions is a bit mind boggling. So for starters, its best to build a simpler tetrahedron that uses only six struts.

Construction

Builder's age
10

Player's age
8+

Materials
☐ 6 full-length unsharpened pencils
☐ 12 pencil-cap erasers
☐ 6 No. 19 rubber bands (3 ½″ x ¹/₁₆″)

Tools
☐ Small file or fine sandpaper

Building instructions

Gather all the materials needed plus some extras. Some rubber bands break more easily than others, and pencil-cap erasers can split.

Begin by making the six identical tensegrity struts.

1. Using the edge of a small file (or a piece of fine sandpaper bent over the square edge of a wood block), cut a shallow groove in both the eraser end and the wood end of a full-length, unsharpened pencil. The two groves should be in line with each other.

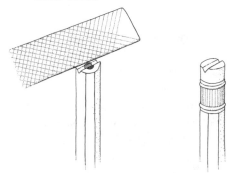

2. Stretch a No. 19 rubber band completely around the length of the pencil so it rests in the grooves cut into the ends. Adjust the rubber band so its tension is about the same on either side of the pencil.

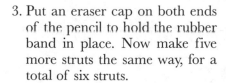

3. Put an eraser cap on both ends of the pencil to hold the rubber band in place. Now make five more struts the same way, for a total of six struts.

Assemble the struts

4. On a flat surface, lay out and attach all six struts exactly as shown in the plan.

   In this layout and in the final structure, the ends of each strut are always attached to the rubber bands of other struts. Notice that the location of the rubber band attachment points from the end of the struts is the same for

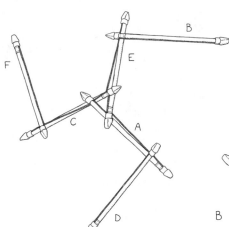

all struts. Only attach strut ends to one of the lengths of rubber band on each pencil. (The length of rubber band on the other side is not used.)

To make an attachment, remove the eraser cap from one end of a strut, being careful that the rubber band stays in the groove. Then, at the point of the attachment, place the rubber band of the other strut into the same groove, and slip the eraser cap back on the pencil end to hold the two rubber bands in place.

5. Follow the illustration carefully and lift the attached struts in the middle of the assembly so they droop down. Now attach the free end of strut A to the rubber band on strut B, being sure the connection location is the correct distance from the pencil end.

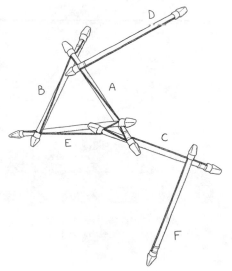

6. In a similar way, connect the end of strut C to the rubber band on strut D. At this point in the construction, the uncompleted form should show two triangular "faces."

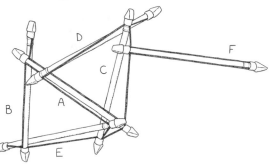

7. Form the third triangular face by connecting the end of strut E to the rubber band on strut F.

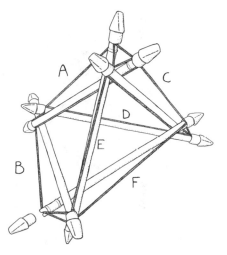

8. To complete the tensegrity structure, connect the remaining free end of strut F to the rubber band on strut B.

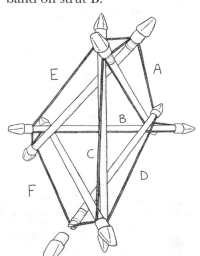

Connect the remaining free end of strut D to the rubber band on strut F.

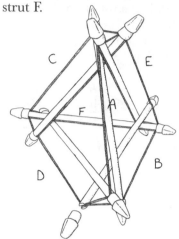

Connect the remaining free end of strut B to the rubber band on strut D.

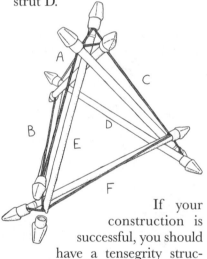

If your construction is successful, you should have a tensegrity structure consisting of six edges, four triangular faces, and four smaller triangles formed by the points of attachment. To create somewhat different tensegrity tetrahedron forms, try reassembling the struts using a different (but consistent) attachment point on the r u b b e r bands.

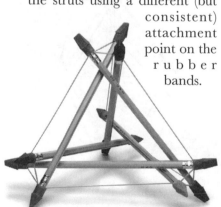

TENSEGRITY

Tensegrity is described as a closed structural system consisting of three or more compression struts positioned within a network of tension cables that allows all the combined parts to support each other in such a way that the struts do not touch one another yet form a firm, triangulated, prestressed, tension and compression unit. But rather than being the work of an engineer or scientist, tensegrity structures were first invented and patented over fifty years ago by a New York artist, Kenneth Snelson, who used the construction method to build both large and small space frame sculptures. It was one of Snelson's college professors, Buckminster Fuller (inventor of the geodesic dome), who later coined the word *tensegrity* to describe the network of cables in tension that maintain the form, or integrity, of the structure. Snelson, however, still prefers to call his sculptures "floating compression."

The idea of designing and building space frame trusses purely for their beauty was the intended application of Snelson's tensegrity building system. After all, people have always admired beautiful truss bridges and structures, and many of Snelson's large works made of stainless steel pipe struts and thin steel cables are as huge as a bridge! But Snelson's inspiration was not engineering, but rather the patterns of the forces found in nature.

"My training is in art and I make art," claimed Snelson. "Engineers make structures for specific uses, to support something, to hold something, to do something. My sculptures serve only to stand up by themselves and to reveal a particular form such as a tower or a cantilever or a geometrical order probably never seen before; all of this because of a desire to unveil, in whatever ways I can, the wondrous essence of elementary structure."

Easy Landing is the name of this thirty-foot-high Kenneth Snelson tensegrity sculpture in Baltimore, Maryland.

UNIVERSAL MODULARITY
BUILDING SYSTEM

The idea of a Universal Modularity building system is simply a way to attach anything to anything else, using a universal connector. There are no specific directions to follow, and no way to do it wrong. Just start connecting everything you can find that's not nailed down and not valuable to anyone else. What you make of all these things attached to each other can be as spontaneous and creative as a sculpture or as planned and complicated as a working mechanical contraption that does something or nothing at all.

All three universal connectors can attach most anything to anything, but each one has its own unique construction features. Deciding which one to use might depend on the type of materials to be attached and how permanent or temporary you want your structure to be.

SYSTEM FEATURES

- Attaches anything to anything
- All scrap material and discards can be used
- Makes quick inventions and sculptures
- Good for large-scale building
- Helps with room cleanup
- Uncovers interesting phenomena
- Pieces cannot be connected incorrectly
- Repairs are easy to make

Construction

Builder's age

6+ for duct-tape and plastic-tie building

9+ for hot-glue building

Materials

☐ Collection of scrap materials, discards, and found objects

☐ Universal connector (Select one or more.)

Duct tape

Plastic ties

Hot glue

Tools

☐ Scissors if using duct tape or plastic ties

☐ Hot-glue gun if using hot glue

Building techniques

After gathering a large resource of materials, select an appropriate Universal Modularity attachment method, and just start building. Which fastening method will work best for your Universal Modularity construction?

Duct tape

Although duct tape is unquestionably the most common and univer-

Twig-frame doghouse fastened with plastic ties

sal way to attach anything to anything, the wide, gray sticky tape suffers from being aesthetically unpleasing and having a reputation for slipshod workmanship. Anything you build using duct tape will be interpreted as a crude construction. Depending on what you build, however, trends and attitudes could change, and so could the image of duct tape. If you want a slightly more pleasing appearance, use black duct tape.

Plastic ties

These quick and easy-to-use fasteners are great for wrapping and tying parts together. Plastic ties come in many lengths and can also be strung together to make even longer ties. Depending on how tightly you close the fastener, plastic ties can create tight fastenings for firm connections, loose fastenings for hinges or movable parts, or loops for hanging parts. And any tie in the structure can be an attachment point for another tie and another part. For a finished appearance, use a sturdy pair of scissors or wire cutters to trim off excess tie material.

Hot glue

If your construction is well-planned right down to the details, or if you have no plan at all but just want to build a "something," a hot-glue gun can be used to make fairly permanent connections between two things made of nearly any materials. This is a truly universal glue that gives your construction a perma-

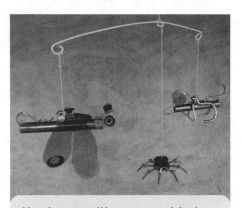

Hardware critters assembled with a hot-glue gun

nent and "engineered" appearance. Hot glue should only be considered if you have been given permission and instructions on how to properly use it. Read the instructions that come with the glue gun for the right kind of hot-glue stick to use.

Blooming flower made from duct-tape petals

RUBE GOLDBERG INVENTIONS

Rube Goldberg was a popular newspaper cartoonist best remembered for his crazy and complicated pseudoscientific inventions meant to make the simplest task (like turning on the toaster or setting off a wake-up alarm) as incredibly complicated as possible. Of course, Goldberg's inventions were only drawings, but the spirit of his nutty and absurd contraptions can be captured in building an actual Rube Goldberg Invention, using Universal Modularity.

Most Rube Goldberg contraptions are action/reaction machines. That is, the movement of one thing causes the movement of something else, which then causes another thing to move, and so on until the last movement successfully achieves the objective of the machine—like ringing a bell, popping a balloon, cracking open a peanut, turning off an alarm clock, turning on a radio, squeezing toothpaste from a tube, or dispensing a jelly bean. The more complicated the process to achieve a simple result, the better.

Setting up the individual ramps, pulleys, pivots, hinges, or whatever is needed will take some clever thinking, and getting everything to work just right takes some time. But presenting your completed contraption to others and watching the sequence of actions run smoothly from start to finish is a very satisfying reward.

Construction

Building system
Universal Modularity

Builder's age
8+ for duct-tape and plastic-tie building

9+ for hot-glue building

Player's age
8+

Materials
☐ Collection of scrap materials, discards, and found objects

☐ Any materials needed for a specific design

☐ Universal connector (Select one or more.)

   Duct tape

   Plastic ties

   Hot glue

PROFESSOR BUTTS GETS HIS THINK-TANK WORKING AND EVOLVES THE SIMPLIFIED PENCIL-SHARPENER.
OPEN WINDOW (A) AND FLY KITE (B). STRING (C) LIFTS SMALL DOOR (D) ALLOWING MOTHS (E) TO ESCAPE AND EAT RED FLANNEL SHIRT (F). AS WEIGHT OF SHIRT BECOMES LESS, SHOE (G) STEPS ON SWITCH (H) WHICH HEATS ELECTRIC IRON (I) AND BURNS HOLE IN PANTS (J). SMOKE (K) ENTERS HOLE IN TREE (L) SMOKING OUT OPOSSUM (M) WHICH JUMPS INTO BASKET (N) PULLING ROPE (O) AND LIFTING CAGE (P), ALLOWING WOODPECKER (Q) TO CHEW WOOD FROM PENCIL (R) EXPOSING LEAD. EMERGENCY KNIFE (S) IS ALWAYS HANDY IN CASE OPOSSUM, OR THE WOODPECKER GETS SICK AND CAN'T WORK.

"Professor Butt's Simplified Pencil Sharpener"

Tools

- ☐ Scissors if using duct tape or plastic ties
- ☐ Hot-glue gun if using hot glue
- ☐ Any tools needed for working with specific materials

Building techniques

If you already have ideas for the Rube Goldberg machine you plan to make, gather the materials needed, select a Universal Modularity universal connector, and start putting parts together. Some builders like to mount their action/reaction mechanisms on a piece of plywood or another type of backing board,

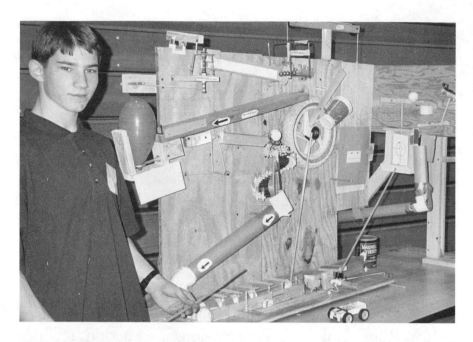

and cord so parts can pivot and swing, things that roll, cups and buckets for catching falling objects, things that make sounds, and whatever else inspires you. Select an appropriate Universal Modularity attachment method, or a combination of methods, and start building.

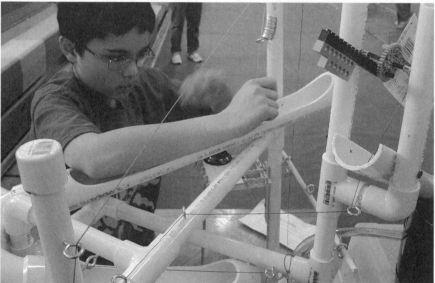

some contraptions are built with all the parts connected to each other like one big kinetic sculpture, and sometimes the individual mechanisms in the chain of actions are arranged in place on a table or the floor.

If you just want to put parts together to see what kind of actions you can create, and then design a Rube Goldberg contraption based on the mechanisms you create, it helps to start with a large resource of materials. Collect tubes and ramps for things to roll down, hinges

GOLDBERG VARIATIONS
AND OTHER AUDIOKINETIC SCULPTURES BY GEORGE RHOADS

George Rhoads is an artist, a toy designer, and one of the first American origami masters. But he is best known for creating large, Rube Goldberg–like mechanical contraptions that he calls "audiokinetic" sculptures because they make sounds as they move. Maybe you have seen one of his colorful rolling-ball sculptures at an airport, science center, museum, hospital, or shopping center.

Each audiokinetic sculpture is a different combination of basic machines that creates a complex course of ball tracks from top to bottom. Balls are typically carried to the top of the sculpture by a chain-driven elevator lift or a rotating screw lift. Then the balls begin a journey down the sculpture, often following several different tracks that may loop, twist, and spiral as the rolling balls activate levers and gates, strike objects, and leap off trampolines.

Along each path there are sound effects created by bells, gongs, chimes, drums, cymbals, and sometimes even a xylophone, all resulting in an intermittent cacophony of sound that most people find quite musical. When the balls reach the bottom, they roll to a lift to be taken back to the top. The ball lifts are driven by motors, but the force of gravity propels the balls' descent and most other actions.

At times there may be several balls in different locations contributing to the unique combination of sounds, but most viewers follow the complete journey of an individual ball before following another. According to the artist, "Each track has its own series of sounds and events. The timing of each series in relation to the others is random, so the overall sequence of events and sounds is never the same."

Just like a true Rube Goldberg invention, each George Rhoads sculpture initially appears to be ultra complex, but a closer examination clearly reveals the simple task of each part. In fact, to honor the Rube Goldberg mechanical approach to design, one Rhoads sculpture at Boston's Logan Airport is named *Goldberg Variations*. The name also intentionally refers to music written by the composer Johann Sebastian Bach. The Rhoads rolling-ball, audiokinetic sculpture shown here is called *Exercise in Fugality*. The sculpture, also at Logan Airport, is enclosed in a huge glass case and always attracts spellbound crowds.

Screw lift and gong

Xylophone

Elevator ball lift

BRICK AND BLOCK STRUCTURES

UNDERSTANDING BRICK
AND BLOCK STRUCTURES

BUILDING WITH BRICKS
AND BLOCKS

UNDERSTANDING BRICK AND BLOCK STRUCTURES

STACKING IS THE SIMPLEST METHOD OF BUILDING

THE STRUCTURAL ELEMENTS OF BRICKS AND BLOCKS

BUILDING BREAKTHROUGHS WITH ARCHES AND DOMES

THE WORLD'S GREAT PYRAMIDS

MEDIEVAL TO MODERN CASTLES

THE ALMOST ALL-AMERICAN LOG CABIN

STACKING IS THE SIMPLEST METHOD OF BUILDING

The simplest way to construct a form is to stack one piece on top another, just like a baby's first attempts at block building. If the two blocks fit closely together and one is balanced on the other, this simple structure will be stable and not fall down. As more blocks are added and the structure begins to grow in all directions, the blocks must be stacked in certain patterns in order for the structure to remain stable. The general rule is that each brick or block must be placed on top of and straddling the two below it. That way, the pieces in the stacked pile are interlocked together, and the structure is less likely to topple.

In very broad terms, a brick is a stackable building unit that can be held in one hand, while a block is defined as a larger building unit that takes at least two hands to lift, though there are many exceptions. The construction is made a lot easier if all the bricks or blocks are the same size with modular dimensions. When working with natural materials like granite or limestone, however, the stones are cut to various shapes and sizes and then tightly fitted together. Still, the stones must be stacked in very specific patterns that help hold the structure together, as well as distribute their own weight and the weight of any load placed upon them. If the stones are tightly fitted and properly balanced, the structure will stand on its own as is. But more often, mortar is used to fill the gaps between the stones and cement them together.

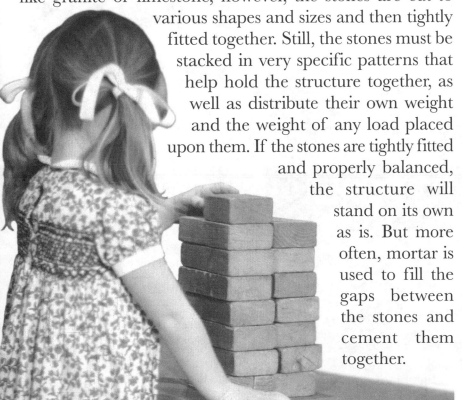

Bricks and Blocks Make Large, Strong Structures

Because bricks and blocks are very strong in compression, they are most often used to make strong walls and columns that can hold up a lot of weight. The Romans built their bridges, buildings, aqueducts, and roadways out of solid stone blocks, and the Egyptians used enormous stone blocks to build pyramids the size of small mountains. While stone is strong in compression, it is very weak in tension, causing it to crack and split apart readily. This property makes it easy to cut a stone to the desired size.

The large stone blocks used to build structures must be cut to shape and tightly fit in a specific pattern.

Many human-made building blocks work just like stone. Bricks in standard shapes and sizes are the most ancient artificial building material, dating back nearly seven thousand years. The first bricks were formed of molded clay and dried in the sun, exactly as adobe bricks are still being made. A few thousand years later, people figured out that burning the clay bricks in a hot fire made them considerably harder and more suitable for larger constructions. In fact, burned clay bricks are so strong in compression that they can be used to build walls or columns up to three hundred feet tall.

When bricks, blocks, or stones are primarily used to build structure and shape, the outer finished surfaces are often covered with plaster or stucco.

The Great Wall of China is a four-thousand-mile-long wall made using millions of bricks, with many sections, each one straddling the two below it.

The fitting together of bricks, blocks, or stones creates patterns that are one of the appealing characteristics of the construction method. Handsome brick houses and stone buildings often celebrate their appearance and draw attention to their details and craftsman-ship, especially around doorways and windows.

In other types of construction, the bricks and blocks are used only to construct the building's structure, which is then covered in another material considered more appealing. The Romans covered their adobe brick homes with a plaster or stucco finish, while they faced their public brick buildings with marble. Most modern adobe-like structures use concrete blocks instead of clay under their skins of stucco.

Because bricks are cast in molds, they can be formed into various standard shapes and sizes. They can also be cast out of several materials, including clay, concrete, and even glass. Building supply centers usually have stacks of different types of bricks and blocks outside. Notice that some are rather fancy in shape or color and are obviously meant to be used for decorative

purposes, while some rougher bricks or concrete blocks are strictly for building strong structures.

The special features of brick and block construction include:

- Brick making is easy, and raw material is plentiful.
- Modular building components make stacking easy.
- Modularity permits a large variety of forms.
- Stacked construction results in pleasing patterns.
- Structures can support heavy loads in compression.
- Heavy and massive structures resist destructive forces.

Buildings made of exposed bricks, blocks, or stones often celebrate the appearance of the material's texture.

HABITAT

Imagine you were going to build a model of a big apartment building, using a lot of empty shoe boxes all the same size, and each shoe box was a complete room. Now suppose you also wanted to arrange the boxes so that some apartments had one room, some two rooms, and some four rooms. And you wanted to arrange the rooms so that no two apartments were exactly alike, plus each had good views of the surrounding landscape and an outdoor deck. What would your structure look like?

That was the same question addressed by Moshe Safdie, a young architect, when he set out to design a big housing project for the Expo 67 International Exhibition in Montreal, Canada. His superb example of modular construction was built right next to the fairgrounds on the banks of the St. Lawrence River and given the name Habitat. Safdie's concept for the design was to use room-sized concrete boxes of identical shape and size and stack them in a way that achieved all the criteria for a good place to live.

The basic shoe box-shaped modules in Habitat differed only in where the window and door holes were located and what was placed inside. Each module was completely built in a factory, using precast reinforced concrete to form the walls and floor. At the construction site, complete bathrooms and kitchens built of molded components were placed inside the appropriate concrete modules, and then the modules were hoisted into position by huge cranes.

The concrete rooms were stacked and arranged according to plan until the finished structure was eleven stories tall. The arrangement of the modules is so clever that each floor of Habitat is considered a neighborhood, and each apartment has an outdoor patio and a private outdoor hallway to get to the stairs. This makes it quite convenient for residents to take a walk or maybe walk their dogs.

Because the outdoor patios needed walls with railings for safety, Safdie designed low windows in the walls so young children also had a good view. Everyone living in Habitat could enjoy the sounds and sights of the water fountains surrounding the building. But rather than just being ornamental, these fountains served a practical purpose by spraying and cooling down the water used to cool certain pipes that ran throughout the building.

For its time, Habitat was considered a radical idea. But Safdie's building-block design proved that factory-built housing could be practical and economical as well as good looking. Now modular concrete structures are found all over the world.

Habitat
Montreal, Canada
Designed by Moshe Safdie, 1967

THE STRUCTURAL ELEMENTS OF BRICKS AND BLOCKS

Bricks and blocks can be used as reliable structural materials for building because they are exceptionally strong in compression, even when many are stacked on top of one another. As long as we can count on gravity to supply the forces of compression, structures made of bricks and blocks will remain intact and stable.

Building Only with Compression

Compression is the force of things pushing together under the effect of gravity. Gravity is what causes almost everything to want to fall to the ground, and gravity is what keeps us all firmly planted on the ground. If you have ever been at the bottom of a "pig pile," you probably know how it feels to be in compression. Just laying on the ground by yourself seems normal enough, but what do you feel when one friend piles on top of you, and then another and another? Pretty soon you begin to feel crushed under the effects of compression. The pressure you feel is the force of gravity pulling each person above you toward the ground. Since you happen to be at the bottom of the pile, the collective force of all their bodies transfers through you on its way toward the ground.

That is exactly what happens to the bricks or blocks that are piled atop one another to build a structure. Imagine how much compression the bottom brick feels in a ten-foot-tall wall. Gravity is pulling each brick an equal amount, but the bottom brick has to pass all that force to the ground, so it feels the total of all the force above it. A brick halfway up to the top of the wall is only under half that amount of force, and a brick at the top feels only its own weight unless another force is placed on top of it.

One problem with brick and block construction is that the bottom pieces can take only so much compression before they crack and crumble. Therefore, most large brick and block constructions must be designed to take the weight of the upper part of the structure and spread it out at the bottom of the structure. That is why so many masonry buildings are bigger at the bottom. A pyramid is one of the strongest forms to build with bricks and blocks, because it has a large, square base and tapers into a point at the top. The tapering effect transfers the forces at any point in the structure to a larger area below.

Another disadvantage of building structures in compression is that the form needs to be nearly solid in order to pass all the forces to the

ground. This means buildings constructed of bricks and blocks cannot have large windows or large, open rooms without massive columns to help support and distribute the forces of the weight above.

TESTING THE LIMITS OF COMPRESSIVE MATERIALS

This simple demonstration illustrates how compressive materials and structures have limits of how much weight they can support before they fail.

Make a short stack of three or four small cubes of cheese, crackers, croutons, sugar cubes, or any cereal that will stack like bricks or blocks. Then put a finger on the top of the stack and press down lightly, gradually applying more and more pressure. How much force do you have to apply before one or all of the pieces in the stack crush or crumble?

Controlling the forces of compression

It is not very difficult to imagine how the forces of compression work in a brick or block wall where the weight of one block presses down on the block below so that each block supports the weight of all the blocks above it. Because of gravity, the forces in a solid wall go directly straight down from top to bottom, and the block at the bottom has to be strong enough to resist being crushed. The entire structure is in compression even when more load is placed on top of the wall. All that limits how large a brick or block wall can be is the compressive strength of the material used to build it. Different materials have different limits of compressibility before they fail. That is why a structure will obviously be stronger if it is built with blocks of stone rather than cardboard boxes.

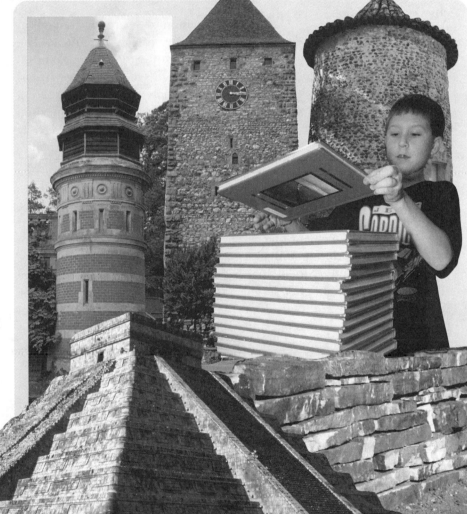

THE MYSTERIES OF BUILDING STONEHENGE

Archaeologists have revealed that about five thousand years ago a cult of people frequently gathered on a large, open field in southern England to celebrate events and perform rituals. That field is now called Stonehenge at Salisbury Plain. During the first eight hundred years of these gatherings, two circular and concentric banks of earth were built with a ditch between them. Such a ditch with a high bank is called a henge. During this same period, fifty-six equally spaced holes were dug in the ground to form a ring.

The purpose of these holes, the henge, and the placement of certain large stones during this first phase of building Stonehenge remains a mystery, although large, standing stones were typical of many prehistoric monuments, and parts of this structure provide some clues. Just outside the only entrance to the outer henge, there is a huge sandstone rock, and for anyone standing at the center of the circle, the midsummer sun rises directly over the big stone. The inner bank of the henge has two entrances that line up with the rising and setting of the moon.

In the second phase of construction, begun about four thousand years ago, two incomplete concentric rings of huge, rectangular

"bluestones" were positioned in the center of the monument. The builders of Stonehenge went to great lengths to import very specific materials for this construction because the kind of bluestone used can be found only in the Prescelly mountains of Wales, over 125 miles away from the building site.

Each of the eighty-two bluestones weighs between four and six tons, and engineers today estimate it would have taken more than five hundred men working every day for over a hundred years just to move the stones from the quarry to the construction site. Why these particular stones with a bluish-gray tint were so important to Stonehenge remains a mystery. Maybe they were believed to possess special powers.

The third and final phase of Stonehenge lasted nearly another thousand years and consisted of building the largest structures of the monument. These builders constructed a circle of thirty upright stones that supported a continuous curved ring of lintels. The ring was about one hundred feet in diameter, and the level top of the lintel ring is about sixteen feet high.

The large stones making up the lintel ring are also known as the sarsen stones. Sarsen is an intensely hard type of sandstone (even harder than granite) that comes from a quarry twenty miles away from Stonehenge. These large outer stones weigh as much as forty tons each and required one thousand workers to haul each one to the site. A nub was carved on the top of each standing stone that

perfectly fit a bowl-shaped cutout in the underside of the lintel. This type of attachment is called either a ball-and-socket or a mortise-and-tenon joint. At each joint where lintels butted together, they were

kept in position by a tongue-and-groove joint.

Five trilithons were then built in the center of the circle, positioned in the form of a horseshoe, with the tallest sitting at the top of the horseshoe and measuring twenty-two feet high. Each trilithon is made of two upright stones that support a horizontal lintel stone. During this period, for unknown reasons, the positions of the bluestones were rearranged from two semicircles around the outside of the trilithons to a horseshoe of stones just inside the trilithons.

Altogether, it took nearly two thousand years to complete Stonehenge, yet in another one thousand years (by around 1000 B.C.), the Stonehenge site had become completely deserted. Although many of the giant stones have survived five thousand years of howling winds, pounding rains, and earth tremors,

several parts of Stonehenge were ruined by a sect of people in the Middle Ages who believed that pushing over giant stones kept the devil away. Only some clues remain to suggest who built Stonehenge and why.

Today, Stonehenge seems to mean different things to different people. The scientist sees the megalithic monument as an instrument to predict the movements of the sun and moon and maybe eclipses, as well as other astronomical events. Archaeologists suggest that Stonehenge was designed to contain the graves

of important men, and perhaps for worshipping their spirits. The architect sees a monument to clever engineering. A member of the clergy sees a shrine. And others think Stonehenge was simply a meeting place where members of distant tribes would gather to celebrate weddings and funerals.

Stonehenge may have been any of these things or something else. Why would thousands of people work their entire lives to build something they would never see finished? What purpose could have been so important?

Stone rings both larger and smaller in diameter can be found throughout England and Ireland. Did these rings maybe serve a purpose similar to Stonehenge?

Adobe Mud Bricks and Blocks

For thousands of years, structures have been built using sun-dried mud molded into bricks and blocks. Part of the Great Wall of China was built with bricks of sun-baked earth, as was history's earliest known city, Jericho; the biblical Tower of Babel; and many rural buildings still being used throughout Europe. In the warm, dry climate of the southwest corner of the United States, and particularly in Arizona and New Mexico, building with sun-dried earthen bricks, called adobe, has long been the most practical material for building structures and is still being used today. However, in humid regions, adobe will decompose and crumble and wash away.

There are many reasons why adobe construction became and has remained so popular in the Southwest. Adobe bricks are made of earth, water, and straw, all of which is plentiful and usually free. Molding the brick shapes is easy, and the bricks can be made right at the construction site if there is an ample supply of earth and water. Assembling adobe bricks requires no special tools or skills, and the thick walls of an adobe structure are durable and very energy efficient.

A well-built adobe house with thick walls can be very comfortable in both winter and summer. Adobe is an excellent thermal regulator that keeps the house cool in the summer by insulating out the heat of the sun, and warm during cold nights by keeping the interior heat from escaping. In dry, arid climates, adobe construction will last almost indefinitely. In New Mexico, some adobe structures in perfect condition are nearly a thousand years old.

Even though the Southwest Native Americans had been building with sun-dried earthen bricks for many centuries, calling the brick material "adobe" began only relatively recently. *Adobe* is an Arabic word meaning "to mix together" and was probably brought to the American Southwest by Spanish explorers.

Casting adobe bricks

Making adobe bricks begins with mixing the right proportions of soil, water, and cut straw. But not all soil will work. The best soil for adobe has almost equal proportions of sand, silt, and clay, and most important, it contains very little or no organic matter. A soil sample can easily be analyzed by putting a handful in a

big glass jar filled with water. Stir the mixture thoroughly, and let it sit undisturbed for a day as the different materials in the soil sink or float to form their own strata, or layers. Sand will sink to the bottom, silt will form the next layer, and clay will form a layer on top of that. Any organic matter will float to the top. The relative thickness of the layers formed shows the approximate proportions of sand, silt, clay, and organic matter in the soil sample tested.

There are two basic methods for molding the brick shapes—casting the bricks in individual molds or casting a large slab and then cutting it up into many bricks. In either method, the muddy mixture is packed into a wooden mold and left to dry in the sun. Individually cast bricks will completely harden in their molds in about two weeks. When using the slab method, the large cast block is removed from its mold after only a few days of drying or when the mud has become hard enough to hold its shape. The slab is then cut into smaller bricks that are left to continue to dry in the sun for about a week.

The adobe building process

The completely hardened adobe building brick is very strong in compression, and the straw embedded in the brick helps provide strength in tension. Though water is used

for making adobe, water is also an adobe brick's worst enemy. Unless an adobe structure gets a thin covering of plaster or concrete, a heavy rain could completely wash it away. Because of this, adobe walls are usually built on top of a foundation made of concrete or stone so groundwater cannot reach and weaken the bricks from underneath.

When building a structure, adobe bricks are stacked in a bond pattern just like other types of brick construction, and adobe mud is used as the mortar between the bricks. Experienced adobe builders don't pile on more than three or four layers of bricks per day so that the mortar can dry and the bricks have a chance to settle.

Exterior adobe walls will last longer if they are protected from rain. Therefore, adobe houses usually have overhanging roofs with drainage systems that lead water far away from the walls. Almost any type of roof can be used with

adobe construction. Older civilizations placed brush and branches across the walls and plastered them over with adobe mud. About a foot of mud made a decent roof, but it required constant care and repair, especially after a rain. Modern adobe houses usually have flat roofs supported by beams and covered with shingles or tiles. But it is not unusual to see an adobe building with a shed roof, a gable roof, or even a turret roof.

ALL ABOUT

MESA VERDE

The stone and adobe structures at Mesa Verde (a Spanish word meaning "green table") have changed very little in the last seven to eight hundred years, since the Anasazi built their homes in the natural sandstone cliffs and caves of an area that is now part of southwestern Colorado. What makes these brick and mortar homes special is that they are built under the overhangs of huge cliffs.

At Mesa Verde, there are several hundred cliff dwelling communities that vary in size from only a few rooms to a few hundred rooms. Spruce Tree House is one of the best-preserved dwellings and contains around 114 rooms that housed a hundred people and included eight ceremonial chambers called kivas. The large, overhanging cliff protected the structures built underneath from the damaging and eroding effects of rain and wind.

Sandstone is a porous stone that allows water to slowly seep down through it. When the moisture in the rock freezes during the cold winter, the ice cracks and loosens the sandstone, causing chunks to break away and fall into the canyon below. Over time, a large overhang of rock is left, and it is beneath the shelter of the overhang that the Anasazi built their cliff dwellings. Archaeologists have pieced together what is left of these dwellings and have discovered some interesting things.

It is believed that all the structures in Mesa Verde were built using the sandstone rubble that resulted from the overhang being formed. The rubble was shaped into rectangular blocks about the size of a loaf of bread, and the mortar used between the blocks was an adobe mix of mud and water. To tighten the joints, the builders forced small stones into the mortar that separates the layers of bricks.

Roofs were made by placing large logs across the tops of the brick walls. Smaller sticks and branches were then used to more thoroughly cover the roof before applying a thick layer of adobe.

The homes in the cliffs were often three or four stories tall, with each room measuring about six feet by eight feet by six feet high. Each

house had a rectangular or T-shaped door that was typically two feet off the ground, making it look more like a large window. These openings had slabs of stone that could be used to close them, or sometimes an animal-hide curtain was used to cover the opening.

Because there are so few windows to let daylight inside, it is likely that the rooms in these multistory houses were used only for sleeping. During the day, people of the community worked outdoors in the courtyards in front of the buildings. Some of the upper stories had an exterior platform or balcony that connected one room to another, just like a hallway, and the platforms could also be used as

workplaces or for looking down at the courtyard activities.

An important part of the cliff dwelling community was the kiva, which is believed to have been a religious room, similar to a church. A kiva is a round room sunk about six feet into the ground, like a circular swimming pool, with a ground-level roof. Just like the roofs of the dwellings, the kiva roof was constructed of beams made of logs, covered by sticks, twigs, and reeds, and a thick layer of adobe mud. Because the kiva roof was level with the courtyard in front of the dwellings, it was a common meeting place for people to work or socialize. An opening in the kiva roof allowed entry and exit by a ladder, and the opening also allowed smoke to escape from the fireplace pit in the center of the kiva floor. To keep the kiva from becoming too smoky, an effective ventilation system brought fresh air down into the round room through a ventilator shaft.

Before building the cliff dwellings, the Anasazi had lived, farmed, and hunted on the mesa plains for over seven hundred years. But as the population became concentrated

into cliff-dwelling communities, and as these communities grew, it is believed the people depleted the farmland, consumed all the available firewood, and reduced the animal populations, forcing hunters to travel farther. To make things worse, a study of tree rings has shown that there was a prolonged drought that may also have contributed to forcing the Anasazi to abandon their cliff dwellings. By 1300, fewer than a hundred years after the Anasazi first started building their cliff communities, Mesa Verde was completely deserted.

Making Bricks, Laying Bricks, and Brick Patterns

In regions where stone and wood were scarce, clay was often plentiful, so bricks could be made and used for building structures. The earliest-made clay bricks were formed by hand and set out in the sun to bake and harden, but for the last eight thousand years or so, bricks have more commonly been made in molds. The molds could also be placed in the sun for the bricks to bake, dry, and harden, but builders quickly learned that the process worked much better when the bricks were baked or fired in a hot oven. The small size of a brick makes it easy to fire quickly, and fired bricks are much more durable than sun-dried bricks.

The size and shape of a regular building brick has not changed much since the Middle Ages. The width of a brick is roughly four and one-half inches, or about the largest size that a human hand can easily pick up and hold. The length is usually twice the dimension of the width. The thickness can vary, but most bricks are about half as thick as they are wide.

half width

twice width

width

Most bricks are red because the clay commonly used to make bricks contains iron. When the clay is baked, the burned iron turns a deep red. The more iron there is in the clay, the deeper the red color.

The walls and structures made from bricks and stone are called masonry. Each layer of brick is called a course, and the pattern created by an arrangement of courses in a brick wall is called the bond. (Don't confuse this with the adhesion of the mortar to the bricks, which is also called a bond.)

Brick bonds create structure and pattern

As a brick wall is built, the courses are laid in rows, one on top another, so the vertical joints between bricks in one course are never directly over the joints in the course below. In other words, each brick must rest on at least two other bricks. The walls of a brick building are usually more than one brick thick, and because

the length of a brick is usually twice its width, the bricks can be arranged in interlocking and weaving patterns that come out square and even when finished. This interlocking of the bond creates a strong wall, and the pattern it creates also has a decorative effect. Look at brick walls to see if you can identify the pattern of the bond. These are some of the most common bond patterns.

American bond

Dutch bond

English bond

English garden wall bond

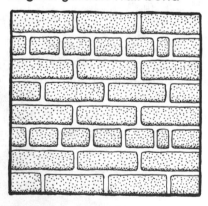

Flemish bond

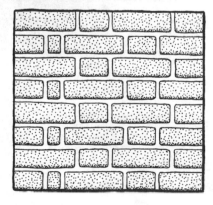

Open bond

Running bond

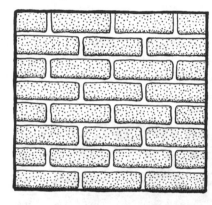

Mortar joints and pointing

Mortar is used to cement the bricks together and lock them in place. The mortar is usually applied with a trowel, and when a brick is placed on top of wet mortar, the excess mortar squeezes out from between the bricks. The process of removing the excess mortar and finishing off the joint is called pointing. Just scraping off the mortar even with the brick face is called a flush joint, but various shapes can be applied to the mortar joints to provide either practical or decorative effects. One benefit of pointing is to compress the mortar into a smooth surface that will better repel water. The outward slope of a joint is especially good at shedding rain. Special pointing tools (or improvised ones) are used to create particular types of pointing. Look at a brick wall to see if you can identify its style of pointing. Here are some common types.

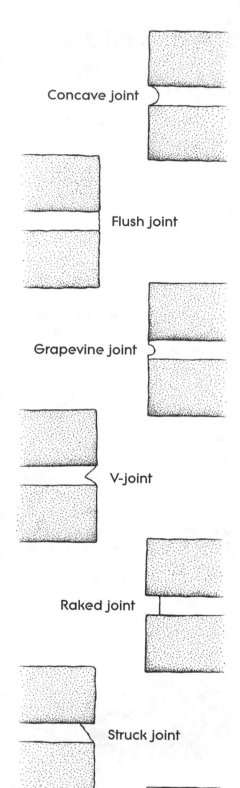

Concave joint

Flush joint

Grapevine joint

V-joint

Raked joint

Struck joint

Weathered joint

Bricks for paving pathways and patios

Bricks are also used for paving pathways, patios, and sometimes streets or roads. Depending on the bricks used, there are several patterns that can be created by arranging the bricks in regular patterns. Using typical building bricks with a width-to-length ratio of 2:1, these are some of the many patterns you may be able to find.

Herringbone 90 degrees

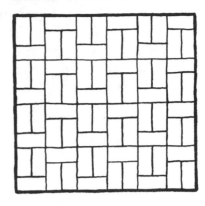

Basket weave No. 2

Whorling square

Herringbone 45 degrees

Basket weave offset with cut

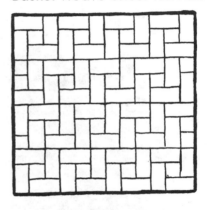

Running bond

Herringbone with cut

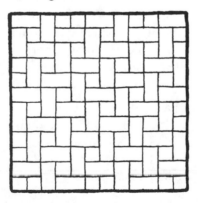

Basket weave variation

Running bond head-on

Basket weave No. 1

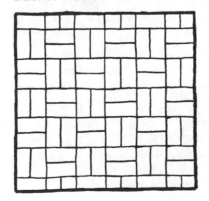

Dan Freitas F Stack

THE STORY OF LEGO

In the late 1940s, a Danish carpenter named Ole Kirk Christiansen began making wooden toy cars, trucks, and animals that quickly became popular throughout Denmark. He called his company Lego, which in Danish means "to play well." Even though Christian-sen's wooden toys were quite successful with a certain age of children, he wanted to create a toy that kids of all ages and interests would like.

Christiansen decided to make sets of wooden blocks that included several new block designs. And, in an attempt to even further improve the design and manufacture of traditional blocks, he started making them in plastic. Still, all was not well. Back then, plastic toys had a reputation for being cheap and flimsy because most manufacturers used thin, low-quality plastic that easily cracked, broke, or shattered. Besides, there was nothing really new or better about the molded plastic blocks except they were not made of wood and therefore they could not splinter.

If Christiansen was going to use plastic, he thought he should use a higher quality plastic and take better advantage of its unique properties, especially plastic's ability to be molded into unique shapes with fine detail. Certain better-quality plastics also could withstand some amount of bend and flex without cracking or breaking. Plus, plastic parts could easily be mass-produced.

It was around this time that Christiansen's Lego company produced a toy truck that could be taken apart into several pieces and then put back together again. Christiansen realized that such a toy added a new dimension to play, and that's when the idea struck him: What if he were to combine the concept of plastic, modular building blocks that snapped together with put-together and take-apart toys?

When a child tired of playing with the toy truck, he or she could take it apart and reassemble the same pieces into something else, like a toy boat, a plane, a house, a bridge, or just about anything a young builder could imagine. This was the universal plaything for all ages and interests he had been trying to develop. Ordinary wooden blocks could only be piled one on top of another, but these new plastic building blocks, designed with special snap-together studs, could be easily locked together to create a sturdy structure. The Automatic Binding Brick, as it was originally called, had been born.

Even though Christiansen's new snap-together plastic blocks became popular in Denmark, they didn't sell well anywhere else. These Automatic Binding Bricks were a big improvement over his earlier designs, except they still didn't hold together as well as Christansen would have liked. Like today's Lego bricks, the early ones had the familiar round studs on the top side. However, there were no individual "sockets" on the other side of the brick to connect with the studs of another brick, just an open recess. That meant the plastic bricks held tightly only when they were connected by four or more studs. Any less, and the bricks fell apart much too easily.

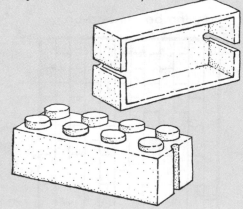

It was when the company re-designed the bottom of the brick with sockets that the Lego bricks, as we now know them, became popular all over the world. The sockets not only made connections between the bricks much more snug, but it was now possible to connect two eight-stud bricks in twenty-four different ways, and just three bricks could be connected in 1060 ways! The universal connectability of Lego bricks made it possible for builders to make intricate constructions of almost anything from a model robot to the model buildings of an entire city.

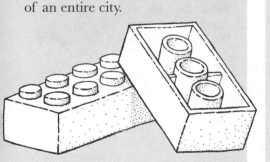

When Christiansen later learned that his company's name, Lego, also means "I build" in Latin, he renamed the plastic bricks. While other pieces like wheels, roof panels, and even a propeller have been added over the years, the simple studded brick is still the universal component of the Lego building system.

WHAT 2-D MODULES FILL A SQUARE?

Have you ever noticed that four identical squares can be put together to form a larger square? Or that two bricks can form a square? How many different individual module shapes can you create so that identical multiples of each module will completely fill a square? Here are a few solutions to get you started.

Smaller squares

4 squares   **9 squares**

16 squares   **25 squares**

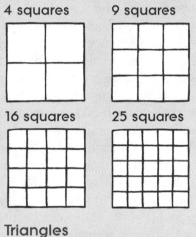

Triangles

4 triangles   **8 triangles**

Rectangles

2 rectangles   **3 rectangles**

4 rectangles   **10 rectangles**

Here's another hint: Use one solution to figure out another. So, after drawing a grid of sixteen small squares (or any other modular shape that works) to fill a large square, trace over the grid, combining the smaller modules into larger ones to come up with other modular shapes that work—like L-shaped, U-shaped, or T-shaped modules.

L shapes

2 Ls   **4 Ls**

By combining various shapes and using clever thinking, you might also try creating asymmetrical modules that fill a square. Just remember that the square must be completely filled by identical shape and size modular pieces. Here are a few examples.

Now that you understand how to combine identical modules of a particular shape to create a square module, here is one last hint: There are hundreds and even thousands of modular shapes that will work.

BUILDING BREAKTHROUGHS WITH ARCHES AND DOMES

It was the discovery of the arch that first allowed brick and block buildings to be larger and stronger, and masonry bridges to span greater distances than any previous method of building. Arches also allowed larger windows and entrances to be built into brick and block walls.

In a solid wall, it is easy to imagine the force of one row of blocks pressing down on the row below it and so on until the combined forces reach solid ground. But what if you put a hole in the wall for a window or doorway? What happens to the forces of the wall pushing down directly above these openings?

In structures with narrow openings, a lintel block often spans the top of each opening. But without having anything to completely support it from underneath, the bottom of the block is in tension. Too much force from above would cause too much tension and the lintel would break, collapsing the wall above. Therefore, openings with lintels were relatively narrow.

The simplest type of arch to allow wider openings was the corbel arch, in which the sides of an opening in a brick or block wall taper inward from the base of the opening until they meet at the top. Each layer, or course, of blocks is laid to overhang the course beneath it. Finally, the projecting corners or corbels of the blocks are smoothed off to make an even inner surface. The corbel arch (like all arches) is a completely compressive structure that transfers all the forces above it directly to the ground or the support below it. However, the proportions and strength of a corbel arch were not always practical for building large structures.

In a corbel arch, each course of blocks is laid to overhang the course beneath it until the tapered sides meet at the top.

Instead of solid lintel stone, this ancient entrance opening uses wedge-shaped stones to form an arch.

Most of the credit for developing the design and construction of arches goes to the Romans of about two thousand years ago. In creating their vast empire, the Romans built over fifty thousand miles of roads that required several thousand bridges. These stone arch bridges were so strong and stable that many are still in use today.

Even the simple arch of a Bermuda moon gate requires a temporary wooden framework to keep the stones in place until the keystone is positioned at the top.

To span the distance over a stream or river with a stone arch bridge, the Roman builders first constructed a half-circle-shaped wooden frame from one riverbank to the other. Blocks of stone called voussoirs were then placed over the framework in a very specific order, working in symmetry from either end toward the top. So a block would be placed leaning against the frame on one end of the frame, then another block just like it would be placed against the frame on the other side in the matching position. As both sides of the arch grew from the sides of the riverbank and curved toward the center, other blocks could be filled in behind them. Just before reaching the middle and top of the arch framework, a slightly tapered space was left for the keystone,

keystone

abutment

voussoirs

the last stone that both halves of the arch would lean against when the wooden framework was removed. A typical Roman bridge consisted of two parallel stone arches with wood beams connecting them, upon which the roadway was built. The largest of these bridges could span a river one hundred feet wide.

However, there was a problem with building a single arch bridge because the forces of its own weight are transferred down both sides, giving the structure a tendency to want to thrust its legs outward, spread apart, and collapse. Therefore, a single arch bridge needed to be built into large embankments on either side of the river, or large stone supports needed to be constructed at either end. The Romans also discovered that by placing a series of arches in a row, end to end, the arcade could be any length without needing heavy supports or buttresses except at the two ends. The Romans used this technique not only to build long bridges,

but also to construct aqueducts that carried water to Rome over distances of hundreds of miles.

The use of the arch continued in the construction of cathedrals and other buildings as well as bridges and is still used in today's architecture. However, more modern arches will likely be constructed of concrete or steel as well as bricks and blocks. Not only has the arch proven to be a useful and enduring element of structure, but its appearance is almost always pleasing.

This section of a Roman aqueduct uses tiered arcades of arches to span two distant hillsides that are also the buttresses at either end.

Compared to earlier masonry construction, arches allowed bridges to be longer, buildings to be taller, and openings to be wider.

Brick and Block Domes

Once you understand the structure of a brick or block arch, it is easier to understand the structure of a brick or block dome. Just imagine rotating an arch in a circle around its vertical center axis. The half-sphere form that the rotating arch makes is the shape of a dome. And that is exactly what a dome is, just a continuous series of arches passing through the same center at the top, all having the same keystone.

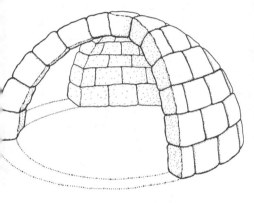

Even though it is convenient to think of a dome as many identical arches placed around a circular base, the resulting half-sphere shape of a dome is so strong that it really needs only about one-tenth of the material it would take to actually build a dome out of arches. An arch requires some type of buttressing on either side to keep its legs from spreading out, but the dome does not need any type of buttressing at all. The circular horizontal sections of a dome act like rigid rings around the structure that resist the forces of spreading out under a load.

Just as the arch is able to span greater distances than a post-and-lintel system, domes can cover larger open areas than any other types of structures—whether the dome is constructed using bricks, stone blocks, concrete, or metal. In

many ways, the dome is a perfect structure because its shape is so enormously strong, yet it uses a minimal amount of material to achieve its shape and size compared to other building methods. A dome is also very stable because

the structure is helped by gravity and affected very little by the forces of wind. The dome is not only a structural masterpiece, but its shape is also very appealing from both the outside and inside. Maybe that is why so many houses of worship and public buildings use a dome in their architecture.

The building of domes followed the development of arches, so the first brick and block domes were formed by corbeling, in which the

bricks or stone blocks are laid so that each course was smaller in diameter than the course below, tapering inward toward the top until the dome shape is formed. In a corbeled dome, each layer is self-

supporting without a temporary framework needed during construction. And, with all the layers overlapping, the shape is somewhat pointed at the top, and the outside and inside surfaces appear as a series of stepped ridges. These projecting edges are usually chipped away to leave a smooth surface.

Later domes were constructed of bricks and concrete or stones fitted over temporary forms to create a true half-sphere shape (or nearly half-sphere shape). Sometimes the bricks were laid in layers of rings that were self-supporting (like in a corbeled arch), so no temporary framework was needed except at the top where the dome's surface approaches horizontal. In some of these domes, it was easier to not complete the dome but rather leave a round hole opening at the top.

EXPERIMENT

TESTING THE STRENGTH OF ARCHES AND DOMES

Here's a simple demonstration that compares the structure of an arch to a dome.

Cut an orange or a grapefruit in half to form two half spheres, then scoop out (and eat) the fruit, leaving only the outer skin shells. From one of the halves, cut an arch out of the middle section. Stand the arch upright on a table and lightly press down at the top of the arch with your finger. As you press harder, notice that the legs of the arch spread outwards away from each other until the entire structure has failed and the arch is completely flat. The force of compression could not go straight down because there was nothing under the middle of the arch. With no buttressing to hold the two bases in place, the arch simply spread out and collapsed.

Place the other scooped-out half sphere of fruit so its circular base is flat on the table. Notice how stable this dome structure is compared to the fruit arch. You can't easily knock a dome off its base. Now place your finger on the top of the dome and start pressing down. Notice that the base doesn't spread at all, and the top of the dome will deform and collapse first. The walls of the dome want to spread out just like in the arch, but the ring shape of the dome base acts like a tightly buckled belt to keep the walls from spreading. In fact, some large domes that need extra strength are built with belts made of iron chain wrapped around their bases.

THE INUIT IGLOO

Contrary to what most people imagine, Inuits living in the frozen Arctic of northern Canada don't usually live in igloo huts. Most of the time, they live in regular looking houses (also called igloos) made of stone and wood, not blocks of snow. The Inuits only build a snow igloo, or igluvigak, as a temporary or emergency shelter when away from home. While hunting for food or traveling across the barren frozen tundra, an Inuit might be caught in a sudden snowstorm or blizzard. But in about an hour, an Inuit can build a lifesaving igloo out of tundra snow, using only a broad-bladed snow knife carved from a long piece of ivory, wood, or bone.

Building with blocks of packed snow and creating the dome shape of the igloo provides many practical advantages and interesting features. First, snow and ice are the only building materials available in the desolate regions away from villages. Ice is heavy and difficult to cut, but the snow on the tundra is the perfect consistency for cutting out

firm, solid blocks of snow. The powerful Arctic winds pack the snow into a dense mass, turning it into a durable building material that can be easily cut and shaped. The best snow comes from a single snowfall so that there is no layering or cracks or differences in density.

Next, a dome-shaped structure is extremely strong and can withstand heavy winds and other strong forces. In fact, the curved surface of an igloo uses wind pressure to make the building stronger and more stable by pressing the dome structure to the ground. A snow-block dome is so strong that polar bears weighing a thousand pounds have been photographed standing on top of an igloo without it collapsing.

The average igloo is about fifteen feet in diameter and nine feet high. The builder begins by marking a circle in the snow and then placing about fifteen blocks of snow around the marked perimeter. These foundation blocks measure about three feet long, two feet wide, and a half foot thick, and weigh about forty pounds each. Instead of

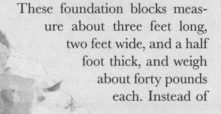

being laid flat like bricks, the snow blocks are laid on their narrow edge. The tops of the foundation blocks are then shaved off at an angle, slant-ing inward and sloping upward.

The next row of snow blocks is stacked on top of the foundation, with each block tilted slightly inward. As rows continue to be added in an inward sloping spiral, the shape of the dome is formed. The last block of snow, the keystone, is fitted at the top, and small chinks of snow are packed in any remaining openings between the blocks.

To make the igloo extra strong, the Inuit builder will then start a small fire inside the structure and let it burn until the inside walls start to melt. When the fire is extinguished, a small hole is carved in the top of the igloo to let out the hot air and to let the cold air in to freeze the melted water. This turns the inner walls to strong, solid ice. The hole is left in the top of the dome for ventilation, and a layer of snow is smoothed over the entire outside of the dome.

The entrance to the igloo is built with more snow blocks in the shape of a low, small tunnel to keep out the wind and cold. Since the coldest air settles to the lowest point, the floor of the tunnel entrance is about one foot lower than the floor inside the igloo, creating a simple cold trap.

Once built, the igloo does a very good job protecting its occupants from cold and wind. The air trapped inside the thick blocks of snow provides excellent insulation, much like the foam used to insulate a conventional home. An emergency igloo made from blocks of wind-packed tundra snow might only be large enough for a few people to huddle inside, but it can get so warm from trapped body heat that to stay comfortable, the inhabitants might need to remove most of their clothing.

On some rare occasions, an Inuit might build an igloo to live in for the whole winter. These homes are usually built as a cluster of several igloos, each one being the size of a small room, and all of them connected by tunnels. These igloos are much more sophisticated dwellings, often with raised sleeping platforms, cooking tables, and maybe a window made from a block of ice or the transparent intestine of a seal.

Making Big Stone Blocks Fit Perfectly

Many ancient stone buildings have remained standing for hundreds or even thousands of years through fierce storms and earthquakes. A close look at these structures will reveal that their massive stone block foundations used no mortar at all. Their strength and rigidity is the result of stacking and fitting the enormous stone blocks so tightly that there is almost no space between the joints—not even enough of a gap to slip a piece of paper through!

It is easier to fit large stone blocks using small chink stones to fill gaps.

How did the builders of these structures get the blocks to fit so tightly together when they had no modern tools? Ancient tools found at building sites suggest that each stone was patiently shaped using very hard hammer stones of different sizes and weights. Workers would tap away at the stone to slowly chip away small amounts, then test the stone in position to see what additional material had to be removed. This process was repeated over and over again, constantly comparing and cutting, until the shape and fit were perfect.

What has not yet been figured out is how the workers kept moving the stones (some being the size of a car) repeatedly in and out of position while testing the fit. Someone once calculated that it would have taken more than two thousand men to move some of the largest stone blocks found in ancient structures.

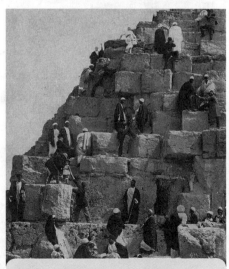

Fitting stone blocks tightly requires much chipping and patience until the shape is exactly right.

THE WORLD'S GREAT PYRAMIDS

The pyramids built by the ancient Egyptians are the oldest stone buildings in the world, and one of human civilization's oldest construction mysteries. For a period of over a thousand years, beginning about 4700 years ago, every Egyptian pharaoh of any importance was buried beneath a pyramid. No one knows exactly how the builders of these massive tombs moved the blocks of granite to the building site at a time when the wheel had not yet been invented. And no one knows how they were able to perfectly carve and stack the huge stone blocks that weighed at least two and a half tons each. Hundreds of pyramids were once built, but today there are fewer than ninety pyramids still standing, and many of them are in Egypt. Some pyramids are also in Central America, but they were built much later and were used as temples rather than tombs.

The Egyptians believed pyramids were ladders to heaven, and the taller the pyramid, the closer their deceased pharaoh could climb to the afterlife they strongly embraced. Most Egyptian pyramids have concealed entrances and false doors, and on the inside, there are secret passageways, hidden rooms, ramps, bridges, airshafts, and a burial chamber. Because the Egyptians believed their king would want his possessions in this heavenly afterlife, all the necessary tools, clothes, food, and wealth were also buried in the pyramid. One reason the pyramids were built to be secure fortresses was to discourage robbers and looting. But the most important reason for building these enormous structures was to display the power and wealth of the deceased occupant.

Building the Pyramids

Some of the largest Egyptian pyramids contain over two million precisely stacked, massive stone blocks. Just moving the blocks around on the ground was a formidable task, but probably not nearly as challenging as lifting a stone block that weighed as much as an elephant almost fifty stories high. It is the sheer magnitude of the building task that creates the most speculation about how the pyramids were built. Since recorded history reveals that it took twenty years to build the Great Pyramid at Giza in Egypt, that means workers had to fit in place over three hundred massive blocks of stone every day, seven days a week. That also means that every single day three hundred blocks of stone had to be quarried, moved to the site, and shaped for positioning. This would require a workforce of thousands, and although the pharaohs had enough wealth to hire all the workers needed, they most likely just ordered citizens and slaves to do much of the work.

The granite blocks used to build the pyramid structure were transported on barges floated down the Nile River from the Aswan quarry six hundred miles upstream. Once on the shore near the pyramid construction site, the blocks weighing up to fifty tons (about as much as fifteen cars) were slid onto wooden sleds that were tugged and rolled over logs using sheer manpower. There were no camels or horses in Egypt at the time.

As with any building, the first step in constructing the pyramids was building a perfectly level foundation. Just like the rest of the pyramid, the foundation was constructed of large stone blocks, and it alone took ten years to build.

The Egyptians were terrific astronomers and surveyors, so the corners of their pyramids are perfectly square, the sides are exactly the same length and are precisely positioned to face north, south, east, and west, and foundations are perfectly level even though the largest pyramid covers an area of over thirteen acres. The geometry of angles is not the same for all pyramids, but many have similar proportions.

The granite blocks arriving at the building site had messages scrawled on them to indicate where the block was meant to fit and the name of the team that had quarried it. It is still a mystery how the Egyptians lifted massive blocks from the ground to the appropriate levels of a growing pyramid. Although a ramp is the most likely solution, there are several other theories that involve various simple mechanical machines. Once lifted to its intended location, each block was slid into place, using a thin layer of mortar as a lubricant. The mortar wasn't needed for cementing because the fit was so tight, and even after

thousands of years, it is still impossible to slip the thickness of a postcard between any two blocks.

The last stage of building a pyramid was completely covering all four outside surfaces with smooth white limestone. The limestone blocks came from a quarry eight miles away and were exactly cut and shaped to perfectly butt against each other even more tightly than the granite blocks beneath. There is also some evidence that the pointed capstone on the top of some pyramids may have been covered in gold, which would have sparkled brilliantly in the sunlight. When completed, these enormous, gleaming, white geometric pyramids rising from the Egyptian desert sands certainly displayed the wealth and power of the king buried inside.

Modern-Day Pyramids

The pyramid shape is so imposing and appealing that it continues to be used in buildings and monumental structures.

The pyramids added to the original buildings of the Louvre museum in Paris are made of space-frame materials and glass, and the largest rises over seven stories high.

The Pyramid Arena in Memphis, Tennessee, is thirty-two stories high and covers an area larger than six football fields.

MEDIEVAL TO MODERN STONE CASTLES

Castles were built all over Europe during the Middle Ages, and most were the fortified private residences of nobles and kings. During that time, people were living under the constant threat of being attacked by hostile armies out to conquer more territory. The castle not only protected the wealthy owner and his family from attackers, but it also provided a refuge for his soldiers and all the townspeople during an assault. Because each castle was meant to be a fortress, many builders came up with clever castle designs, and all were based on a system of defense.

The best castles kept enemies out no matter how they tried to go over, under, or through the castle walls. Inside the castle walls, there were often animal stables, workshops, a great hall for gatherings, a chapel, and a dungeon, plus basement rooms to store plenty of food, water, weapons, and everything else needed to survive a long siege.

The first castles were built in England about a thousand years ago, and their typical "motte and bailey" design consisted of a wooden tower built atop a huge mound of earth (called a motte), surrounded by a fence that also formed a protected pathway down the mound to a stockade for animals (called the bailey). If invaders broke through the fence,

Early stone castle keeps were fortresses designed for protection against attack by flaming arrows, hurled stones, or just tall ladders.

the castle occupants could retreat to the tower to ward off the attack and wait for help. These early castles were not very strong or safe, but a local noble or a successful invader could have one built in only a matter of weeks.

But invaders soon learned that burning arrows could easily set a motte and bailey castle ablaze, so wealthier nobles began using stone for the main structures of their castles. Stone did not rot or burn like wood and could be used to construct taller, stronger, and safer castles. However, unlike a simple wooden castle tower that could be quickly built by local laborers using wood from local forests, it took hundreds of skilled craftspeople and workers many years to build a stone castle. The stone had to be quarried and transported to the site. Stonemasons then cut and fit stones to build the structure, carpenters built the doors, roofs, and many of the furnishings, and blacksmiths were kept busy making nails, hinges, and other hardware items as well as making and fixing the tools used by the other tradespeople.

To create upper floors in the stone structure, wide wooden planks were nailed to large wooden beams that spanned from wall to wall. The ends of the wood beams were supported by corbel stones projecting from the wall, or sometimes the beams were fitted into pocket openings in the walls. The roof structures of most stone castle buildings and towers used wooden trusses covered with slate tiles or wood shingles.

The owner of the castle and his family typically lived in the center section called the keep. As the last stronghold of protection from attack, the keep had stone and mortar walls that were at least ten, and up to twenty, feet thick. There were very few windows in the keep, only narrow vertical slits just wide enough for looking out and shooting arrows while remaining shielded from enemy view.

In naturally protected locations, castles were built on the sides or peaks of hills and sometimes on a small island in the middle of a lake. But most castles were situated in fields or on gentle hills, so for even

Castles were often built in naturally protected locations.

High walls repelled attacking enemies in clever ways.

Additional defensive systems usually protected the entrance.

more protection from would-be invaders, a massive stone curtain wall was built around the entire castle grounds.

The castle's perimeter walls were a first line of defense from enemies. Small towers and platforms often jutted out from the walls so guards could observe the outside grounds and soldiers could fire arrows and drop rocks, fireballs, hot tar, or boiling oil at anyone attempting to scale the fortress. Battlements with wide gaps called crenels were built atop the outer edge of the perimeter walls to protect the castle soldiers from enemy rocks and arrows. The walls were made extra thick at their base to resist battering, and sometimes the thick walls also flared out at their base, which caused dropped rocks from above to ricochet off the flare and onto the attackers.

A deep, wide ditch was often dug just outside and all around the wall to make it difficult for attackers to charge the castle. Where an ample supply of water was available, the ditch was filled to create a wet moat.

But no matter how fortified a castle was, there had to be an entrance through the wall by which to enter and leave. Since the castle entrance was the most vulnerable part of the defensive wall, a fortified gatehouse with guard towers usually protected the entry. The gatehouse often included a pull-up drawbridge for crossing the moat, a heavy pull-down timber and iron gate, and thick wooden doors with locks. In very hostile territories, a few rather nasty systems of defense were also built in and around the gatehouse just in case an invading army actually made it across the moat or through one of the barrier gates. From the top of the gatehouse, hot oil and tar could be poured on invaders, and arrows could be fired up through holes in the gatehouse floor.

It often took weeks or even months for invaders to lay siege to a castle. Using huge mechanical machines, they would catapult rocks and fireballs over the castle walls into the castle grounds. They would attempt to knock down the gatehouse door with battering rams, and they might try to pry stones loose from the castle walls, working under portable sheds for protection. Ambitious invaders would even attempt to tunnel underneath a castle wall or excavate enough earth to cause a section of the wall to collapse. Building a hot fire next to the stone wall would eventually crack and crumble some types of stone to create an opening. The simplest plan, when possible, was to starve the occupants of the castle by preventing the delivery of food and other needed supplies. As a last resort, invaders might try to scale the wall, using ladders, wooden towers, or ropes.

As these primitive methods of attack evolved, many later castles and keeps were built in an octagonal or round plan because it became evident that catapulted rocks and enemy arrows would just glance off a round tower if they didn't score a direct hit. However, cylindrical keeps and towers had less room inside and were harder to build. Besides, this innovation in castle design soon also became obsolete with the invention of gunpowder.

Many later castles were squatter and thicker to defend against gunfire, but ultimately, few castles were a match for large cannons that could hammer holes right through their walls. When stone castles were no longer an effective defense from

Huge mechanical weapons hurled big rocks to knock down castle walls.

Angled and rounded walls helped to deflect projectiles.

Modern castles have large windows and lack a curtain wall or gatehouse.

attacking enemies, they were also no longer suitable accommodations for royalty. Many old castles are now in ruins, yet some still remain standing and are being used today as homes, hotels, museums, and restaurants. The stone castles built in recent centuries were intended to be luxurious private residences and not for protection.

THE ALMOST ALL-AMERICAN LOG CABIN

One of the strongest images associated with early America is the log cabin. President Abraham Lincoln is well-known to have been born in a log cabin over two hundred years ago, and even today, new log-cabin-style homes are being built all across America. But even though Americans like to think of the log cabin as a national symbol, the building design and construction methods were brought to America by immigrants from many different countries.

Depending on the techniques familiar to the builder, some log cabins were built directly on the ground, while others were supported above the ground with stone or wooden post foundations. Some cabins were made of round logs, while others used squared-off logs or grooved logs. At the corners of the cabin where the walls came together, the logs were notched in different ways to overlap at right angles.

Scandinavian settlers used a round notch cut only in the undersides of the logs. This method helped shed water away from the cabin but required great craftsmanship. The V-notch corner joint was popular in the Appalachian Mountains, and the logs could be made to fit using just an ax, without any measuring tools or precise cutting. The tightest fitting corners were made by German immigrants, who used dovetail joints. This technique required careful measuring and cutting of the connecting logs but did not leave the ends of the overlapping logs projecting from the corners. The clean, squared-off corners of their cabins also allowed the entire exterior to be plastered over. The oldest log cabin still standing in America, the Nothnagle cabin in New Jersey, was built around 1638 using dovetail joints.

The construction of a log cabin usually begins with some type of foundation, although some early American cabins were built directly on the ground and had a floor of bare earth. Foundations made of stone or

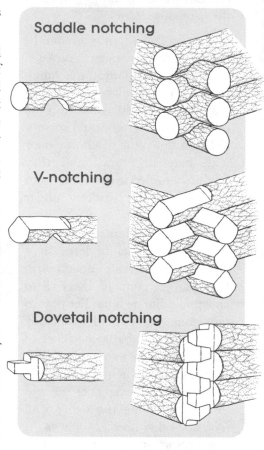

Saddle notching

V-notching

Dovetail notching

wooden piers help protect the logs from termites, carpenter ants, and water rot.

About eighty logs are needed to build an average one-room log cabin. To make construction easier, all the logs ideally should be about the same age, thickness, and length. The logs are usually harvested, cut to shape, and notched during the winter months when the wood is drier, weighs less, and is easier to cut.

Because each log can weigh several hundred pounds, hoisting them into place requires at least two people plus the use of a block and tackle. Unless the logs are cut, carved, and fitted with great care, there will be gaps between the logs that must be caulked with a filler material to make the walls weatherproof. In the traditional construction method,

Rafter roof

Purlin roof

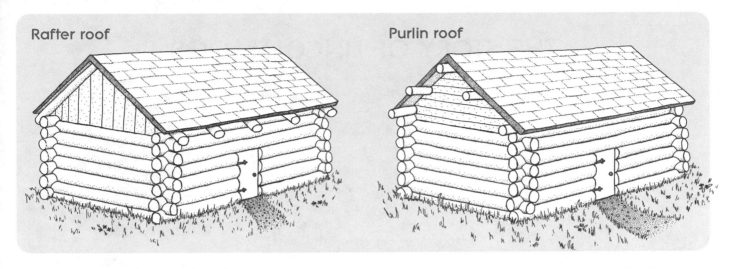

the walls are built solid, then the door and window openings are cut out of the completed wall sections. The floor is made of pine boards supported by joist beams that span the distance between walls. The joists are cut to fit into notches in the bottom logs.

There are two ways to make a log cabin roof. The traditional method uses rafters that lean inwards from the walls and meet at the ridge, very similar to the rafters of a conventional house. The purlin roof uses beams that span the entire length of the structure from end wall to end wall. The end walls use increasingly shorter logs to create the roof pitch and to support the purlin logs. The purlins then support the roof covering, which can be made from overlapping wood shingles, wood board decking, grasses, or tiles.

The log cabins being built today are usually constructed from logs that have been precut and shaped in a factory. Using modern woodworking machinery, the log shapes and notches can be made to fit perfectly. And by using modular lengths and sizes, an entire log-cabin house can be supplied as a kit to be assembled at the building site, much like putting together the pieces of a Lincoln Logs construction toy.

THE STORY OF LINCOLN LOGS

The famous American architect Frank Lloyd Wright had a son named John Lloyd Wright, who was also an architect. In addition to designing buildings and competing with his father, John invented a modular construction toy he named Lincoln Logs. That was in 1918, when many parents were concerned that children living in industrial cities needed more contact with nature, and the idea of

building a model log cabin was the next best thing to living in a real one in the woods. This "back to nature" movement of the time included camping, outdoor adventure activities, and "simple living," and also encouraged children to build crafts using materials from nature, especially wood.

The inspiration for inventing Lincoln Logs began earlier, when Frank Lloyd Wright added a playroom to the family house for young John and his three brothers and two sisters, and filled it with building blocks of all shapes and sizes. Frank Lloyd Wright's designs and architecture had been greatly influenced by the building blocks he played with as a child, and he was determined to teach his children the same appreciation for shape, form, and analytical thinking. By building structures with modular

toy building blocks, the Wright children experimented with the concepts of pattern, rhythm, structure, and construction from interchangeable elements.

Then, in 1917, Frank Lloyd Wright took his son John (now a young architect) to Tokyo, Japan, to help oversee construction of the Imperial Hotel. In designing the hotel, Frank used a structure system in which projecting wooden beams were notched and locked onto other beams. It was this technique that inspired John to create his toy construction system, which used miniature wood logs with notches on either end that allowed them to be stacked at right angles—very much resembling the construction of a log cabin. The image of a log cabin not only reminded American children of the virtues of living with nature, it also was a powerful symbol of President Abraham Lincoln's log-cabin birthplace and the notion that any American, no matter how humble his or her origins, could grow up to be a great leader. So John named his toy

Lincoln Logs. The original Lincoln Logs building set consisted of enough miniature wooden logs to build the model log cabin shown on the box.

As the building toy grew in popularity, later sets became more elaborate and could be used to build forts, towers, bridges, and all sorts of buildings in addition to log cabins. Even wheels were added so builders could construct log-looking vehicles. Once Lincoln Logs became so popular, other toy manufactures tried to capitalize on the success by producing Lincoln Bricks and Lincoln Stones construction sets, but only Lincoln Logs remained a favorite.

BUILDING WITH BRICKS AND BLOCKS

- STACKING BLOCKS AND PILED UP PLAYTHINGS
- BRICKS AND MORTAR BUILDING SYSTEMS
- LOCKING BLOCKS AND BANDED BUNDLES
- BRICK AND BLOCK MOLDING METHODS

STACKING BLOCKS AND PILED UP PLAYTHINGS

You probably started piling up things when you were just a baby, and maybe you were stacking wooden blocks into towers and buildings when you were a toddler. Some kids keep stacking and building with their sets of plastic bricks through all ages, even until they're adults. These Stacking Blocks and Piled Up Playthings are intended to be used by a wide range of builders, although most of the building systems create only the simplest stacked structures.

Babies and toddlers will obviously need a parent or maybe an older brother or sister to construct the blocks they play with. You could make a set of Paper Bag Bedroom Blocks to share with someone younger and maybe show them things to build. A Fruit Face Tasty Totem Pole should be eaten soon after you build it—and it's usually too big for one person to eat. Brothers, sisters, and friends can play Table Game Snacks and also eat the stacked game pieces, or challenge each other to a game of Blocks of Logic that requires both brains and bluffing.

If the instructions require any cutting with a knife or saw, you may need to ask for an adult's help. When carefully sliced just the right way, a bagel can become a simple set of building blocks or be assembled into a bird feeder. And a classic set of Modular Wooden Blocks can be cut from scraps of common-size lumber.

Structures built with Stacking Blocks are almost always temporary and meant to be disassembled (or eaten). Beach Beaux Arts and week-old Stale Bagel Blocks constructions should just be thrown away after play. But some builders may want to keep their Stick and Branch Blocks structures because they often look like true objects of art.

BUILD IT

MODULAR WOODEN BLOCKS 383

BLOCKS OF LOGIC 386

BIG BOX BLOCKS 389

PAPER BAG BEDROOM BLOCKS 391

STALE BAGEL BLOCKS 393

BAGEL BLOCK BIRD BANQUET 395

STICK AND BRANCH BLOCKS 397

BEACH BEAUX ARTS 399

TABLE GAME SNACKS 401

FRUIT FACE TASTY TOTEM POLE 404

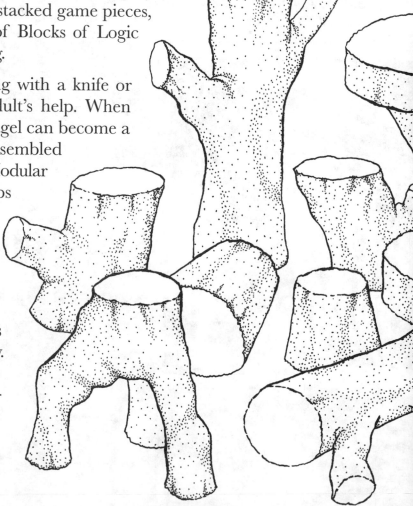

MODULAR WOODEN BLOCKS

BUILDING SYSTEM

Building structures with Modular Wooden Blocks is an all-time favorite kid activity, but making a high-quality set of modular wooden blocks that will last through a few generations requires an adult who has experience working with power tools. You can assist in the block-making project by helping to select the best pieces of wood, helping to lay out the geometric shapes, and sandpapering the cut edges.

Listed on the next page are the suggested shapes and quantities for a good starter set. By making your own blocks, you can easily add pieces to the set as building projects become more elaborate. The most important thing is that there are enough blocks and modular shapes to completely construct your creations.

SYSTEM FEATURES

- Stacking is the easiest type of building
- Modular sizes allow stable structures
- Best for temporary constructions
- Durable modular parts for repeated use

Construction

Builder's age
15+ (with adult supervision)

Player's age
2+

Materials

- ☐ Lumber plank at least 2″ thick by 4″ wide
- ☐ Best woods are maple, oak, birch, and sugar pine
- ☐ Dowel (diameter same thickness as plank)

Tools

- ☐ Table saw with a finish-cut, smooth-cutting blade
- ☐ Band saw or saber saw for cutting curved shapes
- ☐ Sandpaper, 150/medium grit and 220/fine grit
- ☐ White or yellow wood glue
- ☐ Wood clamps
- ☐ Ruler and pencil

Building techniques

Modular Wooden Blocks must be made from hardwoods that do not splinter or need any type of paint, sealer, or other surface finish to keep them from warping. Because very young builders often put things in their mouths, you might want to use woods that taste good. Maple and oak are the most desirable woods for blocks and should be available at your local lumberyard or building supply center. Other woods to consider are birch and sugar pine. Given several choices, you might select one wood over another because of its special attributes. For example, blocks made of maple or oak will be heavy and durable (but also difficult to saw to size), while blocks made from birch or sugar pine will dent rather easily but will be lighter in weight (and sugar pine blocks seem to taste the best).

When selecting the type of wood to use, you will also need to check what sizes are available. A plank of wood measuring an actual two inches by four inches on the end is a good size for making modular blocks. (The plank can be any length.) The four-inch width of the board will become the modular dimension of the set so that all block lengths will be multiples of four inches (4″, 8″, 12″, and 16″) or half the four-inch width, which is two inches. To make unit blocks from a two-inch by four-inch plank, just cut the board to the proper multiple lengths. The two-inch thickness is already exactly half the width of the four-inch board. In addition to making flat shapes, large diameter wooden dowels can also be cut into modular lengths to make cylinder blocks or columns.

Cutting unit blocks from other sizes of lumber may first require "ripping" the boards on a power table saw so that the board thickness is exactly half the width. That will certainly be necessary when using "dimension lumber" that measures

Modular Block Shape	Cut length from actual 2 x 4 lumber	Number of pieces for starter set
Square	4 inches	12
Unit	8	8
Double unit	16	4
Pillar	8	4
Half pillar	4	4
Triangle	8	4
Double unit triangle	16	4
Roman arch	16	4
Half circle	Cut from Roman Arch	4
Quarter circle	8 (two pieces glued up)	4
Column	8 (cut from dowel)	4
Half column	4 (cut from dowel)	4

less that its descriptive size. For example, a 2 x 4 piece of dimension lumber that is commonly used to build house walls actually measures only 1 ½ inches thick by 3 ½ inches wide. In this case, the width would have to be cut down to three inches, which is twice the thickness of 1 ½ inches.

The starting width of the board will determine the scale of the blocks. A full-scale modular block uses a four-inch width, while a two-inch width makes the smallest practical size wooden blocks. Building a set of blocks using any width in between is okay.

You might decide to add other modular shapes, depending on the lumber sizes available or the cutting thickness capacity of the table saw. For example, you can make modular unit blocks in half thickness. These thinner blocks are often used as ramps or roofs.

When measuring for cuts, mark and cut one block at a time so the width of the saw cut doesn't affect the length of the next cut.

After the blocks are cut to shape, sandpaper all block edges, especially the cut edges. Start with medium grit sandpaper to ease, or slightly round, all sharp edges and corners, then use fine sandpaper to smooth the entire block. The finished block should be free of any sharp edges, corners, or splinters. No paint or any type of wood finish is desirable.

Making floor grids for block building

The bare floor is the best place for building with blocks. Although one- and two-year-olds prefer a cushy carpeted floor for most play activities, a carpet is not the most stable base for stacking building blocks. The play floor should be flat and

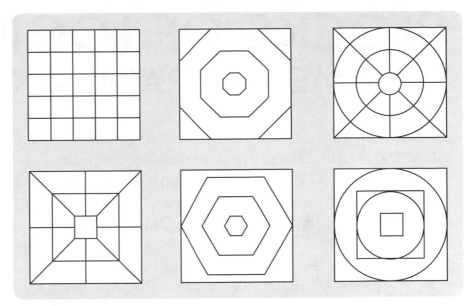

level enough so it won't cause tilting and unstable stacks.

The best floors for block building are made of wood or vinyl tile. Not only are these surfaces good, flat foundations, but they also provide the builder with another significant advantage—the squares of the tiles and the edges of the floor boards help as layout guides for lining up straight block walls or building a square corner.

More experienced block builders will learn to use the grid work of the tiles and the parallel lines of floorboards to lay out the footprints of buildings, the streets of a town, the runways of an airport, the pathways of a maze, or maybe the walls of a castle or fort. And even without realizing it, the modularity of a floor grid will also give you experience in the development of basic math concepts like multiple units, measuring, symmetry, and geometric shapes, angles, and patterns.

If the floor doesn't have floorboards or grid work tiles, then you can make a grid work pattern on an old bedsheet and place it on a flat, hard floor. A permanent-ink type laundry marker works well for drawing grid lines on fabric.

A few special tools may be needed to accurately lay out the grid pattern, including a long straightedge (like a yardstick), something to measure with (like the yardstick or a measuring tape), and some type of right-angle guide for drawing corners. (The right-angle cut of a newspaper page will work fine.) The overall size of the grid work will depend on how ambitious a builder you are. A five-foot by five-foot grid of one-foot squares is fine for one builder age three or four. Group play activities and older builders with grandiose plans will need a larger grid that could be up to ten feet square. Above are a few suggestions for grid pattern layouts.

MODULAR WOODEN BLOCKS
BUILD-IT PROJECT

BLOCKS OF LOGIC

BLOCKS OF LOGIC
A GAME OF BRAINS AND BLUFFING

In the 1950s and 1960s, a Hungarian-born mathematician named Zoltan P. Dienes became well-known around the world for his "blocks of logic" or "attribute blocks." A set consisted of forty-eight pieces, with each block having its own unique combination of four attributes—shape, color, size, and thickness—so that no two blocks shared the same combination. Kids were asked to build things that shared some common attribute—like an all-red house or a tower with only square corners. Dienes also suggested playing games of logic that were both challenging and fun. By making a set of sponge blocks with the specific Dienes attributes, you and one or more challengers can compete in games of logic that require both brains and bluffing. Don't be hesitant to challenge older players. Kids are often much better at this kind of logic than adults.

Construction

Building system
Modular Wooden Blocks

Builder's age
8+

Player's age
6+

Materials

☐ Set of modular blocks, or

☐ Kitchen sponges in three colors

Tools

☐ Color markers (if using modular blocks)

☐ Scissors (if using sponges)

Building instructions

A complete forty-eight-piece set of Blocks of Logic consists of the combinations of shape, color, size, and thickness attributes listed below. There is one piece for every possible combination of values for each attribute. For example, one round block might be yellow, large, and thick. A second round block would be blue, large, and thick. A third round block would be red, large, and thick. A fourth round block would be yellow, small, and thick, and so on.

For younger players, a set of twenty-four blocks will work fine and can be made by eliminating one of the attributes so that the blocks are either all one size (instead of both large and small sizes) or only one thickness.

Adapting a set of building blocks

A collection of building blocks or bricks with enough pieces in four different shapes, three colors, two sizes, and two thicknesses can be used to play these Games of Logic. Sometimes plastic bricks can be combined to make the different pieces, or stickers can be put on wooden blocks to indicate different colors. A full set of game blocks must possess the four attributes. The games can also be played with a half set of twenty-four blocks by eliminating one thickness or one size attribute.

Making a set of sponge blocks

Kitchen sponges typically come in a variety of rectangular sizes and colors that are ideal for making Blocks of Logic. You will need several sponges in two thicknesses and

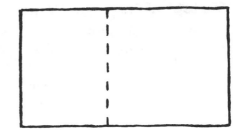

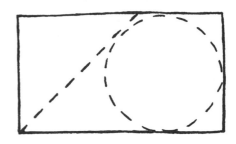

three colors. The four different shapes can easily be cut from the sponges by using scissors.

There are no specific dimensions for making the geometric shapes, but a full set of game blocks must possess the four attributes. The games can also be played with a half set of twenty-four blocks by eliminating one thickness or one size attribute.

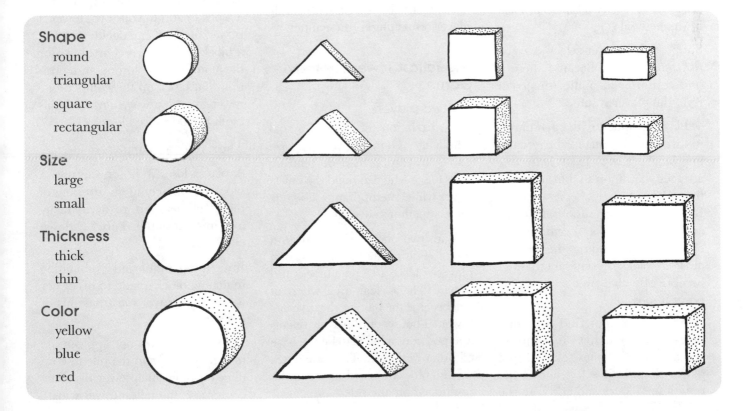

Shape
round
triangular
square
rectangular

Size
large
small

Thickness
thick
thin

Color
yellow
blue
red

The Logical Challenge Game

For two or more players

1. Place the complete set of attribute blocks on the floor (or table) with two or more players sitting around the pile. The first player selects one block from the pile and moves it to a clear area to start a new pile.

Assume, for example, that the block selected was a *small, red, thick triangle*.

2. The second player must now select a block to move to the new pile that has at least one of the attributes of the first block selected. However—and this is very important—the player does not reveal to the other players what the common attribute is.

Suppose the second player selects a *small, red, thin square*. In this case, there are two common attributes—red and small—and the player is "safe."

3. The third player (or the first player again if there are only two players) selects a block to move to the new pile that has at least one attribute of the two blocks already in the new pile.

Suppose this player selects a *large, red, thin triangle*. Because there is one common attribute (the color red), the player is safe.

4. Play continues, with each player in turn selecting one of the remaining blocks that has at least one attribute common to all the blocks that have already been selected. But with fewer common attributes and fewer blocks remaining to choose from, finding the "right" attribute block becomes increasingly more of a challenge and at some point impossible.

If a player cannot find a "right" block that matches a common attribute of the ones selected, the player should still select one of the remaining blocks and add it to the new pile—not revealing to the other players that the block is not a match.

Suppose the player has few choices remaining and selects a *large, yellow, thick, round* block. Since there are no common attributes to the blocks previously selected, this block is "not right," even though the player should pretend it is.

5. At any time in the game, any player who thinks that another player has selected a block that does not match a common attribute of all the blocks already selected can make a challenge by saying, "I challenge you." The player being challenged must now reveal what the common attribute is.

If the player can justify the selection (there is a common attribute), then the challenger loses and is out of the game. Play resumes with the remaining players.

If the player was bluffing and there is no common attribute for the block being played, the challenger wins and the game is over. The first challenger to be correct (or the only player remaining) is the winner.

The Tallest Tower Strategy Game

For two players

This variation of The Logical Challenge Game requires good game strategy instead of bluffing skills to see who can build the tallest tower while attempting to sabotage the competitor's structure.

1. With two players sitting around a pile of attribute blocks, the first player selects any one block and moves it to a clear area where it will become the base of that player's tower. The second player selects and positions a block to be the base of his or her tower. The base block and all blocks stacked on it can be positioned on any side.

2. The first player now selects another block from the pile to stack on top his or her base block. However, the new block must share at least one of the attributes of the block it is touching below it. The second player also selects an appropriate block to stack on the base of his or her tower.

3. The game continues and the two towers begin growing upward as each player in turn selects an appropriate block from the pile with at least one attribute of the block in the tower it will rest on. In a structure where one block rests on two or more blocks below it, the new block must share at least one common attribute with each block it touches.

Remember that the objective is to build the tallest tower—without the tower collapsing. So you must decide which blocks to stack on their flat sides for greater stability and which to stack on an edge for greater height.

4. Here's the catch and the strategy for winning. Instead of selecting a block to add to your own tower, a player, on turn, can decide to select a block with a correct attribute for the competitor's tower, and position that block on the competitor's tower in such a way to make it difficult to add more blocks.

These rules also apply:

A player loses if he or she uses a block not matching an attribute of the block below it, or accidentally (or intentionally) knocks down either tower.

If a player cannot find a remaining matching block to add to his or her tower, that player must pass his or her turn.

When there are no appropriate matching blocks in the pile to continue building either tower, the game is over and the tallest tower wins.

BIG BOX BLOCKS
BUILDING SYSTEM

All it takes to make giant-size structures is a set of giant-size building blocks. Large building blocks are often free and available everywhere. What others might see as an empty corrugated box to be discarded in the trash is actually a perfectly good giant building block. Grocery stores and warehouse-type stores typically give boxes away, you may receive them in the mail, and your family has probably thrown out several good ones.

First, you have to find several complete boxes that still have all six sides and all flaps intact, then convert each empty box into a giant, lightweight building block by following simple instructions for making the empty boxes more sturdy. The finished blocks can be used as is, or they can be painted to build colorful Big Box structures. Just be sure you have a place to store them!

SYSTEM FEATURES

- Big blocks build big kid-size structures
- Block sizes can be modular or arbitrary
- Blocks can be plain, painted, or decorated
- Used corrugated boxes are easily available
- Stacked structures are stable and sturdy

Construction

Builder's age
9+

Player's age
3+

Materials
☐ Corrugated boxes (Collect mostly complete boxes with all flaps attached.)

☐ Kraft packaging tape (Three-inch wide, reinforced-type works best.)

☐ Latex paint (optional)

Tools
☐ Large scissors

☐ Measuring tape or yardstick

☐ Pencil

☐ Paintbrush or roller (if using paint)

Building techniques

Collect several corrugated boxes that still have all their sides and flaps, and are in good shape for making the blocks. You will also need some not-so-good corrugated boxes to make the internal box strengtheners.

Most corrugated boxes, except the smaller ones, will need an inner support structure to keep the sides from crushing in during rough use. For simple stacked constructions, sealed empty boxes will work fine. But Big Box Blocks that will be stepped on and sat on will need more strength.

Strengthening an empty box

A simple way to make a Box Block stronger (and still keep it lightweight) is to add an X-brace, using two pieces of corrugated board cut from reject boxes. Before taping a Box Block closed, measure the diagonal dimension of the opening and the depth of the box. Then cut two identical pieces of corrugated

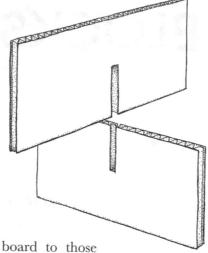

board to those dimensions. Cut a slit halfway through each of the pieces, starting at the middle point on a long side. Insert one slit into the other to form an X, and insert the complete X-brace inside the box. Close and seal the carton with tape.

Taping the box block

Packaging tape is used for resealing the boxes. Reinforced kraft packaging tape is wider, seals better, looks better, and is easier to work with than plastic packaging tape. Kraft tape can also be painted along with the rest of the box. However, it does take a little practice and skill to apply kraft packaging tape correctly.

If the tape is too wet or not wet enough, it will not stick properly. Try this method to get the right amount of water on the tape. Thoroughly wet a kitchen sponge with warm water and then squeeze out about half the water. Cut a piece of tape to the length you need, then pull the tape between the sponge and the side of the sink (with the glue side of the tape facing

the sponge). Immediately apply the tape to the box seam and rub it down with your fingers or a towel.

Here's a tip for taping edge seams and corners. Cut a piece of tape as long as the combined length and width of the box. After wetting the tape, wrap it around one long edge and halfway around each of the two sides. Fold the tape over the long edge and then over the side edges to make neat corners.

Painting and decorating Box Blocks

Latex paint in a satin or semigloss finish can be rolled or brushed on the corrugated box surfaces. Don't apply the paint too thick, or it will soften and curl the corrugated paper surface. The colors you choose can turn the rather bland tan or white corrugated boxes into building blocks that resemble granite, bricks, ice blocks, or just colorful cubes. And you can also choose to paint each face of a block a different color or design.

PAPER BAG BEDROOM BLOCKS
BUILDING SYSTEM

The scale of these blocks is so large that it only takes a few to build a structure that's over your head! Paper Bag Bedroom Blocks may be big, lightweight, and easy to handle, but they are not very strong and should *only* be used for building the walls of play fortresses, castles, and other buildings—*not* for supporting any type of load, like yourself! If you should sit or fall on a Paper Bag Bedroom Block, it will crush and you will have to rebuild it.

Paper Bag Bedroom Blocks can be used anywhere, even outdoors in dry weather. A playroom or your bedroom is probably the safest place indoors for keeping the large blocks from knocking over valuables. What you build will depend on how many blocks you have made, but remember, you will need a pretty big storage place to keep the blocks.

SYSTEM FEATURES

- Blocks are lightweight and safe
- Large scale is fun for young builders
- Modular size makes stacking easy
- Used bags and newspaper are free
- Blocks are easily painted and decorated

Construction

Builder's age
7+

Player's age
3+

Materials
- □ Large paper grocery bags (3 bags needed for each block)
- □ Newspapers
- □ Masking tape
- □ Poster paints or markers (optional)

Tools
- □ Hands only

Building techniques

A good starter set includes at least ten Paper Bag Bedroom Blocks of the same size. Larger sets can include additional blocks in other sizes made from smaller, gusseted-type paper bags.

Most grocery stores offer customers a choice of either plastic or paper bags for packing groceries. If you do not already have a good supply of large paper grocery bags, ask your family to start requesting them, because it takes three paper bags to make each Paper Bag Bedroom Block.

1. Start with three empty grocery bags all the same size and all folded flat. Lay one bag flat on the floor or a table. Fold down the top of the bag a few inches, and crease the bag on the fold.

2. Open the bag completely, and stuff it with between ten and twelve double-page sheets of crumpled newspaper.

3. Fold the top of the bag over on the crease lines you made, and tape the top closed to form a block shape.

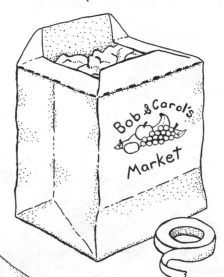

4. Crease the top of the second bag the same way as the first bag, and open the bag completely.

5. Insert the block upside-down into the second bag, fold the top of the second bag over on the crease lines you made, and tape the top closed to retain the block shape.

6. Crease the third bag, open it, and insert the block, taped end first. Fold over the top and tape it closed to complete the block.

You can decorate the blocks with poster paints or markers if you like, or leave the blocks their natural brown kraft color that simulates the look of adobe blocks.

STALE BAGEL BLOCKS
BUILDING SYSTEM

There is finally a good use for stale, hard, day-old bagels—making a set of Stale Bagel Blocks. One bagel can be cut into six or eight building blocks that include free-standing arches, flat-sided slabs, and curved-top slabs. By simply stacking the blocks, the unique shapes will make interesting sculptures as well as architectural forms like arched walls, crenellated castle walls, and corbeled arches and domes. Because bagels aren't exactly symmetrical, nearly every bagel block will have its own character and variation of the block shape. That will also give your bagel block constructions an interesting character, especially if you start mixing poppy seed, onion, salt, sesame seed, garlic, raisin, and other types of bagels. Bagel blocks can be used over and over again and can last for weeks or months—or until they eventually dry up, shrink, and crumble into squirrel food.

SYSTEM FEATURES

- Finally, a use for day-old bagels
- Bagels are the only material needed
- Good for building irregular forms and sculptures
- Fresh bagels can be used to build edible structures
- Parts can be reused. (good until they crumble)

Construction

Builder's age

Adult required for bagel cutting

Player's age

4+

Materials

☐ Bagels, any flavor and as many as possible

Tools

☐ Serrated bread knife

Building techniques

Although anyone can build with Bagel Blocks, only older builders or adults should cut the whole bagel into block pieces. Stale bagels can get rock hard very quickly. That's what makes them so good as blocks, but it also makes them tough to cut. You can cut the bagels under adult supervision if you're old enough and careful enough to use a sharp bread knife. Otherwise, let an adult do the cutting for you.

Start with a bagel that is only a day or two old. If the bagel is too stale, it will be too difficult to cut.

Follow the cutting pattern and first make the five vertical cuts to make six blocks—two curved-top slabs, two flat-sided slabs, and two jumbo arches. If you began with a thick bagel, cut across the arch blocks as shown to make four thinner arches. If you are using more than one bagel, make both jumbo arches and thinner arches.

The Stale Bagel Blocks will continue to harden over the next several days and become somewhat distorted from their original cut shape. These slight twists and curves actually help to hold the stacked block constructions together.

In addition to building recognizable structures like forts and towers, Stale Bagel Blocks are especially good for just stacking. Finding the right block to keep the stack growing is like solving a three-dimensional puzzle. Whatever you build or however you stack the blocks, the resulting design will certainly look whimsical—or maybe even brilliant.

Fresh bagel building

If leftover stale bagels are a rarity at your home, you can still make Bagel Blocks, and the structures you build with them can be firmly bond-ed using your favorite cream cheese or other spread. These constructions, however, are culinary creations that are meant to be eaten soon after building. Think of yourself as a chef creating an elegant presentation in a fancy restaurant.

Cut a fresh bagel into six or eight blocks, and assemble the pieces into an interesting construction on a serving plate. The bagel "course" can then be served and eaten plain, or you might incorporate daubs of cream cheese into your construction, using the spread as a mortar to bond the Bagel Blocks.

Quickly admire what you have built (before the bagel does become stale), then enjoy eating it.

STALE BAGEL BLOCKS
BUILD-IT PROJECT

BAGEL BLOCK BIRD BANQUET

BAGEL BLOCK BIRD BANQUET

Using Stale Bagel Blocks to build a Bird Banquet feeding station is an excellent way to get rid of any leftover bagels, stale or not. The birds (or squirrels) don't really care what this bird-feeder structure or sculpture looks like, but they certainly are attracted to the bagel blocks and peanut butter mortar used to build it. The only functional requirement is that your construction have places for the birds to perch while feeding. And perches will occur just because of the kind of shapes made by stacking bagel blocks.

If you regularly feed the birds, the addition of this special treat may attract a new species. Woodpeckers seem to especially like bagels with peanut butter. And depending on where you hang the Bagel Block Bird Banquet, you might also entice other wildlife to the feeder. Regardless of where you put it, you can be sure the entire structure will be quickly consumed.

Construction

Building system
Stale Bagel Blocks

Builder's age
6+ (Adult required for bagel cutting)

Materials
☐ Day-old bagels, any flavor

☐ Peanut butter, either creamy or chunky

Tools
☐ Serrated bread knife

☐ Table knife

Building instructions

Begin by thinking of the type of feeder you want to design. You may want to place it outside on a windowsill or on a nearby tree stump, hang it from a tree branch, or just find a convenient location on top of something else outdoors where you will be able to watch the feeder from inside your home. Maybe you want to build a portable feeder on a plate, a plastic lid, a piece of board, or on some other base that would allow you to move the feeder to different locations and bring it in at night.

You can either first lay out your sculpture design using Bagel Blocks without the peanut butter mortar, or just begin building from the ground up, laying brick upon brick and spreading peanut butter mortar between each course. Whatever type of structure you build—a castle, a tower, a fly-through tunnel, a space station, or just a free-form sculpture—keep building until the design of your feeder pleases you. Whatever shape your Bagel Block Bird Banquet building takes, you can be sure the birds will love it.

Feeding tips

Many species of birds just happen to like bagels as well as the seeds and other delicacies that cover them. And just about all birds like peanut butter. So the combination should prove irresistible to whatever types of birds are around your neighborhood. However, do remember that if you don't regularly feed the birds, it may take a few days for the local flocks to find your feeder. Unfortunately, squirrels usually find new sources of food much more quickly. In the worst case, you may have to be content with having a squirrel feeder instead of a bird feeder. Many of the other land creatures that could raid your feeder look for food at night, so you may want to take the feeder in at sunset and save your bird feeding and bird watching for the daytime.

Bird nutrition information

Nutrition requirements vary by species, size, season, age, and many other factors, including flying time, which consumes great amounts of energy. However, all birds need the fat, protein, calcium, carbohydrates and vitamins they usually get from eating seeds, grains, fruit, vegetables, nuts, and sometimes worms and insects. A source of fat is especially important in winter when food can be scarce. But there are some foods with high amounts of sugar and fat you should never feed to birds, including chips, doughnuts, avocado, chocolate, fruit pits, and persimmons (which are poisonous to birds).

Of all the varieties available, a whole wheat bagel is most nutritious for birds and often contains barley, sunflower seeds, pumpkin seeds, flaxseeds, and millet in addition to other nutrients and vitamins. Peanut butter, either creamy or chunky, is also a good food for birds. Combined, a whole wheat bagel and peanut butter Bird Banquet is a tasty and nutritional meal for most hungry birds.

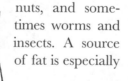

Nutrition Facts
Whole Wheat Bagel and Peanut Butter Bird Banquet

Daily Serving Size -

Small Birds	15 g
Medium Birds	30 g
Large Birds	90 g
Servings Per Feeder	3 to 18

Amount Per Serving – Medium Size Birds*

Calories 99

Calories from Fat   47

Calories from Saturated Fat 1

Total Fat	**6** g
Saturated Fat	**1** g
Trans Fat	**0** g
Cholesterol	**0** mg
Sodium	**110** mg
Total Carbohydrates	**7** g
Protein	**2** g

Iron • Calcium • Thiamin

*Amounts given are for medium birds the size of a house sparrow or a purple finch. Amounts are half as much for small birds including the chickadee or goldfinch. The amounts for very large birds can be up to three times as much.

STICK AND BRANCH BLOCKS
BUILDING SYSTEM

Modular-length sections cut from large sticks and small, dead branches make rather interesting and artful stacking structures. The building pieces can be round, forked-shaped, tripod-shaped, and just weird-shaped. But because they are all cut with parallel ends and in modular lengths, the pieces do stack quite well.

Stick and Branch Blocks provide an opportunity to build block structures that don't have to have square corners. In fact, constructing box shapes and other conventional block-building structures is nearly impossible with this building system. The arbitrary diameters and twists instead inspire fanciful towers and abstract sculptures. The oddly shaped blocks also invite experimentation with balance, proportion, and form. And, because the bark and textures of the blocks are natural, whatever you build looks good.

SYSTEM FEATURES

- Sticks and dead branches are easily found
- Special shapes can be cut from odd pieces
- Modular lengths allow good stacking
- All constructions look good
- Permanent constructions can be glued together

Construction

Builder's age
9+ (with adult supervision)

Player's age
4+

Materials
☐ Sticks and dead branches, 1-inch diameter and larger

Tools
☐ Miter box

☐ Handsaw

☐ Tape measure

☐ Pencil

Building techniques
Gather sticks and dead branches of all shapes from about one to two inches in diameter (and even larger if you like). Look for interesting forks and twists, and make sure you use branches that have not yet begun to decay. The bark can either be left on or peeled off.

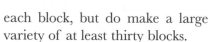

each block, but do make a large variety of at least thirty blocks.

To cut the branch sections so the cut ends are parallel, use a miter box and a handsaw. Use the first cut as a guide to line up the second, parallel cut. You will need to hold the branch firmly when making the second cut so it doesn't slip. You also need to be very careful not to let the saw slip out of the miter box while cutting. Smooth and steady cutting strokes with a sharp saw is the safe way to cut. If an adult is doing the cutting, a power table saw or band saw can be used.

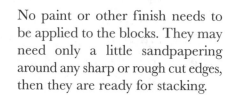

No paint or other finish needs to be applied to the blocks. They may need only a little sandpapering around any sharp or rough cut edges, then they are ready for stacking.

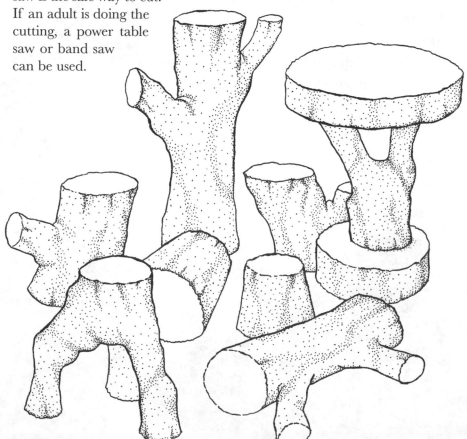

To make modular-length blocks, just cut the most interesting parts of the branches into unit lengths with parallel cuts. For example, you might make some one-inch blocks, two-inch blocks, and four-inch blocks. You can decide what unit length to use and how long to make

BEACH BEAUX ARTS

What if none of the materials available for building were modular but could still be stacked in piles? Maybe you could arrange the piles into patterns and figures that resemble mosaic blocks. One place you might find such a supply of materials is at the beach. Collecting seashells, driftwood, ocean stones, and other objects of nature is a favorite activity for all kids, and turning those objects into a beautiful, or *beaux*, work of art can be even more fun—and it's simple to do! Just draw an outline in the sand—maybe a boat, a fish, a flower, a pattern, or anything else—then fill in the drawing with a collection of found objects to create interesting patterns, textures, and colors.

Using clean debris as well as the natural materials found on the beach can also help keep the beach clean. So, after completing your beaux arts project, and after it has been admired by those passing by, please toss any debris you have gathered into the trash.

Construction

Builder's age

3+

Materials

☐ All natural materials found on the beach, including shells, seaweed, driftwood, stones, and sand

☐ Clean trash and litter found on the beach, including bottle caps, cups, straws, and pieces of plastic

Tools

☐ Beach bucket or pail with a handle for collecting beach objects

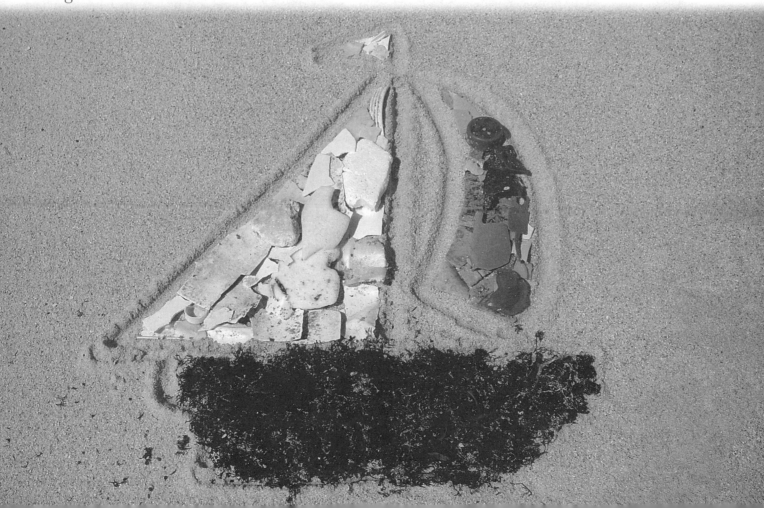

Building instructions

Gather materials

Creating a beaux arts project on the beach requires no prior preparation (other than bringing a bucket or pail for collecting materials), and your artwork can be as simple or complex as you wish.

First, gather a lot of beach materials and debris. Take a walk and collect what you find on the ground or at the edge of the water. Be careful not to take a shell that might still be a home to some living sea creature. You might also look for leaves, seeds, berries, and fruits that have fallen to the ground, but do not pick them from trees or bushes. Be careful when collecting trash. Pieces of plastic and wood that have washed ashore are usually clean and safe, but fresh trash and food left by visitors should be avoided.

You might collect a variety of materials or only one type of object, like shells. But notice that even the same type of object can vary in color, size, shape, and texture. As you gather things, begin to develop ideas of what the materials might become. A collection of white shells might be used to fill in the outline of sails on a ship, darker shells could become the scales of a fish, and seaweed could be used to make flowers or trees.

Draw a picture outline

Use your hands to level an area of sand, then use a finger to draw a simple outline of what you plan to make. Sometimes it is easier to draw in damp sand close to the water. The subject you choose for your picture can be anything—a ship, dragon, whale, shark, fish, dinosaur, bird, house, person, tree, car, boat, dog, cat, or whatever inspires you. Or instead, you might chose to draw an interesting geometric pattern or even an arbitrary design.

Here's a tip: Try to create a drawing made up of a few clearly outlined sections, like a boat that has a hull and two sails, or a house with a roof, a door, a window, and a chimney. That will make the drawing easier to fill in. As you draw, you can make changes or corrections simply by erasing lines with your hand and redrawing part or all of it.

Fill the outlined sections with objects

When you are pleased with your outline drawing, decide which material to use to fill in each part of your drawing. Overlapping clamshells all placed in the same direction look like the scales of a fish. Or a house might have stones for the roof shingles, seashells for siding, and a piece of driftwood for the chimney. Another idea is to fill in areas with different materials that have similar attributes, like a collection of green things for a boat hull and white things for a ship's sails. If it is a breezy day at the beach, any lightweight materials can be pressed a little into the sand to help hold them down.

When you are done and ready for cleanup, put all the debris and trash you have collected into a trash receptacle, or bag it up to take home and throw away, or recycle it properly. You can leave all natural materials on the beach for others to discover.

Backyard Beaux Arts

Beaux arts projects can also be made in your backyard by drawing outline pictures in a sandbox, in the dirt, or on a lawn. For fill-in material, try using collections of leaves, twigs, stones, pinecones, pine needles, grass clippings, acorns, crab apples, berries, ferns, wood chips, or just about anything else you can find.

TABLE GAME SNACKS

Table games and puzzles have always been popular with kids, and many old standards like tic-tac-toe, three in a row, and triangle solitaire are still favorites. Some restaurants even place these games on tables to amuse customers while they wait to be served. With these versions of the table games, however, there is no waiting for food. The game itself is the snack!

Table Game Snacks are played with the same rules as the standard games, except the game boards are made of celery, cereal, and banana slices, and the game pieces are healthy food snacks that include grapes, strawberries, and blueberries. As you play these games and remove pieces from the board, you can eat them. And when the game is over, you can also eat the game board!

Construction

Player's age
5+

Materials
See specific game.

Tools
See specific game.

Building instructions
See specific game.

TIC-TAC-TOE

Materials
☐ Banana or cucumber

☐ 5 strawberries

Tools
☐ Table knife

☐ Large plate

Building instructions

The game is played with banana slices or cucumber slices as the base pieces, representing positions on the game board, and strawberries are the movable game pieces that sit on the banana-slice bases.

Slice a banana into disks about a quarter-inch thick, and position nine discs on the plate in rows of three to form the square tic-tac-toe game board.

Slice five strawberries horizontally across the middle so you have five strawberry tops (the stem end) and five strawberry bottoms (the pointed end)

Rules of the game

Tic-tac-toe is for two players. One player uses the strawberry tops, and the other player uses the strawberry bottoms. As you play the game, place the cut side down on the banana slices.

The first player places one of his or her strawberry pieces on any banana-slice position. Players then alternate turns, placing their game

pieces on empty positions while trying to get three of their pieces in a straight row—horizontally, vertically, or diagonally.

If all the positions become taken and there is no winner, remove the game pieces (but leave the banana slices) and play the game again. When someone does win, he or she gets to decide who eats the game.

For a more difficult version of tic-tac-toe, each player uses only three game pieces. If there is no winner after both players have positioned their pieces, then each player, in turn, gets to move one of his or her pieces to a vacant position until someone wins. The only other rule for this game version is that moves must be either horizontal or vertical, but not diagonal.

THREE IN A ROW

Materials
☐ Celery stalk

☐ Red grapes and green grapes

Tools
☐ Large plate

Building instructions

This game is played with a stalk of celery used for the game board, and the red and green grapes are the movable game pieces that are positioned on the celery stalk.

Place a full stalk of celery across the plate so the channel formed by the stalk is facing up. Spread the leafy portion of the celery over the plate edge to help keep the stalk from rolling to either side.

Select three red grapes and three green grapes to use for game pieces. Set up the game board by placing three red grapes directly next to each other on the channel at one end of the

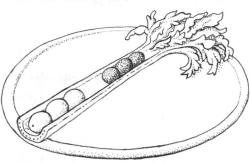

celery stalk. Now put three green grapes at the other end of the stalk, leaving a grape-size space between the two groups.

Rules of the game

This is a solitaire game you play against yourself. The idea is to reverse the positions of the grapes in the least number of moves while following these two rules.

1. The grapes can only move forward toward their new positions—there are no backward moves.

2. A grape can move only into a vacant adjacent space or jump over a grape of the other color to a vacant space.

Play the game once and then again to see if you can better your score. Each time you get a better score, you might reward yourself by eating the game pieces and then build the game again with fresh pieces.

TRIANGLE SOLITAIRE

Materials
☐ Round toasted oat cereal, such as Cheerios

☐ Blueberries

Tools
☐ Large plate

Building instructions
This game is played with round cereal pieces representing positions on the game board, and blueberries as the movable game pieces that sit on the cereal ring bases.

In the center of a plate, arrange fifteen cereal pieces to form a triangle with five cereal pieces per side. Leave about one inch between adjacent pieces. Carefully place one blueberry on each cereal ring except for the middle ring.

Rules of the game
The objective is to remove all the blueberry game pieces from the game board cereal rings except for one remaining piece. A game piece

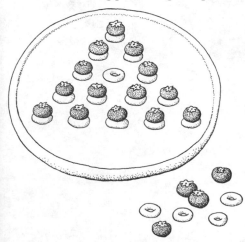

is removed after it is jumped by another piece. Only jumps in a straight line over one game piece are allowed, but you can jump in any direction. You can reward yourself as you play by eating the berries as they are removed from the board. And when you are finished playing, eat the cereal.

OTHER TASTY GAMES

The same tasty foods used for base pieces and game markers in Table Game Snacks can be used to play several other games you may already know. Sometimes you can create a new game by simply changing the game rules, the game board, or both.

Jumbo Tic-Tac-Toe
Have you ever tried playing tic-tac-toe using a twenty-five space game board in a five-by-five grid? The rules and the winning objective are still the same. You and an opponent take turns placing markers on the game bases while trying to be the first player to get three of your own markers straight in a row in any direction. In another version of this game, players continue to alternately place markers on the base pieces until the game board is completely filled. Then the player with the longest row is the winner. In case of a tie, the player with the second longest row wins.

Four by Four Equals Ten
Place sixteen base pieces on a plate, arranged in a four-by-four grid. Place exactly ten game markers on the base pieces to form ten rows with each row having either two or four markers. The rows can be horizontal, vertical, or diagonal from corner to corner.

Here's a clue: The solution is not symmetrical. And don't peek at the solution below.

The Mirror Image
Place six base pieces on a plate to form two rows of three bases each. Arrange five different-looking markers (A, B, C, D, and E) on five of the six base pieces as shown, leaving one base with no marker.

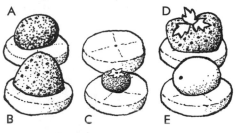

The first challenge is to switch the positions of the two end markers A and B by moving only one piece at a time onto a vacant base. If you eventually solve that puzzle (without looking at the solution below), you might attempt the mind-boggling challenge of also switching the positions of markers D and E, following the same rules. With both ends reversed, the game board should look like a mirror image of its original layout.

Solutions
Four by Four Equals Ten

Ⓧ○○Ⓧ
○○ⓍⓍ
○Ⓧ○Ⓧ
ⓍⓍⓍⓍ

The Mirror Image
Moves to vacant space: A, B, C, A, E, D, A, C, B, E, C, A, D, C, E, B, A.

FRUIT FACE TASTY TOTEM POLE

Totem poles are constructed to tell a story about a person or an event, with each carved figure representing a special quality or spirit that represents the values of its owner. By carving and stacking slices and chunks of tasty fruits on a drinking straw, you can build a Fruit Face Tasty Totem Pole that tells your own story and reflects your own special values of strength, love, happiness, leadership, or whatever characteristics you want to reveal to others. And while you're building the totem pole, you get to snack on the pieces of fruit you carve away. The completed totem pole can be temporarily displayed before it, too, is eaten.

Construction

Builder's age
8+ for carving

3+ for stacking

Materials
☐ Plastic drinking straw

☐ Toothpicks

☐ Several fresh fruits

Tools

- ☐ Kitchen knife for slicing
- ☐ Paring knife for carving
- ☐ Cutting board (optional)
- ☐ Melon baller (optional)
- ☐ Fruit and vegetable peeler (optional)

Building instructions

Select the fruits you want to use based on their seasonal availability, the type of carvings or forms you want to make, and the meanings represented by the particular fruits for the designs you plan to create. Each of the following fruits has its own unique appearance and specific meaning in the totem pole story, and some fruits are easier to carve than others. These descriptions will help you select which fruits to use.

Apples
Knowledge

Apples can be cut into slices or chunks, and designs can easily be carved in the apple skin. Apple rings and apple chunks make good faces, wings, arms, or legs, as well as arrows, hearts, stars, and other recognizable shapes. A large chunk of apple with a wide, flat side makes a good, stable base for the drinking straw. Apples will quickly brown once they are cut open and exposed to the air, but you can preserve their original color by dipping the freshly cut pieces into a little diluted lemon juice or a lemon-lime soft drink.

Pears
Love

Pears can be cut and carved just like apples. Pears will quickly brown once they are cut open and exposed to the air, but you can preserve their original color by dipping the freshly cut pieces into a little diluted lemon juice or a lemon-lime soft drink.

Oranges
Life

The skin of an orange is thick and tough and not easy to carve, and the fruit inside is not very firm, so oranges work best as unpeeled rings or wedges.

Strawberries
Beauty

Large, ripe strawberries, with or without the stem, can be used whole to make heads, bodies, and attachments to other fruit pieces. Simple designs can also be easily carved into the fruit.

Melons
Happiness

Chunks of cantaloupe, watermelon, honeydew, and other melons are perfect for carving all kinds of forms and stacking them on the totem pole straw. First, cut the melon into halves, then quarters, and remove any seeds. Then cut the wedges into the shapes and forms you want. (Large melon wedges make great wings.) Depending on the firmness of the fruit inside, the pieces cut from melons can be used with or without their thick skins.

Peaches and nectarines
Wealth

Before using either of these fruits, you must first remove the pit by cutting all the way around the circumference of the fruit, beginning and ending at the stem. Then pull the two halves apart and remove the pit. The ripe fruit may be too soft for cutting into accurate shapes, but slices, wedges, and chunks with the skin attached are good for carving designs.

Grapes and berries
Abundance

Red and green grapes can be used whole or as halves, peeled or unpeeled. These small fruits and several types of berries make good attachments to larger fruit pieces and can be used to represent parts of faces, appendages, or just decorative elements.

Bananas
Wisdom

Use thick slices of banana either with or without its tough skin. But be warned that a peeled banana can get quite slimy if handled too much. And be careful to keep the banana from splitting apart when placing pieces over the straw.

Pineapple
Comfort

Whole, fresh pineapples make the best totem pole parts, but not the pineapple rings that come in a can. Although the skin of a pineapple cannot be easily carved, it does have a rather interesting texture with spikes that can add character to pieces placed on the totem pole.

Be sure to first rinse all fruits in running water, and always use caution when cutting with knives.

Stacking the totem pole

1. Begin with a large, flat disk of fruit to make a wide, stable base that will keep the completed totem pole from tipping over. Half an apple or half an orange cut so that the core is in the center makes a good base.

2. Position the half-sphere base cut-side down, and push one end of a plastic drinking straw into the center of the base fruit so that the straw is vertical. If the skin of the fruit is too tough for the straw to penetrate, just cut the skin away in the center.

3. To make the individual fruit creatures and features to stack on the totem pole, start with large pieces of fruit and carve them into shape with a sharp kitchen knife. Depending on the fruit, you can remove all the skin and carve only the fruit inside, or try carving into the skin, using the skin color as a contrast to the fruit. A paring knife or other small, pointed knife is best for carving details. Another way to shape or carve patterns into the skin of some fruits is with a fruit and vegetable peeler.

4. After cutting and carving a piece for your totem pole, put it on the straw by gently pushing the piece down over the top of the straw. For some pieces, it may be difficult to start the straw through the fruit's skin side, so plan the design of pieces so that you always push the pieces onto the straw going first through the softer fruit side.

   As pieces of fruit collect inside the straw, you can squeeze them out for a snack.

5. Smaller pieces of fruit, berries, and other attachments can be connected to the larger fruit

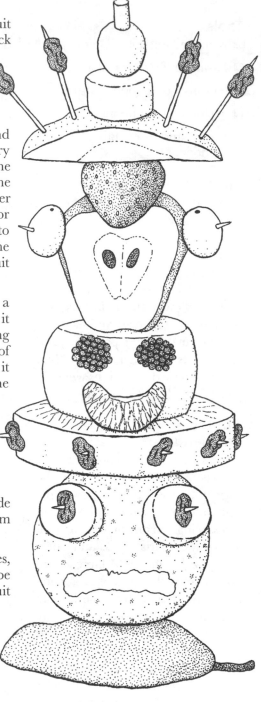

pieces, using toothpicks. Try to stack your carved pieces so that they symbolically tell a story. Continue adding sections of fruit and attachments until you have reached the top of the straw.

BRICKS AND MORTAR BUILDING SYSTEMS

Compared to only stacking, building systems that use mortar to bond bricks and blocks are capable of creating more complex structures with a greater variety of forms. Using bricks and mortar, you can build Roman arches and domes plus curved walls and cantilevers, and the smaller modular bricks allow finer details. However, the structures you build using mortar will harden into a permanent rigid structure, and building them will take a lot longer than just stacking.

If you're a fan of building with plastic bricks, you will probably like building with Mini Marshmallow Sticky Bricks. The small bricks stick together quickly and easily with just a dab of water. Building with Stack and Stick Sugar Cubes is even more like actual modular brick building. A special mortar mix is used to attach the identical and perfectly shaped sugar-cube bricks, and with careful workmanship, the structures you build will look like miniature versions of life-size masonry buildings. You can also use this building system to construct a Sugar-Cube Cube Puzzle that will challenge your ability to think in three dimensions. Both of these building systems are excellent for constructing a wide range of small masonry structures from simple walled forts and castles to Roman arched bridges, to modern monuments and architecture.

If you want to make more primitive-looking masonry structures, try building with Peanut-Shell Bricks and Kitchen-Paste Mortar. Although the peanut-shell halves are modular in general shape and size, no two are exactly alike. This building system is best for constructing walls in layers, using a conventional pattern of one brick over two. However, because the peanut-shell bricks have curved sides, the mortar that oozes out between the bricks is hard to finish flush, so just about anything you build will look somewhat crude but authentically old. And if you're a builder with an artistic flare, Cake Blocks and Frosting Mortar makes super-simple block structures that are meant to be decorated for presentation and then eaten.

BUILD IT

CAKE BLOCKS AND FROSTING MORTAR	408
PEANUT-SHELL BRICKS AND KITCHEN-PASTE MORTAR	411
STACK AND STICK SUGAR CUBES	413
SUGAR-CUBE CUBE PUZZLE	415
MINI MARSHMALLOW STICKY BRICKS	417

CAKE BLOCKS AND FROSTING MORTAR
BUILDING SYSTEM

The best feature of building blocks made of cake and joined with a frosting mortar is getting to eat what you build. By simply slicing a cake into modular-shaped squares, triangles, rectangles, arches, and columns, you will have enough block pieces to build a small castle, an igloo, a statue, or maybe a sculpture. And by using additional frosting to cover the structure, plus some sprinkles, chocolate pieces, powdered sugar, and drizzle, your cake-brick creations can be decorated for birthday parties, holidays, or just-for-fun desserts.

A pound cake, which is dense and finely textured, makes the best building blocks. Most other cakes are too crumbly and don't hold their shape well after being cut. But if you don't like pound cake, chocolate brownies are a reasonably good substitute.

SYSTEM FEATURES

- Perfect for making highly decorative block structures
- The finished structures and leftovers are edible
- Homemade frosting mortar requires no eggs or cooking
- Frosting mortar can be white or mixed with food coloring
- Cake blocks are easily cut and trimmed to any size

Construction

Builder's age
   4+ (with adult assistance preparing the bricks and mortar)

Player's age
   1+

Materials

- [ ] Pound cake (Purchase a ready-made cake or make your own using the recipe in Building techniques.)

- [ ] Cake frosting (Purchase a ready-made cake frosting or make your own using the recipe in Building techniques.)

- [ ] Edible decorations might include sprinkles, chocolate chips, and powdered sugar. (optional)

Tools

- [ ] Serrated cake knife

- [ ] Ruler

- [ ] Table knife or small spatula

- [ ] If making your own cake and frosting mortar:

  2 mixing bowls

  2 mixing spoons

- [ ] Baking pan. A standard 5″ x 9″ loaf pan will make a double-thickness cake that will need to be cut into two layers. To make a single-layer cake, use a larger pan that will hold at least eight cups of batter and make a cake at least two inches thick. An 8″ x 8″ square or a 7″ x 11″ rectangular cake pan works well, as does an 8″ or 9″ round pan.

Building techniques

Making the pound cake

You can either use a ready-made pound cake or bake your own. A store-bought pound cake typically measures about five by seven inches and makes about twenty blocks plus some leftover trimmings. A home-made pound cake baked in a five-by-nine-inch loaf pan yields about thirty bricks plus even more trimmings. The trimmings cut from around the sides of the cake usually don't make full bricks, and can either be saved and used for decorating the structure to be built or just eaten.

To bake a pound cake, you can use a store-bought mix (requiring only the addition of eggs and water and sometimes oil) or do everything from scratch following this recipe:

- [ ] ³⁄₄ cup (1 ½ sticks) butter, softened

- [ ] 1 ½ cups granulated sugar

- [ ] 2 ¼ cups flour (preferably cake flour)

- [ ] ½ teaspoon salt

- [ ] 2 teaspoons baking powder

- [ ] 4 whole eggs

- [ ] ½ cup milk

- [ ] 1 ½ teaspoons vanilla extract

Preheat the oven to 325°F

1. Mix together the flour, salt, and baking powder, and set the mixture aside.

2. In another mixing bowl, cream together the softened butter and granulated sugar until the mixture is light and fluffy. Save a little butter for greasing the baking pan.

3. To the butter and sugar mixture, add and beat in the eggs, one egg at a time. Continue to stir until the mixture is smooth.

4. Add the flour mixture alternately with the milk and vanilla, stirring just enough to blend everything together. Do not mix the batter too much or the cake will be crumbly.

5. Scrape the batter into a baking pan greased with butter, and place it in the preheated oven to bake for approximately 60 minutes for a loaf and 50 minutes for the shallower pans. Oven temperatures can vary, so check the cake at 45 minutes. When done, the top of the cake will be a light golden brown, and a knife inserted into the cake should come out clean without batter stuck to it.

6. Remove the cake from the oven and cool it in the pan for 15 minutes. Then remove the cake from the pan and place it on a wire rack to cool completely before slicing.

Cutting the pound cake blocks

Depending on the shape of the whole pound cake you have bought or baked, these are the suggested cutting patterns to make a set of cake building blocks.

First, trim the cake as necessary to square up all sides into a big rec-

tangular block. To avoid crumbling the cake, use a serrated knife and cut with an even back and forth motion. Use a ruler to lay out the cutting pattern and to guide the knife while making straight cuts.

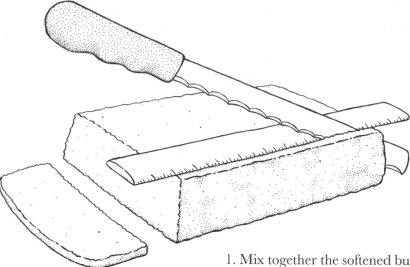

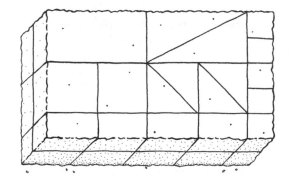

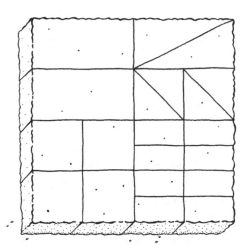

1. Mix together the softened butter and the confectioners sugar, and beat with a mixing spoon until smooth.

2. Add 3 teaspoons of milk and 1 teaspoon of extract and beat for one or two minutes until fluffy. If the frosting is too stiff to spread easily, add a few more drops of milk (or water). If the frosting mortar is too thin, add a teaspoon or two of confectioners sugar. Cover the bowl with a lid or plastic wrap until you are ready to use the mortar.

Stacking and bonding the blocks

Building with Cake Blocks and Frosting Mortar is the same as building with any other type of bricks. The frosting mortar can be spread with a small spatula or a table knife, applying just enough of the frosting to fill the joints between blocks to a consistent thickness.

result should be about thirty to forty 1″ x 1″ x 2″ blocks. Trim any smaller blocks into one-inch cubes.

Making the frosting mortar

You can purchase ready-made frosting to use for the mortar, or mix your own frosting from common kitchen ingredients. Because this special homemade frosting mortar recipe uses no eggs and requires no cooking, it is easy to make, bonds to the cake blocks very well, tastes great, and keeps for weeks in the refrigerator.

☐ ¼ cup butter, softened (½ stick)

☐ 2 cups confectioners sugar

☐ 3 to 4 teaspoons milk

☐ 1 teaspoon vanilla or lemon extract (optional for flavor)

Start with a first-row foundation, then keep adding blocks to build up walls. Remember that each block should straddle at least two bricks below it, and no vertical joints should line up. If you build carefully, a cake block structure can be four or five blocks high before it starts to become wobbly. Within twenty-four hours (if you can wait that long before eating what you built), the homemade mortar will dry and form a reasonably rigid structure.

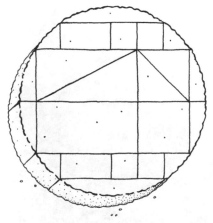

To make modular-size blocks, it may be easiest to first slice the cake into two or three layers, each one inch thick, then cut each layer into strips one inch wide, and finally cut the strips into two-inch lengths. The

PEANUT-SHELL BRICKS AND KITCHEN-PASTE MORTAR
BUILDING SYSTEM

To become a good brick mason takes years of experience, so it shouldn't be surprising that it takes some skill to build neat and sturdy structures from peanut-shell bricks. It also takes a lot of time. This building system is so easy that nearly anyone can construct model structures by simply stacking halves of peanut shells in courses, or layers, just like bricks, and pasting the half shells in place, using a simple and safe mortar you mix up in the kitchen. However, it does take some technique and practice to keep the mortar paste from looking messy and oozing out between the shell bricks.

Once you get the hang of it, try constructing model buildings with walls that have openings for windows and doors, and try to copy several of the standard patterns used in real brick building (see brick patterns on page 363). Using pieces of paperboard and other scrap materials, you can finish off your models with roof panels, doors, and other details.

SYSTEM FEATURES

- Peanut shell halves are laid in courses like real bricks
- Builds any shape structure that can be built with bricks
- Kitchen paste mortar is easy to mix and safe to use
- Structures are permanent and strong once the mortar dries

412   BRICK AND BLOCK STRUCTURES

Construction

Builder's age
8+

Materials
☐ Peanut shell halves (Collect as many as possible.)

☐ 2 cups white flour

☐ 1 cup salt

☐ 1 cup water

☐ Corrugated cardboard, for foundation platforms and roof panels (optional)

Tools
☐ Table knife or butter spreader

☐ Mixing bowl and spoon

☐ Scissors (optional)

Building techniques
One roasted peanut that is shelled by hand yields two peanut-shell brick units. Practice squeezing the shells on their seams to crack them into halves. However, not all peanuts will break evenly into two complete halves. Just discard the incomplete, crumbly, or oddly shaped halves, but save any well-formed, half-brick pieces to use for fill-ins as needed. A one-pound package of peanuts should yield enough shell bricks to build a complete model house, a tall tower, or maybe a fort with tall walls.

Making the mortar
The mortar for peanut-shell bricks is a salt dough made from edible materials, although you would probably find the taste unpleasant. Put the flour, salt, and water in a mixing bowl and thoroughly mix by hand with a spoon. With supervision, you can also do the mixing in a food mixer, blender, or food processor. This mixture of ingredients will form a stiff, yet pliable, paste that should be easy to apply to the bricks. If a softer mortar is

desired, just add a little more water and mix the batch again. If the mortar is too wet and sticky, add more flour.

Applying the mortar
Use the mortar paste to attach one peanut-shell brick at a time to the structure you are building, just like cement mortar used between real bricks. The flat side of the half shell should be facing down and the two shell humps facing up. Use a table knife for a mortar trowel, and apply the paste to the underside cavities of the peanut-shell brick, then position and press the brick in place. If some of the mortar oozes out more than you like, or if you want to "point" your bricks, carefully scrape off any excess with the tip of your table-knife trowel.

The paste will hold the bricks in place while you build, and the complete structure (or the work in progress) can be left to dry hard overnight. If you are in a big hurry and want to harden the mortar in a few hours, the structure can be placed in a warm oven (set at a

low temperature, about 200°). When the mortar hardens, the structure will be very strong and should keep indefinitely. Any leftover paste you want to use again should be placed in a covered container and put in the refrigerator where it will keep for weeks.

How and what to build
Any type of building or structure that is constructed of real bricks can be modeled with peanut-shell bricks. Just remember that to build strong brick walls, one brick should always straddle the two bricks below it. For tall structures, make the walls double thick, and use a few peanut shell bricks across the double wall every few rows to lock or "tie" it together.

Use a piece of corrugated cardboard as a sturdy foundation platform, and draw the footprint of your structure as a building guide. If you plan to harden the mortar in a warm oven, use a cookie sheet or a pie tin as a platform.

Because it takes a long time to lay course upon course of bricks, start with a simple structure like a model of a doghouse or a round wishing well. Once you get the hang of it, try more complex brick structures like a small cottage or a tall, tapered chimney. And when you get really good, try making a peanut-shell brick model of an arched bridge.

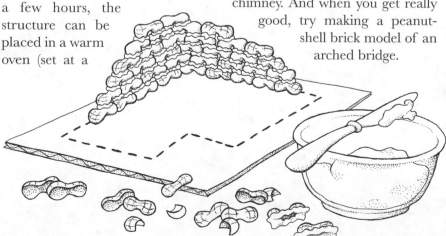

STACK AND STICK SUGAR CUBES
BUILDING SYSTEM

Big cups of individually paper-wrapped sugar cubes were once commonly found on restaurant tables instead of the sugar packets used today. Back then, if enough sugar cubes were available and service was slow, kids would occupy time at the table by stacking the sugar cubes to build simple brick towers, tapered pyramids, long fort walls, or a train of railroad cars.

Sugar cubes may no longer be as common as they once were, but both square and rectangular sugar "cubes" are still available at most grocery stores. Their precise size and modular shape are excellent for building free-standing stacked structures without the need of any glue or mortar to hold the pieces in position. However, you can also stick the sugar cubes together using a special homemade mortar to build curved structures like arches and domes.

SYSTEM FEATURES

- Sugar cubes are inexpensive
- Available in cube and brick sizes
- Pieces of either shape are precision cut and identical
- Test structures can be stack built before rebuilding with mortar
- Mortar dries white to match white sugar cubes
- Completed structures are solid and durable
- Modular sections or units can be prebuilt and assembled later

Construction

Builder's age
5+

Materials
☐ Sugar cubes or sugar tablets

Sugar "cubes" come in two sizes. Cubes are 1/2" square on all sides. Tablets are shaped like bricks, with the dimensions 1" X 1/4" X 3/8"

☐ Flour

☐ Cornstarch

☐ Water

Tools
☐ Mixing bowl

☐ Mixing spoon

☐ Table knife for spreading

☐ Measuring cup

☐ Coarse sandpaper (optional)

Building techniques

If you are not sure what you want to build, you may first want to test build a few constructions dry, without using mortar between them, before permanently joining the cubes and bricks with mortar. Some builders may prefer to just start stacking and bonding bricks while deciding on a design as the construction grows.

Mixing a batch of mortar

This is an exceptionally strong, yet easy-to-make and easy-to-use mortar for bonding sugar cubes.

1. Combine equal amounts of flour, cornstarch, and water in a mixing bowl. Using 1/4 cup of each ingredient should make plenty of mortar for even the largest structures.

2. Blend the mixture with a spoon to form a stiff paste.

Using a little more or less of either

the flour or cornstarch causes little change to the properties of the mortar. However, using too much water will make the mixture too soupy and runny, and too little water makes the mortar too doughy and not sticky enough. Mortar that is too thick or too thin can be easily made right by simply adding a little more water or a little more flour or cornstarch as appropriate.

The perfect mortar paste should be thick, easy to spread, and sticky. At this consistency, the mortar will provide good adhesive qualities while remaining soft enough for an hour or two so that the cubes can be adjusted or rearranged if necessary. The mortar will hold well enough during construction to make walls with doorway and window openings that won't collapse while drying.

After about twenty-four hours, the mortar will dry completely hard and the structure will be rock solid. The mortar will also dry white, nearly perfectly matching the white color of the sugar cubes.

The mortar mixture should last about one to two days at room temperature or up to a week in a sealed container kept in a refrigerator. Saved mortar may need to be thinned or thickened a little when you use it again.

Assembling the sugar cubes and bricks

Keep sugar cubes away from water, moisture, and high humidity that

can cause them to melt.

Here is the conventional way to lay bricks with mortar.

1. Use a table knife to spread a thin layer of the mortar mixture onto the horizontal surface of the sugar cube to which you will be attaching another cube.

2. Spread a thin layer of mortar to the vertical side of the cube you are laying that will be in contact with another cube already positioned.

3. Press the cube into position, slightly squeezing out any excess mortar.

4. Use the knife (or your finger) to scrape away any excess mortar from the joints.

Continue to add more cubes, using standard brick-building bond patterns and stacking techniques.

To build roof panels, floors, and other horizontal or slanted panels, first build the sections flat on a tabletop, then position the prefabricated sections in the construction after the mortar has hardened and the panels are rigid.

If you need to trim a sugar cube to fit a particular space or to round off square edges, use coarse sandpaper.

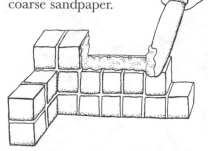

STACK AND STICK SUGAR CUBES BUILD-IT PROJECT

SUGAR-CUBE CUBE PUZZLE

SUGAR-CUBE CUBE PUZZLE

The objective of this puzzle is simple. Just assemble all the puzzle pieces to form a cube. However, there are two different ways to make the puzzle pieces—one using seven shapes that make a difficult puzzle to solve, and one that is very difficult to solve using six shapes. The puzzle pieces can also be assembled in other ways to create figures of animals, structures, and other abstract objects. Fortunately, making the puzzle piece shapes is quite easy using cube-shaped sugar cubes bonded with homemade mortar.

Construction

Building system
Stack and Stick Sugar Cubes

Builder's age
6+

Player's age
Geniuses of any age

Materials
☐ 27 cube-shaped sugar cubes
☐ Flour
☐ Cornstarch
☐ Water

Tools
- ☐ Mixing bowl
- ☐ Mixing spoon
- ☐ Table knife for spreading
- ☐ Measuring cup
- ☐ Coarse sandpaper (optional)

Building instructions
Here is an important practical tip: Remember to keep sugar cubes away from water, moisture, and high humidity that can cause them to melt.

Mixing a batch of mortar
Mix a small batch of sugar-cube mortar using the recipe in Stack and Stick Sugar Cubes. The perfect mortar paste should be thick, sticky, and easy to spread. At this consistency, the mortar will provide good adhesive qualities while remaining soft enough for an hour or two so the cubes can be adjusted if necessary. After about twenty-four hours, the mortar will dry completely hard and the puzzle pieces will be ready to use.

Making the puzzle pieces
The puzzle pieces are easy to make, although you must be careful to attach the sugar cubes squarely to each other so the puzzle will assemble correctly. Unless you are a puzzle wizard, start with the easier, seven-piece puzzle.

These are the forms to make for a seven-piece puzzle. Notice that six of the pieces use four cubes each, and one piece is made from three cubes.

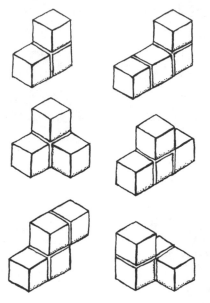

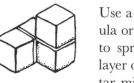

Use a small spatula or table knife to spread a thin layer of the mortar mixture onto a joining surface of a sugar cube, then attach another cube to the mortared surface. When making each puzzle piece, apply the mortar to every side of each cube that is in contact with another cube. Continue to add more cubes with mortar until the puzzle piece is complete. Also use the knife or spatula (or your finger) to scrape away any excess mortar from the joints.

These are the forms to make a six-piece puzzle. Notice that three puzzle pieces use five cubes each, and three pieces use four cubes each.

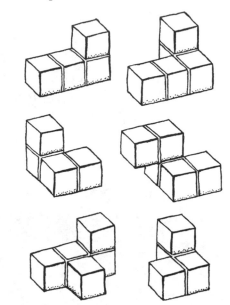

Solving the puzzle
There is more than one way to assemble the puzzle pieces into a perfect cube, and if you don't give up, you should eventually solve the puzzle.

Building figures using the seven puzzle pieces
In addition to forming a cube, the puzzle pieces of the seven-piece puzzle can also be arranged to create all kinds of other geometric forms, familiar objects, and figures. See how many of these forms you can duplicate, then experiment with inventing your own objects and sculptures.

Dinosaur, duck, snake, lobster, swan

MINI MARSHMALLOW STICKY BRICKS
BUILDING SYSTEM

This is an especially unique construction system because it requires only one material—miniature marshmallows—for both the building bricks and the mortar. There are no special brick shapes to make and no special brick mortar to mix. The adhesive for bonding the small marshmallow cylinders to each other is the marshmallow itself. Just slightly wet one brick with water and stick it to another brick. It is that simple—you can quickly build any type of structure that uses conventional brick construction. After the structure dries and hardens overnight, it can easily be decorated with watercolors or markers—or eaten instead!

SYSTEM FEATURES

- Marshmallows are the only material needed
- Modular cylinder shape
- Dries firm and solid overnight
- Constructions can be colored
- Other shapes can be cut to size
- Fast building and easy repairs
- Makes edible novelties for parties

Construction

Builder's age
3+

Materials
☐ Miniature marshmallows

A 10-ounce package typically contains about 500 pieces, each ½″ round by ½″ long.

Tools
☐ Sponge

☐ Plate or bowl

☐ Felt-tip markers or watercolors (optional)

Building techniques

Be sure you have a place to work and a surface to build on that will not be damaged by water. Building a mini marshmallow structure on a stiff paper plate or a piece of corrugated cardboard will make it much easier to move the construction while working or when it needs to be moved somewhere else to dry overnight.

A marshmallow piece will stick to another marshmallow piece when one or both surfaces have been made slightly wet. An easy way to dampen a piece to prepare it for attachment is to gently tap the marshmallow on a wet sponge. Set up a wetting station by placing a wet sponge (but not dripping wet) on a plate or in a shallow bowl.

You only need to dampen the surfaces of the marshmallow piece that will be touching and attached to other pieces. Each time a piece is added to the structure, hold it in position for several seconds to bond before letting go. Until the piece has a chance to start drying, it may have a tendency to slip out of place, so it is best to alternate adding brick pieces to different parts of the construction to give pieces a chance to dry before bearing weight.

As the marshmallow bricks dry and bond together, the pieces become harder, resulting in a fairly firm and strong construction. You can leave your creation its natural marshmallow white—especially if you plan to eat it—or color the bricks as you like.

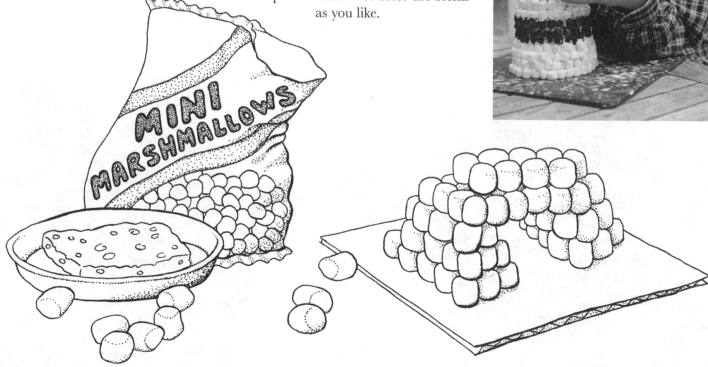

LOCKING BLOCKS AND BANDED BUNDLES

These building systems have a combination of the benefits of both stacking systems and systems using mortar. Parts can quickly be assembled like stacking blocks and rearranged anytime as you build. However, the blocks can also be joined together to form rigid structures, although these methods of attachment do not harden like mortar. And all structures built from Locking Blocks and Banded Bundles can be disassembled and the parts reused to build something else.

BUILD IT

WET SPONGE BLOCKS	420
TP TUBE TOWER BLOCKS	422
LOCKING LOGS AND TIMBER COLUMNS	424
SODA CAN CASTLES	427

Younger builders who also like water play in and out of the bathtub will probably enjoy assembling and reassembling Wet Sponge Blocks into simple and colorful abstract creatures and sculptures. Ambitious builders will find a large supply of empty soda cans can quickly construct crenellated walls that resemble castles or a tall castle tower big enough to stand in. With an even larger number of toilet paper tubes, you will be able to make enough TP Tube Tower Blocks to build structures as tall as you that resemble the world's tallest skyscrapers.

And builders old enough (or with a helper old enough) to fabricate the foam-filled tubes used in Locking Logs and Timber Columns can construct large models of log cabins and buildings that use column and slab construction. You can also attach cardboard panels to the logs and columns, using roofing nails as pushpins.

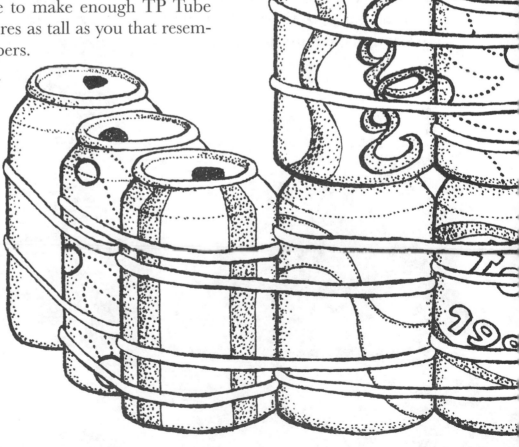

WET SPONGE BLOCKS
BUILDING SYSTEM

A few colorful kitchen sponges right out of the package can be used as simple stacking blocks, or you can cut them into a set of modular interlocking blocks to build more complex forms and structures. Just four kitchen sponges will produce a nine-block building set of seven different shapes. The interlocking modular sponge blocks you build with can be either wet or dry, although wet blocks work best and are more fun. The sponge blocks will float even when completely waterlogged, so simple constructions can be made while in the tub, and pieces won't get lost underwater. Wet or damp sponge constructions can be left to dry in place (which usually takes several days), or the parts can be disconnected, squeezed out, and the separated blocks left to dry. To swell the blocks to their full building sizes and shapes, just dip them in water again.

SYSTEM FEATURES

- Builds simple abstract structures
- Blocks can be used wet or dry
- Makes colorful constructions
- Great building activity for tub soak time
- Blocks and constructions will not sink

Construction

Builder's age
  8+

Player's age
  2+

Materials
- ☐ 4 rectangular kitchen sponges, all the same size in a variety of colors (4″ x 6″ x 1″ is a typical size.)

Tools

- ☐ Felt-tip marker
- ☐ Scissors (that can easily cut through the sponges)

Building techniques

Draw the lines of the pattern to be cut on the first sponge with a marking pen, using one of the other sponges in the set as a modular measuring tool. Mark a square at one end of the first sponge by laying the measuring sponge perpendicular across its end with its long end even with the first sponge's short end.

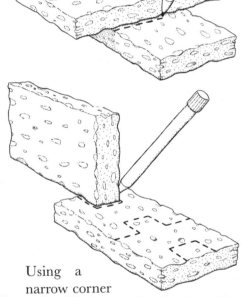

Using a narrow corner of the measuring sponge, measure and mark three small square cutouts to form one "H" block and one "M" block. The small square cutouts should all line up in the middle of the sponge. Now clearly mark the pattern for cutting out the blocks.

Use scissors to cut the two blocks to shape, being careful to follow the cut lines. Don't make the cutouts wider than the lines, or the interlocking connections will be too loose. When cutting inside corners,

first cut straight up to the corner, then fold part of the sponge back while turning the scissors and sponge to make the crossover cut.

Warning: After cutting the two blocks to shape, there will also be two small leftover sponge cubes. Infants and very young kids can choke on small parts, so these sponge pieces should be either discarded or saved in a safe place for some other project.

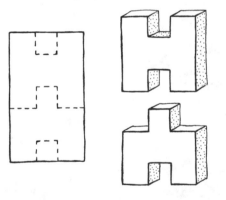

Lay out the cutting pattern for the second sponge to make another "H" connector, plus a "T" block and an "I" block, and cut out the shapes.

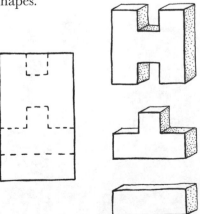

Lay out and cut a third sponge to make a third "H" connector, plus two "L" blocks of different dimensions.

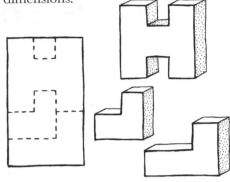

Now the block that was being used for measuring can be converted into a "big H" base block by marking and cutting a square notch at either end.

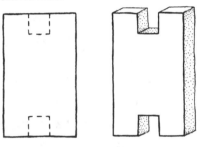

Building tips

The best interlocking connections are made using damp sponge blocks—wet sponges with most of the water squeezed out.

Dried sponge blocks will shrink to a slightly smaller size, and the connections will become loose. Rewetting the blocks will return them to the proper shape and size.

More complex constructions using all the Wet Sponge Blocks need to be built on a flat and water-safe play surface like a kitchen counter.

TP TUBE TOWER BLOCKS
BUILDING SYSTEM

Once you've accomplished the first challenge of collecting at least fifty toilet paper tubes, making the tubular building modules and assembling them into tall towers is fast and easy. The basic one-design module consists of a toilet paper tube with four slits cut into one end. Then identical modules are stacked and interconnected in several ways to quickly form tall kid-size towers.

Tube towers usually begin with a large base structure that can have just about any shape footprint—round, square, rectangular, triangular, polygonal, or arbitrary. As tubes are added and the structure grows taller, it can taper to a spire by using fewer and fewer tubes every few rows. Another way to build is to allow the base structure to grow into two or three separate towers. It's also fun to build individual towers and then arrange them into a tower city, or stack them to create one super-tall tower.

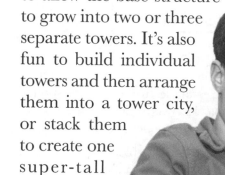

SYSTEM FEATURES

- Discarded toilet paper tubes are always available
- Modular tubes assemble and disassemble quickly
- Builds kid-size towers and sky-scrapers
- Joints can be glued for perma-nent constructions
- Tubes can be left plain, painted, or decorated

Construction

Builder's age
8+

Player's age
6+

Materials
- ☐ Toilet paper tubes
- ☐ Paper tubes from food wraps and paper towels (optional)
- ☐ White glue to make construc-tions permanent (optional)
- ☐ Paints, markers, and deco-rations (optional)

Tools

☐ Scissors

☐ Pencil or any marker

Building techniques

Collect toilet paper tubes. A starter set capable of building a kid-size tower will require at least fifty tubes. You can also include several longer paper tubes from food wraps and paper towels.

All tubes are converted to TP Tube Tower building modules by cutting four slits into one end of each tube to create four tab connectors. The slits should be evenly spaced around the perimeter of the tube and cut down the side to half the length of the tube.

1. Mark the slit locations by positioning an end of each tube on a tracing of the template shown below.

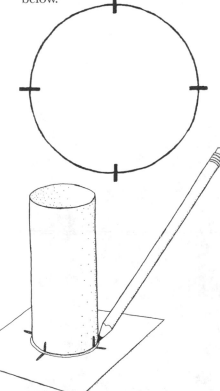

2. To consistently cut the tube slits to half the length of the toilet paper tube, use a small piece of tape, a pencil line, or some other mark as a guide. Make the slits

as parallel to the tube sides as you can. Slits cut into the ends of longer tubes should only be as long as the slits in the toilet paper tubes.

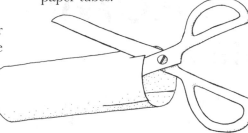

3. To connect the TP Tube Blocks, hook the unslit end of one block over one of the four tabs on another block, and push the two tubes together as far as they will go.

Even though any two modules can only be joined vertically, one on top the other, there are several ways for the structure to grow in all directions. To help you start building, here are a few typical connections. As your tower grows, you will probably discover other ways the tubes can be stacked and interlocked.

Stacking with all slit ends up or all down creates straight, curved, and angled walls.

You can use a single building technique or a combination of stacking methods to build a tower or sky-

Stacking with slit ends interlocking forms an extra-strong foundation or a rigid panel.

Stacking both ways and using different length tubes forms complex structures.

scraper or whatever you imagine. Either plan the structure ahead of time, or just start stacking and see how far up you can get. The blocks can just as easily be disassembled and reused to build something else.

If you do build a masterpiece worthy of keeping, the tubes can be glued together by running short beads of white glue into many of the crevices formed where the tubes attach to each other.

After building, the tan or white color of the toilet-paper tubes can be left as is or decorated with strips of tape, stickers, crayons, markers, and paints. Gray painted tubes might make your Tube Tower look more like a granite fort or stone castle, a tall tower with tubes covered in silver foil or silver paint could become a skyscraper design of the future, and a brown tube construction might resemble a wooden lookout tower.

LOCKING LOGS AND TIMBER COLUMNS
BUILDING SYSTEM

Any round tube and some round containers can be turned into rigid, lightweight, strong, and durable building blocks simply by filling them with expanding-foam insulation. Once the foam has cured and hardened, the logs, rods, columns, and rollers you create can be easily cut, carved, drilled, and sanded just like real wood, only more easily. Foam-filled logs made from paper tubes can be notched on the ends to make a set of Locking Logs that stack at right angles the same way a log cabin is built. Foam-filled logs stood on end also make columns for building towers and big building frameworks. To create walls and floors, you can easily attach cardboard panels and other sheet materials to the logs and columns, using large-headed roofing nails that easily push into the foam logs and hold firmly. And the foam-filled blocks can be decorated to look like wooden logs, marble columns, brick chimneys, or steel girders.

SYSTEM FEATURES

- Makes lightweight, strong, and durable logs and columns
- Quickly builds simple structures
- Paper tubes come in many lengths and diameters
- Blocks can be cut, carved, drilled, sanded, and painted
- Logs are notched for stacking
- Parts cut into modular sizes
- Hard-cured foam is safe

Construction

Builder's age
Adult

Player's age
5+

Materials
- ☐ Paperboard tubes from paper-towels, food wrap, gift wrapping paper, and toilet paper
- ☐ Expanding polyurethane foam sealant (comes in a pressurized can, and is available at hardware stores and building supply centers)
- ☐ Disposable gloves
- ☐ Scraps of cardboard or corrugated board
- ☐ 1″ roofing nails

Tools
- ☐ Serrated kitchen knife or hacksaw
- ☐ Straightedge
- ☐ Pencil
- ☐ Mat knife or utility knife

Building techniques
Collect paper tubes
Foam-filled blocks can be made only with cylindrical paperboard tubes and some round paperboard containers. Paperboard tubes can be almost any size, from short and fat toilet paper tubes to long and thin gift wrap tubes. Some drinking straws and uncoated paper cups with their bottoms cut out can also make good foam-filled logs and columns. Rectangular tubes and boxes do not make good foam-filled blocks because the expanding foam will cause the sides of the container to bulge.

Injecting the foam
Expanding foam sealant comes in a pressurized can and is sold at most hardware stores, paint stores,

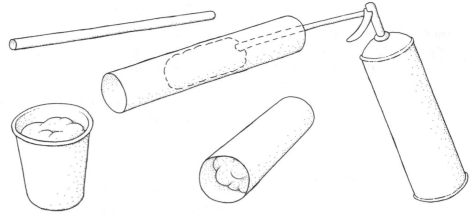

discount stores, and all building supply centers. Just one regular-size can of foam will make nearly one hundred foam-filled blocks. Injecting the sticky, gooey, messy, and smelly foam must be done by an adult, but the results are well worth the effort.

Warning: Expanding foam sealant should be used only by adults. Kid builders can assist in the process by holding the tubes steady while the foam is being injected. Even adults need to take precautions because the foam is very sticky and messy and nearly impossible to remove once it has cured. Make sure everyone participating in the foaming process is wearing disposable gloves and work clothes. Work in a well-ventilated area (outdoors is best), and follow all instructions on the can of foam. Although the foam is flammable and toxic while it is being dispensed, the cured foam is perfectly safe, even if chewed.

Spread newspaper over your work surface just in case the foam drips. Wear a pair of protective disposable gloves (gloves are sometimes supplied with the foam), and hold an empty tube or cup in one hand while holding the can of spray foam in the other hand. Press on the nozzle to inject the foam into the tube. The foam will come out of the nozzle like a foam snake and immediately begin expanding to many times its original volume.

Begin to fill an open tube or any cylinder from both ends, each time starting in the middle and working out. Because the foam will expand greatly and continue to expand for several hours, *only* fill the middle half of the tube. Any foam that eventually expands out the ends of the tube can be sliced off with a serrated kitchen knife once the foam has hardened.

After you stop injecting the foam, it will continue to expand even more, to about twice the volume you have already filled. Different brands of foam expand different amounts, so experiment with foaming one tube or cup cylinder before filling

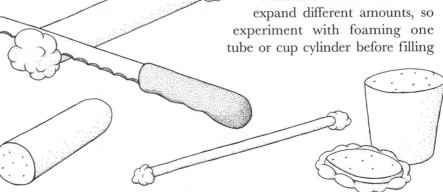

others. Even though the foam will appear to have stopped expanding after an hour or so, it is actually still expanding at a slower rate. So wait at least eight hours to see how much it totally expands. Once cured, the foam-filled blocks are nearly crushproof.

Making Locking Logs

Begin with a starter set of modular Locking Logs, and add more as you discover what you want to build. First, foam ten long tubes collected from paper towels and food wraps, and also foam ten toilet paper tubes. Allow the foam to cure, and trim off any excess foam protruding from the tube ends.

Note the location of the notches close to the ends of the log shown in the illustration. Make a properly shaped notch by first cutting a shallow V shape with a serrated knife (or a hacksaw blade). To prop-

erly shape the notch for perfect stacking, wrap a piece of coarse sandpaper around another foam-filled tube of the same diameter, and sand the V shape notch into a shallow, rounded shape. Make sure the notches at either end of a tube are the same depth and in alignment.

Locking Logs are made to be stacked like the logs of a log cabin. The logs can also be cut and shaped as needed. The completed Locking Logs can be used as is, painted with a satin or semigloss acrylic paint (which is easier to clean than a flat finish), or maybe wrapped with self-adhesive wallpaper or shelf paper.

Building with columns

Foam-filled cylinders can simply be stacked on end to build simple towers and smokestacks, or you can use them as part of a construction system to build more complex structures like the framework of a skyscraper. The foam-filled columns can easily be cut, shaped, and sanded for attaching foam-

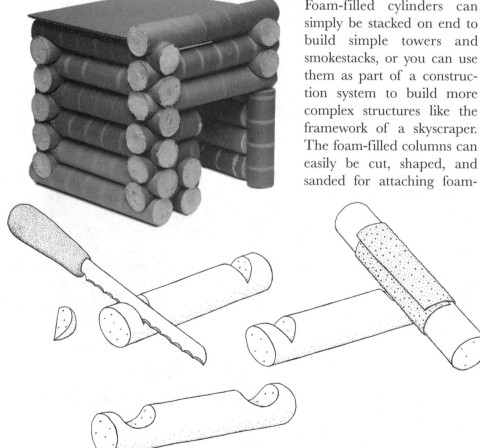

filled beams. The columns can also be drilled to accept drinking-straw rafters and floor joists or maybe axles for building simple vehicles and toy machines.

Attaching panels to logs and columns

Like using a big thumbtack, it is easy to push a large-headed roofing nail through scraps of cardboard and into the sides or ends of foam-filled logs and columns. Adding cardboard panels lets you quickly build (and disassemble) model buildings with side walls and roofs, or long bridge spans, elevated highways, and even sloped ramps for launching balls and racing model cars.

Panels can be cut from scraps of cardboard and corrugated-box board as needed for a planned construction. You can also cut squares, rectangles, circles, ovals, triangles, or any flat shape to create an inventory of panels to select from while building.

Use a pencil and straightedge to lay out the panel sizes you want, and cut corrugated panels to size with a mat knife or a utility knife. Thinner cardboard panels can be cut with a pair of scissors. These panels can now be used as templates for making duplicate panels.

SODA CAN CASTLES
BUILDING SYSTEM

This method of quickly building medium-size to large-scale structures is super simple—once you figure out how to attach one soda can to another without disturbing the positions of the cans already in place. This building system requires good dexterity, takes some practice, and also takes a lot of empty soda cans, so start collecting now.

Soda cans are designed to stack firmly one on top of another, so they easily make tall, cylindrical columns. Using large rubber bands, you can build many columns side by side to construct soda-can walls, and the walls can be connected to make large models of walled structures like castles, play gardens, and forts. And although the building technique is simple, having a helper makes construction a lot easier, as one builder holds a can in place while the other builder attaches the rubber band connectors.

SYSTEM FEATURES

- Soda cans are readily available
- Most soda cans are the same modular shape
- Walls can be straight or curvy
- Good for medium-size to large-scale structures
- Can be reused (or recycled)
- Structures are weatherproof for outdoor play
- Cans come in many colors and graphic designs

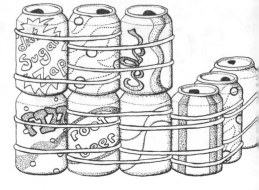

Construction

Builder's age
7+

Player's age
7+

Materials

☐ Empty soda cans

For small- to medium-size constructions, you will need at least one hundred empty cans, and large constructions will take several hundred cans.

☐ No. 33 size rubber bands

This size rubber band measures about 3 1/2″ × 1/8″. You will need about one-and-a-half times as many rubber bands as the number of cans being used.

Tools

☐ Hands only

Building techniques

Collect empty soda cans that are not bent, crushed, or distorted. Push the opening tab flush with the top of each can, or remove the tab by bending it back and forth a few times until it breaks off. And be sure to rinse the cans before using them.

If you want to create a more durable set of reusable soda can blocks, the empty cans can be filled with expanding polyurethane foam sealant to make them uncrushable but still light in weight. See the Locking Logs and Timber Columns building system for foaming instructions.

Although soda cans stack and nest nicely with one atop another, a single column of stacked cans is not very sturdy. To create a more rigid structure, you must build horizontally as well as vertically, using rubber bands as connectors to hold the cans together.

Begin by building a long wall only one can high. The wall can be straight, curved, or even bent at sharp angles. Following the illustrations, connect the cans with rubber bands, being sure that each rubber band is stretched around only two cans. (Trying to stretch the rubber band around three or more cans could crush the cans or cause the rubber band to break.)

After completing the first length of wall, build another just like it, and place the second course, or layer, on top of the first. The two courses are not attached, but should fit and stay together fairly well. You can continue building the wall higher by adding additional courses until the wall becomes wobbly.

To build a more rigid wall, the connected cans will need to be two-cans deep or staggered so they can be connected to each other both horizontally and vertically.

You might find it easier to build a staggered-can wall by starting the construction on a table or floor with the cans laying on their sides, and then standing the wall up when completed. Follow the illustrations for connecting the cans with rubber bands.

Once you have mastered the building technique, try building a walled structure as tall as you are. This building system is especially well suited for building castles with thick walls, peep-window openings, and notched crenellations. Other ideal system structures include a low-wall play garden and a tall, round tower.

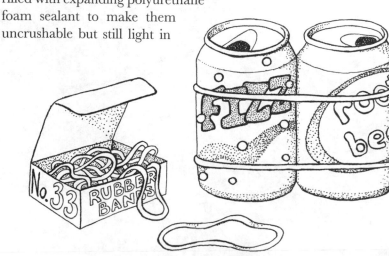

BRICK AND BLOCK MOLDING METHODS

If you haven't found a brick or block that's just right for the model you want to build, these building systems show ways to mold your own bricks and blocks. All the recipes for Kitchen Clay and Concrete Blocks use common ingredients to make a variety of concrete-like substances that can be mixed, molded, and shaped into miniature versions of natural stone, concrete, and many commercial bricks and blocks. Most of these molded bricks and blocks need to dry and harden in an oven or air-dry overnight before they can be used for building. One Kitchen Clay can be mixed and used in minutes because it is meant to stay soft like putty. Depending on what methods you choose, you may need to plan ahead and make a supply of bricks or blocks at least a day in advance of building.

Building with Snow and Sand Mound Molds doesn't require any advance work except for maybe planning a trip to the beach or watching the local forecast for snow. Then all you do need are a few empty containers to use for molds. Deciding what to build with molds of sand or snow seems to always happen instinctively.

Molding Gel-O-Cube Blocks in an ice-cube tray produces modular and uniformly shaped building blocks with two parallel sides and four tapered sides. This unique shape easily allows the slightly sticky stacked blocks to form curves, arches, and domes. With two trays of bricks, you can build a model Gel-O-Cube Igloo that's assembled the same way an Inuit might build a real igloo. And even though the special Gel-O-Cube Blocks formula produces bricks and blocks that are extremely tough and durable for building and play, any special size blocks can be easily cut to shape with a table knife.

BUILD IT

KITCHEN CLAY AND CONCRETE BLOCKS	430
SNOW AND SAND MOUND MOLDS	434
GEL-O-CUBE BLOCKS	437
GEL-O-CUBE IGLOO	439

KITCHEN CLAY AND CONCRETE BLOCKS
BUILDING SYSTEM

Commercial bricks and blocks are molded in a variety of shapes, sizes, and colors for different types of building projects. For building models and small-scale structures, you can mold your own bricks and blocks with the special features you need most, all made with common kitchen ingredients. Using special recipes, you can manufacture soft bricks that can be shaped like clay and colored to resemble red bricks or gray granite. Some Kitchen Clay and Concrete Blocks stay soft and pliable, some air-dry or dry hard in the sun (although it may take days), and one can be baked hard as a rock. Some recipes require cooking, some don't. Some have a smooth surface texture, while another is rough. Some recipes are better for molding small blocks just right for construction details, and others make larger blocks ideal for the youngest builder's hands.

SYSTEM FEATURES

See the specific features listed for each of these building systems:

- Sawdust Clay
- Bread Clay
- Kitchen Concrete
- Funny Flour Putty

Construction

Builder's age
  See building system.

Player's age
  See building system.

Materials

See building system.

Tools

See building system.

Building techniques

(for all building system recipes)

Shaping and molding

Kitchen Clays can be shaped and formed using the same building techniques for modeling store-bought clay. You can press or roll the clay into a flat sheet, then cut out slabs that can be joined at the edges to construct forms. Clay can also be rolled flat and cut into shapes with cookie cutters. Use a drinking straw to poke a string hanging hole through a piece to make it an ornament.

The clay can be rolled back and forth into long "ropes" or "snakes" that can then be coiled and stacked into walls or hollow structures. To form bowls, push with your thumbs together into the center of a large ball of clay, then pull and shape the sides, using your thumbs and fingertips.

A few Kitchen Clays are good for molding into shapes. You might try using gelatin molds, candy molds, decoratively shaped ice-cube trays, marzipan molds, butter molds, or molds you make yourself by forming a piece of aluminum foil. It's a good idea to dust the mold lightly with flour before pressing the clay into place. Depending on the recipe you are using, bake the molded pieces hard, let them air-dry in the sun, or pop them out of the mold while still soft.

Storing

With the exception of Sawdust Clay (which can get moldy if stored damp), store unused and unhardened Kitchen Clay and Concrete in a sealed plastic bag or in an airtight container. Also, keep it stored in a cool place or in the refrigerator. Hardened pieces and constructions do not require any special storage.

Drying

Not all Kitchen Clay and Concrete constructions are meant to harden for keeping. One of the fun features of most clays is that you can build something, squash it back into a ball, and then build something else. If you do want to keep what you've built, it could take at least a week and often longer for the object to air-dry and harden without heat. Air-drying time depends on the humidity and the thickness of the object being dried. Drying time can be shortened a bit by placing the item in direct sunlight or in a warm spot near a stove or a heating vent.

Selecting which clay to use

The different system features of each recipe can help you decide what to build. Sawdust Clay, for example, makes relatively large hand-formed objects without much detail, and Kitchen Concrete is a good choice for producing modular blocks. If you have a construction idea in mind, review the features for all recipes to see which one will work best.

SAWDUST CLAY

This clay is easy to mix and fun to form with your hands and fingers, but it is not the best choice for making small parts or showing details.

SYSTEM FEATURES

- Has a rough, dry texture
- Easy to handle, shape, and mold
- Can be air-dried or sun dried
- Becomes hard when fully dry
- Can be sanded and painted
- Easy cleanup

Construction

Builder's age

7+

Player's age

4+

Materials

☐ Sawdust (Do not use sawdust from chemically treated wood.)

☐ Flour

☐ Water

Tools

☐ Large bowl or small bucket

☐ Wooden mixing spoon

Recipe

1. In a large bowl or bucket, mix together two parts sawdust and one part flour. As you blend the ingredients, remove any large sawdust pieces that could make the clay too lumpy.

2. While stirring, pour in small amounts of water, a little at a time, until the mixture reaches a stiff but squishy consistency. Add small amounts of additional flour or water as needed until the consistency is right.

3. The clay now needs to be kneaded for the gluten in the flour to become elastic and hold the sawdust together. Using your hands, knead the mixture in the mixing bowl or on a protected tabletop. Continue kneading until the clay becomes easy to shape.

4. When dried in the sun, Sawdust Clay becomes very hard and can be smoothed and shaped with sandpaper, as well as painted.

BREAD CLAY

This is a good choice for sculpting small figures, forming small parts, and showing fine details. Bread Clay is especially well suited for making colorful beads of many sizes and mosaic tiles of various shapes.

SYSTEM FEATURES

• Has a stiff and sticky texture
• Easy to handle, but not to mold
• Sticks to most anything
• Can be air dried or sun dried
• Becomes hard when fully dry
• Good for forming small objects
• Keeps for days in a refrigerator

Construction

Builder's age
6+

Player's age
6+

Materials
☐ Dry, stale white bread
☐ White glue
☐ Food coloring (optional)

Tools
☐ Medium-size bowl
☐ Wooden mixing spoon
☐ Tablespoon-size measuring spoon

Recipe

1. Remove the crust from all sides of three or more pieces of stale white bread, and break or crumble the bread into small pieces directly into a medium-size bowl.

2. Add white glue to the bowl, about one tablespoon for each slice of bread. If you choose to add food coloring, mix it thoroughly with the glue first.

3. Mix well with a spoon, then knead with your fingers until the clay is soft and pliable. If the clay is too sticky to work with, add a little more bread. If your clay is too crumbly, add a bit more glue. When the mixture is very stiff and easily stays together, it is ready to use immediately. Bread Clay is very sticky and difficult to handle unless you keep your hands and tools wet while rolling the clay, cutting parts, or molding forms. Also, use a wet finger or utensil to smooth surfaces.

4. Wash the mixing bowl and the utensils before the Bread Clay begins to dry. Any unused clay can be put in a small container with a tight-fitting lid, and stored in the refrigerator for a few days.

KITCHEN CONCRETE

This is an excellent material for making both small and large parts that are cut to exact shapes and especially for making a lot of modular blocks in all shapes, sizes, and thicknesses. Kitchen Concrete mixes well and is easily rolled into flat sheets of any thickness. The sheets can be sliced into panels, strips, blocks, or any shape with a table knife, or you might use a cookie cutter, a melon scooper, or the rim of a glass to stamp out specific shapes. Kitchen Concrete also forms well in molds of any size, as long as the mold can be heated in the oven and the hardened piece be removed. This generous recipe makes enough Kitchen Concrete to try many things.

SYSTEM FEATURES

• Has a soft, smooth texture
• Easy to manipulate and shape
• Molds well into any form
• Becomes hard when baked dry
• Dried pieces can be painted

Construction

Builder's age
6+ (adult required if objects are baked hard)

Player's age
6+

Materials
☐ 2 1/2 cups flour
☐ 1 cup salt
☐ 1 cup water

Tools

- ☐ Large mixing bowl
- ☐ Wooden mixing spoon
- ☐ Baking sheet
- ☐ Table knife, rolling pin, cookie cutters, and molds (optional)

Recipe

1. Combine the flour and salt in a mixing bowl.

2. Add the water and mix thoroughly with a spoon. Do not add extra water to aid in mixing.

3. Using your hands, knead the mixture in the bowl for three to five minutes until it becomes smooth and ready to use.

   You can mold, roll, cut, form, and sculpt with this clay-like substance. If the mixture is a bit sticky, you may need a dusting of flour on the work surface, on the rolling pin, and on your hands. Use cookie cutters or a table knife to cut out shapes you want.

Baking constructions hard

1. Place your Kitchen Concrete creations on a baking sheet, and bake them in the oven for three hours at 250°. Don't bake at a higher temperature or the dried pieces will become misshapen. As the Kitchen Concrete bakes and hardens, it may puff up a little and soften sharp edges and fine details.

2. After removing the tray from the oven, allow the baked objects to cool. Thick objects may need some extra time to air-dry completely.

FUNNY FLOUR PUTTY

Although objects and constructions built with the other Kitchen Clay and Concrete Blocks are meant to eventually dry and permanently harden, Funny Flour Putty uses a recipe that keeps the putty soft and pliable for several weeks. That makes this putty excellent for shaping forms and building structures that can be played with until the putty is squeezed back into a ball to make something else, or saved in a sealed plastic bag for the next play session. Anything you do leave out to dry will harden a little but become brittle.

SYSTEM FEATURES

- Has a stiff, sticky texture
- Easy to handle but not to mold
- Sticks to most anything
- Can be air-dried or sun dried
- Good for forming small objects
- Keeps for days in a refrigerator

Construction

Builder's age

7+ (adult or adult supervision required for cooking)

Player's age

3+

Materials

- ☐ 1 cup flour
- ☐ ½ cup salt
- ☐ 2 teaspoons cream of tartar
- ☐ 1 tablespoon salad oil
- ☐ 1 cup water
- ☐ Food coloring
- ☐ Glitter (optional)

Tools

- ☐ Large saucepan
- ☐ Mixing bowl
- ☐ Wooden mixing spoon
- ☐ Table knife, rolling pin, cookie cutters, and molds (optional)

Recipe

1. In a cold saucepan, combine the flour, salt, and cream of tartar, and mix them well.

2. In a mixing bowl, combine the oil, water, and food coloring, stirring well.

3. Pour the liquid ingredients into the saucepan, and stir everything together thoroughly with a wooden spoon while heating the mixture on medium. Stir constantly to prevent sticking.

4. The mixture will stay soupy for several minutes, then suddenly it will firm up and stick together. When it all thickens into a ball, remove the saucepan from the heat and continue stirring.

5. Dump the hot ball out onto a countertop (use a dusting of flour to keep it from sticking), let it cool just enough for safe handling, then begin kneading the ball as it cools further and becomes a moldable play putty.

   Funny Flour Putty is very much like a store-bought moldable dough, only a little softer. The putty will last for months if kept in a sealed container in a cool place. Small objects left out to be air-dried will stiffen somewhat, but they will eventually crumble.

SNOW AND SAND MOUND MOLDS
BUILDING SYSTEM

Some types of building seem to happen instinctively. Wherever you find a stretch of sand or a mound of snow, most kids can't resist the spontaneous temptation to dig, stack, carve, and mold the material into a castle, fort, igloo, or cave. Sometimes your hands are the only tools you need for building with snow (wearing gloves, of course), but for building snow structures out of snow blocks, you will need a few plastic buckets and containers to use for molds. And for sand play at the beach or in the sandbox, just collect several sand molds, add a supply of water to dampen the sand, and the building can begin. All types of containers can become the forms to mold building blocks from snow or damp sand, and each mold will form its own special type of brick or block.

SYSTEM FEATURES

- Almost any small container can be used as a mold
- Molds are available in many shapes and sizes
- Molds can also be used as part of the structure

Construction

Builder's age
2+

Materials
☐ Snow on the ground, or

☐ A sandy beach or a sandbox

Tools
☐ Molds (See the suggestions listed below for common containers that make good molds.)

☐ Kitchen scissors (optional)

Building techniques

The containers used for Snow and Sand Mound Molds are frequently whatever you find at the beach or sand "construction site" unless you plan ahead and bring them with you. Just make sure each container or other type of mold you use is thoroughly clean and is safe to handle, with no sharp edges or rust.

Most kids already know how to use a mold. Pack it flush to the top with snow or damp sand, flip it over quickly and set it firmly, then carefully lift the mold to reveal the building-block mound. Containers with slightly tapered sides tend to work best, because the taper allows the mold to be easily removed once it has been turned over to set the mound. Only damp sand will hold its molded shape once the mold has been removed. For cold-weather building, snow that makes good snowballs is also the best snow for molding snow blocks.

When choosing or finding the molds you plan to use, think about the size of your construction site and the scale of your planned snow or sand structures. Some small molds, like a 35 mm film canister or an ice-cube tray, are obviously best for making blocks to build small stacked structures or to use as decorations on larger structures. Plastic buckets and other large molds make large-scale castles and forts, but a large bucket of sand can be quite heavy. The easiest-to-use molds are medium-size containers. They also can be found in the greatest variety of forms and make the greatest variety of structures.

These are some common containers that make good Snow and Sand Mound Molds.

Big molds
small trash cans

plastic wastepaper baskets

small buckets

plastic storage boxes

Medium molds
wet-wipes containers

plastic flowerpots

frozen food trays

milk cartons (with an end cut off)

plastic tubs from take-out food

plastic drinking cups

yogurt containers

soup cans

plastic tubs from margarine

cake pans

food storage containers

funnels

Small molds
ice-cube tray

spray-can tops

gelatin molds

muffin tins

film canisters

mini medicine cups

bottle caps

clam shells

Once your snow or sand structure is built, you may want to add drawn decorations to the surfaces. These are a few handy texture tools you might easily find.

Texture tools

- comb
- pinecone
- shoe treads
- plastic fork
- seashells

Building a backyard beach

If you can't make it to the beach, bring the beach to your own backyard. It's easy to designate an area for sand play, or you may want to put up a simple wood barrier or other type of edging to confine the sand play area—and the sand. Here are a few other precautions and suggestions.

Use clean beach sand rather than builder's sand. Both types are inexpensive, good for sand structures, and commonly available at building supply centers. However, builder's sand will dirty clothes.

Don't make the sand play area too small. Several friends will usually want to join you for

play in the sand, and each one will want to have room for building.

Instead of a sandbox, consider making a sand pile that can either be gathered into a mound or spread out. If you live in a windy location, you may need a plastic tarp to cover most of the sand. Just tuck

all the edges of the tarp under the sand to also keep it from being blown away.

To create a more permanent and easily contained sand play area, consider making a sand pit. The size and shape can vary, but do make the pit about two feet deep to allow digging and burrowing down into the sand. If the ground in your area does not drain well, dig the pit another foot deeper and put a one-foot-deep base of stones under the sand. This will act as a holding area for excess water and help keep the sand above from becoming a watery slush. A short wall around the sand pit will not only keep wind from blowing the sand away, it will also serve as a good sand-building workbench.

GEL-O-CUBE BLOCKS
BUILDING SYSTEM

Using a special recipe for preparing a gelatin desert mix plus an ice-cube tray for a mold, you can make small, sticky Gel-O-Cube Blocks that are perfect for stacking and building model structures with curves. The four tapered sides of a Gel-O-Cube Block allow the modular building pieces to be stacked on their sides to quickly create curved, arched, and dome structures. The blocks can also be stacked straight up on their flat, parallel tops and bottoms. And if you need a special shape, the blocks can simply be cut to size using a table knife. The slightly sticky surfaces of the blocks will hold the stacked blocks firmly in position.

Gel-O-Cube Blocks and the structures you build with them will keep for several weeks at room temperature and even longer if stored in the refrigerator. The blocks are surprisingly durable and can be assembled and disassembled over and over again. You can also build and eat Gel-O-Cube Block structures, as long as you eat them right away or refrigerate them right after building to be eaten later.

SYSTEM FEATURES

- Tapered sides help form curves, arches, and domes
- Special shapes are easily cut with a table knife
- The slightly sticky surfaces keep blocks in position
- Blocks can be molded in a variety of gelatin colors
- Blocks are very durable for repeated use
- Structures can be saved or immediately eaten

Construction

Builder's age

7+ (adult supervision required for cooking)

Materials

For each tray of cubes:

☐ Two 3-ounce packages of gelatin dessert mix such as Jell-O, in any flavor

☐ Three ¼-ounce packets (or approximately three tablespoons) clear, unflavored gelatin, such as Knox

☐ 1¼ cups water

Tools

☐ Mixing bowl

☐ Mixing spoon

☐ Measuring cup

☐ Pot or kettle

☐ Plastic ice-cube trays

☐ Table knife

Building techniques

1. Assemble all the ingredients for filling one ice-cube tray. Empty the contents of the gelatin dessert packages and the unflavored gelatin packets into a mixing bowl and stir with a spoon.

2. Heat 1¼ cups of water to a boil in a pot or kettle on the stove (or in an appropriate container in a microwave oven). Add the boiling water to the bowl of ingredients and immediately begin to stir the mixture. Continue to stir slowly (don't make any bubbles) for about three minutes.

3. Pour the mixture into a plastic ice-cube tray, carefully filling each cube mold to the same level, but try not to let the tops of the cubes run all together. It may be easier to first pour the mix-

ture into a measuring cup and then into the tray. Get rid of any bubbles that form on the surface by poking them with any utensil. Warning: The mixture will be very hot.

4. Place the filled ice-cube tray in the refrigerator (not the freezer), and wait at least one hour for the mixture to fully set.

5. To remove the cubes, use your finger or a table knife to push into a corner of a cube and scoop it out. The gelatin in the bricks makes them a bit sticky, so you may have to pry them out. The bricks are rather tough and can take a lot of abuse, so prying should not damage them.

A few more recipe tips

Before making a second batch of cubes, first wash and dry the bowl, tray, and all utensils. Any damaged or badly shaped blocks can be melted in a pot and poured back into the mold.

If you want extra-firm and tough blocks, increase the amount of unflavored gelatin to four packets per batch. However, you will need to work more quickly when stir-

ring the mixture and pouring it into the tray molds because the extra gelatin will cause the mixture to begin turning firm after only a few minutes of mixing.

As an alternative to using a flavored gelatin dessert mix to make colored blocks, you can make clear, rubbery, extra-tough blocks using only unflavored gelatin with no Jell-O added. These clear gelatin bricks can withstand a lot of abuse, and can be bounced around on a table or floor with little or no damage. And they even remain firm when left out of the refrigerator for a long time. For this modified recipe, use four packets of unflavored gelatin and a pinch of sugar to each 1¼ cups of boiling water. The sugar prevents the gelatin from clumping. The clear blocks will have all the features of Gel-O-Cube blocks, except they won't taste very good.

Building tips

If the room temperature is too warm while building, the cubes might begin to soften and sag a little and require refrigeration to make them firm again.

If the cubes become a little wet after being refrigerated in a closed container, simply pat the blocks dry with a towel before using them.

Cubes saved at room temperature for any period of time or in the refrigerator for more than a few days are still fine for building, but not for eating.

GEL-O-CUBE BLOCKS
BUILD-IT PROJECT
GEL-O-CUBE IGLOO

GEL-O-CUBE IGLOO

The miniature blocks formed in an ice-cube tray with tapered sides are the perfect shape needed for building a model igloo. However, ice-cube blocks made of frozen water are just too slippery for stacking and too difficult to shape into smaller sizes. Besides, real igloos are made from blocks of packed snow, not from blocks of ice. Using the blocks from two trays of Gel-O-Cube Blocks, you can build a miniature igloo that is constructed not too differently than a real Inuit igloo. The completed igloo can be used to create an Arctic setting for your small action figures or maybe served for dessert surrounded by whipped-cream "snow."

Construction

Building system
Gel-O-Cube Blocks

Builder's age
7+ (adult supervision required for cooking)

Player's age
5+

Materials
☐ Two ice-cube trays of Gel-O-Cube Bricks
☐ Large plate or cookie sheet

Tools
☐ Table knife

Building instructions

To build a model igloo, you will need at least twenty-eight Gel-O-Cube Blocks, which is about the number of blocks made in two ice-cube trays. Use same-size blocks you have already made or mold two trays of blocks following the recipe and directions for the Gel-O-Cube Blocks building system.

Notice that each molded block has a larger top than bottom, plus two long, tapered sides and two short, tapered sides.

1. Begin by making a ring of blocks on a large plate or any flat surface. All the blocks should be placed lying on their long trapezoidal sides, and the tapered end of each block should be flat against the adjoining blocks on either side. The tapered angle of the block ends will help shape the size of the base ring, which should use about nine to eleven blocks. Because the blocks have a taper on four sides, notice how the top surface of the ring leans slightly inward towards its center.

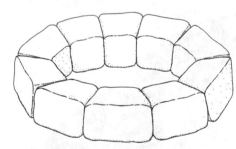

2. Add a second ring of blocks on top the first ring, again laying the blocks on their trapezoidal sides. The second ring will be smaller and lean inward even more, and adjacent blocks will not fit as tightly as they did in the base ring. Don't try to compress the blocks for a better fit or other joints might push apart. If the space for the last block in the second ring is smaller than a full block, use a table knife to trim the block to fit the space.

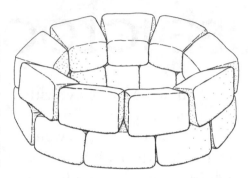

3. Add a third ring on top the second ring. However, as the blocks lean even farther inward, you may have to hold some of these blocks in place until you have added the last block in the ring. Trim the last block as needed to fit.

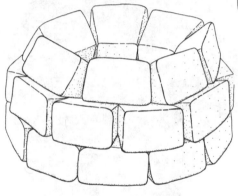

4. Continue to add another row or two until the igloo dome form is complete. The exact number of rows needed will depend on the size of the blocks and the tapered angle of their sides. You have completed the last row when there is space for just one block to fill the opening remaining at the top of the igloo.

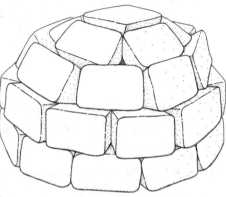

5. In a real igloo, a ventilation hole is left open at the top, and the entrance is built with more blocks in the shape of a low tunnel. If you are an ambitious builder, use a table knife to cut out an arch-shaped opening in the side of the igloo, and try building the entrance tunnel, using smaller cut and shaped blocks.

ROADSIDE IGLOO EATERIES

Beginning in the 1930s when paved roads first connected every state and city in America, roadside gas stations, motels, and diners were built along the way to service travelers. To get the attention of passing motorists, some establishments were built to look like peculiar attractions. A motel cabin might look like a tepee, a caboose, or a tropical hut. Motorists approaching a gas station might first see a giant-size tire with a lookout tower on top. And roadside eateries might resemble anything from a giant hotdog or chuck wagon to an oversize igloo.

Of course, rather than being true igloos made from blocks of packed snow, these commercial buildings were simple domes fabricated from conventional building materials and decorated to look like igloos. However, unlike most other examples of whimsical *autotecture*, the dome structures of these igloo eateries were also designed to be very functional and relatively inexpensive to construct.

Jerry's Catfish House

The temperature in Florence, Mississippi, rarely drops below freezing, so Jerry and Wanda Bridges chose to build an igloo style restaurant in 1985 because the big, snow-white dome would certainly attract attention. They also chose a dome shape, rather than a conventional rectangular building, because it was more resistant to tornados and used less energy for air-conditioning and heat.

The shell structure of the dome is made from a concrete material called gunite that is more typically

used to form the walls of a swimming pool. To construct this dome shape, the gunite was poured over a huge, inflated, canvas balloon, and the outside of the finished building was painted white to resemble an igloo. Inside the igloo, there are two levels that seat nearly three hundred people.

Jerry's Catfish House is still thriving as a popular attraction and eatery. And the igloo dome structure has also become a perennial inspiration for local school science projects.

The Igloo Diner

The inspiration for this long-gone, double-igloo eatery was pure showmanship. When Ralph Grossman and Ernie Hughes decided to build a diner at a busy intersection in Seattle, Washington, they wanted a design that would grab the attention—and business—of passing motorists. Hughes suggested an igloo, and Grossman supposedly responded, "How about two igloos?"

The twin side-by-side domes, each with a row of windows all around, were fabricated from sheets of shiny steel and joined by a stereo-

typical igloo tunnel that served as an entrance. Above the entrance, an ice-blue neon sign displayed the Igloo name, a smiling Eskimo face, and the slogan "Good Food."

The Igloo diner and drive-in restaurant opened on Halloween day in 1940 and almost immediately became a local hangout. For nearly fifteen years, the Igloo served Husky Burgers and Boeing Bombers to faithful local patrons, but by 1955 the diner was out of business. The building was torn down in 1960.

Igloo Soft Freeze

This ice cream stand in Everett, Pennsylvania, is painted to look like a big scoop of vanilla dripping with chocolate sauce, with a red cherry sitting on top. As its name implies, the dome-shaped building is also intended to remind customers of a frozen igloo.

Directly behind the Igloo Soft Freeze building, there is an oval dome structure that originally housed the construction company that built the round igloo eatery. Both domes are fabricated from triangular fiberglass panels that are bolted together, covered with insulation, and sealed with epoxy paint. According to the current occupants, the theme might evoke a chillingly cold igloo, but the dome is toasty warm inside even in the winter.

PANEL AND PLANE STRUCTURES

UNDERSTANDING PANEL
AND PLANE STRUCTURES

BUILDING WITH PANELS
AND PLANES

UNDERSTANDING PANEL AND PLANE STRUCTURES

PANELS AND PLANES FORM
STRENGTH AND BEAUTY

THE STRUCTURAL ELEMENTS OF
PANELS AND PLANES

ALL KINDS OF TENTS WITH ALL
KINDS OF USES

PANELS AND PLANES FORM STRENGTH AND BEAUTY

The simple concept of making a large, flat roof by fabricating a rigid panel or slab has always been a popular method of building shelter. One of the first structures made by early civilizations was a flat-roof canopy used to protect gatherings of people from the rain or sun. This simple roof was usually made by weaving long branches into an open square grid. At each place two branches met or crossed, they were tied tightly together using strings of plant fibers. The rigid grid now formed a flat plane that could be raised up to become a roof. The woven slab was so rigid that it only needed support at the edges. The significant advantage of this type of structure was the unobstructed openness of the entire space under the canopy. To create more shade from the sunlight, smaller branches and twigs could be woven to fill in the open grid. To keep out rain or snow, animal hides could also be draped over the grid.

In modern slab construction, the concept hasn't changed, but the materials available are immensely stronger and more durable. Slabs are often made from reinforced concrete panels that have been formed in molds. Once the concrete has hardened, the slabs are hoisted into place to rest on support columns at the corners. In many of these buildings, the columns are erected first and then the concrete slabs for each floor are added one floor at a time from the top down.

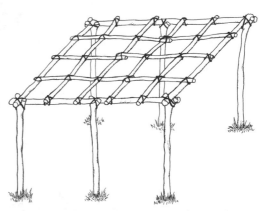

Slab construction has evolved from fabricating flat panels using a grid of branches to molding large panels of reinforced concrete.

Curves and Bends Make Shapes and Shells

The flat, rigid slab provides many advantages in a structure where a flat surface is needed to cover a broad expanse—like the floors of a multistory office building. But in other structures, like a roof where the slab or plane does not have to be flat, simply adding some curvature to the slab will allow it to resist much more force. Adding curvature to any thin, flat sheet of material provides both stiffness and strength, and allows structures to be formed in a large variety of thin shapes and shell forms.

Just look at the curved surfaces of a car's doors, hood, roof, and fenders.

These panels were all formed from thin, flat, flimsy sheets of material, and it is their bends, curves, and twists that make them rigid structures. Not only are these thin-plane shapes very strong structures, but they are also quite pleasant to look at. The shape of curvature that provides the ideal amount of structure also seems to be a pleasing form that mimics the curves found in nature.

Thin-shell panels and curved plane shapes can also be molded in cast iron, reinforced concrete, plastics, and a few other materials to create some immensely strong shapes that are often used as roofs, towers, and other architectural structures. A few have visually descriptive names like the barrel vault roof, which consists of one or a series of thin-shelled, half-barrel-shaped arches, or the saddle roof or the butterfly roof, both of which have elegant shapes and proportions. But most plane shapes are described by their technical names, like a rotational hyperboloid (the typical shape of the large cooling tower at a nuclear power plant) and the pretty common hyperbolic paraboloid (a saddle shape often referred to as a hypar saddle).

The combined architectural strength and beauty of curved- and angled-panel structures has inspired architects and engineers to produce several bold designs. A thin-shell dome can cover a stadium that holds eighty thousand people. Thin-shell structures have been used to construct large

Thin-shell structures are commonly found in nature.

Although constructed from thin materials, these shapes and forms are rigid because of their bends and curves.

dams, spiral stairways, and giant smokestacks, saving both material and weight over most other building methods. A properly curved cantilevered roof, for example, can dramatically extend straight out nearly fifty feet even though it is attached only at one end and is only a few inches thick.

The special features of curved panel and thin-shell construction include:

- Builds extremely lightweight structures in proportion to their size

- Very economical use of material for the size and strength of the structure

- A large variety of strong and rigid forms are possible that cannot be built using any other method of construction

- Structures can cover a large area with support needed only at the perimeter

- Curved forms can be made in a variety of shapes that are pleasing and natural looking

- Shells can be formed, fabricated, or molded using many types of materials

- Offers oppertunities for new shapes and designs

Shell structures are often used in architecture for their combined strength and pleasing appearance.

THE SYDNEY OPERA HOUSE

The spectacular opera house located in Sydney Harbor, Australia, has become one of the most recognizable national symbols in the world. The distinctive overlapping shell shapes of this structure form an impressive and graceful sculpture from whatever angle it is viewed. From the outside, each giant shell appears to be balanced only on two points, without pillars to keep it from falling over. But smaller, barely noticeable shells under the larger shells face in the opposite direction and support the structure with great rigidity.

Beneath the shells that serve as both roof and side walls for three unconnected buildings are five separate halls that include an opera house, a symphony concert hall, a smaller hall for chamber music, a theater for stage performances, and an exhibition hall. Also under the shells are three restaurants, a library, dressing rooms for performers, plus several other rooms and spaces. In fact, the opera house alone has nearly one thousand rooms.

However, building this daring design was far from easy; it required new methods of construction and fourteen years to complete. Along the way there were many problems and controversies that changed the architect's original design, including the use of the spaces inside. The completed structures also cost more than twelve times the original construction estimate.

The project began in 1957 when a little known thirty-eight-year-old Danish architect named Jorn Utzon entered and won a competition to design a performing arts center for the city of Sydney, Australia. Utzon had previously designed only a few private homes and housing projects, but his concepts were more visually exciting than anything else submitted. Most other designs in the competition used conventional methods of construction. Even though Utzon's radical and strikingly original design would certainly be more difficult to construct, the judging committee thought it was the only one that had the potential to become one of the great architectural wonders of the world.

The proposed site for the opera house was a point of land jutting out into Sydney Harbor like a big stage. One of the exciting features of Utzon's proposed design was that the sculptural forms creating the buildings looked like an array of billowing white sails that could be viewed by pedestrians walking around the site, by peo-

The Sydney Opera House
Sydney, Australia
Designed by Jorn Utzon
Completed 1973

ple on boats entering the harbor, and even by passengers in planes flying overhead.

One big problem was that Utzon had submitted only sketches of his idea that did not reveal or explain how the daring shell structures of his proposed design could actually be built. Nonetheless, the design seemed so exciting to government officials that two years later, in 1959, they authorized construction to begin even though Utzon and the engineers hired for the project had still not figured out how to build the structural shells that formed the many roofs and walls of the building.

The exact shapes that Utzon had sketched were too complicated to actually build, so some alterations had to be made. Instead of using

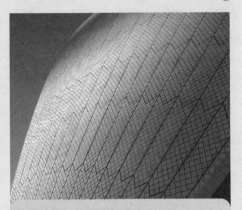

More than one million white ceramic tiles cover the outside of the entire shells.

the conventional method for forming shell structures by building temporary wood or steel molds, then filling them with concrete, engineers decided to try a new technique they thought would be easier, faster, and less expensive. The shell shapes were constructed of many modular prefabricated concrete ribs that were cast in sections on the ground, hoisted into

place by a tower crane, and attached together with steel rods and mortar. Altogether it took more than two thousand ribs to complete the basic shape of the shells.

The giant bare concrete shells were then covered with more than a million ceramic tiles to give the structure a gleaming, bright-white appearance. Instead of laying the tiles in place one at a time, workers prefabricated large sections in curved panels that were hoisted up by a crane and bolted to the concrete shells.

The open ends of the shells were enclosed by large glass walls that formed curved and creased planes. Each glass wall was made of many panels of glass and plastic supported by vertical steel posts, or mullions, with horizontal bronze bars between panels. Altogether there were more than two thousand panes of glass in seven hundred different sizes. The use of plastic sandwiched between two glass panes in each panel helped both to quiet outside noises from being heard inside the building and to reduce the danger of a broken glass pane from falling inside.

By 1966, construction was well under way, but Utzon was being blamed for enormous cost overruns and constant engineering difficulties. The government asked

him to reduce his role in the project, but he refused and quit. He left Australia and never returned to see the finished building.

Although the exterior shapes of the shells were completed much as Utzon had originally envisioned them, a new architectural team formed by the government made many changes to the planned interior spaces. By 1973, the completed building was opened to the public

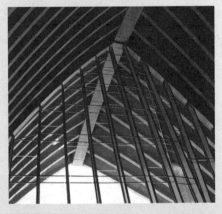

and immediately received praise from architectural critics all over the world. However, only sixteen years later, the building began to deteriorate, with tiles falling off, glass walls leaking rain, and the concrete ribs weakening. Though the cost of repairs nearly equaled the original cost of construction, the people of Australia were determined to maintain the building that had become one of their national symbols at any price.

THE STRUCTURAL ELEMENTS OF PANELS AND PLANES

Straight beams made of any material can span relatively short distances without sagging or breaking. The crossbar of a football goalpost or a log spanning the opposite banks of a stream to form a simple bridge are good examples. To make the log bridge wider, you could just add several more logs side by side and tie them together. Using a lot of straight branches laid flat side by side, you could also make a simple roof or shelter. If all those branches are tied together tightly, you have created a rigid panel called a plane or a plate.

Steel reinforcing rods, commonly called rebar, allow large concrete slabs to be strong in tension and support heavy loads.

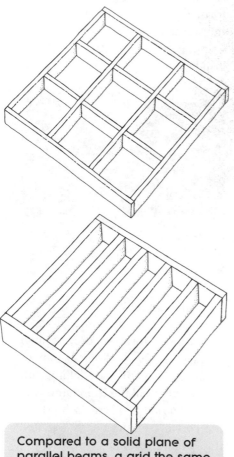

Compared to a solid plane of parallel beams, a grid the same size is stronger, even though they both use the same number of beams and the grid beams are lighter.

A plane constructed as a grid of beams will be stronger than a plane made from beams lined up in the same direction. The intersections of an open grid using beams connected at right angles to form squares create a rigid, strong, and lightweight panel. Compared to a heavier solid plane of parallel beams, the grid does not need to support as much of its own structure weight in addition to other loads placed on it.

When a load is placed anywhere on the grid, the grid will tend to sag, or deflect, at that point. However, if the same load were placed on parallel beams instead of the grid, the beams would tend to sag even more. The rigid grid does a better job of distributing the force of the load to the other beams. That is, all the beams in a grid share in supporting the weight, so the grid can support more weight.

Using modern building materials like concrete and steel, there are now easier ways to make rigid planes. Imagine taking a grid work plane and filling it in solid with more beams and then gluing the whole thing together. What you now have is a solid slab or plate that has all the strength properties of the grid plane. Flat slabs made of poured concrete are commonly used for floors and roofs in big buildings. Large slabs are made using reinforced concrete that has a grid work of steel rods embedded inside.

Besides having the load-distributing properties of a grid work of beams, a solid slab is actually stiffer and stronger than the grid alone because it has a continuous surface on both sides. Just like a beam, the top and bottom surfaces add stiffness and structure. Similarly, the strength of a slab comes from its thickness. If a slab is too thin and flexible, it may barely be able to support its own weight. There is also a limit to how thick a slab can be before it starts behaving more like a building block. Besides, thick slabs are not a very economical use of material.

THE SLAB HOUSES AND GEO DOMES OF ROOSEVELT, NEW JERSEY

At the height of America's industrial revolution in the 1930s, with its smokestack factories, pollution, and congested cities, many people began to long for the country life and clean air they or their parents had left behind before moving to the city. A strong "back-to-the-land movement" began in the big cities of America, and two of its most recognizable advocates were the brilliant scientist Albert Einstein and another immigrant named Benjamin Brown.

Ben Brown, along with several New York City garment-factory workers, decided to do something about improving their unhealthy living conditions. They conceived of a utopian cooperative village that would be built in the fresh air of the New Jersey countryside, away from the congestion of the city. His plan called for a small village with well-designed and affordable homes for families who would earn a living by working in the community's cooperative garment factory and on the five-hundred-acre dairy and poultry farm. The people of the community would also operate their own school and retail stores, and have their own water supply and sewage disposal systems.

Ben Brown applied to the U.S. federal government for a $500,000 loan to construct the Jersey Homesteads Cooperative Development, which would include the factory, the farm, and two hundred homes for homesteader families. Each family would contribute a $500 down payment to make up the total cost of $600,000 for the project. From the wages earned in the factory and on the farm, families could then buy their homes by paying back their portions of the government loan.

However, from the beginning of the project, very little went as planned. The first architect hired submitted designs for building everything out of tamped earth (similar to adobe). After Brown and others rejected the idea, a contractor was hired to build the factory and several houses out of prefabricated concrete slabs, but the first house built soon collapsed and the contractor abandoned the project.

The next architect, Alfred Kastner, then came up with a plan for seven different designs of Bauhaus-style homes that all used modular concrete-block and concrete-slab construction. Kastner was assisted by a young architect named Louis Kahn, who would later become one of America's most famous architects. The plan also included small parks, communal areas, and a green beltway around the entire village.

EVENING JOURNAL

Tugwellville, N. J.   Resettlement Project—
Taxpayer Will Settle Later   By T. E. Powers

The stark geometric look of these slab-roof houses was quite controversial at the time, and some critics made fun of the plan, calling the designs "pool tables," "concrete caves," and "cooking ovens." All two hundred of the Bauhaus-style homes were built, but only 120 were sold to homesteaders, in part because of the controversial style, but mainly because business at the cooperative garment factory was not going well. The other eighty houses were put up for rent. The founders' vision of a self-sufficient utopia was soon abandoned, but the spirit of the community continued to flourish.

Following the death of President Franklin D. Roosevelt in 1945, the Jersey Homesteads community renamed itself Roosevelt, and the small country village quickly gained the reputation of being an artist's colony. Roosevelt soon became the new home of many artists, academics, architects, sculptors, photographers, writers, dancers, musicians, and others who appreciated the simple yet sophisticated architectural heritage of the community. Their attitudes also influenced the next generation of housing design in the town.

In 1975, a small company selling geodesic dome buildings settled in Roosevelt, and soon after, geodesic dome structures from small studios to very large houses began appearing next to their Bauhaus-style neighbors. This revived attempt to establish a successful industry in Roosevelt employed twelve people who could prefabricate the panels for a dome in one day and erect the dome on a site in less than one week.

The company believed the artistic and intellectual community would continue to embrace innovative housing design just as the town founders had accepted the new Bauhaus design forty years earlier.

Their literature claimed that a geodesic dome house "yields more floor space at less cost, withstands greater exterior pressure, has outside walls that are maintenance free, and is easier and less expensive to heat than a conventional house." Dome living was also claimed to be "more fun and more relaxing, because the wide range of window panels available allows for more natural light giving the impression of letting the outside in." But the fad of living in a dome quickly passed, leaving only another reminder of the community's avant-garde thinking.

Not much has changed in Roosevelt since the dome-building spurt of the 1970s, except the addition of a Solar Village complex for senior citizens built in 1983. Today, about nine hundred people live in this small village in central New Jersey. The factory building now contains artist's studios, horses graze on the farmland, and slab houses and geodesic domes all remain standing in excellent condition.

Greater Strength Is Achieved Through Form

No matter what material or method is used to make a flat slab, there are limits to how much distance a particular slab can span before it begins to deflect, sag, and then collapse. However, slabs and other flat sheet materials (like paper or plywood) can be made considerably stiffer and stronger when they are given a curved shape like half a cylinder.

For example, the half-cylinder shape of the barrel vault can structurally act just like an arch when it is supported along the entire length of both its sides. The two bases of the barrel vault exert an outward thrust, so they must either be buttressed to absorb the forces of compression or be tied together with a tension rod. However, when acting as a beam, the legs do not push outward to transfer forces. Instead, the top of the half cylinder is in compression and the bottom in tension, creating a strong structural member that transfers loads straight down through the end supports. Therefore, to support the heaviest loads or to span the greatest distances, the best way to use the barrel shape is as a beam supported at both ends.

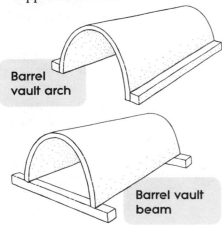

Barrel vault arch

Barrel vault beam

In a similar way, a series of parallel and connected barrel vaults act just like the side-by-side arches in a bridge or an arcade (so they help to buttress each other), and a series of barrel vaults act like structural beams when they are supported only at their ends.

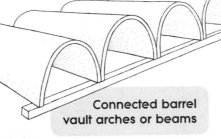

Connected barrel vault arches or beams

Another way to structurally combine two barrel vaults is at right angles, forming a cross vault, or groined vault. The large diagonal arches created by the intersection are the groins. The vault in one direction acts to buttress the vault in the other direction and vice versa, to create a strong self-supporting structure. A groined vault can cover such a large area that some buildings are designed so that their entire structure is the shape of a thin-walled groined vault.

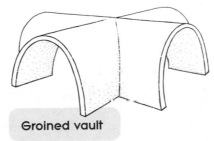

Groined vault

The folded-plate method is a simple variation of a barrel vault and is another way to achieve stiffness and strength. Instead of forming a half-round vault, several long, narrow slabs are connected by their long edges in a zigzag to form valleys and ridges. When used as a structure of connected beams supported only at the ends, the many tension and compression forces

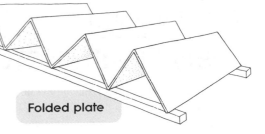

Folded plate

within the stiff structure are transferred straight down through the end supports. And there are no outward thrust forces, so the supports need no buttressing.

In comparison, however, a folded-plate structure is only about half as strong as a barrel-shaped one of the same size and material.

Thin-walled structures with compound curves are even stronger than barrel vaults. In a saddle shape, the curved surfaces go both up and down, just like the shape of a horse saddle. The double curvature of the saddle shape is called a rectangular hyperbolic paraboloid, and because it is especially stiff and strong, saddle-shaped shells can be built with incredibly thin walls that can often be used as the entire outer structure of a large building. Some saddle structures as thin as a half-inch can cover an area the size of half a football field. The structural behavior of the saddle shape is a result of the combination of tension and compression forces. The portion of the saddle that curves downward acts like an arch and is in compression, while the part of the shape that curves upward is in tension. The tension of the upward shape counters the tendency of the downward arch to spread and collapse.

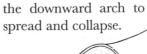

Saddle shape

GIVING STRUCTURE TO A FLAT AND FLOPPY PLANE

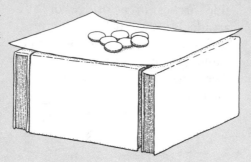

Using a few plain sheets of copier or printer paper and four thick books that are all about the same thickness and size, you can perform some simple experiments that demonstrate how thin, flat, floppy sheets of material get rigid and strong from being folded or curved into structural forms. Most of these experiments are a test of how much weight each type of paper structure can support before collapsing. You might think of each structure as a roof holding up a load of snow, or a bridge supporting itself and the weight of the traffic on it.

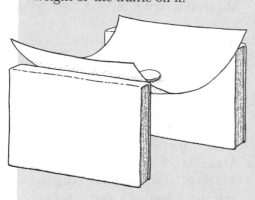

To test the load-bearing capacity of each paper span, use a supply of equal-unit weights like coins. About twenty-five nickels or fifty pennies should be enough for these tests. Carefully place and balance the coins, one at a time, on the middle of the paper structure to see how many it takes to make the span collapse. You might be surprised to find which structural shapes are the strongest.

The flat, paper-plane span test

Begin by trying to support a single sheet of paper lengthwise between two books lying flat and being used as supports at either end. How far apart can you position the books

before the paper sags and collapses? Notice that the paper sheet becomes dished and takes the shape of a curved surface as the books are moved apart. You can also create dishing by pressing down in the middle of the paper. How far apart can you move the books with three nickels paced in the middle of the paper sheet? Now try supporting the paper, using four books, one book on each side, and notice that the paper doesn't sag even if the books are near the edges of the paper. If you press down in the center of the paper, it doesn't want to sag, but instead it wants to stretch. This stretching action actually makes the paper sheet slab even stiffer and stronger. How many nickels can this structure support?

The curved, paper-plane strength test

Try holding a flat sheet of paper only by the edge of one side so that the paper sheet stays horizontal. As long as you keep the sheet flat, it can't be done. If you used a stiff piece of cardboard or a slab the same size, you could probably do it easily because of

their natural stiffness, but not with a thin, flat sheet of paper. Now hold the same sheet by the same edge, using your thumb on the top and first two fingers on the bottom, and give it a gentle bend so the sides turn up. It's easy now to hold the sheet out horizontally without it collapsing. The thin sheet of paper was strengthened simply by curving rather than by adding more material for thickness. See how many nickels this curved-plane structure can support before collapsing. You may have to borrow some extra change!

The curved, paper-plane span test

To span greater distances and support heavier loads (without adding additional thickness or supports in the middle), the flat sheet has to be curved or angled in some way. As before, see how far you can span a flat sheet of paper between two books before the sheet sags and collapses. Now curve the sheet up in the middle like an arch, and buttress each side against the side of another book lying flat. The same sheet of paper with only a slight curve now acts like an arch and has enough stiffness and strength to span its entire length. But, in order to keep its arched shape, the curved paper plane needs to be buttressed by the books. With just a slight curve, the arch probably won't even support one nickel. Move the book buttresses closer together so the sides of the arch are close to vertical, and now see how many nickels the arch will support. (You will need to place the nickels carefully along the top of the arch so they don't slide off.)

The folded-plate paper span test

The same flimsy, flat sheet of paper that was unable to completely support itself between two books can be made into a folded-plate

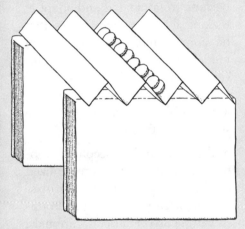

design that acts like a series of beams and will easily support itself and a load equal to a few hundred times the weight of the paper sheet. To make the structure, fold a sheet of paper in half and crease the folded edge. Now fold it again in the same direction, crease the fold, and do the same thing a third time. Unfold the paper and you should have eight long, thin panels between the creases. Refold the paper on the same crease lines, alternating between forward and backward folds to form an accordion, or zigzag, design. (You will have to refold some creases in the opposite direction from their original fold.) Notice that the accordion shape of a folded-plate design has very little strength when pushed or pulled from either side—the accor-

dion shape just collapses when pushed, or returns to a flat sheet when pulled. Now place the structure like a series of beams between two book supports and see how many nickels it will support.

The barrel-vault paper span test

A flimsy sheet of paper unable to resist bending becomes a stiff structure once rolled up into a tube. Roll a paper sheet tightly into a small tube about as thick as your finger. Here's a tip: Roll up the tube as tightly as you can, then use a finger inside the tube to wind the tube even smaller. Notice how rigid the tube shape becomes if used as a beam between two books. The same sheet of paper can be rolled and folded into a series of barrel-vault beams that are also strong and cover a much greater expanse than the tubular beam. It takes some practice to make a series of barrel vault beams from a sheet of paper. Start by folding a sheet of paper in half and crease the folded edge, then fold it again in the same direction and crease the fold. Unfold the sheet and you should have four panels between the creases. Now tightly roll the paper sheet in the same

direction as the folds until it is as thick as your finger. Completely unroll the tightly wound tube so that it retains much of its curl and recrease the center fold to form a double U-shape. Now fold back and recrease each "U" to form a series of four barrel-vault-shaped beams. Place the vaulted beam structure between two book supports and test the structure for strength. Which form supports the most weight—a folded-plate design or a barrel vault?

Making a double-curve saddle shape

To create the geometric shape of a thin-shell saddle, you'll need a square or rectangular piece of cloth (like a cloth napkin, handkerchief, or scarf) and the help of one or two friends. While one person holds two opposite corners of the cloth and pulls down, the other person holds the other two corners and pulls up. The more the cloth is pulled in opposite directions, the more curved and stiff the saddle shape becomes. A third person can feel and test the stiffness of the saddle shape while the other two are doing the holding and pulling. Now imagine that instead of cloth, the saddle shape was made of rigid plastic or some other thin, stiff material. You would then have a thin-walled saddle not only capable of holding its own shape, but capable of supporting considerable weight.

Origami

For nearly two thousand years, the art of origami paper folding has been used to create clever forms, shapes, and designs that represent familiar objects, animals, figures, patterns, and puzzles—all from plain paper. There is no cutting, gluing, drawing, stapling, or taping, just folding.

The word *origami* comes from two Japanese words: *ori*, meaning "to fold" and *kami*, meaning "paper." However, the art of paper folding probably began with the invention of papermaking in China around 100 A.D. Soon the custom in ancient China became to bury deceased people along with paper models of their house and their other important possessions.

It took six hundred more years before the knowledge of papermaking came to Japan, and Japanese people also began to use simple abstract and decorative folded-paper forms in their ceremonies. In one Japanese religion, the word *kami* for *paper* is a homonym for the words *spirit* and *God*, and special folded papers called gohei signify the presence of divine spirits.

In time, Japanese people began to use folded-paper ornaments for other purposes, including good-luck tokens that were attached to a package to signify it was a gift. The art of creating these and other designs were traditionally passed on from mother to daughter until the late 1700s, around the time that books about paper folding were first published. One of those books, *How to Fold a Thousand Cranes*, included detailed folding instructions for making the long-legged bird in every conceivable position.

Another Japanese book on paper folding, *Window on Mid-winter*, was published in the mid-1800s, and it contained a complete collection of traditional Japanese figures including a frog, a crab, and a dragonfly. Unlike current origami figures, many of these early examples of origami allowed slits to be cut in the paper as well as details and decorations to be drawn on the figures.

Soon after Japanese people learned how to make paper, Spanish people did as well, and they too developed a particular style of paper folding. The most well-known (and possibly the oldest known) folded-paper design in Spain is the pajarita, or the sparrow. However, a folded-paper design can often be viewed in different ways, and the folded shape for the Spanish sparrow later became known as a hen in France, a crow in Germany, and a hobbyhorse in England.

In the 1930s, a young Japanese man named Akira Yoshizawa became so fascinated and adept at making folded paper figures that he created tens of thousands of models that included every conceivable subject. He also worked out a diagramming system of lines and arrows to record how the shapes were folded.

Today, origami has become a popular pastime and even a recognized art form. It is not unusual for masters of origami to create anatomically correct insects, animals, and other creatures, as well as origami sculptures, packaging, and even fashion accessories like hats and purses.

THE QUONSET HUT

At the start of World War II, the American Navy needed a multi-purpose building that could be easily transported to any location where a large shelter was quickly needed. The prefabricated structure would also have to be easy to assemble, sturdy and stable in all weather conditions, and quite rugged.

A team of designers at the Quonset Point Naval Air Station in Rhode Island came up with an extremely simple solution: a half-cylinder hut that looked like a giant barrel lying half-buried on its side. The design used a rectangular metal foundation that supported a plywood floor. A framework of semicircular steel ribs was then assembled to arch above the floor, and sheets of curved, corrugated metal were attached to the ribs to form the walls and roof. All the parts were manufactured in a factory and shipped in wooden crates to the building site. The entire structure could be erected in a single day by a team of ten men.

The practical and popular design quickly became known as the Quonset hut, after its place of origin, and the huts were used by the military for everything from housing and hospitals to warehouses and auto repair shops.
The original

design had a foundation footprint that measured sixteen feet by thirty-six feet. But, because both large and small huts were needed, the original design was replaced with two models. The model 20 hut measured twenty feet wide by forty-eight feet long, while the model 40 (also called the Elephant Hut) was a monstrous forty feet by one hundred feet. Often, two or more huts would be joined end to end to create super-long huts, the largest being about the size of fourteen model 40s.

During the war, the design evolved and improved. The original plans required nuts and bolts to attach the sheet-metal panels to the T-shaped steel ribs. Later, designers found that grooves in the ribs could hold the panels in place and nails could be driven through the rib and panel to lock everything together. This new method of assembly, using nails instead of nuts and bolts, allowed a hut to be built in half the time.

Special hut designs were also created for different climates. The design for cold northern regions had insulated wooden walls at each end,

while the designs for southern and tropical areas had screens at either end for flow-through ventilation. On very hot days, a Quonset hut was about four degrees cooler than conventional structures. That was an important difference when there was no air-conditioning.

By the time the war had ended, the military had built about 170,000 Quonset huts all over the world, and the half-cylinder-shaped buildings had become a familiar sight in America. For a short time after the war, the Quonset hut even became popular for civilian uses. Universities built dormitory huts for students. They were also used for movie theaters, department stores, sheds, barns, and artists' studios. There were even some Quonset hut homes, churches, and office buildings. Today, sixty years after most were built, many Quonset huts are still being used for just about everything.

ALL KINDS OF TENTS WITH ALL KINDS OF USES

Ancient humans may have sought shelter in caves or other natural hollows that just happened to be found, but historians believe that the first personal shelters actually built by humans were simple tent structures. These primitive tents, which first appeared nearly ten thousand years ago, were not much different in concept from the tents seen today. Of course, early humans were limited to using what was readily available from nature as tent building materials.

As building materials evolved and building methods improved, so did the understanding of how to make better tents. Stronger and lighter weight framing allowed larger tent

frames, and tightly fitting coverings better resisted the wind. Today, there are tent designs of many shapes and sizes with special features that make each one suited for particular applications—from a small personal tent designed to keep a mountain climber warm in sub-zero weather to a gigantic tent that covers an entire sports stadium.

The earliest tent designs

The first tents were probably invented by nomadic tribes who continually traveled from place to place, often covering great distances that took them over all types of terrain and through varying climates. Their quickly made tempo-

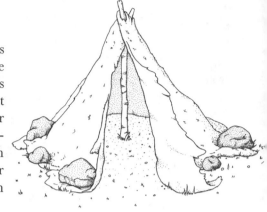

rary structures provided protection from the hot sun when traveling through barren desserts, or from the steady rains of the open plains. These early tents were most likely built by first fastening a few fallen branches into a simple frame and then draping the frame with animal skins. The structure had to be easy to construct from portable parts, but unfortunately these first tents did not work well in the wind.

Because the covering was only draped over the frame and not attached to it, a strong breeze might have caused the covering to begin flapping or even to blow off, and a strong wind would have certainly ripped the tent to shreds. As future generations and civilizations evolved and invented solutions to problems, they also began building more sophisticated structures, including better versions of the tent. The invention of rope and woven fabrics inspired the design of these new tent structures and shapes, and also allowed them to be built much larger and more secure.

Since tents are basically roof structures, they were used as the permanent roof covering on some ancient masonry buildings, or as a temporary cover over the open area of a courtyard, an outdoor market, or a sports arena. The famous col-

iseum in Rome once had a tent-like fabric roof that protected the Roman spectators from the blazing heat of the summer sun. This simple design consisted of ropes up to five hundred feet long that spanned the top of the structure from side to side. The rope framework supported a canvas fabric roof that stretched from end to end across the open stadium. If the roof wasn't needed, it could just be rolled back to let the sun in.

Tents are true tensile structures

Tent makers soon discovered that the secret to building a stronger and more durable structure was to attach the tent covering tightly over the framework. A tight covering not only made the entire structure stronger, but it resisted fluttering and breaking apart in the wind. True tents are tensile structures in

which the tent covering is pulled tightly in tension over a framework and becomes an integral part of the structure's strength.

A good example of this principle is the common umbrella. Before an umbrella is opened, it is merely a flimsy piece of fabric attached to several flimsy struts. But once the umbrella is opened, it becomes a rather rigid domed tent structure

THE BEDOUIN TENT

Elegant design made simple

The tent design used by the Bedouin peoples of the Middle East and North Africa is a wonderful example of elegant design. Bedouin means desert dweller, and these nomadic people travel from place to place in the desert, where

the daytime temperature often exceeds 120 degrees Fahrenheit with no shade and not even a slight breeze. However, their rather simple-looking portable tent functions as a climate control system that accomplishes a remarkable number of things automatically.

First, the tent is black and casts a deep shade, so just being inside the

shade of the tent reduces the temperature somewhat. Yet, because the black fabric of the tent is coarsely woven, it lets in thousands of pinpoints of light to illuminate the shaded interior. As heat inside the tent rises and flows out the top of the tent through the fabric, it draws in air through the bottom of the tent, creating a breeze of its own. All together, the tent has the ability to keep the inside of the tent about thirty degrees cooler than the outside daytime temperature. When it rains, another remarkable thing happens. Instead of allowing the water to come in through the openings in the coarse weave, the fibers swell up, the holes close, and the fabric becomes waterproof. After the rain ends, the fabric dries, the fibers shrink back to their original size, and the tent is once again in cooling mode. That is an elegant design!

that wants to hold its shape. Backpacking tents and family camping tents are other common examples of tensile tent structures in which the framework alone keeps the covering in tension.

Other types of tents, especially large ones, require tie-downs or guy lines

to maintain tension on the covering. Each line tugs on a corner or edge of the covering and is tied to a stake planted firmly in the ground. Some dome-shaped tents and tepee-like tents are pretty stable in winds and do not need guy lines as long as the material covering is taut against the tent frame.

THE UNIVERSALLY VERSATILE YURT

A tent house for all seasons

Imagine your family moved to a new town, but instead of living in a new house, you took your old house with you. If your house was a yurt, you could actually bring it with you wherever you decided to live, no matter what the climate. A yurt is a kind of portable tent structure made of modular folding panels that can be easily erected or dismantled in less than an hour without the use of special tools or equipment. Unlike a portable camping tent, a yurt is cleverly designed to be comfortable in the cold, heat, wind, rain, and snow.

Yurt is a Turkish word that means "dwelling." Even though these tent-like houses seem to have been invented by the nomadic people of Central Asia more than two thousand years ago, since then, the yurt has become a popular form of housing in several cultures, and its basic modular shape has evolved into a variety of interesting designs. A modern yurt might have a stove, electricity, and even plumbing. However, the original features and benefits of the earliest yurts are still a part of every new yurt constructed. It is not unusual for a well-made yurt

to last forty or fifty years and periodically be upgraded with more modern conveniences.

The basic yurt design consists of three parts that include a wall frame, a roof frame, and a felt mat covering. The assembled yurt is a mat-covered cylinder with a dome-shaped roof that provides the maximum amount of structure for the minimum amount of material needed to build it. For a portable tent, this is a great advantage, as fewer materials mean less to carry. A yurt can be erected directly on dry ground or placed on an elevated platform. Either way, the structure's shape and construction provide many useful benefits, including a wide-open interior space sixteen to twenty feet in diameter, good usable height,

a strong domed roof capable of supporting heavy loads without collapsing, and a round shape that forces the wind to move around it instead of knocking the tent down. This feature is especially important to the Mongolian nomads who must deal with tremendous wind, dust, and snowstorms.

Several other features of the yurt's structure are also simple yet quite clever. The wall sections are formed by thin pieces of wood crisscrossed over each other into a lattice and attached with pins where they

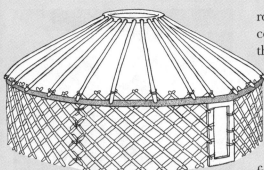

Folding lattice wall panels and pitched roof poles create the domed cylinder form, and a tension band around the framework completes the structure.

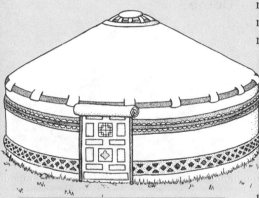

Depending on the climate, the yurt frame may be covered with layers of wool-felt mats for warmth or woven straw mats to let cooling breezes flow through.

intersect. Each latticed wall section is expandable to cover a large area and collapsible for storage or carrying (just like a folding-lattice baby gate). The roof poles, the door, and the crisscrossed latticework are almost always decorated with intricate designs.

When assembling a yurt, the lattice wall sections are expanded open, overlapped at the sides, and lashed together with cords to form a vertical cylinder. One of the wall sections is a wooden door frame with a wooden door. The dome-shaped roof is built from wooden poles that connect the crisscrossed joints at the top of the wall sections to a ring in the middle of the rooftop. The poles keep the walls from collapsing inward, and a tension band that works like a big belt is tied around the top of the wall to prevent the roof poles from pushing the wall outward.

A yurt is adaptable to all but extreme weather conditions and can be used during all four seasons. In cold weather, the traditional Mongolian yurt is covered with as many as eight layers of wool-felt mats. In warm weather, the felt is removed or rolled up to increase air circulation. Hot air then rises out of the opening above the roof ring. Sometimes loosely woven straw mats are used in place of the felt mats to allow airflow through the tent while also providing privacy to the occupants. The roof ring at the top of the dome allows an abundance of natural light to flow into the yurt and also works as a chimney to allow smoke from a fire or stove to escape. During inclement weather, a roof flap or skylight is placed over the roof ring to keep out rain and snow.

Today, commercially manufactured yurts are popular throughout the world. Even the yurts now used by the Mongolians are made in a factory using modern materials and manufacturing technologies, and they often come with wood flooring, stoves, and wires for electricity. If you are ever in Mongolia, remember that it is rude to step on the threshold of a yurt (the bottom of the door frame) or to hold onto any tent ropes when entering.

Also, according to traditional nomad hospitality, anyone stopping outside a yurt is always welcomed inside for a meal.

In other societies, the modern yurt is used for a variety of purposes, including temporary housing, vacation homes, ski huts, backyard spas, art studios, and sometimes guesthouses. When the owner decides to move, even if it's only to another part of the yard, the modern yurt can still be easily packed to travel.

Commercially made yurts are now used as backyard guesthouses and true mobile homes complete with electricity, plumbing, and even a skylight.

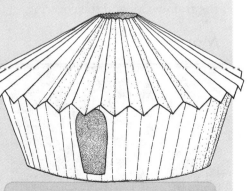

Small huts and sheds inspired by the yurt design are often constructed using large accordion-folded sheets of corrugated cardboard made from paper or plastic.

What Type of Tent Is That?

Tents are everywhere. Temporary tents are instantly erected for weddings, craft fairs, concerts, and auctions. People carry portable tents for shade, picnics, camping, fishing, and hunting, and elaborate permanent tents are designed as shelters in many places people congregate. Here are some of the basic types of tents. Don't be surprised if you see a tent that matches none of these descriptions. Some tents are a combination of designs, and new tent structures are always being invented.

Pavilion

A round tent with a peaked roof that usually requires guy lines for both the framework and the covering.

Marquee

Although the name Marquee refers to the covering of any tent, the term is commonly used to describe a large field tent with more than two main poles.

Bell

A round tent with a dome or pointed roof in which the diameter roof edge is smaller than the diameter of the bottom edge. Some designs do not require guy lines.

Cone

A tent shaped like an inverted cone with a single center pole or multiple poles as used in tepees. Many conical designs do not require guy lines or tie-downs.

Lean-to

A prism-shaped design with one face perpendicular to the ground, a sloped rear roof, and sometimes splayed sides. The perpendicular face is often left open.

Wedge or "A"

A tent with sloping sides in the shape of a triangular prism. The framework is usually made with two uprights connected by a ridgepole.

Dome

A dome-shaped camping tent with a structure typically made of aluminum poles with elastic cords running through them. Some designs use fiberglass rods inserted into pockets on the fabric covering.

Canopy

A simple open framework, self-supporting or guyed, with only a roof covering. The roof is either sloped over a ridgepole or peaked in the middle.

Umbrella canopy

Usually a dome- or cone-shaped roof covering attached to a frame and supported by a center pole. The umbrella may be designed to fold closed for easy storage and setup.

Shade canopy

A piece of fabric held in tension and position by guy lines. Shade canopies are very often formed into a strong saddle shape to resist winds and shed rain.

Pyramid

A square-based pyramid shape using a center pole. The fabric covering is staked at each corner, and the entrance is typically created by an overlapping slit on one side.

DIRECTOR'S CHAIR

The modern look of the ever-popular director's chair is bit deceiving. The X-frame, cross-braced chair design, which provides a perfect balance between tension and compression, has been used in some variation by many cultures going back to ancient China and Egyptian times.

Around 1894, the Racine Gold Medal Company began to manufacture and sell their version of a cross-braced folding chair that used cotton canvas slings nailed to a wooden X-frame for the seat and backrest. A few years later, a competitor, the Telescope Casual Furniture Company, also began selling wood and canvas folding chairs of a very similar design.

These easily portable chairs were quite comfortable, collapsible, and lightweight, and as it turned out, exactly what the Hollywood film industry needed for movie-set locations. By the 1940s, the image of a movie director sitting in an X-frame and canvas chair became so familiar that people began to call the chair a director's chair and its popularity soared.

The simple X-frame and nailed-canvas construction of the director's chair remained mostly unchanged until 1953, when the president of the Telescope Company made a significant design improvement. While sailing as a guest on the U.S. Coast Guard ship *Eagle*, he noticed how the canvas slings in the sleeping quarters were not nailed to their wooden frames, but instead, the canvas had thick edges that slid into grooved rails along the sides of the frame. This design detail provided a more even fit and allowed the canvas to be easily slid out of the frame for cleaning and just as easily replaced.

The Telescope Company immediately adopted the method and began to make their director's chairs with canvas seats and backs that simply slid in and out on rails carved into the wood frame. Buyers could now remove the canvas for cleaning, and they could also just change the canvas for another color or pattern. The Telescope design is still popular today and so is the name director's chair.

To fully appreciate its simple and elegant design, take a close look at the structure of a director's chair while sitting in one. The heavier the load, the more taut the canvas seat becomes to better support the load. The chair's legs are in compression and are trying to spread apart, but they are being held in place by the tension of the canvas seat, creating a perfect balance of forces no matter who sits on the chair.

Modern Materials and Methods Make Bigger Tents

The strong and lightweight construction materials available today have allowed designers, architects, and engineers to create tents that are considerably larger than earlier ones built of only natural materials. Modern materials have also given designers new ways to create some rather unusual shapes with interesting features. Some tent fabrics are opaque or translucent to sunlight, insulating and weatherproof or open to the breeze, fireproof, colorful, tearproof, and even coated with Teflon to be self-cleaning.

Tent frameworks are now fabricated from steel, aluminum, and wire cables and covered tightly with strong fabrics made from nylon, vinyl, and rubber, or space-age reinforced fabrics engineered to be extremely strong and long lasting. Many of the largest tents are meant to be permanent enclosures, covering entire sports stadiums and airport terminals, or grandstands and other places that people gather in the hotter climates.

The structure of Olympic Stadium in Munich, Germany, resembles its nickname "the glass tent."

The Olympic Stadium built in Munich, Germany, in 1972 is called "the glass tent" because it uses 89,700 square yards of a fabric-like covering made from thousands of acrylic-glass panels attached together. The covering is supported by nine huge masts and many steel guy ropes that look like cobwebs.

The highly technical process of tent building today stands in sharp contrast to the simple structures and natural materials of primitive tents. To create these imaginative and functional modern tent designs requires computer-aided engineering tools for determining the precise shapes that have the greatest strength for the least amount of material, and for predicting their behavior in high winds and under heavy loads of rain and snow. If designed correctly, the tent should not collect any snow or allow ponds of water to collect.

By the beginning of the twenty-first century, the largest area to be covered by a tent (actually a system of many tents) was the Haj Terminal located at King Abdul Aziz International Airport in Saudi Arabia. This enormous structure covers an area of over 4.5 million square feet, the size of one hundred football fields!

This airport terminal in Saudi Arabia is the largest tent structure in the world.

BUILDING WITH PANELS AND PLANES

CARDBOARD CARPENTRY
CONSTRUCTIONS

FOLDED PAPER PROJECTS AND
PUZZLES

TENTS, SHELLS, DOMES, AND BOWLS

OTHER PANEL OPTIONS AND
ODDBALLS

CARDBOARD CARPENTRY CONSTRUCTIONS

Building with cardboard can be as simple as playing with a big, empty carton until it shreds to pieces from use, or as specific as accurately fabricating designs for usable furniture. What you build mostly depends on your age and your cardboard carpentry skills, though nearly all the Cardboard Carpentry projects you may build can also be used by younger kids.

Big Box Buildings and the One-Box Puppet Theater both require only folding and decorating. Building the Step-Side Pyramid Toy Box is almost as simple but also involves gluing or taping. However, both of these projects depend on finding empty boxes or cartons that are the right size and type.

Builders who have developed good cutting skills using knives can cut corrugated cardboard into panel shapes and learn how to cut slots into panels for joining pieces together. Try building a One-Box Dollhouse or maybe a set of Slotted Panels for a younger brother or sister. Building the panels for a Panelized Playhouse requires the same good cutting skills, but builders must also be able to carefully measure and lay out specific cutting patterns. Once cut to shape, assembling the pieces for all these projects is easy.

Experienced cardboard carpentry builders might think of building a Laminated Lounge Chair. Although this project uses a lot of corrugated cardboard and takes a long time to build, you will end up with a durable piece of furniture made to perfectly fit you. The Caney Stool might also be considered furniture, but the unique multipurpose design requires the best building skills for laying out the pattern, cutting out the shapes, making the scores for folding, and assembling its two halves to form the stool structure. If you do build it, however, you won't be disappointed.

BUILD IT

CORRUGATED CARDBOARD CARPENTRY	467
ONE-BOX DOLLHOUSE	472
ONE-BOX PUPPET THEATER AND SUPER SIMPLE PUPPETS	474
PANELIZED PLAYHOUSE	479
STEP-SIDE PYRAMID TOY BOX	482
CANEY STOOL	484
BIG BOX BUILDINGS	486
SLOTTED-PANEL STRUCTURES AND SCULPTURES	487
LAMINATED LOUNGE CHAIR	489

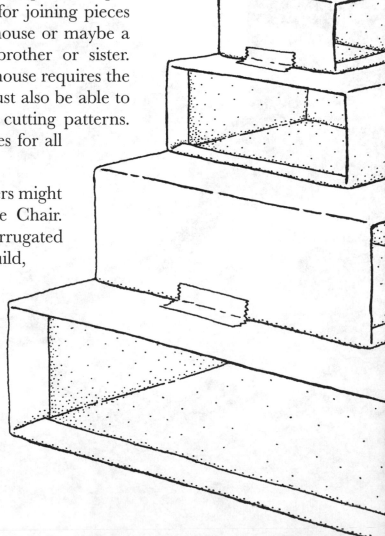

CORRUGATED CARDBOARD CARPENTRY
BUILDING SYSTEM

Corrugated cardboard scavenged from empty boxes is one of the most common and plentiful free building materials you can find. Corrugated cardboard is also easy to work with and quickly builds large kid-size structures that are both strong and lightweight. You can cut, fold, or hinge cardboard. You can fasten pieces with tape, glue, or laces. Structures can be permanent or built for take-apart, and the panel surfaces can be plain, painted, or decorated. And most Corrugated Cardboard Carpentry projects don't require fine craftsmanship, so panels that are a bit out of square or off dimension should still work fine. The things you build with Cardboard Carpentry can be as simple as an empty corrugated box refolded into a puppet theater, or require measuring, cutting, and fastening corrugated cardboard panels to construct a full-scale playhouse and several kinds of furniture you can actually use.

SYSTEM FEATURES

- Scrap cardboard is free and plentiful
- Good for large-scale kid-size structures
- Constructions can be permanent or take-apart
- Corrugated cardboard is easy to cut
- Pieces can be fastened in many ways
- Corrugated cardboard is self-hinging
- Surfaces are easily painted with brush or roller
- Tears and rips are easy to repair

Construction

Builder's age
9+

Materials

☐ Corrugated boxes

☐ Fasteners (See specific fastening method.)

Tools

☐ Carpenter's square

☐ Pencil

☐ Mat knife or utility knife

☐ Wooden mixing spoon (or other tool for scoring)

☐ Scissors (for cutting tape or lacing)

☐ Paintbrush (optional, for applying latex contact cement)

☐ Hole punch, awl, or knitting needle (for making lace holes or bolt holes)

Building techniques

There are several ways to build structures using corrugated cardboard. First, decide what you want to build and what fastening system you will be using, then gather all the materials and tools needed. Most projects require cutting and scoring the corrugated material; practice those skills by cutting a few scraps into straight strips. It's also a good idea to practice taping or gluing or whichever fastening system you plan to use.

Many designs that are typically built with plywood panels can also be made in Cardboard Carpentry, but they just won't be as strong or as durable. So, after practicing these building techniques and constructing a few Corrugated Carpentry projects, think about what else you might build.

Finding a supply of corrugated cardboard

Grocery stores and hardware stores are always good places to ask for empty cartons, and many warehouse-type stores stack empty cartons by the exit, hoping you'll take them away. And for projects requiring really big pieces of corrugated cardboard, you'll find plenty of material free for the taking at furniture stores and appliance dealers. You just need to have a way to get the big boxes back home.

Single-wall corrugated is the most common material used for boxes. Looking at the edge of a box flap, you can see that single-wall corrugated board is actually a sandwich of two pieces of flat paper glued to a fluted sheet of the same paper in between. This construction works like a large, thin truss, and that is why corrugated cardboard is lighter and stronger than a solid piece of paperboard of the same dimensions.

Double-wall corrugated is a sandwich of papers consisting of three flat sheets and two fluted sheets. This material is very strong (but harder to work with) and is commonly used for packaging furniture or machinery. There is even a *triple-wall corrugated* that is over one-half inch thick and exceptionally strong, but it has to be cut with a saw.

Before you begin a project, figure out how much material you will need, and make sure you have some extra. And be sure to find a box with a panel that is big enough for your largest piece, or you will have to attach two or more smaller panels to make it.

Laying out plans and patterns

Find a large, level area of floor space that gives you plenty of room for working. Try not to step or lean your elbows on the corrugated material, which can cause it to crush and lose some of its strength. If you do need to step or lean on the corrugated material while working, use a hardcover book as a cushion between you and the material.

To lay out most plans and patterns, all you need is a carpenter's square

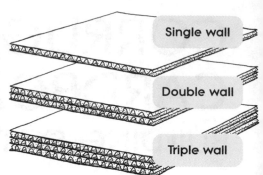

and a pencil. The square is marked in inches, and the 90-degree angle makes it easy to draw perfect square corners. And if you know some geometry, the square can also be used to measure and draw 30-, 45-, and 60-degree angles.

When laying out any plan, remember that single-wall corrugated cardboard has a definite grain, which makes it easy to bend along the length of the corrugations, but the material resists bending across the corrugations. You might be able to use that feature if your design requires bends or hinged pieces.

If your project calls for several or all panel pieces to be the same shape and size, you can lay out and cut out the first piece, then use it as a template to trace the shape of the other similar pieces.

Cutting

Because you will be using a mat knife or utility knife to cut completely through the cardboard, protect the floor or table you are working on. A large sheet of plywood or wall-paneling board is

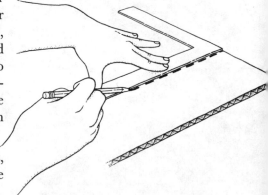

ideal, but with careful cutting, a few scraps of cardboard can also be used. Another technique is to place a wood board or strip under the line to be cut, but that requires even more careful cutting and handling of the material.

For cutting on straight lines, position yourself on the "scrap side" of the cut, and align an edge of the carpenter's square directly next to the line to be cut. It is important that you hold the straight edge of the steel square firmly with one hand (and maybe even a knee) to keep it from sliding while cutting with the knife in your other hand. If the straight edge slips, the line of your cut will wander off track. And for safety, hold the straight edge at a place a little above the start of the cut. That way, if the knife slips, your hand will be out of the way.

Starting at one end of the line to be cut, hold the knife at a low angle with the blade against the edge of the steel square. Make the cut by drawing the knife toward you while pressing the blade down firmly and while keeping it against the edge of the steel square. If the cut wanders off line (sometimes seemingly by itself), try turning the blade slightly towards the straight edge.

Depending on the sharpness of the blade, the thickness of the material, and your strength, it might take more than one pass of the knife to cut completely through. So try not

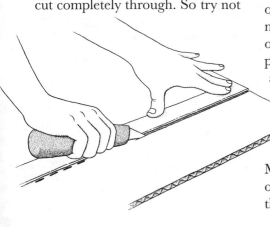

to move the straight edge away from the line until you are sure the cut is made. Some long, straight lines may need to be cut using two or more connecting cuts. Just be sure to cut completely through one section at a time before moving the steel square along the line to the next section.

To cut along a curved line, either find a metal-edge cutting guide that has the same shape (like a lid of a paint can), or make the cut freehand. Sometimes single-wall corrugated cardboard can also be cut with sturdy scissors.

Scoring and folding

Your plan may call for the corrugated board to be folded on a line rather than cut. If the fold line is directly parallel with the corrugations, the material can just be folded on the line, using the carpenter's square or any straight edge as a guide. All other folds that are not parallel to the corrugations will first require scoring.

A score is a shallow crease you make along the fold line (using a straight edge as a guide) that helps start the fold and keeps it straight. All kinds of common things can be used as a tool for making scores, as long as they crease only the corrugated surface and not break or cut through it.

Practice making scores and folds on scrap pieces of corrugated material with tools like the handle of large scissors, a paintbrush, or a paint mixing paddle. Either end of a wooden mixing spoon works well, and an eye bolt screwed into a scrap-wood handle makes a professional scoring tool.

Make the score only on the inside of the fold. (Bend the material over the scored crease.) To make a hinge

that bends both ways, score the material on both sides (the second score directly over the first). You will discover that folds in corrugated cardboard are never quite exact and can affect other dimensions of your plan.

Painting and decorating

Corrugated cardboard is not waterproof and is best suited for indoor play or outdoor play only on dry days. That makes it okay to use any type of paint or marker to decorate your structure.

If you decide to paint an entire surface area on one side, also paint the opposite side of the cardboard piece immediately or it will warp badly. Latex wall paint and a roller are excellent for painting large, flat panels either before assembly (easier) or after.

Other decorating treatments you might try include applying stickers and pieces of tape, making potato print patterns, or even hanging wallpaper (with wallpaper paste or the self-stick kind).

Permanent fastening methods

Corrugated cardboard panels can be permanently fastened to each other using either tape or glue or both. Decide which method has the features best suited for your construction.

Taping

☐ Kraft packaging tape, plastic packaging tape, masking tape, filament tape, or duct tape

Most tapes one inch or more wide are excellent for fastening corrugated cardboard panels edge to edge or edge to surface, although each type of tape has its own advantages and disadvantages. Try using several shorter lengths of tape for

longer joints. A long strip of tape tends to twist and stick to itself before you have finished applying it to the cardboard.

Masking tape is easy to use and strong (and the color matches brown corrugated boxes), but cannot be painted. Plastic packaging tape, duct tape, and filament tape (which is probably stronger than you need) are all a little difficult to handle and cannot be painted, but they do make strong joints.

Kraft packaging tape, especially the reinforced type, makes neat and strong joints, but the tape adhesive must first be wetted with a sponge (a wet sponge, but not dripping). The wetted tape must be

quickly applied and smoothed out before the glue quickly begins to dry. It might take fifteen minutes or more for the tape to fully dry, but it can then be painted along with the corrugated material.

Here is an important safety tip: The raw cut edges of corrugated cardboard are sharp and can cause paper cuts. Although you must be careful while handling the material, you can provide an extra measure of safety by taping over any raw edges on your completed construction.

Gluing

☐ Contact cement, or

☐ Hot-glue gun and adhesive sticks

Contact cement makes fast and permanent surface-to-surface connections, but does not work for attaching edges. Use a safe latex-based contact cement, and apply it to both sides being joined using a one-inch brush. The instructions for most contact cements call for the adhesive to dry for several minutes before the pieces are joined.

A hot-glue gun takes some practice and skill to use properly, but can make very strong bonds between corrugated surfaces as well as edges. A hot-glue gun is especially useful for attaching an edge to a surface.

Take-apart fastening methods

Corrugated Carpentry constructions using take-apart fasteners can be disassembled so the panels can be stored flat and then reassembled into something else when you like.

Slotting

Cardboard pieces with slots can be fastened to other pieces with slots without using glue, tape, or any other material, but what you can build may be limited to having panels joined at right angles to each other. However, slotting

does allow some types of joinery that would be difficult to duplicate using tape or glue.

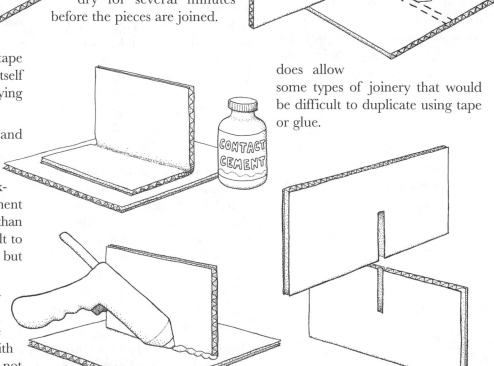

Depending on the particular project you build, the location and depth of slots cut from the cardboard must be carefully planned and marked. Use a straight piece of the same corrugated material placed on edge to trace the width and depth of a slot to be cut, then cut out the long, thin piece of scrap.

Lacing

☐ Heavy string, light cord, shoelaces, or plastic clothesline

Lacing together the edges of adjoining corrugated panels is especially easy for younger builders who are not concerned with making precise constructions. Laced panels can be

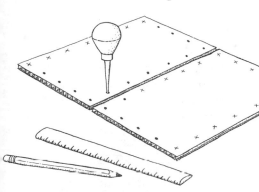

a bit wobbly, and the joints can tear, but large structures made of precut panels go up quickly. However, first you have to mark and punch a row of holes along the edges of all the panels.

So the holes of joined panels line up for easy lacing, use a standard unit of measure between all holes (about three or four inches apart works well) and another consistent distance between the holes and the edges of each panel (no closer than about $^3/_4$ inch). Use an awl or a short, fat knitting needle to punch a hole completely through the cardboard at every location you have marked.

After aligning the holes of two panels, there are a few different materials and a few different techniques that can be used for lacing

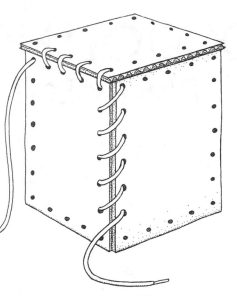

them together. The simplest method is to thread a pipe cleaner through several matching pairs of holes and twist the ends together. You can also lace up the matching holes with long shoelaces. Tie a loop through the first pair of holes, then thread the cord through each other pair of matching holes. Tie off the end of the cord when you have completed lacing all the holes (or come to the end of the cord).

Bolts and nuts

☐ 1″ bolts, fender washers, and wing nuts ($^1/_4$-20 size)

Machine screws with flat washers and wing nuts make a fine fastening system for temporarily attaching panels and tabs together, but the process is time-consuming, and needs a lot of hardware, which could be expensive.

For each point of connection, make a hole in the corrugated material just large enough to accept a $^1/_4$-inch diameter bolt. ($^1/_4$-20 size machine screws and wing nuts are easy to handle.) Hold together the two pieces to be joined, and punch a hole through both using a hole punch, an awl, or a short, fat knitting needle. Wiggle the tool around

to make the hole just a little larger if needed.

Place a washer on a one-inch-long machine screw, put the bolt through both punched holes, add another washer, and thread on a wing nut finger tight. Larger type fender washers work best since they help keep the holes in the cardboard from tearing.

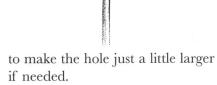

CORRUGATED CARDBOARD
CARPENTRY BUILD-IT PROJECTS

ONE-BOX DOLLHOUSE

ONE-BOX PUPPET THEATER AND
SUPER SIMPLE PUPPETS

PANELIZED PLAYHOUSE

STEP-SIDE PYRAMID TOY BOX

CANEY STOOL

BIG BOX BUILDINGS

SLOTTED-PANEL STRUCTURES
AND SCULPTURES

LAMINATED LOUNGE CHAIR

ONE-BOX DOLLHOUSE
MANY BOX APARTMENT BUILDING

Using just one medium- to large-size corrugated box, you can build a four-room, single-family dollhouse complete with an attic for storage and a large gable roof. With three or more medium-size boxes, you get a multiunit, multistory, dollhouse apartment building with lots of indoor rooms and several outdoor balconies. And the construction is so simple that you could build a whole village of houses or maybe a skyscraper city. Just remember that once construction is complete, you may have to paint the buildings, decorate the walls, and furnish the rooms before your doll family moves in.

Construction

Building system
Corrugated Cardboard Carpentry (slotting and taping)

Builder's age
9+ (younger with an adult doing the cutting)

Player's age
2+

Materials
☐ One or more complete corrugated boxes, medium- to large-size with double flaps on the large sides

☐ Kraft packaging tape or 2″ masking tape

Tools
☐ Carpenter's square

☐ Pencil

☐ Mat knife or utility knife

Building instructions

Making a one-family dollhouse

Find one complete corrugated box that isn't too deep. Keep the flaps on one end folded and taped closed.

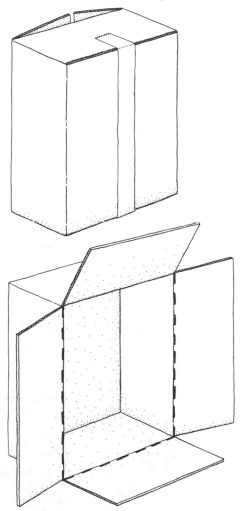

Open all four flaps on the other end and carefully cut off three of them. The flap you leave remaining will determine which side of the box will become the attic and the roof. Now stand the box on its side so the roof is on top.

Complete the gable roof by taping the matching cutoff flap to the remaining box flap. Tape the other long edge to the back of the box to form an inverted "V." The triangular space under the gable roof becomes the attic.

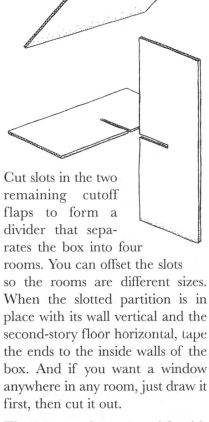

Cut slots in the two remaining cutoff flaps to form a divider that separates the box into four rooms. You can offset the slots so the rooms are different sizes. When the slotted partition is in place with its wall vertical and the second-story floor horizontal, tape the ends to the inside walls of the box. And if you want a window anywhere in any room, just draw it first, then cut it out.

The way you decorate and furnish your dollhouse is up to you. Be as

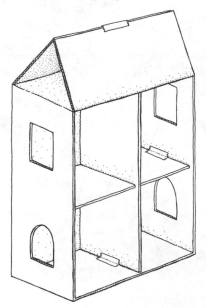

elaborate as you wish with painted outside walls and wallpapered inside walls, or maybe just leave the walls unfinished and let your imagination add what's needed.

Building a multiunit apartment building

Find three or more complete medium-size corrugated boxes that are not too deep. They do not all need to be the same size or depth.

For each box, keep the flaps on one end folded and taped closed, and cut all four flaps off the other end.

Now stack the boxes in a tower, one on top the other, with the openings facing out either all in the same direction or any way you want each apartment to face. If you're stacking a smaller box on top of a larger box, you can create terraces. By slipping a few of the cutoff flaps between stacked boxes, you can create cantilevered balconies. Also, use the cutoff flaps to make a roof, which could be a simple gable design or something more elaborate. And with the remaining cutoff flaps, you can make space dividers to give each apartment a few rooms.

When you get the structure stacked and arranged just right, tape everything together. Kraft packaging tape will make the strongest structure, but masking tape is much faster and easier to use.

ONE-BOX PUPPET THEATER AND SUPER SIMPLE PUPPETS

Building a One-Box Puppet Theater is super easy. Using one medium- to large-size corrugated box and only your hands (no tools and no fasteners are required), you can make a tabletop puppet theater complete with a stage and curtain wings. Just add some decorations, make a simple hand puppet, find a few stage props, and put on a show. With a few modifications, this basic one-box theater can be converted into a stage for finger puppets, and even a screen for shadow puppets. And using three corrugated cartons, you could build a multiplex, multimedia theater with separate stages for each type of puppet performance.

Construction

Building system
Corrugated Box Carpentry (folding)

Builder's age
5+

Player's age
2+

Materials
☐ 1 complete medium- to large-size corrugated box with double end flaps

Tools
☐ Hands only

Building instructions

Select a medium-size corrugated box that has double end flaps and is not missing any pieces. The type and size boxes used to package computers, stereo components, and office equipment all work well.

1. To convert the box into a puppet theater, begin by opening all the flaps. You may need to remove or cut any packaging tape keeping the flaps closed

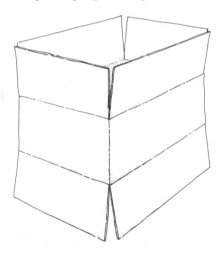

2. Holding the box open, completely fold in the two long flaps on one side (this will be the back of the theater) and the two long flaps at the opposite side (the front).

3. While holding these four flaps flat against the insides of the box, fold in the remaining two flaps on the front end, but don't fold them all the way in. Leaving the two front side flaps at an angle provides the theater stage with the appearance of curtain wings.

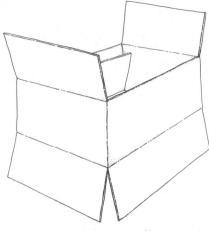

4. The remaining two flaps on the back of the theater can either be folded in against the insides of the box or folded out to the sides at an angle to help hide the puppeteer's hands from the audience.

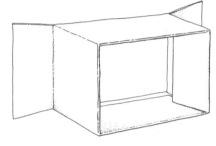

The construction is complete and ready to use. However, you might also consider painting the outside theater walls, drawing curtains on the stage wings, writing the theater name somewhere, and maybe make a clock face to display show times.

Making a Finger-Puppet Theater

The construction of a Finger-Puppet Theater is a simple variation of the One-Box Puppet Theater, except you can use a smaller box made of a thin single-wall corrugated board that usually can be cut with scissors. Young builders, however, will need help cutting the "finger slot" in the corrugated material.

1. Leave the bottom of the box closed and fastened. Completely open the four flaps on the top of the box.

2. Fold both long flaps into the box and against the inside walls to make the stage and ceiling. Fold the remaining two narrower flaps part way in at an angle to make the curtain wings.

3. Cut a finger slot across the bottom panel a few inches from the back of the "stage" (which was once the inside bottom of the box). The slot only needs to be wide enough for your finger puppets to poke through, but it should run most of the width of the exposed stage.

4. To complete the stage set, tape a picture page from a magazine to the back of the stage.

When putting on finger-puppet performances, a small box theater can simply be held in your free hand while you wear the puppets on the fingers of your other hand. For larger box theaters (which let you wear finger puppets on both hands), place the box on a table so that only the slot cut in the bottom hangs over the back edge.

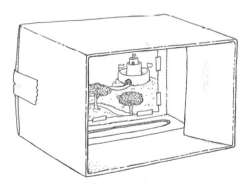

Making a Shadow-Puppet Theater

You may have already discovered the fun of playing with shadows. By placing your hands in the path of a stream of bright light, you can create shadows that mimic your own movements. And with some practice, you can learn to manipulate your hands and fingers to "throw" shadows that can look like talking animals, flying birds, walking dinosaurs, or any kind of animated character you decide to invent.

1. Begin by refolding a corrugated box into a One-Box Puppet Theater.

2. Make the shadow screen by covering the back of the theater box with a white piece of cloth cut from an old sheet or pillow case. Measure the size of the screen to be cut by placing the back of the theater box on the fabric and marking a cut line around the box about two inches away from all sides.

3. Cut out the screen shape with scissors, and tape it taut over the rear of the stage (the back opening of the box). Try to keep the screen from wrinkling as you tape it in place all around its edges. Using strips of masking tape will let you reposition any tape-down points to get rid of screen wrinkles.

4. To create shadows on the screen (in a darkened room), use a lamp with the lamp shade removed so you can see the bare bulb. Warning: Regular incandescent type bulbs can get dangerously hot, so is very important that you only use a lamp with a fluorescent bulb. Use a fluorescent bulb with brightness equivalent to a 100-watt or brighter incandescent bulb.

Put the theater on a table and put the lamp about two feet directly behind it so the lightbulb is at stage level. You may have to use a few thick books to hike up the level of the theater, or find a shorter or taller table for the lamp.

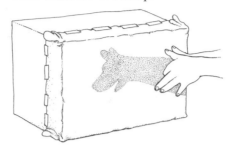

Now practice throwing hand shadows by standing just to the side of the rear of the theater (but not blocking the light with your body) and making hand figures at the rear of the screen. What you see on the back of the screen is the same image your audience will see looking from the front, only turned around the other way.

Putting on a puppet performance

Your one-box, one-performer-size puppet theater should be placed on a tabletop so that it faces the audience with the puppeteer stooping behind the table trying to stay hidden. The effect of the performance is enhanced even more if the tabletop has been covered by a sheet, a blanket, or a tablecloth that drapes over the front and sides to help hide the puppeteer.

It takes only a little practice to learn to make hand puppets perform. To make it seem like the puppet is talking to the audience (or another character on stage), move its head up and down. A drooping head appears sad, and a quick uplifted head appears surprised. Also, practice hand movements so the puppet can learn to pick up and handle props.

You might also learn to speak in the puppet character's voice by disguising your own voice. Everyone will know you are really the one speaking, but if your audience can see only the puppet, the effect will be more convincing. And it isn't always necessary to prepare a puppet-show script. Most kid puppeteers just have their puppets say and do whatever funny things come to mind.

Making super simple puppets

To use your puppet theater, you will of course need a hand puppet. You may already have one or more in your toy collection, or you can easily make a homemade puppet. By controlling the movements of the puppet and creating its voice, you can make the puppet become anyone or anything you choose and even pretend to be in some other place. These are super simple puppets you can make using only a few scrap materials—or nothing but your bare hands.

TENNIS BALL PUPPETS

Construction

Builder's age
9+

Player's age
2+

Materials
- ☐ Tennis ball
- ☐ Cloth handkerchief or napkin
- ☐ Rubber band
- ☐ Magazine with pictures of faces (optional)
- ☐ Transparent mending tape (optional)

Tools
- ☐ Mat knife or pen knife
- ☐ Felt-tip markers or crayons

Building instructions

1. To make the puppet's head, cut a hole in the tennis ball a bit larger in diameter than your index finger. Cutting through the tough rubber can be very difficult, especially with a dull knife. If you have trouble, ask an adult for help.

2. Decide what character your puppet will be, and decorate the ball head, using felt markers, crayons, or paints. Glue on buttons, yarn, or other small items. Remember that the shape and features of the puppet's face create the character's personality.

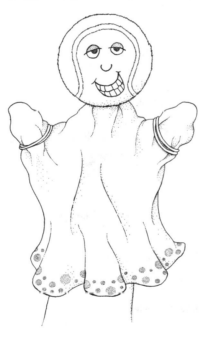

You could draw a clown face, some friendly creature, a not-so-friendly monster, or any character you want to play. Another way to create a face is to cut one out of a magazine and put it on the ball with glue or tape.

3. The body of the puppet is made by draping a colorful cloth handkerchief or napkin over your hand, which is held in the position shown in the illustration. Your index finger will become the puppet's neck, and your thumb and second finger will be the puppet's arms. The remaining two fingers should be folded in your palm. With the cloth draped over your hand, push your index finger into the hole in the tennis ball. Now slip a loose-fitting rubber band over the cloth and around your thumb and another rubber band over the second finger to better define the puppet's hands.

TALKING-HAND PUPPETS

Construction

Builder's age
5+

Player's age
5+

Materials
- ☐ Lipstick
- ☐ Yarn or cloth scraps

Tools
- ☐ Scissors

Building instructions

One of the best ways to achieve a sense of realism is to have the puppet's lips move in rhythm to the words you are speaking. But only specially made (and usually expensive) puppets can do that. There is a way to achieve a similar effect simply by converting your hand into a talking-hand puppet.

1. Hold your hand in the position shown in the illustration. Your thumb should rest on the side of your index finger between the first and second joints. Now try moving your thumb up and down to look like lips opening and closing.

2. To emphasize the effect of talking, use dark lipstick to draw lips on your thumb and pointer finger, then add eyes and maybe

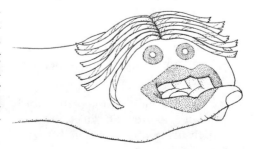

a nose above the lips. As a final touch, make a simple wig from yarn or a hat from a scrap of cloth. You can even entertain your audience by putting on the lipstick and the wig right in front of them.

A simple act for starters (and one that's also good for practicing the puppet's lips) is to have your talking hand "sing" a song you know well. Of course, you will be doing the singing, or you could have the puppet sing to a record or something on the radio. In time, you can create several different talking-hand characters and give each one a particular personality—and maybe an interesting name.

FINGER PUPPETS

Construction

Builder's age
  3+

Player's age
  3+

Materials
☐ Magazine with pictures of faces
☐ Transparent tape

Tools
☐ Scissors

Building instructions
Finger puppets using faces cut from magazine pictures are super fast and easy to make, and you can pretend to be up to ten different characters all at one time.

1. Look through a magazine for small pictures of faces. Faces measuring about one inch high

work well. When you find a face you like, cut it out in a horizontal strip about two inches wide.

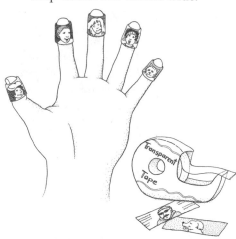

2. Wrap the paper strip around the tip of one of your fingers so that the face is looking out from the pad of your finger (not from the fingernail), and wrap a piece of transparent tape around the strip to make a finger ring. The finger puppet is ready to perform.

HAND SHADOW PUPPETS

Construction

Player's age
  4+

Materials
☐ None

Tools
☐ Hands only

Building instructions
Set up the Shadow Puppet Theater, and place your hands between the light and the back side of the screen. Now form your arms, hands, and fingers to create shadows on the screen.

Before you try to duplicate the hand shadow characters shown in the illustrations, experiment and practice throwing hand shadows onto the theater screen. Just twist your hands and stretch your fingers in all kinds of different ways to experiment with getting the shadows to look the way you want, and making the shadows the right size. Notice that the farther away you move your hands from the theater screen, the larger the shadow figures become, but the shadows also become less sharp.

Once you have mastered creating a few hand shadow puppets, go on to animate the figures by moving your hands and fingers to make wings flap, tails wag, ears wiggle, mouths talk, or legs walk. And to complete your hand shadow show, add voices to your characters and sound effects to your story.

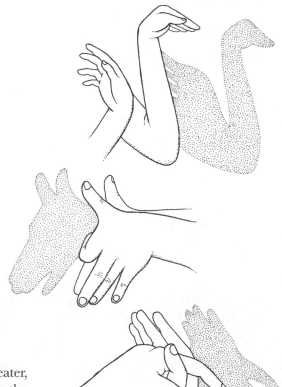

PANELIZED PLAYHOUSE

Some houses are built from prefabricated modular panels that are made in a factory and assembled at the construction site. With enough corrugated cardboard material, you can set up your own "factory" to make a supply of both square- and triangular-shaped panels that can be laced together at your selected site to construct several types of Panelized Playhouses.

Using just four squares and four triangles, you can build a simple one-small-kid play hut with a pyramid roof. And with a set of fifteen squares and ten triangles, you can design and construct a fort with a lookout tower, a shopping center with a flat roof, an apartment building with a gabled roof, a farmhouse with a silo, an airport terminal with a traffic-control tower, or just about any other kind of play building.

It may take a while to cut out the panels and poke through all the lace-up holes, but lacing together (and unlacing) the panels is simple. And the unassembled panels can be conveniently stored flat under a bed.

Construction

Building system
Corrugated Cardboard Carpentry (lacing)

Builder's age
9+

Player's age
3+

Materials
☐ Double-wall corrugated cardboard from several large boxes

☐ Vinyl-covered clothesline or sneaker shoelaces (approximately two laces for each panel with each lace being about twice the length of one edge of a panel)

Tools

☐ Carpenter's square

☐ Pencil

☐ Mat knife or utility knife

☐ Awl (to punch ¼″ diameter holes)

Building instructions

Making the panels

1. Collect several unbent pieces of double-wall corrugated cardboard from appliance boxes and furniture packaging, then figure out what size and how many identical squares and triangles they can make. Both the squares and the triangles in a modular set will have the same dimension for every edge. The smallest practical play space uses twenty-six-inch panels, and thirty-four-inch panels are ideal for building comfortable kid-size Panelized Playhouses.

A basic starter set of six square panels and four triangular panels is enough to build small buildings and towers with either a gable roof or a pyramid roof. To build more elaborate structures, you can make each panel as you need it, or calculate in advance how many squares and triangles (and how much corrugated material) you will need.

2. Using a carpenter's square and a pencil, lay out the pattern of cut lines to make the first square and the pattern of cut lines to make the first equilateral triangle. Remember that you must use the same side-length dimension for both the square and the triangle.

3. With a mat knife and the carpenter's square for a cutting guide, cut out the triangle and the square, and use them as templates for drawing the cut lines of all the additional squares and triangles you will need. Cut out all the additional squares and triangles.

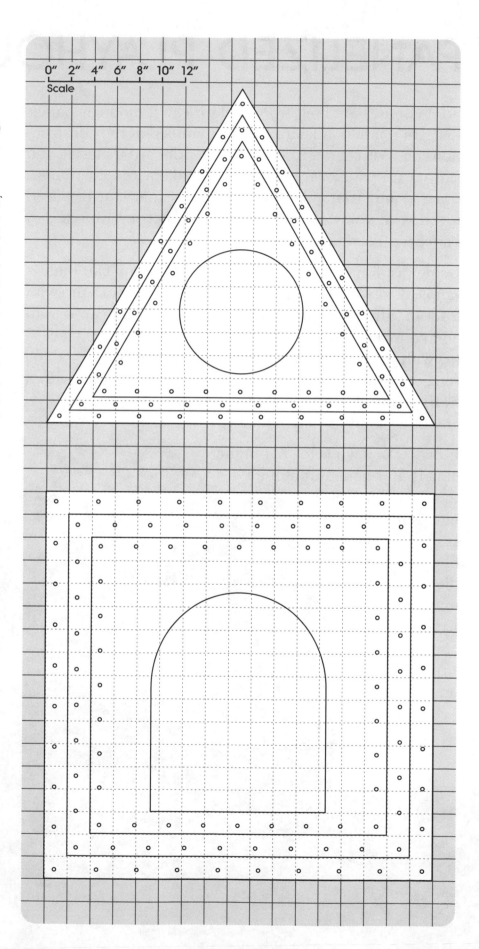

0″ 2″ 4″ 6″ 8″ 10″ 12″
Scale

You can decide to leave all or some panels plain, or decorate them with paint, wallpaper, or markers. You can cut openings in some panels for windows, skylights, and a door, but removing too much material will weaken the panel.

Making a hole-location template and punching the lace-up holes

1. Use a scrap length of corrugated cardboard to make the template. Since all edges of all panels are the same length, you can make one master template for punching the lace-up holes along all edges of both the squares and the triangles.

   All holes should be the same distance from the edges and no closer than one inch. Spacing between holes should be the same but no more than four inches apart or less than three inches apart. You will need to do some calculating to get the template to lay out evenly for the side length you are using.

2. Use an awl to punch holes through the template at each of the lace-hole locations. To protect the work surface from getting gouged by the awl, stack several scraps of corrugated board under the hole you are punching.

3. Now use the template to mark the hole locations along each edge of each panel, then punch the holes completely through to the full diameter of the awl.

Making the laces

Use one lace for each adjoining pair of edges to be laced together. The starting length of each lace should be about twice the length of the edge. For example, you will need a fifty-two-inch long lace to lace a twenty-six-inch panel. You can either use sneaker shoelaces of the correct length or cut laces to length from vinyl-covered clothesline. The plastic clothesline is stiff enough to easily thread through the holes and pliable enough for tying knots.

Assembling the panels

Since all sides of all panels are the same length, you can attach any combination of squares and triangles—square to square, square to triangle, or triangle to triangle.

First, line up the edges of two panels at the angle you want, and check to be sure the punch holes are opposite each other. Loop one end of a lace through a pair of matching holes and tie a knot. Now thread the other end of the lace through the next pair of holes and pull snugly to take up the slack. Continue threading each successive pair of holes the same way until you come to the last pair. After threading the last pair of holes, you can either let any remaining length of lace just hang in place or knot it for a stronger construction.

Playhouses to build

The kind of playhouse you build is up to you. However, here are a few basic assemblies of squares and triangles you may want to use in your construction.

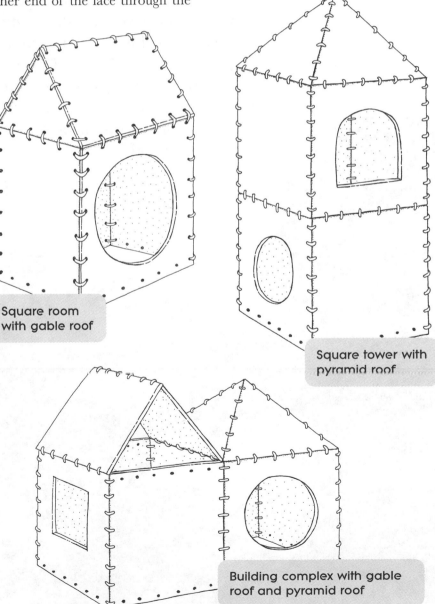

Square room with gable roof

Square tower with pyramid roof

Building complex with gable roof and pyramid roof

STEP-SIDE PYRAMID TOY BOX

A plain stack of boxes might make a nice room organizer and storage system for toys and other stuff, but using three or four boxes that are just the right shapes and sizes makes a special kind of stepped-pyramid toy box with cubbies for storage and step-sides for shelves. And there are a few different ways to stack the boxes to construct the Aztec-like pyramid.

Building the toy-box structure is so simple that you should have plenty of time to paint the pyramid panels in bright colors and maybe draw Aztec patterns. For another pleasing look, the entire structure can be covered with self-stick wallpaper. And when you're done building and decorating, there's still the fun of loading up the cubbies and displaying your favorite stuff on the pyramid steps. There's even one very special place to display a very special possession on the top of the pyramid.

Construction

Building system
Corrugated Cardboard Carpentry (gluing or taping)

Builder's age
5+

Player's age
3+

Materials
☐ 3 or 4 complete corrugated boxes in graduated sizes (See building instructions.)

☐ Latex contact cement or kraft packaging tape

Tools

☐ Paintbrush or paint roller (for applying latex contact cement if used)

☐ Scissors (for cutting kraft tape if used)

Building instructions

1. To create a pleasing stepped pyramid form, it's important to find three or four complete corrugated boxes in graduated sizes like the ones shown. Notice that the box flaps are on the smaller side panels (not the larger top and bottom sides). One of the flap sides of each box will be folded open to form a cubby.

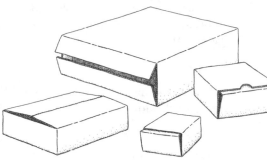

Boxes with flaps on the larger tops and bottoms can be used, but you will need to first tape all the box flaps closed, then cut three edges of a side to make a flap opening.

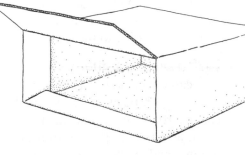

Check to make sure that when the boxes are stacked and centered, from the biggest on the bottom up to the smallest, they create steps that are wide enough to be useful shelves. If you need wider shelves, try stacking the boxes with the back side of the pyramid toy box lined up flush and vertical. For even more shelf

space, try positioning the boxes in a corner so two sides are flush and vertical.

You will also need to decide if you want the cubby openings to all face the same direction or different directions. The top box can have its opening either to the side or facing up.

2. After deciding which stacking method works best, convert each of the boxes into a cubby box. Begin by opening the four flaps on one side of the box. You may need to remove or cut away any packaging tape keeping the flaps closed. The opposite side should remain closed and taped.

Completely fold in the two narrow flaps (flat against the insides of the box), and completely fold in only one of the long flaps. The other long flap can become a hanging door if you want a way to close the cubbies. If you prefer open cubbies, completely fold in both long flaps.

3. Stack the cubby boxes into the type of stepped pyramid you liked best and either tape or glue the boxes in position. Kraft packaging tape creates a smooth stepped appearance. Using latex contact cement is a bit messier and requires careful application, but creates a very strong bond.

Here's a tip for making it easier to apply tape in right-angle corners: Cut the tape to the length needed, then before wetting the strip, fold it lengthwise into a "V" shape, glue-side out, and crease the fold. Flatten the tape open again for wetting with a sponge. Immediately apply the tape to position, using a finger to force

the crease into the corner joint as it is being applied.

Other than any decorating of the boxes you may want to do, the Step-Side Pyramid Toy Box is complete and ready to be loaded.

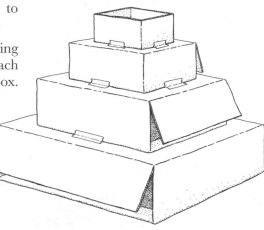

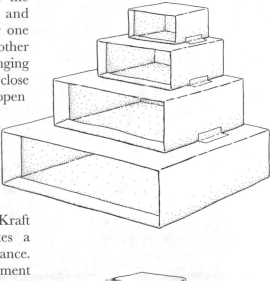

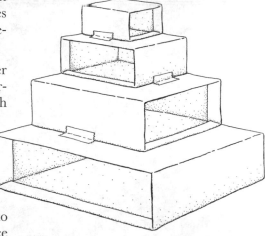

CANEY STOOL

The unique structure and elegant design of this sitting stool is created from two identical shapes that fold and interlock to strengthen and support each other. There are no fasteners, no adhesives, or anything else needed to create the rigid structure. However, you must carefully lay out the panel pattern and exactly cut out and score the shapes so the two halves will fit together correctly.

Since the completed Caney Stool is symmetrical, either square end can be the top or the bottom. The stool can also be used as a small table. You might even draw a checkers board on one square end and another game board on the opposite end.

Construction

Building system
Corrugated Box Carpentry (score, cut, and fold)

Builder's age
9+

Player's age
5+

Materials
☐ 2 large pieces of double-wall corrugated cardboard, each at least 30″ x 47″

Tools
☐ Builder's square or straightedge at least 20″ long

☐ Pencil

☐ Yardstick or measuring tape

☐ Mat knife or utility knife

☐ Scoring tool

Building instructions
One stool is made from two identical folded panels that must be drawn, scored, cut out, and folded exactly according to the plan.

Laying out the pattern
You can either draw the same pattern on both pieces of corrugated cardboard, or make one panel and use it as a tracing pattern to draw the other identical piece. Drawing lightly with a pencil, use a yardstick (or a straightedge and measuring tape) to lay out a grid of two-inch squares on one of the pieces of corrugated board. Using the grid squares as a comparative guide, copy the Caney Stool pattern onto the corrugated board.

Scoring and cutting the shape

Note that solid lines on the pattern are for cutting, and dotted lines get scored for folding. Use the straight edge of a builder's square as a guide for both scoring and cutting. First, score all the dotted lines with a scoring tool, then cut out the shape with a mat knife.

Score and cut the second piece identical to the first. (You can use the first piece to trace the cut lines for the second identical piece, although you will have to measure and draw in the score lines.)

Folding the panels

This is the trickiest part of the construction, and it might be easier to do with a helper. Gently begin to fold each of the eight flaps around the perimeter. Use a straightedge along the score to help the material bend straight on line. Go around the piece several times, bending each flap up a little more each time until it looks like the illustration below.

Note that all scores fold in the same direction except the four small scores radiating from the corners of the square. These scores fold in the opposite direction—and that's the tricky part—getting some scores to fold one way while folding others the opposite way.

Fold the second panel to be identical to the first.

Assembling the stool

Position the two folded pieces as shown so the long "legs" of each piece fit into the short "legs" of the other piece. Push the two pieces together as far as they will go. The long legs of each piece should "bottom out" on the base (or top) of the other. The stool is now ready for sitting.

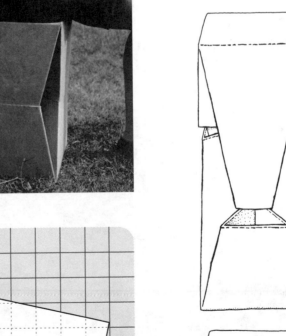

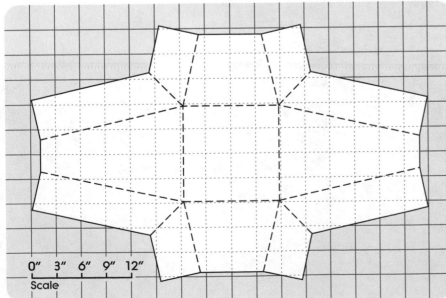

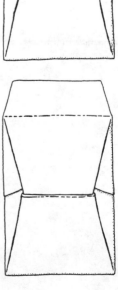

0" 3" 6" 9" 12"
Scale

BIG BOX BUILDINGS

Turning a big box into a building needs very little explanation or instructions. Kids have been doing it ever since delivery drivers have been leaving empty refrigerator cartons and other large boxes behind. What the box then becomes is up to you. One box might go through several transformations from a fortress with peepholes, to the deck of a submarine with a lookout hatch, maybe a country house with window shutters, or a sidewalk stand with a counter, to finally just a tattered cardboard sled for sliding down grassy slopes.

Of course, you do need to start with the biggest box you can find, and the box you get may have some influence on what you build with it. A washing machine carton with a few cutouts in the right locations makes a pretty nice castle tower, and a couch carton easily converts into a school bus. When you do have an inspiration, just let the construction begin and start cutting, scoring, folding, and taping.

Construction

Building system
Corrugated Box Carpentry (cut, score, fold, and tape)

Builder's age
9+

Player's age
3+

Materials
☐ Large corrugated carton

☐ Packaging tape or filament tape

Tools
☐ Mat knife or utility knife

☐ Scoring tool

Building instructions
In the traditional spirit of Big Box Buildings, just start playing with the empty box, then cut, score, fold, or tape it to become whatever you imagine. There is no need for exact measurements and cutting accuracy.

SLOTTED-PANEL STRUCTURES AND SCULPTURES

Maybe you have seen empty cartons at the grocery store that contain slotted vertical dividers made of corrugated cardboard panels that fit together to form a matrix of cells. These cells once kept bottles separated in the shipping carton so they would not bang and break against each other. However, the slotted dividers collected from several of these cartons also make an instant construction system. Simply take them apart and reassemble the slotted panels in new ways. Or you could use Corrugated Box Carpentry to make a stronger and a more modular set of slotted panels. Using either system, the slotted panels can be quickly assembled to build medium- and large-scale fantasy forts, towers, and sculptures, and just as easily be taken apart and reassembled in a different way.

Construction

Building system
Corrugated Cardboard Carpentry (slotting)

Builder's age
9+

Player's age
4+

Materials

☐ Corrugated cardboard from several large boxes

Tools

☐ Carpenter's square

☐ Pencil

☐ Mat knife or utility knife

Building instructions

Although the slotted-panel dividers taken from a shipping carton can often be reassembled into a few other forms, they are usually made from rather thin and weak corrugated material that too easily bends and tears. And slotted panels from different-size boxes may not fit together very well. A more versatile and durable set of modular slotted panels can be made from the stronger corrugated cardboard carton.

Thicker types of single-wall corrugated cardboard may be rigid enough, and heavier double-wall corrugated is better. Use panels of corrugated cardboard cut from the strongest cartons, and make sure all the pieces are the same thickness.

First, lay out and then cut out a starter set of modular slotted panels. Follow the plans above and refer to Corrugated Box Carpentry building techniques for laying out and cutting out the panels and slots. You can add more panels and cut special shapes as needed. To make a smaller set of modular panels for building desktop structures, divide each dimension in half.

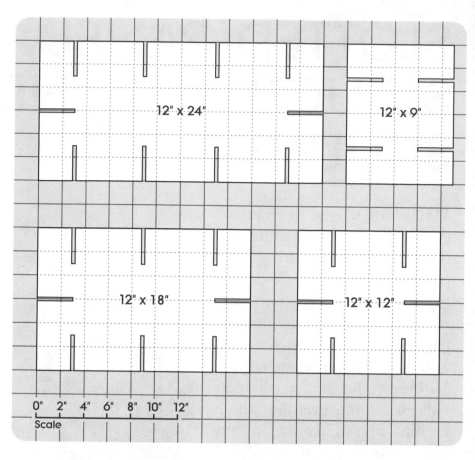

12" x 24"   12" x 9"

12" x 18"   12" x 12"

0" 2" 4" 6" 8" 10" 12"
Scale

Starter Set

Quantity	Size
4	12 x 24
4	12 x 18
2	12 x 12
2	12 x 9

Building with slotted panels

Sometimes it's fun to just begin interlocking the panels to see what you get and then decide what your imagination says it is. You can also plan the assembly to create specific structures—maybe a pretend airport control tower, a real exhibit display system for your artwork, or a sculpture that casts interesting shadows.

The slotted-panel structures and sculptures you build with corrugated cardboard are sturdy, but not strong enough to sit or stand on. And don't place anything on the structure than could fall off and hurt you.

Structures built with these slotted panels are meant to be temporary playthings, but if you build a masterpiece worth keeping,

the panels can be taped at intersecting joints to create a more permanent structure.

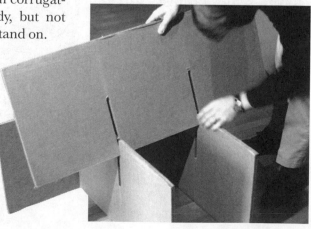

LAMINATED LOUNGE CHAIR

This is a big, time-consuming project that uses an enormous amount of corrugated cardboard, but the result may be worth it. You get to personalize the shape of the chair to both suit your aesthetic taste and the way you like to lounge. Or by building the lounge chair as a group project, you can collectively design the shape that most find pleasing and comfortable, and share the work of collecting large boxes, laying out the plans, cutting out the panels, and gluing them together. The Laminated Lounge Chair is so strong and durable that it can be used every day as a piece of your bedroom or playroom furniture or outdoors on dry ground. And for even more comfort, plus a pleasing effect, drape a large colorful bath towel over the lounge chair.

Construction

Building system
Corrugated Cardboard Carpentry (gluing)

Builder's age
10+

Player's age
2+

Materials
□ Corrugated cardboard panels from at least 40 large boxes

□ Latex contact cement

Tools
□ Carpenter's square or measuring tape

□ Pencil

□ Mat knife or utility knife

□ Paintbrush or paint roller for applying latex contact cement

Building instructions
Design a pattern

Begin by designing a lounge-chair shape and size that best fits you (and probably others about your size). Notice that from a side view, the lounge chair has a few curves meant to comfortably support your legs, your bottom, and your back. Following the plans below, lay out and cut out one base panel with the curves shown, then adjust the shape any way you like. Maybe you prefer to lay back farther or maybe more upright. Maybe you want your legs arched more or maybe lying flat.

Here is one way to determine a shape that fits you. Sit on the floor with your back up against the wall and your legs straight out in front of you. Now place pillows behind your back and under your legs to find a more comfortable position. Keep adding and removing pillows until you are lounging on your back in the most comfortable position. Compare the shape of the base panel you made to the angles and curves of your lounging position, and change the base piece to match them. In addition to cutting away some material, you may also need to add material to create the shape you need. Now use the new shape as a template pattern to trace the cut line for the rest of the base pieces needed.

Make and assemble the pieces

To make the base wide enough (about thirteen to fifteen inches), you will need to trace, cut out, and glue up about sixty-five to eighty identical base panels. Since all the side panels (except the first and last) will be sandwiched between other panels, its easiest if

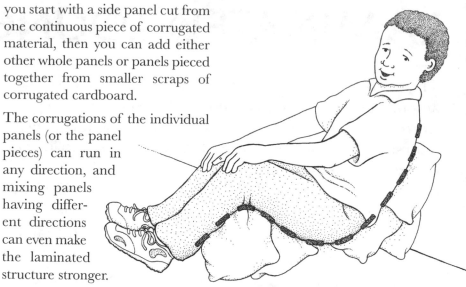

you start with a side panel cut from one continuous piece of corrugated material, then you can add either other whole panels or panels pieced together from smaller scraps of corrugated cardboard.

The corrugations of the individual panels (or the panel pieces) can run in any direction, and mixing panels having different directions can even make the laminated structure stronger.

Follow the directions on the container of latex contact cement, and glue a second panel directly over the first panel. If you use a roller to spread the contact cement, it's probably better to first cut out all the panels needed. If you don't expect to finish the construction all at once, it is easier (less cleanup and wasted glue) to apply the cement with a wide brush.

Be careful to perfectly align one panel over the other before sticking the two together. Contact cement allows only one try at getting it right, and once the two panels make con-

tact, they cannot be taken apart. Building the stack on the floor and up against a perpendicular wall will help keep the stack "square" and the panels aligned. Continue to add panels, one directly on top of the previous one, until the thickness of the laminate stack is about fifteen inches—or wide enough when you test the lounge chair for comfort. All that's left is the decision to paint, decorate, or cover the chair or leave it "natural."

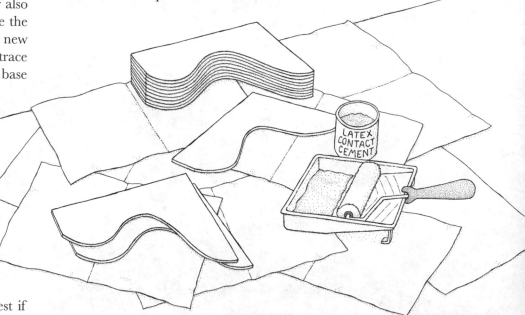

FOLDED PAPER PROJECTS AND PUZZLES

You probably already know how to fold a sheet of paper into a paper airplane or maybe into an origami bird, box, or cootie catcher. Several of these Folded Paper Projects are just as easy to make—including four paper airplanes that were chosen "best flyers" by their kid testers. The performance of the Rain Stick Storm Maker is also truly outstanding. The sound of falling rain is very realistic, and the storm lasts about half a minute.

If you want to make action figures or other characters to use for pretend play or maybe with a dollhouse or model fort, Play-People Stand-Ups shows how to turn magazine pictures of people into three-dimensional stand-up figures. And you can completely furnish your model house or castle with Small-Box Furniture and Appliances.

These paper projects also include two building systems. Stack'n Clip Sawhorses are super simple to make and can be assembled in more ways than may first seem obvious. Rainbow Prisms can be stacked to create complex and colorful sculptures, or the prism shapes can be connected end to end to make a rainbow-colored model of the St. Louis Gateway Arch.

To make several of the Folded Paper Puzzles, you will first need to lay out the puzzle-piece patterns on paper. Ten Simple and Tough Tessellations use various shaped cutouts to form regular geometric designs. The designs created by Octagon Arrow Artwork and Quad Panel Patterns are also geometric, but the number of different designs you can make is in the thousands! Pattern and Puzzle Paper Cubes don't require layouts but do demand accurate paper folding and good dexterity to make the origami harlequin cubes. Solving the Paper Cubes puzzle is also challenging. And for the toughest mental challenge (but requiring the least manual skill), try solving the Paper Puzzle Brain Twisters.

BUILD IT

RAIN STICK STORM MAKER 492

STACK'N CLIP SAWHORSES 495

BEST-FLYER PAPER PLANES 497

RAINBOW PRISMS 501

SMALL-BOX FURNITURE
AND APPLIANCES 504

PLAY-PEOPLE STAND-UPS 506

PATTERN AND PUZZLE
PAPER CUBES 508

OCTAGON ARROW ARTWORK 510

QUAD PANEL PATTERNS 512

PAPER PUZZLE BRAIN TWISTERS 514

TEN SIMPLE AND TOUGH
TESSELLATIONS 516

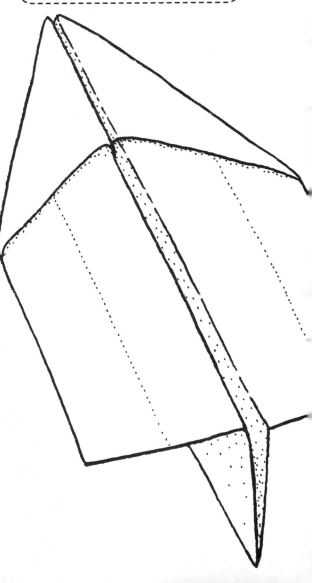

RAIN STICK STORM MAKER

In dry desert climates all over the world, rain sticks have been used in ceremonies to mimic the sound of rain in an attempt to remind the "spirits" that a rainstorm would be welcome. In southwestern Native American cultures, rain sticks were made from long pieces of dead cactus that had dried in the desert sun to become hollow tubes. The long cactus needles were pushed into the entire length of the hollow core so they created a labyrinth of obstructions. A handful of small pebbles were then put inside the tube and both ends sealed closed. Each time the rain stick was flipped over and held vertically, a new rain shower would begin as the pebbles cascaded down through the tube, hitting the protruding needles to create the peaceful and calming sound.

You can build an excellent Rain Stick Storm Maker from a cardboard tube, a few folded strips of paper, and some rice. The sound it makes may remind you of a spring shower, a city rainstorm, or rain falling through the leaves of a forest.

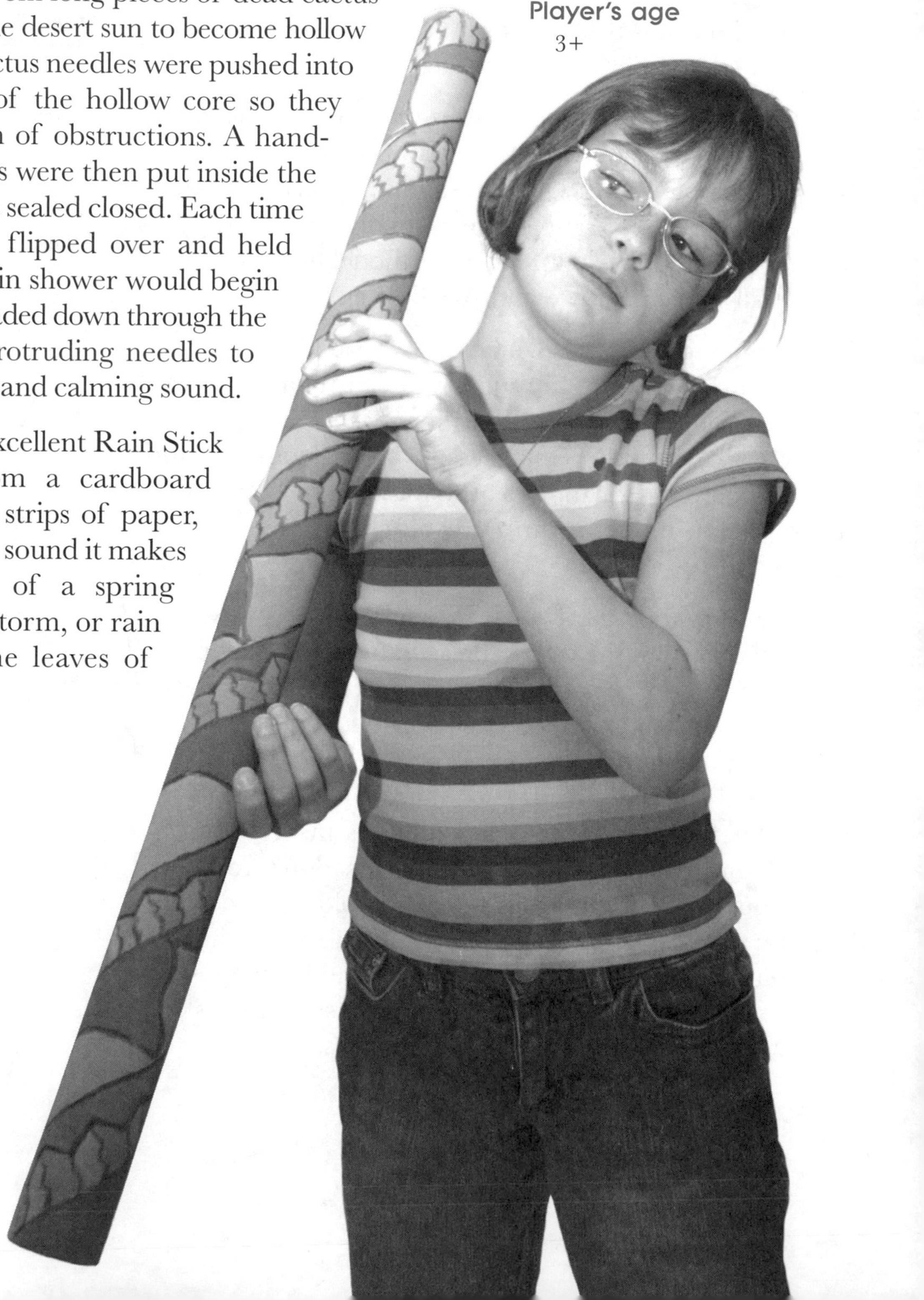

Construction

Builder's age
8+

Player's age
3+

Materials

- ☐ 1 long cardboard tube from gift-wrapping paper, or
- ☐ 3 shorter cardboard tubes from paper towels and food wraps
- ☐ ¼ cup of rice, dried split peas, or lentils, or ½ cup or more of popcorn kernels, sunflower seeds, or dried beans if using a tube larger than 1 ¾ inch diameter
- ☐ Several sheets of heavyweight paper. Construction paper, paper grocery bags, magazine covers, and file folders work well.
- ☐ Masking tape or packaging tape
- ☐ 4 foot length of string

Tools

- ☐ Ruler or yardstick
- ☐ Pencil
- ☐ Scissors
- ☐ Measuring cup (optional)

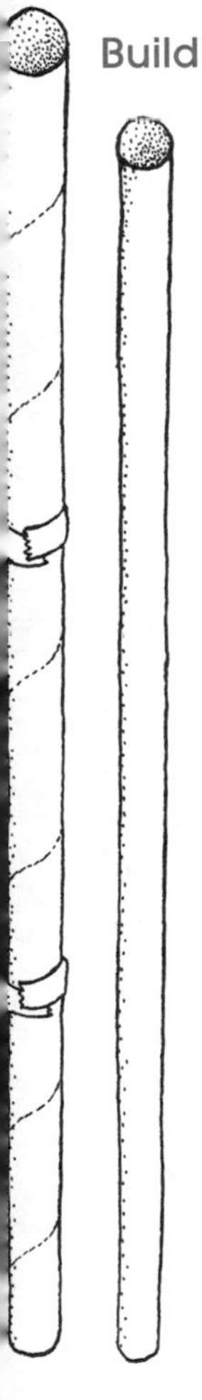

Building instructions

Find or make a long paper tube

Paper tubes left over from gift-wrapping paper are usually thirty inches long and come in several diameters. The smallest 1 ¼ inch inside-diameter tube allows for the fastest construction and uses rice to make a pleasant rain shower sound. Larger gift-wrap tubes with an inside diameter of 1 ⅞ inch or greater use larger seeds or beans to make a sound more like a rainstorm, but the larger tube requires much more material and time to construct. Instead of using one long gift-wrap tube, you can tape together, end to end, three paper-towel tubes or food-wrap tubes to make one thirty-three-inch-long tube.

Construct the folded-paper core

Instead of sticking needles or nails into the tube like those used in traditional and commercial rain sticks, the obstructed pathway through the cardboard tube is made using folded strips of paper. The width of the paper strips you cut and fold must be an exact dimension that depends on the diameter of the tube you use.

1. Measure the inside diameter of your tube, and refer to the chart below to determine the width of the paper strips needed.

Tube diameter	Strip width
1 ¼ inch	⅞ inch
1 ⅝ inch	1 ³⁄₁₆ inch
1 ¾ inch	1 ¼ inch
1 ⅞ inch	1 ⁵⁄₁₆ inch

2. Using a ruler and pencil, measure and mark lines on several sheets of heavyweight paper, indicating the correct width for cutting paper strips. Using scissors, carefully cut the strips on the marked lines you have drawn.

The number of paper strips you will need to cut and attach end to end depends on the length and diameter of the tube and the size of the paper sheets you start with. In general, you will need enough strips to equal a length five to six times the length of the tube being used. That means, for example, if you are cutting eleven inch-long strips (from 8 ½ x 11 inch paper) to make the core for a thirty-inch-long tube, you would need to cut at least fourteen strips.

3. Start with two strips taped together at their ends at a right angle and alternately fold one strip over the other, back and forth, creating an accordion-like stack. When you get near the end of the first two strips, tape another strip onto each, butted end to end and straight in line. Continue to alternately fold one strip over the other, back and forth, and continue to add strips, creating an increasingly taller accordion-like stack.

4. When you have attached and folded all but the last few strips, it's time to test the length of the core. Holding an end of the folded and compressed core in each hand, gently pull and stretch it out to see how long it actually is. As you pull, the

core will twist and get considerably longer. If needed, add more
folded strips until the stretched
core is the length of the tube.

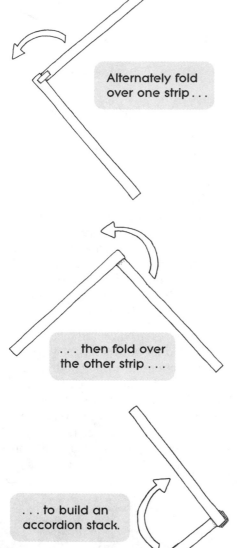

Alternately fold
over one strip . . .

. . . then fold over
the other strip . . .

. . . to build an
accordion stack.

Tape the final fold so the stack
doesn't unfold.

Assemble the rain stick

1. Pull and stretch the folded core to its full length.
   Tie one end of a
   string around one
   end of the core, and drop the
   other end of the string completely through the tube.

2. Gently but firmly pull the string
   to pull the core completely into
   the tube. The fit should be snug,
   and the core should be positioned so its ends are about one
   inch inside the ends of the tube.
   Remove the string.

3. Seal off one end of the tube by
   folding over the edge of the tube
   in a few places and taping the
   folds closed. You can also plug and
   tape the end closed using a disk
   cut from a scrap of cardboard.

4. Pour the measured amount of
   rice, split peas, or lentils into the
   open end of the tube. If you are
   using a tube with a diameter
   larger than 1 3/4 inches, you may
   want to try using popcorn kernels, sunflower seeds, or dried
   beans for a "heavier" rain sound.
   You might experiment with the
   kind and the amount of seeds
   you use to get the right rainfall
   sound—and to be sure they flow
   through the core without getting
   stuck. When you like what you
   hear, seal the remaining open
   end the same way you did the
   other end.

5. Although the rain stick is complete and ready to be used, decorating a rain stick is traditional.
   Most rain sticks were used in
   some type of ceremony, so they
   were always adorned with colors,
   patterns, and whimsical carvings.
   Use whatever markers and materials you like to create designs
   and drawings on the tube. If
   you paint the entire tube,
   the dry paint will slightly harden the card-
   board tube and
   make the sound
   even better.

User tip

To get the longest dura-
tion of rain each time
the rain stick is flipped
over, try holding the rain
stick at slight angles from
straight up and down and
gently shake it back and
forth. You should expect
to get at least a twenty-
to thirty-second shower,
and some Rain Stick
Storm Makers have been
known to produce tor-
rential downpours for up
to one minute.

STACK'N CLIP SAWHORSES

You probably can't imagine all the intricate and interesting structures you can build using identical multiples of a simple folded card. The secret is discovering all the ways this bent-panel module can be oriented for stacking. The results can be a rather complex panel-and-plane structure or maybe a game of challenge you play by yourself or with others. How tall can you build a Saw Horse tower before it topples?

For those builders who prefer to use a fastening system to build with Saw Horse panels (rather than just stacking), bobby pin "clips" work perfectly once you discover the different ways the panels can be attached with clips. Using clips, you have a choice to either attach all the Saw Horses with clips when building a structure, or use clips only to construct different stacking-module designs, like X-shaped and U-shaped modules.

Construction

Builder's age
4+

Player's age
4+

Materials
- 25 or more cards all the same size. Either an old deck of playing cards or 3″ × 5″ index cards work best

- Bobby pins. Figure on using about one bobby pin for each sawhorse

Tools
☐ Hands only

Building instructions

Use at least twenty-five cards for a starter set. All cards must be the same size. A deck of playing cards makes Sawhorses with interesting graphics. Index cards are available in white and a variety of colors. As a less sturdy substitute, you can

also make Sawhorses using paper sheets from a small notepad or even a pad of sticky notes.

To convert a card into a Sawhorse module, simply fold the card in half, rub the folded crease to flatten it, then open the fold to create a "V" or "sawhorse"

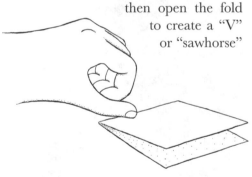

shape. Heavyweight card stock may be difficult to fold and crease smoothly unless you fold the card over the sharp edge of a table or countertop. Make at least twenty-five Sawhorses for a starter set.

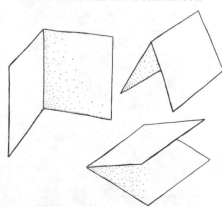

Playing tips

The hardest part of building a stacked structure is getting it started—especially for young builders. The Sawhorse shape is weak because it is missing a third side to become a structural triangle. Beginning builders will find it easiest to start a Sawhorse structure on carpeting. Carpet has enough texture to keep the legs of the base cards from spreading.

It takes a while for most novice Sawhorse builders to discover the many different ways the identical cards can be oriented and stacked. When adding a piece to your structure, try to imagine it oriented in every conceivable position, and try to plan ahead so you prepare a stable base for placing the next card on top.

Here are a few simple structures that illustrate some of the ways the Sawhorse cards can be stacked. Discovering other ways is up to you.

And don't be discouraged if your building suddenly comes crashing down. Sawhorse structures are considered precarious art that is meant to be temporary and only last until an imbalance, a breeze, or a bump causes the entire thing to come crashing down. The idea is not to see how long the structure will stand, but how big and complicated you can make it before the crash occurs. You have to decide if just "one more" Sawhorse will be one too many.

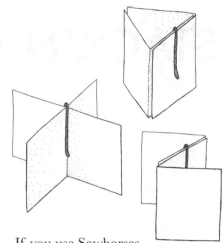

If you use Sawhorses with bobby pin connectors, you will be able to make very different types of shapes including structural X-beams, channels, box beams and triangular sections. Above are a few simple structures that illustrate some of the ways Sawhorse cards can be connected using bobby pins to either build entire structures or to make different shapes of stacking modules.

BEST-FLYER PAPER PLANES

You may already know how to fold and launch a paper plane, but how many different types of paper planes can you make that are guaranteed to dart long distances or perform outstanding aerobatics? These four great-flying paper planes were chosen "best flyers" by a group of kid testers, and they are super easy to make without measuring or cutting. They can all glide for long distances across open spaces, either indoors or outdoors, and with a few adjustments, some models can do loops, flips, dips and landings. Each plane starts as a flat sheet of paper, and with only a few folds and bends, the paper is transformed into a Flying Carpet, a Classic Dart, a Double Dart, or an Acrobat.

Construction

Builder's age
8+

Player's age
4+

Materials

☐ Sheets of paper, approximately 8 1/2″ x 11″. Magazine covers work best.

☐ Transparent mending tape (optional)

Tools
☐ Hands only

Building instructions

In terms of flight aerodynamics, a paper plane is just a miniature version of a real plane. Building and flying paper planes involves the same principles of flight, and many variables will determine how a plane will fly or if it will fly at all. The weight and stiffness of the paper, how the plane is tossed in the air, adjustments to the wings, flying conditions indoors or outdoors, and, of course, the plane design itself will all affect how far the plane will fly, how long it will stay aloft, and whether it will dart straight ahead or swerve, dip, dive, and make U-turns. Most paper plane builders and pilots continually experiment and make adjustments, always trying to fly their planes farther and keep them in flight longer.

According to the rules established by international airplane competitions, a paper airplane must be able to fly a distance of at least fifteen feet or stay aloft for at least three seconds. Award winning flights typically last more than ten seconds and travel distances well over one hundred feet. Some paper plane flyers also attempt to set altitude records. *The Guinness Book of World Records* lists a best indoor distance of nearly two hundred feet and indoor time aloft of over ninety seconds. Here are a few tips for building your Best-Flyer Paper Planes.

Paper selection

All planes start with a full sheet of paper, approximately 8 1/2 x 11 inches. Although any sheet of paper will make a plane that flies, a lightweight and stiff paper is best and will hold its shape better than papers commonly used in copiers and computer printers. The front and back covers of magazines work especially well and add a splash of graphic design.

Making folds

If you have difficulty making straight folds, crease the paper over a straight edge like a ruler or countertop, and complete the fold-over by further creasing the fold with your fingers.

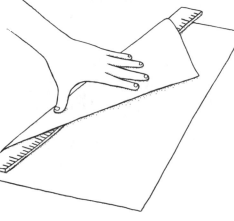

Tossing techniques

The way you hold and toss the plane greatly affects its flight. Some planes require a gentle toss, some should be thrown with force, and some planes will fly quite differently depending on how they are launched. Tossing the plane straight ahead or slightly up or down will also affect flight. Follow the flying tips given for each plane design, and then experiment using different techniques.

Making adjustments

The flight pattern of any paper plane depends on how it is "trimmed" for flight. Just the slightest adjustments can result in big flight changes. These Best-Flyer Paper Planes are designed to be perfectly balanced and soar gracefully through space. You can usually correct any flight problems by slightly bending the angle of the wings or tail up or down. Experiment.

The Flying Carpet

- Ultra simple to make
- One sheet makes a slow-flying plane
- A half sheet makes a faster plane

Folding instructions

1. Start with either a whole sheet or half sheet of paper. Fold the sheet in half in the direction shown and crease it, then open it into two flaps.

2. Fold one of the flaps over to the center and crease the fold flat.

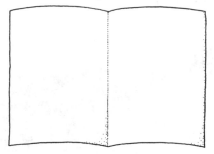

3. Fold the folded flap over again to the center and crease the fold flat.

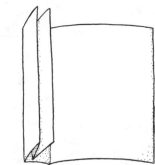

4. Now fold the twice-folded flap over *at* the crease in the center (not *to* the crease).

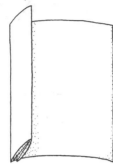

5. Give the flying carpet some curvature (for aerodynamic stability) by drawing the folded flap over the sharp edge of a tabletop as shown.

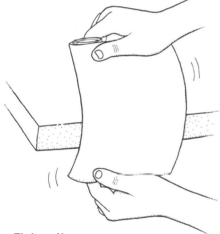

Flying tips

Grasp the back edge of the plane in your fingertips with the folded flap facing forward and curved up. Then just hold the plane up high and release it with a very gentle push.

To correct erratic loops or dives, trim the corners of the tail by curving them either slightly up or down.

The Classic Dart

- Straight and accurate flight
- Short-distance flyer
- Tail trims to do dips and turns

Folding instructions

1. Start with a whole sheet of paper. Fold the sheet in half in the direction shown and crease it, then open the sheet flat.

2. Fold over two corners so they line up close to the center as shown, and crease the folds flat.

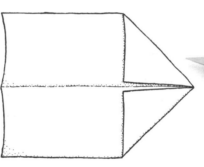

3. Fold over both sides so they line up close to the center as shown, and crease the folds flat.

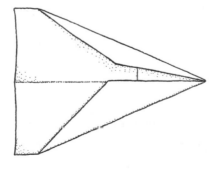

4. Fold over both sides again to the center, then crease the new folds flat.

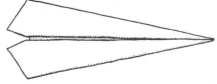

5. Fold the two halves of the plane together along the center crease,

and unfold the wings enough to give the plane its Classic Dart shape. For greater durability, apply a short strip of tape across the two wings.

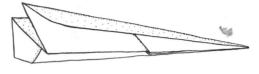

Flying tips

Grasp the center crease along the bottom, and sharply toss the nose of the dart straight forward.

If the dart dives sharply downward, trim the tail by giving it some upward curve.

The Double Dart

- Very smooth flight
- Long-distance flyer
- Makes nice landings

Folding instructions

1. Make a Classic Dart paper plane as shown in the folding instructions.

2. Make a second Classic Dart paper plane, but only through step 3 of the folding instructions as shown.

3. Insert the complete Classic Dart into the folds of the partially completed Dart as shown. For greater strength and durability, apply two short strips of tape where shown to fasten the two plane sections together.

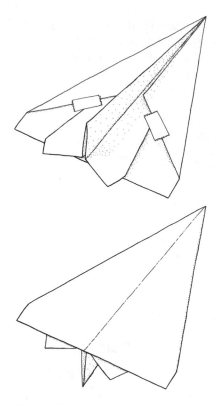

Flying tips

Grasp the center crease along the bottom, and sharply toss the nose of the dart straight forward.

If the dart dives sharply downward, trim the tail by giving it some upward curve.

The Acrobat

- Performs dips, flips, and loops
- Easily adjusts for different stunts
- Refolds for long-distance flights

Folding instructions

1. Fold the sheet in half in the direction shown and crease it. Fold it again in half and crease the fold, then fold it a third time and crease the fold. Open up the sheet flat.

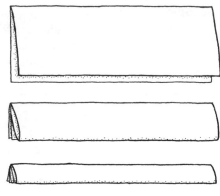

2. Fold over one corner from the center crease so the tip reaches the middle of the opposite half, and crease the fold.

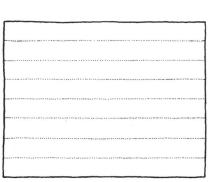

3. Fold over the opposite corner the same way.

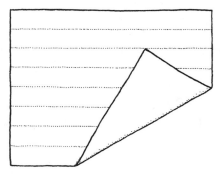

4. Fold over the top of the triangle so its tip lines up with the bottom of the triangle as shown.

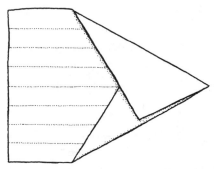

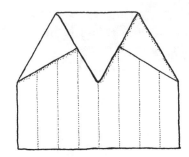

5. Now fold both sides up on the center crease. For acrobatics, fold down each wing on the creases next to the center crease as shown. For distance flight, fold down each wing on the creases located two up from the center crease as shown. Crease the new folds flat.

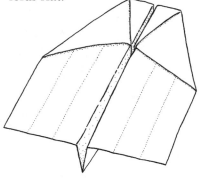

6. Unfold the wings to form the shape of the plane, then fold down each wing tip as shown.

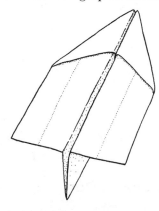

Flying tips

Grasp the underside of the plane, and sharply toss it up, down, or straight ahead and see what path the flight takes.

Make adjustments by trimming both tips of the tail with either a slight upward or downward curve.

RAINBOW PRISMS

Paint stores, hardware stores, and home improvement centers all offer "paint chips" that help customers compare and choose paint colors. These paint chips are often presented on rectangular strips of heavy paper with three, four, or five different color samples on each strip. By simply folding and fastening each strip so any three adjacent color chips form a triangular prism, you can make a very colorful set of building modules that can either be stacked like blocks to create both structures and patterns or joined end to end to form colorful rainbows and an arch similar in structure to the famous St. Louis Gateway Arch.

Construction

Builder's age
7+

Player's age
7+

Materials
- ☐ Lots of paint-chip strips, all the same size and all with the same number of colors per strip (Three or four colors per strip is preferred.)
- ☐ Transparent mending tape or rubber cement

Tools
- ☐ Scissors

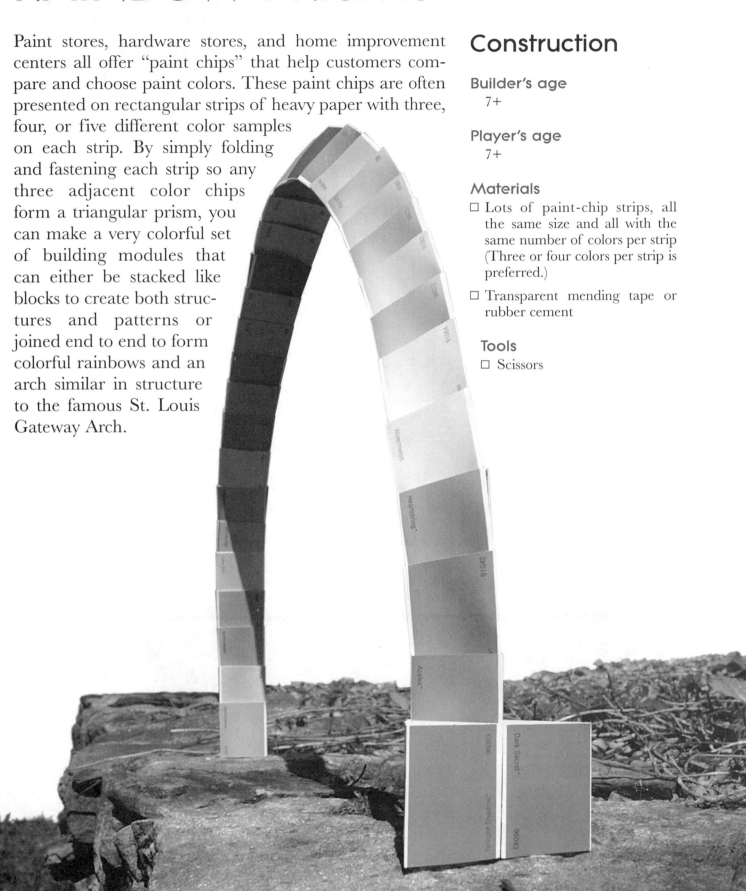

Building instructions

Making Rainbow Prism modules

1. Collect at least thirty paint-chip strips that are all the identical shape and have three or four color chips per strip. Strips having more than four colors can be cut down to three or four color chips with scissors. Note that strips with three color chips are best taped to form prisms, and strips with four color chips should be glued (and are a little easier to make).

Because you will need many paint-chip strips (and probably not buying that much paint), ask someone at the store if they have extra or discontinued color strips you can have. They often do. And if you have a choice, select strips in a range of colors that gradually transition from one color to the next—like the color transitions of a rainbow.

2. Fold each strip into a triangular prism so there is a different paint-chip color on each side. If the strip has three chips, bring the opposite ends of the strip together, and carefully tape the joint with a piece of clear mending tape. If the strip has four chips,

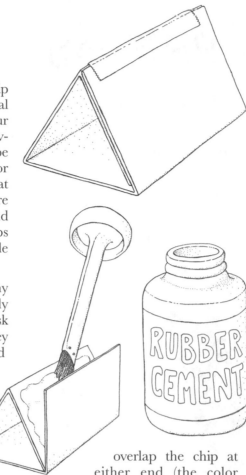

overlap the chip at either end (the color that won't be seen). Use rubber cement to secure the overlapping joint.

Whichever fastening method you use, it is very important that each of the folded triangular prisms be exactly the same size and shape.

Stacking Rainbow Prisms

The hollow triangular shape and identical size of the prism modules permit stacking in some interesting ways that you will quickly discover. And the multicolored structures they build can be a thoughtful juxtaposition of colors to create some special effect (like a rainbow or a checkerboard of light and dark shades), or the prisms can be stacked in any arbitrary arrangement of colors.

Building a Rainbow Prism arch

Most people find the graceful curve of a thin arch to be a very pleasing shape, especially the colorful rainbow that arches across the sky after a thunderstorm. A popular fast-food restaurant uses thin arches as one of its identifying symbols. And anyone who has been to St. Louis, Missouri, (or flown over the city on a clear day) could not have missed seeing the magnificent Gateway Arch that has become the city's most recognizable symbol and its most popular attraction. The stainless-steel structure has an equilateral-triangle cross section throughout its entire length, just like the arches you can build with Rainbow Prisms. Interestingly, the curve of the arch is not a perfect semicircle, but rather the shape you would get (only upside down) if you freely hung a length of rope between two supports.

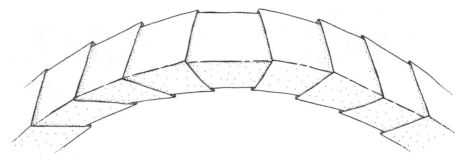

1. To build a complete Rainbow Prism arch, you will need at least thirty prism modules. Consider the order of the colors that will be used for making the arch, and lay out the prisms in the order they will be assembled. Because the triangular prisms have a different color on each side, you will actually get three different color patterns or rainbows in one arch.

2. The arch is built in two halves with each half starting at the base and rising up and towards the other until they meet and join at the top. If you are building the arch by yourself, it is easier to build it flat on a table or the floor and then raise it.

To begin one of the half-arch sections, assemble two prism modules end to end by inserting one module about a quarter-inch into the second module below it. Even though the modules are the same size, if you gently squeeze the three sides of the module to be inserted, it will contract enough to slip into the triangular end of the other module. When you stop squeezing, the connection will become snug.

3. Add one module at a time to the one below it. After inserting each module, slightly offset its joint so that the stack of modules arches in one direction. Continue to add modules (about ten to fifteen, depending on the module proportions) until you have formed half the arch.

4. Build a second arch the same way, starting at the base and using the same number of modules.

5. Assemble the two halves to form a complete arch by inserting the top of each half arch into either end of one more module. The arch is complete except for slight adjustments to the shape.

You may be able to balance the arch to stand on its own, or you can stabilize both bases to keep it from tipping over. Depending on where you plan to display the arch, you might tape it to a piece of cardboard, buttress it between two objects on a table or shelf, or figure out how to attach three more prism modules to each base of the arch to form large, stable, triangular platforms—just like the Gateway Arch!

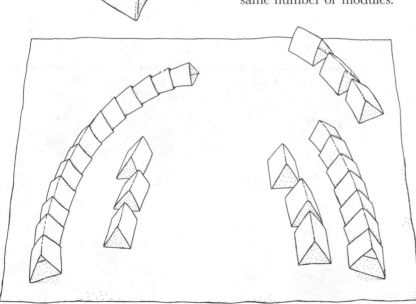

Gateway Arch
St. Louis, Missouri
Designed by Eero Sarinen
Built 1966

SMALL-BOX FURNITURE AND APPLIANCES

Each space in a dollhouse is defined by what you put in it. A bed, dresser, and mirror make a bedroom, just as a refrigerator, sink, and stove turn an empty room into a kitchen. An entire dollhouse could hold quite a lot of furniture and large appliances, including chairs, tables, cabinets, a TV set, and maybe a fireplace. You can make all of these by simply cutting and refolding small boxes—the kind commonly used to package tubes of toothpaste, bars of soap, sticks of butter, and half pints of milk. For example, with two simple cuts, an empty toothpaste box can be refolded into a living room couch. You can also find a picture of the furnishing or appliance in a magazine, cut it out, and tape the image to a small box that's the right size and shape. It's that simple.

Construction

Builder's age
9+

Player's age
3+

Materials
☐ Small boxes used for packaging these and other products: tubes of toothpaste, bars of soap, sticks of butter, half pints of milk, individual servings of cereal, and paper clips

☐ Transparent mending tape

☐ Magazines with pictures of furnishings and appliances

☐ Paint, felt-tip markers, and stickers (optional)

Tools

☐ Scissors

☐ Craft knife (optional)

Building instructions

Collect all the small boxes you can find. Because most packaging is immediately thrown away after the contents have been removed, you may have to ask family, friends, and neighbors to save their small disposable boxes for you.

The shape and size of the box you select for conversion to a piece of furniture or an appliance should be about the right shape for the item and the right size (scale) for the space it will occupy.

Turning the empty packaging into Small-Box Furniture and Appliances can be done a few different ways.

Method 1

Use a sharp, pointed craft knife or scissors to make the appropriate cuts and cutouts needed to refold and reshape the boxes into a

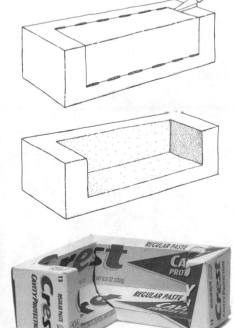

couch, a chair, or a cabinet. A simple rectangular cutout can turn a small box into a refrigerator, an oven, a sink, a TV set, a fireplace, or maybe a washer or dryer.

Method 2

Find pictures of furnishings and appliances in magazines and catalogs, cut them out, and apply them

to the right shape and size box. You may have to look through a lot of magazines to find just the right images. Advertising flyers and manufacturers' catalogs are often good sources. You can either tape the cutout image to the right-size box or use rubber cement to glue it in place.

Method 3

Because small-box packaging is printed only on the outside, the inside of the cartons is usually plain, unprinted cardboard. Many small boxes can easily be unsealed

at their glued seam and refolded into the same box but with the unprinted side on the outside. Use a small knife (a table knife may do) to separate the glued seam at an edge of the box, and use rubber cement or clear mending tape to reseal the refolded box. You can then draw images of furnishings on the unprinted sides of the refolded boxes, using paints and markers.

Sample small-box conversions to furnishings

If you are planning to furnish a dollhouse with Small-Box Furniture and Appliances, here is a shopping list of what you might need. For each item selected, decide which method to use to make it. Also, consider other types of cardboard discards that could be converted into furnishings. A paper drinking cup cut down to half height and turned upside down becomes a round table. A ring cut from a toilet paper tube can be a lamp shade or the base of a table. The cardboard backing of a small notepad can be the tabletop.

Living room

couch, easy chair, table, entertainment center, fireplace, grandfather clock, floor lamp

Kitchen area

refrigerator, stove, microwave, dishwasher, sink, cabinets, table, chairs

Bedroom

bed, dresser, nightstand, chair

Bathroom

bathtub, shower, sink, toilet

Home office

desk, file cabinets, bookshelves

Utility room

clothes washer, clothes dryer, workbench

Outdoor yard

playhouse, swing set, pool

PLAY-PEOPLE STAND-UPS

It's fun to have pretend-play characters to interact with your model structures. If you build a fort, it's fun to have soldiers to protect it from an attack of warships or enemy troops. If you build a model house, it's fun to have all the members of the family that "live" there—including pets. Pictures of all the play people you might want, from babies to grandparents, can usually be found in magazines, and with Play-People Stand-Ups, you can easily convert the cutout magazine people into three-dimensional figures that stand on their own. Cardboard rings cut from a toilet paper tube are cleverly used as bases to hold the figures upright and stable as well as give them curvature for structure and a more realistic appearance.

Construction

Builder's age
  6+

Player's age
  4+

Materials
☐ Magazines and catalogs with pictures of people

☐ Toilet paper tubes, or tubes from food wrap or paper towels

☐ Transparent mending tape

Tools
☐ Scissors

Building instructions

Determine what scale you want

It is okay to mix the relative sizes of the cutouts you create, so the cutout of a dog could be larger than the cutout of a horse. But if you want to find figures that are all about the right scale for a model you have built, you will first need to calculate the scale of your structure to determine the size of the characters to look for in magazines and catalogs.

First, determine how tall you would be if you were to shrink down to the same scale as your model structure. Simply hold a ruler or measuring tape next to your model and imagine how many inches tall you are if you were standing next to it. Then look through magazines and catalogs for pictures of kids about your age that are the same measured height. For example, if you estimated you would be four inches tall, look for pictures of kids your age that measure four inches tall. Now use that figure as a guide to find other characters that look to be the right size in comparison.

Making figure cutouts and ring bases

1. Gather several magazines and catalogs that are full of pictures of people and pets. Look for pictures that show all of the person from head to toe with no parts obscured or missing.

   When you find a picture you like, carefully tear the entire page from the magazine, then cut out the complete picture of the person. You do not have to follow the outline shape

exactly, but you do need to include a long, wide, and straight-bottomed strip of paper at the base of the cutout as shown in the illustration. Continue to find people pictures you like, and cut them out the same way.

2. Make the tube-ring bases by cutting a toilet paper tube into several one- to two-inch lengths. Use scissors to cut across the tube. If the rings flatten while cutting, just reshape them back into rings. To cut rings from a thicker paper tube, first poke a small hole in the tube with the point of the scissors, and use that hole to start cutting around the tube. It is very hard to cut perfectly straight around a tube, so it is okay if your cut is wavy and doesn't quite end up where you started. If that happens, don't use the wavy-cut end as the down side of the base ring or the

stand-up figure will be wobbly. Do use the two end rings from the tube that have square and flush bases.

3. Roll the bottom of the cutout into a cylinder smaller than the diameter of the ring base, then place the rolled figure into the ring. Use the shorter length rings for smaller cutouts and the bigger rings for taller cutouts. The rolled cutout will automatically unroll enough to fit snugly inside the tube ring, and the curved paper figures should stand up rigidly with a three-dimensional appearance.

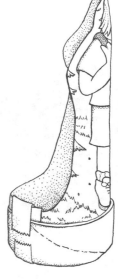

With gentle handling, the cutouts will stay in their tube bases, but you might want to permanently connect the two with a piece of tape as shown.

PATTERN AND PUZZLE PAPER CUBES

Making the origami cubes for this pattern and puzzle game is one of those constructions adults often find baffling, yet many kids seem to understand and do quite easily. Fortunately, playing the game is simple and fun for everyone. The patterns on the sides of the cubes are formed by the paper folds and the colors of the six sheets of paper it takes to make each cube. A set of either four or nine cubes will allow you to arrange them in a square and then rotate each of the cubes into various positions to form patterns within the square. The cubes can also be stacked in a tower to attempt spiral patterns and other visual effects. For an extraordinary challenge, make a set of nine cubes so that each cube has a different non-symmetrical pattern on each side, and no two cubes are exactly alike. Mathematically, that means you can create more than two trillion unique patterns! It's clearly going to take a while to see how many of them you can make.

Construction

Builder's age
8+

Player's age
6+

Materials
☐ 24 square sheets of paper in equal amounts of two to six colors (makes 4 cubes), or

☐ 54 square sheets of paper in equal amounts of two to six colors (makes 9 cubes)

Tools

□ Scissors, for cutting sheets square, otherwise

□ Hands only

Building instructions

Start by making a set of four cubes that form a two-by-two square grid. If you want to make more complex patterns, add five more cubes to form a three-by-three grid.

Making harlequin pattern cubes

Follow each folding step carefully, referring to both the illustrated folding instructions and the photographs of completed cubes.

Each cube uses six sheets of paper and can be made with two, three, or six different colored sheets. However, you must use the same number and combination of colors for each cube in the set. All paper sheets must be square and the same size. If starting with 8 1/2 x 11 inch paper, cut the sheets to 8 1/2 inch squares.

1. Select the six square sheets of paper it will take to make each cube. Decide if you want to use three sheets each of two colors, two sheets each of three colors, or one sheet each of six colors.

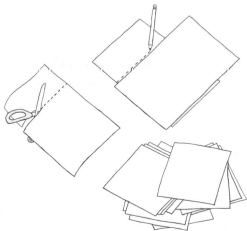

2. Each of the six sheets is first folded to make a trapezoid-shaped "unit." All units are folded exactly the same way.

a. Fold the sheet over exactly in half, lightly crease the fold to mark a middle line, then open the sheet flat again.

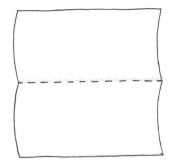

b. Fold each side to the middle line and crease the folds flat.

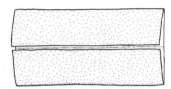

c. Turn the paper with the other side facing up, and fold over two opposite corners to form a trapezoid shape.

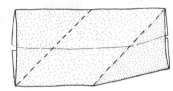

d. Fold over each end of the trapezoid to form a square, crease the folds, then fold open the triangular ends at a right angle to the square.

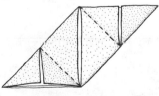

e. Make five more identical units for a total of six units.

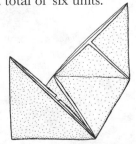

3. Assemble the six units into a cube by inserting the two triangles of each unit into the diagonal slits on the square faces of other units. Begin by assembling three units as shown, then add the remaining three units one at a time.

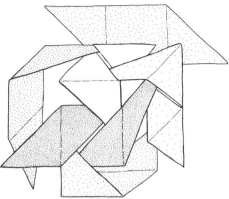

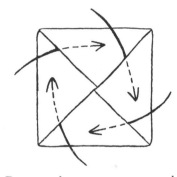

4. Repeat the exact process three (or eight) more times, using the same color combinations in the same order of assembly.

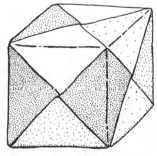

When you have completed making four identical cubes, try arranging them into patterns in a two-by-two square. Then, if you think you want to advance to the expert level, make five more cubes to form a three-by-three square, and see what other interesting patterns you can arrange.

OCTAGON ARROW ARTWORK

Making four octagon-based arrows is simple, and arranging them within a square in over fifty thousand possible patterns is even easier. The results always look like a work of modern art, and your chosen design can be displayed on a table, attached to the refrigerator door, or hung on a wall. Each arrow can be rotated to one of eight different positions and flipped to either one of two different colored sides, so the design can instantly be changed by simply repositioning one or more arrows. And once you've discovered your favorite Octagon Arrow Artwork designs, there are several other sets of octagon-based shapes you can make to create totally new patterns and designs.

Construction

Builder's age
7+

Player's age
5+

Materials
☐ Poster board, foam board, or any sheet material that has a different color or texture on either side

☐ Plain paper for making a pattern

Tools
☐ Ruler, yardstick, or builder's square

☐ Pencil

☐ Scissors, mat knife, or whatever cutting tool is appropriate for the material used

Building instructions
There are several materials you can choose from to make the four arrow panels, but the completed pieces should all be identical and have the same color on one side, and the same second color on the other side. The size of the pieces will depend on the materials available, and whether you want to use the panels for tabletop designs, a wall-hanging object of art, or a refrigerator decoration.

To make octagon arrows of most any size, you can use any type and thickness of rigid flat board—as long as you have the tools and skill to cut the material. Many poster boards and foam boards already have a different color on each side, and they are also easy to cut with a mat knife or utility knife. If the material is all one color, you can use markers, paint, or a laminated sheet of colored paper to change the color of one side or to select the two colors for both sides. You can also create panels with one smooth side and one textured side by carefully peeling the paper surface from one side of a sheet of corrugated board to reveal the corrugated pattern of stripes.

1. Make an accurate pattern of an octagon arrow shape. Start by measuring and cutting a sheet of paper into a perfect square for the size arrow you will be making or to fit the size of the material you will be using. For example, if you plan to use four pieces of poster board, each 8 x 10 inches in size, your octagon pattern can be no larger than 8 x 8 inches.

A set of four 4-inch octagons makes good refrigerator arrows, eight-inch arrows are manageable for table and floor play, and wall-mounted arrows can be any practical size.

2. Using a ruler and pencil, copy the octagon arrow pattern shown on the plan to the paper square and cut out the shape with scissors. Check your pattern to make sure it is based on a perfect octagon by folding the paper arrow in half several different ways to be sure overlapping corners and edges line up.

3. If necessary, prepare the sheet material you are using by coloring one side a different color than the other side. Use markers, paint, or colored paper laminates to differentiate one side from the other. Measure and cut the material into four identical squares.

4. Trace the arrow pattern onto each of the four squares, then cut out the four arrow panel pieces, using the appropriate cutting tool for the material used. For straight cuts, use the straight edge of a ruler or builder's square to guide a cutting blade.

Making artwork

Arrange the four octagon arrows in a two-by-two square. By rotating and flipping each of the arrows to any one of its sixteen possible positions, you can create some rather interesting graphic patterns. In fact, when viewing the square grouping of the arrows from the same perspective, there are over 65,000 different patterns possible (sixteen positions for each of four arrows = $16 \times 16 \times 16 \times 16 = 65,536$ patterns).

It is also possible to mount the four panels on a wall and change the pattern arrangement whenever you like. Depending on the sheet material you choose to use, the arrow panels can be attached, removed, and reattached to most walls, using pushpins. You might even try mounting a small set of arrows on the refrigerator, using magnets to hold them in place.

Once you have made and played with the four arrow shapes, there are several other sets of shapes you can try, all starting with a basic octagon pattern.

QUAD PANEL PATTERNS

The geometric pattern used to make a set of four Quad Panels is based on a regular modular grid within a square. So, when four identical square panels are arranged two-by-two into a larger square, no matter what the orientation of each individual square, the patterns on all four panels will line up and visually connect with the patterns on adjacent panels. The design patterns that result from more than two hundred possible combinations often create the illusion of being three-dimensional. And if you assemble a set of six identical Quad Panels into a cube, the number of different combinations of panel orientations is astronomical—and so is the complexity of the patterns created.

Construction

Builder's age
7+

Player's age
4+

Materials
□ Poster board, foam board, or heavyweight paper
□ White glue (optional)

Tools

- ☐ Ruler, yardstick, or builder's square
- ☐ Pencil
- ☐ Scissors, mat knife, or whatever cutting tool is appropriate for the material used
- ☐ Felt-tip markers, crayons, or poster paints in three colors
- ☐ Sheets of colored paper, foil, or other appliqués (optional)

Building instructions

1. Using poster board, foam board, or heavyweight paper, measure and cut out four six-inch by six-inch square panels. You can make the panels larger if you like, but you will need to recalculate the measurements in step 2.

2. With a ruler and pencil, divide each panel into a six-by-six grid of one-inch squares. Draw the grid lines lightly because many will later be erased.

3. Select one of the geometric patterns shown below, and copy it onto each of the four square panels. Just note where on the grid each line begins and ends, and use the straight edge of a ruler and pencil to draw straight lines between those points. This time, draw the pattern lines dark, and erase all remaining light grid guide lines.

4. Refer to the pattern illustration you have copied, and color each of the four square panels to match the color changes shown. You can use poster paints, markers, crayons, or pieces of appliqué materials cut to fit the design and glued in place. Pick whatever three colors you like, just be sure to follow the color pattern, and make all four panels the same.

The four square panels can now be arranged two-by-two to form one larger square and a complex geometric design. Keep changing the orientation of the squares to see how different combinations create symmetrical and asymmetrical patterns that seem to form three-dimensional shapes.

PAPER PUZZLE BRAIN TWISTERS

Each of the six Paper Puzzle Brain Twisters is a simple cut-and-fold paper sculpture made from a single sheet of note paper. The challenge is simply to re-create each folded-paper sculpture exactly as shown. That objective may be easy to understand, but for most people, finding the solutions can be a major brain twister, especially because there are a few rules you must follow.

1. Each sculpture is folded from a single sheet of notepaper.

2. A maximum of only three cuts (or tears) are allowed.

3. All cuts must be straight (no curves).

4. Each cut must start from an outer edge or from another cut.

5. No paper can be removed.

6. No glue, tape, or staples can be used.

To help you solve these tough puzzles, the number of cuts needed are given for each Brain Twister, and there are no hidden cuts, folds, or panels. Good luck!

Construction

Player's age
8+

Materials
☐ Sheets of note-size paper.

Tools
☐ Scissors (optional)

Playing

Following the rules listed above, try to duplicate each Paper Puzzle Brain Twister. Solutions are shown on page 518, but do try to resist referring to them except in cases of great frustration.

To help get your brain thinking correctly, here is the cut-and-fold pattern and the folds and twists required for solving another (and simpler) Paper Puzzle Brain Twister. The solid line is the cut (or tear) line, and the dotted lines are the fold lines. This folded paper sculpture is started by making only a single straight cut in a single sheet of notepaper.

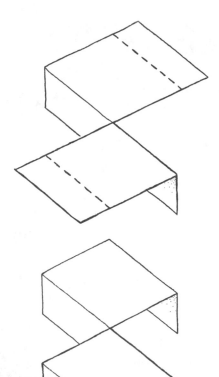

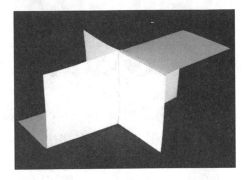

C. Two cuts

D. Two cuts

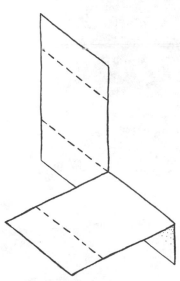

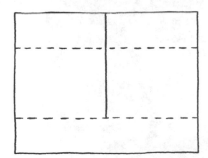

Now try to figure out the cuts and folds needed to duplicate these Brain Twisters. As a clue to the solution, the number of cuts needed is given for each one.

E. Two cuts

A. Three cuts

B. Three cuts

F. Two cuts

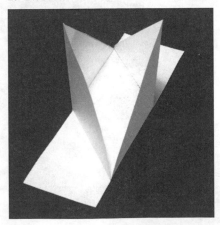

TEN SIMPLE AND TOUGH TESSELLATIONS

A tessellation is a collection of one or more shapes designed to fit together like pieces of a jigsaw puzzle to create geometric patterns. The pieces must completely cover an area without overlapping or leaving any gaps. But unlike a conventional puzzle, a tessellation does not have any "edge" pieces to frame the pattern. So if you have enough multiples of the shapes needed, you could keep building and expanding the pattern indefinitely. Squares, equilateral triangles, hexagons, and other special shapes can all make tessellations. However, in a "regular" tessellation, all the pieces are only one shape and size like the hexagon cells in a honeycomb or the square tiles on a floor. Tessellations that combine two or more shapes to create a repeatable pattern are called semiregular. These patterns are usually more complex and visually interesting and have frequently been used in mosaics.

Construction

Builder's age
7+

Player's age
5+

Materials

☐ Heavyweight construction paper, poster board, or foam board in four different colors

Tools

☐ Pencil

☐ Scissors

Building instructions

To build nine of these ten tessellations, you will need to make several pieces each of four different shapes (triangle, square, hexagon, and octagon) that have two things in common. Every edge on all four shapes is the same length, and all pieces are cut from the same thickness material. However, each of the shapes should be its own unique color, so the patterns you make will clearly stand out. The tenth tessellation is a curved-edge trapezoid and is designed to fit together only with other identically shaped pieces.

Making the tessellation pieces

1. Copy the patterns below and carefully cut them out to make a tracing template for each shape. The heavier the paper or cardboard you use to make the master tracing templates, the easier they will be to trace around and the more accurate your tessellation pieces will be. For the tessellation pieces to properly fit together, all the pieces of each shape must be identical and symmetrical.

2. Select four different color papers (or other sheet material), and assign one color to each of the four geometric shapes. Only the curved-edge trapezoid pieces can be made in a variety of colors.

   For each shape and paper-color combination, trace as many pieces as you can fit on a single sheet. Notice that the sheet layouts themselves can be arranged as regular tessellations to maximize the number of pieces you can get.

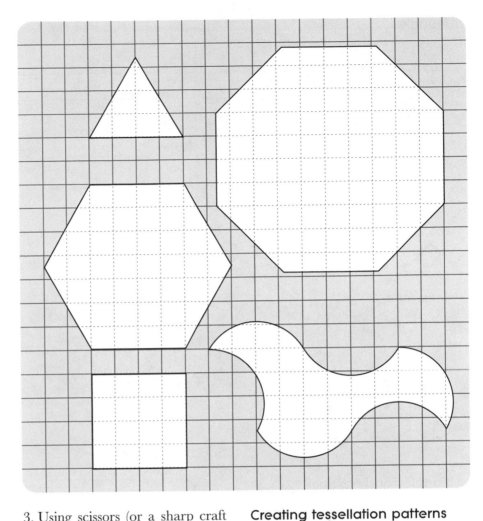

3. Using scissors (or a sharp craft knife and straightedge), carefully cut out all the multiple pieces of each shape.

Because tessellations are puzzles with no specific ending, you may not be able to predict how many pieces of each shape you might use. So if you do need more pieces, just make more of what you need.

Creating tessellation patterns

Working on a tabletop, the floor, or any flat surface, build each of the ten tessellations on the next page. You decide how far you want to build and what overall shape the finished puzzle will take. The examples shown are meant only to get you started.

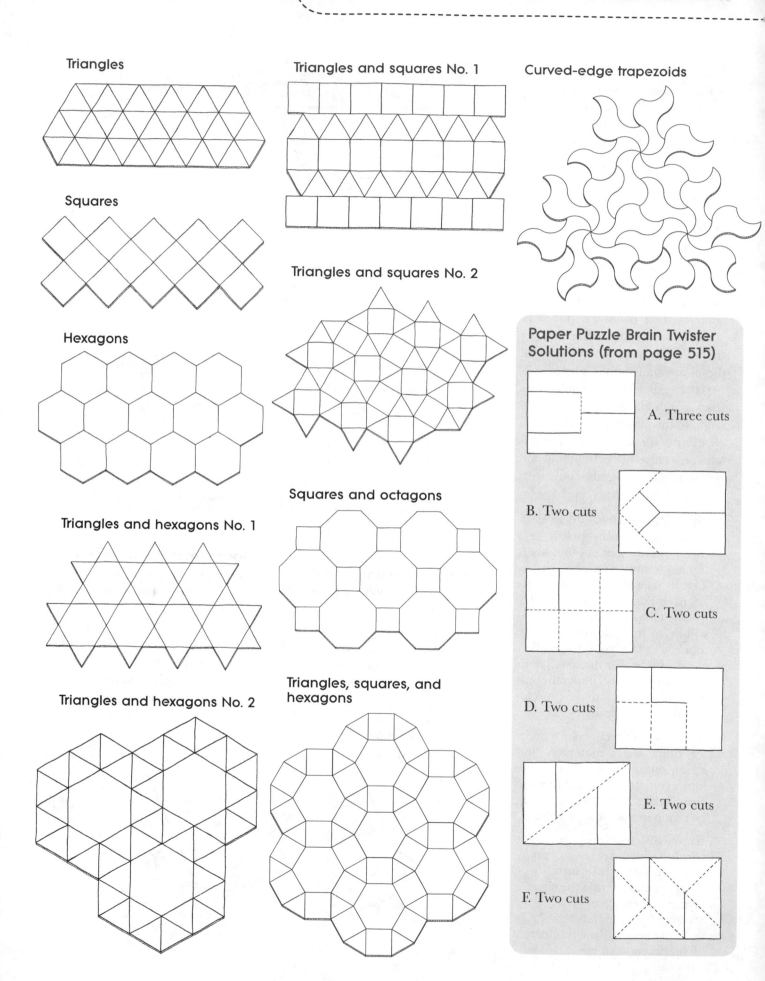

Triangles

Squares

Hexagons

Triangles and hexagons No. 1

Triangles and hexagons No. 2

Triangles and squares No. 1

Triangles and squares No. 2

Squares and octagons

Triangles, squares, and hexagons

Curved-edge trapezoids

Paper Puzzle Brain Twister Solutions (from page 515)

A. Three cuts

B. Two cuts

C. Two cuts

D. Two cuts

E. Two cuts

F. Two cuts

TENTS, SHELLS, DOMES, AND BOWLS

All of these projects use panel and plane structures to create functional products designed to work well and provide other unique benefits. Which ones you decide to build might depend on your own personal play lifestyle. Observers of nature will enjoy the many birds (and squirrels) that flock to the Birdbath and Watering Station. The unique and functional design of this birdbath meets the different drinking requirements of all bird species. If you would rather have your own personal pet, the Hanging Betta Bowl is designed to be an ideal home for one pet betta. The macramé structure that supports the plastic-bag tank also forms bulges that magnify and distort your view of the fish in an entertaining way.

BUILD IT

ONE-TARP TENTS	520
TENNIS BALL POPPERS	523
PAPIER MÂCHÉ SHELLS	525
BIRDBATH AND WATERING STATION	528
HANGING BETTA BOWL	530
WINTER WARMER SOLAR DISH	533

If you love the outdoors, you will probably be interested in learning the many ways to simply and quickly turn a tarp into One-Tarp Tents. These structures come in handy at both sunny and rainy outdoor events. And if you happen to be camping on a cold day with lots of sunshine, the Winter Warmer Solar Dish can provide just enough heat to help thaw your cold hands.

Craftspeople will probably invent clever or even humorous ways to use the structural curved panels and domes that are made with Papier Mâché Shells. Many kid builders seem to enjoy wearing them as hats. And just about everyone, regardless of interests or age, will have fun playing with unpredictable Tennis Ball Poppers.

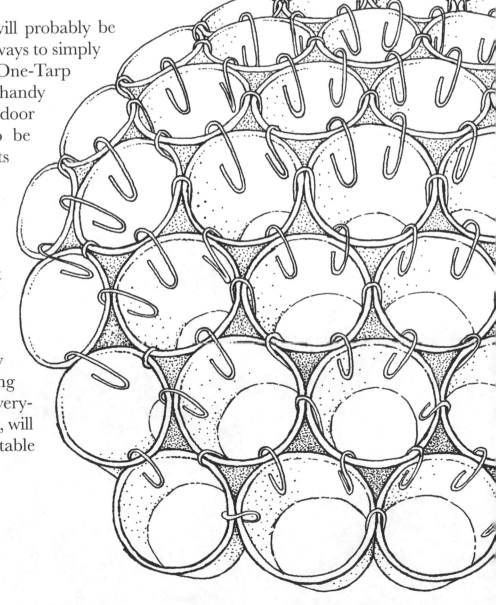

ONE-TARP TENTS

With just one all-purpose tarp, a few garden stakes, and some rope, you have all the materials needed to quickly build several types of backyard tents. And if you happen to have a few trees to tie ropes to, there are even more tent and canopy configurations you can create. All-purpose tarps are an ideal material and size for making variations of the basic pup tent as well as various shade canopies. They are waterproof, there are tie-down grommets at the corners and on the sides, and they come in a variety of sizes and a few colors. A small tarp (6 x 8 feet) is easy to handle and can provide shelter for a couple of kids. An large tarp (8 X 10 feet) makes bigger tents and is a good size for constructing shade canopies.

Construction

Builder's age
8+

Player's age
4+

Materials

□ All-purpose tarp, size 6′ × 8′ or 8′ X 10′

□ Hardwood garden stakes, 4′ and 6′ lengths

□ Rope (Clothesline and polyethylene rope work well.)

□ Tent stakes (or 1′ sections cut from garden stakes)

Tools

☐ Hammer or rock (for pounding stakes into ground)

☐ Scissors or knife (for cutting rope)

Building instructions

Rope supported tents

The type of tarp tent you can build depends on the attachment points you have handy. A rope spanning two sturdy trees located several feet apart can support a simple pup tent. Just hang a tarp over the rope in an upside-down "V" shape and drive a stake through the grommet at each corner. Even if you don't have two convenient trees, consider using other attachment points that might include fence posts, stair or porch railings, or a swing set.

If you happen to have four attachment points in the right locations, tie a rope between each point and a corner of the tarp to create a graceful saddle-shaped shade canopy. Experiment with other attachment points, and tie support ropes to the grommets on the side of the tarp to see what other kind of shell-shaped tents you can create.

Pole supported tents

Most simple tents use poles for support. Hardwood garden stakes make ideal support poles for tarp

Two-pole pup tent

Hanging pup tent

Hanging shade canopy

tents and usually have one pointed end for driving into the ground.

After deciding what type of tent to build, the tarp can be placed in position on the ground to determine the placement of the poles. For a simple pole-supported pup tent, the length of the tent tarp will determine where to hammer the poles into the ground.

For some tents (including a pup tent), you will have to do some figuring to determine exactly how long the poles should be. Remember that part of the pole goes into the ground. A small-tarp pup tent will probably need four-foot-long poles (including the part that goes into the ground), and a little larger tent will need about five-foot-long poles.

To build a pup tent frame, hammer the poles into the ground just far enough so they remain self standing. Following the design shown, tie a length of rope from a stake placed several feet in front of one pole to the top of that pole. After wrapping the rope tightly a few times around the top of the pole, pull the rope tightly across to the top of the

One-pole shelter

Four-pole lean-to

Five-pole blind

Two-pole canopy

Four-pole canopy

other pole, wrap it around the pole, and pull the rope down to another stake positioned several feet behind the other pole.

Both the guy-line ropes and the structural shape of the completed tent itself are what keeps the poles in their vertical positions. So until you have hammered in the last stake and tied off the last rope, the tent structure can be quite flimsy. That is why setting up a tent is much easier if you have a helper.

To complete the tent, drape the tarp over the rope to form an upside-down "V," and drive a tie-down stake through the grommet at each corner. If the grommet holes in the tarp are too small for the stakes to go through, pound the stakes into the earth alongside each grommet (and at an angle away from the tent), and use short lengths of rope to tie the grommets to the stakes.

Using the same basic tent-building techniques, these are some other tent and canopy designs you can make with one tarp. Where to place the poles and how to run the guy-line ropes is shown in the photographs. You can also modify these designs to build your own One-Tarp Tents.

TENNIS BALL POPPERS

This is an interesting phenomenon. Flip a dome-shaped Tennis Ball Popper inside out, place it that way on a hard surface like a table or floor, and in a moment or two, it will suddenly pop back into its original shape and fly a few feet up in the air. When the popper will actually pop up can often come as a surprise, and slightly different-size poppers cut from a tennis ball, as well as the way you flip one inside out, and even the temperature will vary the delay time. With several Tennis Ball Poppers, you can try to quickly set and stack them in a pile before one pops to set off a chain reaction. And with a few strategically placed "demolition poppers," you might attempt to demolish a Card Castle or some other lightweight stacked structure.

Construction

Builder's age
Adult

Player's age
4+

Materials
☐ Tennis ball

Tools
☐ Serrated kitchen knife
☐ Ruler or measuring tape
☐ Cup or can with a 2 1/4″ outside diameter

Building instructions

The most important part of making a Tennis Ball Popper is getting the size of the popper shell just right, and the right size can vary with individual tennis balls. If the popper is too small, it will not hold its inside-out shape for any amount of time, and if it is too large, the flipped shell will not pop back into shape no matter how long you wait. So, to make a successful popper, you may need to experiment.

Start by making one popper according to the directions that follow, then from the remaining piece of tennis ball, make another popper that is either slightly larger or smaller depending on how the first one performed.

1. Use a ruler or measuring tape to find a 2 1/4-inch-diameter template and draw a circle around a tennis ball. For example, you might use a small, empty can; a jar; or a drinking glass that has a 2 1/4-inch outside diameter. You can also make a correct-size template by rolling up a sheet of heavy paper or a magazine cover to a 2 1/4-inch diameter.

2. Use a sharp serrated kitchen knife to slice off the marked piece. Cutting through the tough rubber of a tennis ball can be difficult and should only by done by an adult or with adult supervision. Use a back-and-forth sawing action as if you were slicing through a tomato.

3. Test the popper to see if it will pop after being flipped inside out and placed fuzzy-side down (rubber-side up) on a hard surface. A good popper will wait several seconds or as long as a minute before popping into the air. The popper will not go very high or fast, but you should still be safe and keep your face out of the way.

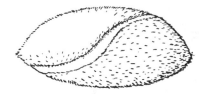

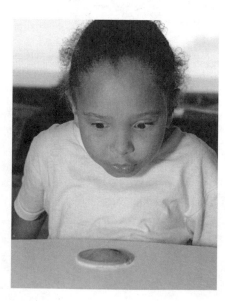

PAPIER MÂCHÉ SHELLS

Shells are remarkable structures. Have you ever tried to break an egg shell by pressing against its ends with the palms of your hands? Some people can't break the shell no mater how hard they push, and an egg shell is only about as thick as a postcard. Using papier mâché, you can make thin shells and domes that will be just as strong or stronger. And everything you need, from making the special paste to finding forms to mold, is probably right in your kitchen. Simply take torn strips of newspaper dipped in a flour-and-water paste, then mold the strips over a temporary form. When the glued strips harden and the form is removed, you will have a thin shell structure that holds its shape and is remarkably strong.

The shell shapes you make will probably inspire ways to use them. A Papier Mâché Shell could become the dome for a model building, the head of a puppet, a hat or a mask, a decorative object of art, or a model that resembles some well-known shell structure.

Construction

Builder's age
6+

Player's age
6+

Materials
☐ Papier mâché paste (The ingredients and recipe are given in the building instructions.)

☐ Newspaper

☐ Forms (See the building instructions for suggestions for finding and making forms.)

☐ Clear plastic food wrap

Tools
☐ Mixing bowl
☐ Mixing spoon
☐ Scissors

Building instructions

Finding forms for shells and domes

The most important part about building a structural shell is to find the right form to mold. Look around the kitchen, the playroom, or in the garage for rounded forms that might work. The forms will be covered in food wrap while you use them, so nothing should get damaged. These are a few suggestions:

    inflated round balloons

    egg shells

    upside-down mixing bowls

    a football

    a basketball and other balls

Making dome-shaped forms

You can make forms by shaping some materials that include:

    formed chicken wire

    reformed thin aluminum pie pans

    freezer bags filled with water

    aluminum foil molded over crumpled paper

Making a saddle form

In addition to molding shells and domes, you can also make saddle-shaped shells by building a special form that requires one all-wire coat hanger and ten No. 19 rubber bands. You will also need clear plastic food wrap to help with construction as well as to cover the form.

1. Bend a standard wire coat hanger into a square.

2. Place the ten rubber bands over the frame, five in each direction.

   Start with the two center bands, one in each direction, then work out to the edges, always alternating directions so the rubber bands "weave" together. Do not use more than ten No. 19 rubber bands or the force will collapse the frame.

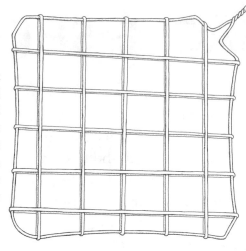

3. Cover the frame all around with plastic wrap. It's okay if the covering has wrinkles and is a bit messy. Sometimes the heat from a hair dryer will shrink the plastic wrap and create a smoother surface.

4. Gently bend the flat form into a saddle shape by bending one set of opposite corners up and the other two corners

down. Use your hands to smooth the plastic wrap into the saddle form.

Making papier mâché paste

There are several recipes for making papier mâché paste. The easiest recipe combines one cup of flour with two cups of water that are mixed in a bowl until the paste becomes thick like glue. Stir well to get out all the lumps, and add a little more flour or water to get the consistency right. Also, add two tablespoons of salt to help prevent mold.

An alternative recipe uses white glue mixed with a little water to thin it out. Warm water makes mixing easier. Start with a mixture of two parts glue to one part water, and adjust the mixture if it seems too thick or too watery.

And as a third alternative, you can use commercial wallpaper paste, and follow the instructions for mixing on the package.

Applying the papier mâché strips

1. Prepare the form by covering the surface to be formed with plastic wrap. The plastic wrap will later make it easy to remove the form from the dried Papier Mâché Shell. Try to smooth the plastic over the form as best you can, although it is impossible to get rid of all the wrinkles.

2. Prepare a bowl of papier mâché paste, and place the paste and the form on a work surface covered with several layers of newspaper. Working with the paste can get sloppy.

3. Tear sheets of newspaper into strips no more than an inch wide and a few inches long. Short, narrow strips work best on rounded molds. Tear the strips by hand, and do not cut them with scissors. There is no need to be exact; smaller and larger pieces will be fine.

4. Dip a newspaper strip into the paste, then while holding it over the bowl, run the strip between two fingers of your other hand to squeeze out the excess paste.

5. Place the wet strip over an area of the form. Continue to dip, wipe, and apply strips until the form is covered by one layer of overlapping strips.

6. You will need to apply at least two more layers of strips to give the shell strength (you can then make the shell as thick as you like), but you should wait until one layer has dried before applying another. Sometimes that can take overnight.

7. When the final layer has dried, carefully remove the form, and peel away the plastic wrap. You can trim any excess material away from the edges with scissors. Leave the shell unfinished, or paint it. And if you have not already done so, decide how you want to use it.

PAPIER MÂCHÉ

It seems natural that China, the country that invented paper, would also be the first to discover ways to recycle and reuse paper. By mixing small scraps of paper with a liquid paste, the wet, pulpy material could be layered and shaped either over or inside a temporary mold until the papier mâché dried into a hard, thin shell. In second-century China, one of the first uses of papier mâché was for making war helmets for soldiers. To give the hardened paper shells even more strength (and to make them more fierce looking), they were coated with layers of lacquer paint that included ornate decorations.

As papermaking spread across the continents, so did the art and popularity of papier mâché. By the middle of the eighteenth century, papier mâché trinkets from elegant little boxes to intricate dolls became very fashionable all over Europe. This light and inexpensive material was also commonly used for mirror frames, trays, clock cases, and other products that had previously been made from more costly woods. And like wood, papier mâché could be easily painted and gilded to look expensive.

The increased strength and versatility of papier mâché soon made it practical for an even wider variety of uses including furniture, tableware, life-size advertising figures, architectural moldings, and all kinds of decorative ornaments. Papier mâché was so fashionable at the time that George Washington requested two rooms at his Mount Vernon home have papier mâché decorated ceilings.

By the nineteenth century, artists and craftspeople were getting pretty creative with new recipes for mixing up batches of papier mâché. Sometimes garlic was added to the paper and paste mixture as an insect repellent, then cinnamon or cloves might be added to eliminate the smell of the garlic. Other ingredients (some for purposes unknown) have included mashed potatoes, broccoli, tobacco leaves, cabbage, and cauliflower. And papier mâché made with scraps of cotton was found to be strong enough to be fastened with screws and nails—just like wood.

By the mid-1800s, however, newer and more practical materials (like plywood) were beginning to replace many of these new-found uses for papier mâché, and it returned to being a craft used mostly by artists. Today, the papier mâché mixture used in crafts is typically made from torn strips of old newspapers dipped into wallpaper paste and formed around balloons and aluminum-foil frameworks. And the most common papier mâché projects seem to be face masks, model boat hulls, and lightweight versions of rocks, trees, and other objects used in theatrical productions.

BIRDBATH AND WATERING STATION

Watching birds playing in water can be fascinating, and a good watering station can attract more birds, and more kinds of birds, than a bird feeder. That's because different kinds of birds like different kinds of foods. Because all birds need to drink clean water for survival, they are attracted to areas where there is a reliable source.

This Birdbath and Watering Station is made by assembling many drinking cups to form a dome. When placed outside, the cups will fill with rainwater, or you can just spray the structure with a hose to fill it up. The cups at the top of the dome can fill completely with water, but the tilted cups towards the lower levels hold less and less water. This design gives different birds a choice of the depth of water they like best for drinking, washing, and playing. And the cup edges make perfect perches. The dome is quite strong and can support the weight of the water-filled cups, but the structure will deteriorate over a few months and will need to be replaced with another one.

Construction

Builder's age
7+

Player's age
Any age

Materials
- ☐ 50+ paper drinking cups, all the same type and size (Any 6-ounce cups or larger work well.)
- ☐ 100+ jumbo paper clips, or staples, or white glue

Tools
- ☐ Hands only (if paper clips are used to fasten the cups)
- ☐ Stapler (if staples are used to fasten the cups)
- ☐ Spring clothespins (if glue is used to fasten the cups)

Building instructions

Choosing a fastening system

There are three types of fasteners that can be used to attach the cups together. Any one will work well for the limited life of the structure. Before deciding on which fastening system to use, you might experiment with each one.

Large paper clips are fast and easy to attach; they "lock" under the lip of the cup and allow for adjustments. And two or more people can be working on the project at the same time.

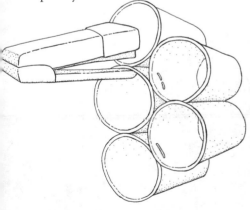

Stapling the cups makes secure connections, but squeezing the stapler takes some strength. Fitting the stapler into smaller cups can be a little difficult, and staples will quickly rust.

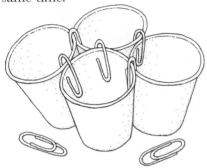

Gluing the cups requires some patience, and clothespin clamps are needed to hold the parts while drying. The result is a more permanent structure especially if you are using sturdy drinking cups that glue well. Glue does not stick well to cups that are coated with wax or plastic.

Building the paper-cup dome

Start with two cups, and attach them together side by side as shown in the illustrations. Continue to add and attach more cups, one cup at a time, trying to build in concentric rings so the form begins to look more and more like a dome. Don't try to build separate groups of cups and then fasten the sections together because it doesn't work well. The Birdbath and Watering Station will be complete when you run out of materials or time, or when the dome becomes a complete hemisphere.

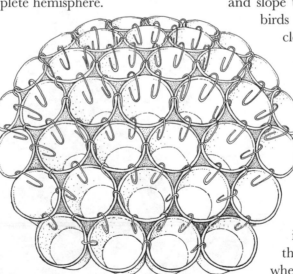

Playing tips

Choosing the right location for the birdbath is very important. A wet bird cannot quickly fly away and is vulnerable to nearby cats and other predators. Find an outdoor location that is in the open but still good for viewing from indoors. The dome can sit directly on the ground or be placed on a table, a garbage can, or some other platform that is ideally about three feet off the ground.

Most birds prefer shallow puddles of water that gradually slope to no more than a few inches deep. The tiers of cups hold more water near the top of the dome and less and less water (and at a shallower angle) at the lower tiers, so birds can find a depth

and slope that pleases them. And birds are attracted only to clean water, so the cup structure will need to be hosed off and refilled when it gets too dirty.

A small dome built the same way but using fewer cups can also be used as a bird feeder when filled with bird seed instead of water. Place the bird feeder somewhere near the birdbath, but be sure to take it inside at night and during rainy weather.

Other uses for a small drinking-cup dome might include a desktop organizer or a place to keep collections of shells, rocks, or anything small. And if you are really ambitious (and have a hundred or more cups), you can build an entire drinking-cup sphere.

HANGING BETTA BOWL

A Hanging Betta Bowl is a unique structure designed to be the home of only a single fish and only one type of fish—a betta. This plastic-bag fish tank is supported by a woven string netting, and the pressure of the water in the bag causes it to bulge between the woven strings, creating magnifiers that make the betta appear larger as it swims close to the sides.

The betta (also called a Siamese fighting fish) is quite beautiful, requires little care, doesn't cost much, and is the only fish that will live happily in this environment. And unlike any other pet fish, a betta can actually learn to recognize when you approach the bowl and will swim to the side to meet you while displaying its colorful fins. With proper care, a betta can live for two to three years.

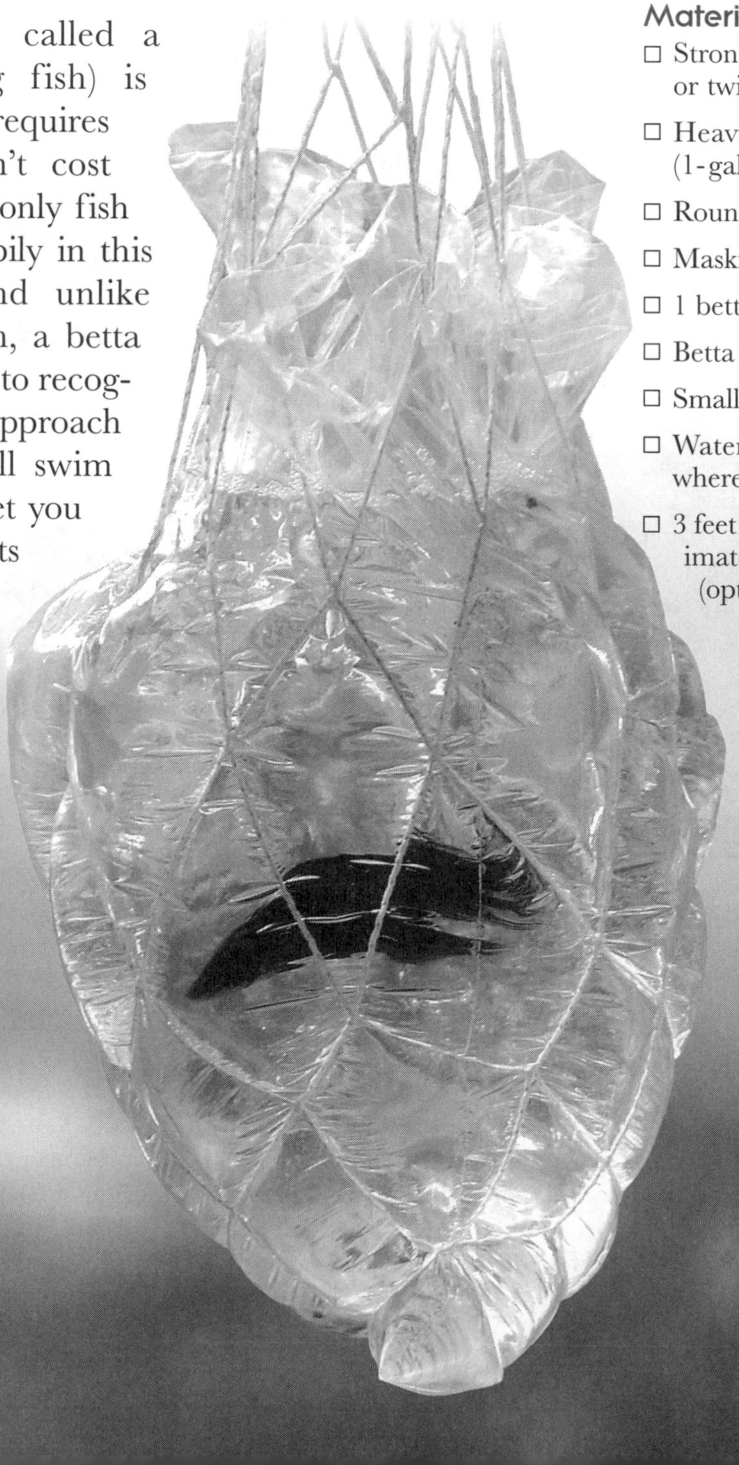

Construction

Builder's age
10+

Player's age
5+

Materials

☐ Strong string, thin nylon cord, or twine

☐ Heavy-duty clear plastic bag (1-gallon size)

☐ Round balloon (12″ party size)

☐ Masking tape

☐ 1 betta fish

☐ Betta food

☐ Small fishnet

☐ Water conditioner (available where pet supplies are sold)

☐ 3 feet clear vinyl tubing, approximately ¼″ inside diameter (optional)

Tools

☐ Scissors

☐ Ruler or tape measure

☐ Felt-tip marker

Building instructions

Building the betta bowl

1. Begin by building a form over which the netting will be woven. Place the balloon inside the plastic bag, and blow up the balloon. As the balloon inflates, make sure it is positioned all the way into the bag, then knot the balloon to keep it inflated. This is the completed form.

2. To keep the form positioned and steady as you weave the netting around it, tape the knot of the balloon to the table where you will be working. Also tape the open edges of the bag to the table.

3. Cut eight equal-length pieces of string, each about four feet long, and lay them out in a long bundle with the ends even. Temporarily wrap a small piece of tape around the exact middle of the bundle, then tie the bundle together with the knot at the middle. (Remove the small piece of tape just before you pull the knot tight.)

4. Using a ruler or tape measure and a felt-tip marker, put a mark on all the strings every 1 ¹/₂ inches from the center. You will only need to mark the strings about half their length from the center. These marks indicate where the strings will be knotted for weaving.

5. Tape the string knot onto the top of the form, centered in the middle, and drape the sixteen hanging strings evenly spaced around the form in eight pairs.

6. To begin the first row of weaving, tie each pair of strings with a square knot at the first mark down from the top center of the form. The knot will form a loop that will later become diamond shaped as the weaving expands.

7. To weave the second row, pair adjacent strings from neighboring loops, then tie each new pair into a square knot at the next markings. This will form a second row of loops around the form.

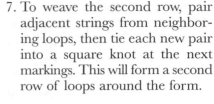

8. Continue weaving more rows of loops the same way by pairing and knotting the adjacent strings of neighboring loops. After a few rows, you will begin to see a netting pattern of diamonds take shape over the form. Stop making loops just before you reach the edge of the plastic bag.

9. Remove all tape holding the form to the table, but leave the tape that centers the netting to the bag.

10. Pull all the remaining string lengths into a bundle, then knot them together close to the ends. Trim off the excess ends.

11. Remove the tape that centers the netting to the bag, then use scissors to pop the balloon and remove it from the bag. The Betta Bowl is now complete and ready to be hung.

12. The Betta Bowl can be hung from a ceiling hook, an angled nail in the wall or a beam, a closet pole, or any other convenient place you find where it will not be accidentally disturbed. Make sure the hanging place you choose can support the weight of the bowl once it is filled with water.

Do not hang the Betta Bowl in direct sunlight. It will promote algae growth and make the water too hot for the fish. Also, do not keep the bowl in a place that gets too cold (by the window in winter). Normal room temperature is perfect.

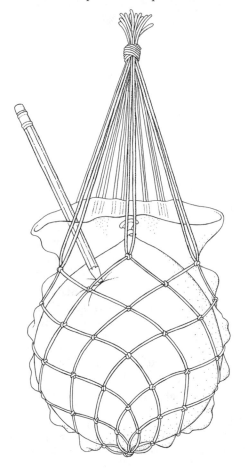

Getting ready for the betta

Bettas are very easy to care for. The water they swim in does not require filtration or aeration, and they live well alone in small tanks. Fill the Betta Bowl about three-quarters full with tap water so the bag fills out and the water has plenty of surface area. Bettas are air breathers and need room to come to the surface.

If your tap water is chlorinated (most city water is), it should be dechlorinated using a water conditioner every time you add tap water to the bowl. Follow the directions on the bottle.

Caring for the betta

Chose a bright, lively looking betta from the selection available at the pet store. Follow the store's instructions for introducing the betta to its new home in your Betta Bowl. After your betta is settled in its new home for a day or two, you will need to feed it and clean its bowl regularly.

Your betta can live well on "betta flakes" from the pet store, but the fish will also occasionally enjoy a variety of live foods (also available at the pet store). Feed the betta about once every few days, but *do not overfeed*. That is very important! A betta's stomach is about the size of one of its eye. Only a tiny pinch of food is necessary at each feeding. The fish should finish most or all of what is fed at any one time.

Clean the bowl every few weeks. There are two ways to do this. If the bowl becomes really dirty, place some of the bowl water into a clean drinking glass, then use a fishnet to temporarily relocate the betta to the glass while you clean the bowl. Dump out all the remaining water (but keep the bag inside the netting), and thoroughly rinse the bag clean. *Do not use soap!* Wipe the inside of the bag with a clean paper towel. Add fresh room-temperature water to the bowl (with water conditioner if needed). Now use the fishnet to place the betta back into its home.

This is the other method: If the bowl is not too dirty and just needs a routine cleaning and change of water, use a length of tubing to siphon out about half the water in the bowl. A two- to three-foot length of clear, flexible plastic tubing with a quarter-inch inside diameter ($1/4''$ ID) works well. First, fill the tubing with tap water, and

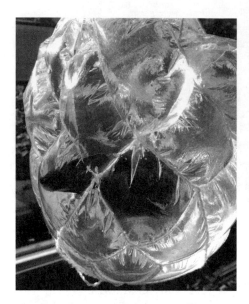

hold both ends of the tubing level with each other so no water spills out. Quickly put one end of the tube into the Betta Bowl water while simultaneously putting the other end into a small bucket or large bowl placed below the fish tank. As the water drains from the bowl (with the betta still in it), you can maneuver the end of the tube around the inside of the bowl to "vacuum" out any waste or algae. Add new room-temperature water to the bowl with water conditioner if needed.

Other uses for a Betta Bowl

If you prefer not to raise a betta right now, here are a few suggestions for other ways to use the hanging bowl.

- Fill the bag bowl with a few inches of soil, plant seeds or small plants in the soil, and you will have a hanging terrarium that shows growth above and below ground.

- Fill the bag bowl with colored water and hang it in a window to create a beautiful light show.

- Collect tadpoles at a local pond, fill the bag bowl with pond water plus the tadpoles, and watch the tadpoles change to frogs in your hanging aquarium.

WINTER WARMER SOLAR DISH

The greatest source of fuel and heat is our own sun, and there are several practical ways to collect and use the sun's energy. One device that collects heat energy from the sun is called a solar furnace and looks like a dish-shaped mirror aimed at the sun. The curved dish acts like a lens to focus a large area of the sun's rays into a smaller area, which becomes much hotter than the air around it. Some large solar furnaces can create enough heat to melt almost anything on earth. The small Solar Dish that you can build will not generate enough heat to hurt you, but it will warm your hands on a cold, sunny day. The Solar Dish is made by attaching ten identical reflector panels to form a round dish shape. Just aim the dish directly at the sun, wait a few minutes, then place your cold hand in the warmer air just in front of the dish.

Construction

Builder's age
9+

Player's age
9+

Materials
☐ Cardboard or poster board
☐ Aluminum foil
☐ White glue, spray glue, or rubber cement
☐ Tracing paper
☐ Paper fasteners

Tools
☐ Pencil
☐ Scissors
☐ Hole punch or awl

Building instructions

The Winter Warmer Solar Dish is made by fastening ten foil-covered panels together to make a dish-shaped reflector.

1. Using a pencil and tracing paper, trace the exact shape of one panel shown in the drawing, including its three holes and two notches. Use scissors and a hole punch to carefully cut out the shape and punch the holes to make a template. You can also poke the holes through the material, using an awl.

2. Find enough scrap pieces of cardboard or poster board to make ten panels. You can use pieces of material cut from shoe boxes, gift boxes, or the backing from notepads, but all pieces must be about the same thickness.

   Use the template to trace ten identical panels, including hole locations, onto the pieces of cardboard.

3. Turn the cardboard over (pattern side down), and glue a piece of aluminum foil (shiny side up) onto each cardboard piece. Use a thin layer of glue, and try to keep the foil flat and free of wrinkles, but it is not critical that the surfaces be mirror smooth.

4. When the glue has dried, cut out the panel shapes and punch out the holes.

5. Stack the panels in an even pile with the foil sides up, and place one paper fastener through all ten panels at the narrow base. Bend out the two legs of the paper fastener to secure the stack.

6. Using the photograph as a guide and starting with the top panel in the stack, fan open the panels and attach each panel to the next in order. Connect the notches at the sides of adjacent panels, and attach the top adjoining holes with paper fasteners. You will need to bend each two adjoining panels to line up the holes and create the concave reflector dish shape.

Using the Solar Dish

When the Solar Dish is aimed directly at the sun, it will concentrate its heat in an area a few inches out from the center of the dish. Prop it up in that position against a rock, a tree, or anything handy so you can have both hands free for warming. However, because the position of the sun changes as the earth turns, you will need to reposition the Solar Dish every fifteen minutes or so to collect the most sunlight.

Experiment to see if you can get more heat by removing one of the panels to create a deeper dish shape. If you are scientifically minded, you might try putting a thermometer in the center of the Solar Dish and compare that temperature to the surrounding ambient air temperature.

By removing all the paper fasteners except the center one, the Solar Dish can be folded closed to a convenient size for carrying in a bag with the loose fasteners.

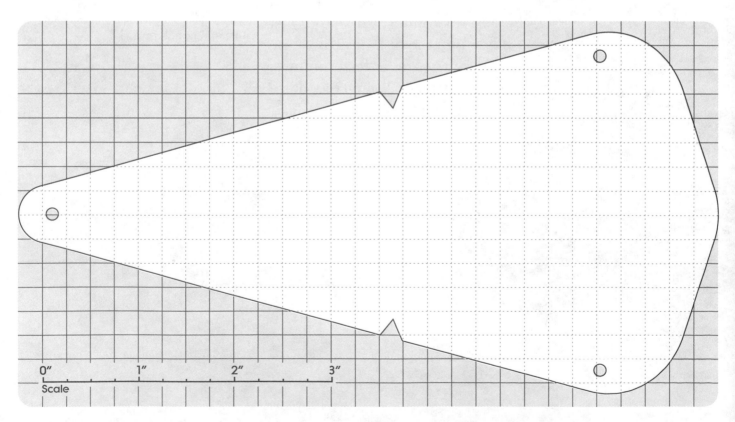

0"   1"   2"   3"
Scale

OTHER PANEL OPTIONS AND ODDBALLS

Some of these panel and plane building systems use modular panels that can be used as found or require only slight modification. A graham cracker conveniently breaks apart to create three different-size modular building panels that you can connect with fluff frosting mortar. Table crackers are available in a large variety of shapes and sizes, all ready to be quickly assembled into edible structures using peanut-butter mortar. A deck of playing cards is all that's needed to build Card Castles, and ordinary paper plates can be converted into a set of polygon building panels that connect with rubber bands.

If you are an advanced builder and want to fabricate accurate or realistic models of panel and plane structures (the way many architects and designers do), consider using the Foam Board Fabrications building system.

The projects considered to be Oddballs are not necessarily odd at all. They are just difficult to categorize as a type or method of building. For example, ESP Mind-Reading Cards could be described as *small decorated panels that are sometimes stacked* while you use them to measure your extrasensory perception abilities. Cookie and Candy Domino Disks is a puzzle you can eat after solving, but the game pieces you build are actually *round cookie panels stacked with candy pieces attached in a frosting mortar*. In a similar way, you could jokingly call the mowed pathway of a Backyard and Field Foot Maze *a single plane incorporating a surface pattern formed by two different lengths of vertical posts (blades of grass) imbedded in a slab of earth*. And if that is difficult to describe, consider Bathtub Barges. These floating and flexible platforms can be almost any size, using a construction method that connects clusters of empty soda-can pontoons with their original plastic six-pack carriers. So just think of the Oddballs as oddballs.

BUILD IT

FOAM BOARD FABRICATIONS	536
PAPER PLATE POLY PANELS	539
GRAHAM CRACKER TRI-PANELS	542
PEANUT BUTTER AND CRACKERS	545
CARD CASTLES	547
ESP MIND-READING CARDS	549
COOKIE AND CANDY DOMINO DISKS	552
BATHTUB BARGES	554
BACKYARD AND FIELD FOOT MAZE	556

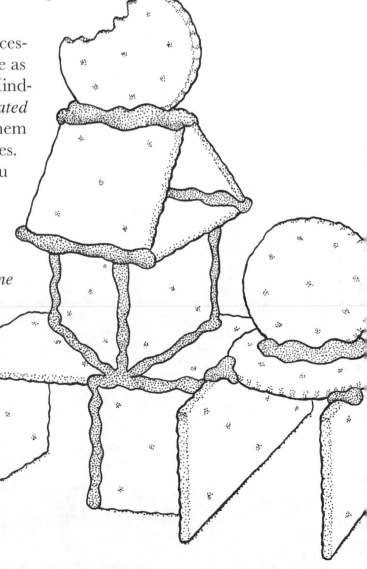

FOAM BOARD FABRICATIONS
BUILDING SYSTEM

Foam board is a favorite building material used by architects and designers to fabricate models of the structures they are designing. It could also be the perfect material for the models you build. The flat, rigid board is very light in weight, easy to cut to any shape, and can be scored, bent, hinged, and fastened in a variety of ways. And unlike cardboard models, foam board is dimensionally stable and will usually not warp in damp weather or after applying paint. The most common foam boards are made like a sandwich with heavyweight paper on the front and back surfaces and a white or black plastic-foam center between the two. The paper facings are usually smooth and white, which is perfect for applying markers and paints. Foam board is also available with surface facings in several colors as well as brown kraft paper, silver foil, and gold foil.

SYSTEM FEATURES

- Builds lightweight, flat-sided structures
- Good for medium- to large-scale models
- Easy to mark and cut straight or curved edges
- Easy to score for bending or to make hinges
- Pieces can be fastened with tape, glue, or pins
- Available in white and many colors
- Surface can be painted or decorated
- Should be used only for indoor projects

Construction

Builder's age
9+

Player's age
Depends on construction (See building techniques.)

Materials
- ☐ Foam board. Available at most office supply stores in 20″ × 30″ sheets approximately 3/16″ thick. Art supply stores may also offer 1/8″, 1/4″, and 3/8″ thick foam boards in sheet sizes up to 4′ × 8′.
- ☐ Fastener. Select one or more.

  Straight pins or "T" pins

  Masking tape (kraft or white)

  Hot glue

  White or yellow glue

Tools
- ☐ Builder's square or other metal straightedge
- ☐ Craft knife with No. 11 blade, or
- ☐ Fine-tooth, hacksaw blade
- ☐ Pencil

Building techniques

Measuring and marking panel pieces

Start with a plan of the foam-board pieces needed to build the model you have designed. While laying out the dimensions of each piece, remember to account for the thickness of the foam board. So wherever pieces join, you will need to figure out what edges butt up against the sides of other panels and which ones overlap others. Some model builders find it easier to measure, cut, and install one panel at a time instead of figuring out the dimensions of all the pieces in advance.

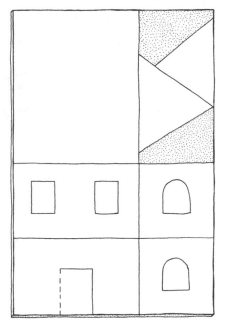

Use a builder's square (or a metal-edge ruler) and pencil to measure and mark all straight lines where you will be cutting. Also, mark any scores with a dotted line. Curved cut lines can be drawn freehand or traced around any convenient object that is the right shape and scale. Try to create an economical layout of the pieces on the board so they share cut lines where possible and leave the least amount of unusable scrap.

Cutting foam boards

Foam boards cut easily with very sharp knife blades. For clean cuts with sharp edges, many professional model builders prefer using a craft knife with a sharp, pointed No. 11 blade. A safer cutting method for younger builders is to use a fine-tooth hacksaw blade with a handle made of duct tape wrapped around one end (the push-to-cut end). You can also cut small pieces of foam board with a heavy-duty pair of scissors, but the cut edge will be crushed and have a "pillow edge" look.

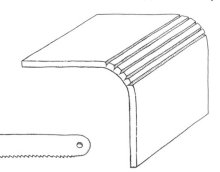

Scoring for bends and hinges

By making shallow scores or very shallow cuts along the score lines, the foam board can be sharply bent to any angle, curved to any radius, or hinged to create movable doors, ramps, and shutters.

For simple scoring and bending (and making hinges), score the foam board on the inside of the bend, then fold the board over, using the straightedge or a sharp table edge as a bending guide. If the paper surface on the unscored side tears while folding, try making two close and parallel scores (on

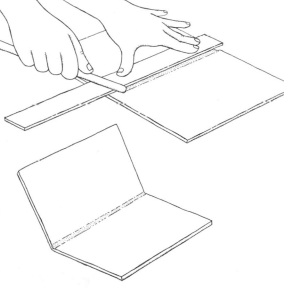

either side of the marked score line) instead of one.

Create curved panels or sections of panels by cutting a series of straight, shallow, parallel slits in one side of the board covering the section to be curved. Then make scores on the uncut side directly opposite the cuts. The panel can now easily be curved with the cuts on the outside radius and the scores on the inside.

Fastening foam board pieces

Use the method of fastening that works best for you and the type of model you are building. Sometimes it's best to use a temporary fastening system like straight pins or small pieces of tape to test the fit of all panels before completely taping or gluing the model together.

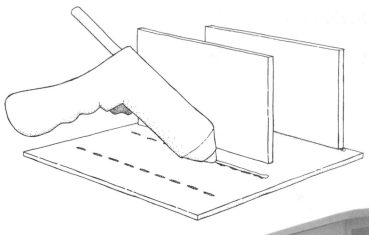

Straight pins and "T" pins (straight pins with a T-shaped head) can be used like nails to quickly fasten panels together or to hold glued panels together while drying. Straight-pin fasteners may be all you need if the model is fairly simple and will be handled very little.

A hot-glue gun is the fastest way to make permanent joints in foam-board constructions, but hot glue does not necessarily make the neatest and best-looking joints. Hot-glue fastening is often best suited for quickly making models for testing things like strength, function, or visual form.

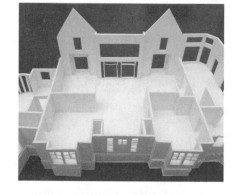

Only water-based liquid adhesives, including white glue and carpenter's yellow glue, will work with foam boards. Plastic glues and other chemical-solvent adhesives will melt the plastic-foam core and provide no joint strength at all. Water-based glues, however, have a relatively long drying time, and a joint should not be disturbed while it is drying. Use straight pins to keep the joints aligned and from separating while you continue working on the model.

Masking tape takes some skill to apply cleanly without wrinkles and twists. For white foam boards, use white masking tape to connect panels along seams and to cover over foam edges. Use kraft masking tape for kraft covered foam boards.

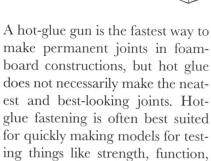

PAPER PLATE POLY PANELS
BUILDING SYSTEM

This modular construction system comes in three shapes for building different types of geometric polyhedrons that can become all kinds of whimsical playthings from a sunhat dome to a galaxy of hanging-mobile globes. Once a set of panels has been constructed, they are easily connected with rubber bands, and they come apart just as easily to be used over again. And the paper plate building panels are easy to decorate either before or after building.

Each of the three polygon-panel shapes—a square, triangle, and pentagon—makes its own unique forms. When all three shapes are made from six-inch paper plates, one shape cannot be connected to another. But with some experimentation, you can discover how to build each Paper Plate Poly Panel shape from a different-size paper plate so that all connecting sides are the same length for fastening. That way, the different shapes can all be combined in one structure to build more complex forms like a rhombicosidodecahedron.

Construction

Builder's age
8+

Player's age
5+

Materials
☐ 6″ round paper plates (Thin plates work best.)

☐ No. 16 rubber bands (2 ½″ × ¹/₁₆″)

Tools
☐ Ruler or other straightedge

☐ Pencil or ballpoint pen

☐ Paper hole punch

☐ Scissors

Building techniques

Although any size paper plate can be used to make Poly Panels, six-inch round paper plates are easy to work with, the least expensive to buy, and they are attached with common 2 ½ inch rubber bands. If you do decide to use a larger size paper plate, use a longer thin rubber band that measures about half the diameter of the plate.

Next, decide which panel shapes to make by determining the kind of forms you want to build. Square panels by themselves can build only cubes and various forms based on combinations of cubes. Triangle panels are the most versatile and can form a simple tetrahedron using only four panels, a more complex octahedron using eight panels, an icosahedron using twenty panels, and several variations. Pentagon panels by themselves make a limited number of forms. It takes twelve panels to build the simplest complete polyhedron, a dodecahedron.

Once you have experience making the six-inch plate Poly Panels and building forms with them, you might experiment with larger diameter paper plates to make square panels and pentagon panels with connecting sides the same length as the six-inch plate triangle panels. If you are successful, you will be able to build some rather complex polyhedral forms, using combinations of

two or all three shapes, like a truncated octahedron and a small rhombicuboctahedron.

Making a tracing template

First, make a square, triangle, or pentagon template for the panel shape selected so you can draw the folding pattern exactly the same way on all the paper plates.

1. Trace the appropriate angle needed on a sheet of paper (a 90-, 60-, or 108-degree angle) and cut the paper on the angle lines.

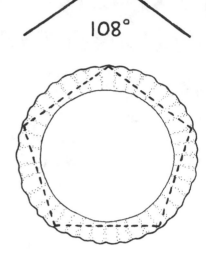

2. Use the paper angle to lay out the polygon shape on one paper plate. You might need to flatten the plate when drawing the angles. Make sure that each corner point of the angles you draw just touches the edge of the plate. You only need to mark each corner point with a pencil mark, and then use a ruler or other straightedge to connect the points with straight lines to create the polygon outline.

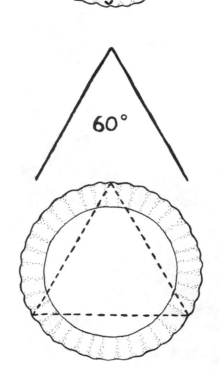

3. Cut out the polygon shape from the paper plate to complete the template. Check to make sure that all sides of the template are the same length—they should be.

Making Poly Panels from paper plates

1. Use the template as a guide, and trace the polygon pattern on the top of all the plates you intend

to turn into Poly Panels. Because some paper plates are dished more than others, it may be easier to use the template to mark only the corners of the shape and then connect the marks, using a ballpoint pen and a straightedge. Press down hard with the pen when drawing lines to score the paper, which will make it easier to fold the plate on the drawn line.

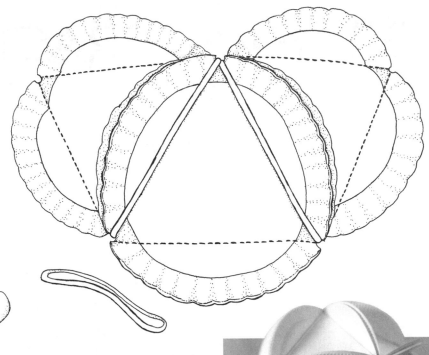

2. Use a paper hole punch to make a notch at each corner point around the edge of each plate.

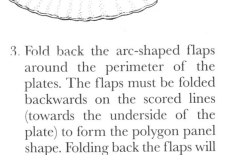

3. Fold back the arc-shaped flaps around the perimeter of the plates. The flaps must be folded backwards on the scored lines (towards the underside of the plate) to form the polygon panel shape. Folding back the flaps will also help flatten the plates.

hooks into the notches at both corners. Continue to add panels the same way until you have completed the form you are building.

Getting ideas for things to make

Each Paper Plate Poly Panel structure you build can become a different plaything just by deciding how to use it and maybe applying some decoration. To make a Tiffany-style lamp shade, cut shapes out of the centers of the panels and glue pieces of colorful wrapping paper behind the openings. Make a photo display by gluing or taping pictures on the panels. Or make a fortune-telling globe by writing "YES, NO, MAYBE, SOMETIMES, A L W A Y S, NEVER, ASK AGAIN" on the panel faces, and roll the Poly Panel globe to get answers to your most personal questions.

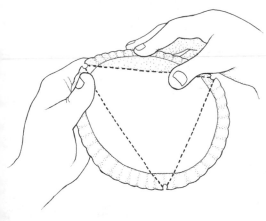

4. To connect Poly Panels, hold two panels together, flap to flap, and stretch a rubber band over the flaps so that the rubber band

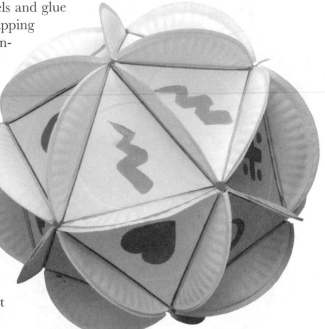

GRAHAM CRACKER TRI-PANELS
BUILDING SYSTEM

Graham crackers make excellent building pieces because they already come as prescored panels in three modular sizes. Start with the whole rectangular cracker for one size, break it in half to get two square panels, and break a square in half to get two small rectangular panels. Using all three modular sizes of Graham Cracker Tri-Panels with fluff frosting as a mortar, you can easily and quickly build a model of most any type of building, from a simple gable-roof cottage to a modern panel-clad office tower. And what you build can be saved and displayed as the centerpiece for a party table or the decoration on a birthday cake, or just be eaten immediately after others have admired your work.

SYSTEM FEATURES

- Builds edible structures
- Modular sizes scored on crackers
- Odd-shaped pieces can be nibbled to size
- Fast and easy constructions
- Frosting mortar allows repositioning while working
- Frosting mortar hardens overnight
- Good for medium-scale models

Construction

Builder's age
6+

Materials
☐ Graham crackers

☐ Inspect the box for any damage or corner crumpling while at the store to be sure the crackers inside are not broken.

☐ Marshmallow fluff (or make homemade fluff frosting mortar, using the recipe and ingredients given)

☐ Corrugated cardboard panel to build on

Tools
☐ Table knife to spread the frosting mortar

Building techniques

Making three sizes of modular panels

Before you begin building, it is helpful to have a ready supply of modular panels in all three sizes. Whole crackers (large rectangular panels) are ready to use as is. Half crackers (square panels) are made by breaking a whole cracker in half. And quarter crackers (small rectangular panels) are made by breaking a half cracker in half again.

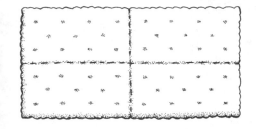

Knowing where to break the crackers is easy because graham crackers are already scored for breaking. But breaking the crackers cleanly on the score lines takes a little technique and practice, and some brands of graham crackers seem to break more evenly than others. If you have trouble breaking whole crackers by hand, try breaking the cracker over the sharp edge of a table—with the score line just over the table edge.

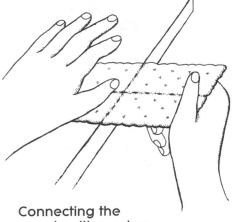

Connecting the panels with mortar

Marshmallow fluff from a grocery store can be used straight from the jar at room temperature and works perfectly as a mortar for assembling the graham crackers. It is easy to apply, holds the pieces firmly, stays flexible while building, dries hard overnight, and is edible. If a commercial fluff frosting is not available, you can make your own using the recipe given.

Playing with frosting mortar can get messy, so build your structure on a piece of corrugated cardboard. To assemble the modular graham cracker panels, use a table knife, a popsicle stick, or whatever works best for you to spread the frosting mortar on the edges of a cracker panel where it will

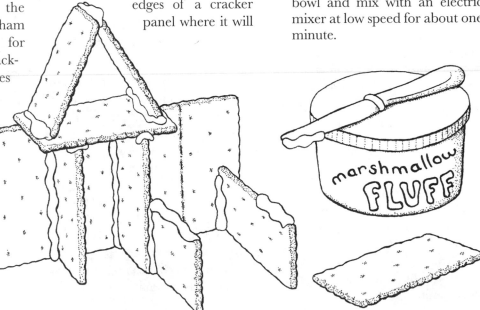

be attached to other crackers in the structure, and gently press the panel into place.

Panels can attach edge to edge, edge to face, or face to face. Because the panels are modular in their dimensions, constructions tend to fit together nicely. However, if you want to build with irregular-shaped panels, just break or nibble the cracker to whatever shape you want.

The frosting mortar bond will stick and hold instantly and will stay flexible for several hours, so you can make adjustments to the panels as you build. After a while, the mortar will begin to harden, and after twelve to twenty-four hours (depending on the temperature and humidity), the mortar will completely harden and hold the panels firmly in place.

Making fluff frosting mortar

This recipe makes about two cups of mortar, which should be plenty for even the largest structures. First, gather these ingredients.

☐ 1 pound confectioners sugar

☐ 3 egg whites at room temperature

☐ ½ teaspoon cream of tartar

1. Put all the ingredients in a large bowl and mix with an electric mixer at low speed for about one minute.

2. Gradually increase the mixer speed to high and mix for another five minutes or longer. The mortar is ready to use when the frosting can stand up in peaks.

If you don't plan to use the mortar right away, cover the bowl or put the frosting in a container with a tight-fitting lid. Homemade frosting mortar dries hard very quickly when exposed to air, but that is what makes it so good for building with graham crackers.

Making a squeeze-tube mortar dispenser

Instead of using a table knife to apply the mortar, you can make a squeeze-tube mortar dispenser out of a plastic bag to neatly apply a ribbon of frosting mortar directly along the edge of a cracker.

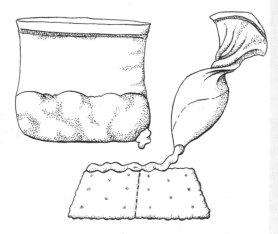

Fill a small plastic sandwich bag about one-third full with frosting mortar, and cut off one bottom corner of the bag. The size of the opening you make in the corner will determine the size of the mortar ribbon you squeeze out. So start by snipping off only a tiny piece of the corner and make the opening larger if you need to. To squeeze out the mortar, hold the cut corner of the bag in one hand while twisting the top of the bag with your other hand. Keep twisting until you want the ribbon to stop coming out.

INVENTION

GRAHAM CRACKERS

Each year, American kids and adults eat more than two billion graham crackers. That is enough crackers to cover the entire surface of the United States at least twice! Not only do graham crackers taste good, but they are also nutritious and considered one of America's original health foods.

During the 1800's, many Americans began to move away from rural farmlands to the cities. However, most jobs in the city didn't involve the same amount of physical exercise, and in the heavily populated cities, people were also exposed to a lot more germs. Some people soon became overweight, and many caught colds as well as more serious illnesses. In those days, doctors considered raw fruits and vegetables to be a source of germs and therefore too dangerous to be eaten too often. To stay healthy, city dwellers believed they should eat a diet of cooked meat, potatoes, and alcohol. Then along came Sylvester Graham who had completely different ideas about personal health and hygiene.

Sylvester Graham was born in 1794, the last of seventeen children. His own frequent illnesses eventually led him to study nutrition as he tried to discover what was good (and not so good) for the human body. As his own health improved, he became convinced that good health was a result of regular exercise and a diet rich in fresh fruits and green vegetables. Not only were these ideas contrary to popular thinking, but he also tried to convince others that their health would actually improve by consuming less meat, coffee, tea, chocolate, tobacco, and alcohol.

Many doctors thought him to be eccentric, but Graham was so sure of his findings that he traveled from city to city, persuading others to follow his prescribed diet. He also encouraged others to brush their teeth daily, take regular baths, get plenty of fresh air and exercise, and sleep seven hours each night. And in addition to his diet and lifestyle rules, Graham believed that baked goods should be made only with whole grains containing both the bran and germ of the grain.

At that time (as well as today), most of the breads made by commercial bakeries used refined flour with the bran and the germ removed. But Sylvester Graham's influence on good health became so widespread and popular that some bakeries began making graham breads using a finely ground whole wheat flour.

As the Graham health craze grew, so did the popularity of Graham bakeries, as well as Graham restaurants and Graham boarding houses that served healthy foods and breads made of whole wheat flour. And in 1829, Sylvester Graham introduced the graham cracker as a healthy food snack for guests.

The graham crackers you can buy today come in a wide variety of flavors, and most contain salt and fat, which Sylvester Graham disliked. But at least they still contain some percent of the healthy graham flour from which they originated.

PEANUT BUTTER AND CRACKERS
BUILDING SYSTEM

Crackers come in a wide variety of geometric shapes and sizes that make excellent building panels, and peanut butter not only tastes good with crackers, it makes the perfect mortar for sticking the cracker panels together. Using a combination of round, square, triangular, rectangular, and oval crackers, the kinds of structures you build will take on interesting sculptural forms that can be admired for a short time and then eaten.

And because structures built with Peanut Butter and Crackers should always be eaten soon after construction, you can play some interesting challenge games with friends or family at snack time. For example, who can build the tallest, the longest, or the strongest cracker structure using only six crackers? Or who can build the most interesting structure when each snacker uses the same combination of cracker shapes?

SYSTEM FEATURES

- Builds edible structures
- Crackers come in many shapes and sizes
- Crackers can be nibbled to odd-shaped panels
- Fast and easy constructions
- Peanut butter mortar allows repositioning while working
- Good for snack time because structures must be eaten

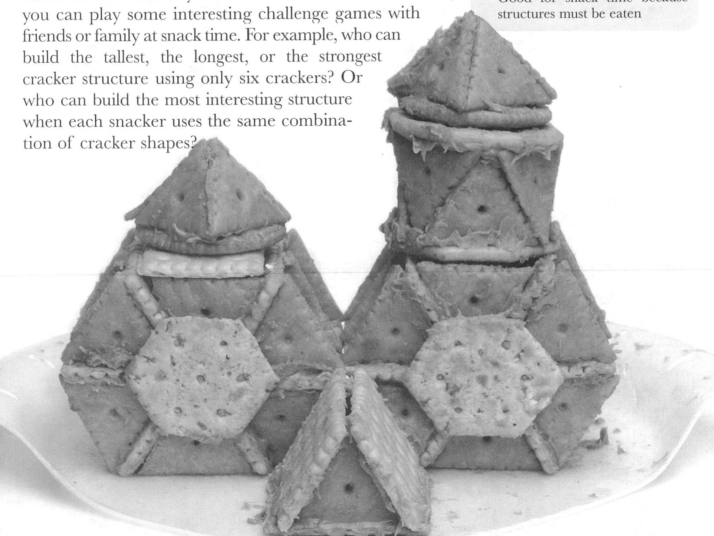

Construction

Builder's age
4+

Materials
□ Crackers of all shapes and sizes

□ Creamy peanut butter

Tools
□ Table knife to spread the peanut butter

□ Plate to build on

Building techniques

Building with peanut butter and crackers can get messy, so build your edible structures on a plate. And depending on what's in your kitchen cabinet, you might choose to build with a selection of crackers or just one kind.

To assemble the cracker panels, use a table knife to spread the peanut butter mortar on the cracker panel where it will be attached to other crackers in the structure,

and gently press the panel into place. The cracker panels can be attached edge to edge, edge to face, or face to face, depending on their shape and what you want to build. You can just mess around attaching crackers to crackers in designs that seem "right" to you, or you might plan your construction based on the shape of the crackers you have. You could build a dome of triangles, a house of squares, a sculpture of circles, or some other structure based on a geometric cracker shape.

CARD CASTLES

When first learning to build with a deck of playing cards, you may need a little help or at least a little patience. Leaning, stacking, and balancing a lot of playing cards to create a panel structure demands exacting "handsmanship" and concentration. At first, it may seem difficult to construct a simple tower only two card-levels high, but with a little practice and growing self-confidence, you will develop a mastery of the coordination and delicate handling needed to build whatever size Card Castles you like. Although you also might build a sprawling factory, a tall skyscraper, or a whimsical sculpture, it just happens that most playing-card structures look like castles anyway.

Construction

Player's age
4+

Materials
☐ Playing cards (does not have to be a complete deck)

Tools
☐ Hands only

Playing instructions

All you need for building Card Castles is one or more decks of playing cards. The hardest part is building a stable base structure. The three basic constructions shown in the illustrations should get you started, and from there the rest is up to you.

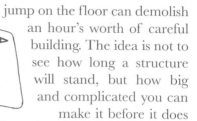

You will quickly discover that it is much easier to build on a carpeted floor than on a smooth surface where the cards will slip. It might take a while to get the knack, but once you have learned to delicately balance two or three cards against each other, the rest will seem quite easy. You can build out across the floor, or your castle can go up two, three, or even four stories high.

Don't be discouraged if your entire building comes crashing down. Building with cards is a precarious art, and even a slight breeze or a

jump on the floor can demolish an hour's worth of careful building. The idea is not to see how long a structure will stand, but how big and complicated you can make it before it does collapse. You have to decide if just "one more card" will be one card too many.

ESP MIND-READING CARDS

Maybe you have ESP, or extrasensory perception. Can you read minds? Have you ever thought you knew what someone else was thinking? Maybe you've had a premonition that something was going to happen, and it did. Or when picking a card in a game, have you had the feeling you knew which card was the "right" one? There are people who seem to have clairvoyance (the ability to see hidden things), telepathy (the ability to read minds), or precognition, (the ability to foretell events).

One way to find out if you do have ESP is to test yourself with a deck of ESP Mind-Reading Cards. Not only can you find out what kinds of ESP you might have, but you can also determine just how much of each force is present. All of these tests resemble simple guessing games in which you try to predict the symbol on cards one after the other. However, these games are based on actual ESP tests conducted by psychologists who study ESP.

Construction

Builder's age
7+

Player's age
7+

Materials
☐ 30 blank, white, square cards. Index cards can be cut to squares, or squares can be cut from heavyweight paper. Cards may be any convenient size—3″ squares work well.

Tools
☐ Black felt-tip marker

☐ Scissors, ruler, and pencil (to cut cards to shape)

Building instructions

Making the ESP cards

This easy-to-make deck of cards contains six cards each of five different symbols.

1. Make a set of thirty identical blank cards. The cards must be square, white, and opaque enough so that writing with a felt-tip marker on one side of a card will not show through (in any way) on the other side.

2. Using a black felt-tip marker, draw each of these symbols on six of the blank cards. The ESP card deck is complete.

Taking ESP tests

When you take the ESP card tests, it doesn't make any difference whether you think you do or do not have ESP—that is what you are going to find out. All that is required

is guessing the symbols on the cards. Your guesses should be quick, calling out the first thought or hunch that comes to mind. ESP is often thought of as intuition. Being too self-conscious can block your ESP energy, so relax, breathe deeply, and free your mind of all other thoughts. The harder someone tries to have ESP, the less the chance of actually demonstrating it!

Also, it is common for someone to be very strong in one type of ESP and weak in another. So try each test several times to see where you consistently perform well and where you do not.

If you want to perform these tests in a scientific way, keep score of your results by making a score sheet. The card symbols can be filled in on the score sheet as shown.

Testing for clairvoyance

The ability to see hidden things

Taking the test

This game uses twenty-five ESP cards, five cards each of the five symbols, and requires two people sitting opposite each other at a desk, table, or on the floor. One person is the subject to be tested, and the other is the tester.

The tester thoroughly shuffles the card deck and places it facedown (symbols down) in front of the subject. The subject tries to guess the symbol of each of the cards in order from top to bottom—without touching the deck and without turning over any cards. Each of the guesses, in the order guessed, is recorded on the record sheet along side the numbers 1 through 25.

After the subject has made all his or her guesses, the tester then turns the cards over, one by one, and records the actual card symbols in order on the record sheet from 1 through 25. The guesses and actual results are then matched to determine the number of correct guesses.

Calculating the results

You can use the score results to calculate how much ESP you do or do not have. This method of calculation can also be used for all the other ESP card games that follow.

There is a score that you would expect to get only by chance. Since the twenty-five card deck has five different symbols, you can easily calculate that for each guess there are five possible choices, but only one that can be correct. So the probability of making a correct guess is one in five. For the entire deck of twenty-five cards, therefore, there is an expected probability that just by arbitrarily guessing, you will guess correctly five times. Any score greater than five correct guesses may be an indication of ESP.

The greater the score above five, the more ESP is probably working. However, sometimes luck is a factor, so the more times you test yourself on a particular game, the more accurate your results will be.

More testing for clairvoyance

Taking the test

This card-matching test can be played as a solitaire game using the twenty-five card ESP deck plus the five remaining cards you made (one of each symbol). You will also need a pencil and paper for recording total scores—a record sheet is not necessary.

To begin, the five extra cards, called "key" cards, are laid out in a row, faceup. The deck of twenty-five cards is then thoroughly shuffled, and the deck placed facedown. Without looking at the face of the cards, take the cards from the deck, one by one, and place each card on the symbol you think it matches. The guesses should be spontaneous, and you should not be concerned about getting exactly five cards in each pile.

When all the cards have been assigned to piles, turn over the cards guessed, and count the total number of correct matches to the key cards.

Testing for telepathy

The ability to read minds

Taking the test

This game uses twenty-five ESP cards, five cards each of the five symbols, and requires two people. One person is the subject to be tested, and the other is the tester.

Some subjects may be better at reading minds than cards. In this game, the tester starts with a shuffled deck placed facedown. The tester then picks up each card in order and concentrates on the face symbol. While the tester is concentrating, the subject tries to guess what the symbol is. After each guess, the tester writes it down on the score sheet, listing both the card symbol guessed and the actual card symbol for each trial.

It is very important in this game that the subject go through all the cards before learning what they really are. While guessing, the subject should not see the card at all, either before of after the guess. To be certain, the tester should sit behind the subject. As the tester picks up each card, he or she signals the subject by calling "ready." In no way should the tester's voice or expressions ever indicate whether a guess by the subject is correct or not.

When all twenty-five cards have been used, the guesses and the actual card symbols are checked for matches, and the score is listed on the record sheet.

Testing for precognition

The ability to foretell events

Taking the test

This game uses twenty-five ESP cards, five cards each of the five symbols, and requires two people sitting opposite each other at a desk, table, or on the floor. One person is the subject to be tested, and the other is the tester.

In this game, the subject attempts to guess what the identity of the card symbols will be in the shuffled deck before the deck is shuffled. The subject starts by imagining what the symbols will be in order, and records those guesses on the record sheet for trials one through twenty five. The guesses should be spontaneous, and the subject should

not be concerned about listing exactly five cards of each suit.

The tester then thoroughly shuffles the deck and turns the cards over one by one in order. The results are listed on the record sheet, and the score is calculated.

More testing for precognition

Taking the test

This test is similar to clairvoyant card matching, except to start the game, the subject should put aside the five key cards. Shuffle the card deck and place it facedown. The subject now takes each card from the deck, one at a time, and places it in one of five imaginary piles. The only guessing should be in which pile to place a card. Again, no attempt should be made to distribute the cards evenly.

The subject then shuffles the five key cards and places them one at a time, faceup, at the head of each pile. The subject can either place the key cards in sequence from left to right or assign them randomly. The cards in each pile are turned faceup, and each pile is compared to the key card above it. The test results are compiled, and the number of correct guesses is recorded.

COOKIE AND CANDY DOMINO DISKS

This solitaire game is guaranteed to be challenging, but the reward for solving the puzzle (or even if you give up) is getting to eat the game. And being made of sandwich cookies and M&M candies, you can imagine how good the game pieces taste. Each of seven cookie disks has six different color candies embedded in the cream filling and arranged in a specific order around their perimeters. The idea is to arrange the Cookie and Candy Domino Disks in a round cluster so that the colors of all adjacent candies match. After trying for a while you might not believe it, but this puzzle can be solved.

Construction

Builder's age
6+

Player's age
6+

Materials
☐ 7 cream-filled sandwich cookies. Oreo, Hydrox, or any round cream-filled cookie will do.

☐ Small bag of M&M candies

Tools
☐ Hands only

Building instructions

The seven game pieces are made from the split halves of sandwich cookies that have kept all the cream filling. Each cookie disk has six M&M candies in six specific colors arranged in a circle exactly as shown in the illustration.

1. Carefully separate the two halves of a cookie so that all the cream filling remains on one of the halves. The plain half is not used, so you can eat it right now.

2. Using the correct color M&M candy pieces, copy the pattern of colors shown for game piece No. 1 by embedding each M&M into the cream filling around the perimeter of the cookie. Just pressing the candy into the filling will cause it to stay in place well enough. Continue to make the other six game pieces in the same way, being sure to follow the exact color pattern for each piece.

Playing tips

Arrange the seven disks so that six disks make a circle around one disk. Then, by rotating the disks and swapping their positions, try to find an arrangement in which all adjacent colors match. Remember that even though you can pick up and move the disks, the arrangement must always be six disks in a circle around one disk. Good luck and good eating!

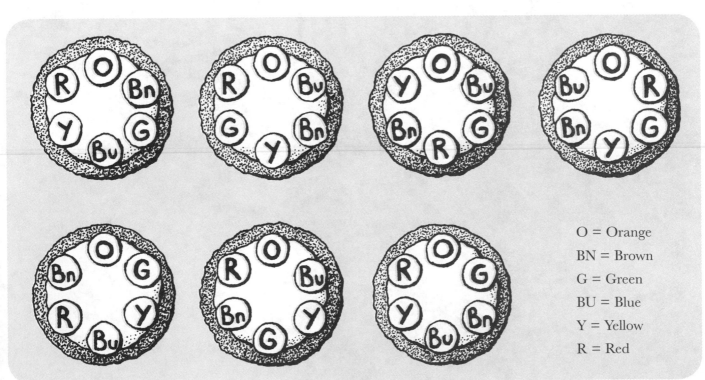

O = Orange
BN = Brown
G = Green
BU = Blue
Y = Yellow
R = Red

BATHTUB BARGES

Using empty soda cans, plus the six-pack plastic tops that held them together and a plastic trash bag, you can make a floating barge that will support a lot of cargo while drifting down a stream, across a small pond, or just across the bathtub. The larger you make the barge, the more it will hold, and if you made one big enough, it could support you. However, the most practical application for this floating-panel construction system is building a Bathtub Barge play platform just wide enough to fit across the inside width of the tub. Then while you soak, the barge can be used for doing many types of "on-shore" tabletop activities.

Construction

Builder's age
9+

Player's age
3+ (with adult supervision)

Materials
☐ Empty soda cans

☐ Soda six-pack tops (plastic ring carriers)

☐ Heavy-duty plastic trash bag

Tools
☐ Scissors

Building instructions

Soda can barges can be made to any size depending on the number of six-pack floating modules you join together. Each module consists of six empty soda cans covered with a piece of plastic trash bag and reconnected together with their original six-pack, plastic-ring carrier.

A one-module barge (six cans) will not be very stable, a four-module barge makes a good bathtub play platform, and a nine-module barge is large enough to navigate gentle streams and still ponds.

1. Start with six empty soda cans and remove the opening tabs by bending each one back and forth several times until it breaks off. Arrange the six cans in two rows with the opened ends up, the same way the six cans were originally positioned in the six-pack.

2. Cut a single thickness of plastic from a heavy-duty trash bag, making the plastic sheet several inches larger all around than the size of the barge you plan to build.

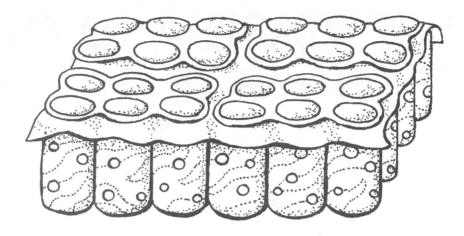

3. Place a corner section of the plastic sheet over the six cans and then place a six-pack, plastic-ring carrier top over the plastic bag and snap it onto each of the six cans. You may have to push or pull hard to get the plastic rings to pull over the plastic bag and snap onto the can tops.

4. Continue to add more six-packs to the same piece of plastic bag sheeting until the barge is the size you planned, however, do make sure all six-pack modules arc snugly positioncd ncxt to each other.

Your completed barge is now ready for christening and launching.

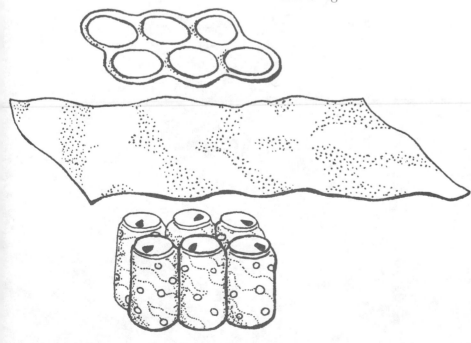

BACKYARD AND FIELD FOOT MAZE

A maze is a puzzle with a specific starting point and ending point and a confusing choice of pathways between the two. A player has to figure out the right path to get from start to finish, but along the way there are several intersections that may lead to dead ends—and force the player to double back to try a different route.

Walking mazes are especially popular and often built by farmers in the fall after the harvest to entertain their families and neighbors. Some farmers use a tractor to cut the maze pathways through their picked-over fields, and others mark the pathway design by turning up the sod with a shovel or by laying down sheaves of wheat. You may not have a farm field, but anyone with an overgrown lawn or backyard and a lawn mower can make his or her own Backyard and Field Foot Maze.

Construction

Builder's age
12+ (with adult supervision)

Player's age
3+

Materials
☐ An overgrown big backyard, lawn, or field

☐ General purpose white flour

Tools
☐ Lawn mower

Building instructions

Finding a place to make a maze

An overgrown lawn or field is the perfect place to make a temporary foot maze. The grass should be tall enough so that pathways cut through it are easily seen and followed. Since most lawn mowers cut a swath nearly two feet wide, you'll need a pretty big lawn to make an interesting maze. Your maze pathways can wend around trees and rocks (and even your house), but you will need a total area at least equal to the size of six parking spaces for cars.

If you only have a smaller area to work with (or no grassy area at all), just lay out the maze pattern on the outdoor ground using flour, and just use the flour trail as the pathway. If you have no outdoor area available, you might use masking tape to mark a maze on the floor. And if its winter, you can trample a maze in the snow.

Planning the maze design

Whatever location you plan to use or whatever size maze you choose to build, it's a good idea to plan the maze pathway configuration on paper before you begin the actual cutting. Begin by sketching the shape of the overall space, then sketch the maze within the shape.

All mazes have a starting point somewhere around the outside perimeter, but the finish point can be in the middle of the puzzle or anywhere else—including another location back to the outside perimeter. The simplest mazes have only one correct pathway for getting from start to finish. The more turns, twists, and dead ends, the more difficult the maze. And the most complicated mazes often have detours that make lots of twists and turns but eventually return to the same pathway a person detoured from. Here are a few maze puzzle patterns to give you some ideas.

When you are satisfied with the maze you have planned, use the sketch as a guide to lay out the pathway design on the lawn or field. Lines can be drawn using small amounts of white flour. If you want to change a line, simply erase it with your hand and draw a new one.

Cutting the maze pathways

Now it's time to get adult help or supervision and cut the pathways through the grass with a lawn mower. Follow the white flour lines, making sure to leave all surrounding areas uncut. To show the pathways clearly against the uncut grass, the lawn mower wheels may need to be adjusted to lower the cutting height.

It's a good idea to mark the finish point of the maze with a flag, a rock, or anything clearly visible so that each player will know where he or she eventually wants to end up.

Since you built the maze, you probably remember the way to solve it. So invite friends to walk your Backyard Foot Maze to see how simple or difficult it really is. If you want to build a different maze, you'll have to cut the rest of the lawn even, and then wait a few weeks for the grass to grow tall again.

MAZES

Going on four thousand years of popularity

Mazes have been popular for thousands of years in many regions throughout the world. The earliest mazes were found on rock carvings that date from about 1600 B.C. Some societies used puzzle mazes as religious symbols meant to signify "the journey of life," and some mazes were known to have been used in ceremonies of superstition, but most mazes were (and still are) built just for fun. Archaeologists have discovered maze puzzles painted on the walls of houses, designed into floor mosaics, and marked on the ground with trails of seashells.

In recent centuries, the British became well-known for designing and building some of the world's most elaborate lawn and garden mazes (sometimes called turf mazes). These maze puzzles were often intricate pathways cut through tall hedges, and with tall hedges that players could not see over (or be seen over), it was common for players to actually get lost and not be able to find their way out. And because getting lost in a closed-in space was too scary for younger children, some garden mazes were built low to the ground, using pathways lined with low hedges, shrubs, or flower beds.

The popularity of maze puzzles came to America with the Puritans, and building mazes became such a big fad that many elders considered it to be a serious distraction from productive work. So by the late sixteenth century, all maze puzzles and games in the American colonies were banned by law. Fortunately, the ban has long been forgotten, and you can now build any kind of maze you like without fear of violating any laws.

Today, mazes come in all types from pencil-maze puzzles printed on paper, to mazes carved into wood that you follow with a finger, to molded plastic mazes with a steel ball bearing that runs in a grooved pathway, and the ever-popular garden mazes defined by tall hedges or other plantings.

THE DRAGONFLY MAZE
DESIGNED BY KIT WILLIAMS
CAN YOU REACH THE GOAL AND
DISCOVER THE GOLDEN DRAGONFLY
Puzzle and Maze in one
◀ ENTRANCE ▶
AVERAGE TIME 20 mins FOR THE BRAINY

Show me the structures you build.
buildingbook@caneybooks.com

APPENDIX
FOR PARENTS AND OTHER TEACHERS

BUILDING IS AN IMPORTANT PART OF PLAY

THE BUILDING YEARS ARE SPECIAL

BUILDING INVITES ALL TYPES OF PLAY

CREATE AN IDEAL ENVIRONMENT FOR BUILDING

THE MAGIC OF MODULAR WOODEN BLOCKS

TOY BUYING MADE BETTER

BUILDING IS AN IMPORTANT PART OF PLAY

One of the earliest and most significant ways a child can communicate is through the "language" of building. Long before most kids can read or write, they are expressing themselves physically and tactually through art and building activities. A kid's pictures, constructions, and fantasy play reflect his reactions to what he sees around him. Playthings help children respond to new experiences by suggesting new avenues of interpretation and discovery. As a child's world of experience opens, grows, and changes, there are ever more things to watch, compare, prod, lift, collect, build, and understand.

Through building, kids begin to understand how individual parts combine to form a whole object. Through building, they learn the satisfaction of making things with materials that respond to their own skills and intuitions rather than being disappointed trying to mimic those of adults. Through building, kids make their own discoveries, which are more thrilling than any spoon-fed knowledge. And through self-mastery of building skills, kids develop confidence. Learning and discovery become much more powerful and meaningful when it is self-directed and self-willed. Kids who experience, exercise, and master these sensory ways of communicating through building and fantasy play will develop a greater sensitivity and awareness to everything they approach. These are the kids that will be able to see ideas and create solutions where others cannot.

Creativity is an automatic part of building. Each new experience must be visualized and expressed in order to be figured out. Building with blocks, trucks, and play people not only leads kids to discoveries about their community, it gives them the opportunity to rebuild the world as they see it. It also provides practice in the skills of counting, estimating, and measuring. A varied assortment of building projects can help develop interests in music, science and the arts, as well as promote social relationships and exercise fantasy play.

Play Is the First Step in a Child's Life Education

Play is most easily described as child's work, pleasure, and early education. When children are playing, they are most absorbed and most involved in working hard at their tasks and tackling their jobs with great enthusiasm. Kids' play is a time of intense concentration when a child can get lost in what he is doing. It is the time to create, discover, and experiment in a half-serious and half-playful attitude. The child is in charge of dreaming up new ideas, making plans, deciding what to do, acting out fantasies, and building new creations.

Play at its best embodies all the characteristics of a good educational process. Good play is building a completed object out of parts and changing it to make it better. Good play is mastering materials and the tools to manipulate them. Good play is developing physical coordination and mental curiosity, discovering adventures in nature and science, asking questions, and finding answers. Good play helps define character and influences social adjustment. In play, a child learns about himself—what he can do, what he likes, how he relates to others, what his weaknesses are, and how he sees himself. Good play is essential to growing up, and good playthings are a child's tools for getting there.

Playing with toys and building materials are extensions of children's natural curiosities and the need to control a part of their own lives. Kids are most interested in the immediate world around them where they can experience the shapes, colors, textures, and structures of natural and human-made objects. Building play provides the tools for a child's perceptual apprenticeship. Children first learn their world through their senses—they touch it, smell it, taste it, hear it, see it, and then try to make some sense out of the experience. Watch kids build something and notice how seriously they go about manipulating the materials in an uninhibited way. It is this intense personal involvement that provides the educational value of play.

Kids will build things and learn from the experience whether they are taught to or not. But what they do learn will be greatly influenced by the variety of materials, the richness of the environment, and encouragement that surrounds them. All this will stimulate children to explore and discover new relationships among the objects in their immediate physical world and also to learn the behavior and attributes of those objects and how to manage them.

Although for kids it is the actual manipulating of materials and objects that is so important and exciting in play, children are also learning to plan construction projects and discovering the need to observe and measure. Kids in play learn that it is easier to move a collection of things in a wheeled cart rather than to move them individually or drag heavy objects across the ground. A child in play learns to experiment with different ways to solve construction problems, and he also learns to practice and reinforce the lessons of earlier building successes. A child will practice a new skill over and over again with great pleasure until he can accomplish it more easily and eventually master it. But if the experience proves to be too difficult, too simple, or just disappointing, the child will just move on to something else. Sometimes that something else is the child's own conception of how the plaything should work.

New Life Experiences Provide Essential Inspirations

This ongoing exposure to new sights, sounds, and experiences will help a child hold on to that special feeling of discovery, and with enough stimulation, that feeling can be drawn upon for a lifetime. Exposure to new experiences is an essential condition for developing gifted eyes, ears, or hands that will then create original work. It is our responsibility as adults to make these experiences available to children. You might think of everything in a child's world as his or her museum, and we adults as the curators. The curator's job is to make each exhibit meaningful; it is our job to make a child's environment curious, exciting, and varied. And it is our job to help a child discover likes and passions.

Building can provide continuous exposure to an unlimited range of exciting, new topics, and homemade constructions used for play and learning have a personality that no store-bought toy can ever acquire. Building a space frame bird feeder will demonstrate several principles of structure and also certainly lead to observations and discussions about the behavior of birds. Build a marble roll and experience laws of physics; explore magnification under a polyhedron magnifying water lens; or build a trestle bridge of drinking straws and a satisfying curiosity will develop about the way things work.

From these varied experiences with building, a child becomes more confident about expressing and applying creativity and more willing to take risks to do things his or her own way. Out of that confidence grows an adult who is better equipped to take on any problem or task, and who is comfortable exercising his or her creativity.

Creativity Comes with Childhood

Parents now consider their child's creative endeavors on an even par with traditionally recognized intelligences like excellence in math or science. In addition to getting good grades, children are expected to develop and display creativity. As long as children do not feel pressured into proving their creativity to others, this renewed emphasis on the benefits of creative thinking is quite healthy. A child who feels comfortable expressing creative ideas is well on the path to learning how to initiate and effect change for the better rather than to assume or accept limitations. And kids who practice creativity and hold on to

their creative attitudes through adolescence into adulthood often emerge as the business and society leaders who are most receptive to new ideas and most capable of recognizing the best ones.

Creativity is no longer associated only with the arts, and anyone can apply creative thinking to just about any activity. Artists, engineers, businesspeople, kids, and parents apply creative thinking as a catalyst for innovation. Along with developing creativity comes an instinctive search for problems in need of solutions, a process for generating lots of ideas, a willingness to postpone judgment, an intuitive sense for recognizing solutions others have overlooked, a passion for finding the best, the most elegant, the simplest way to do something, and a confidence in expectations for success.

Creativity must be encouraged and practiced

Like so many other potential skills in need of encouragement and enhanced during early development, creativity must be practiced to become realized, and the earlier a kid's creativity is encouraged the better. Getting started is automatic. Every infant and toddler naturally experiences and displays creativity when trying to mimic and understand new things encountered. Some may argue that an infant isn't aware of being creative, but it is the experience, not the conscious awareness of being creative, that is preparing the child for further development. Even as an infant begins to make simple stacks of two or more objects, the foundation of creativity is being exercised in choice.

Unless this early natural creativity is encouraged, practiced, and rewarded, the ability to further develop creative skills will wither, as will an attitude of curiosity. The good news is that because everyone was once creative, almost anyone can be coached into regaining some of the creativity they may have left behind in childhood. It just takes a few learned skills and lots of practice. Adults who share their own creativity with children set excellent examples that will surely be mimicked.

Should anyone ever claim not to possess even "an ounce of creativity," they just need to be reminded that they have dreams, and dreams are a kind of creativity that everyone has experienced. Dreams try to create logical explanations out of things that are often quite illogical. Trying to figure out what a dream might mean is like figuring out all the ways an object can be used. This process of coming up with several potential explanations and then choosing the one that works best is the very essence of being creative.

Creativity is giving yourself choices

How can you tell if a child's constructions are an expression of real creativity or just arbitrary? Sometimes a kid's construction is called creative only because its appearance is strange or its purpose isn't recognized. In some cases, "creative" is even used as a euphemism and a redeeming feature for something considered ugly. We may have opinions as to what we each like and what we each think is creative work, but only the creator of the work knows if it was conceived, constructed, or applied in a conscious attempt to achieve a result. Anyone's work, child or adult, can only be judged creative after understanding the process that was applied. Was the builder

attempting to achieve some result? Were several options considered or tried? And was the objective accomplished?

The best measure of creative thinking is how easily a child can generate ideas one after the next so that there is always something new to try and always an attempt to improve upon past successes. Think of it this way. Creativity is the ability to generate lots of ideas until you find the one that works best. Sometimes that means continuing past the first few good ideas and coming up with maybe ten, fifty, or even a hundred more ideas before picking the best one. To someone who has good creative thinking skills, that's not too hard to do. In fact, creativity means never running out of ideas. So maybe a more practical definition is this: Creativity is being able to continually give yourself new clues that lead to more ideas, and also having some criteria or "gut feeling" to recognize the idea you like best.

To be a good creative thinker requires practice that begins with the earliest stages of building and further develops with some learned techniques. And with enough encouragement, guidance, and practice, creative thinking becomes an automatic response a child will learn to count on. In time, creative thinking will become so automatic that when confronted with a problem to solve, idea after idea will keep coming to mind. The creative thinker will then instinctively match each idea to the problem at hand to see which one is the best "fit" for the best solution.

Coming up with ideas is the divergent-thinking part of the creativity process, while picking the best idea is the convergent part. Both divergent and convergent thinking are

needed to ultimately achieve a workable idea or an effective solution. It doesn't do much good to only come up with ideas and not be able to select one based on some criteria. Therefore, creative people must have the ability and the discipline to think both divergently and convergently, but only one way at a time. When coming up with ideas, there should be no judgment of any idea until all ideas are generated. That's because even a bad or silly idea can inspire another idea that may be a brilliant one.

An example of a creative divergent-thinking process is brainstorming. Suppose you were shown a round dot drawn in the middle of a white sheet of paper and were asked, "What is it?" Well, since the drawing could represent anything round, you might immediately come up with ideas like a basketball, an orange, the full moon, a car tire, a button, and so on until the flow of ideas begins to stop. To get the ideas flowing again, just look back to the categories of the ideas you already thought of and ask, "What other kind of ball could it be? What other kind of fruit? What else in space? What other part of a car? What else that is worn?" That should generate at least a hundred more ideas of what the round dot could be. But keep on going by making up some additional categories. Maybe it's something that looks round when seen from an end view, like a pen or a soup can, or maybe a baseball bat. And what if it could be something that floats, or something that you might keep in a pocket, and so on. As long as you keep giving yourself clues, you can continue to generate new ideas. The more ideas you think of, the better chance you will have of finding the best one.

The convergent part of creative

thinking should be easy. If the builder has an objective in mind, then the best solution will become obvious compared to the other ideas. Given a choice of ideas, most people will readily migrate towards the one that best matches their personal preferences or their own logic of what will work best. So the best technique of convergent thinking in the creative process is to choose the idea that excites you the most. That is the idea with the most energy and at that moment the idea most likely to prove successful. Given a list of ideas or options for any situation, it is this personal choice that makes each individual's creativity so unique.

All Kids Need Encouragement

Many kids, even very young kids, can successfully organize themselves to build a project without the help of an adult. These kids have a sense of ownership, they are motivated, and they are in charge of what is going on. You can probably remember your early attempts at making a playhouse or a fort in the bedroom closet, or a tent from a blanket and chairs. Maybe you even figured out a way to set up your own lemonade stand.

Even though kids may be able to initiate and organize their own constructions and to make leaps in discovery and learning, they still need to be involved in meaningful projects with adults. Kids need to develop skills in understanding the characteristics of materials, in learning how to manipulate materials with tools, in following plans and procedures, and in exercising their creative thinking. And we need to learn how to successfully provide those experiences without interfer-

ing in the child's own building and learning process.

Maybe the most important help you can provide young builders is your approval and encouragement. Kids need to know it is okay to be creative, to experiment with a new idea, and maybe not get it right the first time. Encouragement can come from just a smile, by helping discover solutions, by supplying new materials, or by sharing a skill.

Although adult encouragement is a critical component in a child's feeling of success, resist the temptation to take over the construction even though it may be messy or out of whack. The child will only become discouraged because you can do it so much better. Rather than compete with you (and fail), the child gives up trying and just stands back to watch. More important than the quality of the construction is the process of building and creating, and acquiring many new skills and interests along the way.

The role of the adult is to be the catalyst. A child's understanding of a structure's concept or of how to manipulate a particular construction technique is best accomplished by letting the child play. Kids need time—lots of time—to explore their environment and the variety of materials and structures within it. Kids will discover amazing relationships on their own that would have been missed if they had been rushed to a conclusion. In time, kids will willingly, if not anxiously, reveal their discoveries in the structures they build and play with.

But at the same time, don't just stand back and watch a disaster about to happen when a suggestion would prevent real disappointment and failure. Be sure to approach a building project with a positive attitude about accidental spills, breaks, and damage. It is a normal consequence of building and learning. And when things do work, or when a problem has been solved, don't forget to provide that important "pat on the back"

THE BUILDING YEARS ARE SPECIAL

Between the ages of one and adolescence, building play provides different experiences and skills for children at different stages of their development. For most kids, the process is almost automatic. However, their interests can be encouraged by providing appropriate building materials and tools, a good play environment, and some occasional help and praise.

The ages for building that follow are general time frames with the understanding that each child develops interests at his or her own pace. A parent usually knows when a child is ready to do more, and kids are not shy about displaying their latest constructions and announcing what they're going to build next. But a general overview of what to expect from each age group can help a parent present options that exercise certain skills or interests.

Toddler and Preschool Years

During the preschool years, construction toys help develop hand-eye coordination. This is the age when all kids are hands-on everything. They want to manipulate materials, form shapes, create patterns, and take things apart—but not necessarily put them back together. In building play, preschool kids exercise placing, stacking, pushing together, taking apart, and balancing. As kids handle the materials of building, they experience the concepts of large and small, thick and thin, wide and narrow, light and heavy, smooth and rough, and straight and curved. They also experience many simple scientific and mathematical principles, but

without necessarily understanding them in a formal sense. Nonetheless, the kids will be better equipped to later understand these principles more easily if they are simply introduced now.

From the one- to two-year-old builder, don't expect much more than simple stacking and sorting play, and maybe some primitive-looking structures. A one-year-old delights in knocking down stacks that others have built, and is soon building and knocking down her own stacks. Even at this very early age of building, it is important to remember to introduce a large variety of stacking materials that could include foam or sponge blocks; small, empty cartons; and paper tube cylinders. Before kids can go beyond stacking and sorting to turning out finished products, they need to experience firsthand what type of structures different materials want to make.

The typical two- and three-year-old is not necessarily trying to build a preconceived structure or plaything; he is just enjoying the process of building. These kids use all available objects for making bigger and bigger stacks, they squeeze and roll clay into arbitrary shapes, and they begin to use simple tools to create new effects like pounding clay with a block, scooping and piling sand with a hand shovel, transporting water in a small bucket, or applying paints with a brush.

Between ages three and five, children learn that one thing can stand for another, that symbols can represent actual objects, and that they can first draw what they later intend to build. During this phase, children are at their most creative growth spurt. They are usually

pleased with their finished projects and don't really care what their peers think.

By the ages of four and five, kids have become avid explorers and are building models of their homes and communities. Kids this age have a healthy curiosity about their environment, and they like to practice interacting with all sorts of people and situations. Much of this interaction is done in fantasy play through imaginative role-playing. And because their self-confidence is high, this is the perfect time to encourage building to help strengthen their developing hand skills and creative thinking. Block building, transportation toys, small people figures, or any construction that substitutes for the real thing and mimics the community drama around them can be safe and satisfying play.

But most four-year-olds are still not ready for projects that require long periods of time or precise handwork. An attention span of about fifteen minutes is best filled with quick and easy projects that do not require cutting accuracy, the fitting of small pieces, or other tasks that frustrate the child's limited motor skills. Don't avoid these tasks altogether. Kids do need to practice and develop the skills of tracing, cutting, and assembling. Just make sure the task is not too far beyond the child's short-term potential.

Some four- or five-year-olds almost feel compelled to figure out how things work. They will innately take something apart, but their skills to assemble complex components is only beginning to develop. As these kids mature both physically and mentally, they exhibit finer dexterity, more creativity, and become better at problem solving.

Children five and older are increasingly able to work well in groups, although some may still prefer to work individually. Building as a group activity helps kids learn by watching others and also exercises creativity. Seeing their peers use the same materials in different ways helps convey the important concept that there is always more than one way to do something. And the open-ended quality of building provides the direct experience kids need to learn that trying new ideas eventually brings better results. The creativity skills kids exercise at this early age will give them a head start for the approaching school years.

Six to Nine Years

By the age of six, most kids have already developed firm ideas and preferences for the playthings they enjoy and the types of building they like to do. It is also an age when a child becomes less dependent on adults and far more influenced by peers. Over the next few years, kids will tend to do more of their building working with others on some communal effort.

By age eight or nine, creativity may appear to slump for some kids. Instead of uninhibited building with little concern for the result actually "working," these kids are trying to incorporate greater realism into building projects. This isn't an abandoning of the creative concepts and tools learned during the previous years; it is only a shifting of these skills to problem solving and invention activities.

Kids this age have started experimenting with spatial concepts, so their sketches may show objects drawn from various angles with attempts at correct perspectives and proper dimensions. The model buildings they construct now have insides as well as outsides, backs as well as fronts, and multiple levels instead of only one floor. These builders have figured out how to make hinges for the doors so they actually work and wheels for a vehicle so it actually rolls. Fine motor skills are now well-developed, and craftsmanship begins to show.

But not every kid will learn to cut straight, glue neatly, and do finely detailed work.

The Preteens

From about age ten up through the preteens, kids are forming personal preferences that strongly influence not only what they want to build, but also the building skills that get further developed. Whatever the child's current interests (and they may change often), there are building projects that can both support each new passion and become bridges to new learning. This is an age when some kids become avid model builders, budding carpenters, weavers and knitters, and tinkering inventors. This is also an age when builders focus more on realistic and practical constructions rather than just putting pieces together to mess around. Sophisticated and sometimes profound concepts become integrated in their constructions as young builders empirically figure out the laws of mechanics, physics, and nature, and learn how to exercise control over them all

BUILDING INVITES ALL TYPES OF PLAY

Even though most of the projects and playthings described in this book can be called "construction" toys, they cover almost all categories of play. Building a cardboard box puppet theater will foster fantasy play, building a milk carton bathtub boat will lead directly to water play, and building a polygon space frame drum will generate an attempt at banging out rhythms. But don't think that leading a child in the direction of certain types of play or projects is a rehearsal for becoming an adult. Building toys and structures will not cause a child to become an engineer, an architect, or a construction worker. However, a child's readiness for further learning can be strongly influenced by these early build-and-play experiences. Here are the basic types of playthings and their play characteristics.

Fantasy and Pretend Play

In order to understand what they see and hear in the everyday world, kids need to act out experiences, events, and the actions of others through fantasy role-playing. By impersonating others during these impressionable years, kids develop an understanding of different people's roles, feelings, and needs. Fantasy and pretend play help a kid explain the present, reflect on the past, and anticipate the future.

The toys of fantasy play include miniature versions of everyday objects, toy vehicles, playhouses, and dolls. Dolls and stuffed toys are especially appealing in fantasy play because they empower a child to mimic the role, the personality, and

the appearance of anyone, to go anywhere, and to do anything. Simple structures can be built that can be readily transformed into a puppet theater, general store, lemonade stand, playhouse, or fort. The structure doesn't need much detail. A sign that says STORE instantly turns a pile of empty boxes into a Wal-Mart or McDonald's. A simple curtain says theater, and with a piece of hose, you have a gas station. A kid's natural sense of drama in "playing parts" and experimenting with his perceptions of life will complete the scenario.

Tub Tube Toys   273

Rotelle Rattler and Other
Pasta Snakes   282

Personal Pyramid Play Space   301

One-Kid Two-Kid Teepee   303

Plastic Pipe Playhouse   320

Big Box Blocks
Building System   389

Paper Bag Bedroom Blocks
Building System   391

Soda Can Castles
Building System   427

One-Box Dollhouse   472

One-Box Puppet Theater and
Super Simple Puppets   474

Panelized Playhouse   479

Big Box Buildings   486

Play-People Stand-Ups   506

Construction Play

Building bridges, towers, and castles not only provides experience with design and assembly, but it helps explain why structures stand up or fall down. For young budding builders, disassembly of simple

structures and objects is good preparation for learning to assemble things. As skills and imagination develop, kids graduate from simple stacking constructions to more complex structures, to more lifelike buildings, and to more useful contraptions. Constructions can be anything from amorphous sculptures that are built up and torn down to building toys and objects that are then meant to be played with.

String and Straw Sticks
Building System   209

Polygon Puzzles and
Polyhedron Playthings   232

Punch and Poke Sticks
Building System   235

Tinker Toothpicks
Building System   251

Quick Sticks
Building System   263

Tub Tubes
Building System   271

Pasta Pieces and Paste
Building System   275

Clip Grippers and Straw Struts
Building System   290

Newspaper Struts and Poles
Building System   298

Indoor Circle Dome   307

Plastic Pipe Dreams
Building System   309

Pipe Chables   325

Cozy Cat Playground   327

Caney Trihanger Module
Building System   333

Trihanger Pyramids, Spheres,
Domes, and Trusses   336

Modular Wooden Blocks
Building System   383

Stick and Branch Blocks
Building System   397

Peanut-Shell Bricks and
Kitchen-Paste Mortar 411

Stack and Stick Sugar Cubes
Building System 413

Mini Marshmallow Sticky Bricks
Building System 417

TP Tube Tower Blocks
Building System 422

Locking Logs and Timber Columns
Building System 424

Gel-O-Cube Blocks
Building System 437

Corrugated Cardboard Carpentry
Building System 467

Caney Stool 484

Slotted-Panel Structures
and Sculptures 487

Laminated Lounge Chair 489

Stack'n Clip Sawhorses 495

Rainbow Prisms 501

Foam Board Fabrications
Building System 536

Card Castles 547

Bathtub Barges 554

Crafts

Craft work typically includes things built primarily for appearance and sometimes also to be used in play. Craft projects can expose a child to the elements of art and design, and can also exercise dexterity and crafting skills. But many crafts that come in kits can be too limiting because they are meant to be done only the one way shown in the directions. The few craft projects in this book give some suggested designs, but the instructions encourage the builder to experiment and create original designs.

Cake Blocks and Frosting Mortar
Building System 408

Step-Side Pyramid Toy Box 482

Paper Plate Poly Panels
Building System 539

Graham Cracker Tri-Panels
Building System 542

Peanut Butter and Crackers
Building System 545

Games

Action games, skill games, card games, board games, and strategy games all offer opportunities for social interaction and good ways to develop competitive feelings, decision-making skills, and self-esteem. Games of chance, physical skill, and mental strategy all help prepare a child for the competitions of everyday life. The best games include action, variety, surprise, and some level of skill or strategy instead of just plain luck.

Sticky Triangle Dominos 226

Toothpick Tantalizers 259

Magnetic Battle Bugs 294

3-D Blind Marble Maze 318

Table Game Snacks 401

Sugar-Cube Cube Puzzle 415

Pattern and Puzzle
Paper Cubes 508

Paper Puzzle Brain Twisters 514

Cookie and Candy
Domino Disks 552

Art, Design, and Self-Expression

In the preschool years, art is a spontaneous event that leads to creation, discovery, and a sense of achievement. Through artwork, kids both express their feelings and develop their creativity. Each experience with art and design provides the young artist with practice leading to greater skills, and in time to an awareness of line, color, shape, texture, space, light, shadow, balance, proportion, motion, pattern, scale, composition, and unity of design.

The continuous sharpening of art sensitivity skills and artistic techniques results from easy access to a variety of art materials as well as exposure to new subjects. So to keep artistic expression alive in later years, kids need both new materials and ideas that are suitable to the developmental level they have reached.

Sticky Q-Sticks
Building System 224

Clip Hooks and Hangers 292

Four-Poster
Roof-Canopy Beds 305

Plastic Pipe Art Easel 312

Moth Magnet Movies 338

Tensegrity Thing 340

Universal Modularity
Building System 343

Stale Bagel Blocks
Building System 393

Beach Beaux Arts 399

Fruit Face Tasty Totem Pole 404

Wet Sponge Blocks
Building System 420

Octagon Arrow Artwork 510

Quad Panel Patterns 512

Ten Simple and
Tough Tessellations 516

Rhythm and Music

Babies respond to music from birth. They seem pleased by the sounds of rattles and continue their interest in making noises and then music as they grow up. Well before age two, most babies have developed a natural love of music, and they move and dance to its rhythms. Even at this young age, babies know what music they like and are eager to have it repeated to learn the melody. In the years that follow, young children continue to practice and develop their rhythm and music skills through chanting games, skipping rope, and dancing.

A child's natural interest in music can be supported and sharpened by providing simple rhythm instruments to accompany the melody. These require very little learning and can include rhythm sticks, tambourines, jingle bells, drums, cymbals, castanets, tone blocks, whistles, and horns. These simple musical instruments allow a child to improvise sounds and experiment with high and low pitch, with long, short, and staccato rhythms, and with all other aspects of music awareness that later provide a basis for making his or her own original music and trying to re-create familiar tunes.

Music-Making Materials   97

Outdoor Play and Sports

Throughout childhood, kids have a need to exercise basic motor skills, improve muscle tone, learn body control and coordination, and express an emotional release through physical activity. Outdoor play and sports help kids discover their physical abilities as they follow natural impulses to run, jump, and climb. They learn to conquer height and master their own self in a balance between courage and caution. And competitive play fosters the social values of fairness and good sportsmanship.

Kids like the challenges of outdoor play and doing things in large scale. Early on, kids learn the fun of sliding down anything, and going faster becomes a child-long challenge. And the outdoors provides the space to build kid-size structures, although many of the outdoor play projects in this book can also be used indoors.

Polyform Kickball and
Indoor Golf   211

Butterfly Net   267

Tri-Stick Stool   269

Classic Lemonade Stand   315

Pipe Sculpture Sprinkler   330

Snow and Sand Mound Molds
Building System   434

One-Tarp Tents   520

Backyard and
Field Foot Maze   556

Power and Propulsion

Kids get a feeling of mastery when they can control a toy's action by winding up a "motor" to make something go, releasing a lever to see something drop, or just folding a piece of paper to make it fly. This category includes toy boats, cars, planes, parachutes, and kites, as well as riding toys that use muscle power. In adding power to a homemade project, kids learn to make rubber-band motors, air foils that catch the wind, gravity racers, kitchen chemistry jet engines, and simple do-nothing contraptions. They also experience the force of gravity, speed, acceleration, and momentum.

Marble Coaster
Tracks and Trestles   237

Classic Kites   244

Wind Whirlies   249

Rube Goldberg Inventions   345

Rain Stick Storm Maker   492

Best-Flyer Paper Planes   497

Tennis Ball Poppers   523

Science and Nature

Science exploration quite naturally becomes part of childhood play and adventure. Just by handling a variety of materials, kids gain experience in learning why things feel and behave differently. With building materials at hand, children will devise experiments out of curiosity, make predictions, try out assumptions, experiment with ways to fix what doesn't work, and record the experience in memory for future reference.

Some constructions provide good learning examples of more sophisticated attributes like the action of pulleys and levers, inclined planes, wheels, friction, volume, and so on. And some constructions generate new interests beyond the structure itself. If a kid builds a space frame bug house, he learns something about the science of structure and the bugs he collects to put in it. The same is true for building a bird feeding station or a windowsill garden terrarium. A kid who builds a tensegrity kite learns something about flexible structure techniques along with the aerodynamics of flying a kite. By experiencing the mathematical concepts and laws of the physical world through building play, kids may not be gaining a thorough understanding of the principles, but they are being prepared for a more formal science education that is to come.

Pyramid Power	213
Water Lens Magnifier	216
Portable Pocket Scope	218
Space Frame Terrarium	221
Bubble Frames and 3-D Planes	229
Bird Feeder Space Station Platform	242
Geodesic Dome Bug House	254
Mosquito Chamber of Doom	256
Gardener's Greenhouse	322
Blocks of Logic	386
Bagel Block Bird Banquet	395
Birdbath and Watering Station	528
Hanging Betta Bowl	530
Winter Warmer Solar Dish	533
ESP Mind-Reading Cards	549

Model Building

As kids become fascinated with discovering new parts of their neighborhood, they also begin an interest in building miniatures of the structures around them. Using whatever pieces and parts are available, kids will build recognizable shapes like skyscrapers, forts, vehicles, and airplanes, and sometimes attempt to create accurate scale models. When life-size objects are scaled down into playthings, a child is better able to deal with the concept of totality. Miniature objects permit large layouts of cities, towns, airports, or factories, all with buildings, roadways, rivers, bridges, and whatever else the builder has imagined should be there.

Kids have always made miniature facsimiles of the objects and structures they like most. And in building a full-size replica or a scaled-down version of the real thing, a child can better understand how the item works and its relationship to other things. They re-create and imitate their perception of the real world—dolls are babies, block buildings become the neighborhood, and anything with wheels is a car, truck, bus, tractor, or whatever type of vehicle is currently of interest.

Most kid constructions are a child's simplified transformation of an object that merely suggests rather than replicates the original. By reducing scale, a child is not only eliminating complexity, he is making the object correspond to his sense of scale in relation to adults. Sometimes, however, a younger child will prefer an enlarged version of the object that better suits his limited dexterity. In these instances, building with wooden pegs is easier than using nails, and making a huge scale model of a bug is a lot easier and provides more information than trying to make a real-size tiny version.

Model building should certainly be encouraged, but realism and detail should not. Young builders exhibit an uninhibited spontaneity that results in their constructions being free and imaginative in both form and interpretation. A kid's imagination can go a long way in turning a single block into a miniature house, and that easily makes up for the detail and craftsmanship adults seem to crave. A child's age, dexterity, and building skills will often determine how realistic the construction becomes. The older the child, the more she will become concerned with creating an exact scaled-down copy of the original. In time, the child builder will want more realism and begin adding doors, windows, roofs, and chimneys, and then fences, sidewalks, streets, cars, a school, and so on.

The progression to greater detail should be natural and hopefully not influenced by a parent's request and praise for a photographic likeness of the original. When an adult points out that the young builder's model house should have windows or that the door needs a handle, some kids become inhibited at furthering the construction for fear of not meeting the adult's expectations. A young builder is most comfortable with her own interpretations of reality. Being overly pressured to produce a precision likeness will cause some children to abandon their creative efforts in favor of collecting commercially available models and miniatures.

Triangle Truss Bridges Model Building	279
Noodle Novelty Twisters	285
Kitchen Clay and Concrete Blocks Building System	430
Gel-O-Cube Igloo	439
Small-Box Furniture and Appliances	504
Papier Mâché Shells	525

CREATE AN IDEAL ENVIRONMENT FOR BUILDING

Materials Are the Inspiration to Build

Materials, materials, and more materials all by themselves have the almost magical ability to turn a kid's ideas and fantasies into reality—and become the inspirations for new ones. Given nothing else but available materials and a space to play, any age child will spontaneously start to build. Even without the benefit of construction sets and toys, children will interpret their ideas in mud, snow, ice, clay, sand, water, rocks, twigs, or with whatever other "natural" materials might be available. By playing with any material, a child soon discovers its attributes and then it becomes obvious what kind of structure the material wants to be.

Many commercial building toys using modular rods, bricks, or special connectors may provide good play value, but the learning possibilities multiply when a child gathers or makes his own modular building pieces and then uses them to construct new playthings. When building with a plentiful supply of common household materials and everyday throwaways, there isn't any limit to what can be built or what size it can become. And there is nothing stopping the inspired child from immediately beginning to build whatever construction might come to mind. The builder doesn't have to follow plans in an instruction book or have just the right number of special parts and fasteners.

Many of the projects in this book are meant to be played with over and over again just like commer-cial toys. But some of the projects kids build are not intended to last—at least in the child's mind. Even if the completed construction project has only limited play value, there is another positive experience and lesson taking place. Just the act of transforming seemingly worthless scrap materials into something, whatever it is, teaches kids that building leads to successful conclusions.

Build with Scrap Materials and Discards

If you want to see the building process take place automatically and produce everything from wonderful solutions to weird constructions, just place a kid in the middle of a lot of scrap materials. Then, depending on the child's age, maybe add a few tools, some tape, or adhesive, and watch spontaneous building and creativity take place. Building homemade playthings gives kids early successes and the repeated experience of taking a project from beginning to end, from conception, to construction, to play, to improvement, to fixing what breaks. Kids who learn to expect these successful conclusions are much more likely to approach life's projects the same way.

Many of the toys and games that really turn out to be the most fun are those that kids build themselves from the materials readily at hand. The independence of making playthings from scrap empowers a child with the ability to create his own

entertainment. In a process that is almost instinctive, the child will select a project, gather the necessary materials and tools, build it, play with it, and show it off to others. And once the child gains confidence that what he makes works for him and is appreciated by others, he will lose any inhibitions about failing and want to experiment even more.

Materials from nature are a great resource for kids' constructions, but sticks, stones, and shells are not always available and not always suited for modular building systems. Human-made materials are usually better for building structures, especially for younger children who need flatter surfaces for building stable stacks and unit length pieces for building accurate shapes. Fortunately, much of the best building material available to kids comes from common everyday materials and discards like paper plates and paper tubes, paper clips and rubber bands, drinking straws and paper cups, old magazines and newspapers, and the parts and fasteners redeemed from broken toys and appliances.

Whatever the source, no material should be so precious or valuable to cause the builder to feel guilty if it was to get broken. On the contrary, the material should encourage the child to tear it, break it, paint it, or change it in any way that is needed.

Building structures from scrap materials is similar to assembling the parts in a construction set or model kit—but with one big difference. Although there are instructions to be followed for both kinds of building, very few kids strictly adhere exactly to what is shown. To vary from the prescribed plan with most model kits means doing it "wrong." If the final product doesn't look like the picture on the box, then the builder must have made a mistake. By building with scrap materials, it is expected that the variety of materials or the open-ended nature of the construction system will purposely distract the builder with inspirations for new ideas to try. And instead of the precision snap-together quality of plastic brick or rod construction sets, structures made from scrap materials have a much greater latitude in the way parts can go together. The builder can change the pieces as needed because there is no one way to do it right. To the builder, some constructions will just seem more successful than others.

The Entire Home Is a Child's Workspace

To support creative building requires very little besides lots of building materials, some tools for manipulating the material, and a space for building that can take the abuse of hammers and glue. Then spice the area with plenty of pictures for reference, and you have created an ideal environment for kid constructions.

Depending on the builder's age and what is being built, a kid's building space can be anything from a clearing on the floor to a well-equipped workshop. Playrooms, bedrooms, basements, kitchens, backyards, and garages—when occupied by building play, all easily transform into childhood laboratories.

All building begins on the floor as infants and toddlers make their simple stacks of blocks and strings of beads. For the first few years, creative building and play can take place anywhere as long as there is a large enough and safe enough play area. But as kids grow older and their constructions become more sophisticated, the spaces they require may also need to be more specialized. An inventor-type builder would probably prefer a basement or garage workshop surrounded by lots of scrap parts. For a builder who likes to experiment with boats, bubble makers, or water-play concoctions, the kitchen sink or the bathroom tub might become a temporary laboratory. And making outdoor play structures, like tents, kites, or maybe a greenhouse, requires a backyard environment, at least for testing.

Some special projects may dictate temporary workshop locations, but everyday creative building, play, and learning requires a regular everyday space in which the young builder feels in charge. That means a carefully planned and equipped environment that addresses the child's abilities and interests. At the age when young builders begin using tools, they need to be provided with lots of table or floor space that is resistant to the potential damages of glue, paint, hammering, and cutting. If you don't have a large work table, you can inexpensively make one by nailing a piece of plywood to the top of two sawhorses.

The well-equipped building space has open shelves or stacking bins for easy review and access to materials and tools. A large bulletin board displays the child's two-dimensional works or maybe pictures of buildings and structures for reference, and a chalkboard or

white board can be helpful in sketching out ideas. Also, include a builder's reference library of product catalogs that contain pictures for building inspirations. Books about building and repairing with diagrams that show how things work help builders get ideas about solving problems. And don't forget to include this book!

The space should be organized well enough to have things readily available, but not so neat as to discourage messy experiments. Some building projects will take time, and some projects may want to be kept in place for another day or two. Kids like to know they can leave a project undisturbed for a while and come back to it later.

A Safe Workspace Is Essential

Certain spaces around the home typically used for building and play require careful attention to potential dangers, and younger builders may need supervision. This is especially important when building in the kitchen.

Some kitchen safety rules are just good common sense and apply to everyone, both kids and adults. For example, baggy sleeves can catch things, overturn pots, and maybe catch fire when reaching over the stove. Hands can be burned if you don't use a pot holder, and be aware that steam and boiling liquids also can cause serious burns. And never use an electrical appliance near the sink or anywhere there is water, or you could get a severe electric shock. But just in case there is an accident, the builder should know where the first-aid materials are kept. Its also a good idea to keep emergency numbers near the phone

THE MAGIC OF MODULAR WOODEN BLOCKS

The Universal Building Toy

Among all the types of building toys that may be available, a set of wooden blocks is often given the highest priority by two- to twelve-year-olds. A child's first set of blocks is a powerful invitation to spontaneous and open-ended play. Even one-year-olds will repeatedly enjoy attempts to stack and balance one block on top of another, although they seem to get much more pleasure knocking down someone else's stack. A two-year-old can confidently build a tower six or seven blocks high, or string a line of blocks horizontally end to end to make a train. Preschoolers like to build simple houses or maybe a garage for a toy car. Six-year-olds can build tall skyscrapers and elaborate streetscapes, and the block constructions of older kids begin to reveal the builder's sense of design as well as any architectural skills. And it is not unusual for some adult designers and architects to still use wooden blocks to help them create. The famous architect Frank Lloyd Wright once called blocks "the finest material that came into my house."

Blocks are an easy, open-ended way for kids to manipulate their play environment, to try out and test new ideas, and to challenge themselves at each stage of their development. Block builders come to understand or at least be aware of cause-and-effect relationships. They establish confidence in their building skills and themselves, they experiment with form, record visual impressions for later reference,

and improve coordination. And as a consequence of what they build, kids often develop spontaneous verbal and physical dramatizations, which reflect their growing awareness of reality and the outside world.

In fact, many educators believe that playing with ideas prepares children to conceptually master them later. By building and arranging block structures to represent complex real-life situations, the young builder is beginning to learn the basis for all social, scientific, and mathematical thinking. A child with a background of block-building experience will more readily recognize many of the mathematical and scientific ideas presented at school and much more easily grasp their concepts. This head start to formal learning also becomes evident in the young builder's extended vocabulary. In block building, kids must learn words to describe and explain things to others. They inadvertently practice and then begin to understand the meaning of long and short, high and low, wide and narrow, far and near, up and down, and so on. To encourage this development, an adult need only talk to the young builder about what he has built.

But don't be fooled into thinking that a set of blocks alone will suggest what a child will build. As powerful a plaything as blocks may be, their real play value comes from the child's own experience and personality. The abstract quality of block play just happens to be one of the best and most fun ways for young builders to give form and substance to their ideas, to feel

some control over their environment, and to express their feelings about anything within it. The adult's role is to help provide new experiences that are appropriate for the child's age and interests. The young builder will then take care of both the fun and learning parts of play by imitating in block constructions what she has observed and how she thinks it works.

For some kids or at some ages, this type of block building fantasy play requires solitude and quiet so the builders can concentrate on inventing their own personal interpretations of life. But just as blocks are ideal for solitary play, they are equally suited for cooperative play, even if the young builders are all different ages. And because blocks have such a common appeal among all ages and all levels of conceptualization, group play helps kids build social relationships with other builders whatever their ages or interests.

Building with modular wooden blocks is so appealing mostly because of their simple abstract quality. Unlike using interlocking plastic building pieces, wooden blocks allow a young builder to quickly interpret an idea in a block structure, maybe play with it, and then knock it down to use the parts to build something else. In block play, there is no construction so precious that it can't be knocked down for another idea. Sometimes this spontaneity progresses from individual buildings and structures to whole layouts. To better model the builder's perceptions, all kinds of extras can be added like model cars, trees, and people figures. And at the end of play, kids find it quite reasonable to take their structures down and put the blocks away until next time.

Through block building, kids develop a quest for learning how to make things work, they experience the reward of concentration and persistence in finding answers and solutions by themselves and with others, and they gain new knowledge while having fun. This is play at its best.

The Ages and Influence of Block Play

A simple set of modular wooden blocks probably has the longest life of any toy because of their strong play value over the broadest age range. Wooden blocks just also happen to be a very powerful and versatile learning tool for any age. Along with the inherent fun of playing with blocks and building things, block play gives kids a lot of practice in developing many useful skills from a very early age. Just which skills are practiced depends on the child's age.

The youngest builders may only be trying to pick up one block and place it on top of another, but this is valuable practice in hand and eye coordination. Just in handling blocks, kids learn about their physical properties, in building, they learn about structure, space, form, and function, and in solving construction problems, they learn to compare dimensions, understand systems, and think creatively. By planning to build something, or in figuring what something already built may happen to be, young builders are also practicing conceptual thinking skills and developing

a host of good intuitions.

Here is the kind of play and learning you can expect at each age of block building.

Nine months old

A nine-month-old will work at grasping at a block until it is under control and then celebrate the achievement by banging it on the floor. This is also an age when just about anything picked up is brought to the mouth, so avoid small blocks that could choke or painted blocks that could chip. A few unpainted natural-wood blocks are fine (raw wood even tastes good), or a set of cloth-covered foam blocks can be introduced into play.

One year old

By age one, block play may have progressed to holding a block in each hand and then banging the blocks together. Blocks are now closely inspected, carried around, pushed, pulled, lifted, and dropped. Block play at this age is mostly solitary with much repetition. These builders are gaining tactile experience as they try to stack blocks one on top of the other without knocking down the pile—until ready to do so. Three or four modular cloth blocks or plain wooden blocks are all that is needed at this age to inspire and exercise building skills. The wooden blocks must be large enough and have enough weight to build stable structures, yet small enough to be handled securely.

Two years old

A child of two is mastering the ability to position blocks and construct simple structures. At first, the novice builder will simply pile up blocks to create wobbly towers or string them in a row to make a "train." Using just a few blocks, the builder will repeatedly stack a

tower and knock it down. When this skill is mastered, add another block or two for building (and knocking down) even taller towers. Building will soon progress from towers and trains, to making a simple bridge (by setting one block across two others), to decorative or symmetrical patterns, to making constructions that symbolize actual objects. The awareness that something new can be intentionally created from a number of building pieces is a major discovery and a critical part of learning.

Three years old

By age three, block building has become a regular part of play. Three-year-olds begin building more sophisticated structures, but only if they are given enough blocks to build things their own way. Three-year-olds typically build all types of simple block enclosures representing familiar structures for people, animals, and vehicles, as well as simple roads, bridges, and towers. This becomes the perfect setting for fantasy play as the young builders add people figures, vehicles, and other playthings to their block structures. This is also the time to introduce more complex building pieces. To adequately build a small block village or neighborhood takes a set of at least sixty blocks made up of several modular shapes. It is important that the blocks fit together well so that the large blocks are multiples of the small blocks. This allows the blocks to fit together in a large variety of ways and makes building less frustrating. It also helps introduce the concepts of volume, size, and simple mathematics.

Four years old

The four-year-old builder will arrange blocks and buildings with a definite plan in mind, although the structure will be vague and probably change several times as it is being built. Four-year-olds are also able to handle larger blocks, so it is a good age for introducing large-scale, lightweight blocks that give kids the opportunity to build full-scale structures they can actually get inside of or climb on—either inside or outdoors. A pile of big blocks immediately suggests a wall to hide behind or an enclosed set of walls to build a kid-sized building. At this point, the structure itself begins to suggest and stimulate several types of social and imaginative play—and also provides a sense of security.

Five years old

By age five, kids have become aware of many more types of structures as well as much more detail, so they need more blocks and more shapes to build highway systems with cloverleafs, airport terminals and runways, shopping centers and malls, and skyscraper cityscapes. Much block play is now done in a group setting where kids both mimic each other's structures and learn to share. A set of over a hundred blocks in all shapes and sizes will encourage some pretty impressive structures. At this age, the visualization of what the builder is making is also more precise, and he knows exactly which shapes fit together and what forms the blocks will create.

Six years old

The six-year-old block builder makes elaborate structures and loves to build contraptions that "do things" or that show off some building skills to prove competence. But the six-year-old also begins to become critical of her own work. Some planned projects can become overly complicated and overwhelming to the point that the project is abandoned without the intervention of someone to help. At about this age, kids begin to master simple hand tools and may want to use some blocks to practice hammering nails and screwing screws.

Seven years old and up

At age seven, the block builder has become quite sophisticated in both building methods and learning to represent familiar structures more accurately. Each year following, the block builder's structures take on more personal style and clearly represent a better understanding of structural concepts. However, the key to sustaining block building now lies in the variety and quantity of blocks available. It can be very discouraging and frustrating for the "older" young builder to run out of blocks at the finale of a grand design. So for this age group, a set of two hundred blocks of all modular shapes and sizes is an ideal minimum

TOY BUYING MADE BETTER

Meeting the Child's Needs Comes First

The first crucial issue in toy buying is matching the plaything to the child's development and interests. Adults trying to match the right toy with the right child have the seemingly paradoxical responsibility of finding something that is both full of fun and full of learning. Make your search easier by not starting the purchase process at the toy store. The shelves of toy superstores are cluttered with an overwhelming range of things from traditional rubber balls and crayons to the latest electronic marvels. The perfect toy for a particular child may be somewhere on the shelves, but browsing isn't the best way to find it.

And don't start by asking the child what toy to buy. The child's realm of toy experience is often limited to TV hype and the possessions of their friends. As kids get older, they are deluged with promotions for snazzy looking toys that promise to be everlasting fun. But good play is more than just entertaining amusement. A good plaything should certainly be appealing in design, color, and content, and it must also invite the use of hands and involve problem solving. Kids really want to manipulate and use playthings, not just look at them.

Before shopping for a toy, learn about the child's recent interests and attitudes about play. Talk with a child about the kind of play he likes most, the fun play experiences and projects he remembers most, and his fantasies about new encounters in life. In addition to what you may already know about a child's interests and curiosities, every discussion on the topic will yield more clues about what interests to support next.

With a knowledge of the child's budding interests in mind, you now have the first essential criterion for finding just the right plaything—a fun toy that matches the child's current needs that may also help develop a lifelong interest or skill. Be assured, however, that while parents should influence the child's play experience, overexposure to a particular interest will not necessarily lead directly to a life profession. Supporting an interest in puppets and fantasy play does not mean a predisposition to acting, nor will a passion for construction sets turn a kid toward a future in building or architecture. Toys can both introduce new types of play to see if a lasting interest develops and reinforce attitudes and interests that the child has already begun to form through social interactions.

Look for Open-Ended Playthings with High Play Value

The second most important consideration in selecting a plaything is estimating its play value or open-ended qualities. A toy that is meant to be played with in only one specific way will soon become boring once that way has been mastered. The special-purpose doll that can walk or talk or wet is more than likely to restrict, if not dull, the child's imagination. The classic "do-nothing special" doll, on the other hand, can be anything or do anything the child's imagination dictates. In a similar way, a detailed fire truck with ladders and hoses may inspire firefighter play, but that's all. A less detailed truck can be any work vehicle the child imagines—a police car, fuel truck, ambulance, or maybe a delivery van with packages.

Open-ended toys with high play value invite participation in any way the child can imagine and therefore they encourage creativity. There are no predictable results. A younger child, for example, may not be ready to play dominoes by the game rules, but may find that the pieces make a neat modular brick-building set. Using the parts to play a game of dominoes will come later when the child is ready for game rules.

Construction sets and building toys should encourage and allow the child builder to construct not only the structures and themes suggested in their accompanying booklets, but they should also invite open-ended play. The modular construction components should assemble quickly and in a variety of configurations to test building ideas, easily make changes, and be a catalyst to inventive thinking and fantasy play.

But to achieve the full benefits of any toy's potential for open-ended play often requires some interaction. Don't just hand over the gift-wrapped toy and let the child go at it alone. Helping a child understand a toy's real play value should be an essential extra. An adult might explain the "official" instructions or show how the toy is supposed to work, but also understand that the child's own experimentation and exploration is an important part of open-ended creative play. Kids need to know that their "unofficial" play outside the rules is not only okay, but encouraged!

Know the Ingredients of Good Building Toys

By definition, most construction toys using modular building components are open-ended playthings with high play value. The best construction sets are capable of enticing a broad range of ages into building a variety of projects that reflect current interests. And to have that appeal, a good building toy must provide the structural materials necessary not only to fabricate what the builder has designed or imagined, but the building system must also satisfy the builder's needs for the right amount of realism or abstractness, simplicity or complexity, operation, and function. Good building toys offer great opportunities for exercising the skills that help develop creativity and understanding. In many ways, not to the exclusion of other types of play, construction toys promise to be the best educational toys you can purchase.

There is always a large variety of modular-construction building toys available, and the perennial favorites still include classics like Lincoln Logs, TinkerToy, and Lego. Most building systems are based on a few basic construction methods, which include plastic bricks that stack, flat shapes and cylinders that interconnect in their own unique ways, and rods, sticks, and structural members that join in various ways, using cleverly designed connectors.

Still, every year at least one new building toy appears in stores and catalogs showing yet another unique way its parts are meant to fit together. There are modular connectors for attaching empty soda cans in columns and clusters, clip connectors for building with pennies, and plastic plug-in connectors for building with drinking straws. And several high-tech building toys offer sophisticated computer-controlled modules to operate the kinetic structures they build.

With so many building sets available, the choice of which one or ones to buy becomes even more confusing because very few kits have parts that mix and match. Each brand and building system imparts its own distinct character and scale on the structures it can build. And since each system is so uniquely different, it is difficult for kids to mix the structures of one system with another. This is not just because the parts from different systems are not interchangeable, but also because children have difficulty transferring their perception of reality from one abstract system to another.

Beginning with the large, soft stacking cubes that often introduce infants to building, the construction materials needed to support building interests will certainly change. However, when given a choice at any age of the building years, a young builder will quickly discover which building system best matches his or her needs—and then play only with that system (often building a huge collection) at the exclusion of all others.

Many toys that are called construction kits or building projects are meant to build just a single plaything that is usually appropriate only to a specific age or interest.

Most of these kits confine play experience to a single purpose, so they rob the builder of creativity and inventiveness. In trying to be both model kits and construction toys, some kits present a conflict between the exacting precision and specialized shape of the parts they include for "realism" and the more abstract structures the remaining modular parts are meant to create.

Some theme toys may be built from modular components, but they are just disassembled toys that must be put together again, and there is only one "right" way to do it right. These model kits disguised as construction systems represent the opposite of open-ended building, and although some may provide exercise in developing dexterity, they do little to exercise and develop creativity. They are just too limited in play value to encourage planning and building of one's own ideas. And if the limited way in which the pieces must be assembled is too difficult or too easy, the young builder will just walk away from the project or maybe make something else out of the parts that came in the kit.

Doing something differently than described on the box or in the instructions is just fine and sometimes even more desirable as long as the child is not made to feel that different is wrong. But walking away from a construction is discouraging, leaving the builder less likely to work out the next difficult problem.

Even if the prospect of building the pirate ship, spaceship, castle, or fort shown on the package seems exciting to the young builder, there are much better kits available intended only for building scale models. Theme construction kits are only meant to be put together once or twice before the builder wants to move on to build something else, which is often another theme kit.

Young builders need to create their own challenges and successes, and building play is much more rewarding and beneficial when the builder is in charge of the final result.

Classic Modular Construction Toys Are Still Fun

Building with modular bricks and blocks has captivated children for thousands of years, and modular construction toys and model building kits with specially shaped interlocking pieces have been popular with a wide range of ages for over a hundred years. It may be no surprise then that many of today's most popular construction toys have been best sellers ever since they were introduced several generations ago, and there are several reasons why they will probably be just as popular for many generations to come.

The basic versions of most classic modular construction toys are not much different today than when they were first invented, and they continue to prove their high play value in a toy market dominated by ever new themes and associations with popular characters. The main benefit of a construction kit is that the large variety of modular pieces go together easily to build things quickly. These kits encourage experimenting and make complex structures seem more manageable than building with raw materials.

Many of these classic construction sets do double duty as fun playthings and educational tools, allowing a hands-on approach to understanding structures. Each one of these classic commercial toys, as well as others, offers and encourages certain types of open-ended building and fantasy play. Erector Set building mimics a kind of engineering approach, the large-size, kid-scale structures of Duplo empower young builders with confidence, and kids playing with Lego are planning and designing buildings and cities. The most significant limitation of construction toys is that kits from different manufacturers are not interchangeable.

These classic construction kits are still available and popular today, and some kits have been updated to include power modules, gearing systems, and even computer controls. These are some of the features and attributes of each kit to be considered when matching a construction toy to the builder's interests and capabilities.

Lego

- Plastic parts assemble very easily but also come apart easily

- Builds and demonstrates brick and block building

- Many specialty parts and specific model kits are available but not necessary for school-age builders

- Suited for young builders starting at three years and interesting for all age builders

Duplo

- Large-scale version of basic Lego bricks are easily handled and manipulated

- Plastic parts assemble very easily but also come apart easily

- Some modular pieces include images depicting everyday objects to aide in imaginative play

- Some specialty parts are molded as popular characters, animals, and everyday objects

- Best suited for very young builders starting at twelve to eighteen months

Tinkertoy

- Rods and spool connectors originally made of wood but are now plastic and assemble somewhat easily

- Builds and demonstrates very limited types of space frame structures and vehicles

- Best suited for free-form building projects by young builders who have developed good manipulation skills

Lincoln Logs

- Interlocking notched wooden logs in modular lengths are stacked

- Only suited for building log cabin structures and similar log buildings such as forts

- Kit accessories include plastic roof slats, windows, and doors, plus people and animals

- Delicate stacking assembly for very young builders and too limited for older builders

K'NEX

- Builds simple or complex, large or small structures

- Plastic parts are easy to assemble and take apart

- Bright, colorful parts consist mostly of rods and disk connectors plus wheels and other special accessories

- Limited modular sizes require some "work arounds" to build certain type structures

- Suitable for preschoolers, and interesting for all age builders

Erector Set

- Builds rigid space frame, post and beam, and other girder type structures

- Metal parts are fastened together with small machine screws and nuts that require delicate manipulation plus using a screwdriver and wrench
- Accessories include wheels, axles, motors, gears, and pulleys
- Building and disassembly can be very time-consuming
- Theme kits that primarily build a single project are not as versatile as older sets containing quantities of all type parts
- Not suited for most young builders

Meccano

- Builds rigid space frame structures (similar to Erector set and called "Erector Meccano")
- Metal parts are fastened together with small machine screws and nuts that require using a screwdriver and wrench
- Accessories include wheels, axles, motors, gears, and pulleys
- Building can be time-consuming
- Not suited for young builders

Fischertechnik

- Best for building and demonstrating mechanical and technology devices
- Plastic building blocks and other parts lock solidly together
- Suited for older builders and even adults
- A large variety of accessories is available to add power, gears, pneumatics, lights, and even computer controls with software

Guidelines to Use at the Toy Store

When selecting or shopping for good building toys, it is sometimes too easy to get carried away with the hoopla of claims made on the box. Not all building sets or projects meet all the criteria that help kids understand and learn, but the absence of too many "good toy" attributes should be a warning that the toy will probably turn out to be quickly discarded. Read the information on the toy package, look carefully at the contents, and review the toy based on the following values. Then use common-sense judgment to decide whether or not to buy the toy.

Consider the child's age and abilities.

Does the construction system have lasting play value to be used in different ways by different ages? Is it also capable of creating more complex structures that will still interest kids as they grow older? Are the pieces easy and fun to manipulate, and are the structures they build sturdy? Manufacturers have an obvious interest in suggesting the widest possible age range for the use of their products. Thus the minimum age suggested is a sure caution against use of the toy by a younger child. Beyond that, however, the suggestions on the box offer a very rough guide, which must be tempered by knowledge of the child's habits and abilities.

Give top preference to toys with open-ended qualities.

Can the set construct objects that are general enough in detail to leave room for a young child's imagination to transform it into something else? Does the building system arouse curiosity and invite the player to experiment—without using the instruction book? And does the plaything build structures with appealing shape and color? Toys that can be used in many different ways encourage kids to apply imagination or strategy, and help develop their ability to think in terms of choices and alternatives. A construction set with specific realistic pieces to build a fire truck is ultimately less desirable and of less play value than building a whole host of different vehicles, using more generalized building pieces. Of course the difference in realism is easily made up in the child's imagination.

Thoroughly inspect a toy before you buy it.

Do the contents fulfill the promise of what is claimed on the package? Unfortunately, most retail stores don't put out display samples, and they discourage customers from opening sealed boxes. All the information available to the consumer is what is printed on the box, and often the box top doesn't even display a picture of the product inside. The consumer should then assume (most often correctly) that nothing shown on the outside means nothing worthwhile inside. This rule especially applies to products embellished with pictures of popular television characters and little else.

Use common sense in judging toy safety.

Are the parts well made from quality materials and free from sharp edges, toxic paints, or other potential dangers? The child who takes toys to bed at night can do without sharp edges, poking corners, or protrusions. The child who is a habitual chewer or sucker should not be given toys made up of little pieces or breakable parts. Attention to toy safety by manufacturers has improved considerably in recent years. Under a self-regulated code, toy manufacturers are obligated to eliminate all hidden dangers and to warn clearly of any inherent dangers in the toy's use. But these warning labels don't mean much if they are only read by an adult. The first rule of toy safety is making the child aware of any potential dangers.

Check Toys for Choking Hazards

The most dangerous playthings for babies and young children are small toys and other small objects that pose a choking hazard. It is normal for young children to pick up and bring things to their mouths. Choking occurs when food, a toy, or some other object is swallowed and goes down the "wrong way," blocking the airway. A person of any age can choke, but choking is an especially serious problem for children under the age of three, and it is important for older family members to keep all choking hazards well out of their reach.

Just about anything that can fit inside a young child's mouth can block breathing. Young children who are learning to eat solid foods often choke on hard candies, nuts, grapes, carrots, popcorn, and hot dogs. And after foods, the most common choking hazards are toys.

Some toy stores sell a "no-choke tester tube" designed to measure small toys and parts to determine which ones are too small. If the object can fit completely within the tube, it should be considered a potential danger. Unfortunately, these plastic-cylinder testers generally measure only 1 3/8 inches in diameter and are not quite large enough to include many known hazards, including balls. The Child Safety Protection Act requires toy balls to be larger than 1 3/4 inches in order to be safe for young chil-

dren. In fact, the Consumer Product Safety Commission recommends that all small toys and removable parts be larger than 1 3/4 inches.

A toilet paper tube makes the best choke tester.

A toilet paper tube is exactly 1 3/4 inches across its opening and makes a perfect choke tester. It's also free. To test any item, try to insert it into a standard toilet paper tube. If it doesn't fit one way, try the item at several different angles. Can the object be bent or twisted to fit into the tube? If it completely fits within the tube in any way, the part or toy is small enough to fit in a young child's mouth and should be considered a choking danger.

Use the toilet paper tube to check balls, rattles, puzzle pieces, xylophone mallets, and toys intended for older siblings, as well as anything you think is questionable. Check (or avoid) small toys sold from vending machines and bins, because they are rarely labeled with warnings. Inspect how a toy is designed and the quality of the construction. Read labels for warnings. Are there any parts that might break off? Especially check

eyes on dolls and stuffed animals, squeakers attached to toys, car wheels, and any toy parts that might be removed or pulled off by accident. Also, be on the lookout around your home for small, easy-to-reach common household items such as loose change, buttons, jewelry, batteries, nuts, popcorn, and balloons.

There are many other common-sense precautions that can be taken to protect children from choking. And most importantly, take a Child First Aid and CPR class through your local American Red Cross or American Heart Association. Choking can and does happen despite the best efforts to remove hazards.

Ignore the Instruction Booklet

When trying to decide what to build with a modular-part construction set, try not to be overly influenced by the instruction booklet packed in the container or the photographs of completed structures shown on the box. The illustrated examples of what presumably can be built typically show everything exciting to kids from tractors and airplanes to Ferris wheels, skyscrapers, and spacecraft. The payoff these pictures promise may even have influenced the purchase of the set. But in terms of maximizing play value, the instruction booklet is probably the least creative thing about nearly all modular construction toys.

Too often the instruction booklet transforms the inherent open-ended quality of a modular construction set into a closed-ended, model-making toy. Duplicating the models shown in the instruction booklet is just like filling in the predrawn outlined pictures in a coloring book. The exercise may help practice a young child's dexterity and fine motor skills, but it does very little to encourage the builder's creativity, invention, and design skills.

Still, it's okay if a young builder wants to copy a project from the instruction booklet for the satisfaction of figuring out the construction "puzzle." A child trying to "do it right" will attempt to copy the construction piece for piece, exactly as it is shown in the booklet. But what if there are not enough long red parts or angled corner pieces in the set to complete the construction? Even if there are plenty of long blue parts to substitute for the missing red ones, the builder may see any alteration as different or "wrong," and the disappointing project will soon be abandoned.

Sometimes the box cover, the instruction book, or a display in the toy store window will show an enormous layout of buildings and structures to suggest what the construction set is capable of making. But this also suggests that these complex structures should be built for keeping and putting on display. That may be fine for homemade construction projects built from inexpensive household materials and discards. But except for those few kids who might become collectors of a particular construction system, not many children will ever have enough pieces to build more than a few small buildings at one time. And besides, the real play value and purpose of a modular construction set is not in keeping what is built, but rather in repeating the cycle of building and taking apart so the pieces can be used to build something else.

In addition to the projects shown by the toy manufacturer, the modular parts of a construction set are certainly capable of being used to build anything the young builder imagines. And without the instruction booklet, there are no such constraints as the wrong color, the wrong size, or an insufficient supply of pieces. The builder can just go about conceiving the next step in the construction, using whatever parts are available to interpret his idea.

Most kids will build recognizable shapes such as skyscrapers, towers, forts, vehicles, and airplanes. Some will just want to create sculpture. Some will enjoy competing to solve building challenges, like who can construct the tallest free-standing structure, build the longest "bridge" between two chairs, or maybe make a structure that will support the builder's own weight.

Sometimes the builder will start by connecting one modular part to another and so on without any apparent plan of what is being built. This is not the time for an adult to interrupt and interfere by suggesting what the child seems to be building. Left alone, the builder will almost always find a time during the construction for her own revelation, deciding what the structure looks like and therefore what it will become. And even if an experiment doesn't work as well as planned, the fun of building is improving on past constructions by trying new ideas until one does work better.

Consider a Toy Store Alternative

Sometimes the toy store may not be the best place to find the perfect toy to support a developing interest. Excellent playthings can also

be found in the adult marketplace. Kids at play often try to emulate what adults do, so unless there is some danger or safety issue that cannot be handled by the child, there is no reason kids cannot use the "real" tools and materials that adults use rather than simulated or scaled-down "kid" versions. Play is always enhanced by materials that work well.

For a preschooler or an older kid who shows interest or promise as a builder of things, a suitable plaything might include a few basic hand tools from the hardware store and a small toolbox to put them in. These functional and durable tools (with your instruction in using them properly) are likely to mean far more to the child than any toy-store tool set with a saw that cuts nothing and a hammer hardly adequate for driving thumbtacks.

Play tools are usually either tools that aren't meant to do real work in the first place, or cheaply made tools that don't do their jobs very well. But the biggest reason not to buy these fake tools is that they are much more dangerous to use than the real tools they represent. A cheaply made or toy screwdriver does not have a precision ground blade, so it tends to slip out of the groove in the head of the screw, and that can pose a danger to hands and damage materials. A toy saw is relatively dull and requires more pressure, so it has a tendency to slip out of the cut. And even though the saw teeth are not really sharp enough to easily cut through wood, they can create nasty gashes in hands and fingers.

A good starter set of basic hand tools might include a light hammer and some nails, a screwdriver and some screws, an adjustable wrench with several sizes of nuts and bolts, and a measuring tape. And to gain experience using the tools (and not on your household possessions), the kit should also provide an assortment of wood scraps and other materials.

A child captivated by a parent's cooking might enjoy a personal set of cooking utensils, a special place in the pantry to keep his or her own utensils and ingredients, and a junior cookbook that includes "cold cooking" recipes, assuming the child is still too young to risk the hazards of the kitchen stove.

The musically inspired child deserves the real thing. Most homemade instruments are fine for discovering and learning the fun of making sounds and music. But the cheap toy instruments you can purchase at toy stores are likely to keep playtime out-of-tune and discouraging. Toy-store guitars, for example, are almost impossible to tune, awkward to play, and terrible to hear. But that doesn't mean you must spend a bundle to get a decent quality instrument. Support a musical interest with a used but real instrument. And some real instruments, like a harmonica or a recorder, are inexpensive to buy new and easy to play.

Alternative toys can show up almost anywhere. Here is a list of places where you might do some looking.

- Arts and crafts shop
- Bookstore
- Building materials and supplies
- Camera shop
- Carpet store
- Computer software store
- Convenience store
- Electronic parts store
- Fabric and sewing shop

- Gift shops
- Hardware store
- Hobby shop
- Kitchenware store
- Lawn and garden shop
- Museum store
- Music store
- Office supply store
- Pet shop
- Sporting goods store
- Supermarket
- General variety store
- Thrift shop
- Yard sale

Look for Toy and Play Perennials

Some toys and types of play are perennial. They were popular when parents were kids, they are popular now, and they will probably always be an important part of play. Just think about what was the most fun when you were a kid. What kind of playthings did you like best—dolls, model cars, blocks, kites, pets, or maybe dinosaurs? What games and puzzles did you play by yourself or with others? What kind of tents, forts, castles, and other personal spaces did you make for yourself? And what kind of inventions and contraptions did you like to build?

These perennial toys and types of play fill many of a child's needs through the growing years. Homemade forts, tents, and "caves" in the closet will appear at an age when a child needs to play away from the prying eyes and interference of adults. Water play may begin with baths and continue with bubbles and boats. And a quickly

crafted "bug house" will be invented when a child discovers nature.

Use this list of toy and play perennials to help identify a young builder's special interests. Most parents get strong clues from kids about what interests them and especially what doesn't. Then review the projects in this book to suggest those building activities that might further develop their interests.

- Art and sculpture
- Balancing
- Balloons
- Balls and marbles
- Bikes, trikes, and wagons
- Birds and butterflies
- Block building
- Books
- Bubbles
- Bugs and insects
- Building structures
- Cameras
- Camping
- Candy
- Card games
- Cars, trains, and planes
- Climbing
- Clothes, costumes, and dress up
- Collecting
- Contests and competition
- Cooking and kitchens
- Crafts
- Dancing
- Dinosaurs
- Dolls
- Drawing and painting
- Farm animals
- Finger paints
- Fishing

- Flags and banners
- Flowers, plants, and gardens
- Golf
- Hiding places
- Inventing
- Jobs
- Jokes and riddles
- Kites
- Magic
- Magnifiers
- Markers and crayons
- Masks and disguises
- Miniatures
- Mirrors
- Mobiles
- Model kits
- Movies
- Music
- Nature
- Parachutes
- Parties
- Pets
- Playhouses
- Posters and pictures
- Pottery
- Printing patterns
- Puppets and pretend
- Puzzles and patterns
- Racing and competition
- Riding vehicles
- Rocks and shells
- Roller coaster
- Sand and beaches
- Science discoveries
- Shadows
- Snow
- Sports
- Stars and planets
- Stores and selling
- Stories
- Target games
- Tents, forts, caves, and personal spaces
- Tools
- Tops and spinners
- Trips
- Water play
- Weaving and knitting
- Wind wheels
- All things that go by themselves

GLOSSARY

Basic Shapes and Forms

circle
A closed curve equally distant from a single center point

semicircle
Half a circle

ellipse
A flattened circle similar to an angled slice of a cone

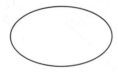

arc
An unbroken segment of a circle

equilateral triangle
All sides are the same length, and all inside angles are the same

isosceles triangle
Two sides are the same length, and two inside angles are the same

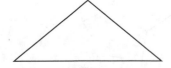

right-angle triangle
One inside angle is a right angle

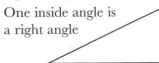

scalene triangle
All sides are different lengths, and all inside angles are different

square
All four sides are the same length, and all angles are right angles

kite
Adjacent sides are equal length, and diagonals intersect at right angles

parallelogram
Opposite sides are the same length and parallel to each other, but none of the angles are right angles

rectangle
Opposite sides are the same length, and all angles are right angles

rhombus
All sides are the same length, but none of the angles are right angles

trapezoid
One pair of opposite sides are parallel

swiss cross
Five equal squares making a cross

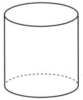

cylinder
A surface that rotates around a circle

cone
Sides taper up from a circular base to a point

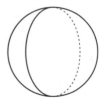

sphere
A ball with its surface being a given distance from a center

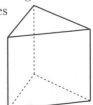

triangular prism
Identical triangular ends and rectangular sides

Regular Polygons

In addition to an equilateral triangle with three equal-length sides and three equal angles, and a square with four equal-length sides and four equal angles, all other regular polygon shapes have equal length sides and angles. All regular polygons fit within a circle with their angles touching the circle.

triangle
3 sides

square
4 sides

pentagon
5 sides

hexagon
6 sides

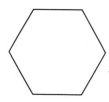

heptagon
7 sides

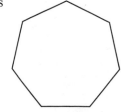

octagon
8 sides

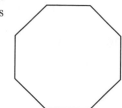

nonagon
9 sides

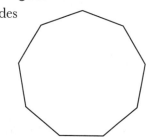

decagon
10 sides

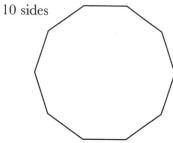

undecagon
11 sides

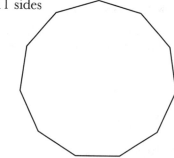

dodecagon
12 sides

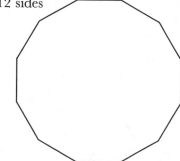

Basic Polyhedrons

tetrahedron
4 triangles

cube
6 squares

octahedron
8 triangles

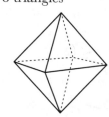

icosahedron
20 triangles

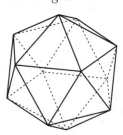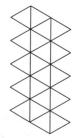

dodecahedron
12 pentagons

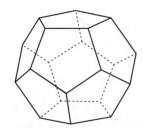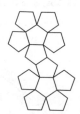

Other Geometric Forms

square pyramid
4 triangles, 1 square

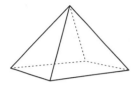

triangular dipyramid
6 triangles

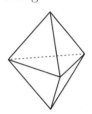

square antiprism
8 triangles, 2 squares

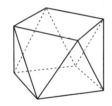
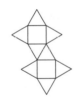

cuboctahedron
8 triangles, 6 squares

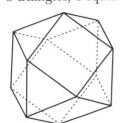

truncated octahedron
6 squares, 8 hexagons

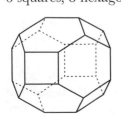

rhombicuboctahedron
8 triangles, 18 squares

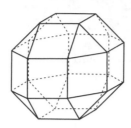
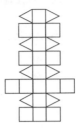

truncated icosahedron
12 pentagons, 20 hexagons

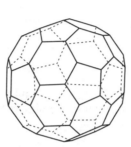

pentagonal dome
6 pentagons

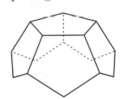

hexagonal dome
4 triangles, 3 squares

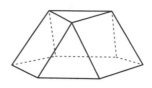

octagonal dome
4 triangles, 5 squares

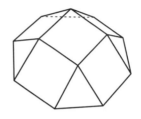

decagonal dome
10 triangles, 6 pentagons

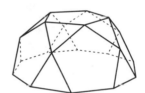

Common Angles

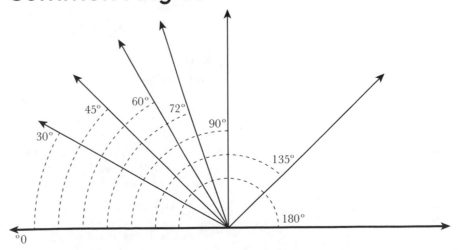

Symbols Used in Building

inch
″

foot
′

plus or positive
+

minus or negative
−

plus or minus
±

multiply by or times
X

percent
%

equals
=

does not equal
≠

less than
<

more than
>

right angle
∟

degree
°

centerline

Words Used in Building

acoustics
The sound qualities and characteristics of a room or space

adobe
A sun dried brick made of earth and straw

airfoil
A surface affected by air currents to provide control, stability, direction, or lift

anchor
A tie rod to prevent bulging or separation. Also a metal fastener attachment imbedded in masonry

angle
An amount of turn or rotation measured in degrees with 360 degrees being one complete rotation. A *right angle* is exactly 90 degrees, an *acute angle* is a turn of less than 90 degrees, an *obtuse angle* is greater than 90 degrees, and a reflex angle is greater than 180 degrees

apex
The top or peak of a pyramid or cone shaped form

asymmetry
The lack of symmetry

arc
Any section of a curve

arch
A self supporting curved structure made of wedge-shaped blocks that span an opening. Arches can be semicircular or pointed.

area
The amount of surface covered by a shape

backfill
Earth and stone used to refill the excavation between the foundation wall and the grade

baffle
A partial obstruction of the flow usually in a pipe or duct

ballast
Added weight to provide stability

beam
A horizontal structural member that spans the distance between two supports.

benchmark
A fixed point of reference from which things are measured or reckoned

bevel
A sloped surface edge of a horizontal or vertical surface

break
The change in direction of a wall or other element

brittle
Likely to break or shatter

buckle
To curve or bend from the normal shape when under strain or load

butt
The meeting of two members squarely end to end

buttress
A support structure usually of masonry built up against the side of a wall to give it additional strength.

cantilever
A horizontal structural member (like a beam) that is firmly secured at one end only, and completely

unsupported at the other (like a swimming pool diving board).

capacity
The amount something will hold or support

ceiling
The part of a building attached to the underside of a floor or roof which creates the upper surface of a room.

chord
A straight line joining any two points on a circle

circumference
The distance around a circle

colonnade
A line of several identical columns evenly spaced and lined up side by side in a row to hold up beams or arches

column
Columns are posts that hold up building sections and can be made of any material.

compression
Squeezing together

concave
Curving inward

convex
Curving outward

corbel
A type of stacking and overlapping construction using bricks or stone in successively projecting rows or rings to create a stable arch or dome structure.

cornice
On the exterior of a building, the cornice is an ornamented horizontal band between the top of a wall and the roof. On the interior, the cornice is any molding at the top of a wall, usually between the wall and the ceiling.

counter balance
A weight used to balance a load on the other end of a lever arm

cross section
The plane created when cutting through a solid

deck
Roadway or platform of a bridge

density
The mass of a material in a given volume. The more mass, the more dense

diameter
The distance across a circle, going straight through the middle

dome
A hemispherical shaped roof that may be made from a variety of structure systems including blocks, space frames, reinforced concrete, or inflatables

drag
A force working against the movement of something

eaves
The underside of a roof where it overhangs the building's walls

energy
The capacity to perform work and create a force

entry
The door opening or passageway into a building

equilibrium
Everything is in balance

erosion
A natural process due to wind, water, or weather that moves material from one place to another on the earth's surface

facade
The front side of a building

flexible
The ability to be bent or flexed

force
The ability to do work or cause change

foundation
A flat platform or a walled perimeter used to firmly secure a structure to the earth and to carry and spread its weight over a larger area

frame
The skeletal framework of a structure that is sometimes covered with an outer skin and sometimes left bare

frequency
The number of times an event occurs in a given amount of time

friction
A stopping force with physical contact

fulcrum
The support on which a lever turns

gable
The triangular end portion of a pitched roof

girder
A supporting beam made of iron or steel

gradient
An amount of slope or how steep an incline is

gravity
The force generated by the earth

which everything is subject to according to its mass. The force of gravity on the mass of an object creates the weight of an object.

guy lines
Ropes or cables used to steady poles, tents, and towers

hypotenuse
The longest side of a right-angle triangle

joint
The connection between two or more structural members

joist
A beam specifically meant to support a floor

keystone
The topmost stone of an arch or the tapered center stone of a lintel which holds the rest of the arch structure in place

lever
A rigid bar resting on a fulcrum or wedge that can be used to magnify force

lift
An upward force generated when air passes over an airfoil

lintel
A horizontal beam that is placed across two upright posts. Lintels are usually placed across the top of window and door openings

membrane
A thin, flexible layer covering surfaces or separating two regions

modules
Parts of regular shapes that are joined together in a system to build larger or more complicated structures

obelisk
A tall pointed block of stone

parallel
Lines or planes, straight or curved, that are the same distance apart along their length

percentage
A part of 100, so that 30 percent (%) means 30 out of 100, 75% means 75 out of 100, and so on

perpendicular
Lines or planes at right angles (90 degrees) to each other

plane
A flat surface

pressure
A force that one body generates on another, either by gravitational force or by restricting the area that the second body occupies

radius
The distance from the center of a complete or partial circle to the outside edge

rafter
The sloping structural beams that form the frame structure used to support a roof

ratio
A comparison of two amounts so that something three times longer than its width would have a length

to width ratio of 3 to 1

resistance
A force that opposes.

roof
A covering over all or some of the structure to keep out rain, wind, snow, or sun

tensile strength
Strength that is generated by stretching a membrane in tension

tension
A pulling or stretching force

ties
A beam, rod, or cable used to in tension to keep two parts of a structure from separating

truss
A rigid framework of beams and braces incorporating triangular structures

volume
The amount of space occupied by a form or inside a form

walls
The portion of the structure that contains openings for windows and doors

wheel
An object, usually circular, which rotates around an axle

winch
A machine used to lift or pull loads by winding up a cable or chain attached to the load

window

INDEX

A

Additive design, 142
Adhesives, 103-107
Adjustable wrench, 124-125
Adobe bricks, 358-360
Air-inflated structures, 72-73
Air-supported radome, 73
Airplane models, 114, 497-500
American-style house, 34-35
Angles, 587
Animal architects, 77-89
Ants, 84, 86-87
Arch bridges, 182-183, 189-191
Arches, 366-368, 370, 453-455,
    457, 503
Architects, 27, 156
Architectural designs, 19-22,
    140-145
Architectural terms, 22-25, 588-590
Architecture
    elements of, 19-22
    in nature, 77-89
    and roof types, 32-34, 54
    terms of, 22-25, 588-590
    and workers, 27-28
    see also Structures
Art projects, 569
Asymmetry, 149
Augustine, Margaret, 176

B

Backyard and Field Foot Maze,
    556-558
Bagel Block Bird Banquet, 395-396
Bailey bridges, 188
Bailey, Donald, 188
Balance, 148
Balls, 156, 477, 523-524
Barns, 36-37. See also Silos
Barrel vault arches, 453-455
Bathtub Barges, 554-555
Beach Beaux Arts, 399-400
Beam bridges, 182-187
Beams, 25-26, 65, 183, 185-186
Beavers, 80-82
Bedouin tent, 459
Bees, 84, 87-89

Bell, Alexander Graham, 172-173
Bench vise, 131
Bends, 445-447
Best-Flyer Paper Planes, 497-500
Big Box Blocks Building System,
    389-390
Big Box Buildings, 486
Biosphere II, 176
Bird Feeder Space Station
    Platform, 242-243
Bird nests, 78-79, 82-83
Birdbath and Watering Station,
    528-529
Block arches, 366-368
Block construction, 351-380.
    See also Brick and Block
    Structures
Blocks, 157-158, 574-576
Blocks of Logic, 386-388
Bob houses, 38-39
Bolts, 111-112
Bowls, 519
Box wrenches, 134-135
Bread Clay, 432
Brick and Block Molding
    Methods, 429
Brick and Block Structures
    arches, 366-368
    building, 349-441
    cabins, 378-379
    castles, 375-377
    domes, 369-372
    elements of, 354-355
    fitting stone blocks, 372
    patterns for, 361-363
    pyramids, 373-374
    understanding, 56, 350-380
Brick arches, 368
Bricks and Mortar Building
    Systems, 407
Bridges
    categories of, 182-194
    covered bridges, 179-181
    early bridges, 178-179
    of the future, 74
    making, 184
    Merritt Parkway, 143
    parts of, 183
    of steel, 65
    types of, 177-195
Brown, Benjamin, 451

Bubble Frames and 3-D Planes,
    229-231
Builder's square, 127
Building blocks, 157-158
Building designs, 20-22
Building jobs, 27-28. See also
    Structures
Building materials
    and creativity, 152-155, 563-565
    for fastening, 103-114
    gathering, 92-121, 572-573
    purchasing, 100-102
    resources for, 95-99
    types of, 47-76
Building skills
    ages for, 566-567, 575-576
    and creativity, 1-5, 151-161,
        563-565
    encouraging, 565
    environment for, 1-2, 572-573
    and new experiences, 563
    and playtime, 562-584
Building terms, 22-25, 588-590
Buildings
    history of, 46-76
    styles of, 28-35
    types of, 47-76
    understanding, 7-45
    see also Architecture;
        Structures
Bus-stop shelters, 139
Butterfly Net, 267-268

C

Cabins, 378-379
Cable bridges, 186, 192-194
Cake Blocks and Frosting Mortar
    Building System, 408-410
Caney Stool, 484-485
Caney Trihanger Module
    Building System, 333-335
Cantilever bridge, 186
Card Castles, 547-548
Cardboard Carpentry Building
    System, 467-471
Cardboard Carpentry
    Constructions, 466
Carpenter's pencil, 129
Cast iron, 61
Castles, 375-377
Caves, 47-48

Chimneys, 57
Christiansen, Ole Kirk, 364-365
Clamps, 129
Classic Kites, 244-248
Classic Lemonade Stand,
    315-317
Clay, 161
Clip Grippers and Straw Struts
    Building System, 290-291
Clip Hooks and Hangers,
    292-293
Coat hangers, 335
Compact rotary tool, 136
Compass saw, 130
Compression, 13-14, 351, 354-355
Concrete, 70
Construction play, 568-569
Construction toys, 578-580
Contractors, 27-28
Contrast, 148, 150
Cookie and Candy Domino
    Disks, 552-553
Coping saw, 126
Corrugated Cardboard
    Carpentry Building System,
    467-471
Cozy Cat Playground, 327-329
Craft projects, 569
Cranes, 174-175
Creativity, 1-5, 151-161, 563-565
Crosscut saw, 130-131
Cubes, 157, 173
Curves, 445-447
Cutting paper, 159
Cylinders, 157

D

Dams, 80-82
Design, 4-5, 137-150
Design attributes, 146-150
Design elements, 140-142
Design preferences, 138
Design projects, 569
Designers, 28
Designs, from nature, 144-145
Designs, in architecture, 20-22
Director's chair, 463
Disney World, 205, 206
Dollhouse, 472-473, 504-505
Domes, 203-206, 307-308,
    336-337, 369-372, 451, 519

Drawbridges, 186
Drawing, 159
Drills, 126-127, 136
Drinking Straws, 220
Dunkelberger, George, 143
Duplo bricks, 579

E

Einstein, Albert, 451
Encouragement, 565
Engineers, 27
Epcot Center, 205, 206
Erector Set, 195, 579-580
ESP Mind-Reading Cards, 549-551
Experiences, 563

F

Fantasies, 74-76, 568
Farm silos, 71
Fastening hardware, 113
Fastening materials, 53, 103-114
Fences, 40-42
Files, 133
Finger puppets, 478
Finishes, 115-121
Fischertechnik, 580
Fishing houses, 38-39
Foam Board Fabrications
    Building System, 536-538
Folded Paper Projects and
    Puzzles, 491
Folding paper, 160, 456
Folding wooden rule, 127
Form and function, 19, 137-139
Forster, Charles, 261-262
Four-Poster Roof-Canopy Beds,
    305-306
Frame barns, 36-37
Frame construction, 165-166.
    See also Space frame structures
Frame houses, 34-35
Free play, 156-161
Froebel Gifts, 156-161
Froebel System of Kindergarten,
    156
Fruit Face Tasty Totem Pole,
    404-406
Fuller, Buckminster, 75, 144,
    203-204, 342
Funny Flour Putty, 433
Futuristic structures, 74-76

G

Games, 569
Gardener's Greenhouse, 322-324
Gel-O-Cube Blocks Building
    System, 437-438
Gel-O-Cube Igloo, 439-440
Geodesic Dome Bug House,
    254-255
Geodesic dome home, 451-452
Geodesic domes, 203-206
Geometric forms, 585-587
Gerstenzang, Leo, 234
Gilbert, Alfred Carlton, 195
Glossary, 585-590
Glues, 103-107
Goggles, 129
Goldberg, Rube, 345, 347
Golden rectangle, 141-142
Graham Cracker Tri-Panels
    Building System, 542-544
Graham Crackers, 544
Graham, Sylvester, 544
Graves, Michael, 74
Great Pyramid, 373-374

H

Habitat, 353
Hacksaw, 130
Hammers, 125
Hand drill, 126-127
Hand measures, 128
Hand puppets, 477-478
Hanging Betta Bowl, 530-532
Hangers, 335
Hardware, 113
Herron, Ron, 74
Hideouts, 43-45
Honeybees, 87-88
House-building lessons, 15-17
House designs, 21-22
House styles, 28-31
Howe, John Ireland, 296
Howe, William, 180

I

Ice-fishing houses, 38-39
Icosahedron, 204
Ideas, finding, 152-155
Igloos, 371-372, 441
Indoor Circle Dome, 307-308
Industrial designers, 28

Inflatables, 72-73
Insects, 84-89
Inspiration, 153-154
Instruction booklets, 581-582
Instruments, 97-99, 569-570
Interior designers, 28
Interlacing, 160
International Space Station, 167
Inuit igloo, 371-372
Invention, 1-5, 151-161
Inventors, 152-153
Iron, 61

J

Jefferson, Thomas, 289
Jointed slats, 160

K

Kahn, Louis, 75, 451
Kastner, Alfred, 451
Keyhole saw, 130
"Kinder-Garten Gifts," 156-161
Kitchen Clay and Concrete
    Blocks Building System, 430-433
Kitchen Concrete, 432-433
Kites, 172-173, 244-248
K'NEX, 579
Knife, 131-134
Knife-sharpening tip, 134

L

Laminated Lounge Chair,
    489-490
Lego bricks, 364-365, 579
Level, 131
Lighthouses, 62-64
Lincoln, Abraham, 378, 380
Lincoln Logs, 380, 579
Locking Blocks and Banded
    Bundles, 419
Locking Logs and Timber Columns
    Building System, 424-426
Log cabins, 378-379
Longhouse, 51-52
Lumber, 100-102

M

Magnetic Battle Bugs, 294-295
Marble Coaster Tracks and
    Trestles, 237-240
Materials, gathering, 92-121,

572-573.
    See also Building materials
Mazes, 556-558
Measuring tape, 127
Measuring tips, 128
Meccano structures, 580
Medieval castles, 375-377
Merritt Parkway bridges, 143
Merritt, Schuyler, 143
Mesa Verde, 359-360
Metal file, 133
Middlebrook, William, 296
Mind-Reading Cards, 549-551
Mini Marshmallow Sticky Bricks
    Building System, 417-418
Model airplanes, 114
Model building projects, 571
Modeling clay, 161
Modular construction toys,
    579-580
Modular parts, 93-94
Modular wooden blocks, 574-576
Modular Wooden Blocks Building
    System, 383-385
Monuments, 66-69
Mosquito Chamber of Doom,
    256-258
Motels, 140
Moth Magnet Movies, 338-339
Moving bridges, 186
Music-making materials,
    97-99, 569-570

N

Nails, 110-111
Native American structures, 49-52
Nature designs, 144-145
Nature projects, 570-571
Nature structures, 78-89
Nests, 78-83, 86-89
New and Novel Space Frame
    Systems, 332-347
Newspaper Struts and Poles
    Building System, 298-300
Noodle Novelty Twisters, 285-288
Nuts, 111-112

O

Octagon Arrow Artwork, 510-511
Octahedron, 204

One-Box Dollhouse, 472-473
One-Box Puppet Theater, 474-478
One-Kid Two-Kid Tepee, 303-304
One-Tarp Tents, 520-522
Open-end wrenches, 134-135
Order, 146-147
Origami, 160, 456
Otis, Elisha, 197
Outdoor playthings, 570

P

Paint cleanup, 121
Paint rollers, 115, 118-120
Paintbrushes, 115, 118-120
Painting techniques, 116, 119-121
Paints, 115-121
Pajeau, Charles, 169
Palmer, Timothy, 179-180
Panel and Plane Structures
    and arches, 453-455, 457
    building with, 465-558
    elements of, 450
    stability for, 454-455
    understanding, 443-464
Panel Options and Oddballs, 535
Panelized playhouse, 479-481
Paper Bag Bedroom Blocks
    Building System, 391-392
Paper clips, 290-291, 296
Paper-cutting, 159
Paper-folding, 160, 456
Paper Planes, 497-500
Paper Plate Poly Panels
    Building System, 539-541
Paper Puzzle Brain Twisters,
    514-515
Papier Mâché, 527
Papier Mâché Shells, 525-527
Parent resource, 561-584
Parkhouse, Albert J., 335
Parquetry, 158
Pasta, 277-278, 289
Pasta Pieces and Paste Building
    System, 275-278
Pasta Snakes, 282-284
Paste, 106, 275-278
Pattern, 147-148
Pattern and Puzzle Paper Cubes,
    508-509
Peanut Butter and Crackers
    Building System, 545-546

Peanut-Shell Bricks and Kitchen-Paste Mortar Building System, 411-412

Peas work, 160-161

Penaud, Alphonse, 114

Pencil, 129

Pentagons, 204-205

Perennial playthings, 583-584

Perry, Stephen, 114

Personal Pyramid Play Space, 301-302

Personal-Size Space Frames, 297-331

Piano, Renzo, 32

Pipe Chables, 325-326

Pipe Sculpture Sprinkler, 330-331

Plastic Pipe Art Easel, 312-314

Plastic Pipe Dreams Building System, 309-311

Plastic Pipe Playhouse, 320-321

Play-People Stand-Ups, 506-507

Play perennials, 583-584

Play Places, 297-331

Playhouses, 320-321, 479-481, 486

Playthings, buying, 577-584

Playtime, 562-584

Pliers, 124

Pneumatics, 72-73

Polyform Kickball and Indoor Golf, 211-212

Polygon Puzzles, 232-233

Polygons, 586

Polyhedrons, 204, 586

Pompidou Center, 32

Portable Pocket Scope, 218-220

Post-and-beam construction, 36-37

Post-and-lintel construction, 54

Power drill, 136

Power tools, 136

Pretend play, 568

Pricking, 159

Proportion, 149-150

Propulsion projects, 570

Pueblo, 52

Punch and Poke Sticks Building System, 235-236

Puppets, 474-478

Pyramid Power, 213-215

Pyramids, 213-215, 301-302, 336-337, 373-374

Q

Q-Tips, 224-225, 234

Quad Panel Patterns, 512-513

Quick Sticks Building System, 263-266

Quonset hut, 457

R

Rain Stick Storm Maker, 492-494

Rainbow Prisms, 501-503

Rectangles, 141-142

Reinforced concrete, 70

Rhoads, George, 347

Rhythm, 569-570

Rings, 158-159

Rodgers, Richard, 32

Rods and connectors, 207-347

Roebling, John A., 192

Roller Coasters, 241

Roof types, 32-34, 54

Roosevelt, Franklin D., 452

Rotary tool, 136

Rotelle Rattler, 282-284

Rubber bands, 114

Rube Goldberg Inventions, 345-347

Rule, 127

S

Saber saw, 136

Safdie, Moshe, 353

Safety goggles, 129

Safety tips, 123, 125, 129, 136, 573, 580-581

Sandpaper, 133, 134, 135

Sawdust Clay, 431-432

Saws, 126, 130-131, 136

Scaffolds, 170

Scale, 150

Science projects, 570-571

Scissors, 127

Scrap materials, 18, 93-94, 572-573

Screwdrivers, 124

Screws, 111

Self-expression projects, 569

Sewing, 159

Shadow puppets, 478

Shapes, 516-518, 585-587

Shell structures, 445-449, 519, 525-527

Sidewalk Superintendent, 18-19

Silos, 71

Skyscrapers, 76, 196-202

Slab construction, 445, 450

Slab houses, 451-452

Slats, 160

Slotted-Panel Structures and Sculptures, 487-488

Small-Box Furniture and Appliances, 504-505

Snelson, Kenneth, 342

Snow and Sand Mound Molds Building System, 434-436

Socket wrenches, 135

Soda Can Castles Building System, 427-428

Soleri, Paolo, 75

Solvents, 115-116

Space frame structures
building, 208-347
elements of, 168-176
materials for, 165-166
types of, 168-206
understanding, 163-167

Space Frame Terrarium, 221-223

Space Station, 167

Spaceship Earth dome, 205, 206

Spheres, 157, 204-205, 336-337

Spider webs, 84-86

Sports projects, 570

Spray painting, 118, 119

Square, 127

Square shape, 170-171, 365

Stack and Stick Sugar Cubes Building System, 413-414

Stack 'n Clip Sawhorses, 495-496

Stacking, 351, 382, 495-496

Stains, 115-117

Stale Bagel Blocks Building System, 393-394

Steel beams, 25-26, 65

Step-Side Pyramid Toy Box, 482-483

Stick and Branch Blocks Building System, 397-398

Stick-built houses, 34-35

Sticks, 158, 397-398

Sticky Q-Sticks Building System, 224-225

Sticky Triangle Dominos, 226-228
Stone arches, 366-368
Stone castles, 375-377
Stone construction, 351-380. *See also* Brick and Block Structures
Stone, Marvin, 220
Stone rings, 356-357
Stone walls, 59-60
Stonehenge, 356-357
Stoneworking, 58
Straws, 209-210, 220, 290-291
String and Straw Sticks Building System, 209-210
Structures
    elements of, 19-22
    explanation of, 9-10
    history of, 46-76
    in nature, 78-89
    roofs of, 32-34, 54
    styles of, 28-35
    for survival, 78
    types of, 9-12, 47-76
    understanding, 7-45
    and workers, 27-28
    see also Architecture
Style, 138
Subcontractors, 27-28
Subtractive design, 142
Sugar-Cube Cube Puzzle, 415-416
Suspension bridges, 182-183, 192-194
Sydney Opera House, 448-449
Symbols, 588
Symmetry, 149

T
Table Game Snacks, 401-403
Tape, 107-109
Tape measures, 127
Teacher resource, 561-584
Ten Simple and Tough Tessellations, 516-518
Tennis Ball Poppers, 523-524
Tennis Ball Puppets, 477
Tensegrity Thing, 340-342
Tension, 13-14, 351
Tents, 301-302, 458-464, 519-522
Tepee, 49-51, 303-304

Termites, 84, 86-87
Tessellations, 516-518
Tetrahedron, 172-173, 204
Tetrahedron kites, 172-173
Thatching, 54
Thompson, LaMarcus Adna, 241
Three-D Blind Marble Maze, 318-319
Three in a Row, 402-403
"Three Little Pigs," 15-17
Tic-Tac-Toe, 402
Timber frame barns, 36-37
Tinker Toothpicks Building System, 251-253
Tinkertoy, 169, 579
Toolboxes, 124-125, 129
Tools, 122-136. *See also* Safety tips
Toothpick Building System, 251-253
Toothpick Tantalizers, 259-260
Toothpicks, 261-262
Towers, 66-69
Town, Ithiel, 180-181
Toy Box, 482-483
Toy buying tips, 577-584
Toy favorites, 583-584
Toy stores, 580-583
TP Tube Tower Blocks Building System, 422-423
Tree houses, 43-45
Tri-Stick Stool, 269-270
Triangle shape, 170-171
Triangle Solitaire, 403
Triangle Truss Bridges Model Building, 279-281
Triangles, 204-205
Triangulation, 168, 170
Trihanger Pyramids, Spheres, Domes, and Trusses, 336-337
Truss beam, 183, 185-186
Truss Bridges Model Building, 279-281
Trusses, 171, 185-186, 336-337
Tub Tube Toys, 273-274
Tub Tubes Building System, 271-272

U
Universal Modularity Building System, 343-344

Utility knife, 133
Utzon, Jorn, 448-449

V
Varnishes, 115-117
Vise, 131
Visual vocabulary, 146-150
Visualization, 3-4

W
Walls, 59-60
Walt Disney World Resort, 205-206
Washers, 111-112
Wasps, 88-89
Water Lens Magnifier, 216-217
Waterwheels, 55
Weaving, 54, 160
Webs, 84-86
Wet Sponge Blocks Building System, 420-421
Whittling tip, 132
Wigwams, 51
Wildwood Vacation Resort, 140
Wind Whirlies, 249-250
Winter Warmer Solar Dish, 533-534
Wire coat hangers, 335
Wood, 100-102
Wood file, 133
Wood grain, 100
Wooden blocks, 574-576
Wooden Blocks Building System, 383-385
Wooden toothpicks, 261-262
Woodworkers, 84, 86-87
Workspace, 573
Wrenches, 124-125, 134-135
Wright, Anna Lloyd, 156
Wright, Frank Lloyd, 76, 144, 156, 380
Wright, John Lloyd Wright, 380

Y
Yoshizawa, Akira, 456
Yurts, 460-461

CREDITS

pp. 5 (left section: left & right bottom), 22 (left), 27 (right), 44 (center bottom), 45 (center top), 86 (right top & bottom), 88 (right top), 138 (top right), 171 (left & right bottom), 175 (right top, left bottom, right bottom), 178 (center), 184 (left bottom), 185 (left bottom), 186 (center center), 187 (left top), 190 (center bottom), 194 (2nd from top), 200 (left top & bottom), 257 (bottom section: right), 296 (left), 352 (right top, left bottom), 366 (left top), 370 (top section: left bottom), 373 (top, left center), 374 (bottom section: left top, right bottom), 375 (left & center top), 376 (all except right top), 377 (middle section: left top & bottom; bottom section: all), 383, 436 (right top, bottom), 445 (left bottom), 446 (top section: bottom left & right; bottom section: left top & bottom), 456 (center, left, right bottom), 458 (bottom section: left & right top, right center), 459 (right top, left bottom & bottom), 460 (left, right top), 462 (right top, center top, center center, right center, left bottom), 527: © iStockphoto International

pp. 29 (top right), 79 (bottom left), 80 (bottom left), 81 (right), 86 (left), 87 (right), 88 (left), 192 (left), 196, 365 (bottom left), 446 (top section: top left; bottom section: bottom right), 447 (bottom left), 456 (top right), 503 (bottom right): © morgueFile

pp. 10 (3rd row from top, center), 72 (top section: bottom left), 458 (left side, 2nd from top): Nemo Equipment

p. 43 (left bottom): © Hulton Archive/Getty Images

p. 44 (left center): © John Fowler/The Image Finders

p. 45 (bottom right & left): Courtesy of TreeHouse Workshop, Inc.

p. 48 (center bottom): © Jeff Schultz/AlaskaStock.com

pp. 63 (left top & bottom), 64 (left bottom): © Kraig Anderson www.lighthousefriends.com

pp. 63 (center bottom), 64 (right top): Photos courtesy of the U.S. Coast Guard Historian's Office, Washington, D.C.

p. 66 (right top): U.S. Geological Survey Library, Denver, Colorado

p. 66 (right bottom): Courtesy of The CN Tower, Copyright of Canada Lands Company CLC Limited

p. 66 (left top): © Walter Bibikow/Taxi/Getty Images

p. 72 (bottom): AP Images

p. 73: Maine Historical Society

p. 74 (bottom): Courtesy of Michael Graves and Associates

p. 75 (top): Image provided by Milton Academy Archives, Milton, Massachusetts. Image

courtesy, The Estate of R. Buckminster Fuller

p. 75 (left bottom): © Cosanti Foundation, drawing by Junji Shirai, photographed by H.S. Anaya

p. 75 (right bottom): © 1977 Louis I. Kahn Collection, University of Pennsylvania and Pennsylvania Historical and Museum Commission

p. 76: Copyright © 1956 The Frank Lloyd Wright Foundation, Taliesin West, Scottsdale, AZ

p. 87 (center top): Courtesy of USDA, ARS, IS Photo Unit. Photo by Scott Bauer. Image Number K5860-1

p. 87 (left bottom): image100/Fotosearch

p. 144 (left bottom): Library of Congress, Prints and Photographs Division, Historic American Buildings Survey or Historic American Engineering Record, Reproduction Number: HABS, WIS,51-RACI,5-22

p. 145 (left, 2nd from top): © Edward Chamberlain/Emporis

p. 166 (right bottom): Corbis/Fotosearch

p. 167: International Space Station graphics courtesy of National Aeronautics and Space Administration, Johnson Space Center

pp. 169 (left) & 296 (center top): United States Patent and Trademark Office

pp. 172 (right bottom), 173 (right top): Parks Canada/Alexander Graham Bell National Historic Site of Canada

p. 176 (left): © E.R. Degginger/Color-Pic, Inc.

p. 176 (right top): © Dan Budnik/Woodfin Camp Associates

p. 176 (bottom): Camerique/robertstock.com

p. 190 (right top): fotoLibra

p. 191 (right top): Library of Congress, Prints and Photographs Division, Historic American Buildings Survey or Historic American Engineering Record, Reproduction Number: HAER NJ, 9-BAYO,1-1

p. 192 (right bottom): Library of Congress Prints and Photographs Division Digital ID: cph 3b26128, Reproduction Number: LC-USZ62-79048

p. 192 (center top): Newburyport, Massachusetts Historical Society

p. 193 (right center): Library of Congress, Prints and Photographs Division, Historic American Buildings Survey or Historic American Engineering Record, Reproduction Number: HAER, NY,31-NEYO,90-6

p. 193 (bottom): Library of Congress, Prints and Photographs Division, Historic American Buildings Survey or Historic American Engineering Record, Reproduction Number: HAER, NY,31-NEYO,161-8

p. 194 (3rd from top): © Jeremy Bright/Robert Harding World Imagery/Getty Images

p. 197 (right): Courtesy of the Frances Loeb Library, Harvard Design School

p. 198 (top): Courtesy of the Otis Elevator Company

pp. 198 (left), 199 (center & right): © Battman Studios, New York City

p. 199 (left): © John Slaughter/Emporis

p. 200 (right): AP Images

p. 201 (top): Courtesy of Kohn Pedersen Fox Associates PC, rendering by KPF

p. 201 (bottom): Courtesy of Skidmore, Owings & Merrill LLP; Steinkamp Ballogg Photography

p. 202 (right bottom): © Peter Pearson/Stone/Getty Images

p. 203 (left top): Creatas/Fotosearch

p. 203 (center): Flat Earth/Fotosearch

p. 206 (left): © Disney Enterprises, Inc.

p. 206 (right): Used by permission from Disney Enterprises, Inc.

p. 234: (credit tk)

p. 261 (bottom): Courtesy of Strong, Maine, Fire Department

p. 289 (top): Library of Congress, LC-MSS-27748-180

p. 335 (bottom): Photograph courtesy of Gary Mussell, www.vcnet.com/garym/hanger1.html

p. 342 (right bottom): Courtesy of Kenneth Snelson, Easy Landing, 1977, stainless steel, 30 x 85 x 65 ft., Collection, City of Baltimore, Baltimore, MD

p. 352 (left top): © Michael Townsend/Photographer's Choice/Getty Images

p. 371: Photo compliments of Grand Shelters, Inc., www.grandshelters.com

p. 373 (bottom): © Richard Nowitz/Digital Vision/Getty Images

p. 400 (bottom left): Ginger Brown Illustrations

p. 462 (left top & bottom center): Tentsmiths

p. 464 (bottom right): Courtesy of SOM/Aga Khan Trust for Culture

p. 464 (right top): © Sebastian Willnow/AFP/Getty Images

p. 464 (top section: left bottom): © Donald Corner & Jenny Young/GreatBuildings.com

All other photos provided by Steven Caney.